THE HARVARD CLASSICS

The Five-Foot Shelf of Books

THE HARVARD CLASSICS
EDITED BY CHARLES W. ELIOT, LL.D.

I Promessi Sposi

(THE BETROTHED)

By Alessandro Manzoni

With Introduction and Notes
Volume 21

P. F. Collier & Son Corporation
NEW YORK

MANUFACTURED IN U. S. A.

CONTENTS

I

2 CONTENTS

INTRODUCTORY NOTE

Count Alessandro Manzoni was born at Milan, Italy, March 7, 1785. He was educated at Lugano, Milan, and Pavia, and after taking his degree he joined his mother in Paris, where he found her in the circle of Mme. Condorcet and the surviving rationalists of the eighteenth century. These associations led him for a time into scepticism, but he was later converted to Catholicism, and remained a steadfast adherent of that faith till his death, defending it in his writings against the Protestant historian Sismondi. Manzoni was a warm sympathizer with the aspirations of his country toward political independence, but he took no very active part in public agitation. When Italy was at last free, he was made a Senator and awarded a pension. He died at Milan, May 22, 1873.

Manzoni's most important literary productions are in poetry, drama, and the novel. In the first group he wrote some hymns, notable for the warmth of their religious sentiment, and two odes, "Il cinque maggio" and "Marzo 1821." The former of these, on the death of Napoleon, first brought him fame. His dramatic compositions, "Il Conte di Carmagnola" and "Adelchi," represent an attempt to free Italian drama from the restraints of the classical conventions, but neither met with general approval in Italy. Goethe, however, reviewed the earlier in the most favorable terms. In a prefatory essay Manzoni made an important contribution to the romantic protest against the restrictions of the dramatic "unities" of the classical drama. But the Italians were not yet prepared to accept truth in the treatment of human nature in place of stylistic polish and conventional form.

The reception given to Manzoni's masterpiece, "I Promessi Sposi" (1825–26) was very different. In form a historical novel, written at a time when the vogue of the Waverley Novels had stimulated the production of this form of fiction throughout Europe, the interest of "The Betrothed," as it is usually called in England, is rather psychological and sentimental than external. The scene is laid in Lombardy between 1628 and 1631, and the plot deals with the thwarting of the love of two peasants by a local tyrant. The manners of the time are presented with great vividness and picturesqueness; one of the most notable elements being the elaborate description of the plague which devastated Milan in 1630 (see Chaps. xxxi–xxxvii). The novel has taken a place as the most

3

distinguished novel of modern Italy, and has been translated into nearly all the literary languages.

The age-long dispute as to which dialect should be used as the standard language of Italian prose engaged the interest of Manzoni in his later years; and, becoming convinced of the claims of Tuscan, he rewrote the entire novel in order to remove all traces of non-Tuscan idiom, and published it in 1840. This proceeding had the effect of rekindling the discussion on the question of a national Italian literary language—a discussion which still goes on. Along with the revised edition of "I Promessi Sposi," he published a kind of sequel, "La Storia della Colonna infame," written more than ten years before; but this work, overloaded with didacticism, is universally regarded as inferior. Both at home and abroad, Manzoni's fame rests mainly on the novel here printed, a work which has taken its place among the great novels of the world, not merely for its admirable descriptions of Italian life in the seventeenth century, but still more for its faithful and moving presentation of human experience and emotion.

Mention has been made above of a so-called sequel to "I Promessi Sposi"; and since this publication is less easily accessible than Manzoni's more famous works, being properly regarded as unworthy of a place beside his great novel, it may interest the reader to have some account of its contents.

At the end of Chapter xxxii of "I Promessi Sposi," Manzoni refers to the affair of the anointers of Milan, men who were suspected of smearing the walls of the houses with poison intended to spread the pestilence; but he relegates to another place a full account of the incident. It is this matter which he takes up in "La Storia della Colonna infame."

One morning in June, 1630, a woman standing at a window in Milan saw a man enter the street della Vetra de Cittadini. He carried a paper on which he appeared to be writing, and from time to time he drew his hands along the walls. It occurred to her that he was perhaps an "anointer," and she proceeded to spread her suspicion, with the result that the man was arrested. He was found to be one Piazza, a Commissioner of the Tribunal of Health, who was able to give such an account of himself as, in ordinary times, would have led to his immediate acquittal. Both the populace and the judges, however, were panic-stricken, and eager to vent on any victim the fear and anguish into which the ravages of the plague had plunged them. Piazza was accordingly tortured, and after repeated and horrible sufferings was induced to make a false confession and to implicate an innocent barber, who, he said, had given him the ointment and promised him money if he spread it on the houses. Mora, the barber, was next arrested and submitted to a similar illegal and infamous process, until he also confessed, throwing the burden of blame in turn upon Piazza. Under false promises of immunity and suggestions of what was wanted from them, they alleged that several other persons were their accomplices or principals, and these also were thrown into jail. The evidence of Mora and Piazza was mutually contradictory on many points and was several times retracted, but the judges ignored these matters, broke their promise of immunity, and condemned both to death. They were placed on a car to be carried to the place of execution; as they proceeded, their bodies were gashed with a hot iron; their right hands were struck off as they passed Mora's shop; their bones were broken on the wheel; they were bound alive to the wheel and raised from the ground, and after six hours were put to death. This they bore with fortitude, having previously declared their innocence, retracted their confessions, and absolved their alleged accomplices. Mora's house was demolished, and a pillar, called the Column of Infamy, was erected on the spot, where it stood till 1778.

After the murder of these two miserable men, the judges proceeded to press the cases against the others whose names had been dragged into the matter, one of whom was an officer called Padilla, son of the Commandant of the Castle of Milan. Several of these suffered the same tortures and death as Mora and Piazza; but Padilla's case dragged on for two years, at the end of which he was acquitted.

The story of this terrible example of judicial cruelty had been to some extent cleared up by Verri in his book on Torture, but Manzoni was anxious to show that, evil as were the laws which permitted the use of the rack, it was not they but the judges who were responsible. For even the laws of torture prohibited the methods by which these men were made to inculpate themselves, and the illegality and monstrosity of the whole proceeding were attributable to a court eager for a conviction at all costs to gratify the thirst for blood of a maddened and ignorant populace.

The incident is related by Manzoni with considerable diffuseness and much technical argument; but the frightful nature of the events and the exhibition of the psychology of a panic-stricken mob give the production a gruesome interest.

I PROMESSI SPOSI

CHAPTER I

THAT branch of the lake of Como, which extends towards the south, is enclosed by two unbroken chains of mountains, which, as they advance and recede, diversify its shores with numerous bays and inlets. Suddenly the lake contracts itself, and takes the course and form of a river, between a promontory on the right, and a wide open shore on the opposite side. The bridge which there joins the two banks seems to render this transformation more sensible to the eye, and marks the point where the lake ends, and the Adda again begins—soon to resume the name of the lake, where the banks receding afresh, allow the water to extend and spread itself in new gulfs and bays.

The open country, bordering the lake, formed of the alluvial deposits of three great torrents, reclines upon the roots of two contiguous mountains, one named San Martino, the other, in the Lombard dialect, *Il Resegone,* because of its many peaks seen in profile, which in truth resemble the teeth of a saw so much so, that no one at first sight, viewing it in front (as, for example, from the northern bastions of Milan), could fail to distinguish it by this simple description, from the other mountains of more obscure name and ordinary form in that long and vast chain. For a considerable distance the country rises with a gentle and continuous ascent; afterwards it is broken into hill and dale, terraces and elevated plains, formed by the intertwining of the roots of the two mountains, and the action of the waters. The shore itself, intersected by the torrents, consists for the most part of gravel and large flints; the rest of the plain, of fields and vineyards, interspersed with towns, villages, and hamlets: other parts are clothed with woods, extending far up the mountain.

Lecco, the principal of these towns, giving its name to the territory, is at a short distance from the bridge, and so close upon the shore, that, when the waters are high, it seems to stand in the lake itself. A large town even now, it promises soon to become a city. At the time the events happened which we undertake to recount, this town, already of considerable importance, was also a place of defence, and for that reason had the honour of lodging a commander, and the advantage of possessing a fixed garrison of Spanish soldiers, who taught modesty to the damsels and matrons of the country; bestowed from time to time marks of their favour on the shoulder of a husband or a father; and never failed, in autumn, to disperse themselves in the vineyards, to thin the grapes, and lighten for the peasant the labours of the vintage.

From one to the other of these towns, from the heights to the lake, from one height to another, down through the little valleys which lay between, there ran many narrow lanes or mule-paths, (and they still exist,) one while abrupt and steep, another level, another pleasantly sloping, in most places enclosed by walls built of large flints, and clothed here and there with ancient ivy, which, eating with its roots into the cement, usurps its place, and binds together the wall it renders verdant. For some distance these lanes are hidden, and as it were buried between the walls, so that the passenger, looking upwards, can see nothing but the sky and the peaks of some neighbouring mountain: in other places they are terraced: sometimes they skirt the edge of a plain, or project from the face of a declivity, like a long staircase, upheld by walls which flank the hillsides like bastions, but in the pathway rise only the height of a parapet—and here the eye of the traveller can range over varied and most beautiful prospects. On one side he commands the azure surface of the lake, and the inverted image of the rural banks reflected in the placid wave; on the other, the Adda, scarcely escaped from the arches of the bridge, expands itself anew into a little lake, then is again contracted, and prolongs to the horizon its bright windings; upward,—the massive piles of the mountains, overhanging the head of the gazer; below,—the cultivated terrace, the champaign, the bridge; opposite,—the further bank of the lake, and, rising from it, the mountain boundary.

Along one of these narrow lanes, in the evening of the 7th of November, in the year 1628, Don Abbondio . . . , curate of one of the towns alluded to above, was leisurely returning home from a walk, (our author does not mention the name of the town—two blanks already!) He was quietly repeating his office, and now and then, between one psalm and another, he would shut the breviary upon the fore-finger of his right hand, keeping it there for a mark; then, putting both his hands behind his back, the right (with the closed book) in the palm of the left, he pursued his way with down-cast eyes, kicking, from time to time, towards the wall the flints which lay as stumbling-blocks in the path. Thus he gave more un-disturbed audience to the idle thoughts which had come to tempt his spirit, while his lips repeated, of their own accord, his evening prayers. Escaping from these thoughts, he raised his eyes to the mountain which rose opposite; and mechanically gazed on the gleaming of the scarcely set sun, which, making its way through the clefts of the opposite mountain, was thrown upon the projecting peaks in large unequal masses of rose-coloured light. The breviary open again, and another portion recited, he reached a turn, where he always used to raise his eyes and look forward; and so he did to-day. After the turn, the road ran straight forward about sixty yards, and then divided into two lanes, Y fashion—the right hand path ascended towards the mountain, and led to the parsonage: the left branch descended through the valley to a torrent: and on this side the walls were not higher than about two feet. The inner walls of the two ways, instead of meeting so as to form an angle, ended in a little chapel, on which were depicted certain figures, long, waving, and terminating in a point. These, in the intention of the artist, and to the eyes of the neighbouring inhabitants, represented flames. Alternately with the flames were other figures—indescribable, meant for souls in purgatory, souls and flames of brick-colour on a grey ground enlivened with patches of the natural wall, where the plaster was gone. The curate, having turned the corner, and looked forward, as was his custom, towards the chapel, beheld an unexpected sight, and one he would not willingly have seen. Two men, one opposite the other, were stationed at the confluence, so to say, of the two ways: one of them was sitting across the low wall, with one

leg dangling on the outer side, and the other supporting him in the
path: his companion was standing up, leaning against the wall,
with his arms crossed on his breast. Their dress, their carriage, and
so much of their expression as could be distinguished at the distance
at which the curate stood, left no doubt about their condition. Each
had a green net on his head, which fell upon the left shoulder, and
ended in a large tassel. Their long hair, appearing in one large lock
upon the forehead: on the upper lip two long mustachios, curled
at the end: their doublets, confined by bright leathern girdles, from
which hung a brace of pistols: a little horn of powder, dangling
round their necks, and falling on their breasts like a necklace: on
the right side of their large and loose pantaloons, a pocket, and
from the pocket the handle of a dagger: a sword hanging on the
left, with a large basket-hilt of brass, carved in cipher, polished and
gleaming:—all, at a glance, discovered them to be individuals of
the species *bravo*.

This order, now quite extinct, was then most flourishing in Lombardy, and already of considerable antiquity. Has any one no clear
idea of it? Here are some authentic sketches, which may give him
a distinct notion of its principal characteristics, of the means put
in force to destroy it, and of its obstinate vitality.

On the 8th of April, 1583, the most Illustrious and Excellent Signor
Don Carlo d'Aragon, Prince of Castelvetrano, Duke of Terranuova,
Marquis of Avola, Count of Burgeto, grand Admiral, and grand
Constable of Sicily, Governor of Milan, and Captain-General of His
Catholic Majesty in Italy, *being fully informed of the intolerable
misery in which this city of Milan has lain, and does lie, by reason
of bravoes and vagabonds,* publishes a ban against them, *declares
and defines all those to be included in this ban, and to be held
bravoes and vagabonds who, whether foreigners or natives, have
no occupation, or having it do not employ themselves in it . . . but
without salary, or with, engage themselves, to any cavalier or
gentleman, officer or merchant . . . to render them aid and service,
or rather, as may be presumed, to lay wait against others . . .* all
these he commands, that, within the term of six days, they should
evacuate the country, threatens the galleys to the refractory, and
grants to all officials the most strangely ample and indefinite power

of executing the order. But the following year, on the 12th of April, this same Signor, perceiving *that this city is completely full of the said bravoes . . . returned to live as they had lived before, their customs wholly unchanged, and their numbers undiminished,* issues another hue and cry, more vigorous and marked, in which, among other ordinances, he prescribes—*That whatsoever person, as well as inhabitant of this city as a foreigner, who by the testimony of two witnesses, should appear to be held and commonly reputed a bravo, and to have that name, although he cannot be convicted of having committed any crime . . . for this reputation of being a bravo alone, without any other proof, may, by the said judges, and by every individual of them, be put to the rack and torture, for process of information . . . and although he confess no crime whatever, notwithstanding, he shall be sent to the galleys for the said three years, for the sole reputation and name of bravo, as aforesaid.* All this and more which is omitted, because *His Excellency is resolved to be obeyed by every one.*

At hearing such brave and confident words of so great a Signor, accompanied too with many penalties, one feels much inclined to suppose that, at the echo of their rumblings, all the bravoes had disappeared for ever. But the testimony of a Signor not less authoritative, nor less endowed with names, obliges us to believe quite the contrary. The most Illustrious and most Excellent Signor Juan Fernandez de Velasco, Constable of Castile, Grand Chamberlain of his Majesty, Duke of the city of Frias, Count of Haro and Castelnovo, Lord of the House of Velasco, and that of the Seven Infantas of Lara, Governor of the State of Milan, &c., on the 5th of June, 1593, he also, fully informed of *how much loss and destruction . . . bravoes and vagabonds are the cause, and of the mischief such sort of people effects against the public weal, in despite of justice,* warns them anew, that within the term of six days, they are to evacuate the country, repeating almost word for word, the threats and penalties of his predecessor. On the 23rd of May, in a subsequent year, 1598, *being informed, with no little displeasure of mind, that . . . every day, in this city and state, the number of these people* (bravoes and vagabonds) *is on the increase, and day and night nothing is heard of them but murder, homicide, robbery, and crimes of every kind, for which there is greater facility, because these bravoes are confident of being supported by their great employers* . . . he prescribes anew the same remedies, increasing the dose, as men do in obstinate maladies. *Let every one, then,* he concludes, *be wholly on his guard against contravening in the least the present proclamation; for, instead of experiencing the clemency of His Excellency, he will experience the rigour of his anger* . . . *he being resolved and determined that this shall be the last and peremptory admonition.*

Not, however, of this opinion was the most Illustrious and most Excellent Signor, Il Signor Don Pietro Enriquez de Acevedo, Count of Fuentes, Captain and Governor of the State of Milan; not of this opinion was he, and for good reasons. *Being fully informed of the misery in which this city and state lies by reason of the great number of bravoes which abound in it* . . . *and being resolved wholly to extirpate a plant so pernicious,* he issues, on the 5th of December, 1600, a new admonition, full of severe penalties, *with a firm purpose, that, with all rigour, and without any hope of remission, they shall be fully carried out.*

We must believe, however, that he did not apply himself to this matter with that hearty good will which he knew how to employ in contriving cabals and exciting enemies against his great enemy, Henry IV. History informs us that he succeeded in arming against that king the Duke of Savoy, and caused him to lose a city. He succeeded also in engaging the Duke of Biron on his behalf, and caused him to lose his head; but as to this pernicious plant of bravoes, certain it is that it continued to blossom till the 22nd of September, 1612. On that day the most Illustrious Signor Don Giovanni de Mendosa, Marquis of Hynojosa, Gentleman, &c., Governor, &c., had serious thoughts of extirpating it. To this end he sent the usual proclamation, corrected and enlarged, to Pandolfo and Marco Tullio Molatesti, associated printers to His Majesty, with orders to print it to the destruction of the bravoes. Yet they lived to receive on the 24th of December, 1618, similar and more vigorous blows from the most Illustrious and most Excellent Signor, the Signor Don Gomez Suarez di Figueroa, Duke of Feria, &c., Governor, &c. Moreover, they not being hereby done to death, the most Illustrious and most Excellent Signor, the Signor Gonzala Fernandez di Cordova, (under whose government these events happened to Don Abbondio,) had found himself obliged to recorrect and republish the usual proclamation against the bravoes, on the 5th day of October, 1627; *i. e.* one year one month and two days before this memorable event.

Nor was this the last publication. We do not feel bound, how-ever, to make mention of those which ensued, as they are beyond the period of our story. We will notice only one of the 13th of February, 1632, in which the most Illustrious and most Excellent Signor *the Duke of Feria,* a second time governor, signifies to us *that the greatest outrages are caused by those denominated bravoes.*

This suffices to make it pretty certain, that at the time of which we treat, there was as yet no lack of bravoes.

That the two described above were on the lookout for some one, was but too evident; but what more alarmed Don Abbondio was, that he was assured by certain signs that he was the person expected; for, the moment he appeared, they exchanged glances, raising their heads with a movement which plainly expressed that both at once had exclaimed, 'Here's our man!' He who bestrode the wall got up, and brought his other leg into the path: his companion left leaning on the wall, and both began to walk towards him. Don Abbondio, keeping the breviary open before him, as if reading, directed his glance forward to watch their movements. He saw them advancing straight towards him: multitudes of thoughts, all at once, crowded upon him; with quick anxiety he asked himself, whether any pathway to the right or left lay between him and the bravoes; and quickly came the answer,—no. He made a hasty examination, to discover whether he had offended some great man, some vindictive neighbour; but even in this moment of alarm, the consoling testimony of conscience somewhat reassured him. Meanwhile the bravoes drew near, eyeing him fixedly. He put the fore finger and middle finger of his left hand up to his collar, as if to settle it, and running the two fingers round his neck he turned his head backwards at the same time, twisting his mouth in the same direction, and looked out of the corner of his eyes as far as he could, to see whether any one was coming; but he saw no one. He cast a glance over the low wall into the fields—no one; another, more subdued, along the path forward—no one but the bravoes. What is to be done? turn back?

It is too late. Run? It was the same as to say, follow me, or worse. Since he could not escape the danger, he went to meet it. These moments of uncertainty were already so painful, he desired only to shorten them. He quickened his pace, recited a verse in a louder tone, composed his face to a tranquil and careless expression, as well as he could, used every effort to have a smile ready; and when he found himself in the presence of the two good men, exclaiming mentally, 'here we are!' he stood still. 'Signor Curato!' said one, staring in his face.

'Who commands me?' quickly answered Don Abbondio, raising his eyes from the book, and holding it open in both hands.

'You intend,' continued the other, with the threatening angry brow of one who has caught an inferior committing some grievous fault, 'you intend, to-morrow, to marry Renzo Tramaglino and Lucia Mondella!'

'That is . . .' replied Don Abbondio, with a quivering voice,— 'That is . . . You, gentlemen, are men of the world, and know well how these things go. A poor curate has nothing to do with them. They patch up their little treaties between themselves, and then . . . then, they come to us, as one goes to the bank to make a demand; and we . . . we are servants of the community.'

'Mark well,' said the bravo, in a lower voice but with a solemn tone of command, 'this marriage is not to be performed, not to-morrow, nor ever.'

'But, gentlemen,' replied Don Abbondio, with the soothing, mild tone of one who would persuade an impatient man, 'be so kind as put yourselves in my place. If the thing depended on me . . . you see plainly that it is no advantage to me . . .'

'Come, come,' interrupted the bravo; 'if the thing were to be decided by prating, you might soon put our heads in a poke. We know nothing about it, and we don't want to know more. A warned man . . . you understand.'

'But gentlemen like you are too just, too reasonable . . .'

'But,' (this time the other companion broke in, who had not hitherto spoken)—'but the marriage is not to be performed, or . . .' here a great oath—'or he who performs it will never repent, because he shall have no time for it . . .' another oath.

'Silence, silence,' replied the first orator: 'the Signor Curato knows the way of the world, and we are good sort of men, who don't wish to do him any harm, if he will act like a wise man. Signor Curato, the Illustrious Signor Don Rodrigo, our master, sends his kind respects.'

To the mind of Don Abbondio this name was like the lightning flash in a storm at night, which, illuminating for a moment and confusing all objects, increases the terror. As by instinct he made a low bow, and said, 'If you could suggest . . .'

'Oh! *suggest* is for you who know Latin,' again interrupted the bravo, with a smile between awkwardness and ferocity; 'it is all very well for you. But, above all, let not a word be whispered about this notice that we have given you for your good, or . . . Ehem! . . . it will be the same as marrying them.—Well, what will your Reverence that we say for you to the Illustrious Signor Don Rodrigo?'

'My respects.'

'Be clear, Signor Curato.'

'. . . Disposed . . . always disposed to obedience.' And having said these words, he did not himself well know whether he had given a promise, or whether he had only sent an ordinary compliment. The bravoes took it, and showed that they took it, in the more serious meaning.

'Very well—good evening, Signor Curato,' said one of them, leading his companion away.

Don Abbondio, who a few moments before would have given one of his eyes to have got rid of them, now wished to prolong the conversation and modify the treaty;—in vain they would not listen, but took the path along which he had come, and were soon out of sight, singing a ballad, which I do not choose to transcribe. Poor Don Abbondio stood for a moment with his mouth open, as if enchanted: and then he too departed, taking that path which led to his house, and hardly dragging one leg after the other, with a sensation of walking on crab-claws, and in a frame of mind which the reader will better understand, after having learnt somewhat more of the character of this personage, and of the sort of times in which his lot was cast.

Don Abbondio—the reader may have discovered it already—was not born with the heart of a lion. Besides this, from his earliest years, he had had occasion to learn, that the most embarrassing of all conditions in those times, was that of an animal, without claws, and without teeth, which yet, nevertheless, had no inclination to be devoured.

The arm of the law by no means protected the quiet inoffensive man, who had no other means of inspiring fear. Not, indeed, that there was any want of laws and penalties against private violence. Laws came down like hail; crimes were recounted and particularized with minute prolixity; penalties were absurdly exorbitant; and if that were not enough, capable of augmentation in almost every case, at the will of the legislator himself and of a hundred executives; the forms of procedure studied only how to liberate the judge from every impediment in the way of passing a sentence of condemnation; the sketches we have given of the proclamations against the bravoes are a feeble but true index of this. Notwithstanding, or rather in great measure for this reason, these proclamations, republished and reenforced by one government after another, served only to attest most magniloquently the impotence of their authors; or if they produced any immediate effect, it was for the most part to add new vexations to those already suffered by the peaceable and helpless at the hands of the turbulent, and to increase the violence and cunning of the latter. Impunity was organized and implanted so deeply that its roots were untouched, or at least unmoved, by these proclamations. Such were the asylums, such were the privileges of certain classes, privileges partly recognized by law, partly borne with envious silence, or decried with vain protests, but kept up in fact, and guarded by these classes, and by almost every individual in them, with interested activity and punctilious jealousy. Now, impunity of this kind, threatened and insulted, but not destroyed by the proclamations, was naturally obliged, on every new threat and insult, to put in force new powers and new schemes to preserve its own existence. So it fell out in fact; and on the appearance of a proclamation for the restraint of the violent, these sought in their power new means more apt in effecting that which the proclamations forbade. The proclamations, indeed, could accomplish at every step the molestation of a good sort of men, who had neither power themselves nor protection from others; because, in order to have every person under their hands, to prevent or punish every crime, they subjected every movement of private life to the arbitrary will of a thousand magistrates and executives. But whoever, before committing a crime, had taken measures to secure his escape in time to a convent or a palace, where the *birri*[1] had never dared to enter; whoever (without any other measures) bore a livery which called to his defence the vanity and interest of a powerful family or order, such an one was free to do as he pleased, and could set at nought the clamour of the proclamations. Of those very persons to whom the enforcing of them was committed, some belonged by birth to the privileged class, some were dependent on it, as clients; both one and the other by education, interest, habit, and imitation, had embraced its maxims, and would have taken good care not to offend it for the sake of a piece of paper pasted on the corners of the streets. The men entrusted with the immediate execution of the decrees, had they been enterprising as heroes, obedient as monks, and devoted as martyrs, could not have had the upper hand, inferior as they were in number to those with whom they would have been engaged in battle, with the probability of being frequently abandoned, or even sacrificed, by those who abstractedly, or (so to say) in theory, set them to work. But besides this, these men were, generally, chosen from the lowest and most rascally classes of those times: their office was held base even by those who stood most in fear of it, and their title a reproach. It was therefore but natural that they, instead of risking, or rather throwing away, their lives in an impracticable undertaking, should take pay for inaction, or even connivance at the powerful, and reserve the exercise of their execrated authority and diminished power for those occasions, where they could oppress, without danger, *i. e.* by annoying pacific and defenceless persons.

The man who is ready to give and expecting to receive offence every moment, naturally seeks allies and companions. Hence the tendency of individuals to unite into classes was in these times carried to the greatest excess; new societies were formed, and each man strove to increase the power of his own party to the greatest

[1] *i. e.,* the armed police.

degree. The clergy were on the watch to defend and extend their immunities; the nobility their privileges, the military their exemptions. Tradespeople and artisans were enrolled in subordinate confraternities, lawyers constituted a league, and even doctors a corporation. Each of these little oligarchies had its own peculiar power; in each the individual found it an advantage to avail himself, in proportion to their authority and vigour, of the united force of the many. Honest men availed themselves of this advantage for defence; the evil-disposed and sharp-witted made use of it to accomplish deeds of violence, for which their personal means were insufficient, and to ensure themselves impunity. The power, however, of these various combinations was very unequal; and especially in the country, a rich and violent nobility, having a band of bravoes, and surrounded by a peasantry accustomed by immemorial tradition, and compelled by interest or force, to look upon themselves as soldiers of their lords, exercised a power against which no other league could have maintained effectual resistance.

Our Abbondio, not noble, not rich, not courageous, was therefore accustomed from his very infancy to look upon himself as a vessel of fragile earthenware, obliged to journey in company with many vessels of iron. Hence he had very easily acquiesced in his parents' wish to make him a priest. To say the truth, he had not reflected much on the obligations and noble ends of the ministry to which he was dedicating himself: to ensure something to live upon with comfort, and to place himself in a class revered and powerful, seemed to him two sufficient reasons for his choice. But no class whatever provides for an individual, or secures him, beyond a certain point: and none dispenses him from forming his own particular system.

Don Abbondio, continually absorbed in thoughts about his own security, cared not at all for those advantages which risked a little to secure a great deal. His system was to escape all opposition, and to yield where he could not escape. In all the frequent contests carried on around him between the clergy and laity, in the perpetual collision between officials and the nobility, between the nobility and magistrates, between bravoes and soldiers, down to the pitched battle between two rustics, arising from a word, and decided with fists or poniards, an unarmed neutrality was his chosen position. If he were absolutely obliged to take a part, he favoured the stronger, always, however, with a reserve, and an endeavour to show the other that he was not willingly his enemy. It seemed as if he would say, 'Why did you not manage to be stronger? I would have taken your side then.' Keeping a respectful distance from the powerful; silently bearing their scorn, when capriciously shown in passing instances; answering with submission when it assumed a more serious and decided form; obliging, by his profound bows and respectful salutations, the most surly and haughty to return him a smile, when he met them by the way; the poor man had performed the voyage of sixty years without experiencing any very violent tempests.

It was not that he had not too his own little portion of gall in his disposition: and this continual exercise of endurance, this ceaseless giving reasons to others, these many bitter mouthfuls gulped down in silence, had so far exasperated it, that had he not an opportunity sometimes of giving it a little of its own way, his health would certainly have suffered. But since there were in the world, close around him, some few persons whom he knew well to be incapable of hurting, upon them he was able now and then to let out the bad humour so long pent up, and take upon himself (even he) the right to be a little fantastic, and to scold unreasonably. Besides, he was a rigid censor of those who did not guide themselves by his rules; that is, when the censure could be passed without any, the most distant, danger. Was any one beaten? he was at least imprudent;—any one murdered? he had always been a turbulent meddler. If any one, having tried to maintain his right against some powerful noble, came off with a broken head, Don Abbondio always knew how to discover some fault; a thing not difficult, since right and wrong are never divided with so clean a cut, that one party has the whole of either. Above all, he declaimed against any of his brethren, who, at their own risk, took the part of the weak and oppressed against the powerful oppressor. This he called paying for quarrels, and giving one's legs to the dogs: he even pronounced with severity upon it, as a mixing in profane things, to the loss of dignity to the sacred ministry. Against such men he discoursed (always, however, with his eyes about him, or in a retired corner) with greater vehemence in proportion as he knew them to be strangers to anxiety about their personal safety. He had, finally, a favourite sentence, with which he always wound up discourses on these matters, that a respectable man who looked to himself, and minded his own business, could always keep clear of mischievous quarrels.

My five-and-twenty readers may imagine what impression such an encounter as has been related above would make on the mind of this pitiable being. The fearful aspect of those faces; the great words; the threats of a Signor known for never threatening in vain; a system of living in quiet, the patient study of so many years, upset in a moment; and, in prospect, a path narrow and rugged, from which no exit could be seen,—all these thoughts buzzed about tumultuously in the downcast head of Don Abbondio. 'If Renzo could be dismissed in peace with a mere *no,* it is all plain; but he would want reasons; and what am I to say to him? and —and—and he is a lamb, quiet as a lamb if no one touches him, but if he were contradicted . . . whew! and then—out of his senses about this Lucia, in love over head and . . . These young men, who fall in love for want of something to do, *will* be married, and think nothing about other people, they do not care anything for the trouble they bring upon a poor curate. Unfortunate me! What possible business had these two frightful figures to put themselves in *my* path, and interfere with *me?* Is it I who want to be married? Why did they not rather go and talk with . . . Let me see: what a great misfortune it is that the right plan never comes into my head till it is too late! If I had but thought of suggesting to them to carry their message to . . .' But at this point it occurred to him that to repent of not having been aider and abettor in iniquity, was itself iniquitous; and he turned his angry thoughts upon the man who had come, in this manner, to rob him of his peace. He knew Don Rodrigo only by sight and by report; nor had he had to do with him further than to make a lowly reverence when he had chanced to meet him. It had fallen to him several times to defend this Signor against those who, with subdued voice and looks of fear, wished ill to some of his enterprises. He had said a hundred times that he was a respectable cavalier; but at this moment he bestowed upon him all those epithets which he had never heard applied by others without an exclamation of disapprobation. Amid the tumult of these thoughts he reached his own door—hastily applied the key which he held in his hand, opened, entered, carefully closed it behind him, and anxious to find himself in trust-worthy company, called quickly, 'Perpetua, Perpetua!' as he went towards the dining-room, where he was sure to find Perpetua laying the cloth for supper.

Perpetua, as every one already knows, was Don Abbondio's servant, a servant affectionate and faithful, who knew how to obey and command in turn as occasion required—to bear, in season, the grumblings and fancies of her master, and to make him bear the like when her turn came; which day by day recurred more frequently, since she had passed the sinodal age of forty, remaining single, because, as she said herself, she had refused all offers, or because she had never found any one goose enough to have her, as her friends said.

'I am coming,' replied Perpetua, putting down in its usual place a little flask of Don Abbondio's favourite wine, and moving leisurely. But before she reached the door of the dining-room, he entered, with a step so unsteady, with an expression so overcast, with features so disturbed, that there had been no need of Perpetua's experienced eye to discover at a glance that something very extraordinary had happened.

'Mercy! what has happened to you, master?'

'Nothing, nothing,' replied Don Abbondio, sinking down breathless on his arm-chair.

'How nothing! Would you make me believe this, so disordered as you are? Some great misfortune has happened.'

'Oh, for Heaven's sake! When I say nothing, either it is nothing, or it is something I cannot tell.'

'Not tell, even to me? Who will take care of your safety, sir? who will advise you?'

'Oh, dear! hold your tongue, and say no more; give me a glass of my wine.'

'And you will persist, sir, that it is nothing!' said Perpetua, filling the glass; and then holding it in her hand, as if she would give it in payment for the confidence he kept her waiting for so long.

'Give it here, give it here,' said Don Abbondio, taking the glass from her with no very steady hand, and emptying it hastily, as if it were a draught of medicine.

'Do you wish me, then, sir, to be obliged to ask here and there, what has happened to my master?' said Perpetua, right opposite him, with her arms akimbo, looking steadily at him, as if she would gather the truth from his eyes.

'For Heaven's sake! let us have no brawling—let us have no noise: it is . . . it is my life!'

'Your life!'

'My life.'

'You know, sir, that whenever you have told me any thing sincerely in confidence, I have never . . .'

'Well done! for instance, when . . .'

Perpetua saw she had touched a wrong chord; wherefore, suddenly changing her tone, 'Signor, master,' she said, with a softened and affecting voice, 'I have always been an affectionate servant to you, sir; and if I wish to know this, it is because of my care for you, because I wish to be able to help you, to give you good advice, and to comfort you.'

The fact was, Don Abbondio was, perhaps, just as anxious to get rid of his burdensome secret, as Perpetua was to know it. In consequence, after having rebutted, always more feebly, her reiterated and more vigorous assaults, after having made her vow more than once not to breathe the subject, with many sighs and many doleful exclamations, he related at last the miserable event. When he came to the terrible name, it was necessary for Perpetua to make new and more solemn vows of silence; and Don Abbondio, having pronounced this name, sank back on the chair, lifting up his hands in act at once of command and entreaty—exclaiming, 'For heaven's sake!'

'Mercy!' exclaimed Perpetua, 'Oh, what a wretch! Oh, what a tyrant! Oh, what a godless man!'

'Will you hold your tongue? or do you wish to ruin me altogether?'

'Why, we're all alone: no one can hear us. But what will you do, sir? Oh, my poor master!'

'You see now, you see,' said Don Abbondio, in an angry tone, 'what good advice this woman can give me! She comes and asks me what shall I do, what shall I do, as if she were in a quandary, and it were my place to help her out.'

'But I could even give my poor opinion; but then . . .'

'*But then,* let us hear.'

'My advice would be, since, as everybody says, our Archbishop is a saint, a bold-hearted man, and one who is not afraid of an ugly face, and one who glories in upholding a poor curate against these tyrants, when he has an opportunity,—I should say, and I do say, that you should write a nice letter to inform him how that . . .'

'Will you hold your tongue? will you be silent? Is this fit advice to give a poor man? When a bullet was lodged in my back, (Heaven defend me!) would the Archbishop dislodge it?'

'Why! bullets don't fly in showers like comfits.[2] Woe to us if these dogs could bite whenever they bark. And I have always taken notice that whoever knows how to show his teeth, and makes use of them, is treated with respect; and just because master will never give his reasons, we are come to that pass, that every one comes to us, if I may say it to . . .'

'Will you hold your tongue?'

'I will directly; but it is, however, certain, that when all the world sees a man always, in every encounter, ready to yield the . . .'

'Will you hold your tongue? Is this a time for such nonsensical words?'

'Very well: you can think about it to-night; but now, don't be doing any mischief to yourself; don't be making yourself ill—take a mouthful to eat.'

'Think about it, shall I?' grumbled Don Abbondio, 'to be sure I shall think about it. I've got it to think about;' and he got up, going on; 'I will take nothing, nothing: I have something else to do. I know, too, what I ought to think about it. But, that this should have come on *my* head!'

---

[2] It is a custom in Italy, during the carnival, for friends to salute each other with showers of comfits, as they pass in the streets.

'Swallow at least this other little drop,' said Perpetua, pouring it out; 'you know, sir, this always strengthens your stomach.'

'Ah, we want another strengthener—another—another—'

So saying, he took the candle, and constantly grumbling, 'A nice little business to a man like me! and to-morrow, what is to be done?' with other like lamentations, went to his chamber, to lie down. When he had reached the door, he paused a moment, turned round and laid his finger on his lips, pronouncing slowly and solemnly, 'For Heaven's sake!' and disappeared.

CHAPTER II

IT is related that the Prince Condé slept soundly the night before the battle of Rocroi. But, in the first place, he was very tired, and, secondly, he had given all needful previous orders, and arranged what was to be done on the morrow. Don Abbondio, on the other hand, as yet knew nothing, except that the morrow would be a day of battle: hence great part of the night was spent by him in anxious and harassing deliberations. To take no notice of the lawless intimation, and proceed with the marriage, was a plan on which he would not even expend a thought. To confide the occurrence to Renzo, and seek with him some means . . . he dreaded the thought! 'he must not let a word escape . . . otherwise . . . *ehm!*': thus one of the bravoes had spoken, and at the re-echoing of this *ehm!* Don Abbondio, far from thinking of transgressing such a law, began to repent of having revealed it to Perpetua. Must he fly! Whither? And then, how many annoyances, how many reasons to give! As he rejected plan after plan, the unfortunate man tossed from side to side in bed. The course which seemed best to him was to gain time, by imposing on Renzo. He opportunely remembered that it wanted only a few days of the time when weddings were prohibited.[1]—'And if I can only put him off for these few days, I have then two months before me, and in two months great things may be done.'—He ruminated over various pretexts to bring into play: and though they appeared to him rather slight, yet he reassured himself with the thought that his authority added to them would make them appear of sufficient weight, and then his practised experience would give him great advantage over an ignorant youth. 'Let us see,' he said to himself, 'he thinks of his love, but I of my life; I am more interested than he: beside that I am cleverer. My dear child, if you feel your back smarting, I know not what to say; but I will not put my foot in it.' —His mind being thus a little settled to deliberation, he was able

[1] *i. e.* Lent.

at last to close his eyes; but what sleep! What dreams! Bravoes,
Don Rodrigo, Renzo, pathways, rocks, flight, chase, cries, muskets!

The moment of first awaking after a misfortune, while still in
perplexity, is a bitter one. The mind scarcely restored to consciousness, returns to the habitual idea of former tranquillity: but the
thought of the new state of things soon presents itself with rude
abruptness; and our misfortune is most trying in this moment of
contrast. Dolefully Don Abbondio tasted the bitterness of this
moment, and then began hastily to recapitulate the designs of the
night, confirmed himself in them, arranged them anew, arose, and
waited for Renzo at once with fear and impatience.

Lorenzo, or, as every one called him, Renzo, did not keep him
long waiting. Scarcely had the hour arrived at which he thought he
could with propriety present himself to the Curate, when he set
off with the light step of a man of twenty, who was on that day to
espouse her whom he loved. He had in early youth been deprived
of his parents, and carried on the trade of silk-weaver, hereditary,
so to say, in his family; a trade lucrative enough in former years,
but even then beginning to decline, yet not to such a degree, that a
clever workman was not able to make an honest livelihood by it.
Work became more scarce from day to day, but the continual
emigration of the workmen, attracted to the neighbouring states
by promises, privileges, and large wages, left sufficient occupation
for those who remained in the country. Renzo possessed, besides,
a plot of land, which he cultivated, working in it himself when he
was disengaged from his silk-weaving, so that in his station he
might be called a rich man. Although this year was one of greater
scarcity than those which had preceded it, and real want began
to be felt already, yet he, having become a saver of money ever
since he had cast his eyes upon Lucia, found himself sufficiently
furnished with provisions, and had no need to beg his bread. He
appeared before Don Abbondio in gay bridal costume, with feathers
of various colours in his cap, with an ornamental-hilted dagger in
his pocket; and with an air of festivity, and at the same time of defiance, common at that time even to men the most quiet. The
hesitating and mysterious reception of Don Abbondio formed a
strange contrast with the joyous and resolute bearing of the young

He must have got some notion in his head, thought Renzo to himself, and then said: 'I have come, Signor Curate, to know at what hour it will suit you for us to be at church.'

'What day are you speaking of?'

'How! of what day? Don't you remember, sir, that this is the day fixed upon?'

'To-day?' replied Don Abbondio, as if he now heard it spoken of for the first time. 'To-day, to-day . . . don't be impatient, but to-day I cannot.'

'To-day you cannot! What has happened, sir?'

'First of all, I do not feel well, you see.'

'I am very sorry, but what you have to do, sir, is so soon done, and so little fatiguing . . .'

'And then, and then, and then . . .'

'And then what, Signor Curate?'

'And then, there are difficulties.'

'Difficulties! What difficulties can there be?'

'You need to stand in our shoes, to understand what perplexities we have in these matters, what reasons to give. I am too soft-hearted, I think of nothing but how to remove obstacles, and make all easy, and arrange things to please others; I neglect my duty, and then I am subject to reproofs, and worse.'

'But in Heaven's name, don't keep me so on the stretch—tell me at once what is the matter?'

'Do you know how many, many formalities are necessary to perform a marriage regularly?'

'I ought to know a little about it,' said Renzo, beginning to be warm, 'for you, sir, have puzzled my head enough about it, the last few days back. But now is not everything made clear? Is not everything done that had to be done?'

'All, all, on your part: therefore, have patience; an ass I am to neglect my duty that I may not give pain to people. We poor curates are between the anvil and the hammer; you are impatient; I am sorry for you, poor young man; and the great people . . . enough, one must not say everything. And *we* have to go between.'

'But explain to me at once, sir, what this new formality is, which has to be gone through, as you say; and it shall be done soon.'

'Do you know what the number of absolute impediments is?'

'What would you have me know about impediments, sir?'

'*Error, conditio, votum, cognatio, crimen, cultus disparitas, vis, ordo . . . Si sit affinis . . .*'

'Are you making game of me, sir? What do you expect me to know about your latinorum?'

'Then, if you don't understand things, have patience, and leave them to those who do.'

'*Or sù! . . .*'

'Quiet, my dear Renzo, don't get in a passion, for I am ready to do . . . all that depends on me. I, I wish to see you satisfied; I wish you well. Alas! . . . when I think how well off you were; what were you wanting? The whim of getting married came upon you . . .'

'What talk is this, Signor mio,' interrupted Renzo, with a voice between astonishment and anger.

'Have patience, I tell you. I wish to see you satisfied.'

'In short . . .'

'In short, my son, it is no fault of mine. I did not make the law; and before concluding a marriage, it is our special duty to certify ourselves that there is no impediment.'

'But come, tell me once for all what impediment has come in the way?'

'Have patience, they are not things to be deciphered thus at a standing. It will be nothing to us, I hope; but, be the consequence great or little, we must make these researches. The text is clear and evident; *antequam matrimonium denunciet . . .*'

'I have told you, sir, I will have no Latin.'

'But it is necessary that I should explain to you . . .'

'But have you not made all these researches?'

'I tell you, I have not made them all, as I must.'

'Why did you not do it in time, sir? Why did you tell me that all was finished? Why wait . . .'

'Look now! you are finding fault with my over-kindness. I have facilitated everything to serve you without loss of time: but . . . but now I have received . . . enough, I know.'

'And what do you wish me to do, sir?'

'To have patience for a few days. My dear son, a few days are not eternity: have patience.'

'For how long?'

—We are in good train now, thought Don Abbondio to himself: and added with a more polite manner than ever: 'Come now, in fifteen days I will endeavour to do . . .'

'Fifteen days! This indeed is something new! You have had everything your own way, sir; you fixed the day; the day arrives; and now you go tell me I must wait fifteen days. Fifteen . . .' he began again, with a louder and more angry voice, extending his arm and striking the air with his fist; and nobody knows what shocking words he would have added to this number fifteen, if Don Abbondio had not interrupted him, taking his other hand with a timid and anxious friendliness: 'Come, come, don't be angry, for Heaven's sake. I will see, I will try whether in one week . . .'

'And Lucia, what must I say to her?'

'That it has been an oversight of mine.'

'And what will the world say?'

'Tell them too, that I have made a blunder through overhaste, through too much good nature: lay all the fault on me. Can I say more? Come now, for one week.'

'And then will there be no more impediments?'

'When I tell you . . .'

'Very well: I will be quiet for a week; but I know well enough that when it is passed, I shall get nothing but talk. But before that I shall see you again.' Having so said he retired, making a bow much less lowly than usual, to Don Abbondio, and bestowing on him a glance more expressive than reverent.

Having reached the road, and walking with a heavy heart towards the home of his betrothed, in the midst of his wrath, he turned his thoughts on the late conversation, and more and more strange it seemed to him. The cold and constrained greeting of Don Abbondio; his guarded and yet impatient words, his grey eyes, which, as he spoke, glanced inquisitively here and there, as if afraid of coming in contact with the words which issued from his mouth, the making a new thing, as it were, of the nuptials so expressly determined, and above all, the constant hinting at some great occurrence, without

ever saying anything decided,—all these things put together made
Renzo think that there was some overhanging mystery, different
from that which Don Abbondio would have had him suppose. The
youth was just on the point of turning back, to oblige him to speak
more plainly; but raising his eyes, he saw Perpetua a little way before
him, entering a garden[2] a few paces distant from the house. He
gave her a call to open the garden door for him, quickened his pace,
came up with her, detained her in the door-way, and stood still to
have a conversation with her, intending to discover something more
positive.

'Good morning, Perpetua: I hoped we should have been merry
to-day altogether.'

'But! as Heaven wills, my poor Renzo . . .'

'I want you to do me a kindness. The Signor Curate has been
making a long story of certain reasons, which I cannot understand;
will you explain to me better why he cannot or will not marry us
to-day?'

'Oh! is it likely I know my master's secrets?'

—I said there was some hidden mystery, thought Renzo; and to
draw it forth to the light, he continued: 'Come, Perpetua, we are
friends; tell me what you know, help an unfortunate youth.'

'It is a bad thing to be born poor, my dear Renzo.'

'That is true,' replied he, still confirming himself in his suspicions,
and seeking to come nearer the question, 'that is true; but is it for
a priest to deal hardly with the poor?'

'Listen, Renzo, I can tell you nothing; because . . . I know nothing; but what you may assure yourself of, is, that my master does not
wish to ill-treat you, or anybody; and it is not his fault.'

'Whose fault is it then?' demanded Renzo, with an air of indifference, but with an anxious heart, and ears on the alert.

'When I tell you I know nothing . . . In defence of my master
I can speak; because I can't bear to hear that he is ready to do ill
to any one. Poor man! if he does wrong, it is from too good
nature. There certainly are some wretches in the world, overbearing
tyrants, men without the fear of God . . .'

---

[2] To understand this scene fully, the reader must bear in mind that the Italian
gardens are, almost invariably, surrounded by a wall seven or eight feet high.

—Tyrants! wretches! thought Renzo: are not these the great men? 'Come,' said he, with difficulty hiding his increasing agitation, 'come, tell me who it is.'

'Oh, oh! you want to make me speak; and I cannot speak, because . . . I know nothing: when I know nothing, it is the same as if I had taken an oath not to tell. You might put me to the rack, and you would get nothing from my mouth. Good-bye; it is lost time for you and me both.'

So saying, she quickly entered the garden, and shut the door. Renzo, having returned her farewell, turned back, with a quiet step, that she might not hear which way he took; but when he got beyond reach of the good woman's ears, he quickened his pace; in a moment he was at Don Abbondio's door, entered, went straight to the room in which he had left him, found him there, and went towards him with a reckless bearing, and eyes glancing anger.

'Eh! eh! what new thing is this?' said Don Abbondio.

'Who is that tyrant,' said Renzo, with the voice of a man who is determined to obtain a precise reply, 'who is the tyrant who is unwilling that I should marry Lucia?'

'What? what? what?' stammered the astonished poor man, his face in a moment becoming pale, and colourless as a rag just emerged from the washing-tub: then, still stammering, he made a start from his arm-chair, to dart towards the door. But Renzo, who might have expected this movement, was on the alert, sprang there before him, locked it, and put the key in his pocket.

'Ah! ah! Will you speak *now,* Signor Curato? Everybody knows my affairs, except myself. But, by Bacchus, I too will know. What is his name?'

'Renzo! Renzo! for charity, take care what you are about; think of your soul.'

'I *am* thinking that I will know it quickly, in a moment.' And as he spoke, perhaps without being aware of it, he laid his hand on the hilt of the dagger which projected from his pocket.

'*Misericordia!*' exclaimed Don Abbondio, in a feeble voice.

'I will know it.'

'Who has told you? . . .'

'No, no; no more trickery. Speak positively and quickly.'

'Do you wish me to be killed?'

'I wish to know what I have a right to know.'

'But if I speak, I'm a dead man! Surely I'm not to trample on my own life?'

'*Then* speak.'

This *then* was pronounced with such energy, and Renzo's face became so threatening, that Don Abbondio could no longer entertain a hope of the possibility of disobedience.

'Promise me—swear to me,' said he, 'not to speak of it to any one, never to tell . . .'

'I promise you, sir, that I will do an ill deed, if you don't tell me quick—quick, his name!'

At this new adjuration, Don Abbondio, with the face and look of a man who has the pincers of the dentist in his mouth, articulated, 'Don . . .'

'Don?' repeated Renzo, as if to help the patient to utter the rest; while he stood bending forward, his ear turned towards the open mouth of Don Abbondio, his arms stretched out, and his clinched fists behind him.

'Don Rodrigo!' hastily uttered the compelled curate, making a rush at these few syllables, and gliding over the consonants, partly through excitement, partly because exercising the little judgment that was left him, to steer his way betwixt the two fears, it appeared that he wished to withdraw the word and make it invisible at the very moment he was constrained to give utterance to it.

'Ah, dog!' shouted Renzo; 'and how has he done it? And what has he said to . . .?'

'How, eh? how?' replied Don Abbondio, in an indignant voice, as it were; feeling after so great a sacrifice, that he had, in a manner, become a creditor, 'How, eh? I wish it had happened to you, as it has to me, who have not put my foot in it for nothing; for then, certainly, you would not have so many crotchets in your head.' And here he began to depict in dreadful colours the terrible encounter. As he proceeded in the description, he began to realize the wrath which hitherto had been concealed, or changed into fear; and perceiving at the same time that Renzo, between anger and confusion, stood motionless, with his head downwards, he continued triumphantly: 'You have done a pretty deed! Nice treatment you have given me! To serve such a trick to an honest man, to your curate —in his own house—in a sacred place! You have done a fine action, to force from my lips my own ruin and yours, that which I concealed from you in prudence for your own good! And now, when you do know it, how much wiser are you? I should like to know what you would have done to me! No joking here, no question of right and wrong, but mere force. And this morning, when I gave you good advice . . . eh! in a rage directly. I had judgment enough for myself, and you too; but how does it go now? Open the door, however; give me my key.'

'I may have been wrong,' replied Renzo, with a voice softened towards Don Abbondio, but in which suppressed rage against his newly discovered enemy might be perceived; 'I may have been wrong; but put your hand to your heart, and think whether in my case . . .'

So saying, he took the key from his pocket, and went to open the door. Don Abbondio stood behind; and while Renzo turned the key in the lock, he came beside him, and with a serious and anxious face, holding up three fingers of his right hand, as if to help him in his turn, 'Swear at least . . .' said he.

'I may have been wrong, and I beg your pardon, sir,' answered Renzo, opening the door, and preparing to go out.

'Swear . . .' replied Don Abbondio, seizing him by the arm with a trembling hand.

'I may have been wrong,' repeated Renzo, as he extricated himself from him, and departed with vehement haste, thus cutting short a discussion which, like many a question of philosophy, or literature, or something else, might have been prolonged six centuries, since each party did nothing but repeat his own arguments.

'Perpetua!—Perpetua!' cried Don Abbondio, after having in vain called back the fugitive. Perpetua answered not: Don Abbondio then lost all consciousness of where he was.

It has happened more than once to personages of much greater importance than Don Abbondio, to find themselves in extremities so trying to the flesh, in such perplexity of plans, that it has appeared to them their best resource to go to bed with a fever. This resource

Don Abbondio had not to seek for, because it offered itself to him of its own accord. The fright of the day before, the harassing sleeplessness of the night, the additional fright in the morning, anxiety about the future, had produced this effect. Perplexed and bewildered, he rested himself on his arm-chair: he began to feel a certain quaking of the bones; he looked at his nails and sighed, and called from time to time, with a tremulous and anxious voice—'Perpetua!' Perpetua arrived at length, with a great cabbage under her arm, and a business-like face, as if nothing had been the matter. I spare the reader the lamentations, condolences, accusations, defences, the—'You only can have spoken,' and the—'I have not spoken' —all the recriminations, in short, of this colloquy. Let it suffice to say, that Don Abbondio ordered Perpetua to fasten the doors well: not to put foot outside; and if any one knocked, to answer from the window, that the curate was confined to his bed with a fever. He then slowly ascended the stairs, repeating at every third step, 'I have caught it!' and really went to bed, where we will leave him.

Renzo, meanwhile, walked with an excited step towards home, without having determined what he ought to do, but with a mad longing to do something strange and terrible. The unjust and oppressive, all those, in fact, who wrong others, are guilty, not only of the evil they do, but also of the perversion of mind they cause in those whom they offend. Renzo was a young man of peaceful disposition, and averse to violence; sincere, and one who abhorred deceit; but at this moment, his heart panted for murder: his mind was occupied only in devising a plot. He would have wished to hasten to Don Rodrigo's house, to seize him by the throat, and . . . but he remembered that his house was like a fortress, garrisoned with bravoes within, and guarded without; that only friends and servants, well known, could enter freely, without being searched from head to foot; that an artisan, if unknown, could not put foot within it without an examination; and that he, above all . . . he probably would be too well known. He then fancied himself taking his fowling-piece, planting himself behind a hedge, looking out whether his enemy would ever, ever pass by, unaccompanied; and dwelling with ferocious complacency on this thought, he imagined the sound of a step; at this sound he raises his head without noise; recognizes the wretch, raises the fowling-piece, takes aim—fires; sees him fall and struggle, bestows a malediction on him, and escapes in safety beyond the borders.—And Lucia?—Scarcely had this word come across these dreadful phantasies, when the better thoughts, with which Renzo was familiarized, crowded into his mind. He recalled the dying charge of his parents. The thought of God, of the Blessed Virgin, and of the saints, returned upon him; he remembered the consolation he had so often experienced from the recollection that he was free from crimes; he remembered the horror with which he had so often received the news of a murder; and he awoke from this dream of blood with fear, with remorse, and yet with a sort of joy that he had but imagined it. But the thought of Lucia —how many thoughts it brought along with it! So many hopes, so many promises, a future so bright, so secure, and this day so longed for! And how, with what words announce to her such news? And afterwards, what was to be done? How were their plans to be accomplished, in spite of this powerful and wicked enemy? Along with all this, not a defined suspicion, but a tormenting shadow flitted every moment through his mind. This overbearing act of Don Rodrigo could have no motive but a lawless passion for Lucia. And Lucia! could she have given him the smallest encouragement, the most distant hope? It was a thought which could not dwell for an instant in his mind. But was she aware of it? Could he have conceived this infamous passion without her perceiving it? Could he have carried matters so far, without having made an attempt in some other manner? And Lucia had never mentioned a word of it to him, her betrothed!

Overcome by these thoughts, he passed by his own house, which was situated in the middle of the village, and proceeding through it, came to that of Lucia, which stood at the opposite end. This cottage had a little garden in front, which separated it from the road; and the garden was surrounded by a low wall. As Renzo entered the garden, he heard a confused and continual murmur of voices from an upper room. He supposed it was friends and companions come to greet Lucia; and he did not wish to show himself to this company with the sad news he had to communicate visible in his face. A little girl, who happened to be in the garden, ran to meet him, crying, 'The bridegroom! the bridegroom!'

'Gently, Bettina, gently!' said Renzo. 'Come here; go up to Lucia, take her on one side and whisper in her ear . . . but mind no one hears, or suspects . . . tell her I want to speak to her, and that I'm waiting in the down-stairs room, and that she must come immediately.' The child ran quickly up-stairs, delighted and proud to be entrusted with a secret.

Lucia had just come forth adorned from head to foot by the hands of her mother. Her friends were stealing glances at the bride, and forcing her to show herself; while she, with the somewhat warlike modesty of a rustic, was endeavouring to escape, using her arms as a shield for her face, and holding her head downwards, her black pencilled eyebrows seeming to frown, while her lips were smiling. Her dark and luxuriant hair, divided on her forehead with a white and narrow parting, was united behind in many-circled plaitings, pierced with long silver pins, disposed around, so as to look like an aureola, or saintly glory, a fashion still in use among the Milanese peasant-girls. Round her neck she had a necklace of garnets, alternated with beads of filigree gold. She wore a pretty bodice of flowered brocade, laced with coloured ribbons, a short gown of embroidered silk, plaited in close and minute folds, scarlet stockings, and a pair of shoes also of embroidered silk. Besides these, which were the special ornaments of her wedding-day, Lucia had the every-day ornament of a modest beauty, displayed at this time, and increased by the varied feelings which were depicted in her face: joy tempered by a slight confusion, that placid sadness which occasionally shows itself on the face of a bride, and without injuring her beauty, gives it an air peculiar to itself. The little Bettina made her way among the talkers, came close up to Lucia, cleverly made her understand that she had something to communicate, and whispered her little message in her ear. 'I am going for a moment, and will be back directly,' said Lucia to her friends, and hastily descended the stairs.

On seeing the changed look and the unquiet manner of Renzo, 'What is the matter?' she exclaimed, not without a presentiment of terror.

'Lucia!' replied Renzo, 'it is all up for to-day; and God knows when we can be man and wife.'

'What?' said Lucia, altogether amazed. Renzo briefly related to her the events of the morning; she listened in great distress; and when she heard the name of Don Rodrigo, 'Ah!' she exclaimed, blushing and trembling, 'has it come to this point!'

'Then you knew it? . . .' said Renzo.

'Indeed too well,' answered Lucia, 'but to this point!'

'What did you know about it?'

'Don't make me speak now, don't make me cry. I will run and call my mother, and send away the girls. We must be alone.'

While she was going, Renzo murmured, 'You never told me anything about it.'

'Ah, Renzo!' replied Lucia, turning round for a moment without stopping. Renzo understood very well that his name so pronounced by Lucia, at that moment, in such a tone, meant to say, Can *you* doubt that I could be silent, except on just and pure motives?

By this time the good Agnese—(so Lucia's mother was named), incited to suspicion and curiosity by the whisper in her ear,—had come down to see what was the matter. Her daughter, leaving her with Renzo, returned to the assembled maidens, and, composing her voice and manner as well as she could, said, 'The Signor Curate is ill, and nothing will be done to-day.' This said, she hastily bid them good-bye, and went down again. The company departed, and dispersed themselves through the village, to recount what had happened, and to discover whether Don Abbondio was really ill. The truth of the fact cut short all the conjectures which had already begun to work in their minds, and to be discovered undefined and mysteriously in their words.

CHAPTER III

WHILE Renzo was relating with pain what Agnese with pain listened to, Lucia entered the room. They both turned towards her: she indeed knew more about it than they, and of her they awaited in explanation which could not but be distressing. In the midst of their sorrow they both, according to the different nature of the love they bore Lucia, discovered in their own manner a degree of anger that she had concealed anything from them, especially of such a nature. Agnese, although anxious to hear her daughter speak, could not refrain from a slight reproof, 'To say nothing to your mother in such a case!'

'Now I will tell you all,' answered Lucia, as she dried her eyes with her apron.

'Speak, speak!—Speak, speak!' at once cried both mother and lover.

'Most Holy Virgin!' exclaimed Lucia, 'who could have believed it would have come to this!' Then with a voice tremulous with weeping, she related how, as she was returning from her spinning, and had loitered behind her companions, Don Rodrigo, in company with another gentleman, had passed by her; that he had tried to engage her in foolish talk, as she called it; but she, without giving him an answer, had quickened her pace, and joined her companions; then she had heard the other gentleman laugh loudly, and Don Rodrigo say, 'I'll lay you a wager.' The next day they were again on the road, but Lucia was in the midst of her companions with her eyes on the ground; when the other gentleman laughed, and Don Rodrigo said, 'We shall see, we shall see.' 'This day,' continued Lucia, 'thank God, was the last of the spinning. I related immediately . . .'

'Who was it you told it to?' demanded Agnese, waiting, not without a little displeasure, for the name of the confidante who had been preferred.

'To father Cristoforo, in confession, mamma,' replied Lucia, with

38

a sweet tone of apology. 'I related the whole to him, the last time we went to church together, at the convent: and if you noticed, that morning I kept putting my hand to one thing and another, to pass the time till other people were on the road, that we might go in company with them; because, after that meeting, the roads make me so frightened.'

At the reverend name of father Cristoforo, the wrath of Agnese subsided. 'You did well,' said she; 'but why not tell all to your mother also?'

Lucia had had two good reasons: one not to distress and frighten the good woman, about an event against which she could have found no remedy; the other not to run the risk of a story travelling from mouth to mouth, which she wished to be kept with jealous silence; the more so because Lucia hoped that her marriage would have cut short at the beginning this abominated persecution. Of these two reasons she alleged only the first. 'And to you,' said she, turning to Renzo, with that tone which reminds a friend that he is unreasonable: 'And to you *could* I speak about this? Surely you know too much of it now!'

'And what did the father say to you?' asked Agnese.

'He told me that I must try to hasten the wedding as much as I could, and in the mean time to keep myself within-doors; that I should pray to the Lord; and he hoped that this man, if he did not see me, would not care any more about me. And it was then that I forced myself,' continued she, turning again towards Renzo, without however raising her eyes, and blushing to the temples, 'it was then that I put on a too-bold face, and begged you to get it done soon, and have it concluded before the fixed time. Who knows what you must have thought of me! But I did it for good, and it was advised me, and I thought for certain . . . and this morning I was so far from thinking . . .'

Here Lucia's words were cut short by a violent burst of tears.

'Ah, rascal! wretch! murderer!' exclaimed Renzo, striding backwards and forwards across the room, and grasping from time to time the hilt of his dagger.

'Oh, heavens, what a fury!' exclaimed Agnese. The young man suddenly drew himself up before Lucia, who was weeping, looked at her with an anxious and embittered tenderness, and said, 'This is the last deed this assassin shall do.'

'Ah, no, Renzo, for Heaven's sake!' cried Lucia; 'no, no, for Heaven's sake! God is on the side of the poor, and how can we expect him to help us if we do wrong?'

'No, no, for Heaven's sake!' echoed Agnese.

'Renzo,' said Lucia, with an air of hope and more tranquil resolution, 'you have a trade, and I know how to work; let us go so far off that this man will hear no more about us.'

'Ah, Lucia! and what then? We are not yet man and wife! Will the curate give us a certificate of no impediment, such a man as he is? If we were married, oh then! . . .'

Lucia began to weep again, and all three remained silent, giving signs of depression which contrasted strangely with the festive gaiety of their dress.

'Listen, my children; attend to me,' said Agnese, after some moments; 'I came into the world long before you; and I know something about the world. You need not frighten yourselves too much: things are not so bad as people make out. To us poor people the skein seems more entangled because we cannot get hold of the right end; but sometimes a piece of good advice, a little talk with a man who has got learning . . . I know well enough what I would say. Do as I tell you, Renzo; go to Lecco, seek for Dr Azzecca-Garbugli,[1] tell him all about it,—but mind you don't call him so, for Heaven's sake: it's a nick-name. You must tell the Signor Doctor—What in the world do they call him? Oh dear! I don't know his right name: everybody calls him so. Never mind, seek for this doctor; he is tall, thin, bald, with a red nose and a raspberry-coloured mole on his cheek.'

'I know him by sight,' said Renzo.

'Well,' continued Agnese, 'he *is* a man! I have seen more than one person, bothered like a chicken in a bundle of hemp, and who did not know where to put his head, and after being an hour nose to nose with the Dr Azzecca-Garbugli, (take good care *you* don't call him so)—I have seen him, I say, make a joke of it. Take these four capons, poor creatures! whose necks I ought to have wrung for to-

[1] *i. e.,* a picker of quarrels.

night's supper, and carry them to him; because we must never go empty-handed to these gentlemen. Relate to him all that has happened, and you'll see he will tell you, in a twinkling, things which would not come into our heads if we were to think about them for a year.'

Renzo willingly embraced this counsel; Lucia approved it; and Agnese, proud of having given it, took the poor creatures one by one from the hen-coop, united their eight legs, as one makes up a bunch of flowers, tied them up with a piece of string, and consigned them to the hands of Renzo, who, after giving and receiving words of encouragement and hope, went out by a little gate from the garden, that he might escape the observation of the boys, who would have run after him, crying, 'The bridegroom! the bridegroom!' Thus, having crossed the fields, or, as they call them there, *the places,* he continued his route along narrow lanes, giving utterance to his bitter thoughts, as he reflected on his misfortune, and considering what he must say to the Dr Azzecca-Garbugli. I leave it to the reader to think how the journey was enjoyed by those poor creatures, so bound together, and held by the feet with their heads downwards, in the hand of a man who, agitated by so many passions, accompanied with appropriate gestures the thoughts which rushed tumultuously through his mind; and in moments of anger or determination, suddenly extending his arm, inflicted terrible shocks upon them, and caused those four pendent heads to *bob* violently, if we may be allowed the expression; they, meanwhile, vigorously applying themselves to peck each other, as too often happens among friends in adversity.

Arriving at the village, he inquired for the Doctor's house, and when it was pointed out to him, quickly made his way thither. On approaching it, however, he began to feel that bashfulness so usual with the poor and ignorant in the presence of a gentleman or man of learning, and forgot all the fine speeches he had prepared; but a glance at the chickens he carried in his hand restored his courage. He went into the kitchen, and asked the maid-servant if he could see the Signor Doctor. The woman looked at the birds, and, as if accustomed to such presents, was about to take them in her hand, but Renzo held them back, because he wanted the Doctor to see he

had brought something with him. Just at this moment, the wished-
for personage made his appearance, as the servant was saying, 'Give
them here, and go forward to the study.' Renzo made a low bow
to the Doctor, who graciously bid him 'Come in, my son,' and took
him into his study. It was a large room, decorated on three sides
with portraits of the twelve Cæsars; the remaining wall was hidden
by a large bookcase, filled with old and dusty books: in the middle
of the room stood a table covered with extracts, petitions, libels, and
proclamations: three or four chairs were scattered around, and on
one side was a large arm-chair, with a high square back, terminating
at the corners in two horn-shaped ornaments of wood, and covered
with leather, fastened down with large nails. Some of these had
fallen out, so that the leather curled up here and there at pleasure,
leaving the corners unencumbered. The Doctor was in his dressing-
gown; that is to say, he had on a faded robe, which had served him
for many years to harangue in on days of state, when he went to
Milan on any important cause. Having shut the door, he re-animated
the young man's confidence with these words: 'Tell me your case,
my son.'

'I wish to speak a word to you in confidence.'

'I'm ready—speak,' replied the Doctor, seating himself on his arm-
chair.

Renzo stood before the table, and twirling his hat with his right
hand round the other, continued: 'I want to know from you, who
have studied . . .'

'Tell the case as it is,' interrupted the Doctor.

'Excuse me, Signor Doctor: we poor people don't know how to
speak properly. I want, then, to know . . .'

'Blessed set you are! You are all alike. Instead of relating your
case, you ask questions, because you've already made up your minds.'

'I beg your pardon, Signor Doctor. I want to know if there's any
punishment for threatening a curate, and forbidding him to celebrate
a marriage?'

'I understand,' muttered the doctor, who in truth had not understood; 'I understand.' He then put on a serious face; but it was a
seriousness mingled with an air of compassion and importance; and,
pressing his lips, he uttered an inarticulate sound, betokening a sen-

timent, afterwards more clearly expressed in his first words. 'A serious case, my son. There are laws to the point. You have done well to come to me. It is a clear case, recognized in a hundred proclamations, and . . . stay! in an edict of the last year, by the present Signor Governor. I'll let you see it and handle it directly.'

So saying, he rose from his seat, and hunted through the chaos of papers, *shovelling* the lower ones uppermost with his hands, as if he were throwing corn into a measure.

'Where can it be? Come nearer, come nearer. One is obliged to have so many things in hand! But it must surely be here, for it is a proclamation of importance. Ah! here it is, here it is!' He took it, unfolded it, looked at the date, and with a still more serious face, continued, 'The fifteenth of October, 1627. Certainly; it is last year's; a fresh proclamation; it is these that cause such fear. Can you read, my son?'

'A little, Signor Doctor.'

'Very well, follow me with your eye, and you shall see.' And holding the edict displayed in the air, he began to read, rapidly muttering some passages, and pausing distinctly, with marked emphasis, upon others, as the case required.

'*Although in the proclamation published by order of the Signor Duke of Feria, the 14th December, 1620, and confirmed by the Most Illustrious and Most Excellent Signor, the Signor Gonzalo Fernandez de Cordova, &c., there was provision made, by extraordinary and rigorous measures, against oppressions, commotions, and tyrannical acts that some persons dare to commit against the devoted subjects of his Majesty; nevertheless, the frequency of crimes and violences, &c., has increased to such a degree, that his Excellency is under the necessity, &c. Wherefore, with the concurrence of the Senate and a Council, &c., he has resolved to publish the present edict.*

'*And, to begin with tyrannical acts, experience showing, that many, as well in cities, as in the country,* Do you hear? *excite commotions in this state by violence, and oppress the weak in various ways, as, for example, by compelling them to make hard bargains in purchases, rents, &c.,* where am I? ah! here! look—*to perform or not to perform marriages;* eh!'

'That is my case,' said Renzo.

'Listen, listen; there is plenty more; and then we shall see the penalty. *To give evidence, or not to give evidence; compelling one to leave his home, &c., another to pay a debt:* all this has nothing to do with us. Ah! we have it here; *this priest not to perform that to which he is obliged by his office, or to do things which do not belong to him.* Eh!'

'It seems as if they had made the edict exactly for me.'

'Eh! is it not so? listen, listen: *and similar oppressions, whether perpetrated by feudatories, the nobility, middle ranks, lower orders, or plebeians.* No one escapes: they are all here: it is like the valley of Jehoshaphat. Listen now to the penalty. *All these, and other such like criminal acts, although they are prohibited, nevertheless, it being necessary to use greater rigour, his Excellency, not relenting in this proclamation, &c., enjoins and commands that against all offenders under any of the above-mentioned heads, or the like, all the ordinary magistrates of the state shall proceed by pecuniary and corporal punishment, by banishment or the galleys, and even by death* . . . a mere bagatelle! *at the will of his Excellency or of the Senate, according to the character of the cases, persons and circumstances. And this* IR-RE-MIS-SI-BLY, *and with all rigour,* &c. There's plenty of it here, eh? And see, here's the signature: *Gonzalo Fernandez de Cordova:* and lower down; *Platonus;* and here again: *Vidit Ferrer:* there's nothing wanting.'

While the Doctor was reading, Renzo slowly followed him with his eye, trying to draw out the simple meaning, and to behold for himself those blessed words, which he believed were to render him assistance. The Doctor, seeing his client more attentive than alarmed, was greatly surprised. He must be matriculated, said he to himself—'Ah! ah!' added he aloud; 'you have been obliged to shave off the lock. You have been prudent; however you need not have done so, when putting yourself under my hands. The case is serious; but you don't know what I have courage to do in a time of need.'

To understand this mistake of the Doctor's, it must be known, that at that time, bravoes by profession, and villains of every kind, used to wear a long lock of hair, which they drew over the face like a visor on meeting any one, when the occasion was one which rendered disguise necessary, and the undertaking such as required both force and circumspection.

The proclamation had not been silent with regard to this matter. '*His Excellency* (the Marquis of La Hynojosa) *commands that whosoever shall wear his hair of such a length as to cover his forehead as far as the eyebrows only, or shall wear tresses either before or behind the ears, shall incur the penalty of three hundred crowns; or in case of inability, three years in the galleys for the first offence, and for the second, besides the above, a severer penalty still, at the will of his Excellency.*

'*However, in case of baldness or other reasonable cause, as a mark or wound, he gives permission to such, for their greater decorum or health, to wear their hair so long as may be necessary to cover such failings, and no more; warning them well to beware of exceeding the limits of duty and pure necessity, that they may not incur the penalty imposed upon other dissemblers.*

'*And he also commands all barbers, under penalty of a hundred crowns, or three stripes, to be given them in public, and even greater corporal punishment, at the will of his Excellency, as above, that they leave not on those whom they shave, any kind of the said tresses, locks, curls, or hair, longer than usual, either on the forehead, temples, or behind the ears; but that they shall be all of equal length, as above, except in case of baldness, or other defects, as already described.*' The lock, then, might almost be considered a part of the armour, and a distinctive mark of bravoes and vagabonds; so that these characters very commonly bore the name of *Ciuffi*.[2] This term is still used, with a mitigated signification, in the dialect of the country; and, perhaps, there is not one of our Milanese readers who does not remember hearing it said of him, in his childhood, either by his relatives, his tutor, or some family friend, 'He is a *Ciuffo;* he is a *Ciuffetto.*'

'On the word of a poor youth,' replied Renzo, 'I never wore a lock in my life.'

'I can do nothing,' replied the Doctor, shaking his head, with a smile between malice and impatience. 'If you don't trust me, I can do nothing. He who tells lies to the lawyer, do you see, my son, is

[2] *i. e.,* Locks.

a fool who will tell the truth to the judge. People must relate matters clearly to the advocate: it is our business to make them intricate. If you wish me to help you, you must tell me all from *a* to *z*, with your heart in your hand, as if to your confessor. You must name the person who has employed you. He will most likely be a person of consequence; and, in that case, I will go to him to perform an act of duty. I shan't, however, tell him, do you see, that *you* told me he had sent you, trust me. I will tell him I come to implore his protection for a poor slandered youth, and will take all necessary measures with him to finish the affair commendably. You understand, that, in securing himself, he will also secure you. Even if the scrape be all your own, I won't go back; I have extricated others from worse predicaments. And if you have not offended a person of quality, you understand, I will engage to get you out of the difficulty —with a little expense, you understand. You must tell me who is the offended party, as they say; and according to the condition, rank, and temper of the person, we shall see whether it will be better to bring him to reason by offers of protection, or, in some way, to criminate him, and put a flea in his ear; because, you see, I know very well how to manage these edicts; no one must be guilty, and no one must be innocent. As to the curate, if he has any discretion, he will keep in the back-ground; if he is a simpleton, we will dispose of him too. One can escape from any intrigue; but it requires one to act like a man; and your case is serious—serious, I say, serious; the edict speaks clearly; and if the matter were to be decided between justice and you, to say the truth, it would go hard with you. I speak to you as a friend. One must pay for pranks; if you wish to get off clear, money and frankness—trust yourself to one who wishes you well; obey, and do all that is suggested to you.'

While the Doctor poured forth this rhapsody, Renzo stood looking at him, with the spell-bound attention of a labouring man watching a juggler in the street, who, after thrusting into his mouth handful after handful of tow, draws forth thence ribbon—ribbon—ribbon—seemingly without end. When, at last, he understood what the Doctor was saying, and the strange mistake he had made, he cut short the ribbon in his mouth with these words: 'Oh, Signor Doctor, how have you understood me? The case is exactly the other way. I have threatened no one; I never do such things, not I; ask all my neighbours, and you will hear I have never had anything to do with the law. The trick has been played upon *me;* and I came to ask you what I must do to get justice, and I am very glad that I have seen this edict.'

'Hang him!' exclaimed the Doctor, opening his eyes. 'What a medley you have made! So it is: you are all alike; is it possible you don't know how to tell things plainly?'

'I beg your pardon, Signor Doctor, you didn't give me time; now I will relate the case as it is. You must know, then, that I was to have married to-day,' and here Renzo's voice became tremulous—'I was to have married to-day a young woman to whom I have paid my addresses since the beginning of summer; and this was the day, as I said, that was fixed with the Signor Curate, and everything was ready. Well, this morning, the Signor Curate began to throw out some excuses . . . however, not to tire you, I will only say, I made him speak, as was but just; and he confessed that he had been forbidden under pain of death, to celebrate this marriage. This tyrant of a Don Rodrigo . . .'

'Get you gone!' quickly interrupted the Doctor, raising his eyebrows, wrinkling his red nose, and distorting his mouth; 'get you gone! Why do you come here to rack my brain with these lies? Talk in this way to your companions, who don't know the meaning of words, and don't come and utter them to a gentleman who knows well what they are worth. Go away, go away; you don't know what you are talking about; I don't meddle with boys; I don't want to hear talk of this sort: talk in the air.'

'I will take an oath . . .'

'Get you gone, I tell you; what do I care for your oaths! I won't enter into the business; I wash my hands of it.' And he began rubbing and twirling them one over the other, as if he were really washing them. 'Learn how to speak; and don't come and take a gentleman thus by surprise.'

'But listen—but listen,' vainly repeated Renzo. The Doctor, fuming all the time, pushed him towards the door, and, on reaching it, set it wide open, called the servant, and said, 'Be quick and give this man what he brought. I want nothing, I want nothing.' The woman

had never before executed a similar order all the time she had been
in the Doctor's service; but it was pronounced in so resolute a manner, that she did not hesitate to obey. So, taking the four poor birds,
she gave them to Renzo, with a look of contemptuous compassion,
which seemed to say, 'you must indeed have made a grand blunder.'
Renzo tried to be ceremonious, but the Doctor was inexorable; and
the unhappy wight, astonished and bewildered, and more wrathful
than ever, was compelled to take back the restored victims, and
return to the country to relate the pleasing result of his expedition
to Agnese and Lucia.

During his absence, after sorrowfully changing their nuptial robes
for the humble daily dress, they had set themselves to consult anew,
Lucia sobbing, Agnese sighing mournfully, from time to time.
When Agnese had sufficiently enlarged upon the great effects they
might hope for from the Doctor's advice, Lucia remarked, that they
ought to try every method likely to assist them; that Father Cristoforo was a man not only to advise, but also to render more effectual
assistance, where it concerned the poor and unfortunate; and that
it would be a good thing if they could let him know what had
happened.

'It would, indeed,' replied Agnese; and they began immediately
to contrive together some plan to accomplish it; since, to go themselves to the convent, distant, perhaps, two miles, was an undertaking they would rather not risk *that* day; and, certainly, no one
with any judgment would have advised them to do so. While, however, they were thus engaged in weighing the different sides of the
question, they heard a knock at the door; and at the same moment,
a low but distinct *Deo Gratias*. Lucia, wondering who it could be,
ran to open it, and immediately, making a low bow, there entered
a lay Capuchin collector, his bag hanging over his left shoulder, and
the mouth of it twisted and held tight in his two hands, over his
breast. 'Oh, brother Galdino!' exclaimed the two women. 'The
Lord be with you,' said the friar; 'I have come to beg for the
nuts.'

'Go and fetch the nuts for the Fathers,' said Agnese. Lucia arose,
and moved towards the other room; but, before entering it, she
paused behind the friar's back, who remained standing in exactly
the same position; and putting her fore-finger on her lips, gave her

mother a look demanding secrecy, in which were mingled tenderness, supplication, and even a certain air of authority.

The collector, inquisitively eying Agnese at a distance, said, 'And this wedding? I thought it was to have been to-day; but I noticed a stir in the neighbourhood, as if indicating something new. What has happened?'

'The Signor Curate is ill, and we are obliged to postpone it,' hastily replied Agnese. Probably the answer might have been very different, if Lucia had not given her the hint. 'And how does the collection go on?' added she, wishing to change the conversation.

'Badly, good woman, badly. They are all here.' And so saying, he took the wallet off his shoulders and tossed it up between his hands into the air. 'They are all here; and to collect this mighty abundance, I have had to knock at ten doors.'

'But the year is scarce, brother Galdino; and when one has to struggle for bread, one measures everything according to the scarcity.'

'And what must we do, good woman, to make better times return? Give alms. Don't you know the miracle of the nuts that happened many years ago in our Convent of Romagna?'

'No, indeed! tell me.'

'Well, you must know, then, that in our convent, there was a holy Father, whose name was Father Macario. One day, in winter, walking along a narrow path, in a field belonging to one of our benefactors—a good man also—Father Macario saw him standing near a large walnut-tree, and four peasants, with axes upraised, about to fell it, having laid bare its roots to the sun. "What are you doing to this poor tree?" asked Father Macario. "Why, Father, it has borne no fruit for many years, so now I will make firing of it." "Leave it, leave it," said the Father; "be assured this year it will produce more fruit than leaves." The benefactor, knowing who it was that had uttered these words, immediately ordered the workmen to throw the soil upon the roots again; and calling to the Father, who continued his walk, said, "Father Macario, half of the crop shall be for the convent." The report of the prophecy spread, and every one flocked to see the tree. Spring, in very truth, brought blossoms without number, and then followed nuts—nuts without number. The good benefactor had not the happiness of gathering them, for he went before the harvest to receive the reward of his charity. But the miracle was, in consequence, so much the greater, as you will hear. This worthy man left behind him a son of very different character. Well, then, at the time of gathering, the collector went to receive the moiety belonging to the convent; but the son pretended perfect ignorance of the matter, and had the temerity to reply, that he had never heard that Capuchins knew how to gather nuts. What do you think happened then? One day, (listen to this,) the knave was entertaining a party of his friends, of the same genus as himself, and while making merry, he related the story of the walnuts, and ridiculed the friars. His jovial friends wished to go see this wonderful heap of nuts, and he conducted them to the store house. But listen now; he opened the door, went towards the corner where the great heap had been laid, and while saying, "Look," he looked himself, and saw—what do you think?—a magnificent heap of withered walnut-leaves! This was a lesson for him! and the convent, instead of being a loser by the denied alms, gained thereby; for, after so great a miracle, the contribution of nuts increased to such a degree, that a benefactor, moved with pity for the poor collector, made a present to the convent of an ass, to assist in carrying the nuts home. And so much oil was made, that all the poor in the neighbourhood came and had as much as they required; for we are like the sea, which receives water from all quarters, and returns it to be again distributed through the rivers.'

At this moment Lucia returned, her apron so laden with nuts, that it was with difficulty she could manage it, holding the two corners stretched out at arm's length, while the friar Galdino lifted the sack off his shoulders, and putting it on the ground, opened the mouth for the reception of the abundant gift. Agnese glanced towards Lucia a surprised and reproachful look for her prodigality; but Lucia returned a glance which seemed to say, 'I will justify myself.' The friar broke forth into praises, prognostications, promises, and expressions of gratitude, and replacing his bag, was about to depart. But Lucia, recalling him, said, 'I want you to do me a kindness; I want you to tell Father Cristoforo that we earnestly wish to speak to him, and ask him to be so good as to come to us poor people quickly—directly; for I cannot go to the church.'

'Is this all? It shall not be an hour before Father Cristoforo knows your wish.'

'I believe you.'

'You need not fear.' And so saying, he departed, rather more burdened and a little better satisfied than when he entered the house.

Let no one think, on hearing that a poor girl sent to ask with such confidence for Father Cristoforo, and that the collector accepted the commission without wonder and without difficulty—let no one, I say, suppose that this Cristoforo was a mean friar—a person of no importance. He was, on the contrary, a man who had great authority among his friends, and in the country around; but, such was the condition of the Capuchins, that nothing appeared to them either too high or too low. To minister to the basest, and to be ministered to by the most powerful; to enter palaces or hovels with the same deportment of humility and security; to be sometimes in the same house the object of ridicule and a person without whom nothing could be decided; to solicit alms everywhere, and distribute them to all those who begged at the convent:—a Capuchin was accustomed to all these. Traversing the road, he was equally liable to meet a noble who would reverently kiss the end of the rope round his waist, or a crowd of wicked boys, who, pretending to be quarrelling among themselves, would fling at his beard dirt and mire. The word *frate* was pronounced in those days with the greatest respect, and again with the bitterest contempt; and the Capuchins, perhaps, more than any other order, were the objects of two directly opposite sentiments, and shared two directly opposite kinds of treatment; because, possessing no property, wearing a more than ordinarily distinctive habit, and making more open professions of humiliation, they exposed themselves more directly to the veneration, or the contumely, which these circumstances would excite, according to the different tempers and different opinions of men.

As soon as the friar had left,—'All those nuts!' exclaimed Agnese: 'and in such a year too!'

'I beg pardon, mother,' replied Lucia: 'but if we had only given like others, brother Galdino would have had to go about no one knows how long, before his wallet would have been filled; and we cannot tell when he would have returned to the convent; besides,

what with chatting here and there, he would very likely have forgotten . . .'

'Ah! you thought wisely; and, after all, charity always brings a
good reward,' said Agnese, who, spite of her little defects, was a good
woman; and would have given everything she owned for this only
daughter, whom she loved with the tenderest affection.

At this moment Renzo arrived, and, entering with an irritated
and mortified countenance, threw the chickens on the table; and
this was the last sad vicissitude the poor creatures underwent that
day.

'Fine advice you gave me!' said he to Agnese. 'You sent me to a
nice gentleman, to one who really helps the unfortunate!' And he
began immediately to relate his reception at the Doctor's. Poor
Agnese, astonished at his ill success, endeavoured to prove that her
advice had been good, and that Renzo had not gone about the business cleverly; but Lucia interrupted the question, by announcing
that she hoped they had found a better helper. Renzo welcomed the
hope as most people do who are in misfortune and perplexity. 'But if
the Father,' said he, 'does not find us a remedy, I will find one some-
how or other.' The women recommended peace, patience, and prudence. 'To-morrow,' said Lucia, 'Father Cristoforo will certainly
come, and you'll see he will find some help that we poor people
can't even imagine.'

'I hope so,' said Renzo; 'but in any case I will get redress, or find
some one to get it for me. There must be justice in the end, even
in this world!'

In such melancholy discourse, and in such occurrences as have been
described, the day wore away, and began to decline.

'Good night,' said Lucia, sorrowfully, to Renzo, who could not
make up his mind to leave her. 'Good night,' replied he, still more
mournfully.

'Some saint will help us,' added she. 'Be prudent, and try to be
resigned.' Agnese added other advice of the same kind, and the
bridegroom went away with fury in his heart, repeating all the while
those strange words, 'There must be justice at last, even in this
world!' So true is it that a man overwhelmed with great sorrows
knows not what he is saying.

CHAPTER IV

THE sun had scarcely risen above the horizon, when Father Cristoforo left the convent of Pescarenico, and proceeded towards the cottage where he was expected. Pescarenico is a little town on the left bank of the Adda, or rather, we should say, of the lake, a few paces below the bridge; a group of houses, inhabited for the most part by fishermen, and adorned here and there with nets hung out to dry. The convent was situated (and the building still remains) outside the town, facing the entrance, on the road that leads from Lecco to Bergamo. The sky was serene, and as the sun gradually emerged from behind the mountain, the light descended from the summit of the opposite range, spreading itself rapidly over the steeps and through the valleys; while a soft autumnal breeze, shaking from the boughs the withered leaves of the mulberry, carried them away to fall at some distance from the tree. In the vineyards on either hand, the red leaves of various shades glittered on the still festooned branches; and the newly made nets appeared dark and distinct among the fields of white stubble sparkling in the dew. The scene was bright; but the occasional sight of a human figure moving therein dispelled the cheerful thoughts which the scene was calculated to inspire. At every step one met with pale and emaciated beggars, either grown old in the business, or reduced by the necessity of the times to ask alms. They looked piteously at Father Cristoforo as they silently passed him; and although, as a Capuchin never had any money, they had nothing to hope from him, yet they gave him a bow of gratitude for the alms which they had received, or were going to solicit, at the convent. The sight of the labourers scattered over the fields had in it something still more mournful. Some were sowing seed, but niggardly and unwillingly, like a man who risks something he highly prizes: others could with difficulty use the spade, and wearily overturned the sods. The half-starved child, holding by a cord the thin meagre cow, and looking narrowly around, hastily stooped to steal from it

53

some herb as food for the family, which hunger had taught them could be used to sustain life. Such sights as these at every step increased the sadness of the friar, who even now had a presentiment in his heart that he was going to hear of some misfortune.

But why did he take so much thought for Lucia? And why, at the first intimation of her wish, did he attend to it so diligently, as if it were a call from the Father Provincial? And who was this Father Cristoforo?—It will be necessary to answer all these inquiries.

Father Cristoforo of * * * was a man nearer sixty than fifty years of age. His shaven head, circled with a narrow line of hair, like a crown, according to the fashion of the Capuchin tonsure, was raised from time to time with a movement that betrayed somewhat of disdain and disquietude, and then quickly sank again in thoughts of lowliness and humility. His long, gray beard, covering his cheeks and chin, contrasted markedly with the prominent features of the upper part of his face, to which a long and habitual abstinence had rather given an air of gravity, than effaced the natural expression. His sunken eyes, usually bent on the ground, sometimes brightened up with a momentary fire, like two spirited horses, under the hand of a driver whom they know by experience they cannot overcome; yet occasionally they indulge in a few gambols and prancings, for which they are quickly repaid by a smart jerk of the bit.

Father Cristoforo had not always been thus: nor had he always been Cristoforo: his baptismal name was Ludovico. He was the son of a merchant of * * *, (these asterisks are all inserted by the circumspection of our anonymous author,) who, in his latter years, being considerably wealthy, and having only one son, had given up trade, and retired as an independent gentleman.

In his new state of idleness he began to entertain a great contempt for the time he had spent in making money, and being useful in the world. Full of this fancy, he used every endeavour to make others forget that he had been a merchant; in fact, he wished to forget it himself. But the warehouse, the bales, the journal, the measure, were for ever intruding upon his mind, like the shade of Banquo to Macbeth, even amidst the honours of the table and the smiles of flatterers. It is impossible to describe the care of these poor mortals to avoid every word that might appear like an allusion to the former condition of their patron. One day, to mention a single instance, towards the end of dinner, in the moment of liveliest and most unrestrained festivity, when it would be difficult to say which was the merriest, the company who emptied the table, or the host who filled it, he was rallying with friendly superiority one of his guests, the most prodigious eater in the world. He, meaning to return the joke, with the frankness of a child, and without the least shade of malice, replied, 'Ah, I'm listening like a merchant.'[1] The poor offender was at once conscious of the unfortunate word that had escaped his lips; he cast a diffident glance towards his patron's clouded face, and each would gladly have resumed his former expression; but it was impossible. The other guests occupied themselves, each in his own mind, in devising some plan of remedying the mistake, and making a diversion; but the silence thus occasioned only made the error more apparent. Each individual endeavoured to avoid meeting his companion's eye; each felt that all were occupied in the thought they wished to conceal. Cheerfulness and sociability had fled for that day, and the poor man, not so much imprudent as unfortunate, never again received an invitation. In this manner, Ludovico's father passed his latter years, continually subject to annoyances, and perpetually in dread of being despised; never reflecting that it was no more contemptuous to sell than to buy, and that the business of which he was now so much ashamed, had been carried on for many years before the public without regret. He gave his son an expensive education, according to the judgment of the times, and as far as he was permitted by the laws and customs of the country; he procured him masters in the different branches of literature and in exercises of horsemanship, and at last died, leaving the youth heir to a large fortune. Ludovico had acquired gentlemanly habits and feelings, and the flatterers by whom he had been surrounded had accustomed him to be treated with the greatest respect. But when he endeavoured to mix with the first men of the city, he met with very different treatment to what he had been accustomed to, and he began to perceive that, if he would be admitted into their society, as he desired, he must learn, in a new

---

[1] *'Io faccio orecchie da mercante.'* A proverbial expression, meaning, 'I pay no attention to you,' which quite loses its point when translated into English.

school, to be patient and submissive, and every moment to be looked down upon and despised.

Such a mode of life accorded neither with the education of Ludovico, nor with his disposition, and he withdrew from it, highly piqued. Still he absented himself unwillingly; it appeared to him that these ought really to have been his companions, only he wanted them to be a little more tractable. With this mixture of dislike and inclination, not being able to make them his familiar associates, yet wishing in some way to be connected with them, he endeavoured to rival them in show and magnificence, thus purchasing for himself enmity, jealousy, and ridicule. His disposition, open and at the same time violent, had occasionally engaged him in more serious contentions. He had a natural and sincere horror of fraud and oppression—a horror rendered still more vivid by the rank of those whom he saw daily committing them—exactly the persons he hated. To appease or to excite all these passions at once, he readily took the part of the weak and oppressed, assumed the office of arbitrator, and intermeddling in one dispute, drew himself into others; so that by degrees he established his character as a protector of the oppressed, and a vindicator of injuries. The employment, however, was troublesome; and it need not be asked whether poor Ludovico met with enemies, untoward accidents, and vexations of spirit. Besides the external war he had to maintain, he was continually harassed by internal strifes; for, in order to carry out his undertakings, (not to speak of such as never were carried out,) he was often obliged to make use of subterfuges, and have recourse to violence which his conscience could not approve. He was compelled to keep around him a great number of bravoes; and, as much for his own security as to ensure vigorous assistance, he had to choose the most daring, or, in other words, the most unprincipled, and thus to live with villains for the sake of justice. Yet on more than one occasion, either discouraged by ill success, or disquieted by imminent danger, wearied by a state of constant defence, disgusted with his companions, and in apprehension of dissipating his property, which was daily drawn upon largely, either in a good cause or in support of his bold enterprises,—more than once he had taken a fancy to turn friar; for in these times, this was the commonest way of escaping difficulties. This idea would probably have been only a fancy all his life, had it not been changed to a resolution by a more serious and terrible accident than he had yet met with.

He was walking one day along the streets, in company with a former shopkeeper, whom his father had raised to the office of steward, and was followed by two bravoes. The steward, whose name was Cristoforo, was about fifty years old, devoted from child-hood to his master, whom he had known from his birth, and by whose wages and liberality he was himself supported, with his wife and eight children. Ludovico perceived a gentleman at a distance, an arrogant and overbearing man, whom he had never spoken to in his life, but his cordial enemy, to whom Ludovico heartily re-turned the hatred; for it is a singular advantage of this world, that men may hate and be hated without knowing each other. The Signor, followed by four bravoes, advanced haughtily with a proud step, his head raised, and his mouth expressive of insolence and contempt. They both walked next to the wall, which (be it ob-served) was on Ludovico's right hand; and this, according to cus-tom, gave him the right (how far people will go to pursue the *right* of a case!) of not moving from the said wall to give place to any one, to which custom at that time, great importance was attached. The Signor, on the contrary, in virtue of another custom, held that this right ought to be conceded to him in consideration of his rank, and that it was Ludovico's part to give way. So that in this, as it happens in many other cases, two opposing customs clashed, the question of which was to have the preference remaining undecided, thus giving occasions of dispute, whenever one hard head chanced to come in contact with another of the same nature. The foes ap-proached each other, both close to the wall, like two walking figures in bas-relief, and on finding themselves face to face, the Signor, eye-ing Ludovico with a haughty air and imperious frown, said, in a corresponding tone of voice, 'Go to the outside.'

'You go yourself,' replied Ludovico; 'the path is mine.'

'With men of your rank the path is always mine.'

'Yes, if the arrogance of men of your rank were a law for men of mine.'

The two trains of attendants stood still, each behind its leader, fiercely regarding each other with their hands on their daggers prepared for battle, while the passers-by stopped on their way and withdrew into the road, placing themselves at a distance to observe the issue; the presence of these spectators continually animating the punctilio of the disputants.

'To the outside, vile mechanic! or I'll quickly teach you the civility you owe a gentleman.'

'You lie: I am not vile.'

'You lie, if you say I lie.' This reply was pragmatical. 'And if you were a gentleman, as I am,' added the Signor, 'I would prove with the sword that you are the liar.'

'That is a capital pretext for dispensing with the trouble of maintaining the insolence of your words by your deeds.'

'Throw this rascal in the mud,' said the Signor, turning to his followers.

'We shall see,' said Ludovico, immediately retiring a step, and laying his hand on his sword.

'Rash man!' cried the other, drawing his own, 'I will break this when it is stained with your vile blood.'

At these words they flew upon one another, the attendants of the two parties fighting in defence of their masters. The combat was unequal, both in number, and because Ludovico aimed rather at parrying the blows of, and disarming his enemy than killing him, while the Signor was resolved upon his foe's death at any cost. Ludovico had already received a blow from the dagger of one of the bravoes in his left arm, and a slight wound on his cheek, and his principal enemy was pressing on to make an end of him, when Cristoforo, seeing his master in extreme peril, went behind the Signor with his dagger, who, turning all his fury upon his new enemy, ran him through with his sword. At this sight Ludovico, as if beside himself, buried his own in the body of his provoker, and laid him at his feet, almost at the same moment as the unfortunate Cristoforo. The followers of the Signor, seeing him on the ground, immediately betook themselves to flight: those of Ludovico, wounded and beaten, having no longer any one to fight with, and not wishing to be mingled in the rapidly increasing multitude, fled the other way, and Ludovico was left alone in the midst of the crowd, with these two ill-fated companions lying at his feet.

'What's the matter?—There's one,—There are two.—They have pierced his body.—Who has been murdered?—That tyrant.—Oh, Holy Mary, what a confusion!—Seek, and you shall find.—One moment pays all.—So he is gone!—What a blow!—It must be a serious affair.—And this other poor fellow!—Mercy! what a sight! —Save him, save him!—It will go hard with him too.—See how he is mangled! he is covered with blood.—Escape, poor fellow, escape!—Take care you are not caught.'

These words predominating over the confused tumult of the crowd, expressed their prevailing opinion, while assistance accompanied the advice. The scene had taken place near a Capuchin convent, an asylum in those days, as every one knows, impenetrable to bailiffs and all that complication of persons and things which went by the name of justice. The wounded and almost senseless murderer was conducted, or rather carried by the crowd, and delivered to the monks with the recommendation, 'He is a worthy man who has made a proud tyrant cold; he was provoked to it, and did it in his own defence.'

Ludovico had never before shed blood, and although homicide was in those times so common that every one was accustomed to hear of and witness it, yet the impression made on his mind by the sight of one man murdered *for* him, and another *by* him, was new and indescribable;—a disclosure of sentiments before unknown. The fall of his enemy, the sudden alteration of the features, passing in a moment from a threatening and furious expression to the calm and solemn stillness of death, was a sight that instantly changed the feelings of the murderer. He was dragged to the convent almost without knowing where he was, or what they were doing to him; and when his memory returned, he found himself on a bed in the infirmary, attended by a surgeon-friar, (for the Capuchins generally had one in each convent,) who was applying lint and bandages to the two wounds he had received in the contest. A father, whose special office it was to attend upon the dying, and who had frequently been called upon to exercise his duties in the street, was quickly summoned to the place of combat. He returned a few minutes afterwards, and entering the infirmary, approached the bed where Ludovico lay. 'Comfort yourself,' said he, 'he has at least died calmly, and has charged me to ask your pardon, and to convey his to you.' These words aroused poor Ludovico, and awakened more vividly and distinctly the feelings which confusedly crowded upon his mind; sorrow for his friend, consternation and remorse for the blow that had escaped his hand, and at the same time a bitterly painful compassion for the man he had slain. 'And the other?' anxiously demanded he of the friar.

'The other had expired when I arrived.'

In the mean while, the gates and precincts of the convent swarmed with idle and inquisitive people; but on the arrival of a body of constables, they dispersed the crowd, and placed themselves in ambush at a short distance from the doors, so that none might go out unobserved. A brother of the deceased, however, accompanied by two of his cousins and an aged uncle, came, armed *cap-à-pié,* with a powerful retinue of bravoes, and began to make the circuit of the convent, watching with looks and gestures of threatening contempt the idle by-standers, who did not dare say, He is out of your reach, though they had it written on their faces.

As soon as Ludovico could collect his scattered thoughts, he asked for a Father Confessor, and begged that he would seek the widow of Cristoforo, ask forgiveness in his name for his having been the involuntary cause of her desolation, and at the same time assure her that he would undertake to provide for her destitute family. In reflecting on his own condition, the wish to become a friar, which he had often before revolved in his mind, revived with double force and earnestness; it seemed as if God himself, by bringing him to a convent just at this juncture, had put it in his way, and given him a sign of His will, and his resolution was taken. He therefore called the guardian, and told him of his intention. The superior replied, that he must beware of forming precipitate resolutions, but that if, on consideration, he persisted in his desire he would not be refused. He then sent for a notary, and made an assignment of the whole of his property (which was no insignificant amount) to the family of Cristoforo, a certain sum to the widow, as if it were an entailed dowry, and the remainder to the children.

The resolution of Ludovico came very *apropos* for his hosts, who were in a sad dilemma on his account. To send him away from the convent, and thus expose him to justice, that is to say, to the vengeance of his enemies, was a course on which they would not for a moment bestow a thought. It would have been to give up their proper privileges, disgrace the convent in the eyes of the people, draw upon themselves the animadversion of all the Capuchins in the universe for suffering their common rights to be infringed upon, and arouse all the ecclesiastical authorities, who at that time considered themselves the lawful guardians of these rights. On the other hand, the kindred of the slain, powerful themselves, and strong in adherents, were prepared to take vengeance, and denounced as their enemy any one who should put an obstacle in their way. The history does not tell us that much grief was felt for the loss of the deceased, nor even that a single tear was shed over him by any of his relations: it merely says that they were all on fire to have the murderer, dead or living, in their power. But Ludovico's assuming the habit of a Capuchin settled all these difficulties; he made atonement in a manner, imposed a penance on himself, tacitly confessed himself in fault, and withdrew from the contest; he was, in fact, an enemy laying down his arms. The relatives of the dead could also, if they pleased, believe and make it their boast that he had turned friar in despair, and through dread of their vengeance. But in any case, to oblige a man to relinquish his property, shave his head, and walk barefoot, to sleep on straw, and to live upon alms, was surely a punishment fully equivalent to the most heinous offence.

The Superior presented himself with an easy humility to the brother of the deceased, and after a thousand protestations of respect for his most illustrious house, and of desire to comply with his wishes as far as was possible, he spoke of Ludovico's penitence, and the determination he had made, politely making it appear that his family ought to be therewith satisfied, and insinuating, yet more courteously, and with still greater dexterity, that whether he were pleased or not, so it would be. The brother fell into a rage, which the

Capuchin patiently allowed to evaporate, occasionally remarking that he had too just cause of sorrow. The Signor also gave him to understand, that in any case his family had it in their power to enforce satisfaction, to which the Capuchin, whatever he might think, did not say no; and finally he asked, or rather required as a condition, that the murderer of his brother should immediately quit the city. The Capuchin, who had already determined upon such a course, replied that it should be as he wished, leaving the nobleman to believe, if he chose, that his compliance was an act of obedience: and thus the matter concluded to the satisfaction of all parties. The family were released from their obligation; the friars had rescued a fellow-creature, and secured their own privileges, without making themselves enemies; the dilettanti in chivalry gladly saw the affair terminated in so laudable a manner; the populace rejoiced at a worthy man's escaping from danger, and at the same time marvelled at his conversion; finally, and above all, in the midst of his sorrow, it was a consolation to poor Ludovico himself, to enter upon a life of expiation, and devote himself to services, which, though they could not remedy, might at least make some atonement, for his unhappy deed, and alleviate the intolerable pangs of remorse. The idea that his resolution might be attributed to fear pained him for a moment, but he quickly consoled himself by the remembrance that even this unjust imputation would be a punishment for him, and a means of expiation. Thus, at the age of thirty, Ludovico took the monastic habit, and being required, according to custom, to change his name, he chose one that would continually remind him of the fault he had to atone for—the name of friar Cristoforo.

Scarcely was the ceremony of taking the religious habit completed, when the guardian told him that he must keep his novitiate at * * *, sixty miles distant, and that he must leave the next day. The novice bowed respectfully, and requested a favour of him. 'Allow me, Father,' said he, 'before I quit the city where I have shed the blood of a fellow-creature, and leave a family justly offended with me, to make what satisfaction I can by at least confessing my sorrow, begging forgiveness of the brother of the deceased, and so removing, please God, the enmity he feels towards me.' The guardian, thinking that such an act, besides being good in itself, would also serve still more to reconcile the family to the convent, instantly repaired to the offended Signor's house, and communicated to him Friar Cristoforo's request. The Signor, greatly surprised at so unexpected a proposal, felt a rising of anger, mingled perhaps with complacency, and after thinking a moment, 'Let him come to-morrow,' said he, mentioning the hour, and the Superior returned to the monastery to acquaint the novice with the desired permission.

The gentleman soon remembered that the more solemn and notorious the submission was, the more his influence and importance would be increased among his friends and the public; and it would also, (to use a fashionable modern expression,) make a fine page in the history of the family. He therefore hastily sent to inform all his relatives, that the next day at noon they must hold themselves engaged to come to him, for the purpose of receiving a common satisfaction. At midday the palace swarmed with the nobility of both sexes and of every age; occasioning a confused intermingling of large cloaks, lofty plumes, and pendent jewels; a vibrating movement of stiffened and curled ribbons, an impeded trailing of embroidered trains. The ante-rooms, court-yards, and the roads overflowed with servants, pages, bravoes, and inquisitive gazers. On seeing all this preparation, Friar Cristoforo guessed the motive, and felt a momentary perturbation; but he soon recovered himself, and said:—'Be it so; I committed the murder publicly, in the presence of many of his enemies; that was an injury; this is reparation.'—So, with the Father, his companion, at his side, and his eyes bent on the ground, he passed the threshold, traversed the court-yard among a crowd who eyed him with very unceremonious curiosity, ascended the stairs, and in the midst of another crowd of nobles, who gave way at his approach, was ushered, with a thousand eyes upon him, into the presence of the master of the mansion, who, surrounded by his nearest relatives, stood in the centre of the room with a downcast look, grasping in his left hand the hilt of his sword, while with the right he folded the collar of his cloak over his breast.

There is sometimes in the face and behaviour of a person so direct an expression, such an effusion, so to speak, of the internal soul, that in a crowd of spectators there will be but one judgment and opinion of him. So was it with Friar Cristoforo; his face and behaviour plainly expressed to the by-standers that he had not become a friar, nor submitted to that humiliation, from the fear of man; and the discovery immediately conciliated all hearts. On perceiving the offended Signor, he quickened his steps, fell on his knees at his feet, crossed his hands on his breast, and bending his shaved head, said, 'I am the murderer of your brother. God knows how gladly I would restore him to you at the price of my own blood, but it cannot be: I can only make inefficacious and tardy excuses, and implore you to accept them for God's sake.' All eyes were immovably fixed upon the novice and the illustrious personage he was addressing; all ears were attentively listening; and when Friar Cristoforo ceased, there was a murmur of compassion and respect throughout the room. The gentleman, who stood in an attitude of forced condescension and restrained anger, was much moved at these words, and bending towards the supplicant, 'Rise,' said he, in an altered tone. 'The offence—the act certainly—but the habit you bear—not only so, but also yourself—Rise, Father—My brother—I cannot deny it—was a cavalier—was rather a—precipitate man—rather hasty. But all happens by God's appointment. Speak of it no more . . . But, Father, you must not remain in this posture.' And taking him by the arm, he compelled him to rise. The friar, standing with his head bowed, and his eyes fixed on the ground, replied, 'I may hope then that I have your forgiveness? And if I obtain it from *you,* from whom may I not hope it? Oh! if I might hear from your lips that one word—pardon!'

'Pardon!' said the gentleman. 'You no longer need it. But since you desire it, certainly . . . certainly, I pardon you with my whole heart, and all . . .'

'All! all!' exclaimed the by-standers, with one voice. The countenance of the friar expanded with grateful joy, under which, however, might be traced an humble and deep compunction for the evil which the forgiveness of men could not repair. The gentleman, overcome by this deportment, and urged forward by the general feeling, threw his arms round Cristoforo's neck, and gave and received the kiss of peace.

'Bravo! well done!' burst forth from all parts of the room: there was a general movement, and all gathered round the friar. Servants immediately entered, bringing abundance of refreshment. The Signor, again addressing Cristoforo, who was preparing to retire, said, 'Father, let me give you some of these trifles; afford me this proof of your friendship;' and was on the point of helping him before any of the others; but he, drawing back with a kind of friendly resistance, 'These things,' said he, 'are no longer for me; but God forbid that I should refuse your gifts. I am about to start on my journey! allow me to take a loaf of bread, that I may be able to say I have shared your charity, eaten of your bread, and received a token of your forgiveness.' The nobleman, much affected, ordered it to be brought, and shortly a waiter entered in full dress, bearing the loaf on a silver dish, and presented it to the Father, who took it with many thanks, and put it in his basket. Then, obtaining permission to depart, he bade farewell to the master of the house and those who stood nearest to him, and with difficulty made his escape as they endeavoured for a moment to impede his progress; while, in the ante-rooms, he had to struggle to free himself from the servants, and even from the bravoes, who kissed the hem of his garment, his rope, and his hood. At last he reached the street, borne along as in triumph, and accompanied by a crowd of people as far as the gate of the city, from whence he commenced his pedestrian journey towards the place of his novitiate.

The brother and other relatives of the deceased, who had been prepared in the morning to enjoy the sad triumph of pride, were left instead full of the serene joy of a forgiving and benevolent disposition. The company entertained themselves some time longer, with feelings of unusual kindness and cordiality, in discussions of a very different character to what they had anticipated on assembling. Instead of satisfaction enforced, insults avenged, and obligations discharged, praises of the novice, reconciliation, and meekness, were the topics of conversation. And he who, for the fiftieth time, would have recounted how Count Muzio, his father, had served the Marquis Stanislao, (a violent, boastful man, as every one is aware,) in a well-known encounter of the same kind, related, instead, the penitence and wonderful patience of one Friar Simone, who had died many years before. When the party had dispersed, the Signor, still considerably agitated, reconsidered with surprise what he had heard and had himself expressed, and muttered between his teeth, 'The devil of a friar!' (we must record his exact words) 'The devil of a friar!—if he had knelt there a few moments longer, I should almost have begged *his* pardon for his having murdered my brother.'—Our story expressly notes that from that day forward he became a little less impetuous, and rather more tractable.

Father Cristoforo pursued his way with a peace of mind such as he had never experienced since that terrible event, to make atonement for which his whole life was henceforth to be consecrated. He maintained the silence usually imposed upon novices without difficulty, being entirely absorbed in the thought of the labours, privations, and humiliations he would have to undergo for the expiation of his fault. At the usual hour of refreshment, he stopped at the house of a patron, and partook almost voraciously of the bread of forgiveness, reserving, however, a small piece, which he kept in his basket as a perpetual remembrancer.

It is not our intention to write the history of his cloistral life: it will suffice to say, that while he willingly and carefully fulfilled the duties customarily assigned to him, to preach and to attend upon the dying, he never suffered an opportunity to pass of executing two other offices which he had imposed upon himself—the composing of differences, and the protection of the oppressed. Without being aware of it, he entered upon these undertakings with some portion of his former zeal, and a slight remnant of that courageous spirit which humiliation and mortifications had not been able entirely to subdue. His manner of speaking was habitually meek and humble; but when truth and justice were at stake, he was immediately animated with his former warmth, which, mingled with and modified by a solemn emphasis acquired in preaching, imparted to his language a very marked character. His whole countenance and deportment indicated a long-continued struggle between a naturally hasty, passionate temper, and an opposing and habitually victorious will, ever on the watch, and directed by the highest principles and motives. One of the brotherhood, his friend, who knew him well, likened him, on one occasion, to those too-expressive words—too expressive, that is, in their natural state, which some persons, well-behaved enough on ordinary occasions, pronounce, when overcome by anger, in a half-and-half sort of way, with a slight change of letters—words which even thus transformed bear about them much of their primitive energy.

If one unknown to him, in Lucia's sad condition, had implored the aid of Father Cristoforo, he would immediately have attended to the request; when it concerned Lucia, however, he hastened to her with double solicitude, since he knew and admired her innocence. He had already trembled for her danger, and felt a lively indignation at the base persecution of which she was the object. Besides this, he feared that by advising her to say nothing about it, and keep quiet, he might have been the cause of some sad consequences; so that in this case there was added to the kind solicitude, which was, as it were, natural to him, that scrupulous perplexity which often torments the innocent.

But while we have been relating the early history of Father Cristoforo, he has arrived at the village, and reached the door; and the women, leaving the harsh-toned spinning-wheel at which they were engaged, have risen and exclaimed with one voice, 'Oh, Father Cristoforo! God reward you!'

CHAPTER V

FATHER CRISTOFORO stopped on the threshold, and quickly perceived, by a glance at the women, that his presentiments had not been unfounded. While raising his beard, by a slight movement of the head backwards, he said, in that interrogative tone which anticipates a mournful reply, 'Well?' Lucia answered by a flood of tears. Her mother began to apologize for having dared . . . but he advanced and seated himself on a three-legged stool, and cut short all her excuses, by saying to Lucia, 'Calm yourself, my poor daughter. And you,' continued he, turning to Agnese, 'tell me what has happened.' The good woman related the melancholy story as well as she could, while the friar changed colour a thousand times, at one moment raising his eyes to heaven, the next, kicking his heels on the ground. At the conclusion of the recital, he covered his face with his hands, and exclaimed, 'Oh, blessed Lord! how long! . . .' But, without finishing the sentence, he turned again to the women. 'Poor things!' said he, 'God has indeed visited you. Poor Lucia!'

'You will not forsake us, Father?' sobbed Lucia.

'Forsake you!' replied he. 'Great God! with what face could I again make request to Him, if I should forsake you? You in this state! You whom He confides to me! Don't despair: He will help you. He sees all: He can make use even of such an unworthy instrument as I am to confound a . . . Let us see: let me think what I can do for you.'

So saying, he leaned his left elbow on his knee, laid his forehead on his hand, and with the right grasped his beard and chin, as if to concentrate and hold fast all the powers of his mind.

But the most attentive consideration only served to show more distinctly the urgency and intricacy of the case, and how few, how uncertain, and how dangerous were the ways of meeting it. 'Instil shame into Don Abbondio, and make him sensible of how much he is failing in his duty? Shame and duty are nothing to him, when

68

overwhelmed with fear. Inspire him with fears? How can I suggest one that would overbalance the dread he already has of a musket? Inform the Cardinal-Archbishop of all, and invoke his authority? This requires time, and in the mean while what might
not happen? And afterwards, supposing even this unhappy innocent
were married, would that be a curb to such a man? . . . Who knows
to what length he might proceed? And resist him? How? Ah! if
I could,' thought the poor friar: 'if I could but engage in this cause
my brethren here and at Milan! But it is not a common affair, and
I should be abandoned. Don Rodrigo pretends to be a friend to
the convent, and professes himself a favourer of the Capuchins; and
his followers have more than once taken refuge with us. I should
find myself alone in the undertaking; I should be opposed by med-
dling, quarrelsome persons; and, what is worse, I should, perhaps,
by an ill-timed endeavour, only render the condition of this poor
girl more hopeless.' Having considered every view of the question,
the best course seemed to be to confront Don Rodrigo himself, and
try, by entreaties, the terrors of the life to come, and even of this
world, if that were possible, to dissuade him from his infamous
purpose. At least, he could by this means ascertain whether he continued obstinately bent on his wicked design, discover something
more of his intentions, and act accordingly. While the friar was
thus engaged, Renzo, who for reasons that every one can divine,
could not long absent himself, made his appearance at the door;
but seeing the Father absorbed in thought, and the women beckoning to him not to interrupt him, he stood silent on the threshold.
Raising his head to communicate his design to the women, the friar
perceived Renzo, and saluted him with his usual affection, increased
and rendered more intense by compassion.

'Have they told you . . . Father?' asked Renzo, in an agitated
tone.

'Only too much: and for that reason I am here.'

'What do you say to the rascal?'

'What do you wish me to say of him? He is far away, and my
words would be of no use. But I say to you, my Renzo, trust in
God, and He will not forsake you.'

'What blessed words!' exclaimed the youth. 'You are not one of those who always wrong the poor. But the Signor Curate, and that Signor Doctor . . .'

'Don't recall those scenes, Renzo, which only serve to irritate you uselessly. I am a poor friar; but I repeat what I have said to these poor women: poor as I am, I will not forsake you.'

'Ah! you are not like the world's friends! Good-for-nothing creatures that they are! You would not believe the protestations they made me in prosperity. Ha! ha! They were ready to give their lives for me; they would have defended me against the devil. If I had had an enemy . . . I had only to let them know it, and I should have been quickly rid of him! And now, if you were to see how they draw back . . .' At this moment Renzo perceived, on raising his eyes to those of his auditor, that the good friar's face was clouded, and he felt that he had uttered something wrong. He only added to his perplexities, however, and made matters worse, by trying to remedy them: 'I meant to say . . . I don't at all mean . . . that is, I meant to say . . .'

'What did you mean to say? Have you, then, begun to spoil my work before I have undertaken it? It is well for you that you have been undeceived in time. What! you went in search of friends . . . and such friends! . . . who could not have helped you, had they been willing; and you forgot to seek the only One who can and will assist you! Do you not know that God is the friend of the afflicted who put their trust in Him? Do you not know that threatening and contention gain nothing for the weak? And even if . . .' Here he forcibly grasped Renzo's arm: his countenance, without losing any of its authority, expressed a solemn contrition; he cast his eyes on the ground, and his voice became slow and almost sepulchral: 'Even if they did, it is a terrible gain! Renzo! will you trust to me? To me, did I say—a feeble mortal, a poor friar? No; but will you trust in God?'

'Oh yes!' replied Renzo; 'He is in truth the Lord.'

'Very well; promise me that you will not attack—that you will not provoke—any one; that you will be guided by me.'

'I promise you.'

Lucia drew a long breath, as if she were relieved from a great weight; and Agnese exclaimed, 'Bravo, my son!'

'Listen, my children,' continued Friar Cristoforo; 'I will go to-day and speak to this man. If it please God to touch his heart, and give force to my words, well; but, if not, He will show us some other remedy. You, in the mean while, be quiet and retired; avoid gossip, and don't show yourselves. To-night, or to-morrow morning, at the latest, you shall see me again.' So saying, he cut short all their thanks and benedictions, and departed. He returned first to the convent, where he arrived in time to join the chorus in chanting, dined, and then set off on his way towards the den of the wild beast he had undertaken to tame.

The small but elegant palace of Don Rodrigo stood by itself, rising like a castle from the summit of one of the abrupt cliffs by which the shore of the lake was broken and diversified. Our anonymous author only adds to this indication, that the site (it would have been better to have given the name in full) was rather on the side adjoining the country of the Betrothed, about three miles distant from them, and four from the convent. At the base of the cliff, on the side looking towards the lake, lay a group of cottages, inhabited by the peasantry in the service of Don Rodrigo, the diminutive capital of his little kingdom. It was quite sufficient to pass through it to be assured of the character and customs of the country. Casting a glance into the lower rooms, should a door happen to be open, one saw hanging on the wall, fowling-pieces, spades, rakes, straw hats, nets, and powder-flasks, in admired confusion. Everywhere might be seen powerful, fierce-looking men, wearing a large lock, turned back upon their head, and enclosed in a net; old men, who, having lost their teeth, appeared ready, at the slightest provocation, to show their gums; women, of masculine appearance, with strong, sinewy arms, prepared to come in to the aid of their tongues on every occasion. Even the very children, playing in the road, displayed in their countenances and behaviour a certain air of provocation and defiance.

Father Cristoforo passed through this hamlet, and ascended a winding foot-path to a small level plot of ground, in front of the palace. The door was shut—a sign that the master of the mansion was dining, and would not be disturbed. The few small windows that looked into the road, the frameworks of which were disjointed, and decayed with age, were defended by large iron bars; and those of the ground-floor were so high, that a man could scarcely reach them by standing on the shoulders of another. Perfect silence reigned around; and a passer-by might have deemed it a deserted mansion, had not four creatures, two animate, and two inanimate, disposed opposite each other, outside, given some indication of inhabitants. Two great vultures, with extended wings and pendent heads—one stripped of its feathers, and half consumed by time; the other still feathered, and in a state of preservation, were nailed, one on each post of the massive door-way; and two bravoes, stretched at full length on the benches to the right and left, were on guard, and expecting their call to partake of the remains of the Signor's table. The Father stood still, in the attitude of one who was prepared to wait; but one of the bravoes rose, and called to him: 'Father, Father, come forward, we don't make Capuchins wait here; we are friends of the convent; and I have sometimes been within it when the air outside was not very good for me, and when, if the door had been closed upon me, I should have fared badly.' So saying, he gave two strokes of the knocker, which were answered immediately from within, by the howling and yelling of mastiffs, and curs, and in a few moments by an old grumbling servant; but seeing the Father, he made him a low bow, quieted the animals with hand and voice, introduced the visitor into a narrow passage, and closed the door again. He then conducted him into a small apartment, and, regarding him with a surprised and respectful look, said, 'Are you not . . . Father Cristoforo of Pescarenico?'

'I am.'

'You here?'

'As you see, my good man.'

'It must be to do good, then. Good,' continued he, muttering between his teeth, as he still led the way; 'good may be done anywhere.'

Having passed through two or three dark apartments, they at last reached the door of the dining-room, where they were greeted with a loud and confused noise of knives, forks, glasses, pewter dishes, and, above all, of discordant voices alternately endeavouring to take the lead in conversation. The friar wished to withdraw, and was debating at the door with the servant, and begging permission to wait in some corner of the house till dinner was over, when the door opened. A certain Count Attilio, who was sitting opposite, (he was a cousin of Don Rodrigo, and we have already mentioned him without giving his name,) seeing a shaved head and monk's habit, and perceiving the modest intentions of the good friar, exclaimed, 'Aha! aha! You sha'n't make your escape, reverend Father; forward, forward!' Don Rodrigo, without precisely divining the object of this visit, had a sort of presentiment of what awaited him, and would have been glad to avoid it; but since Attilio had thoughtlessly given this blunt invitation, he was obliged to second it, and said, 'Come in, Father, come in.' The friar advanced, making a low bow to the host, and respectfully responded to the salutations of the guests.

It is usual (I do not say invariable) to represent the innocent in the presence of the wicked with an open countenance, an air of security, an undaunted heart, and a ready facility of expression. In reality, however, many circumstances are required to produce this behaviour, which are rarely met with in combination. It will not, therefore, be wondered at, that Friar Cristoforo, with the testimony of a good conscience, and a firm persuasion of the justice of the cause he had come to advocate, together with a mingled feeling of horror and compassion for Don Rodrigo, stood, nevertheless, with a certain air of timidity and submissiveness, in the presence of this same Don Rodrigo, who was seated before him in an arm-chair, in his own house, on his own estate, surrounded by his friends, and many indications of his power, with every homage paid to him, and with an expression of countenance that would at once prohibit the making of a request, much more the giving advice, correction, or reproof. On his right, sat Count Attilio, his cousin, and, it is needless to say, his companion in libertinism and oppression, who had come from Milan to spend a few days with him. To his left, and on the other side of the table, was seated, with a profound respect, tempered, however, with a certain air of security, and even arrogance, the Signor Podestà;[1] the person whose business it was, professedly, to administer justice to Renzo Tramaglino, and

[1] The governor, or magistrate of the place—a dignitary corresponding to the mayor of an English town; but less dignified in this instance, because exercising power in a smaller territory.

inflict upon Don Rodrigo one of the appointed penalties. Opposite the Podestà, in an attitude of the purest, most unbounded servility, sat our Doctor, *Azzecca-Garbugli,* with his black cap, and more than usually red nose; and facing the cousins were two obscure guests, of whom our story merely records that they did nothing but eat, bow their heads, and smile approval at everything uttered by a fellow-guest, provided another did not contradict it.

'Give the Father a seat,' said Don Rodrigo. A servant presented a chair, and Father Cristoforo sat down, making some excuse to the Signor for coming at so inopportune an hour.

'I wish to speak with you alone, on a matter of importance,' added the friar, in a lower voice, in Don Rodrigo's ear.

'Very well, I will attend you,' replied he; 'but in the mean while, bring the Father something to drink.'

The Father tried to excuse himself; but Don Rodrigo, raising his voice above the re-commencing tumult, cried, 'No, no, you shall not do me this wrong; it shall never be said that a Capuchin left this house without tasting my wine, nor an insolent creditor the wood of my forests.' These words were followed by a general laugh, and, for a moment, interrupted the question that was being warmly agitated among the guests. A servant then brought in a bottle of wine, on a tray, and a tall glass, in the shape of a chalice, and presented them to the Father, who, unwilling to refuse the pressing invitation of one he so much wished to propitiate, did not hesitate to pour some out, and began slowly to sip the wine.

'The authority of Tasso will not serve your purpose, respected Signor Podestà; it even militates against you,' resumed Count Attilio, in a thundering voice; 'for that learned, that great man, who perfectly understood all the rules of chivalry, has made the messenger of Argante ask leave of the pious Buglione, before delivering the challenge to the Christian knights . . .'

'But this,' replied the Podestà, vociferating no less vehemently, 'this is a liberty, a mere liberty, a poetical ornament; since an ambassador is, in his nature, inviolable by the law of nations, *jure gentium.* But, without seeking so far, the proverb says, *Ambasciator non porta pena;* and proverbs, you know, contain the wisdom of the

human race. Besides, the messenger having uttered nothing in his
own name, but only presented the challenge in writing . . .'

'But when will you understand that this messenger was an inconsiderate ass, who didn't know the first? . . .'

'With your leave, gentlemen,' interrupted Don Rodrigo, who was
afraid of the question being carried too far, 'we will refer it to
Father Cristoforo, and abide by his sentence.'

'Well—very well,' said Count Attilio, highly pleased at the idea
of referring a question of chivalry to a Capuchin: while the more
eager Podestà with difficulty restrained his excited feelings, and a
shrug of contempt, which seemed to say—Absurdity!

'But, from what I have heard,' said the Father, 'these are matters
I know nothing of.'

'As usual, the modest excuses of the Fathers,' said Don Rodrigo;
'but you shall not get off so easily. Come, now, we know well
enough you did not come into the world with a cowl on your head,
and that you are no stranger to its ways. See here; this is the
question . . .'

'The case is this,' began Count Attilio.

'Let me tell it, who am neutral, cousin,' replied Don Rodrigo.
'This is the story. A Spanish cavalier sent a challenge to a Milanese
cavalier; the bearer, not finding him at home, delivered the summons to his brother, who, after reading it, gave the bearer in reply
a good thrashing. The dispute is . . .'

'One good turn deserves another,' cried Count Attilio. 'It was
really inspiration . . .'

'Of the devil,' added the Podestà. 'To beat an ambassador!—a
man whose person is sacred! Even you, Father, will say whether
this was a knightly deed.'

'Yes, Signor, knightly,' cried the Count, 'and you will allow *me*
to say so, who ought to understand what relates to a cavalier. Oh,
if they had been blows, it would be another matter; but a cudgel
defiles nobody's hands. What puzzles me is, why you think so
much of the shoulders of a mean scoundrel.'

'Who said anything about his shoulders, Signor Count? You
would make out I had talked nonsense such as never entered my

mind. I spoke of his office, not of his shoulders; and am now considering the laws of *chivalry*. Be so good as to tell me whether the heralds that the ancient Romans sent to bid defiance to other nations asked leave to announce their message; and find me one writer who mentions that a herald was ever beaten.'

'What have the officers of the ancient Romans to do with us—a simple nation, and in these things far, far behind us? But, according to the laws of modern chivalry, which are the only right ones, I affirm and maintain that a messenger who dared to place a challenge in the hand of a knight without having asked his permission, is an incautious fool, who may be beaten, and who richly deserves it.'

'Answer me this syllogism . . .'

'No, no, nothing.'

'But listen, listen. To strike an unarmed person is a treacherous act. *Atqui* the messenger *de quo* was without arms. *Ergo* . . .'

'Gently, gently, Signor Podestà.'

'Why gently?'

'Gently, I say: what are you talking about? It is an act of treachery to give a man a blow with a sword behind him, or to shoot him in the back; and to this even there are certain exceptions . . . but we will keep to the point. I allow that this may generally be called an act of treachery; but to bestow four blows on a paltry fellow like him! It would have been a likely thing to say: Take care I don't beat you, as one says to a gentleman: Draw your sword. And you, respected Signor Doctor, instead of smiling at me there, and giving me to understand you are of my opinion, why don't you support my position with your capital powers of argument, and help me to drive some reason into the head of this Signor?'

'I . . .' replied the Doctor, in confusion. 'I enjoy this learned dispute, and am glad of the accident that has given occasion to so agreeable a war of genius. But it does not belong to me to give sentence: his illustrious lordship has already delegated a judge . . . the Father here . . .'

'True,' said Don Rodrigo; 'but how is the judge to speak when the disputants will not be silent?'

'I am dumb,' said Count Attilio. The Podestà made a sign that he would not speak.

'Ah, at last! What do you say, Father?' asked Don Rodrigo with half-jesting gravity.

'I have already excused myself by saying I don't understand the matter,' replied Friar Cristoforo, returning the wine-glass to a servant.

'Poor excuses,' cried the two cousins. 'We must have your sentence.'

'Since you wish it, my humble opinion is that there should be neither challenges, bearers, nor blows.'

The guests interchanged looks of unfeigned astonishment.

'Oh, this is too bad!' exclaimed Count Attilio. 'Pardon me, Father, but this *is* too bad. It is easy to see you know nothing of the world.'

'He?' said Don Rodrigo. 'Ha! ha! he knows it, cousin, as well as you do: isn't it true, Father?'

Instead of replying to this courteous interrogation, the Father said to himself:—This is aimed at you; but remember, friar, that you are not here for yourself; and that which affects you only is not to be taken into the account.

'It may be,' said the cousin; 'but the Father . . . what is his name?'

'Father Cristoforo,' replied more than one.

'But, Father Cristoforo, most reverend Father, with your principles you would turn the world upside down. Without challenges! Without blows! Farewell to the point of honour; impunity for all villains. Fortunately, however, the supposition is impossible.'

'Up, Doctor, up,' broke in Don Rodrigo, who always tried to divert the argument from the original disputants. 'You are the man to argue on any matter. Let us see what you will do in discussing this question with Father Cristoforo.'

'Really,' replied the Doctor, brandishing his fork in the air, and turning to the Father, 'really I cannot understand how Father Cristoforo, who is at once the perfect devotee and a man of the world, should not remember that his sentence, good, excellent, and of just weight, as it is in the pulpit, is of no value (with due respect be it spoken) in a question of chivalry. But the Father knows, better than I, that everything is good in its place; and I think that this time he has only endeavoured the escape by a jest from the difficulty of giving sentence.'

What can one reply to reasonings deduced from a wisdom so ancient, yet so new? Nothing; and so thought our friar.

But Don Rodrigo, wishing to cut short this dispute, proceeded to suggest another. 'Apropos,' said he; 'I hear there are rumours of an accommodation at Milan.'

The reader must know that, at this time, there was a contest for the succession to the Duchy of Mantua, which, on the death of Vincenzo Gonzaga, who left no male issue, had fallen into the possession of the Duke of Nevers, Gonzaga's nearest relation. Louis XIII., or rather Cardinal Richelieu, wished to support him on account of his being well-disposed toward the French. Philip IV., or rather the Count D'Olivares, commonly called the Count Duke, opposed him for the same reason, and had declared war against him. As the Duchy was a fief of the empire, the two parties made interest, by intrigue, threats, and solicitations, at the court of the Emperor Ferdinand II.; the former urging him to grant the investiture to the new Duke, the latter to refuse it, and even assist in banishing him from the State.

'I am inclined to think,' said Count Attilio, 'that matters may be adjusted. I have certain reasons . . .'

'Don't believe it, Signor Count, don't believe it,' interrupted the Podestà; 'even in this corner of the world I have means of ascertaining the state of things; for the Spanish governor of the castle, who condescends to make me his friend, and who being the son of one of the Count Duke's dependents, is informed of everything. . . .'

'I tell you, I have opportunity every day at Milan of talking with great men; and I know, on good authority, that the Pope is highly interested in the restoration of peace, and has made propositions . . .'

'So it ought to be, the thing is according to rule, and his Holiness does his duty; a Pope ought always to mediate between Christian Princes; but the Count Duke has his own policy, and . . .'

'And, and, and—do you know, my good Signor, what the Emperor thinks of it at this moment? Do you think there is no other place in the world besides Mantua? There are many things to be looked after, my good Signor. Do you know, for example, how far the

Emperor can, at this moment, confide in that Prince Valdistano, or Vallestai, or whatever they call him; and whether . . .'

'His right name in German,' again interrupted the Podestà, 'is Vagliensteino, as I have often heard it pronounced by our Spanish Signor, the governor of the castle. But be of good courage, for . . .'

'Will you teach me?' exclaimed the Count, angrily; but Don Rodrigo motioned to him with his knee, for his sake, to cease contradiction. He therefore remained silent; and the Podestà, like a vessel disengaged from a sand-bank, continued, with wide-spread sails, the course of his eloquence. 'Vagliensteino gives me little concern, because the Count Duke has his eyes on everything, and in every place; and if Vagliensteino chooses to play any tricks, he will set him right with fair words or foul. He has his eye everywhere, I say, and long arms; and if he has resolved, as he justly has, like a good politician, that the Signor Duke of Nevers shall not take root in Mantua, the Signor Duke of Nevers will not take root there, and the Cardinal Richelieu will sink in the water. It makes me smile to see this worthy Signor Cardinal contending with a Count Duke—with an Olivares. I should like to rise again, after a lapse of two hundred years, to hear what posterity will say of these fine pretensions. It requires something more than envy: there must be a head; and of heads like that of a Count Duke there is but one in the world. The Count Duke, my good Signors,' continued the Podestà, sailing before the wind, and a little surprised at not encountering one shoal, 'the Count Duke is an aged fox, (speaking with all respect,) who can make anybody lose his track; when he aims at the right, we may be sure he will take the left; so that no one can boast of knowing his intentions; and even they who execute them, and they who write his despatches, understand nothing of them. I can speak with some knowledge of the circumstances; for that worthy man, the Governor of the Castle, deigns to place some confidence in me. The Count Duke, on the other hand, knows exactly what is going forward in all the other Courts, and their great politicians—many of whom, it cannot be denied, are very upright men—have scarcely imagined a design before the Count Duke has discovered it, with that clever head of his, his underhand ways, and his nets everywhere spread. That poor man, the Cardinal

Richelieu, makes an attempt *here,* busies himself *there;* he toils, he strives; and what for? When he has succeeded in digging a mine, he finds a countermine already completed by the Count Duke . . .'

No one knows when the Podestà would have come ashore, had not Don Rodrigo, urged by the suggestions of his cousin, ordered a servant to bring him a certain bottle of wine.

'Signor Podestà,' said he, 'and gentlemen; a toast to the Count Duke; and you will then tell me whether the wine is worthy of the person.' The Podestà replied by a bow, in which might be discerned an expression of particular acknowledgment; for all that was said or done in honour of the Duke, he received, in part, as done to himself.

'Long live Don Gasparo Guzman, Count of Olivares, Duke of San Lucar, grand Private of the King, Don Philip the Great, our Sovereign!' exclaimed Don Rodrigo, raising his glass.

Private (for the information of those who know it not) was the title used in those days to signify the favourite of a prince.

'Long live the Count!' replied all.

'Help the Father,' said Don Rodrigo.

'Excuse me,' replied the Father; 'but I have already been guilty of a breach of discipline, and I cannot . . .'

'What!' said Don Rodrigo; 'it is a toast to the Count Duke. Will you make us believe that you hold with the Navarrines?'

Thus they contemptuously styled the French Princes of Navarre, who had begun to reign over them in the time of Henry IV.

On such an adjuration, he was obliged to taste the wine. All the guests broke out in exclamations and encomiums upon it, except the Doctor, who, by the gesture of his head, the glance of his eyes, and the compression of his lips, expressed much more than he could have done by words.

'What do *you* say of it, eh, Doctor?' asked Don Rodrigo.

Withdrawing from the wine-glass a nose more ruddy and bright than itself, the Doctor replied, with marked emphasis upon every syllable: 'I say, pronounce, and affirm that this is the Olivares of wines; *censui, et in eam ivi sententiam,* that its equal cannot be found in the twenty-two kingdoms of the King, our Sovereign, whom God defend! I declare and determine that the dinners of the most noble Signor Don Rodrigo excel the suppers of Heliogabalus, and that famine is perpetually banished and excluded from this place, where splendour reigns and has its abode.'

'Well said! well defined!' cried the guests, with one voice; but the word *famine,* which he had uttered by chance, at once directed the minds of all to this mournful subject, and every one spoke of the famine. In this matter they were all agreed, at least on the main point; but the uproar was greater, perhaps, than if there had been a diversity of opinion. All spoke at once. 'There is no famine,' said one; 'it is the monopolists . . .'

'And the bakers,' said another, 'who hide the grain. Hang them, say I.'

'Yes, yes, hang them without mercy.'

'Upon fair trial,' cried the Podestà.

'Trial?' cried Count Attilio, more loudly. 'Summary justice, I say. Take three or four, or five or six, of those who are acknowledged by the common voice to be the richest and most avaricious, and hang them.'

'Examples! examples!—without examples, nothing can be done.'

'Hang them! hang them! and grain will flow out in abundance.'

Whoever, in passing through a fair, has had the pleasure of hearing the harmony produced by a party of fiddlers, when, between one air and another, each one tunes his instrument, making it sound as loud as possible, that he may the more distinctly hear it in the midst of, and above, the surrounding uproar, may imagine what would be the harmony of these (if one may so say) discourses. The party continued pouring out and drinking the wine, while the praises of it were mingled, as was but just, with sentences of economical jurisprudence; so that the loudest, and most frequently heard, words were—*nectar,* and *hang them.*

Don Rodrigo, in the mean while, glanced from time to time towards the friar, and always saw him in the same station, giving no signs of impatience or hurry, without a movement tending to remind him that he was waiting his leisure, but with the air of one who was determined not to depart till he had had a hearing. He would gladly have sent him away, and escaped the interview; but to dismiss a Capuchin without having given him audience, was not according to the rules of his policy. However, since the annoying duty could not be avoided, he resolved to discharge it at once, and free himself from the obligation. He therefore rose from the table, and with him all the excited party, without ceasing their clamour. Having asked leave of his guests, he advanced in a haughty manner towards the friar, who had immediately risen with the rest; and saying to him, 'At your command, Father,' conducted him into another apartment.

CHAPTER VI

H OW can I obey you?' said Don Rodrigo, standing in the middle of the room. His words were these; but the tone in which they were pronounced, clearly meant to say, remember before whom you are standing, take heed to your words, and be expeditious.

There was no surer or quicker way of inspiring Friar Cristoforo with courage, than to address him with haughtiness. He had stood waveringly, and at a loss for words, passing through his fingers the beads of the rosary that hung at his girdle, as if he hoped to find in some of them an introduction to his speech; but at this behaviour of Don Rodrigo's, there instantly rose to his mind more to say than he had want of. Immediately, however, recollecting how important it was not to spoil his work, or, what was far worse, the work he had undertaken for others, he corrected and tempered the language that had presented itself to his mind, and said, with cautious humility; 'I come to propose to you an act of justice, to supplicate a deed of mercy. Some men of bad character have made use of the name of your illustrious lordship, to alarm a poor curate, and dissuade him from performing his duty, and to oppress two innocent persons. You can confound them by a word, restore all to order, and relieve those who are so shamefully wronged. You are able to do it; and being able . . . conscience, honour . . .'

'You will be good enough to talk of my conscience when I ask your advice about it. As to my honour, I beg to inform you, I am the guardian of it, and I only; and that whoever dares intrude himself to share the guardianship with me, I regard as a rash man, who offends against it.'

Friar Cristoforo, perceiving from these words that the Signor sought to put a wrong construction on all he said, and to turn the discourse into a dispute, so as to prevent his coming to the main point, bound himself still more rigidly to be patient, and to swallow every insult he might please to offer. He therefore replied, in a sub-dued tone, 'If I have said anything to offend you, I certainly did not intend it. Correct me, reprove me, if I do not speak becomingly, but deign to listen to me. For Heaven's sake—for the sake of that God in whose presence we must all appear . . .' and in saying this, he took between his hands the little cross of wood appended to his rosary, and held it up before the eyes of his frowning auditor; 'be not obstinately resolved to refuse an act of justice so easy and so due to the poor. Remember that God's eye is ever over them, and that their imprecations are heard above. Innocence is powerful in his . . .'

'Aha! father!' sharply interrupted Don Rodrigo: 'the respect I bear to your habit is great; but if anything could make me forget it, it would be to see it on one who dares to come as a spy into my house.'

These words brought a crimson glow upon the cheeks of the friar; but with the countenance of one who swallows a very bitter medicine, he replied, 'You do not think I deserve such a title. You feel in your heart that the act I am now performing is neither wicked nor contemptible. Listen to me, Signor Don Rodrigo; and Heaven grant a day may not come in which you will have to repent of not having listened to me! I will not lessen your honour.—What honour, Signor Don Rodrigo! what honour in the sight of men! what honour in the sight of God! You have much in your power, but . . .'

'Don't you know,' said Don Rodrigo, interrupting him in an agitated tone, the mingled effect of anger and remorse, 'don't you know that when the fancy takes me to hear a sermon, I can go to church like other people? But in my own house! Oh!' continued he, with a forced smile of mockery: 'You treat me as though I were of higher rank than I am. It is only princes who have a preacher in their own houses.'

'And that God who requires princes to render an account of the word preached to them in their palaces, that God who now bestows upon you a token of His mercy, by sending *His* minister, though indeed a poor and unworthy one, to intercede for an innocent . . .'

'In short, father,' said Don Rodrigo, preparing to go, 'I don't know what you mean: I can only suppose there must be some young girl you are concerned about. Make confidants of whom you please, but don't have the assurance to annoy a gentleman any longer.'

On the movement of Don Rodrigo, the friar also advanced, reverently placed himself in his way, raised his hands, both in an attitude of supplication, and also to detain him, and again replied, 'I am concerned for her, it is true, but not more than for yourself: there are two persons who concern me more than my own life. Don Rodrigo! I can only pray for you; but this I will do with my whole heart. Do not say "no" to me; do not keep a poor innocent in anguish and terror. One word from you will do all.'

'Well,' said Don Rodrigo, 'since you seem to think I can do so much for this person; since you are so much interested for her . . .'

'Well?' said Father Cristoforo, anxiously, while the behaviour and countenance of Don Rodrigo forbade his indulging in the hope which the words appeared to warrant.

'Well; advise her to come and put herself under my protection. She shall want for nothing, and no one shall dare molest her, as I am a gentleman.'

At such a proposal, the indignation of the friar, hitherto with difficulty confined within bounds, burst forth without restraint. All his good resolutions of prudence and patience forsook him, the old nature usurped the place of the new; and in these cases Father Cristoforo was indeed like two different men.

'Your protection!' exclaimed he, retiring a step or two, and fiercely resting on his right foot, his right hand placed on his hip, his left held up, pointing with his fore-finger towards Don Rodrigo, and two fiery-glancing eyes piercingly fixed upon him: 'your protection! Woe be to you that have thus spoken, that you have made me such a proposal. You have filled up the measure of your iniquity, and I no longer fear you.'

'How are you speaking to me, friar?'

'I speak as to one who is forsaken by God, and who can no longer excite fear. I knew that this innocent was under God's protection; but you, you have now made me feel it with so much certainty, that I have no longer need to ask protection of you. Lucia, I say—see how I pronounce this name with a bold face and unmoved expression.'

'What! in this house!'

'I pity this house; a curse is suspended over it. You will see whether the justice of God can be resisted by four walls, and four bravoes at your gates. Thought you that God had made a creature in his image, to give you the delight of tormenting her? Thought you that He would not defend her? You have despised His counsel, and you will be judged for it! The heart of Pharaoh was hardened, like yours, but God knew how to break it. Lucia is safe from you; I do not hesitate to say so, though a poor friar: and as to you, listen what I predict to you. A day will come . . .'

Don Rodrigo had stood till now with a mingled feeling of rage and mute astonishment; but on hearing the beginning of this prediction, an undefined and mysterious fear was added to his anger. Hastily seizing the Father's outstretched arm, and raising his voice to drown that of the inauspicious prophet, he exclaimed, 'Get out of my sight, rash villain—cowled rascal!'

These definite appellations calmed Father Cristoforo in a moment. The idea of submission and silence had been so long associated in his mind with that of contempt and injury, that at this compliment every feeling of warmth and enthusiasm instantly subsided, and he only resolved to listen patiently to whatever Don Rodrigo might be pleased to subjoin.

Quietly, then, withdrawing his hand from the Signor's grasp, he stood motionless, with his head bent downwards, as an aged tree, in the sudden lulling of an overbearing storm, resumes its natural position, and receives on its drooping branches the hail as Heaven sends it.

'Vile upstart!' continued Don Rodrigo; 'you treat me like an equal: but thank the cassock that covers your cowardly shoulders for saving you from the caresses that such scoundrels as you should receive, to teach them how to talk to a gentleman. Depart with sound limbs for this once, or we shall see.'

So saying, he pointed with imperious scorn to a door opposite the one they had entered; and Father Cristoforo bowed his head and departed, leaving Don Rodrigo to measure, with excited steps, the field of battle.

When the friar had closed the door behind him, he perceived some one in the apartment he had entered, stealing softly along the wall, that he might not be seen from the room of conference; and he instantly recognized the aged servant who had received him at the door on his arrival. This man had lived in the family for forty years, that is, since before Don Rodrigo's birth, having been in the service of his father, who was a very different kind of man. On his death, the new master dismissed all the household, and hired a fresh set of attendants, retaining, however, this one servant, both because he was old, and because, although of a temper and habits widely different from his own, he made amends for this defect by two qualifications—a lofty idea of the dignity of the house, and long experience in its ceremonials; with the most ancient traditions and minute particulars of which he was better acquainted than any one else. In the presence of his master, the poor old man never ventured a sign, still less an expression, of his disapprobation of what he saw around him every day; but at times he could scarcely refrain from some exclamation—some reproof murmured between his lips to his fellow-servants. They, highly diverted at his remarks, would sometimes urge him to conversation, provoking him to find fault with the present state of things, and to sound the praises of the ancient way of living in the family. His censures only came to his master's ears accompanied by a relation of the ridicule bestowed upon them, so that they merely succeeded in making him an object of contempt without resentment. On days of ceremony and entertainment, however, the old man became a person of serious importance.

Father Cristoforo looked at him as he passed, saluted him, and was about to go forward; but the old man approached with a mysterious air, put his fore-finger on his lips, and then beckoned to him, with the said fore-finger, to accompany him into a dark passage, where in an under tone, he said, 'Father, I have heard all and I want to speak to you.'

'Speak up then, at once, my good man.'

'Not here! woe to us if the master saw us! But I can learn much, and will try to come to-morrow to the convent.'

'Is there some project?'

'Something's in the wind, that's certain: I had already suspected it; but now I will be on the watch, and will find out all. Leave it to me. I happen to see and hear things . . . strange things! I am in a house! . . . But I wish to save my soul.'

'God bless you!' said the friar, softly pronouncing the benediction, as he laid his hand on the servant's head, who, though much older than himself, bent before him with the respect of a son. 'God will reward you,' continued the friar: 'don't fail to come to me to-morrow.'

'I will be sure to come,' replied the servant; 'but do you go quickly, and . . . for Heaven's sake . . . don't betray me.' So saying, and looking cautiously around, he went out, at the other end of the passage, into a hall that led to the court-yard; and seeing the coast clear, beckoned to the good friar, whose face responded to the last injunction more plainly than any protestations could have done. The old man pointed to the door, and the friar departed without further delay.

This servant had been listening at his master's door. Had he done right? And was Father Cristoforo right in praising him for it? According to the commonest and most generally received rules, it was a very dishonest act; but might not this case be regarded as an exception? And are there not exceptions to the most-generally-received rules?

These are questions which we leave the reader to resolve at his pleasure. We do not pretend to give judgment: it is enough that we relate facts.

Having reached the road, and turned his back upon this wild beast's den, Father Cristoforo breathed more freely, as he hastened down the descent, his face flushed, and his mind, as every one may imagine, agitated and confused by what he had recently heard and said. But the unexpected proffer of the old man had been a great relief to him; it seemed as if Heaven had given him a visible token of its protection. Here is a clue, thought he, that Providence has put into my hands. In this very house, too! and without my even dreaming of looking for one! Engaged in such thoughts, he raised his eyes towards the west, and seeing the setting sun already touching the summit of the mountain, was reminded that the day was fast drawing to a close. He therefore quickened his steps, though weary and weak, after the many annoyances of the day, that he might have time to carry back his intelligence, such as it was, to his protégés and arrive at the convent before night; for this was one of the most absolute and strictly-enforced rules of the Capuchin discipline.

In the mean time, there had been plans proposed and debated in Lucia's cottage, with which it is necessary to acquaint the reader. After the departure of the friar, the three friends remained some time silent; Lucia, with a sorrowful heart, preparing the dinner; Renzo, irresolute, and changing his position every moment, to avoid the sight of her mournful face, yet without heart to leave her; Agnese, apparently intent upon the reel she was winding, though, in fact, she was deliberating upon a plan; and when she thought it sufficiently matured, she broke the silence with these words:—

'Listen, my children. If you have as much courage and dexterity as is required; if you will trust your mother, (this *your mother,* addressed to both, made Lucia's heart bound within her,) I will undertake to get you out of this difficulty, better, perhaps, and more quickly than Father Cristoforo, though he is a man.' Lucia stopped and looked at her mother with a face more expressive of wonder than of confidence in so magnificent a promise; and Renzo hastily exclaimed, 'Courage? dexterity?—tell me, tell me, what can we do?'

'If you were married,' continued Agnese, 'it would be the great difficulty out of the way—wouldn't it? and couldn't we easily find a remedy for all the rest?'

'Is there any doubt?' said Renzo: 'if we were married . . . One may live anywhere; and, at Bergamo, not far from here, a silk-weaver would be received with open arms. You know how often my cousin Bortolo has wanted me to go and live with him, that I might make a fortune as he has done; and if I have never listened to him, it is . . . you know, because my heart was here. Once married, we would all go thither together, and live in blessed peace, out of this villain's reach, and far from temptation to do a rash deed. Isn't it true, Lucia?'

'Yes,' said Lucia; 'but how? . . .'

'As I have told you,' replied Agnese. 'Be bold and expert, and the thing is easy.'

'Easy!' at the same moment exclaimed the two lovers, to whom it had become so strangely and sadly difficult.

'Easy, if you know how to go about it,' replied Agnese. 'Listen attentively to me, and I will try and make you understand it. I have heard say, by people who ought to know, and I have seen it myself in one case, that to solemnize a marriage, a curate, of course, is necessary, but not his good-will or consent; it is enough if he is present.'

'How can this be?' asked Renzo.

'Listen, and you shall hear. There must be two witnesses, nimble and well agreed. They must go to the priest; the point is to take him by surprise, that he mayn't have time to escape. The man says, "Signor Curate, this is my wife;" the woman says, "Signor Curate, this is my husband." It is necessary that the curate and the witnesses hear it, and then the marriage is just as valid and sacred as if the Pope had blessed it. When once the words are spoken, the curate may fret, and fume, and storm, but it will do no good; you are man and wife.'

'Is it possible?' exclaimed Lucia.

'What!' said Agnese, 'do you think I have learnt nothing in the thirty years I was in the world before you? The thing is just as I told you; and a friend of mine is a proof of it, who, wishing to be married against the will of her parents, did as I was saying, and gained her end. The curate suspected it, and was on the watch; but they knew so well how to go about it, that they arrived just at the right moment, said the words, and became man and wife; though she, poor thing! repented of it before three days were over.'

It was, in fact, as Agnese had represented it; marriages contracted in this manner were then, and are even to this day, acknowledged valid. As, however, this expedient was never resorted to but by those who had met with some obstacle or refusal in the ordinary method, the priest took great care to avoid such forced co-operation;

and if one of them happened to be surprised by a couple, accompanied with witnesses, he tried every means of escape, like Proteus in the hands of those who would have made him prophesy by force.

'If it were true, Lucia!' said Renzo, fixing his eyes upon her with a look of imploring expectation.

'What! if it were true?' replied Agnese. 'You think, then, I tell lies. I do my best for you, and am not believed: very well; get out of the difficulty as you can: I wash my hands of it.'

'Ah, no! don't forsake us,' cried Renzo. 'I said so because it appeared too good a thing. I place myself in your hands, and will consider you as if you were really my mother.'

These words instantly dispelled the momentary indignation of Agnese, and made her forget a resolution which, in reality, had only been in word.

'But why, then, mother,' said Lucia, in her usual gentle manner, 'why didn't this plan come into Father Cristoforo's mind?'

'Into his mind?' replied Agnese; 'do you think it didn't come into his mind? But he wouldn't speak of it.'

'Why?' demanded they both at once.

'Because . . . because, if you must know it, the friars think that it is not exactly a proper thing.'

'How can it help standing firm, and being well done, when it *is* done!' said Renzo.

'How can I tell you?' replied Agnese. 'Other people have made the law as they pleased, and we poor people can't understand all. And then, how many things . . . See; it is like giving a Christian a blow. It isn't right, but when it is once given, not even the Pope can recall it.'

'If it isn't right,' said Lucia, 'we ought not to do it.'

'What!' said Agnese, 'would I give you advice contrary to the fear of God? If it were against the will of your parents, and to marry a rogue . . . but when I am satisfied, and it is to wed this youth, and he who makes all this disturbance is a villain, and the Signor Curate . . .'

'It is as clear as the sun,' said Renzo.

'One need not speak to Father Cristoforo, before doing it,' continued Agnese; 'but when it is once done, and has well succeeded, what do you think the Father will say to you?—Ah, daughter! it was a sad error, but it is done. The friars, you know, must talk so. But trust me, in his heart he will be very well satisfied.'

Without being able to answer such reasoning, Lucia did not think it appeared very convincing; but Renzo, quite encouraged, said, 'Since it is thus, the thing is done.'

'Gently,' said Agnese. 'The witnesses, where are they to be found? Then, how will you manage to get at the Signor Curate, who has been shut up in his house two days? And how make him stand when you do get at him? for though he is weighty enough naturally, I dare venture to say, when he sees you make your appearance in such a guise, he will become as nimble as a cat, and flee like the devil from holy water.'

'I have found a way—I've found one,' cried Renzo, striking the table with his clenched hand, till he made the dinner-things quiver and rattle with the blow; and he proceeded to relate his design, which Agnese entirely approved.

'It is all confusion,' said Lucia; 'it is not perfectly honest. Till now we have always acted sincerely; let us go on in faith, and God will help us; Father Cristoforo said so. Do listen to his advice.'

'Be guided by those who know better than you,' said Agnese, gravely. 'What need is there to ask advice? God bids us help ourselves, and then He will help us. We will tell the Father all about it when it is over.'

'Lucia,' said Renzo, 'will you fail me now? Have we not done all like good Christians? Ought we not now to have been man and wife? Didn't the Curate himself fix the day and hour? And whose fault is it, if we are now obliged to use a little cunning? No, no; you won't fail me. I am going, and will come back with an answer.' So saying, he gave Lucia an imploring look, and Agnese a very knowing glance, and hastily took his departure.

It is said that trouble sharpens the wit; and Renzo, who, in the upright and straightforward path he had hitherto followed, had never had occasion to sharpen his in any great degree, had, in this instance, planned a design that would have done honour to a lawyer. He went directly, as he had purposed, to a cottage near at hand, belonging to a certain Tonio, whom he found busy in the kitchen, with one knee resting on the stand of a chafing-dish, holding in his right hand the handle of a saucepan, that stood on the burning embers, and stirring with a broken rolling-pin, a little grey *polenta*,[1] of Turkey flour. The mother, brother, and wife of Tonio, were seated at the table; and three or four little children stood around, waiting, with eyes eagerly fixed on the saucepan, till the gruel should be ready to pour out. But the pleasure was wanting which the sight of dinner usually gives to those who have earned it by hard labour. The quantity of the *polenta* was rather in proportion to the times than to the number and inclinations of the household; and each one eyeing the common food with envious looks of strong desire, seemed to be measuring the extent of appetite likely to survive it. While Renzo was exchanging salutations with the family, Tonio poured out the *polenta* into the wooden trencher that stood ready to receive it, and it looked like a little moon in a large circle of vapour. Nevertheless, the women courteously said to Renzo, 'Will you take some with us?'—a compliment that the Lombard peasant never fails to pay to any one who finds him at a meal, even though the visitor were a rich glutton just risen from table, and he were at the last mouthful.

'Thank you,' replied Renzo; 'I only came to say a word or two to Tonio; and if you like, Tonio, not to disturb your family, we can go dine at the inn, and talk there.' This proposal was as acceptable to Tonio as it was unexpected; and the women, not unwilling, saw one competitor for the *polenta* removed, and that the most formidable. Tonio did not require a second asking, and they set off together.

Arrived at the village inn, they sat down at their ease, perfectly alone, since the prevailing poverty had banished all the usual frequenters of this scene of mirth and joviality. They called for the little that was to be had, and having emptied a glass of wine, Renzo addressed Tonio with an air of mystery; 'If you will do me a small favour, I will do you a great one.'

'What is it?—tell me! I'm at your service,' replied Tonio, pour-

---

[1] A thick gruel, made of flour and water, boiled together.

ing out another glass; 'I'm ready to go into the fire for you to-day.'

'You are in debt twenty-five livres to the Signor Curate for the rent of his field that you worked last year.'

'Ah, Renzo, Renzo! you've spoiled your kindness. Why did you remind me of it now? You've put to flight all my good will towards you.'

'If I reminded you of your debt,' said Renzo, 'it is because I intend, if you like, to give you the means of paying it.'

'Do you really mean so?'

'I do really. Well, are you content?'

'Content? I should think so, indeed! if it were for no other reason than to get rid of those tormenting looks and shakes of the head the Signor Curate gives me every time I meet him. And then it is always—"Tonio, remember: Tonio, when shall I see you to settle this business?" He goes so far, that, when he fixes his eyes upon me in preaching, I'm half afraid he will say publicly: Those twenty-five livres! I wish the twenty-five livres were far away! And then he will have to give me back my wife's gold necklace, and I could change it into so much *polenta*. But . . .'

'But, if you'll do me a little service, the twenty-five livres are ready.'

'With all my heart; go on.'

'But! . . .' said Renzo, laying his finger across his lips.

'Need you tell me that? You know me.'

'The Signor Curate has been starting some absurd objections, to delay my marriage. They tell me for certain, that if we go before him with two witnesses, and I say, This is my wife; and Lucia, This is my husband; the marriage is valid. Do you understand me?'

'You want me to go as a witness?'

'Yes.'

'And you will pay the twenty-five livres for me?'

'That is what I mean.'

'He's a goose that would fail.'

'But we must find another witness.'

'I have him! That young clownish brother of mine, Gervase,

will do anything I bid him. You'll pay him with something to drink?'

'And to eat, too,' replied Renzo. 'We'll bring him here to make merry with us. But will he know what to do?'

'I'll teach him. You know I have got his share of brains.'

'To-morrow . . .'

'Well.'

'Towards evening . . .'

'Very well.'

'But! . . .' said Renzo, again putting his finger on his lips.

'Poh!' replied Tonio, bending his head on his right shoulder, and raising his left hand, with a look that seemed to say, Do you doubt me?

'But if your wife questions you, as without doubt she will . . .'

'I owe my wife some lies, and so many, that I don't know if I shall ever manage to balance the account. I'll find some idle story to put her heart at rest, I warrant you.'

'To-morrow,' said Renzo, 'we will make arrangements, that everything may go on smoothly.'

So saying, they left the inn, Tonio bending his steps homewards, and contriving some tale to relate to the women, and Renzo to give an account of the concerted arrangements.

In the mean while, Agnese had been vainly endeavouring to convince her daughter. To every argument, Lucia opposed one side or other of her dilemma; either the thing is wrong, and we ought not to do it, or it is not wrong, and why not tell it to Father Cristoforo?

Renzo arrived quite triumphant, and reported his success, finishing with a *ahn?*—a Milanese interjection which signifies—Am I a man or not? can you find a better plan? would it ever have entered your head? and a hundred other such things.

Lucia shook her head doubtfully; but the other two enthusiasts paid little attention to it, as one does to a child when one despairs of making it understand all the reasons of a thing, and determines to induce it by entreaties or authority to do as it is required.

'It goes on well,' said Agnese, 'very well; but . . . you haven't thought of everything.'

'What is wanting?' replied Renzo.

'Perpetua!—you haven't thought of Perpetua! She will admit Tonio and his brother well enough, but you—you two—just think! You will have to keep her at a distance, as one keeps a boy from a pear-tree full of ripe fruit.'

'How shall we manage?' said Renzo, beginning to think.

'See, now! I have thought of that, too; I will go with you; and I have a secret that will draw her away, and engage her, so that she sha'n't see you, and you can go in. I'll call her out, and will touch a chord . . . You shall see.'

'Bless you!' exclaimed Renzo; 'I always said you are our help in everything.'

'But all this is of no use,' said Agnese, 'unless we can persuade Lucia, who persists in saying it is a sin.'

Renzo brought in all his eloquence to his aid, but Lucia continued immovable.

'I cannot answer all your arguments,' said she; 'but I see that, to do what you want, we shall be obliged to use a great deal of disguise, falsehood, and deceit. Ah, Renzo! we didn't begin so. I wish to be your wife'—and she could never pronounce this word, or give expression to this desire, without a deep flush overspreading her cheek—'I wish to be your wife, but in the right way—in the fear of God, at the altar. Let us leave all to Him who is above. Do you think He cannot find means to help us better than we, with all these deceitful ways? And why make a mystery of it to Father Cristoforo?'

The dispute was still prolonged, and seemed not likely to come to a speedy conclusion, when the hasty tread of sandals, and the sound of a rustling cassock, resembling the noise produced by repeated gusts of wind in a slackened sail, announced the approach of Father Cristoforo. There was instant silence, and Agnese had scarcely time to whisper in Lucia's ear, 'Be sure you say nothing about it.'

CHAPTER VII

FATHER CRISTOFORO arrived with the air of a good general, who having lost an important battle, without any fault on his part,—distressed, but not discouraged; thoughtful, but not confounded; retreating, but not put to flight; turns his steps where necessity calls for his presence, fortifying threatened quarters, regulating his troops, and giving new orders.

'Peace be with you!' said he, as he entered. 'There is nothing to hope from man; you have therefore more need to trust in God, and I have already had a pledge of His protection.'

Although none of the party had anticipated much from Father Cristoforo's attempt, (since, to see a powerful nobleman desist from an act of oppression, unless he were overcome by a superior power, from regard to the entreaties of a disarmed suppliant, was rather an unheard-of, than a rare, occurrence,) yet the melancholy certainty came as a blow upon them all. Their heads involuntarily drooped, but anger quickly prevailed over depression in Renzo's mind. The announcement found him already wounded and irritated by a succession of painful surprises, fallacious attempts, and disappointed hopes, and, above all, exasperated at this moment by the repulses of Lucia.

'I should like to know,' said he, gnashing his teeth and raising his voice as he had never before done in the presence of Father Cristoforo; 'I should like to know what reasons this dog gives for asserting . . . for asserting that my bride should not be my bride?'

'Poor Renzo!' replied the friar, with a look and accent of pity that kindly recommended peaceableness; 'if the powerful who do such deeds of injustice, were always obliged to give their reasons, things would not be as they are.'

'Did the dog then say that he would not, *because* he would not?'

'He didn't even say that, my poor fellow! It would be something, if so commit iniquity, they were obliged openly to confess it.'

'But he must have told you something; what did this infernal firebrand say?'

'I heard his words, but I cannot repeat them to you. The words of a powerful wicked man are violent, but contradictory. He can be angry that you are suspicious of him, and at the same time make you feel that your suspicions are well-founded; he can insult you, and call himself offended; ridicule you, and ask your opinion; threaten, and complain; be insolent, and irreprehensible. Ask no more. He neither mentioned the name of this innocent, nor your own; he did not even appear to know you, nor did he say he designed anything; but . . . but I understood too well that he is immovable. However, confidence in God, you poor creatures!' turning to Agnese and Lucia, 'don't give up in despair! And you, Renzo . . . oh! believe me, I can put myself in your place; I can feel what passes in your heart. But, patience; it is a poor word, a bitter one to those who have no faith; but you—will you not allow God one day, two days, or whatever time He may please to take to clear you and give you justice? The time is His; and He has promised us much. Leave Him to work, Renzo; and . . . believe me, I already have a clue that may lead to something for your help. I cannot tell you more at present. To-morrow I shall not come here; I must be at the convent all day, for you. You, Renzo, try to come to me; or if, by any unforeseen accident, you cannot, send a trustworthy man, or a lad of discretion, by whom I may let you know what may happen. It grows dark; I shall have to make haste to reach the convent. Faith, courage, and good night.'

Having said this, he hastily left them, and made his way rapidly along a crooked, stony by-path, that he might not be late at the convent, and run the risk of a severe reprimand, or, what would have grieved him more, the infliction of a penance, which might have disabled him on the morrow from any undertaking which the service of his protégés might require.

'Did you hear what he said about . . . I don't know what . . . about a clue that he held in hand to help us?' said Lucia. 'It is best to trust in him; he is a man who, if he promises ten . . .'

'I know there is not his like,' interrupted Agnese; 'but he ought to have spoken more clearly, or, at least, taken me aside and told me what it was.'

'Idle prating! I'll put an end to it, that I will!' interrupted Renzo,

in his turn, as he paced furiously up and down the room, with a
look and tone that left no doubt as to the meaning of his words.

'Oh, Renzo!' exclaimed Lucia.

'What do you mean?' cried Agnese.

'Why need I tell you? I'll put an end to it! Though he has a
hundred, a thousand devils in his soul, he's flesh and blood, after
all.'

'No, no! for Heaven's sake! . . .' began Lucia, but tears choked
her utterance.

'This is not proper language, even in jest,' replied Agnese.

'In jest!' cried Renzo, planting himself directly before Agnese,
as she sat, and fixing on her two fearful-looking eyes. 'In jest!
you shall see whether I am in jest or not.'

'Ah, Renzo!' said Lucia, scarcely able to articulate for sobs, 'I
never saw you so before.'

'Don't talk so, for Heaven's sake!' replied Agnese, hastily, lowering her voice. 'Don't you remember how many arms he has at his
bidding? And then, there is always justice to be had against the
poor . . . God defend them!'

'I will get justice for myself, I will. It is time now. The thing
isn't easy, I know. The ruffian is well defended, dog that he is!
I know how it is: but never mind. Patience and resolution . . .
and the time will soon arrive. Yes, I will get justice. I'll free the
country, and people will bless me! And then in four bounds . . .'

The horror of Lucia at these explicit declarations repressed her
sobs, and inspired her with courage to speak. Raising from her
hands her face bathed in tears, she addressed Renzo in a mournful,
but resolute tone: 'You no longer care, then, about having me
for your wife? I promised myself to a youth who had the fear of
God: but a man who has . . . were he safe from all justice and
vengeance, were he the son of a king . . .'

'Very well!' cried Renzo, his face more than ever convulsed with
fury; 'I won't have you, then; but he sha'n't either. I will be here
without you, and he in the abode of . . .'

'Ah, no, for pity's sake, don't say so; don't look so furious! No,
no, I cannot bear to see you thus,' exclaimed Lucia, weeping, and
joining her hands in an attitude of earnest supplication; while

Agnese repeatedly called him by name, and seized hold of his shoulders, his arms, and his hands, to pacify him. He stood immovable, thoughtful, almost overcome at the sight of Lucia's imploring countenance; then, suddenly gazed at her sternly, drew back, stretched out his arm, and pointing with his finger towards her, burst forth: 'Her! yes, he wants *her!* He must die!'

'And *I,* what harm have I done you, that you should kill *me?*' said Lucia, throwing herself on her knees.

'You!' said he, with a voice expressive of anger, though of a far different nature; 'you! what good do you wish me? What proof have you given me? Haven't I begged, and begged, and begged? . . . Have I been able to obtain . . .'

'Yes, yes,' replied she, precipitately; 'I will go to the Curate's to-morrow; I will go now, if you like. Only be yourself again, I will go.'

'You promise me?' said Renzo, his voice and expression rendered in an instant more human.

'I promise you.'

'You have promised me?'

'Thanks be to Thee, O Lord!' exclaimed Agnese, doubly satisfied.

Did Renzo, in the midst of his anger, discern the advantage that might be taken of Lucia's terror? And did he not practise a little artifice to increase it, that he might use this advantage? Our author protests he knows nothing about the matter; nor, I think, did even Renzo himself know very well. At any rate, he was undoubtedly enraged beyond measure with Don Rodrigo, and ardently desired Lucia's consent; and when two powerful passions struggle together in a man's mind, no one, not even the most patient, can always clearly discern one voice from the other, or say, with certainty, which of them predominates.

'I *have* promised you,' replied Lucia, with an accent of timid and affectionate reproof; 'but you have also promised not to make any disturbance—to submit yourself to Father . . .'

'Come, now, for whose sake did I get into a passion? Do you want to draw back? And will you oblige me to do a rash thing?'

'No, no,' said Lucia, ready to relapse into her former fears. 'I have promised, and I will not draw back. But see how you have made me promise; God forbid that . . .'

'Why will you prophesy evil, Lucia? God knows we do no wrong to anybody.'

'Promise me, at least, this shall be the last time.'

'I promise you, upon my word.'

'But this once you will stand by him,' said Agnese.

Here the author confesses his ignorance of another matter, and that is, whether Lucia was absolutely, and on every account, dissatisfied at being obliged to give her consent. We follow his example, and leave the point undecided.

Renzo would willingly have prolonged the conversation, and allotted their several parts in the proceedings of the morrow; but it was already dark, and the women wished him good night, as they thought it scarcely decorous that he should remain any longer with them at so late an hour.

The night was passed by all three as well as could be expected, considering that it followed a day of such excitement and misfortune, and preceded one fixed upon for an important undertaking of doubtful issue. Renzo made his appearance early next morning, and concerted with the women, or rather with Agnese, the grand operations of the evening, alternately suggesting and removing difficulties, foreseeing obstacles, and both beginning, by turns, to describe the scene as if they were relating a past event. Lucia listened; and, without approving in words what she could not agree to in her heart, promised to do as well as she was able.

'Are you going down to the convent to see Father Cristoforo, as he bid you, last night?' said Agnese to Renzo.

'Not I,' replied he; 'you know what discerning eyes the Father has; he will read in my looks, as if it were written in a book, that there's something in the wind; and if he begins to question me, I can't get off it easily. And, besides, I must stay here to arrange matters. It will be better for you to send somebody.'

'I will send Menico.'

'Very well,' replied Renzo; and he set off to arrange matters, as he had said.

Agnese went to a neighbouring cottage to ask for Menico, a sprightly and very sensible lad for his age, who, through the medium of cousins and sisters-in-law, came to be a sort of nephew to the dame. She asked his parents for him, as for a loan, and begged she might keep him the whole day, 'for a particular service,' said she. Having obtained permission, she led him to her kitchen, gave him his breakfast, and bid him go to Pescarenico, and present himself to Father Cristoforo, who would send him back with a message at the right time. 'Father Cristoforo, that fine old man, you know, with a white beard, who is called the Saint . . .'

'I understand,' said Menico; 'he who speaks so kindly to the children, and sometimes gives them pictures.'

'Just so, Menico. And if he bids you wait some time at the convent, don't wander away; and be sure you don't go with other boys to the lake to throw stones into the water, nor to watch them fish, nor to play with the nets hung up to dry, nor . . .'

'Poh, aunt; I am no longer a child.'

'Well, be prudent; and when you come back with the answer . . . look; these two fine new *parpagliole* are for you.'

'Give me them now, that . . .'

'No, no, you will play with them. Go, and behave well, that you may have some more.'

In the course of this long morning many strange things happened which roused not a little suspicion in the already-disturbed minds of Agnese and Lucia. A beggar, neither thin nor ragged, as they generally were, and of somewhat dark and sinister aspect, came and asked alms, in God's name, at the same time looking narrowly around. A piece of bread was given him, which he received, and placed in his basket, with ill-dissembled indifference. He then loitered, and made many inquiries, with a mixed air of impudence and hesitation, to which Agnese endeavoured to make replies exactly contrary to the truth. When about to depart, he pretended to mistake the door, and went to that at the foot of the stairs, glancing hastily upwards, as well as he could. On their calling him back— 'Hey! hey! where are you going, my good man?—this way!' he turned and went out by the door that was pointed out to him, excusing himself with a submission, and an affected humility, that ill accorded with the fierce and hard features of his face. After his departure, they continued to mark, from time to time, other suspicious and strange figures. It was not easy to discern what kind of men they were; yet still they could not believe them to be the unpretending passers-by they wished to appear. One would enter under pretence of asking the way; others, arriving at the door, slackened their pace, and peeped through the little yard into the room, as if wishing to see without exciting suspicion. At last, towards noon, these annoying and alarming appearances ceased. Agnese got up occasionally, and crossed the little yard to the street-door, to reconnoitre; and after looking anxiously around on either side, returned with the intelligence, 'There's nobody;' words which she uttered with pleasure, and Lucia heard with satisfaction, neither one nor the other knowing exactly the reason why. But an undefined disquietude haunted their steps, and, with Lucia especially, in some degree cooled the courage they had summoned up for the proceedings of the evening.

The reader, however, must be told something more definite about these mysterious wanderers; and to relate it in order, we must turn back a step or two, and find Don Rodrigo, whom we left yesterday after dinner by himself, in one of the rooms of his palace, after the departure of Father Cristoforo.

Don Rodrigo, as we have said, paced backwards and forwards with long strides in this spacious apartment, surrounded on all sides by the family portraits of many generations. When he reached the wall and turned round, his eye rested upon the figure of one of his warlike ancestors, the terror of his enemies, and of his own soldiers; who, with a stern grim countenance, his short hair standing erect from his forehead, his large sharp whiskers covering his cheeks, and his hooked chin, stood like a warrior, clothed in a complete suit of steel armour, with his right hand pressing his side, and the left grasping the hilt of his sword. Don Rodrigo gazed upon it, and when he arrived beneath it, and turned back, beheld before him another of his forefathers, a magistrate, and the terror of litigants, seated in a high chair, covered with crimson velvet, enveloped in an ample black robe, so that he was entirely black, excepting for a white collar, with two large bands, and a lining of sable, turned wrong side outwards, (this was the distinctive mark of senators, but only worn in winter; for which reason the picture of a senator in summer-clothing is never met with,) squalid, and frowning; he held in his hand a memorial, and seemed to be saying, 'We shall see.' On the one hand was a matron, the terror of her maids; on the other, an abbot, the terror of his monks; in short, they were all persons who had been objects of terror while alive, and who now inspired dread by their likenesses. In the presence of such remembrancers, Don Rodrigo became enraged and ashamed, as he reflected that a friar had dared to come to him with the parable of Nathan; and his mind could find no peace. He would form a plan of revenge, and then abandon it; seek how, at the same time, to satisfy his passion, and what he called his honour; and sometimes, hearing the beginning of the prophecy resounding in his ears, he would involuntarily shudder, and be almost inclined to give up the idea of the two satisfactions. At last, for the sake of doing something, he called a servant, and desired him to make an apology for him to the company, and to say that he was detained by urgent business. The servant returned with the intelligence that the gentlemen, having left their compliments, had taken their leave.

'And Count Attilio?' asked Don Rodrigo, still pacing the room.

'He left with the gentlemen, illustrious Signor.'

'Very well; six followers to accompany me—quickly! my sword, cloak and hat, immediately!'

The servant replied by a bow and withdrew, returning shortly with a rich sword, which his master buckled on, a cloak which he threw over his shoulders, and a hat, ornamented with lofty plumes, which he placed on his head, and fastened with a haughty air. He then moved forward, and found the six bravoes at the door, completely armed, who, making way for him, with a low bow, followed as his train. More surly, more haughty, and more supercilious than usual, he left his palace, and took the way towards Lecco, amidst the salutations and profound bows of the peasants he happened to meet; and the ill-mannered wight who would have ventured to pass without taking off his hat, might consider he had purchased the exemption at a cheap rate, had the bravoes in the train been contented merely to enforce respect by a blow on the head. To these salutations Don Rodrigo made no acknowledgment; but to men of higher rank, though still indisputably inferior to his own, he replied with constrained courtesy. He did not chance this time, but when he did happen to meet with the Spanish Signor, the Gov-

ernor of the Castle, the salutations were equally profound on both
sides; it was like the meeting of two potentates, who have nothing to
share between them, yet, for convenience sake, pay respect to each
other's rank. To pass away the time, and, by the sight of far different
faces and behaviour, to banish the image of the friar, which continually haunted his mind, Don Rodrigo entered a house where a
large party was assembled, and where he was received with that
officious and respectful cordiality reserved for those who are greatly
courted, and greatly feared. Late at night he returned to his own
palace, and found that Count Attilio had just arrived; and they sat
down to supper together, Don Rodrigo buried in thought, and
very silent.

'Cousin, when will you pay your wager?' asked Count Attilio,
in a malicious, and at the same time rallying, tone, as soon as the
table was cleared, and the servants had departed.

'St. Martin has not yet passed.'

'Well, remember you will have to pay it soon; for all the saints
in the calendar will pass before . . .'

'This has to be seen yet.'

'Cousin, you want to play the politician; but I understand all; and
I am so certain of having won my wager, that I am ready to lay
another.'

'What?'

'That the Father . . . the Father . . . I mean, in short, that this
friar has converted you.'

'It is a mere fancy of your own.'

'Converted, cousin; converted, I say. I, for my part, am delighted
at it. What a fine sight it will be to see you quite penitent, with
downcast eyes! And what triumph for this Father! How proudly
he must have returned to the convent! You are not such fish as
they catch every day, nor in every net. You may be sure they will
bring you forward as an example; and when they go on a mission
to some little distance, they will talk of your acts. I can fancy I
hear them.' And, speaking through his nose, accompanying the
words with caricatured gestures, he continued, in a sermon-like tone,
"In a certain part of the world, which from motives of high respect
we forbear to name, there lived, my dear hearers, and there still

lives, a dissolute gentleman, the friend of women rather than of good men, who, accustomed to make no distinctions, had set his eyes upon . . ."

'That will do . . . enough,' interrupted Don Rodrigo, half amused and half annoyed: 'If you wish to repeat the wager, I am ready, too.'

'Indeed! perhaps, then, *you* have converted the Father?'

'Don't talk to me about him: and as to the bet, Saint Martin will decide.' The curiosity of the Count was aroused; he put numberless questions, but Don Rodrigo contrived to evade them all, referring everything to the day of decision, and unwilling to communicate designs which were neither begun nor absolutely determined upon.

Next morning, Don Rodrigo was himself again. The slight compunction that *'a day will come'* had awakened in his mind, had vanished with the dreams of the night; and nothing remained but a feeling of deep indignation, rendered more vivid by remorse for his passing weakness. The remembrance of his late almost-triumphant walk, of the profound salutations, and the receptions he had met with, together with the rallying of his cousin, had contributed not a little to renew his former spirit. Hardly risen, he sent for Griso.—Something important,—thought the servant to whom the order was given; for the man who bore this assumed name was no less a personage than the head of the bravoes, to whom the boldest and most dangerous enterprises were confided, who was the most trusted by his master, and was devoted to him, at all risks, by gratitude and interest. Guilty of murder, he had sought the protection of Don Rodrigo, to escape the pursuit of justice; and he, by taking him into his service, had sheltered him from the reach of persecution. Here, by engaging in every crime that was required of him, he was secured from the punishment of the first fault. To Don Rodrigo the acquisition had been of no small importance; for this Griso, besides being undoubtedly the most courageous of the household, was also a specimen of what his master had been able to attempt with impunity against the laws; so that Don Rodrigo's power was aggrandized both in reality and in common opinion.

'Griso!' said Don Rodrigo, 'in this emergency it will be seen what you are worth. Before to-morrow, Lucia must be in this palace.'

'It shall never be said that Griso shrank from the command of his noble protector.'

'Take as many men as you want, dispose and order them as you think best, only let the thing succeed well. But, above all, be sure you do her no harm.'

'Signor, a little fright, that she may not make too much noise . . . one cannot do less.'

'Fear . . . I see . . . is inevitable. But don't you touch a hair of her head; and, above all, treat her with the greatest respect. Do you understand?'

'Signor, I could not pluck a flower from its stalk, and bring it to your lordship, without touching it a little. But I will do no more than is necessary.'

'Beware you do not. And . . . how will you manage?'

'I was thinking, Signor. It is fortunate that the house is at the end of the village. We shall want a place to conceal ourselves in; and at a little distance there's that uninhabited building in the middle of the fields, that house . . . but your lordship knows nothing of these things . . . a house that was burnt down a few days ago; and there have been no funds to rebuild it, so it is forsaken, and is haunted by witches; but it is not Saturday, and I don't care for them. The villagers are so superstitious, they wouldn't enter it any night of the week for a treasure, so we may safely dispose ourselves there, without any fear of being disturbed in our plans.'

'Very good: and what then?'

Here Griso went on to propose, and Don Rodrigo to discuss, till they had, together, concerted a way to bring the enterprise to an end without a trace of its authors remaining. They even contrived means to turn all the suspicions, by making false indications, upon another quarter; to impose silence upon poor Agnese; to inspire Renzo with such fear as would overbalance his grief, efface the thought of having recourse to the law, and even the wish to complain; and arranged all the other minor villainies necessary to the success of this principal one. We will omit the account of these consultations, however, because, as the reader will perceive, they are not necessary to the comprehension of the story, and it will only be tedious, both to him and us, to entertain ourselves for any length of time with the discussions of these two detestable villains. It will suffice to say that, as Griso was on the point of leaving the room, to go about the execution of his undertaking at once, Don Rodrigo called him back, and said, 'Listen: if by any chance this rash clown should molest you to-night, it would not be amiss if you were to give him something to remember, on his shoulders, by way of anticipation. By this means, the command to keep quiet, which shall be intimated to him to-morrow, will more surely take effect. But don't go to look for him, lest you should spoil what is of more importance. Do you understand me?'

'Leave it to me,' replied Griso, bowing with an obsequious and ostentatious air, as he departed.

The morning was spent in reconnoitring the neighbourhood. The feigned beggar who had intruded himself so pertinaciously into Agnese's humble cottage, was no other than Griso, who had come to get an idea of the plan of the house by sight; the pretended passengers were his vile followers, who, operating under his orders, required a less minute acquaintance with the place. Their observations being made, they withdrew from notice, lest they should excite too much suspicion.

When they returned to the palace, Griso made his report, arranged definitely the plan of the enterprise, assigned to each his different part, and gave his instructions. All this could not be transacted without the old servant's observation, who, with his eyes and ears constantly on the alert, discovered that they were plotting some great undertaking. By dint of watching and questioning, getting half a hint here, and another half there, commenting in his own mind on ambiguous inferences, and interpreting mysterious departures, he at length came to a pretty clear knowledge of all the designs of the evening. But when he was assured of them, it was very near the time, and already a small detachment of bravoes had left the palace, and set off to conceal themselves in the ruined building. The poor old man, although he well knew what a dangerous game he was playing, and feared, besides, that he was doing no efficient service, yet failed not to fulfil his engagement. He went out, under pretence of taking the air, and proceeded in great haste to the convent, to give Father Cristoforo the promised information.

Shortly afterwards, a second party of bravoes were sent out, one or two at a time, that they might not appear to be one company. Griso made up the rear, and then nothing remained behind but a litter, which was to be brought to the place of rendezvous after dark. When they were all assembled there, Griso despatched three of them to the inn in the village; one was to place himself at the door, to watch the movements in the street, and to give notice when all the inhabitants had retired to rest; the other two were to remain inside, gaming and drinking, as if enjoying themselves, but were also to be on the lookout, if anything was to be seen. Griso, with the body of the troop, waited in ambuscade till the time of action should arrive.

The poor old man was still on his way, the three scouts had arrived at their post, and the sun was setting, when Renzo entered the cottage, and said to the women, 'Tonio and Gervase are here outside: I am going with them to sup at the inn; and at the sound of the Ave-Maria, we will come to fetch you. Come, Lucia, courage; all depends upon a moment.' Lucia sighed, and replied, 'Oh yes, courage!' with a tone that belied her words.

When Renzo and his two companions reached the inn, they found the bravo already there on the watch, leaning with his back against one of the jambs of the doorway, so as to occupy half its width, his arms folded across his breast, and glancing with a prying look to the right and left, showing alternately the blacks and whites of two griffin-like eyes. A flat cap of crimson velvet, put on sideways, covered half the lock of hair which, parted on a dark forehead, terminated in tresses confined by a comb at the back of the head. He held in one hand a short cudgel; his weapons, properly speaking, were not visible, but one had only to look at his face, and even a child would have guessed that he had as many under his clothes as he could carry. When Renzo, the foremost of the three, approached him and seemed prepared to enter, the bravo fixed his eyes upon him, without attempting to make way; but the youth, intent on avoiding any questions or disputes, as people generally are who have an intricate undertaking in hand, did not even stop to say 'make room;' but grazing the other door-post, pushed, side-foremost, through the opening left by this Caryatides. His companions were obliged to practise the same manœuvre, if they wished to enter. When they got in, they saw the others whose voices they had heard outside, sitting at a table, playing at Mora,[1] both exclaiming at once, and alternately pouring out something to drink from a large flask placed between them. They fixed their eyes steadily on the new comers; and one of them, especially, holding his right hand extended in the air, with three enormous fingers just *shot* forth, and his mouth formed to utter the word 'six,' which burst forth at the moment, eyed Renzo from head to foot, and glanced first at his companion, and then at the one at the door, who replied with a nod of his head. Renzo, suspicious and doubtful, looked at his friends, as if seeking in their countenances an interpretation of all these gestures; but their countenances indicated nothing beyond a good appetite. The landlord approached to receive his orders, and Renzo made him accompany him into an adjoining room, and ordered some supper.

'Who are those strangers?' asked he, in a low voice, when his host returned with a coarse table-cloth under his arm, and a bottle in his hand.

'I don't know them,' replied the host, spreading the table-cloth.

'What! none of them?'

'You know,' replied he, again smoothing the cloth on the table with both his hands, 'that the first rule of our business is not to pry into other people's affairs; so that even our women are not in-quisitive. It would be hard work, with the multitude of folk that come and go; always like a harbour—when the times are good, I mean; but let us cheer up now, for there may come better days. All we care for is whether our customers are honest fellows; who they are or are not, beyond that, is nothing to us. But, come! I will bring you a dish of hash, the like of which you've never tasted.'

'How do you know . . .?' Renzo was beginning; but the land-lord, already on his way to the kitchen, paid no attention to his

---

[1] This is a game between two, played by one of them suddenly extending any num-ber of fingers he may choose, and calling at the same moment for some number under eleven, which the opponent must make up at once, by producing such a number of fingers, that the number called for may be summed up exactly on the extended fingers of the four hands. If he succeed in making up the right number, he wins; if otherwise, the speaker. The bystanders keep count. This is a very exciting, lively game, and a great favourite among the Roman peasantry.

inquiry. Here, while he was taking up the stewing-pan in which was the above-mentioned hash, the bravo who had eyed our youth so closely accosted the host, and said, in an under-tone, 'Who are those good men?'

'Worthy people of the village,' replied he, pouring the hash into the dish.

'Very well; but what are they called? Who are they?' insisted he, in a sharp tone.

'One is called Renzo,' replied the host, speaking in a low voice; 'a worthy youth reckoned—a silk weaver, who understands his business well. The other is a peasant of the name of Tonio, a good jovial comrade; pity he has so little; he'd spend it all here. The third is a simpleton, who eats willingly whatever is set before him. By your leave.'

With these words and a slight bow, he passed between the stove and the interrogator, and carried the dish into the next room. 'How do you know,' resumed Renzo, when he saw him reappear, 'that they are honest men, if you don't know them?'

'By their actions, my good fellow—men are known by their actions. Those who drink wine without criticizing it; who show the face of the King upon the counter without prating; who don't quarrel with other customers; and if they owe a blow to any one, go outside and away from the inn to give it, so that the poor landlord isn't brought into the scrape:—these are honest men. However, if one could know everybody to be honest, as we four know one another, it would be better. But why are you so inquisitive on these matters, when you are a bridegroom, and ought to have other things in your head? and with this hash before you, enough to make the dead rise again?' So saying, he returned to the kitchen.

Our author, remarking upon the different manner in which the landlord satisfied these various inquiries, says he was one who in words made great professions of friendship for honest men in general, but who in practice paid much more attention to those who had the character and appearance of knaves. He was, as every one must perceive, a man of singular character.

The supper was not very blithesome. The two invited guests would have deliberately enjoyed the unusual gratification, but the inviter, pre-occupied by—the reader knows what—anxious and uneasy at the strange behaviour of these incognitos, was impatient for the time of departure. He spoke in an undertone, out of respect to the strangers, and in broken and hurried words.

'What a fine thing,' suddenly exclaimed Gervase, 'that Renzo wants to marry, and is obliged . . .!' Renzo gave him a savage look, and Tonio exclaimed, 'Hold your tongue, simpleton!' accompanying the epithet with a knock of his elbow. The conversation flagged till the end of the meal. Renzo, observing the strictest sobriety, managed to help his guests with so much discretion as to inspire them with sufficient boldness, without making them giddy and bewildered. Supper being over, and the bill having been paid by the one who had done the least execution, they had again to pass under the scrutinizing eyes of the three bravoes, who gazed earnestly at Renzo, as they had done on his entrance. When he had proceeded a few paces from the inn, he looked round, and saw that he was followed by the two bravoes whom he had left sitting in the kitchen; so he stood still with his companions, as much as to say, 'Let us see what these fellows want with me.' On perceiving, however, that they were observed, they also stopped short, and speaking to each other in a suppressed voice, turned back again. Had Renzo been near enough to have heard their words, the following would have struck him as very strange: 'It will be a fine thing, however, without counting the drinking-money,' said one of the villains, 'if we can relate, on our return to the palace, that we made them lay down their arms in a hurry;—by ourselves, too, without Signor Griso here to give orders!'

'And spoil the principal business!' replied the other. 'See, they've discovered something; they are stopping to look at us. Oh, I wish it was later! Let us turn back, or they'll surely suspect us! Don't you see people are coming in every direction? Let us wait till they've all gone to bed.'

There was, in fact, that stirring—that confused buzz—which is usually heard in a village on the approach of evening, and which shortly afterwards gives place to the solemn stillness of night. Women arrived from the fields, carrying their infants on their backs, and holding by the hand the elder children, whom they were hearing repeat their evening prayers; while the men bore on their shoulders their spades, and different implements of husbandry. On the opening of the cottage doors, a bright gleam of light sparkled from the fires, that were kindled to prepare their humble evening meal. In the street might be heard salutations exchanged, together with brief and sad remarks on the scarcity of the harvest, and the poverty of the times; while, above all, resounded the measured and sonorous tolls of the bell, which announced the close of day. When Renzo saw that his two indiscreet followers had retired, he continued his way amid the increasing darkness, occasionally, in a low tone, refreshing the memories of one or other of the brothers on some point of their duties they might be likely to forget. When he arrived at Lucia's cottage, the night had quite closed in.

> 'Between the acting of a dreadful thing,'

says a foreign writer, who was not wanting in discernment,

> 'And the first motion, all the interim is
> Like a phantasma, or a hideous dream.'

Lucia had suffered for several hours the horrors of such a dream; and Agnese—Agnese herself, the author of the design, was buried in thought, and could scarcely find words to encourage her daughter. But at the moment of awaking, at the moment when one is called upon to begin the dreaded undertaking, the mind is instantly transformed. A new terror and a new courage succeed those which before struggled within; the enterprise presents itself to the mind like a fresh apparition; that which at first sight, was most dreaded, seems sometimes rendered easy in a moment; and, on the other hand, an obstacle which, at first, was scarcely noticed, becomes formidable; the imagination shrinks back alarmed, the limbs refuse to fulfil their office, and the heart revokes the promises that were made with the greatest confidence. At Renzo's smothered knock, Lucia was seized with such terror, that, at the moment, she resolved to suffer anything, to be separated from him for ever rather than execute the resolutions she had made; but when he had stood before her, and had said, 'Here I am, let us go'—when all were ready to accompany him without hesitation, as a fixed and irrevocable thing, Lucia had neither time nor heart to interpose difficulties; and, almost dragged along, she tremblingly took one arm of her mother, and one of her betrothed, and set off with the venturesome party.

Very softly, in the dark, and with slow steps, they passed the threshold, and took the road that led out of the village. The shortest way would have been to have gone through it, to reach Don Abbondio's house, at the other end; but they chose the longer course, as being the most retired. After passing along little narrow roads that ran between gardens and fields, they arrived near the house, and here they divided. The two lovers remained hidden behind a corner of the building; Agnese was with them, but stood a little forwarder, that she might be able to run in time to meet Perpetua, and take possession of her. Tonio, with his blockhead of a brother, Gervase, who knew how to do nothing by himself, and without whom nothing could be done, hastened boldly forward, and knocked at the door.

'Who's there, at such an hour?' cried a voice from a window, that was thrown open at the moment: it was the voice of Perpetua. 'There's nobody ill, that I know of. But, perhaps, some accident has happened?'

'It is I,' replied Tonio, 'with my brother; we want to speak to the Signor Curate.'

'Is this an hour for Christians?' replied Perpetua, sharply. 'You've no consideration. Come again to-morrow.'

'Listen; I'll come again, or not, just as you like; I've scraped together nobody knows how much money, and came to settle that little debt you know of. Here, I had five-and-twenty fine new *berlinghe;* but if one cannot pay, never mind; I know well enough how to spend these, and I'll come again, when I've got together some more.'

'Wait, wait! I'll go, and be back in a moment. But why come at such an hour?'

'If you can change the hour, I've no objection; as for me, here I am; and if you don't want me, I'll go.'

'No, no; wait a moment; I'll be back with the answer directly.'

So saying, she shut the window again. At this instant, Agnese left the lovers, and saying, in a low voice to Lucia, 'Courage! it is but a moment; it's only like drawing a tooth,' joined the two brothers at the door, and began gossiping with Tonio, so that, when Perpetua should return and see her, she might think she was just passing by, and that Tonio had detained her for a moment.

CHAPTER VIII

CARNEADES! who was he?—thought Don Abbondio to himself, as he sat in his arm-chair, in a room upstairs, with a small volume lying open before him, just as Perpetua entered to bring him the message.—Carneades! I seem to have heard or read this name; it must be some man of learning—some great scholar of antiquity; it is just like one of their names; but whoever was he?—So far was the poor man from foreseeing the storm that was gathering over his head.

The reader must know that Don Abbondio was very fond of reading a little every day; and a neighbouring Curate, who possessed something of a library, lent him one book after another, always taking the first that came to hand. The work with which Don Abbondio was now engaged (being already convalescent, after his fever and fears, and even more advanced in his recovery from the fever than he wished should be believed) was a panegyric in honour of San Carlo, which had been delivered with much earnestness, and listened to with great admiration, in the Cathedral of Milan, two years before. The saint had been compared, on account of his love of study, to Archimedes; and so far Don Abbondio had met with no stumbling-block; because Archimedes has executed such great works, and has rendered his name so famous, that it required no very vast fund of erudition to know something about *him*. But after Archimedes, the orator also compares his saint to Carneades, and here the reader met with a check. At this point, Perpetua announced the visit of Tonio.

'At this hour!' exclaimed Don Abbondio, also, naturally enough.

'What would you have, sir? They have no consideration, indeed; but if you don't take him when you can get him . . .'

'If I don't take him now, who knows when I can? Let him come in . . . Hey! hey!—Perpetua, are you quite sure it *is* Tonio?'

'Diavolo!' replied Perpetua; and going down-stairs, she opened the door, and said, 'Where are you?' Tonio advanced, and, at the same moment, Agnese showed herself, and saluted Perpetua by name.

'Good evening, Agnese,' said Perpetua; 'where are you coming from at this hour?'

'I am coming from * * * mentioning a neighbouring village. 'And if you knew . . .' continued she; 'I've been kept late just for your sake.'

'What for?' asked Perpetua; and turning to the two brothers, 'Go in,' said she, 'and I'll follow.'

'Because,' replied Agnese, 'a gossiping woman, who knows nothing about the matter . . . would you believe it? persists in saying that you were not married to Beppo Suolavecchia, nor to Anselmo Lunghigna, because they wouldn't have you! I maintained that you had refused both one and the other . . .'

'To be sure. Oh, what a false-tongued woman! Who is she?'

'Don't ask me; I don't want to make mischief.'

'You shall tell me; you must tell me. I say she's a false body.'

'Well, well . . . but you cannot think how vexed I was that I didn't know the whole history, that I might have put her down.'

'It is an abominable falsehood,' said Perpetua—'a most infamous falsehood! As to Beppo, everybody knows, and might have seen . . . Hey! Tonio; just close the door, and go up-stairs till I come.'

Tonio assented from within, and Perpetua continued her eager relation. In front of Don Abbondio's door, a narrow street ran between two cottages, but only continued straight the length of the buildings, and then turned into the fields. Agnese went forward along this street, as if she would go a little aside to speak more freely, and Perpetua followed. When they had turned the corner, and reached a spot whence they could no longer see what happened before Don Abbondio's house, Agnese coughed loudly. This was the signal; Renzo heard it, and re-animating Lucia by pressing her arm, they turned the corner together on tiptoe, crept very softly close along the wall, reached the door, and gently pushed it open; quiet, and stooping low, they were quickly in the passage; and here the two brothers were waiting for them. Renzo very gently let down the latch of the door, and they all four ascended the stairs, making scarcely noise enough for two. On reaching the landing, the two brothers advanced towards the door of the room at the side of the staircase, and the lovers stood close against the wall.

'*Deo gratias,*' said Tonio, in an explanatory tone.

'Eh, Tonio! is it you? Come in!' replied the voice within.

Tonio opened the door, scarcely wide enough to admit himself and his brother one at a time. The ray of light that suddenly shone through the opening, and crossed the dark floor of the landing, made Lucia tremble, as if she were discovered. When the brothers had entered, Tonio closed the door inside; the lovers stood motionless in the dark, their ears intently on the alert, and holding their breath; the loudest noise was the beating of poor Lucia's heart.

Don Abbondio was seated, as we have said, in an old armchair, enveloped in an antiquated dressing-gown, and his head buried in a shabby cap, the shape of a tiara, which, by the faint light of a small lamp, formed a sort of cornice all round his face. Two thick locks, which escaped from beneath his head-dress, two thick eye-brows, two thick mustachios, and a thick tuft on the chin, all of them grey, and scattered over his dark and wrinkled visage, might be compared to bushes covered with snow, projecting from the face of a cliff, as seen by moonlight.

'Aha!' was his salutation, as he took off his spectacles, and laid them on his book.

'The Signor Curate will say I am come very late,' said Tonio, with a low bow, which Gervase awkwardly imitated.

'Certainly, it is late—late every way. Don't you know I am ill?'

'I'm very sorry for it.'

'You must have heard I was ill, and didn't know when I should be able to see anybody ... But why have you brought this—this boy with you?'

'For company, Signor Curate.'

'Very well; let us see.'

'Here are twenty-five new *berlinghe,* with the figure of Saint Ambrose on horseback,' said Tonio, drawing a little parcel out of his pocket.

'Let us see,' said Don Abbondio; and he took the parcel, put on his spectacles again, opened it, took out the *berlinghe,* turned them over and over, counted them, and found them irreprehensible.

'Now, Signor Curate, you will give me Tecla's necklace.'

'You are right,' replied Don Abbondio; and going to a cup-board, he took out a key, looking round as if to see that all prying spectators were at a proper distance, opened one of the doors, and filling up the aperture with his person, introduced his head to see, and his arm to reach, the pledge; then drawing it out, he shut the cupboard, unwrapped the paper, and saying, 'Is that right?' folded it up again, and handed it to Tonio.

'Now,' said Tonio, 'will you please to put it in black and white?'

'Not satisfied yet!' said Don Abbondio. 'I declare they know everything. Eh! how suspicious the world has become! Don't you trust me?'

'What! Signor Curate! Don't I trust you? You do me wrong. But as my name is in your black books, on the debtor's side . . . then, since you have had the trouble of writing once, so . . . from life to death . . .'

'Well, well,' interrupted Don Abbondio; and muttering between his teeth, he drew out one of the table-drawers, took thence pen, ink, and paper, and began to write, repeating the words aloud, as they proceeded from his pen. In the mean time, Tonio, and at his side, Gervase, placed themselves standing before the table in such a manner as to conceal the door from the view of the writer, and began to shuffle their feet about on the floor, as if in mere idleness, but, in reality, as a signal to those without to enter, and, at the same time, to drown the noise of their footsteps. Don Abbondio, intent upon his writing, noticed nothing else. At the noise of their feet, Renzo took Lucia's arm, pressing it in an encouraging manner, and went forward, almost dragging her along; for she trembled to such a degree, that, without his help, she must have sunk to the ground. Entering very softly, on tiptoe, and holding their breath, they placed themselves behind the two brothers. In the mean time, Don Abbondio, having finished writing, read over the paper attentively, without raising his eyes; he then folded it up, saying, 'Are you content now?' and taking off his spectacles with one hand, handed the paper to Tonio with the other, and looked up. Tonio, extending his right hand to receive it, retired on one side, and Gervase, at a sign from him, on the other; and behold! as at the shifting of a scene, Renzo and Lucia stood between them. Don Abbondio saw indistinctly—saw clearly—was terrified, astonished, enraged, buried in thought, came to a resolution; and all this, while Renzo uttered the words, 'Signor Curate, in the presence of these witnesses, this is my wife.' Before, however, Lucia's lips could form the reply, Don Abbondio dropped the receipt, seized the lamp with his left hand, and raised it in the air, caught hold of the cloth with his right, and dragged it furiously off the table, bringing to the ground in its fall, book, paper, inkstand, and sandbox; and, springing between the chair and the table, advanced towards Lucia. The poor girl, with her sweet gentle voice, trembling violently, had scarcely uttered the words, 'And this . . .' when Don Abbondio threw the cloth rudely over her head and face, to prevent her pronouncing the entire formula. Then, letting the light fall from his other hand, he employed both to wrap the cloth round her face, till she was well nigh smothered, shouting in the mean while, at the stretch of his voice, like a wounded bull: 'Perpetua! Perpetua!—treachery—help!' The light, just glimmering on the ground, threw a dim and flickering ray upon Lucia, who, in utter consternation, made no attempt to disengage herself, and might be compared to a statue sculptured in chalk, over which the artificer had thrown a wet cloth. When the light died away, Don Abbondio quitted the poor girl, and went groping about to find the door that opened into an inner room; and having reached it, he entered and shut himself in, unceasingly exclaiming, 'Perpetua! treachery, help! Out of the house! out of the house!'

In the other room all was confusion: Renzo, seeking to lay hold of the Curate, and feeling with his hands, as if playing at blind-man's buff, had reached the door, and kicking against it, was crying, 'Open, open; don't make such a noise!' Lucia, calling to Renzo, in a feeble voice, said, beseechingly, 'Let us go, let us go, for God's sake.' Tonio was crawling on his knees, and feeling with his hands on the ground to recover his lost receipt. The terrified Gervase was crying and jumping about, and seeking for the door of the stairs, so as to make his escape in safety.

In the midst of this uproar, we cannot but stop a moment to make a reflection. Renzo, who was causing disturbance at night in another person's house, who had effected an entrance by stealth, and who had blockaded the master himself in one of his own rooms, has all the appearance of an oppressor; while in fact he was the oppressed. Don Abbondio, taken by surprise, terrified and put to flight, while peaceably engaged in his own affairs, appears the victim; when in reality it was he who did the wrong. Thus frequently goes the world . . . or rather, we should say, thus it went in the seventeenth century.

The besieged, finding that the enemy gave no signs of abandoning the enterprise, opened a window that looked into the churchyard, and shouted out: 'Help! help!' There was a most lovely moon; the shadow of the church, and, a little beyond, the long, sharp shadow of the bell-tower, lay dark, still, and well-defined, on the bright grassy level of the sacred enclosure: all objects were visible, almost as by day. But look which way you would, there appeared no sign of living person. Adjoining the lateral wall of the church, on the side next the Parsonage, was a small dwelling where the sexton slept. Aroused by this unusual cry, he sprang up in his bed, jumped out in great haste, threw open the sash of his little window, put his head out with his eyelids glued together all the while, and cried out: 'What's the matter?'

'Run, Ambrogio! help! people in the house!' answered Don Abbondio. 'Coming directly,' replied he, as he drew in his head and shut the window; and although half asleep and more than half terrified, an expedient quickly occurred to him that would bring more aid than had been asked, without dragging *him* into the affray, whatever it might be. Seizing his breeches that lay upon the bed, he tucked them under his arm like a gala hat, and bounding downstairs by a little wooden ladder, ran to the belfry, caught hold of the rope that was attached to the larger of the two bells, and pulled vigorously.

Ton, ton, ton, ton; the peasant sprang up in his bed; the boy stretched in the hay-loft listened eagerly, and leapt upon his feet. 'What's the matter? what's the matter? The bell's ringing! Fire? Thieves? Banditti?' Many of the women advised—begged their husbands not to stir—to let others run; some got up and went to the window; those who were cowards, as if yielding to entreaty, quietly slipped under the bed-clothes again; while the more inquisitive and courageous sprang up and armed themselves with pitchforks and pistols, to run to the uproar; others waited to see the end.

But before these were all ready, and even before they were well awake, the noise had reached the ears, and arrested the attention, of some others not very far distant, who were both dressed and on their feet; the bravoes in one place; Agnese and Perpetua in another. We will first briefly relate the movements of the bravoes since we left them;—some in the old building, and some at the inn.

The three at the inn, as soon as they saw all the doors shut and the street deserted, went out, pretending to be going some distance; but they only quietly took a short turn in the village to be assured that all had retired to rest; and in fact, they met not one living creature, nor heard the least noise. They also passed, still more softly, before Lucia's little cottage, which was the quietest of all, since there was no one within. They then went direct to the old house, and reported their observations to Signor Griso. Hastily putting on a slouched hat, with a pilgrim's dress of sackcloth, scattered over with cockle-shells, and taking in his hand a pilgrim's staff, he said: 'Now let us act like good bravoes; quiet, and attentive to orders.' So saying, he moved forward, followed by the rest, and in a few moments reached the cottage by the opposite way to the one our little party had taken when setting out on their expedition. Griso ordered his followers to remain a few paces behind, while he went forward alone to explore; and finding all outside deserted and still, he beckoned to two of them to advance, ordered them quietly to scale the wall that surrounded the court-yard, and when they had descended, to conceal themselves in a corner behind a thick fig-tree that he had noticed in the morning. This done, he knocked gently at the door, with the intention of saying that he was a pilgrim who had lost his way, and begged a lodging for the night. No one replied; he knocked a little more loudly; not a whisper. He therefore called a third bravo, and made him descend into the yard as the other two had done, with orders to unfasten the bolt inside very carefully, so that he might have free ingress and egress. All was executed with the greatest caution and the most prosperous success. He then went to call the rest, and bidding them enter with him, sent them to hide in the corner with the others, closed the door again very softly, placed two sentinels inside, and went up to the door of the house. Here also he knocked—waited; and long enough he might wait. He then as gently as possible opened this door; nobody within said, Who's there; no one was to be heard. Nothing could be better. Forward then; 'Come on,' cried he to those behind the fig-tree, and he entered with them into that very room where in the morning he had so basely obtained the piece of bread. Drawing from his pocket a piece of steel, a flint, some tinder and a few matches, he lit a small lantern he had provided, and stepped into the next room to assure himself that all was quiet: no one was there. He returned, went to the foot of the stairs, looked up, listened; all was solitude and silence. Leaving two more sentinels in the lower room, he bid Grignapoco follow him, a bravo from the district of Bergamo, whose office it was to threaten, appease, and command; to be, in short, the spokesman, so that his dialect might give Agnese the idea that the expedition came from his neighbourhood. With this companion at his side, and the rest behind him, Griso very slowly ascended the stairs, cursing in his heart every step that unluckily creaked, every tread of these villains that made the least noise. At last he reaches the top. Here is the danger. He gently pushes the door that leads into the first room; it yields to his touch; he opens it a little and looks in; all is dark; he listens attentively, perchance he may hear a snoring, a breath, a stirring within; nothing. Forward then; he puts the lantern before his face, so as to see without being seen, he opens the door wide; perceives a bed; looks upon it; the bed is made and smooth, with the clothes turned down and arranged upon the pillow. He shrugs his shoulders, turns to his companions, beckons to them that he is going to look in the other room, and that they must keep quiet where they were; he goes forward, uses the same precautions, meets with the same success. 'Whatever can this mean?' exclaimed he boldly: 'some traitorous dog must have been acting as spy.' They then began to look about them with less caution, and to pry into every corner, turning the house upside down.

While the party up-stairs were thus engaged, the two who were on guard at the street-door heard hasty and repeated footsteps ap-

proaching along the road that led into the village, and imagining
that whoever it was, he would pass by, they kept quiet, their ears,
however, attentively on the watch. But behold! the footsteps stopped
exactly at the door. It was Menico arriving in great haste, sent by
Father Cristoforo to bid the two women, for Heaven's sake, to
make their escape as quickly as possible from their cottage, and
take refuge in the convent, because . . . the 'because' the reader
knows. He took hold of the handle of the latch, and felt it shake
in his hand, unfastened and broken open. What is this? thought
he, as he pushed open the door in some alarm; and putting one
foot inside with considerable suspicion, he felt himself seized in a
moment by both arms, and heard two smothered voices, on his
right and left, saying to him, in a threatening tone: 'Hush! hold
your tongue, or you die.' On the contrary, however, he uttered a
shrill cry, upon which one of them struck him a great blow on the
mouth, and the other took hold of a large knife to terrify him. The
poor child trembled like a leaf, and did not attempt a second cry;
but all at once, in his stead, and with a far different tone, burst
forth the first sound of the bell before described, and immediately
after many thundering peals in quick succession. 'If the cap fits,
put it on,' says a Milanese proverb; each of the villains seemed to
hear in these peals his name, surname, and nick-name; they let go
of Menico's arms, hastily dropped their own, gazed at each other's
faces in mute astonishment, and then ran into the house where was
the bulk of their companions. Menico took to his legs, and fled,
by way of the fields, towards the belfry, where he felt sure there
would be some people assembled. On the other ruffians, who were
rummaging the house from top to bottom, the terrible bell made
the same impression; confused and alarmed, they ran against one
another, in attempting, each one for himself, to find the shortest
way of reaching the street-door. Though men of approved courage,
and accustomed never to turn their backs on known peril, they
could not stand against an indefinite danger, which had not been
viewed at a little distance before coming upon them. It required
all the authority of Griso to keep them together, so that it might be
a retreat and not a flight. Just as a dog urging a drove of pigs,
runs here and there after those that break the ranks, seizes one by

the ears, and drags him into the herd, propels another with his nose,
barks at a third that leaves the line at the same moment, so the
pilgrim laid hold of one of his troop just passing the threshold, and
drew back, detained with his staff some who were flying they knew
not whither, and finally succeeded in assembling them all in the
middle of the court-yard. 'Halt! halt! pistols in hand, daggers in
readiness, all together, and then we'll begone. We must march in
order. What care we for the bells ringing, if we are all together,
you cowards? But if we let them catch us one by one, even the
villagers will give us it. For shame! Fall behind, and keep together.' After this brief harangue, he placed himself in the front,
and led the way out. The cottage, as we have said, was at the
extremity of the village: Griso took the road that led out of it, and
the rest followed him in good order.

We will let them go, and return a step or two to find Agnese
and Perpetua, whom we had just conducted round the corner of a
certain road. Agnese had endeavoured to allure her companion as
far away from Don Abbondio's house as possible, and up to a certain point had succeeded very well. But all on a sudden the servant
remembered that she had left the door open, and she wanted to
go back. There was nothing to be said: Agnese, to avoid exciting
any suspicion in her mind, was obliged to turn and walk with her,
trying however to detain her whenever she saw her very eager in
relating the issue of such and such courtships. She pretended to
be paying very great attention, and every now and then, by way
of showing that she was listening, or to animate the flagging conversation, would say: 'Certainly: now I understand: that was capital: that is plain: and then? and he? and you?' while all the time
she was keeping up a very different discourse in her own mind.—
'I wonder if they are out by this time? or will they be still in the
house? What geese we all were not to arrange any signal to let me
know when it was over! It was really very stupid! But it can't
be helped: and the best thing I can do now is to keep her loitering
here as long as I can: let the worst come to the worst, it will only
be a little time lost.'—Thus, with sundry pauses and various devia-
tions from the straight path, they were brought back again to within
a very short distance from Don Abbondio's house, which, how-

ever, could not be seen on account of the corner intercepting the view, and Perpetua finding herself at an important part of her narration, had suffered herself to be detained without resistance, and even without being aware of it, when they suddenly heard, echoing through the vacant extent of the atmosphere, and the dead silence of night, the loud and disordered cry of Abbondio: 'Help! help!'

'Mercy! what has happened?' cried Perpetua, beginning to run.

'What is it? what is it?' said Agnese, holding her back by the gown.

'Mercy! didn't you hear?' replied she, struggling.

'What is it? what is it?' repeated Agnese, seizing her by the arm.

'Wretch of a woman!' exclaimed Perpetua, pushing her away to free herself and to run. At this moment, more distant, more shrill, more instantaneous, was heard the scream of Menico.

'Mercy!' cried Agnese also; and they ran off together. They had scarcely, however, gone a step, when the bell sounded one stroke, then two, three and a succession of peals, such as would have stimulated them to run had there been no other inducement. Perpetua arrived first by two steps; while she raised her hand to the door to open it, behold! it was opened from within, and on the threshold stood, Tonio, Gervase, Renzo, and Lucia, who having found the stairs had come down more rapidly than they went up; and at the sound of that terrible bell, were making their escape in haste to reach a place of safety.

'What's the matter? what's the matter?' demanded the panting Perpetua of the brothers; but they only replied with a violent push, and passed on. 'And you! How! what are you doing here?' said she to the other couple on recognizing them. But they too made their escape without answering her. Without, therefore, asking any more questions, and directing her steps where she was most wanted, she rushed impetuously into the passage, and went groping about as quickly as she could to find the stairs.

The betrothed, still only betrothed, now fell in with Agnese, who arrived weary and out of breath. 'Ah! here you are!' said she, scarcely able to speak. 'How has it gone? What is the bell ringing for? I thought I heard . . .'

'Home! home!' cried Renzo, 'before anybody comes.' And they

moved forward; but at this moment Menico arrived, running as fast as his legs could carry him; and recognizing them, he threw himself in their way, and still all in a tremble and scarcely able to draw his breath, exclaimed: 'Where are you going? back, back! This way, to the convent.'

'Are you? . . .' began Agnese.

'What is it?' asked Renzo. Lucia stood by, trembling and silent, in utter dismay.

'There are devils in your house,' replied Menico, panting. 'I saw them myself: they wanted to murder me: Father Cristoforo said so; and even you, Renzo, he said, were to come quickly:—and besides, I saw them myself:—it's providential you are all here:—I will tell you the rest when we get out of the village.'

Renzo, who had more of his senses about him than the rest, remembered that they had better make their escape one way or another before the crowds assembled; and that the best plan would be to do as Menico advised, nay, commanded with the authority of one in terror. When once on their way, and out of the tumult and danger, he could ask a clearer explanation from the boy. 'Lead the way,' said he to Menico; and addressing the women, said, 'Let us go with him.' They therefore quickly turned their steps towards the church, crossed the churchyard, where, by the favour of Heaven, there was not yet a living creature, entered a little street that ran between the church and Don Abbondio's house, turned into the first alley they came to and then took the way of the fields.

They had not perhaps gone fifty yards, when the crowd began to collect in the church-yard, and rapidly increased every moment. They looked inquiringly in each other's faces; every one had a question to ask, but no one could return an answer. Those who arrived first, ran to the church-door; it was locked. They then ran to the belfry outside; and one of them, putting his mouth to a very small window, a sort of loop-hole, cried, 'What ever is the matter?' As soon as Ambrogio recognized a known voice, he let go of the bell-rope, and being assured by the buzz that many people had assembled, replied: 'I'll open the door.' Hastily slipping on the apparel he had carried under his arm, he went inside the church, and opened the door.

'What is all this hubbub?—What is it?—Where is it?—Who is it?'

'Why, who is it?' said Ambrogio, laying one hand on the door-post, and with the other holding up the habiliment he had put on in such haste: 'What! don't you know? People in the Signor Curate's house. Up, boys: help!' Hearing this, they all turned to the house, looked up, approached it in a body, looked up again, listened: all was quiet. Some ran to the street-door; it was shut and bolted; they glanced upwards: not a window was open; not a whisper was to be heard.

'Who is within?—Ho! Hey!—Signor Curate!—Signor Curate!'

Don Abbondio who, scarcely aware of the flight of the invaders, had retired from the window, and closed it, and who at this moment was reproaching Perpetua in a low voice for having left him alone in this confusion, was obliged, when he heard himself called upon by the voice of the assembled people, to show himself again at the window; and when he saw the crowds that had come to his aid, he sorely repented having called them.

'What has happened?—What have they done to you?—Who are they?—Where are they?' burst forth from fifty voices at once.

'There's nobody here now; thank you: go home again.'

'But who has been here?—Where are they gone?—what has happened?'

'Bad people, people who go about by night; but they're gone: go home again: there is no longer anything: another time, my children: I thank you for your kindness to me.' So saying, he drew back, and shut the window. Some of the crowd began to grumble, some to joke, others to curse; some shrugged their shoulders and took their departure: when one arrived, endeavouring but scarcely able to speak from want of breath. It was the person who lived in the house opposite Agnese's cottage, who having gone to the window at the noise, had seen in the court-yard the assembly of bravoes, when Griso was striving to re-unite his scattered troops. On recovering his breath, he cried: 'What are you doing here, my good fellows? the devil isn't here; he's down at the end of the village, at Agnese Mondella's house; armed men are within, who seem to be murdering a pilgrim; who knows what the devil is doing!'

'What?—what?—what?' and a tumultuous consultation began. 'We must go.—We must see.—How many are there?—How many are we?—Who are we?—The constable! the constable!'

'I'm here,' replied the constable from the middle of the crowd: 'I'm here; but you must help me, you must obey. Quick: where is the sexton? To the bell, to the bell. Quick! Somebody to run to Lecco for help: all of you come here . . .'

Some ran, some slipped between their fellows and made their escape; and the tumult was at its greatest height, when another runner arrived who had seen Griso and his party going off in such haste, and cried in turn: 'Run, my good fellows: thieves or banditti, who are carrying off a pilgrim: they are already out of the village. On! after them!' At this information, they moved off in a body in great confusion towards the fields, without waiting their general's orders, and as the crowd proceeded, many of the vanguard slackened their pace, to let the others advance, and retired into the body of the battalion, those in the rear pushing eagerly forward, until at last the disorderly multitude reached their place of destination. Traces of the recent invasion were manifest: the door opened, the locks torn off; but the invaders had disappeared. The crowd entered the courtyard, and went to the room door; this, too, was burst open: they called: 'Agnese! Lucia! the Pilgrim! Where is the pilgrim? Stefano must have been dreaming about the pilgrim.—No, no: Carlandrea saw him also. Ho! hey! pilgrim!—Agnese! Lucia!' No one replied. 'They've run away with them! They've run away with them!' There were then some who raised their voices and proposed to follow the robbers; said it was a heinous crime, and that it would be a disgrace to the village, if every villain could come and carry off women with impunity, as a kite carries off chickens from a deserted barn-floor. Then rose a fresh and more tumultuous consultation; but somebody, (and it was never certainly known who,) called out in the crowd that Agnese and Lucia were in safety in a house. The rumour spread rapidly; it gained belief, and no one spoke again of giving chase to the fugitives; the multitude dispersed, and every one went to his own house. There was a general whispering, a noise, all over the village, a knocking and opening of doors, and appearing and disappearing of lights, a questioning of women from the windows, an answering from the streets. When all outside was deserted and quiet, the conversation continued in the houses, and ended at last in slumber, only to be renewed on the morrow. However, no other events took place, excepting that on the morning of that morrow, the constable was standing in his field, with his chin resting on his hands, his hands on the handle of the spade, which was half stuck into the ground, and one foot on the iron rest affixed to the handle; speculating in his mind, as he thus stood, on the mysteries of the past night, on what would reasonably be expected of him, and on what course it would be best for him to pursue, he saw two men approaching him with very fierce looks, wearing long hair, like the first race of French kings, and otherwise bearing a strong resemblance to the two who, five days before, had confronted Don Abbondio, if, indeed they were not the same men. These with still less ceremony than had been used towards the Curate, intimated to the constable that he must take right good care not to make a deposition to the *Podestà* of what had happened, not to tell the truth in case he was questioned, not to gossip, and not to encourage gossiping among the villagers, as he valued his life.

Our fugitives walked a little way at a quick pace in silence, one or other occasionally looking back to see if they were followed, all of them wearied by the fatigue of the flight, by the anxiety and suspense they had endured, by grief at their ill-success, and by confused apprehensions of new and unknown danger. Their terror, too, was increased by the sound of the bell which still continued to follow them, and seemed to become heavier and more hoarse the further they left it behind them, acquiring every moment something more mournful and ominous in its tone. At last the ringing ceased. Reaching then a deserted field, and not hearing a whisper around, they slackened their pace, and Agnese, taking breath, was the first to break the silence, by asking Renzo how matters had gone, and Menico, what was the demon in their house. Renzo briefly related his melancholy story; and then, all of them turning to the child, he informed them more expressly of the Father's advice, and narrated what he had himself witnessed and the hazards he had run, which too surely confirmed the advice. His auditors, however, understood more of this than did the speaker; they were seized with new horror at the discovery, and for a moment paused in their walk, exchanging mutual looks of fear; then with an unanimous movement they laid their hands, some on the head, others on the shoulders of the boy, as if to caress him, and tacitly to thank him for having been to them a guardian angel; at the same time signifying the compassion they felt for him, and almost apologizing for the terror he had endured and the danger he had undergone on their account. 'Now go home, that your family may not be anxious about you any longer,' said Agnese; and remembering the two promised *parpagliole,* she took out four, and gave them to him, adding: 'That will do; pray the Lord that we may meet again soon; and then . . .' Renzo gave him a new *berlinga,* and begged him to say nothing of the message he had brought from the Father: Lucia again caressed him, bade him farewell with a sorrowful voice, and the boy, almost overcome, wished them good-bye, and turned back. The melancholy trio continued their walk, the women taking the lead, and Renzo behind to act as guard. Lucia clung closely to her mother's arm, kindly and dexterously avoiding the proffered assistance of the youth at the difficult passes of this unfrequented path; feeling ashamed of herself, even in such troubles, for having already been so long and so familiarly alone with him, while expecting in a few moments to be his wife. Now that this vision had been so sorrowfully dispelled, she repented having proceeded thus far; and, amidst so many causes of fear, she feared even for her modesty, —not such modesty as arises from the sad knowledge of evil, but for that which is ignorant of its own existence;—like the dread of a child who trembles in the dark, he knows not why.

'And the house?' suddenly exclaimed Agnese. But however important the object might be which extorted this exclamation, no one replied, because no one could do so satisfactorily. They therefore continued their walk in silence, and, in a little while, reached the square before the church of the convent.

Renzo advanced to the door of the church, and gently pushed it open. The moon that entered through the aperture, fell upon the pale face and silvery beard of Father Cristoforo, who was standing here expecting them; and having seen that no one was missing, 'God be praised!' said he, beckoning to them to enter. By his side stood another Capuchin, the lay sexton, whom he had persuaded, by prayers and arguments, to keep vigil with him, to leave the door ajar, and to remain there on guard to receive these poor threatened creatures; and it required nothing short of the authority of the Father, and of his fame as a saint, to persuade the layman to so inconvenient, perilous, and irregular a condescension. When they were inside, Father Cristoforo very softly shut the door. Then the sexton could no longer contain himself, and taking the Father aside, whispered in his ear; 'But Father, Father! at night . . . in church . . . with women . . . shut . . . the rule . . . but Father!' And he shook his head, while thus hesitatingly pronouncing these words. Just see! thought Father Cristoforo; if it were a pursued robber, Friar Fazio would make no difficulty in the world; and a poor innocent escaping from the jaws of a wolf . . . *'Omnia munda mundis,'* added he, turning suddenly to Friar Fazio, and forgetting that he did not understand Latin. But this forgetfulness was exactly what produced the right effect. If the Father had begun to dispute and reason, Friar Fazio would not have failed to urge opposing arguments; and no one knows how and when the discussion would have come to an end; but at the sound of these weighty words of a mysterious signification, and so resolutely uttered, it seemed to him that in them must be contained the solution of all his doubts. He acquiesced, saying, 'Very well; you know more about it than I do.'

'Trust me, then,' replied Father Cristoforo; and by the dim light of the lamp burning before the altar, he approached the refugees, who stood waiting in suspense, and said to them, 'My children, thank God, who has delivered you from so great a danger! Perhaps at this moment . . .' and here he began to explain more fully what he had hinted by the little messenger, little suspecting that they knew more than he, and supposing that Menico had found them quiet in their own house, before the arrival of the ruffians. Nobody undeceived him, not even Lucia, whose conscience, however, was all the while secretly reproaching her for practising such dissimulation with so good a man; but it was a night of embarrassment and dissimulation.

'After this,' continued he, 'you must feel, my children, that the village is no longer safe for you. It is yours, you were born there, and you have done no wrong to any one; but God wills it so. It is a trial, my children; bear it with patience and faith, without indulging in rancour, and rest assured there will come a day when you will think yourselves happy that this has occurred. I have thought of a refuge for you, for the present. Soon, I hope, you may be able to return in safety to your own house; at any rate, God will provide what is best for you; and I assure you, I will be careful not to prove unworthy of the favour He has bestowed upon me, in choosing me as His minister, in the service of you, His poor, yet loved afflicted ones. You,' continued he, turning to the two women, 'can stay at * * *. Here you will be far enough from every danger, and at the same time not far from your own home. There seek out our convent, ask for the guardian, and give him this letter; he will be to you another Father Cristoforo. And you, my Renzo, must put yourself in safety from the anger of others, and your own. Carry this letter to Father Bonaventura da Lodi, in our convent of the Porta Orientale, at Milan. He will be a father to you, will give you directions, and find you work, till you can return and live more peaceably. Go to the shore of the lake, near the mouth of the Bione, a river not far from this monastery. Here you will see a boat waiting; say "Boat!" it will be asked you "For whom?" And you must reply, "San Francesco." The boat will receive you, and carry you to the other side, where you will find a cart, that will take you straight to * * *.'

If any one asks how Father Cristoforo had so quickly at his disposal these means of transport by land and water, it will show that he does not know the influence and power of a Capuchin held in reputation as a saint.

It still remained to decide about the care of the houses. The Father received the keys, pledging himself to deliver them to whomsoever Renzo and Agnese should name. The latter, in delivering up hers, heaved a deep sigh, remembering that, at that moment, the house was open, that the devil had been there, and who knew what remained to be taken care of!

'Before you go,' said the Father, 'let us pray all together that the Lord may be with you in this your journey, and for ever; and, above all, that He may give you strength, and a spirit of love, to enable you to desire whatever He has willed.' So saying, he knelt down in the middle of the church, and they all followed his example. After praying a few moments in silence, with low but distinct voice he pronounced these words: 'We beseech Thee, also, for the unhappy person who has brought us to this state. We should be unworthy of Thy mercy, if we did not, from our hearts, implore it for him; he needs it, O Lord! We, in our sorrow, have this consolation, that we are in the path where Thou hast placed us; we can offer Thee our griefs, and they may become our gain. But he is Thine enemy! Alas, wretched man! he is striving with Thee! Have mercy on him, O Lord; touch his heart; reconcile him to Thyself, and give him all those good things we could desire for ourselves.'

Rising then in haste, he said, 'Come, my children, you have no time to lose; God defend you; His angel go with you;—farewell!' And while they set off with that emotion which cannot find words, and manifests itself without them, the Father added, in an agitated tone, 'My heart tells me we shall meet again soon.'

Certainly, the heart, to those who listen to it, has always something to say on what will happen; but what did his heart know? Very little, truly, of what had already happened.

Without waiting a reply, Father Cristoforo retired with hasty steps; the travellers took their departure; and Father Fazio shut the door after them, bidding them farewell with even his voice a little faltering.

The trio slowly made their way to the shore they had been directed to; where they espied the boat, and exchanging the password, stepped in. The waterman, planting one oar on the land, pushed off; then took up the other oar, and rowing with both hands, pulled out and made towards the opposite beach. Not a breath of wind was stirring; the lake lay bright and smooth, and would have appeared motionless but for the tremulous and gentle undulation of the moonbeams, which gleamed upon it from the zenith. No sounds were heard but the muffled and slowly measured breaking of the surge upon the pebbly shore, the more distant gurgling of the troubled waters dashing among the piles of the bridge, and the even plash of the light sculls, as, rising with a sharp sound of the dripping blade, and quickly plunged again beneath, they cut the azure surface of the lake. The waves, divided by the prow, and reuniting behind the little bark, tracked out a curling line, which extended itself to the shore. The silent travellers, with their faces turned backwards, gazed upon the mountains and the country, illumined by the pale light of the moon, and diversified here and there with vast shadows. They could distinguish the villages, the houses, and the little cabins: the palace of Don Rodrigo, with its square tower, rising above the group of huts at the base of the promontory, looked like a savage standing in the dark, and meditating some evil deed, while keeping guard over a company of reclining sleepers. Lucia saw it and shuddered; then drawing her eye along the declivity till she reached her native village, she fixed her gaze on its extremity, sought for her own cottage, traced out the thick head of the fig-tree which towered above the wall of the court-yard, discovered the window of her own room; and, being seated in the bottom of the boat, she leaned her elbow on the edge, laid her forehead on her arm, as if she were sleeping, and wept in secret.

Farewell, ye mountains, rising from the waters, and pointing to the heavens! ye varied summits, familiar to him who has been brought up among you, and impressed upon his mind as clearly as the countenance of his dearest friends! ye torrents, whose murmur he recognizes like the sound of the voices of home! ye villages, scattered and glistening on the declivity, like flocks of grazing sheep! farewell! How mournful is the step of him who, brought up amidst your scenes, is compelled to leave you! Even in the imagination of one who willingly departs, attracted by the hope of making a fortune elsewhere, the dreams of wealth at this moment lose their charms; he wonders he could form such a resolution, and could even now turn back, but for the hope of one day returning with a rich abundance. As he advances into the plain, his eye becomes wearied with its uniform extent; the atmosphere feels heavy and lifeless; he sadly and listlessly enters the busy cities, where houses crowded upon houses, and streets intersecting streets, seem to take away his breath; and, before edifices admired by the stranger, he recalls with restless longing the fields of his own country, and the cottage he had long ago set his heart upon, and which he resolves to purchase when he returns enriched to his own mountains.

But what must he feel who has never sent a passing wish beyond these mountains, who has arranged among them all his designs for the future, and is driven far away by an adverse power! who, suddenly snatched away from his dearest habits, and thwarted in his dearest hopes, leaves these mountains to go in search of strangers whom he never desired to know, and is unable to look forward to a fixed time of return!

Farewell! native cottage, where, indulging in unconscious thought, one learnt to distinguish from the noise of common footsteps, the approach of a tread expected with mysterious timidity! Farewell! thou cottage, still a stranger, but so often hastily glanced at, not without a blush, in passing, in which the mind took delight to figure to itself the tranquil and lasting home of a wife! Farewell! my church, where the heart was so often soothed while chanting the praises of the Lord; where the preparatory rite of betrothal was performed; where the secret sighing of the heart was solemnly blessed and love was inspired, and one felt a hallowing influence around, farewell! He who imparted to you such gladness is everywhere; and He never disturbs the joy of his children, but to prepare them for one more certain and durable.

Of such a nature, if not exactly these, were the reflections of Lucia; and not very dissimilar were those of the two other wanderers, while the little bark rapidly approached the right bank of the Adda.

CHAPTER IX

THE striking of the boat against the shore aroused Lucia, who, after secretly drying her tears, raised her head as if she were just awaking. Renzo jumped out first, and gave his hand successively to Agnese and Lucia; and then they all turned, and sorrowfully thanked the boatman. 'Nothing, nothing; we are placed here to help one another,' answered he; and he withdrew his hand, almost with a movement of horror, as if it had been proposed to him to rob, when Renzo tried to slip in one or two of the coins he had about him, and which he had brought in his pocket with the intention of generously requiting Don Abbondio, when he should, though against his will, have rendered the desired assistance. The cart stood waiting for them; the driver saluted the three expected travellers, and bid them get in; and then, with his voice and a stroke of the whip, he started the animal and set forward.

Our author does not describe this nocturnal journey, and is silent as to the name of the town to which the little company were directing their steps; or rather, he expressly says, he will not give the name. In the course of the story, the reason of all this mystery appears. The adventures of Lucia in this abode involve a dark intrigue of a person belonging to a family still powerful, as it appears, at the time our author wrote. To account for the strange conduct of this person in the particular instance he relates, he has been obliged chiefly to recount her early life; and there the family makes the figure which our readers will see. Hence the poor man's great circumspection. And yet (how people sometimes forget themselves!) he himself, without being aware of it, has opened a way of discovering, with certainty, what he had taken such great pains to keep concealed. In one part of the account, which we will omit as not being necessary to the integrity of the story, he happens to say that this place was an ancient and noble borough, which wanted nothing but the name to be a city; he then inadvertently mentions that the river Lambro runs through it: and, again, that it was the seat of an arch-presbyter. With these indications, there is not in all Europe a moderately-learned man, who will not instantly exclaim, 'Monza!' We could also propose some very well-founded conjectures in the name of the family; but, although the object of our conjectures has been some time extinct, we consider it better to be silent on this head, not to run the risk of wronging even the dead, and to leave some subject of research for the learned.

Our travellers reached Monza shortly after sun-rise; the driver turned into an inn, and, as if at home in the place and well acquainted with the landlord, ordered a room for the newly-arrived guests, and accompanied them thither. After many acknowledgments, Renzo tried to induce him to receive some reward; but he, like the boatman, had in view another, more distant, but more abundant recompense: he put his hands behind him, and making his escape went to look after his horse.

After such a night as we have described, and as every one may imagine, the greatest part spent in mournful thoughts, with the constant dread of some unforeseen misfortune, in the melancholy silence of night, in the sharpness of a more than autumnal air, and amid the frequent jolts of the incommodious vehicle, which rudely shook the weary frames of our travellers, they soon felt themselves overpowered with sleep, and availed themselves of a sofa that stood in an adjoining room to take a little repose. They then partook together of a frugal meal, such as the poverty of the times would allow, and scanty in proportion to the contingent wants of an uncertain future, and their own slender appetite. One after another they remembered the banquet which, two days before, they had hoped to enjoy; and each in turn heaved a deep sigh. Renzo would gladly have stayed there, at least for that day, to have seen the two women provided for, and to have given them his services, but the Father had recommended them to send him on his way as quickly as possible. They alleged, therefore, these orders, and a hundred other reasons;—people would gossip—the longer the separation was delayed, the more painful it would be—he could come again soon, to give and learn news;—so that, at last, the youth determined to go. Their plans were then more definitely arranged; Lucia did not attempt to hide her tears; Renzo could scarcely restrain his; and, warmly pressing Agnese's hand, he said, in an almost choked voice, 'Farewell, till we meet again!' and set off.

The women would have found themselves much at a loss, had it not been for the good driver, who had orders to guide them to the convent, and to give them any direction and assistance they might stand in need of. With this escort, then, they took their way to the convent, which, as every one knows, was a short distance outside the town of Monza. Arrived at the door, their conductor rang the bell, and asked for the guardian, who quickly made his appearance, and received the letter.

'Oh brother Cristoforo!' said he, recognizing the handwriting, the tone of his voice and the expression of his face evidently indicating that he uttered the name of an intimate friend. It might easily be seen, too, that our good friar had in this letter warmly recommended the women, and related their case with much feeling, for the guardian kept making gestures of surprise and indignation, and raising his eyes from the paper, he would fix them upon the women with a certain expression of pity and interest. When he had finished reading it, he stood for a little while thoughtful, and then said to himself, 'There is no one but the Signora—if the Signora would take upon herself this charge.' He then drew Agnese a few steps aside in the little square before the convent; asked her a few questions, which she answered satisfactorily, and then, turning towards Lucia, addressed them both: 'My good women, I will try; and I hope I shall be able to find you a retreat more than secure, more than honourable, until it shall please God to provide for you in some better way. Will you come with me?'

The women reverently bowed assent, and the friar continued: 'Come with me to the convent of the Signora. Keep, however, a few steps behind me, because people delight to speak evil, and no one knows what fine stories they would make out, if they were to see the Father-guardian walking with a beautiful young girl . . . with women, I mean to say.'

So saying, he moved forward. Lucia blushed, their guide smiled, and glanced at Agnese, who betrayed, also, a momentary smile, and when the friar had gone a few steps, they followed him at about ten yards distance. The women then asked their guide what they did not dare say to the Father-guardian, who was the Signora.

'The Signora,' replied he, 'is a nun; but she is not like the other nuns. Not that she is either the Abbess, or the Prioress; for, from what they say, she is one of the youngest there: but she is from Adam's rib, and she is of an ancient and high family in Spain, where some of them now are princes; and therefore they call her the Signora, to show that she is a great lady: and all the country call her by this name, for they say there never was her equal in this monastery before; and even now, down at Milan, her family ranks very high, and is held in great esteem; and in Monza still more so, because her father, though he does not live here, is the first man in the country; so that she can do what she pleases in the convent; and all the country-people bear her a great respect; and if she undertakes a business she is sure to succeed in it; so that if this good monk before us is fortunate enough to get you into her hands, and she takes you under her protection, I dare venture to say you will be as safe as at the altar.'

On reaching the gate of the town, flanked at that time by an ancient ruined tower, and a fragment of a demolished castle, which, perhaps, some few of my readers may still remember to have seen standing, the guardian stopped, and looked behind to see if they were following; he then passed through, and went on to the convent, and when he reached it, stopped again at the doorway, and waited for the little party. He then begged the guide to come again to the convent, to take back a reply; he promised to do so, and took his leave of the women, who loaded him with thanks and messages to Father Cristoforo. The guardian, bidding them go into the first court of the monastery, ushered them into the apartments of the portress, to whom he recommended them, and went forward alone to make his request. After a few moments, he returned, and, with a joyful manner, told them to come with him; and his reappearance was just à-propos, for they were beginning to find it difficult to ward off the pressing interrogations of the portress. While traversing the inner court, the Father instructed the women how they must behave to the Signora. 'She is well-disposed towards you,' said he, 'and

may be of much service to you. Be humble and respectful, reply
with frankness to the questions she may please to put; and when
you are not questioned, leave it to me.' They then passed through
a lower room to the parlour of the convent; and before entering,
the guardian, pointing to the door, said to the women in an under-
tone, 'She is there;' as if to remind them of the lessons he had been
giving. Lucia, who had never before seen a monastery, looked
round the room, on entering, for the Signora to whom she was
to make obeisance, and perceiving no one, she stood perplexed; but
seeing the Father advance, and Agnese following, she looked in that
direction, and observed an almost square aperture, like a half-win-
dow, grated with two large thick iron bars, distant from each other
about a span, and behind this a nun was standing. Her countenance, which showed her to be about twenty-five years old, gave
the impression, at a first glance, of beauty, but of beauty worn, faded,
and, one might almost say, spoiled. A black veil, stiffened and
stretched quite flat upon her head, fell on each side and stood out a
little way from her face; under the veil, a very white linen band half
covered a forehead of different but not inferior whiteness; a second
band, in folds, down each side of the face, crossed under the chin, encircled the neck, and was spread a little over the breast to conceal the
opening of a black dress. But this forehead was wrinkled every now
and then, as if by some painful emotion, accompanied by the rapid
movement of two jet-black eyebrows. Sometimes she would fix two
very dark eyes on another's face with a piercing look of haughty investigation, and then again would hastily lower them, as if seeking a
hiding-place. One moment, an attentive observer would imagine
they were soliciting affection, intercourse, pity; at another, he would
gather thence a momentary revelation of ancient and smothered
hatred—of some indescribable, fierce disposition; and when they
remained immovably fixed without attention, some might have
imagined a proud indifference, while others would have suspected
the labouring of some secret thought, the overpowering dominion
of an idea familiar to her mind, and more engrossing than
surrounding objects. Her pale cheeks were delicately formed, but
much altered and shrunk by a gradual extenuation. Her lips, though
scarcely suffused with a faint tinge of the rose, stood out in con-

trast with this paleness, and, like her eyes, their movements were sudden, quick, and full of expression and mystery. The well-formed tallness of her figure disappeared in the habitual stoop of her carriage, or was disfigured by certain quick and irregular starts, which betrayed too resolute an air for a woman, still more for a nun. In her very dress, there was a display of either particularity or negligence, which betokened a nun of singular character; her head-dress was arranged with a kind of worldly carefulness, and from under the band around her head the end of a curl of glossy black hair appeared upon her temple, betraying either forgetfulness, or contempt of the rule which required them always to keep the hair closely shaven. It was cut off first at the solemn ceremony of their admission.

These things made no impression on the minds of the two women; inexperienced in distinguishing nun from nun; and the Father-guardian had so frequently seen the Signora before, that he was already accustomed, like many others, to the singularities in manner and dress which she displayed.

She was standing, as we have said, near the grated window, languidly leaning on it with one hand, twining her delicately-white fingers in the interstices, and with her head slightly bent downwards, surveying the advancing party. 'Reverend mother and most illustrious Signora,' said the guardian, bowing his head, and laying his right hand upon his breast, 'this is the poor young girl to whom you have encouraged me to hope you will extend your valuable protection; and this is her mother.'

Agnese and Lucia reverently curtseyed: the Signora beckoning to them with her hand that she was satisfied, said, turning to the Father, 'It is fortunate for me that I have it in my power to serve our good friends the Capuchin Fathers in any matter. But,' continued she, 'will you tell me a little more particularly the case of this young girl, so that I may know better what I ought to do for her?'

Lucia blushed, and held down her head.

'You must know, reverend mother . . .' began Agnese; but the guardian silenced her with a glance, and replied, 'This young girl, most illustrious lady, has been recommended to me, as I told you, by a brother friar. She has been compelled secretly to leave her country to avoid great dangers, and wants an asylum for some time where she may live retired, and where no one will dare molest her, even when . . .'

'What dangers?' interrupted the Signora. 'Be good enough, Father, not to tell me the case so enigmatically. You know that we nuns like to hear stories minutely.'

'They are dangers,' replied the guardian, 'which scarcely ought to be mentioned ever so delicately in the pure ears of the reverend mother . . .'

'Oh, certainly!' replied the Signora, hastily, and slightly colouring. Was it modesty? One who would have observed the momentary expression of vexation which accompanied this blush might have entertained some doubt of it, especially if he had compared it with that which diffused itself from time to time on the cheeks of Lucia.

'It is enough,' resumed the guardian, 'that a powerful noble-man . . . not all of the great people of the world use the gifts of God to his glory and for the good of their neighbours, as your illus-trious ladyship has done . . . a powerful cavalier, after having for some time persecuted this poor girl with base flatteries, seeing that they were useless, had the heart openly to persecute her by force, so that the poor thing has been obliged to fly from her home.'

'Come near, young girl,' said the Signora to Lucia, beckoning to her with her hand. 'I know that the Father-guardian is truth itself; but no one can be better informed in this business than your-self. It rests with you to say whether this cavalier was an odious persecutor.'

As to approaching, Lucia instantly obeyed, but to answer, was another matter. An inquiry on this subject even when proposed by an equal, would have put her into confusion; but made by the Signora, and with a certain air of malicious doubt, it deprived her of courage to reply. 'Signora . . . mother . . . reverend . . .' stam-mered she, but she seemed to have nothing more to say. Agnese, therefore, as being certainly the best informed after her, here thought herself authorized to come to her succour. 'Most illustrious Signora,' said she, 'I can bear full testimony that my daughter hated this cavalier, as the devil hates holy water. I should say, he is the devil himself; but you will excuse me if I speak improperly, for we are poor folk, as God made us. The case is this: that my poor girl was betrothed to a youth in her own station, a steady man, and one who fears God; and if the Signor-Curato had been what he ought to be . . . I know I am speaking of a religious man, but Father Cristoforo, a friend here of the Father-guardian, is a religious man as well as he; and that's the man that's full of kindness; and if he were here he could attest . . .'

'You are very ready to speak without being spoken to,' interrupted the Signora, with a haughty and angry look, which made her seem almost hideous. 'Hold your tongue! I know well enough that parents are always ready with an answer in the name of their children!'

Agnese drew back, mortified, giving Lucia a look which meant to say, See what I get by your not knowing how to speak. The guardian then signified to her, with a glance and a movement of his head, that now was the moment to arouse her courage, and not to leave her poor mother in such a plight.

'Reverend lady,' said Lucia, 'what my mother has told you is exactly the truth. The youth who paid his addresses to me' (and here she coloured crimson) 'I chose with my own good will. Forgive me, if I speak too boldly, but it is that you may not think ill of my mother. And as to this Signor, (God forgive him!) I would rather die than fall into his hands. And if you do us the kindness to put us in safety, since we are reduced to the necessity of asking a place of refuge, and of inconveniencing worthy people, (but God's will be done!) be assured, lady, that no one will pray for you more earnestly and heartily than we poor women.'

'I believe you,' said the Signora, in a softened tone. 'But I should like to talk to you alone. Not that I require further information, nor any other motives to attend to the wishes of the Father-guardian,' added she, hastily, and turning towards him with studied politeness. 'Indeed,' continued she, 'I have already thought about it; and this is the best plan I can think of for the present. The portress of the convent has, a few days ago, settled her last daughter in the world. These women can occupy the room she has left at liberty, and supply her place in the trifling services she performed in the monastery.

In truth . . .' and here she beckoned to the guardian to approach the grated window, and continued, in an under-voice: 'In truth, on account of the scarcity of the times, it was not intended to substitute any one in the place of that young woman; but I will speak to the Lady Abbess; and at a word from me . . . at the request of the Father-guardian . . . in short, I give the place as a settled thing.'

The guardian began to return thanks, but the Signora interrupted him: 'There is no need of ceremony: in a case of necessity I should not hesitate to apply for the assistance of the Capuchin Fathers. In fact,' continued she, with a smile, in which appeared an indescribable air of mockery and bitterness; 'in fact, are we not brothers and sisters?'

So saying, she called a lay-sister, (two of whom were, by a singular distinction, assigned to her private service,) and desired her to inform the Abbess of the circumstance; then sending for the portress to the door of the cloister, she concerted with her and Agnese the necessary arrangements. Dismissing her, she bade farewell to the guardian, and detained Lucia. The guardian accompanied Agnese to the door, giving her new instructions by the way, and went to write his letter of report to his friend Cristoforo. 'An extraordinary character, that Signora!' thought he, as he walked home: 'Very curious! But one who knows the right way to go to work, can make her do whatever he pleases. My good friend Cristoforo certainly does not expect that I can serve him so quickly and so well. That noble fellow! There is no help for it: he must always have something in hand. But he is doing good. It is well for him this time, that he has found a friend who has brought the affair to a good conclusion in a twinkling, without so much noise, so much preparation, so much ado. This good Cristoforo will surely be satisfied, and see that even we here are good for something.'

The Signora, who, in the presence of a Capuchin of advanced age, had studied her actions and words, now, when left *tête-à-tête* with an inexperienced country girl, no longer attempted to restrain herself; and her conversation became by degrees so strange, that, instead of relating it, we think it better briefly to narrate the previous history of this unhappy person: so much, that is, as will suffice to account for the unusual and mysterious conduct we have witnessed in her, and to explain the motives of her behaviour in the facts which we shall be obliged to relate.

She was the youngest daughter of the Prince * * *, a Milanese nobleman, who was esteemed one of the richest men of the city. But the unbounded idea he entertained of his title made his property appear scarcely sufficient, nay, even too limited to maintain a proper appearance; and all his attention was turned towards keeping it, at least, such as it was, in one line, so far as it depended upon himself. How many children he had does not appear from history: it merely records that he had designed all the younger branches of both sexes for the cloister that he might leave his property entire to the eldest son, destined to perpetuate the family: that is, bring up children that he might torment himself in tormenting them after his father's example. Our unhappy Signora was yet unborn when her condition was irrevocably determined upon. It only remained to decide whether she should be a monk or a nun, a decision, for which, not her assent, but her presence, was required. When she was born, the Prince, her father, wishing to give her a name that would always immediately suggest the idea of a cloister and which had been borne by a saint of high family, called her Gertrude. Dolls dressed like nuns were the first playthings put into her hands; then images in nuns' habits, accompanying the gift with admonitions to prize them highly, as very precious things, and with that affirmative interrogation, 'Beautiful, eh?' When the Prince, or the Princess, or the young prince, the only one of the sons brought up at home, would represent the happy prospects of the child, it seemed as if they could find no other way of expressing their ideas than by the words, 'What a lady-abbess!' No one, however, directly said to her, 'You must become a nun.' It was an intention understood and touched upon incidentally in every conversation relating to her future destiny. If at any time the little Gertrude indulged in rebellious or imperious behaviour, to which her natural disposition easily inclined her, 'You are a naughty little girl,' they would say to her: 'this behaviour is very unbecoming. When you are a lady-abbess, you shall then command with the rod: you can then do as you please.' On another occasion, the Prince reproving her for her too

free and familiar manners, into which she easily fell: 'Hey! hey!'
he cried; 'they are not becoming to one of your rank. If you wish
some day to engage the respect that is due to you, learn from henceforth to be more reserved: remember you ought to be in everything
the first in the monastery, because you carry your rank wherever
you go.'

Such language imbued the mind of the little girl with the implicit
idea that she was to be a nun; but her father's words had more effect
upon her than all the others put together. The manners of the
Prince were habitually those of an austere master, but when treating
of the future prospects of his children, there shone forth in every
word and tone an immovability of resolution which inspired the idea
of a fatal necessity.

At six years of age, Gertrude was placed for education, and still
more as a preparatory step towards the vocation imposed upon her,
in the monastery where we have seen her; and the selection of the
place was not without design. The worthy guide of the two women
has said that the father of the Signora was the first man in Monza;
and, comparing this testimony, whatever it may be worth, with
some other indications which our anonymous author unintentionally
suffers to escape here and there, we may very easily assert that he
was the feudal head of that country. However it may be, he enjoyed
here very great authority, and thought that here, better than elsewhere, his daughter would be treated with that distinction and deference which might induce her to choose this monastery as her perpetual abode. Nor was he deceived: the then abbess and several
intriguing nuns, who had the management of affairs, finding themselves entangled in some disputes with another monastery, and
with a noble family of the country, were very glad of the acquisition
of such a support, received with much gratitude the honour bestowed
upon them, and fully entered into the intentions of the Prince concerning the permanent settlement of his daughter; intentions on
every account entirely consonant with their interests. Immediately on
Gertrude's entering the monastery, she was called by Antonomasia,
the Signorina.[1] A separate place was assigned her at table, and a
private sleeping apartment; her conduct was proposed as an example

[1] The young lady.

to others; indulgences and caresses were bestowed upon her without end, accompanied with that respectful familiarity so attractive to children when observed in those whom they see treating other children with an habitual air of superiority. Not that all the nuns had conspired to draw the poor child into the snare; many there were of simple and undesigning minds, who would have shrunk with horror from the thought of sacrificing a child to interested views; but all of them being intent on their several individual occupations, some did not notice all these manœuvres, others did not discern how dishonest they were; some abstained from looking into the matter, and others were silent rather than give useless offence. There was one, too, who, remembering how she had been induced by similar arts to do what she afterwards repented of, felt a deep compassion for the poor little innocent, and showed that compassion by bestowing on her tender and melancholy caresses, which she was far from suspecting were tending towards the same result; and thus the affair proceeded. Perhaps it might have gone on thus to the end, if Gertrude had been the only little girl in the monastery; but among her school-fellows, there were some who knew they were designed for marriage. The little Gertrude, brought up with high ideas of her superiority, talked very magnificently of her future destiny as abbess and principal of the monastery; she wished to be an object of envy to the others on every account, and saw with astonishment and vexation that some of them paid no attention to all her boasting. To the majestic, but circumscribed and cold, images the headship of a monastery could furnish, they opposed the varied and bright pictures of a husband, guests, routs, towns, tournaments, retinues, dress, and equipages. Such glittering visions roused in Gertrude's mind that excitement and ardour which a large basket-full of freshly gathered flowers would produce if placed before a bee-hive. Her parents and teachers had cultivated and increased her natural vanity, to reconcile her to the cloisters; but when this passion was excited by ideas so much calculated to stimulate it, she quickly entered into them with a more lively and spontaneous ardour. That she might not be below her companions, and influenced at the same time by her new turn of mind, she replied that, at the time of the decision, no one could compel her to take the veil without her consent; that she too, could marry, live in a palace, enjoy the world, and that better than any of them; that she *could* if she wished it, that she *would* if she wished it; and that, in fact, she *did* wish it. The idea of the necessity of her consent, which hitherto had been, as it were, unnoticed, and hidden in a corner of her mind, now unfolded and displayed itself in all its importance. On every occasion she called it to her aid, that she might enjoy in tranquillity the images of a self-chosen future. Together with this idea, however, there invariably appeared another; that the refusal of this consent involved rebellion against her father, who already believed it, or pretended to believe it, a decided thing; and at this remembrance, the child's mind was very far from feeling the confidence which her words proclaimed. She would then compare herself with her companions, whose confidence was of a far different kind, and experienced lamentably that envy of their condition which, at first, she endeavoured to awaken in them. From envy she changed to hatred; which she displayed in contempt, rudeness, and sarcastic speeches; while, sometimes, the conformity of her inclinations and hopes with theirs, suppressed her spite, and created in her an apparent and transient friendship. At times, longing to enjoy something real and present, she would feel a complacency in the distinctions accorded to her, and make others sensible of this superiority; and then, again, unable to tolerate the solitude of her fears and desires, she would go in search of her companions, her haughtiness appeased, almost, indeed, imploring of them kindness, counsel, and encouragement. In the midst of such pitiable warfare with herself and others, she passed her childhood, and entered upon that critical age at which an almost mysterious power seems to take possession of the soul, arousing, refreshing, invigorating all the inclinations and ideas, and sometimes transforming them, or turning them into some unlooked-for channel. That which, until now, Gertrude had most distinctly figured in these dreams of the future, was external splendour and pomp; a something soothing and kindly, which, from the first, was lightly, and, as it were, mistily, diffused over her mind, now began to spread itself and predominate in her imagination. It took possession of the most secret recesses of her heart, as of a gorgeous retreat; hither she retired from present objects; here she entertained various personages strangely compounded of the confused remembrances of childhood, the little she had seen of the external world, and what she had gathered in conversations with her companions; she entertained herself with them, talked to them, and replied in their name; here she gave commands, and here she received homage of every kind. At times, the thoughts of religion would come to disturb these brilliant and toilsome revels. But religion, such as it had been taught to this poor girl, and such as she had received it, did not prohibit pride, but rather sanctified it, and proposed it as a means of obtaining earthly felicity. Robbed thus of its essence, it was no longer religion, but a phantom like the rest. In the intervals in which this phantom occupied the first place, and ruled in Gertrude's fancy, the unhappy girl, oppressed by confused terrors, and urged by an indefinite idea of duty imagined that her repugnance to the cloister, and her resistance to the wishes of her superiors in the choice of her state of life, was a fault; and she resolved in her heart to expiate it, by voluntarily taking the veil.

It was a rule, that, before a young person could be received as a nun, she should be examined by an ecclesiastic, called the vicar of the nuns, or by some one deputed by him; that it might be seen whether the lot were her deliberate choice or not; and this examination could not take place for a year after she had, by a written request, signified her desire to the vicar. Those nuns who had taken upon themselves the sad office of inducing Gertrude to bind herself for ever with the least possible consciousness of what she was doing, seized one of the moments we have described to persuade her to write and sign such a memorial. And, in order the more easily to persuade her to such a course, they failed not to affirm and impress upon her, what, indeed, was quite true, that, after all, it was a mere formality, which could have no effect, without other and posterior steps, depending entirely upon her own will. Nevertheless the memorial had scarcely reached its destination, before Gertrude repented having written it. Then she repented of these repentances; and thus days and months were spent in an incessant alternation of wishes and regrets. For a long while she concealed this act from her companions; sometimes from fear of exposing her good resolution to opposition and contradiction, at others from shame at revealing her error; but, at last, the desire of unburdening her mind, and of seeking advice and encouragement, conquered.

Another rule was this: that a young girl was not to be admitted to this examination upon the course of life she had chosen, until she had resided for at least a month out of the convent where she had been educated. A year had almost passed since the presentation of this memorial; and it had been signified to Gertrude that she would shortly be taken from the monastery, and sent to her father's house, for this one month, there to take all the necessary steps towards the completion of the work she had really begun. The Prince, and the rest of the family, considered it an assured thing, as if it had already taken place. Not so, however, his daughter; instead of taking fresh steps, she was engaged in considering how she could withdraw the first. In her perplexity, she resolved to open her mind to one of her companions, the most sincere and always the readiest to give spirited advice. She advised Gertrude to inform her father, by letter, that she had changed her mind, since she had not the courage to pronounce to his face, at the proper time, a bold *I will not*. And as gratuitous advice in this world is very rare, the counsellor made Gertrude pay for this by abundance of raillery upon her want of spirit. The letter was agreed upon with three or four confidantes, written in private, and despatched by means of many deeply-studied artifices. Gertrude waited with great anxiety for a reply; but none came; excepting that, a few days afterwards, the Abbess, taking her aside, with an air of mystery, displeasure, and compassion, let fall some obscure hints about the great anger of her father, and a wrong step she must have been taking; leaving her to understand, however, that if she behaved well, she might still hope that all would be forgotten. The poor young girl understood it, and dared not venture to ask any further explanation.

At last, the day so much dreaded, and so ardently wished for, arrived. Although Gertrude knew well enough that she was going to a great struggle, yet to leave the monastery, to pass the bounds of those walls in which she had been for eight years immured, to traverse the open country in a carriage, to see once more the city and her home, filled her with sensations of tumultuous joy. As to the struggle with the direction of her confidantes, she had already taken her measures, and concerted her plans. Either they will force me, thought she, and then I will be immovable—I will be humble and respectful, but will refuse; the chief point is not to pronounce another 'Yes,' and I will not pronounce it. Or they will catch me with good words; and I will be better than they; I will weep, I will implore, I will move them to pity; at last, will only entreat that I may not be sacrificed. But, as it often happens in similar cases of foresight, neither one nor the other supposition was realized. Days passed, and neither her father, nor any one else, spoke to her about the petition, or the recantation; and no proposal was made to her, with either coaxing or threatening. Her parents were serious, sad, and morose, towards her, without ever giving a reason for such behaviour. It was only to be understood that they regarded her as faulty and unworthy; a mysterious anathema seemed to hang over her, and divide her from the rest of her family, merely suffering so much intercourse as was necessary to make her feel her subjection. Seldom, and only at certain fixed hours, was she admitted to the company of her parents and elder brother. In the conversations of these three there appeared to reign a great confidence, which rendered the exclusion of Gertrude doubly sensible and painful. No one addressed her; and if she ventured timidly to make a remark, unless very evidently called for, her words were either unnoticed, or were responded to by a careless, contemptuous, or severe look. If unable any longer to endure so bitter and humiliating a distinction, she sought and endeavoured to mingle with the family, and implored a little affection; she soon heard some indirect but clear hint thrown out about her choice of a monastic life, and was given to understand that there was one way of regaining the affection of the family; and since she would not accept of it on these conditions, she was obliged to draw back, to refuse the first advances towards the kindness she so much desired, and to continue in her state of excommunication; continue in it, too, with a certain appearance of being to blame.

Such impressions from surrounding objects painfully contradicted the bright visions with which Gertrude had been so much occupied, and which she still secretly indulged in her heart. She had hoped that, in her splendid and much-frequented home, she should have enjoyed at least some real taste of the pleasures she had so long imagined; but she found herself woefully deceived. The confinement was as strict and close at home as in the convent; to walk out for recreation was never even spoken of; and a gallery that led from the house to an adjoining church, obviated the sole necessity there might have been to go into the street. The company was more uninteresting, more scarce, and less varied than in the monastery. At every announcement of a visitor, Gertrude was obliged to go upstairs, and remain with some old woman in the service of the family; and here she dined whenever there was company. The domestic servants concurred in behaviour and language with the example and intentions of their master; and Gertrude, who by inclination would have treated them with lady-like unaffected familiarity; and who, in the rank in which she was placed, would have esteemed it a favour if they had shown her any little mark of kindness as an equal, and even have stooped to ask it, was now humbled and annoyed at being treated with a manifest indifference, although accompanied by a slight obsequiousness of formality. She could not, however, but observe, that one of these servants, a page, appeared to bear her a respect very different to the others, and to feel a peculiar kind of compassion for her. The behaviour of this youth approached more nearly than anything she had yet seen to the state of things that Gertrude had pictured to her imagination, and more resembled the doings of her ideal characters. By degrees, a strange transformation was discernible in the manners of the young girl; there appeared a new tranquillity, and at the same time a restlessness, differing from her usual disquietude; her conduct was that of one who had found a treasure which oppresses him, which he incessantly watches, and hides from the view of others. Gertrude kept her eyes on this page more closely than ever; and, however it came to pass, she was surprised one unlucky morning by a chamber-maid, while secretly folding up a letter, in which it would have been better had she written nothing. After a brief altercation, the maid got possession of the letter, and carried it to her master. The terror of Gertrude at the sound of his footsteps, may be more easily imagined than described. It was *her* father; he was irritated, and she felt herself guilty. But when he stood before her with that frowning brow, and the ill-fated

At the end of four or five long days of confinement, Gertrude, disgusted and exasperated beyond measure by one of these sallies of her guardian, went and sat down in a corner of the room, and covering her face with her hands, remained for some time secretly indulging her rage. She then felt an overbearing longing to see some other faces, to hear some other words, to be treated differently. She thought of her father, of her family; and the idea made her shrink back in horror. But she remembered that it only depended upon her to make them her friends; and this remembrance awakened a momentary joy. Then there followed a confused and unusual sorrow for her fault, and an equal desire to expiate it. Not that her will was already determined upon such a resolution, but she had never before approached it so near. She rose from her seat, went to the table, took up the fatal pen, and wrote a letter to her father, full of enthusiasm and humiliation, of affliction and hope, imploring his pardon, and showing herself indefinitely ready to do anything that would please him who alone could grant it.

CHAPTER X

THERE are times when the mind, of the young especially, is so disposed, that any external influence, however slight, suffices to call forth whatever has the appearance of virtuous self-sacrifice; as a scarcely expanded flower abandons itself negligently to its fragile stem, ready to yield its fragrance to the first breath of the zephyrs that float around. These moments, which others should regard with reverential awe, are exactly those which the wily and interested eagerly watch for, and seize with avidity, to fetter an unguarded will.

On the perusal of this letter the Prince * * * instantly saw a door opened to the fulfilment of his early and still cherished views. He therefore sent to Gertrude to come to him, and prepared to strike the iron while it was hot. Gertrude had no sooner made her appearance, than, without raising her eyes towards her father, she threw herself upon her knees, scarcely able to articulate the word 'Pardon.' The Prince beckoned to her to rise, and then, in a voice little calculated to reassure her, replied, that it was not sufficient to desire and solicit forgiveness, for that was easy and natural enough to one who had been convicted of a fault, and dreaded its punishment; that, in short, it was necessary she should deserve it. Gertrude, in a subdued and trembling voice, asked what she must do. To this question the Prince (for we cannot find in our heart at this moment to give him the title of father) made no direct reply, but proceeded to speak at some length on Gertrude's fault, in words which grated on the feelings of the poor girl like the drawing of a rough hand over a wound. He then went on to say, that even if . . . supposing he ever . . . had had at the first any intention of settling her in the world, she herself had now opposed an insuperable obstacle to such a plan; since a man of honour, as he was, could never bring himself to give to any gentleman a daughter who had shown such a specimen of her character. His wretched auditor was completely overwhelmed; and then the Prince, gradually softening his voice and language, proceeded to say, that for every fault there was a remedy and a hope of mercy; that hers was one the remedy for which was very distinctly indicated; that she ought to see in this sad event a warning, as it were, that a worldly life was too full of danger for her . . .

'Ah, yes!' exclaimed Gertrude, excited by fear, subdued by a sense of shame, and overcome at the instant by a momentary tenderness of spirit.

'Ah; you see it too,' replied the Prince, instantly taking up her words. 'Well, let us say no more of what is past: all is cancelled. You have taken the only honourable and suitable course that remained for you; but, since you have chosen it willingly and cheerfully, it rests with me to make it pleasant to you in every possible way. I have the power of turning it to your advantage, and giving all the merit of the action to yourself, and I'll engage to do it for you.' So saying, he rang a little bell that stood on the table, and said to the servant who answered it,—'The Princess and the young Prince immediately.' Then turning to Gertrude, he continued: 'I wish them to share in my satisfaction at once; and I wish you immediately to be treated by all as is fit and proper. You have experienced a little of the severe parent, but from henceforth you shall find me an affectionate father.'

Gertrude stood thunderstruck at these words. One moment she wondered how that 'yes,' which had escaped her lips, could be made to mean so much: then she thought, was there no way of retracting—of restricting the sense; but the Prince's conviction seemed so unshaken, his joy so sensitively jealous, and his benignity so conditional, that Gertrude dared not utter a word to disturb them in the slightest degree.

The parties summoned quickly made their appearance, and, on seeing Gertrude, regarded her with an expression of surprise and uncertainty. But the Prince, with a cheerful and loving countenance, which immediately met with an answering look from them, said, —'Behold the wandering sheep: and I intend this to be the last word that shall awaken sad remembrances. Behold the consolation of the family! Gertrude no longer needs advisers, for she has voluntarily chosen what we desired for her good. She has determined—she has given me to understand that she has determined

. . .' Here Gertrude raised towards her father a look between terror and supplication, as if imploring him to pause, but he continued boldly: 'that she has determined to take the veil.'

'*Bravo!* well done!' exclaimed the mother and son, turning at the same time to embrace Gertrude, who received these congratulations with tears, which were interpreted as tears of satisfaction. The Prince then expatiated upon what he would do to render the situation of his daughter pleasant, and even splendid. He spoke of the distinction with which she would be regarded in the monastery and the surrounding country: that she would be like a princess, the representative of the family; that, as soon as ever her age would allow of it, she would be raised to the first dignity, and in the mean while would be under subjection only in name. The Princess and the young Prince renewed their congratulations and applauses, while poor Gertrude stood as if possessed by a dream.

'We had better fix the day for going to Monza to make our request of the Abbess,' said the Prince. 'How pleased she will be! I venture to say that all the monastery will know how to estimate the honour which Gertrude does them. Likewise . . . but why not go this very day? Gertrude will be glad to take an airing.'

'Let us go, then,' said the Princess.

'I will go and give orders,' said the young Prince.

'But . . .' suggested Gertrude, submissively.

'Softly, softly,' replied the Prince, 'let her decide: perhaps she does not feel inclined to-day, and would rather delay till to-morrow. Tell me, would you prefer to-day or to-morrow?'

'To-morrow,' answered Gertrude, in a faint voice, thinking it something that she could get a little longer respite.

'To-morrow,' pronounced the Prince, solemnly; 'she has decided that we go to-morrow. In the mean while I will go and ask the vicar of the nuns to name a day for the examination.'

No sooner said than done; the Prince took his departure, and absolutely went himself (no little act of condescension) to the vicar, and obtained a promise that he would attend her the day after to-morrow.

During the remainder of this day Gertrude had not two moments of quiet. She wished to have calmed her mind after so many scenes of excitement, to clear and arrange her thoughts, to render an account to herself of what she had done, and of what she was about to do, determine what she wished, and, for a moment at least, retard that machine, which, once started, was proceeding so precipitously; but there was no opening. Occupations succeeded one another without interruption—one treading, as it were, upon the heels of another. Immediately after this solemn interview, she was conducted to her mother's dressing-room, there, under her superintendence, to be dressed and adorned by her own waiting-maid. Scarcely was this business completed when dinner was announced. Gertrude was greeted on her way by the bows of the servants, who expressed their congratulations for her recovery; and, on reaching the dining-room, she found a few of their nearest friends, who had been hastily invited to do her honour, and to share in the general joy for the two happy events,—her restored health, and her choice of a vocation.

The young bride—(as the novices were usually distinguished, and Gertrude was saluted on all sides by this title on her first appearance)—the young bride had enough to do to reply to all the compliments that were addressed to her. She was fully sensible that every one of these answers was, as it were, an assent and confirmation; yet how could she reply otherwise? Shortly after dinner came the driving hour, and Gertrude accompanied her mother in a carriage, with two uncles who had been among the guests. After the usual tour, they entered the Strada Marina, which crossed the space now occupied by the public gardens, and was the rendezvous of the gentry who drove out for recreation after the labours of the day. The uncles addressed much of their conversation to Gertrude, as was to be expected on such a day; and one of them, who seemed to be acquainted with everybody, every carriage, every livery, and had every moment something to say about Signor this and Lady that, suddenly checked himself, and turning to his niece—'Ah, you young rogue!' exclaimed he; 'you are turning your back on all these follies,—you are one of the saints; we poor worldly fellows are caught in the snare, but you are going to lead a religious life, and go to heaven in your carriage.'

As evening approached they returned home, and the servants,

hastily descending to meet them with lights, announced several visitors who were awaiting their return. The rumour had spread, and friends and relations crowded to pay their respects. On entering the drawing-room the young bride became the idol—the sole object of attention—the victim. Every one wished to have her to himself; one promised her pleasures,—another visits; one spoke of *Madre* this, her relation,—another of *Madre* that, an acquaintance; one extolled the climate of Monza,—another enlarged with great eloquence upon the distinctions she would there enjoy. Others, who had not yet succeeded in approaching Gertrude while thus besieged, stood watching their opportunity to address her, and felt a kind of regret until they had discharged their duty in this matter. By degrees the party dispersed, and Gertrude remained alone with the family.

'At last,' said the Prince, 'I have had the pleasure of seeing my daughter treated as becomes her rank. I must confess that she has conducted herself very well, and has shown that she will not be prevented making the first figure, and maintaining the dignity of the family.' They then went to supper, so as to retire early, that they might be ready in good time in the morning.

Gertrude, annoyed, piqued, and at the same time a little puffed up by the compliments and ceremonies of the day, at this moment remembered all she had suffered from her jailer; and, seeing her father so ready to gratify her in everything but one, she resolved to make use of this disposition for the indulgence of at least one of the passions which tormented her. She displayed a great unwillingness again to be left alone with her maid, and complained bitterly of her treatment.

'What!' said the Prince; 'did she not treat you with respect? To-morrow I will reward her as she deserves. Leave it to me, and I will get you entire satisfaction. In the mean while, a child with whom I am so well pleased must not be attended by a person she dislikes.' So saying, he called another servant, and gave her orders to wait upon Gertrude, who, though certainly enjoying the satisfaction she received, was astonished at finding it so trifling, in comparison with the earnest wishes she had felt beforehand. The thought that, in spite of her unwillingness, predominated in her imagination, was the remembrance of the fearful progress she had this day made towards her cloistral life, and the consciousness that to draw back now would require a far, far greater degree of courage and resolution than would have sufficed a few days before, and which, even *then,* she felt she did not possess.

The woman appointed to attend her was an old servant of the family, who had formerly been the young Prince's governess, having received him from the arms of his nurse, and brought him up until he was almost a young man. In him she had centred all her pleasures, all her hopes, all her pride. She was delighted at this day's decision, as if it had been her own good fortune; and Gertrude, at the close of the day, was obliged to listen to the congratulations, praises, and advice of this old woman. She told her of some of her aunts and near relations who had been very happy as nuns, because, being of so high a family, they had always enjoyed the first honours, and had been able to have a good deal of influence beyond the walls of the convent; so that, from their parlour, they had come off victorious in undertakings in which the first ladies of the land had been quite foiled. She talked to her about the visits she would receive; she would some day be seeing the Signor Prince with his bride, who must certainly be some noble lady; and then not only the monastery, but the whole country would be in excitement. The old woman talked while undressing Gertrude; she talked after she had lain down, and even continued talking after Gertrude was asleep. Youth and fatigue had been more powerful than cares. Her sleep was troubled, disturbed, and full of tormenting dreams, but was unbroken, until the shrill voice of the old woman aroused her to prepare for her journey to Monza.

'Up, up, Signora bride; it is broad day-light, and you will want at least an hour to dress and arrange yourself. The Signora Princess is getting up; they awoke her four hours earlier than usual. The young Prince has already been down to the stables and come back, and is ready to start whenever you are. The creature is as brisk as a hare! but he was always so from a child: I have a right to say so who have nursed him in my arms. But when he's once set a-going, it won't do to oppose him; for, though he is the best-tempered creature in the world, he sometimes gets impatient and storms. Poor fellow! one must pity him; it is all the effect of his temperament; and besides, this time there is some reason in it, because he is going to all this trouble for you. People must take care how they touch him at such times! he minds no one except the Signor Prince. But some day he will be the Prince himself; may it be as long as possible first, however. Quick, quick, Signorina, why do you look at me as if you were bewitched? You ought to be out of your nest at this hour.'

At the idea of the impatient Prince, all the other thoughts which had crowded into Gertrude's mind on awaking, vanished before it, like a flock of sparrows on the sudden appearance of a scarecrow. She instantly obeyed, dressed herself in haste, and, after submitting to the decoration of her hair and person, went down to the saloon, where her parents and brother were assembled. She was then led to an arm-chair, and a cup of chocolate was brought to her, which in those days was a ceremony similar to that formerly in use among the Romans, of presenting the *toga virilis*.

When the carriage was at the door, the Prince drew his daughter aside, and said: 'Come, Gertrude, yesterday you had every attention paid you; to-day you must overcome yourself. The point is now to make a proper appearance in the monastery and the surrounding country, where you are destined to take the first place. They are expecting you.' (It is unnecessary to say that the Prince had despatched a message the preceding day to the Lady Abbess.) 'They are expecting you, and all eyes will be upon you. You must maintain dignity and an easy manner. The Abbess will ask you what you wish, according to the usual form. You must reply that you request to be allowed to take the veil in the monastery where you have been so lovingly educated, and have received so many kindnesses, which is the simple truth. You will pronounce these words with an unembarrassed air; for I would not have it said that you have been drawn in, and that you don't know how to answer for yourself. These good mothers know nothing of the past: it is a secret which must remain for ever buried in the family. Take care you don't put on a sorrowful or dubious countenance, which might excite any suspicion. Show of what blood you are: be courteous and modest;

but remember that there, away from the family, there will be nobody above you.'

Without waiting for a reply, the Prince led the way, Gertrude, the Princess, and the young Prince, following; and, going downstairs, they seated themselves in the carriage. The snares and vexations of the world, and the happy, blessed life of the cloister, more especially for young people of noble birth, were the subjects of conversation during the drive. On approaching their destination the Prince renewed his instructions to his daughter, and repeated over to her several times the prescribed form of reply. On entering this neighbourhood, Gertrude felt her heart beat violently; but her attention was suddenly arrested by several gentlemen, who stopped the carriage and addressed numberless compliments to her. Then continuing their way, they drove slowly up to the monastery, amongst the inquisitive gazes of the crowds who had collected upon the road. When the carriage stopped before these well-known walls, and that dreaded door, Gertrude's heart beat still more violently. They alighted between two wings of bystanders, whom the servants were endeavouring to keep back, and the consciousness that the eyes of all were upon her, compelled the unfortunate girl closely to study her behaviour; but, above all, those of her father kept her in awe; for, spite of the dread she had of them, she could not help every moment raising her eyes to his, and, like invisible reins, they regulated every movement and expression of her countenance. After traversing the first court, they entered the second, where the door of the interior cloister was held open, and completely blockaded by nuns. In the first row stood the Abbess, surrounded by the eldest of the sisterhood; behind them the younger nuns promiscuously arranged, and some on tip-toe; and, last of all, the lay-sisters mounted on stools. Here and there among them were seen the glancing of certain bright eyes and some little faces peeping out from between the cowls: they were the most active and daring of the pupils, who, creeping in and pushing their way between nun and nun, had succeeded in making an opening where *they* might also see something. Many were the acclamations of this crowd, and many the hands held up in token of welcome and exultation. They reached the door, and Gertrude found herself standing before the Lady Abbess. After the first compliments, the superior, with an air between cheerfulness and solemnity, asked her what she wanted in that place, where there was no one who would deny her anything.

'I am here . . .' began Gertrude; but, on the point of pronouncing the words which would almost irrevocably decide her fate, she hesitated a moment, and remained with her eyes fixed on the crowd before her. At this moment she caught the eye of one of her old companions, who looked at her with a mixed air of compassion and malice which seemed to say: ah! the boaster is caught. This sight, awakening more vividly in her mind her old feelings, restored to her also a little of her former courage; and she was on the point of framing a reply far different to the one which had been dictated to her, when, raising her eyes to her father's face, almost, as it were to try her strength, she encountered there such a deep disquietude, such a threatening impatience, that, urged by fear, she continued with great precipitation, as if flying from some terrible object: 'I am here to request permission to take the religious habit in this monastery, where I have been so lovingly educated.' The Abbess quickly answered, that she was very sorry in this instance that the regulations forbade her giving an immediate reply, which must come from the general votes of the sisters, and for which she must obtain permission from her superiors; that, nevertheless, Gertrude knew well enough the feelings entertained towards her in that place, to foresee what the answer would be; and that, in the mean while, no regulation prevented the Abbess and the sisterhood from manifesting the great satisfaction they felt in hearing her make such a request. There then burst forth a confused murmur of congratulations and acclamations. Presently, large dishes were brought filled with sweetmeats, and were offered first to the bride, and afterwards to her parents. While some of the nuns approached to greet Gertrude, others complimenting her mother, and others the young Prince, the Abbess requested the Prince to repair to the grate of the parlour of conference, where she would wait upon him. She was accompanied by two elders, and on his appearing, 'Signor Prince,' said she; 'to obey the regulations . . . to perform an indispensable formality, though in this case . . . nevertheless I must tell you . . .

that whenever a young person asks to be admitted to take the veil, . . . the superior, which I am unworthily . . . is obliged to warn the parents . . . that if by any chance . . . they should have constrained the will of their daughter, they are liable to excommunication. You will excuse me . . .'

'Oh! certainly, certainly, reverend mother. I admire your exactness; it is only right . . . But you need not doubt . . .'

'Oh! think, Signor Prince . . . I only spoke from absolute duty . . . for the rest . . .'

'Certainly, certainly, Lady Abbess.'

Having exchanged these few words, the two interlocutors reciprocally bowed and departed, as if neither of them felt willing to prolong the interview, each retiring to his own party, the one outside, the other within the threshold of the cloister. 'Now then let us go,' said the Prince: 'Gertrude will soon have plenty of opportunity of enjoying as much as she pleases the society of these good mothers. For the present, we have put them to enough inconvenience.' And, making a low bow, he signified his wish to return: the party broke up, exchanged salutations, and departed.

During the drive home Gertrude felt little inclination to speak. Alarmed at the step she had taken, ashamed at her want of spirit, and vexed with others as well as herself, she tried to enumerate the opportunities which still remained of saying no, and languidly and confusedly resolved in her own mind that in this, or that, or the other instance she *would* be more open and courageous. Yet, in the midst of these thoughts, her dread of her father's frown still held its full sway; so that once, when, by a stealthy glance at his face, she was fully assured that not a vestige of anger remained, when she even saw that he was perfectly satisfied with her, she felt quite cheered, and experienced a real but transient joy.

On their arrival, a long toilette, dinner, visits, walks, a *conversazione* and supper, followed each other in rapid succession. After supper the Prince introduced another subject—the choice of a godmother. This was the title of the person who, being solicited by the parents, became the guardian and escort of the young novice, in the interval between the request and the admission; an interval frequently spent in visiting churches, public palaces, *conversazioni.*

villas, and temples; in short, everything of note in the city and its
environs; so that the young people, before pronouncing the irrevocable vow, might be fully aware of what they were giving up.

'We must think of a godmother,' said the Prince; 'for to-morrow
the vicar of the nuns will be here for the usual formality of an
examination, and shortly afterwards Gertrude will be proposed in
council for the acceptance of the nuns.'

In saying this he turned towards the Princess, and she, thinking
he intended it as an invitation to her to make some proposal, was
beginning: "There should be . . .' But the Prince interrupted her.

'No, no, Signora Princess; the godmother should be acceptable
above all to the bride; and though universal custom gives the selection to the parents, yet Gertrude has so much judgment, and such
excellent discernment, that she richly deserves to be made an exception.' And here, turning to Gertrude, with the air of one who was
bestowing a singular favour, he continued: 'Any one of the ladies
who were at the *conversazione* this evening possesses all the necessary qualifications for the office of godmother to a person of your
family; and any one of them, I am willing to believe, will think it
an honour to be made choice of. Do you choose for yourself.'

Gertrude was fully sensible that to make a choice was but to
renew her consent; yet the proposition was made with so much
dignity, that a refusal would have borne the appearance of contempt,
and an excuse, of ignorance or fastidiousness. She therefore took
this step also, and named a lady who had chiefly taken her fancy
that evening; that is to say, one who had paid her the most attention,
who had most applauded her, and who had treated her with those
familiar, affectionate, and engaging manners, which, on the first
acquaintanceship, counterfeit a friendship of long standing. 'An
excellent choice,' exclaimed the Prince, who had exactly wished and
expected it. Whether by art or chance, it happened just as when a
card-player, holding up to view a pack of cards, bids the spectator
think of one, and then will tell him which it is, having previously
disposed them in such a way that but one of them can be seen.
This lady had been so much with Gertrude all the evening, and had
so entirely engaged her attention, that it would have required an
effort of imagination to think of another. These attentions, how-

ever, had not been paid without a motive; the lady had for some time fixed her eyes upon the young Prince as a desirable son-in-law; hence she regarded everything belonging to the family as her own; and therefore it was natural enough that she should interest herself for her dear Gertrude, no less than for her nearest relatives.

On the morrow, Gertrude awoke with the image of the approaching examination before her eyes; and, while she was considering if and how she could seize this most decisive opportunity to draw back, she was summoned by the Prince. 'Courage, my child,' said he: 'until now you have behaved admirably, and it only remains to-day to crown the work. All that has been done hitherto has been done with your consent. If, in this interval, any doubts had arisen in your mind, any misgivings, or youthful regrets, you ought to have expressed them; but at the point at which we have now arrived, it is no longer the time to play the child. The worthy man who is coming to you this morning, will ask you a hundred questions about your election, and whether you go of your own good will, and why, and how, and what not besides. If you tantalize him in your replies, he will keep you under examination I don't know how long. It would be an annoyance and a weariness to you; and it might produce a still more serious effort. After all the public demonstrations that have been made, every little hesitation you may display will risk my honour, and may make people think that I have taken a momentary fancy of yours for a settled resolution —that I have rushed headlong into the business—that I have . . . what not? In this case, I shall be reduced to the necessity of choosing between two painful alternatives; either to let the world form a derogatory judgment of my conduct—a course which I absolutely cannot take in justice to myself—or to reveal the true motive of your resolution, and . . .' But here, observing that Gertrude coloured crimson, that her eyes became inflamed, and her face contracted like the petals of a flower in the sultry heat that precedes a storm, he broke off this strain, and continued with a serene face: 'Come, come, all depends upon yourself—upon your judgment. I know that you are not deficient in it, and that you are not a child, to go spoil a good undertaking just at the conclusion; but I must foresee and provide for all contingencies. Let us say no more about it;

only let me feel assured that you will reply with frankness so as not to excite suspicion in the mind of this worthy man. Thus you, also, will be set at liberty the sooner.' Then, after suggesting a few answers to the probable interrogations that would be put, he entered upon the usual topic of the pleasures and enjoyments prepared for Gertrude at the monastery, and contrived to detain her on this subject till a servant announced the arrival of the examiner. After a hasty repetition of the most important hints, he left his daughter alone with him, according to the usual custom.

The good man came with a slight pre-conceived opinion that Gertrude had a strong desire for a cloistral life, because the Prince had told him so, when he went to request his attendance. It is true that the good priest, who knew well enough that mistrust was one of the most necessary virtues of his office, held as a maxim that he should be very slow in believing such protestations, and should be on his guard against pre-conceptions; but it seldom happens that the positive affirmations of a person of such authority, in whatever matter, do not give a bias to the mind of those who hear them. After the usual salutations: 'Signorina,' said he, 'I am coming to act the part of the tempter; I have come to excite doubts where your request expresses certainty, to place difficulties before your eyes, and to assure myself whether you have well considered them. Will you allow me to ask you some questions?'

'Proceed,' replied Gertrude.

The worthy priest then began to question her in the usual pre-scribed forms. 'Do you feel in your heart a free, voluntary resolution to become a nun? Have no threatenings, no flatteries been resorted to? Has no authority been made use of to persuade you to this step? Speak without reserve and with perfect sincerity to a man whose duty it is to ascertain your unbiased will, that he may prevent your being compelled by any exercise of force to take such a course.'

The true answer to such a demand rose up before Gertrude's mind with fearful distinctness. But to make that reply, she must come to an explanation; she must disclose what she had been threatened with, and relate a story . . . The unhappy girl shrank back in horror from such an idea, and tried to find some other reply, which would more speedily release her from this unpleasant inter-

view. 'I wish to take the veil,' said she, concealing her agitation—
'I wish to take the veil at my own desire, voluntarily.'

'How long have you had this desire?' again demanded the good
priest.

'I have always felt it,' replied Gertrude, rendered after this first
step more unscrupulous about speaking the truth.

'But what is the principal motive that induces you to become a
nun?'

The good priest little knew what a terrible chord he was touching;
and Gertrude had to make a great effort not to betray in her countenance the effect which these words produced on her mind, as she
replied: 'My motive is to serve God, and to fly the perils of the world.'

'May there not have been some disgust? Some . . . excuse me . . .
some caprice? There are times when a passing cause may make an
impression that seems at the moment sure to be lasting; but afterwards, when the cause is removed, and the mind calmed, then . . .'

'No, no,' replied Gertrude, precipitately, 'the reason is exactly
what I have told you.'

The vicar, rather to discharge his duty faithfully than because he
thought it necessary, persisted in his inquiries; but Gertrude was
resolved to deceive him. Besides the horror she felt at the thought
of making him acquainted with her weakness, when he seemed
so far from suspecting her of anything of the kind, the poor girl
thought that though he could certainly easily prevent her taking
the veil, yet that there was the end of his authority over her, or his
power of protection. When once he had gone, she would be left
alone with the Prince, and of what she would then have to endure
in that house, the worthy priest could know nothing; or, even if he
did, he could only pity her. The examiner was tired of questioning,
before the unfortunate girl of deceiving him; and, finding her
replies invariably consistent, and having no reason to doubt their
sincerity, he at last changed his tone, and said all he could to
confirm her in her good resolution; and, after congratulating her,
he took his leave. Passing through one of the apartments, he met
with the Prince, who appeared to fall in with him accidently, and
congratulated him on the good dispositions his daughter had displayed. The Prince had been waiting in a very wearisome state of

suspense, but, on receiving this account, he breathed more freely, and, forgetting his usual gravity, he almost ran to Gertrude, and loaded her with commendations, caresses, and promises, with cordial satisfaction, and a tenderness of manner to a great degree sincere. Such a strange medley is the human heart!

We will not follow Gertrude in her continual round of sights and amusements, nor will we describe, either generally or particularly, the feelings of her mind during this period; it would be a history of sorrows and fluctuations too monotonous, and too much resembling what we have already related. The beauty of the surrounding seats, the continual variety of objects, and the pleasant excursions in the open air, rendered the idea of the place where she must shortly alight for the last time, more odious to her than ever. Still more painful were the impressions made upon her by the assemblies and amusements of the city. The sight of a bride, in the more obvious and common sense of the word, aroused in her envy and anguish, to a degree almost intolerable; and sometimes the sight of some other individual made her feel as if to hear that title given to herself would be the height of felicity. There were even times when the pomp of palaces, the splendour of ornaments, and the excitement and clamorous festivity of the *conversazione,* so infatuated her, and aroused in her such an ardent desire to lead a gay life, that she resolved to recant, and to suffer anything rather than turn to the cold and death-like shade of the cloister. But all these resolutions vanished into air, on the calmer consideration of the difficulties of such a course, or on merely raising her eyes to the Prince's face. Sometimes, too, the thought that she must for ever abandon these enjoyments, made even this little taste of them bitter and wearisome to her; as the patient, suffering with thirst, eyes with vexation, and almost refuses with contempt, the spoonful of water the physician unwillingly allows him. In the meanwhile, the vicar of the nuns had despatched the necessary attestation, and permission arrived, to hold the conference for the election of Gertrude. The meeting was called; two-thirds of the secret votes, which were required by the regulations, were given, as was to be expected, and Gertrude was accepted. She herself, wearied with this long struggle, begged for immediate admission into the monastery, and no one came forward to oppose such a request. She was therefore gratified in her wish; and, after being pompously conducted to the monastery, she assumed the habit. After twelve months of novitiate, full of alternate regret and repentings, the time of public confession arrived; that is to say, the time when she must either utter a 'no,' more strange, more unexpected, and more disgraceful than ever; or pronounce a 'yes,' already so often repeated: she pronounced it, and became a nun for ever.

It is one of the peculiar and incommunicable properties of the Christian religion, that she can afford guidance and repose to all who, under whatever circumstances, or in whatever exigence, have recourse to her. If there is a remedy for the past, she prescribes it, administers it, and lends light and energy to put it in force, at whatever cost; if there is none, she teaches how to do that effectually and in reality, which the world prescribes proverbially,—make a virtue of necessity. She teaches how to continue with discretion what is thoughtlessly undertaken; she inclines the mind to cleave steadfastly to what was imposed upon it by authority; and imparts to a choice which, though rash at the time, is now irrevocable, all the sanctity, all the advisedness, and, let us say it boldly, all the cheerfulness of a lawful calling. Here is a path so constructed that, let a man approach it by what labyrinth or precipice he may, he sets himself, from that moment, to walk in it with security and readiness, and at once begins to draw towards a joyful end. By this means, Gertrude might have proved a holy and contented nun, however she had become one. But, instead of this, the unhappy girl struggled under the yoke, and thus felt it heavier and more galling. An incessant recurrence to her lost liberty, abhorrence of her present condition, and a wearisome clinging to desires which could never be satisfied: these were the principal occupations of her mind. She recalled, over and over again, the bitterness of the past, rearranged in her mind all the circumstances by which she had reached her present situation, and undid in thought a thousand times what she had done in act. She accused herself of want of spirit, and others of tyranny and perfidy, and pined in secret: she idolized and, at the same time, bewailed her beauty; deplored a youth destined to struggle in a prolonged martyrdom; and envied, at times, any woman, in whatever rank, with whatever acquirements, who could freely enjoy these gifts in the world.

The sight of those nuns who had co-operated in bringing her hither was hateful to her: she remembered the arts and contrivances they had made use of, and repaid them with incivilities, caprices, and even with open reproaches. These they were obliged to bear in silence; for though the Prince was willing enough to tyrannize over his daughter when he found it necessary to force her into the cloister, yet having once obtained his purpose, he would not so willingly allow others to assume authority over one of his family; and any little rumour that might have reached his ears would have been an occasion of their losing his protection, or perhaps, unfortunately, of changing a protector into an enemy. It would seem that she might have felt some kind of leaning towards those other sisters who had not lent a hand in this foul system of intrigue, and who, without having desired her for a companion, loved her as such; and, always good, busy, and cheerful, showed her, by their example, that here too, it was possible not only to live, but to be happy: but these, also, were hateful to her, for another reason: their consistent piety and contentment seemed to cast a reproof upon her disquietude and waywardness; so that she never suffered an opportunity to escape of deriding them behind their backs as bigots, or reviling them as hypocrites. Perhaps she would have been less averse to them, had she known, or guessed, that the few black balls found in the urn which decided her acceptance, had been put there by these very sisters.

She sometimes felt a little satisfaction in commanding, in being courted by those within the monastery and visited most flatteringly by those without, in accomplishing some undertaking, in extending her protection, in hearing herself styled the Signora; but what consolations were these? The mind which feels their insufficiency would gladly, at times, add to them, and enjoy with them, the consolations of religion: yet the one cannot be obtained by renouncing the other; as a shipwrecked sailor, who would cling to the plank which is to bring him safely to shore, must relinquish his hold on the unsubstantial sea-weed which natural instinct had taught him to grasp.

Shortly after finally taking the veil, Gertrude had been appointed teacher of the young people who attended the convent for education, and it may easily be imagined what would be their situation under such discipline. Her early companions had all left, but the passions called into exercise by them still remained; and, in one way or the other, the pupils were compelled to feel their full weight. When she remembered that many of them were destined to that course of life of which she had lost every hope, she indulged against the poor children a feeling of rancour, which almost amounted to a desire of vengeance. This feeling she manifested by keeping them under, irritating them, and depreciating in anticipation the pleasures which they one day hoped to enjoy. Any one who had heard with what arrogant displeasure she rebuked them at such times for any little fault, would have imagined her a woman of undisciplined and injudicious temper. On other occasions, the same hatred for the rules and discipline of the cloister was displayed in fits of temper entirely different: then, she not only supported the noisy diversions of her pupils, but excited them; she would mingle in their games, and make them more disorderly; and, joining in their conversations, would imperceptibly lead them far beyond their intended limits. If one of them happened to allude to the Lady Abbess's love of gossiping, their teacher would imitate it at length, and act it like a scene in a comedy; would mimic the expression of one nun and the manners of another; and on these occasions would laugh immoderately; but her laughter came not from her heart. Thus she passed several years of her life, with neither leisure nor opportunity to make any change, until, to her misfortune, an occasion unhappily presented itself.

Among other privileges and distinctions accorded to her as a compensation for her not being abbess, was the special grant of a bed-chamber in a separate part of the monastery. This side of the building adjoined a house inhabited by a young man of professedly abandoned character; one of the many who, in those days, by the help of their retinues of bravoes, and by combinations with other villains, were enabled, up to a certain point, to set at defiance public force, and the authority of the laws. Our manuscript merely gives him the name of Egidio. This man, having, from a little window

which overlooked the court-yard, seen Gertrude occasionally passing, or idly loitering there, and allured, rather than intimidated, by
the dangers and impiety of the act, ventured one day to address
her. The miserable girl replied. At first she experienced a lively,
but not unmixed satisfaction. Into the painful void of her soul was
infused a powerful and continual stimulus; a fresh principle, as it
were, of vitality; but this enjoyment was like the restorative draught
which the ingenious cruelty of the ancients presented to a condemned criminal, to strengthen him to bear the agonies of martyrdom. A great change, at the same time, was observable in her
whole deportment; she became all at once more regular and tranquil,
less bitter and sarcastic, and even showed herself friendly and
affable; so that the sisters congratulated each other on the happy
change; so far were they from imagining the real cause, and from
understanding that this new virtue was nothing else than hypocrisy
added to her former failings. This improvement, however, this
external cleansing, so to speak, lasted but a short time, at least with
any steadiness or consistency. She soon returned to her accustomed
scorn and caprice, and renewed her imprecations and raillery against
her cloistral prison, expressed sometimes in language hitherto unheard in that place, and from those lips. Nevertheless, a season of
repentance succeeded each outbreak, and an endeavour to atone for
it and wipe out its remembrance by additional courtesies and kindness. The sisters were obliged to bear all these vicissitudes as they
best could, and attributed them to the wayward and fickle disposition
of the Signora.

For some time no one seemed to think any longer about these
matters; but one day the Signora, having had a dispute with a lay-
sister for some trifling irregularity, continued to insult her so long
beyond her usual bounds, that the sister, after having for some time
gnawed the bit in silence, could no longer keep her patience, and
threw out a hint that she knew something, and would reveal it
when an opportunity occurred. From that moment the Signora
had no peace. It was not long after that, one morning, the sister was
in vain expected at her usual employment; she was sought in her
cell, but fruitlessly; she was called loudly by many voices, but there
was no reply; she was hunted and sought for diligently, here and

there, above, below, from the cellar to the roof; but she was nowhere to be found. And who knows what conjectures might have been made, if, in searching for her, it had not happened that a large hole was discovered in the garden wall, which induced every one to think that she had made her escape thence. Messengers were immediately despatched in various directions to overtake her and bring her back; every inquiry was made in the surrounding country; but there was never the slightest information about her. Perhaps they might have known more of her fate, had they, instead of seeking at a distance, dug up the ground near at hand. After many expressions of surprise, because they never thought her a likely woman for such a deed; after many arguments, they concluded that she must have fled to some very great distance; and because a sister happened once to say, 'She must certainly have taken refuge in Holland,' it was ever after said and maintained in the monastery that she had fled to Holland. The Signora, however, did not seem to be of this opinion. Not that she manifested any disbelief, or opposed the prevailing idea with her particular reasons; if she had any, certainly never were reasons better concealed; nor was there anything from which she more willingly abstained, than from alluding to this event, nor any matter in which she was less desirous to come to the bottom of the mystery. But the less she spoke of it, the more did it occupy her thoughts. How often during the day did the image of the ill-fated nun rush unbidden into her mind, and fix itself there, not easily to be removed! How often did she long to see the real and living being before her, rather than have her always in her thoughts, rather than be day and night in the company of that empty, terrible, impassible form! How often would she gladly have listened to her real voice, and borne her rebukes, whatever they might threaten, rather than be for ever haunted in the depths of her mental ear by the imaginary whisperings of that same voice, and hear words to which it was useless to reply, repeated with a pertinacity and an indefatigable perseverance of which no living being was ever capable!

It was about a year after this event, that Lucia was presented to the Signora, and had the interview with her which we have described. The Signora multiplied her inquiries about Don Rodrigo's persecution, and entered into particulars with a boldness which must have appeared worse than novel to Lucia, who had never imagined that the curiosity of nuns could be exercised on such subjects. The opinions also which were mingled with these inquiries, or which she allowed to appear, were not less strange. She seemed almost to ridicule Lucia's great horror for the nobleman, and asked whether he were deformed, that he excited so much fear; and would have esteemed her retiring disposition almost irrational and absurd, if she had not beforehand given the preference to Renzo. And on this choice, too, she multiplied questions which astonished the poor girl, and put her to the blush. Perceiving, however, afterwards, that she had given too free expression to her imagination, she tried to correct and interpret her language differently; but she could not divest Lucia's mind of a disagreeable wonder, and confused dread. No sooner did the poor girl find herself alone with her mother, than she opened her whole mind to her; but Agnese, being more experienced, in a very few words quieted her doubts, and solved the mystery. 'Don't be surprised,' said she; 'when you know the world as well as I, you'll not think it anything very wonderful. Great people—some more, some less, some one way, and some another,—have all a little oddity. We must let them talk, particularly when we have need of them; we must pretend to be listening to them seriously, as if they were saying very bright things. Didn't you hear how she silenced me, almost as if I had uttered some great nonsense? I was not a bit surprised at it. They are all so. However, Heaven be praised, that she seems to have taken such a fancy to you, and will really protect us. As to the rest, if you live, my child, and it falls to your lot to have anything more to do with gentlemen, you'll understand it, you'll understand it.'

A desire to oblige the Father-guardian; the pleasure of extending protection; the thought of the good opinions that would result from so charitable an exercise of that protection; a certain inclination for Lucia, added to a kind of relief she would feel in doing a kindness to an innocent creature, and in assisting and comforting the oppressed, were the inducements which had really inclined the Signora to take an interest in the fate of these two poor fugitives. In obedience to the orders she gave, and from regard to the anxiety she displayed, they were lodged in the apartments of the portress, adjoining the cloister, and treated as if they were admitted into the service of the monastery. Both mother and daughter congratulated themselves on having so soon found a secure and honourable asylum, and would gladly have remained unknown by every one; but this was not easy in a monastery, more especially when there was a man determined to get information about one of them; in whose mind vexation at having been foiled and deceived was added to his former passions and desires. Leaving the two women, then, in their retreat, we will return to this wretch's palace, while he was waiting the result of his iniquitous undertaking.

CHAPTER XI

A S a pack of hounds, after in vain tracking a hare, return desponding to their master, with heads hung down, and drooping tails, so, on this disastrous night, did the bravoes return to the palace of Don Rodrigo. He was listlessly pacing to and fro, in an unoccupied room up-stairs that overlooked the terrace. Now and then he would stop to listen, or to peep through the chinks in the decayed window-frames, full of impatience, and not entirely free from disquietude—not only for the doubtfulness of success, but also for the possible consequences of the enterprise: this being the boldest and most hazardous in which our valiant cavalier had ever engaged. He endeavoured, however, to reassure himself with the thought of the precautions he had taken that not a trace of the perpetrator should be left. 'As to suspicions, I care nothing for them. I should like to know who would be inclined to come hither, to ascertain if there be a young girl here or not. Let him dare to come—the rash fool—and he shall be well received! Let the friar come, if he pleases. The old woman? She shall be off to Bergamo. Justice? Poh! Justice! The *Podestà* is neither a child nor a fool. And at Milan? Who will care for these people at Milan? Who will listen to them? Who knows even what they are? They are like lost people in the world,—they haven't even a master: they belong to no one. Come, come, never fear. How Attilio will be silenced to-morrow! He shall see whether I am a man to talk and boast. And then . . . If any difficulty should ensue . . . What do I know? Any enemy who would seize this occasion . . . Attilio will be able to advise me; he is pledged to it for the honour of the whole family.' But the idea on which he dwelt most, because he found it both a soother of his doubts and a nourisher of his predominating passion, was the thought of the flatteries and promises he would employ to gain over Lucia. 'She will be so terrified at finding herself here alone, in the midst of these faces, that . . . in troth, mine is the most human among them . . . that she will look to me, will throw herself upon her knees to pray; and if she prays . . .'

While indulging in these fine anticipations, he hears a footstep, goes to the window, opens it a little, and peeps through: 'It is they. And the litter!—Where is the litter? Three, five, eight; they are all there; there's Griso too; the litter's not there:—Griso shall give me an account of this.'

When they reached the house, Griso deposited his staff, cap, and pilgrim's habit, in a corner of the ground-floor apartment, and, as if carrying a burden which no one at the moment envied him, ascended to render his account to Don Rodrigo. He was waiting for him at the head of the stairs; and on his approaching with the foolish and awkward air of a deluded villain, 'Well,' said, or rather vociferated, he, 'Signor Boaster, Signor Captain, Signor *Leave-it-to-me?*'

'It is hard,' replied Griso, resting one foot on the top step, 'it is hard to be greeted with reproaches after having laboured faithfully, and endeavoured to do one's duty, at the risk of one's life.'

'How has it gone? Let us hear, let us hear,' said Don Rodrigo; and, turning towards his room, Griso followed him, and briefly related how he had arranged, what he had done, seen and not seen, heard, feared, and retrieved; relating it with that order and that confusion, that dubiousness and that astonishment, which must necessarily have together taken possession of his ideas.

'You are not to blame, and have done your best,' said Don Rodrigo. 'You have done what you could; but . . . but, if under this roof there be a spy! If there be, if I succeed in discovering him (and you may rest assured I'll discover him if he's here), I'll settle matters with him; I promise you, Griso, I'll pay him as he deserves.'

'The same suspicion, Signor,' replied he, 'has crossed my mind; and if it be true, and we discover a villain of this sort, my master should put it into my hands. One who has diverted himself by making me pass such a night as this; it is *my* business to pay him for it. However, all things considered, it seems likely there may have been some other cross purposes, which now we cannot fathom. To-morrow, Signor, to-morrow we shall be in clear water.'

'Do you think you have been recognized?'

Griso replied that he hoped not; and the conclusion of the interview was, that Don Rodrigo ordered him to do three things next day, which he would have thought of well enough by himself. One was, to despatch two men, in good time in the morning, to the constable, with the intimation which we have already noticed; two others to the old house, to ramble about, and keep at a proper distance any loiterer who might happen to come there, and to conceal the litter from every eye till nightfall, when they would send to fetch it, since it would not do to excite suspicion by any further measures at present; and lastly, to go himself on a tour of discovery, and despatch several others, of the most dexterity and good sense, on the same errand, that he might learn something of the causes and issue of the confusion of the night. Having given these orders, Don Rodrigo retired to bed, leaving Griso to follow his example, bidding him good night, and loading him with praises, through which appeared an evident desire to make some atonement, and in a manner to apologize for the precipitate haste with which he had reproached him on his arrival.

Go, take some rest, poor Griso, for thou must surely need it. Poor Griso! Labouring hard all day, labouring hard half the night, without counting the danger of falling into the hands of villains, or of having a price set upon thy head *for the seizure of an honest woman,'* in addition to those already laid upon thee, and then to be received in this manner! but thus men often reward their fellows. Thou mightest, nevertheless, see in this instance, that sometimes people judge according to merit, and that matters are adjusted even in this world. Go, rest awhile; for some day thou mayest be called upon to give another and more considerable proof of thy faithfulness.

Next morning, Griso was again surrounded with business on all hands, when Don Rodrigo rose. This nobleman quickly sought Count Attilio, who, the moment he saw him approach, called out to him, with a look and gesture of raillery, 'Saint Martin!'

'I have nothing to say,' replied Don Rodrigo, as he drew near: 'I will pay the wager; but it is not this that vexes me most. I told you nothing about it, because, I confess, I thought to surprise you this morning. But . . . stay, I will tell you all.'

'That friar has a hand in this business,' said his cousin, after having listened to the account with suspense and wonderment, and with more seriousness than could have been expected from a man of his temperament. 'I always thought that friar, with his dissembling and out-of-the-way answers, was a knave and a hypocrite. And you never opened yourself to me,—you never told me plainly what happened to entertain you the other day.' Don Rodrigo related the conversation. 'And did you submit to that?' exclaimed Count Attilio. 'Did you let him go away as he came?'

'Would you have me draw upon myself all the Capuchins of Italy?'

'I don't know,' said Attilio, 'whether I should have remembered, at that moment, that there was another Capuchin in the world except this daring knave; but surely, even under the rules of prudence, there must be some way of getting satisfaction even on a Capuchin! We must manage to redouble civilities cleverly to the whole body, and then we can give a blow to one member with impunity. However, the fellow has escaped the punishment he best deserved; but I'll take him under my protection, and have the gratification of teaching him how to talk to gentlemen such as we are.'

'Don't make matters worse for me.'

'Trust me for once, and I'll serve you like a relation and a friend.'

'What do you intend to do?'

'I don't know yet; but rest assured I'll pay off the friar. I'll think about it, and . . . my uncle, the Signor Count of the Privy Council, will be the man to help me. Dear uncle Count! How fine it is, when I can make a politician of his stamp do all my work for me! The day after to-morrow I shall be at Milan, and, in one way or other, the friar shall be rewarded.'

In the mean while breakfast was announced, which, however, made no interruption in the discussion of an affair of so much importance. Count Attilio talked about it freely; and though he took that side which his friendship to his cousin and the honour of his name required, according to his ideas of friendship and honour, yet he could not help occasionally finding something to laugh at in the ill-success of his relative and friend. But Don

Rodrigo, who felt it was his own cause, and who had so signally failed when hoping quietly to strike a great blow, was agitated by stronger passions, and distracted by more vexatious thoughts. 'Fine talk,' said he, 'these rascals will make in the neighbourhood. But what do I care? As to justice, I laugh at it: there is no proof against me, and even if there were, I should care for it just as little: the constable was warned this morning to take good heed, at the risk of his life, that he makes no deposition of what has happened. Nothing will follow from it; but gossiping, when carried to any length, is very annoying to me. It's quite enough that I have been bullied so unmercifully.'

'You did quite rightly,' replied Count Attilio. 'Your Podestà . . . an obstinate, empty-pated, prosing fellow, that Podestà . . . is nevertheless a gentleman, a man who knows his duty; and it is just when we have to do with such people, that we must take care not to bring them into difficulties. If that rascal of a constable should make a deposition, the Podestà, however well-intentioned, would be obliged . . .'

'But you,' interrupted Don Rodrigo, with some warmth, 'you spoil all my affairs by contradicting him in everything, by silencing him, and laughing at him on every occasion. Why cannot a Podestà be an obstinate fool, when at the same time he is a gentleman?'

'Do you know, cousin,' said Count Attilio, glancing towards him a look of raillery and surprise; 'do you know that I begin to think you are half afraid? In earnest, you may rest assured that the Podestà . . .'

'Well, well, didn't you yourself say that we must be careful . . .?'

'I did: and when it is a serious matter, I'll let you see that I'm not a child. Do you know all that I have courage to do for you? I am ready to go in person to this Signor Podestà. Aha! how proud he will be of the honour! And I am ready, moreover, to let him talk for half an hour about the Count Duke, and the Spanish Signor, the governor of the castle, and to give an ear to everything, even when he talks so mightily about these people. Then I will throw in a few words about my uncle, the Signor Count of the Privy Council, and you will see what effect these words in the ear of the Signor Podestà will produce. After all, he has more need of our protection than you of his condescension. I will do my best, and will go to him, and leave him better disposed towards you than ever.'

After these, and a few similar words, Count Attilio set off on his expedition, and Don Rodrigo remained awaiting with anxiety Griso's return. Towards dinner-time he made his appearance, and reported the success of his reconnoitering tour.

The tumult of the preceding night had been so clamorous, the disappearance of three persons from a village was so strange an occurrence, that the inquiries, both from interest and curiosity, would naturally be many, eager, and persevering; and, on the other hand, those who knew something were too numerous to agree in maintaining silence on the matter. Perpetua could not set foot out of doors without being assailed by one or another to know what it was that had so alarmed her master, and she herself, reviewing and comparing all the circumstances of the case, and perceiving how she had been imposed upon by Agnese, felt so much indignation at the act of perfidy, that she was ever ready to give vent to her feelings. Not that she complained to this or that person of the manner in which she was imposed upon: on this subject she did not breathe a syllable; but the trick played upon her poor master she could not altogether pass over in silence; especially as such a trick had been concerted and attempted by that gentle creature, that good youth, and that worthy widow. Don Abbondio, indeed, might positively forbid her, and earnestly entreat her to be silent; and she could easily enough reply that there was no need to urge upon her what was so clear and evident; but certain it is that such a secret in the poor woman's breast was like very new wine in an old and badly hooped cask, which ferments, and bubbles, and boils, and if it does not send the bung into the air, works itself about till it issues in froth, and penetrates between the staves, and oozes out in drops here and there, so that one can taste it, and almost decide what kind of wine it is. Gervase, who could scarcely believe that for once he was better informed than his neighbours, who thought it no little glory to have been a sharer in such a scene of terror, and who fancied himself a man like the others, from having lent a hand in an enterprise that bore the appearance of criminality, was dying to make a boast of it. And though Tonio, who thought with some dread of the inquiries, the possible processes, and the account that would have to be rendered, gave him many injunctions with his finger upon his lips, yet it was not possible to silence every word. Even Tonio himself, after having been absent from home that night at an unusual hour, and returning with an unusual step and air, and an excitement of mind that disposed him to candour,—even he could not dissimulate the matter with his wife; and she was not dumb. The person who talked least was Menico; for no sooner had he related to his parents the history and the object of his expedition, than it appeared to them so terrible a thing that their son had been employed in frustrating an undertaking of Don Rodrigo's, that they scarcely suffered the boy to finish his narration. They then gave him most strenuous and threatening orders to take good heed that he did not give the least hint of anything; and the next morning, not yet feeling sufficiently confident in him, they resolved to keep him shut up in the house for at least that day, and perhaps even longer. But what then? They themselves afterwards, in chatting with their neighbours, without wishing to show that they knew more than others, yet when they came to that mysterious point in the flight of the three fugitives, and the how, and the why, and the where, added, almost as a well-known thing, that they had fled to Pescarenico. Thus this circumstance also was generally noised abroad.

With all these scraps of information, put together and compared as usual, and with the embellishments naturally attached to such relations, there were grounds for a story of more certainty and clearness than common, and such as might have contented the most criticizing mind. But the invasion of the bravoes—an event too serious and notorious to be left out, and one on which nobody had any positive information—was what rendered the story dark and perplexing. The name of Don Rodrigo was whispered about; and so far all were agreed; but beyond, everything was obscurity and dissension. Much was said about the two bravoes who had been seen in the street towards evening, and of the other who had stood at the inn door; but what light could be drawn from this naked fact? They inquired of the landlord, 'Who had been there the night before?' but the landlord could not even remember that he had seen anybody that evening; and concluded his answer, as usual, with the remark that his inn was like a sea-port. Above all, the pilgrim seen by Stefano and Carlandrea puzzled their heads and disarranged their conjectures—that pilgrim whom the robbers were murdering, and who had gone away with them, or whom they had carried off—what could he be doing? He was a good spirit come to the aid of the women; he was the wicked spirit of a roguish pilgrim-impostor, who always came by night to join such companions, and perform such deeds, as he had been accustomed to when alive; he was a living and true pilgrim, whom they attempted to murder, because he was preparing to arouse the village; he was (just see what they went so far as to conjecture!) one of these very villains, disguised as a pilgrim; he was this, he was that; he was so many things, that all the sagacity and experience of Griso would not have sufficed to discover who he was, if he had been obliged to glean this part of the story from others. But, as the reader knows, that which rendered it so perplexing to others, was exactly the clearest point to him; and serving as a key to interpret the other notices, either gathered immediately by himself, or through the medium of his subordinate spies, it enabled him to lay before Don Rodrigo a report sufficiently clear and connected. Closeted with him, he told him of the blow attempted by the poor lovers, which naturally accounted for his finding the house empty, and the ringing of the bell, without which they would have been obliged to suspect traitors (as these two worthy men expressed it) in the house. He told him of the flight; and for this, too, it was easy to find more than one reason—the fear of the lovers on being taken in a fault, or some rumour of their invasion, when it was discovered, and the village roused. Lastly, he told him that they had gone to Pescarenico, but further than this his knowledge did not extend. Don Rodrigo was pleased to be assured that no one had betrayed him, and to find that no traces remained of his enterprise; but it was a light and passing pleasure. 'Fled together!' cried he: 'together! And that rascally friar!—that friar!' The word burst forth hoarsely from his throat, and half-smothered between his teeth, as he bit his nails with vexation: his countenance was as brutal as his passion. 'That friar shall answer for it. Griso, I am not myself . . . I must know, I must find out . . . this night I must know where they are. I have no peace. To

Pescarenico directly, to know, to see, to find . . . Four crowns on the spot, and my protection for ever. This night I must know. And that villain! . . . that friar . . .'

Once more Griso was in the field; and in the evening of that same day he could impart to his worthy patron the desired information, and by this means.

One of the greatest consolations of this world is friendship, and one of the pleasures of friendship is to have some one to whom we may entrust a secret. Now, friends are not divided into pairs, as husband and wife: everybody, generally speaking, has more than one; and this forms a chain of which no one can find the first link. When, then, a friend meets with an opportunity of depositing a secret in the breast of another, he, in his turn, seeks to share in the same pleasure. He is entreated, to be sure, to say nothing to anybody; and such a condition, if taken in the strict sense of the words, would immediately cut short the chain of these gratifications: but general practice has determined that it only forbids the entrusting of a secret to everybody but one equally confidential friend, imposing upon him, of course, the same conditions. Thus, from confidential friend to confidential friend, the secret threads its way along this immense chain, until, at last, it reaches the ear of him or them whom the first speaker exactly intended it should never reach. However, it would, generally, have to be a long time on the way, if everybody had but two friends, the one who tells him, and the one to whom he repeats it with the injunction of silence. But some highly favoured men there are who reckon these blessings by the hundred, and when the secret comes into the hands of one of these, the circles multiply so rapidly that it is no longer possible to pursue them.

Our author has been unable to certify through how many mouths the secret had passed which Griso was ordered to discover, but certain it is that the good man who had escorted the women to Monza, returning in his cart to Pescarenico, towards evening, happened, before reaching home, to light upon one of these trustworthy friends, to whom he related, in confidence, the good work he had just completed, and its sequel; and it is equally certain that, two hours afterwards, Griso was able to return to the palace, and inform Don

Rodrigo that Lucia and her mother had found refuge in a convent at Monza, and that Renzo had pursued his way to Milan.

Don Rodrigo felt a malicious satisfaction on hearing of this separation, and a revival of hope that he might at length accomplish his wicked designs. He spent great part of the night in meditating on his plans, and arose early in the morning with two projects in his mind, the one determined upon, the other only roughly sketched out. The first was immediately to despatch Griso to Monza, to learn more particular tidings of Lucia, and to know what (if anything) he might attempt. He therefore instantly summoned this faithful servant, placed in his hand four crowns, again commended him for the ability by which he had earned them, and gave him the order he had been premeditating.

'Signor . . .' said Griso, feeling his way.

'What? haven't I spoken clearly?'

'If you would send somebody . . .'

'How?'

'Most illustrious Signor, I am ready to give my life for my master: it is my duty; but I know also you would not be willing unnecessarily to risk that of your dependents.'

'Well?'

'Your illustrious lordship knows very well how many prices are already set upon my head; and . . . here I am under the protection of your lordship; we are a party; the Signor Podestà is a friend of the family; the bailiffs bear me some respect; and I, too . . . it is a thing that does me little honour—but to live quietly . . . I treat them as friends. In Milan, your lordship's livery is known; but in Monza *I* am known there instead. And is your lordship aware that—I don't say it to make a boast of myself—that any one who could hand me over to justice, or deliver in my head, would strike a great blow. A hundred crowns at once, and the privilege of liberating two banditti.'

'What!' exclaimed Don Rodrigo, with an oath: 'you showing yourself a vile cur that has scarcely courage to fly at the legs of a passer-by, looking behind him for fear they should shut the door upon him, and not daring to leave it four yards!'

'I think, Signor patron, that I have given proof . . .'

'Then!'

'Then,' frankly replied Griso, when thus brought to the point, 'then your lordship will be good enough to reckon as if I had never spoken: heart of a lion, legs of a hare, and I am ready to set off.'

'And I didn't say you should go alone. Take with you two of the bravest . . . lo Sfregiato,[1] and il Tiradritto:[2] go with a good heart, and be our own Griso. What! three faces like yours, quietly passing by, who do you think wouldn't be glad to let them pass? The bailiffs at Monza must needs be weary of life to stake against it a hundred crowns in so hazardous a game. And, besides, don't you think I am so utterly unknown there, that a servant of mine would be counted as nobody.'

After thus shaming Griso a little, he proceeded to give him more ample and particular instructions. Griso took his two companions, and set off with a cheerful and hardy look, but cursing, in the bottom of his heart, Monza, and interdicts, and women, and the fancies of patrons; he walked on like a wolf which, urged by hunger, his body emaciated, and the furrows of his ribs impressed upon his grey hide, descends from the mountains, where everything is covered with snow, proceeds suspiciously along the plain, stops, from time to time, with uplifted foot, and waves his hairless tail;

'Raises his nose, and snuffs the faithless wind.'

if perchance it may bring him the scent of man or beast; erects his sharp ears, and rolls around two sanguinary eyes, from which shine forth both eagerness for the prey and terror of pursuit. If the reader wishes to know whence I have got this fine line, it is taken from a small unpublished work on Crusaders and Lombards, which will shortly be published, and make a great stir; and I have borrowed it because it suited my purpose, and told where I got it, that I might not take credit due to others: so let no one think it a plan of mine to proclaim that the author of this little book and I are like brothers, and that I rummage at will among his manuscripts.

The other project of Don Rodrigo's, was the devising of some plan to prevent Renzo's again rejoining Lucia, or setting foot in that part of the country. He therefore resolved to spread abroad rumours of threats and snares, which, coming to his hearing through

----

[1] Cut-face.　　[2] Aim-well.

some friend, might deprive him of any wish to return to that neigh-bourhood. He thought, however, that the surest way of doing this would be to procure his banishment by the state; and to succeed in his project, he felt that law would be more likely to answer his pur-pose than force. He could, for example, give a little colouring to the attempt made at the parsonage, paint it as an aggressive and seditious act, and, by means of the doctor, signify to the Podestà that this was an opportunity of issuing an apprehension against Renzo. But our deliberator quickly perceived that it would not do for him to meddle in this infamous negotiation; and, without pondering over it any longer, he resolved to open his mind to Doctor Azzecca-Garbugli; so far, that is, as was necessary to make him acquainted with his desire.—There are so many edicts! thought Don Rodrigo: and the Doctor's not a goose: he will be sure to find something to suit my purpose—some quarrel to pick with this rascally fellow of a weaver: otherwise he must give up his name.—But (how strangely matters are brought about in this world!) while Don Rodrigo was thus fixing upon the doctor, as the man most able to serve him, another person, one that nobody would imagine, even Renzo himself, was labouring, so to say, with all his heart, to serve him, in a far more certain and expeditious way than any the doctor could possibly have devised.

I have often seen a child, more active, certainly, than needs be, but at every movement giving earnest of becoming, some day, a brave man: I have often, I say, seen such a one busied, towards evening, in driving to cover a drove of little Indian pigs, which had been allowed all day to ramble about in a field or orchard. He would try to make them all enter the fold in a drove; but it was labour in vain: one would strike off to the right, and while the little drover was running to bring him back into the herd, another, or two, or three, would start off to the left, in every direction. So that, after getting out of all patience, he at last adapted himself to their ways, first driving in those which were nearest to the entrance, and then going to fetch the others, one or two at a time, as they hap-pened to have strayed away. A similar game we are obliged to play with our characters;—having sheltered Lucia, we ran to Don Rodrigo, and now we must leave him to receive Renzo, who meets us in our way.

After the mournful separation we have related, he proceeded from Monza towards Milan, in a state of mind our readers can easily imagine. To leave his own dwelling; and, what was worse, his native village; and, what was worse still, Lucia; to find himself on the high road, without knowing where he was about to lay his head, and all on account of that villain! When this image presented itself to Renzo's mind, he would be quite swallowed up with rage and the desire of vengeance; but then he would recollect the prayer which he had joined in offering up with the good friar in the church at Pescarenico, and repent of his anger; then he would again be roused to indignation; but seeing an image in the wall, he would take off his hat, and stop a moment to repeat a prayer; so that during this journey he had killed Don Rodrigo, and raised him to life again, at least twenty times. The road here was completely buried between two high banks, muddy, stony, furrowed with deep cart-ruts, which, after a shower, became perfect streams; and where these did not form a sufficient bed for the water, the whole road was inundated and reduced to a pool, so as to be almost impassable. At such places, a steep foot-path, in the form of steps, up the bank, indicated that other passengers had made a track in the fields. Renzo mounted by one of these passes to the more elevated ground, and, looking around him, beheld the noble pile of the cathedral towering alone above the plain, not as if standing in the midst of a city, but rather as though it rose from a desert. He paused, forgetful of all his sorrows, and contemplated thus at a distance that eighth wonder of the world, of which he had heard so much from his infancy. But turning round, after a moment or two, he beheld along the horizon that rugged ridge of mountains: he beheld, distinct and elevated among these, his own *Resegone,* and felt his blood curdle within him; then indulging for a few minutes in a mournful look in that direction, he slowly and sadly turned round, and continued his way. By degrees, he began to discern belfries and towers, cupolas and roofs; then descending into the road, he walked forward for a long time; and, when he found that he was near the city, accosted a passenger, and making a low bow, with the best politeness he was master of, said to him, 'Will you be kind enough, Signor . . .?'

'What do you want, my brave youth?'

'Can you direct me the shortest way to the Capuchin Convent where Father Bonaventura lives?'

The person to whom Renzo addressed himself was a wealthy resident in the neighbourhood, who having been that morning to Milan on business, was returning without having done anything, in great haste to reach his home before dark, and therefore quite willing to escape this detention. Nevertheless, without betraying any impatience, he courteously replied: 'My good friend, there are many more convents than one; you must tell me more clearly which one you are seeking.' Renzo then drew from his bosom Father Cristoforo's letter, and showed it to the gentleman, who having read the address; 'Porta Orientale,' said he, returning it to him; 'you are fortunate, young man; the convent you want is not far hence. Take this narrow street to the left; it is a by-way; not far off you will come to the corner of a long and low building: this is the Lazaretto; follow the moat that surrounds it, and you will come out at the Porta Orientale. Enter the gate, and three or four hundred yards further, you will see a little square surrounded by elms; there is the convent, and you cannot mistake it. God be with you, my brave youth.' And, accompanying the last words with a courteous wave of the hand, he continued his way. Renzo stood surprised and edified at the affable manners of the citizens towards strangers, and knew not that it was an unusual day—a day in which the Spanish cloak had to stoop before the doublet. He followed the path that had been pointed out, and arrived at the Porta Orientale. The reader, however, must not allow the scene now associated with this name to present itself to his mind: the wide and straight street flanked with poplars, outside; the spacious opening between two piles of building, begun, at least, with some pretensions; on first entering these two lateral mounds at the base of the bastions, regularly sloped, levelled at the top, and edged with trees; that garden on one side, and further on, those palaces on the right and left of the principal street of the suburb. When Renzo entered by that gate, the street outside ran straight along the whole length of the Lazaretto, it being impossible for it, for that distance, to do otherwise; then it continued crooked and narrow between the two hedges. The gate consisted of two pillars with a roofing above to protect the door-posts, and on one side a small cottage for the custom-house officers. The bases of the bastions were of irregular steepness, and the pavement was a rough and unequal surface of rubbish and fragments of broken vessels thrown there by chance. The street of the suburb which opened to the view of a person entering the Porta Orientale, bore no bad resemblance to that now facing the entrance of the Porta Tosa. A small ditch ran along the middle, till within a few yards of the gate, and thus divided it into two winding narrow streets, covered with dust or mud, according to the season. At the spot where was, and now is, the little street called the Borghetto, this ditch emptied itself into a sewer, and thence into the other ditch that washes the walls. Here stood a column surmounted by a cross, called the Column of San Dionigi: on the right and left were gardens enclosed by hedges, and at intervals a few small cottages, inhabited chiefly by washerwomen. Renzo entered the gate, and pursued his way; none of the custom-house officers spoke to him, which appeared to him the more wonderful, since the few in this country who could boast of having been at Milan, had related marvellous stories of the examinations and inter-rogations to which all those who entered were subjected. The street was deserted; so much so, that had he not heard a distant buzz indicating some great movement, he would have fancied he was entering a forsaken town. Advancing forward, without knowing what to make of this, he saw on the pavement certain white streaks, as white as snow; but snow it could not be, since it does not fall in streaks, nor usually at this season. He advanced to one of these, looked at it, touched it, and felt assured that it was flour.—A great abundance, thought he, there must be in Milan, if they scatter in this manner the gifts of God. They gave us to understand that there was a great famine everywhere. See how they go about to make us poor people quiet.—Going a few steps further, and coming up to the column, he saw at its foot a still stranger sight; scattered about on the steps of the pedestal were things which certainly were not stones, and, had they been on a baker's counter, he would not have hesitated a moment to call them loaves. But Renzo would not so readily trust his eyes; because, forsooth! this was not a likely place for bread. —Let us see what these things can be,—said he again to himself;

and, going to the column, he stooped down, and took one in his hand: it was really a round, very white loaf, and such as Renzo was unaccustomed to eat, except on holy days.—It is really bread! said he aloud, so great was his astonishment:—is this the way they scatter it in this country? in such a year too? and don't they even give themselves the trouble to pick up what falls? this must be the land of the Cuccagna![3] After ten miles' walk in the fresh morning air, this bread, when he had recovered his self-possession, aroused his appetite.—Shall I take it? deliberated he: poh! they have left it here to the discretion of dogs, and surely a Christian may taste it. And, after all, if the owner comes forward, I will pay him.—Thus reasoning, he put the loaf he held in his hand into one pocket, took up a second and put it into the other, and a third, which he began to eat, and then proceeded on his way, more uncertain than ever, and longing to have this strange mystery cleared up. Scarcely had he started, when he saw people issuing from the interior of the city, and he stood still to watch those who first appeared. They were a man, a woman, and, a little way behind, a boy; all three carrying a load on their backs which seemed beyond their strength, and all three in a most extraordinary condition. Their dress, or rather their rags, covered with flour, their faces floured, and, at the same time, distorted and much heated; they walked not only as if wearied by their load, but trembling as if their limbs had been beaten and bruised. The man staggered under the weight of a large sack of flour, which, here and there in holes, scattered a shower around at every stumble, at every disturbance of his equilibrium. But the figure of the woman was still more awkward: an unwieldy bulk, two extended arms which seemed to bear it up with difficulty, and looked like two carved handles from the neck to the widest part of a large kilderkin, and beneath this enormous body, two legs, naked up to the knees, which could scarcely totter along. Renzo gazed steadily at this great bulk, and discovered that it was the woman's gown turned up around her, with as much flour in it as it could hold, and rather more, so that from time to time it was scattered in handfuls over the ground. The boy held with both hands a basket full of bread upon his head; but, from having shorter

[3] The name of an ideal country, affording all sorts of pleasure.

legs than his parents, he kept falling behind by degrees, and in running forward to overtake them, the basket lost its balance, and a few loaves fell.

'If you let another fall, you vile, helpless . . .' said the mother, gnashing her teeth at the child.

'I don't let them fall; they fall themselves. How can I help it?' replied he.

'Eh! it's well for you that I have my hands engaged,' rejoined the woman, shaking her fist, as if she would have given the poor child a blow; and with this movement she sent forth a fresh cloud of flour, enough to have made more than the two loaves the boy had let fall.

'Come, come,' said the man, 'we will go back presently to pick them up, or somebody will do it for us: we have been a long while in want: now that we have got a little abundance, let us enjoy it in blessed peace.'

In the mean time people arrived from without; and one of them, accosting the woman, 'Where must we go to get bread?' asked he. 'Forward, forward,' was her reply; and when they were a few yards past, she added, muttering, 'These blackguard peasants will come and sweep all the bake-houses and magazines, and there will be nothing left for us.'

'There's a little for everybody, magpie,' said the husband; 'plenty, plenty.'

From this and similar scenes which Renzo heard and witnessed, he began to gather that he had come to a city in a state of insurrection, and that this was a day of victory; that is to say, when every one helped himself in proportion to his inclination and power, giving blows in payment. However we may desire to make our poor mountaineer appear to the best advantage, yet historical accuracy obliges us to say, that his first feeling was that of satisfaction. He had so little to rejoice at in the ordinary course of things, that he was inclined to approve of anything that might make a change, whatever it might be. And besides, not being a man superior to his age, he entertained the common opinion, or prejudice, that the scarcity of bread was produced by monopolists and bakers; and readily did he esteem every method justifiable of rescuing from their grasp the food, which they, according to this opinion, so cruelly denied to the hunger of a whole people. He resolved, however, to get out of the tumult, and rejoiced at being directed to a Capuchin, who would give him shelter and good advice. Engaged in such thoughts, and looking about him at the fresh victors who appeared, laden with spoil, he took the short road that still remained to reach the convent.

On the present site of a noble palace, with its beautiful portico, there was formerly, and till within a very few years, a small square, and at the furthest side of this, the church and convent of the Capuchins, with four large elms standing before them. We congratulate, not without envy, those of our readers who have not seen Milan as thus described: that is, because they must be very young, and have not had much time to commit many follies. Renzo went straight to the door, put into his bosom the remaining half loaf, took out his letter and held it ready in his hand, and rang the bell. A small wicket was opened at the summons, and the face of the porter appeared at the grate to ask who was there.

'One from the country, bringing an important letter to Father Bonaventura from Father Cristoforo.'

'Give it me,' said the porter, putting his hand through the grate.

'No, no,' said Renzo, 'I must give it into his own hands.'

'He is not in the Convent.'

'Let me come in, then, and I will wait for him,' replied Renzo.

'Follow my advice,' rejoined the friar: 'go and wait in the church, where you may be employing yourself profitably. You cannot be admitted into the convent at present.' So saying, he closed the wicket.

Renzo stood irresolute, with the letter in his hand. He then took a few steps towards the door of the church, to follow the advice of the porter, but thought he would first just give another glance at the stir outside. He crossed the square, reached the side of the road, and stood with his arms crossed on his breast to watch the thickest and most noisy part of the crowd that was issuing from the interior of the city. The vortex attracted our spectator.—Let us go and see thought he; and again taking out the piece of bread, he began to eat, and advanced towards the crowd. While he was walking thither, we will relate, as briefly as possible, the causes and beginnings of this uproar.

CHAPTER XII

THIS was the second year of the scarcity. In the preceding year, the surplus remaining from former seasons had more or less supplied the deficiency; and the people, neither satiated nor famished, but certainly sufficiently unprovided for, had reached the harvest of 1628, in which our story finds us. Now, this harvest, so long and eagerly looked forward to, proved still less productive than the former, partly on account of the adverse character of the season (and that not only at Milan, but, in great measure, in the surrounding country), and partly by the agency of man. Such were the ravages and havoc of the war—that amiable war to which we have already alluded—that in the parts of the country bordering on its scene, much more land than usual remained uncultivated and deserted by the peasants, who instead of working to provide food for themselves and others, were obliged to wander about as beggars. I have said, more than usual, because the insupportable taxes, levied with unequalled cupidity and folly—the habitual conduct, even in perfect peace, of the stationary troops,—conduct which the mournful documents of the age compare to that of an invading enemy—and other reasons, which this is not the place to enumerate, had for some time been producing this sad effect throughout the whole of the Milanese: the particular circumstances, of which we are now speaking, being but the sudden exacerbation of a chronic disease. No sooner had this deficient harvest been gathered in, than the provisions for the army, and the waste which always accompanies them, made such a fearful void in it, that scarcity quickly made itself felt, and with scarcity its melancholy, but profitable, as well as inevitable, effect, a rise of prices.

But when the price of food reaches a certain point, there always arises (at least, hitherto it has always arisen; and if it is so still, after all that has been written by so many learned men, what must it have been in those days!)—there always arises an opinion among the many that it is not the effect of scarcity. They forget that they had foreseen and predicted such an issue; they suddenly fancy that there is plenty of corn, and that the evil proceeds from there not being as much distributed as is required for consumption; propositions sufficiently preposterous, but which flatter both their anger and their hopes. Corn monopolists, either real or imaginary, large landholders, the bakers who purchased corn, all, in short, who had either little or much, or were thought to have any, were charged with being the causes of the scarcity and dearness of provisions; they were the objects of universal complaint, and of the hatred of the multitude of every rank. The populace could tell with certainty where there were magazines and granaries full and overflowing with corn, and even requiring to be propped up; they indicated most extravagant numbers of sacks; they talked with certainty of the immense quantities of grain secretly despatched to other places, where, probably, it was asserted with equal assurance and equal excitement, that the corn grown there was transported to Milan. They implored from the magistrates those precautions which always appear, or at least, have always hitherto appeared, so equitable, so simple, so capable of drawing forth the corn which they affirm to be secreted, walled up, or buried, and of restoring to them abundance. The magistrates, therefore, busied themselves in fixing the highest price that was to be charged upon every commodity; in threatening punishment to any one who should refuse to sell; and making other regulations of a similar nature. As, however, all human precautions, how vigorous soever, can neither diminish the necessity of food, nor produce crops out of season: and as these individual precautions offered no very inviting terms to other countries where there might be a superabundance, the evil continued and increased. The multitude attributed such an effect to the scarcity and feebleness of the remedies, and loudly solicited some more spirited and decisive measures. Unfortunately, they found a man after their own heart.

In the absence of the governor, Don Gonzalo Fernandez de Cordova, who was encamped over Casale del Monferrato, the High Chancellor Antonio Ferrer, also a Spaniard, supplied his place at Milan. This man saw (and who could help seeing it?) that a moderate price on bread is in itself a most desirable thing; and he thought (here was his mistake) that an order from him would suffice to produce it. He fixed the limit (*la meta,* by which name the tariff was distinguished in articles of food,) at the price that bread would have had, if the corn had been generally sold at thirty-three livres the bushel, and they sold it as high as eighty. He acted like the old woman who thought to make herself young again by changing her baptismal faith.

Regulations less irrational and less unjust had, on more than one occasion, by the resistance of actual circumstances, remained un-executed; but that this should be carried into effect was undertaken by the multitude, who, seeing their demands at last converted into a law, would not suffer it to be a mere form. They immediately ran to the bake-houses, to demand bread at the fixed price; and they required it with that air of threatening resolution which passion, force, and law united could impart. It need not be asked if the bakers resisted. With sleeves turned up, they were busied in carry-ing, putting into the oven, and taking out thence, without inter-mission; for the people, having a confused idea that it was too violent an attempt to last long, besieged the bake-houses incessantly, to enjoy their temporary good fortune; and every reader can imagine what a pleasure it must have been to drudge like a slave, and expose one's self more than usually to an attack of pleurisy, to be, after all, a loser in consequence. But with magistrates on one side threaten-ing punishments, and the people on the other importunate, murmur-ing at every delay that was interposed in serving them, and in-definitely menacing some one or other of their chastisements, which are always the worst that are inflicted in this world—there was no help for it; drudge they must; they were forced to empty and replenish their ovens, and sell. However, to keep them up to such employment, it was of little avail to impose strict orders, and keep them in constant fear: it was a question of absolute practicability; and had the thing lasted a little longer, they *could* have done no more. They remonstrated incessantly against the iniquitous and insupportable weight of the burden laid upon them, and protested they would willingly throw the shovel into the oven, and take their departure; and yet they continued to persevere as they could, long-ing, hoping, that some day or other, the High Chancellor would come to his senses. But Antonio Ferrer, who was what would now be called a man of character, replied that the bakers had made enormous profits in past times; that they would equally make great gains in better times to come, that, therefore, it was both reasonable and necessary they should make some compensation to the public, and that, in the mean while, they must get on as they could. Whether he were really convinced of the truth of those reasons he alleged to others, or whether, perceiving, from its effects, the impossibility of maintaining this regulation, he was willing to leave to others the odium of revoking it; for who can now look into Antonio Ferrer's mind? yet certain it is he did not relax one iota of what he had established. At length, the *decurioni* (a municipal magistracy composed of nobles, which lasted till the ninety-sixth year of the last century) informed the Governor, by letter, of the state in which matters stood, hoping he might be able to suggest some remedy.

Don Gonzalo, buried over head in the affairs of war, did what the reader will certainly imagine: he nominated a Council, which he endowed with full authority to fix such a price upon bread as could become current, thus doing justice to both parties. The deputies assembled, or it was expressed, after the Spanish fashion, in the jargon of those days, the junta met; and, after a hundred bowings, compliments, preambles, sighs, whisperings, airy propositions, and subterfuges, urged, by a necessity which all felt, to come to some determination, conscious that they were casting an important die, but aware that there was no other course to be taken, they at length agreed to augment the price of bread. The bakers once more breathed, but the people raved.

The evening preceding the day in which Renzo arrived at Milan, the streets and squares swarmed with men, who, transported with indignation, and swayed by a prevailing opinion, assembled— whether acquaintances or strangers—in knots and parties without any previous concert, and almost without being aware of it, like rain-drops on a hillside. Every conversation increased the general belief, and roused the passions of both hearer and speaker. Amongst the many excited ones, there were some few of cooler temperament, who stood quietly watching with great satisfaction the troubling of the water, who busied themselves in troubling it more and more, with such reasonings and stories as rogues know how to invent, and agitated minds are so ready to believe, and who determined not to let it calm down without first catching a little fish. Thousands went to rest that night with an indeterminate feeling that something must and would be done. Crowds assembled before day-break: children, women, men, old people, workmen, beggars, all grouped together at random; here was a confused whispering of many voices; there, one declaimed to a crowd of applauding bystanders; this one asked his nearest fellow the same question that had just been put to himself; that other repeated the exclamation that he heard resounding in his ears; everywhere were disputes, threats, wonderings; and very few words made up the materials of so many conversations.

There only wanted something to lay hold of: some beginning, some kind of impetus to reduce words to deeds, and this was not long wanting. Towards daybreak, little boys issued from the bakers' shops, carrying baskets of bread to the houses of their usual customers. The first appearance of one of these unlucky boys in a crowd of people, was like the fall of a lighted squib in a gunpowder magazine. 'Let us see if there's bread here!' exclaimed a hundred voices, in an instant. 'Ay, for the tyrants who roll in abundance, and would let us die of hunger,' said one, approaching the boy; and, raising his hand to the edge of the basket, he snatched at it, and exclaimed, 'Let me see!' The boy coloured, turned pale, trembled, and tried to say, 'Let me go on;' but the words died between his lips, and slackening his arms, he endeavoured to disengage them hastily from the straps.

'Down with the basket!' was the instantaneous cry. Many hands seized it, and brought it to the ground; they then threw the cloth that covered it into the air. A tepid fragrance was diffused around. 'We, too, are Christians; we must have bread to eat,' said the first. He took out a loaf, and, raising it in the view of the crowd, began to eat: in an instant all hands were in the basket, and in less time than one can relate it, all had disappeared. Those who had got none of the spoil, irritated at the sight of what the others had gained, and animated by the facility of the enterprise, moved off by parties in quest of other straying baskets, which were no sooner met with than they were pillaged immediately. Nor was it necessary to attack the bearers: those who unfortunately were on their way, as soon as they saw which way the wind blew, voluntarily laid down their burdens, and took to their heels. Nevertheless, those who remained without a supply were, beyond comparison, the greater part; nor were the victors half satisfied with such insignificant spoil; and some there were mingled in the crowds who had resolved upon a much better regulated attack. 'To the bake-house, to the bake-house!' was the cry.

In the street called *La Corsia de' Servi* was a bake-house, which is still there, bearing the same name,—a name that, in Tuscan, means 'The Bakery of the Crutches,' and, in Milanese, is composed of words so extravagant, so whimsical, so out-of-the-way, that the alphabet of the Italian language does not afford letters to express its sound.[1] In this direction the crowd advanced. The people of the shop were busy questioning the poor boy who had returned unladen, and he, pale with terror, and greatly discomposed, was unintelligibly lating his unfortunate adventure, when, suddenly, they heard a of a crowd in motion; it increases and approaches; the fore- he crowd are in sight.

up; quick, quick:' one runs to beg assistance from the thers hastily shut up the shop, and bolt and bar the The multitudes begin to increase without, and the of—'Bread! bread! Open! open!'

ure the sheriff arrived, in the midst of a troop of ake room, make room, my boys; go home, go home: r the sheriff!' cried he. The throng, not too much e way a little, so that the halberdiers could advance ose to the door of the shop, though not in a very orderly r. 'But, my friends,' said the sheriff, addressing the people om thence, 'what are you doing here? Go home, go home. Where is your fear of God? What will our master the King say? We don't wish to do you any harm, but go home, like good fellows. What in the world can you do here, in such a crush? There is nothing good to be got here, either for the soul or body. Go home,

[1] El prestin di scanse.

go home!' But how were those next the speaker, who saw his face and could hear his words, even had they been willing to obey— how were they to accomplish it, urged forward as they were, and almost trampled upon by those behind; who, in their turn, were trodden upon by others, like wave upon wave, and step upon step, to the very edge of the rapidly increasing throng? The sheriff began to feel a little alarmed. 'Make them give way, that I may get a little breath,' said he to his halberdiers; 'but don't hurt anybody. Let us try to get into the shop. Knock; make them give way!'

'Back! back!' cried the halberdiers, throwing themselves in a body upon their nearest neighbours, and pushing them back with the point of their weapons. The people replied with a grumbling shout, and retreated as they could, dispersing blows on the breast and stomach in profusion, and treading upon the toes of those behind; while such was the general rush, the squeezing and trampling, that those who were in the middle of the throng would have given anything to have been elsewhere. In the mean while, a small space was cleared before the house; the sheriff knocked and kicked against the door, calling to those within to open it: these, seeing from the window how things stood, ran down in haste and admitted the sheriff, followed by the halberdiers, who crept in one after another, the last repulsing the crowd with their weapons. When all were secured, they re-bolted the door, and, running up-stairs, the sheriff displayed himself at the window. We leave the reader to imagine the outcry!

'My friends!' cried he: many looked up. 'My friends! go home. A general pardon to all who go home at once!'

'Bread! bread! Open! open!' were the most conspicuous words in the savage vociferations the crowd sent forth in reply.

'Justice, my friends! take care; you have yet time given you. Come, get away; return to your houses. You shall have bread; but this is not the way to get it. Eh! . . . eh! what are you doing down there? Eh! at this door? Fie, fie upon you! I see, I see: justice! take care! It is a great crime. I'm coming to you. Eh! eh! away with those irons; down with those hands! Fie! you Milanese, who are talked of all over the world for peaceableness! Listen! listen! you have always been good sub . . . Ah, you rascals!'

This rapid transition of style was caused by a stone, which, coming from the hands of one of these good subjects, struck the forehead of the sheriff, on the left protuberance of his metaphysical profundities. 'Rascals! rascals!' continued he, shutting the window in a rage, and retiring from view. But though he had shouted to the extent of the powers of his throat, his words, both good and bad, had vanished and consumed in thin air, repulsed by the cries which came from below. The objects that now, as he afterwards described, presented themselves to his view, were stones and iron bars, (the first they could lay hold of by the way,) with which they tried to force open the doors and windows; and they already had made considerable progress in their work.

In the mean time, the masters and shop-boys appeared at the upper windows, armed with stones, (they had probably unpaved the yard,) and crying out to those below, with horrible looks and gestures, to let them alone, they showed their weapons, and threatened to let fly among them. Seeing that nothing else would avail, they began to throw at them in reality. Not one fell in vain, since the press was such that even a grain of corn, as the saying was, could not have reached the ground.

'Ah! you great vagabonds! you great villains! Is this the bread you give to poor people? Ah! alas! oh! Now, now, at us?' was raised from below. More than one was injured, and two boys were killed. Fury increased the strength of the people; the doors and bars gave way; and the crowd poured into the passages in torrents. Those within, perceiving their danger, took refuge in the garrets: the sheriff, the halberdiers, and a few of the household gathered together here in a corner, under the slates; and others, escaping by the sky-lights, wandered about on the roof like cats.

The sight of the spoil made the victors forget their designs of sanguinary vengeance. They flew upon the large chests, and instantly pillaged them. Others, instead, hastened to tear open the counter, seized the tills, took out by handfuls, pocketed and set off with, the money, to return for bread afterwards, if there remained any. The crowd dispersed themselves through the interior magazines. Some laid hold of the sacks and drew them out; others turned them wrong side upwards, and untying the mouth, to reduce them to a weight which they could manage to carry, shook out some of the flour; others crying out, 'Stay, stay!' came underneath to prevent this waste, by catching it in their clothes and aprons; others, again, fell upon a kneading-trough, and seized the dough, which ran over their hands and escaped their grasp on every side: here, one who had snatched up a meal-sieve, came brandishing it in the air. Some come, some go, some handle: men, women, children, swarm around; pushes, blows, and cries are bandied about; and a white powder that rises in clouds and deposits itself in every direction, involves the whole proceeding in a thick mist. Outside, is a crowd composed of two reverse processions, which alternately separate and intermingle, some going out with their prey, others entering to share the spoil.

While this bake-house was being thus plundered, none of the others were quiet and free from danger; but at none had the people assembled in such numbers as to be very daring. In some, the masters had collected a few auxiliaries, and stood upon their defence: others, less strong in numbers, or more terrified, came to some kind of agreement; they distributed bread to those who had begun to crowd around their shops, if they would be content with this and go away. Those who did withdraw, did so not so much because they were contented with their acquisitions, as because the halberdiers and police, keeping at a distance from the tremendous scene at the Bake-house of the Crutches, appeared, nevertheless, elsewhere in sufficient force to keep in awe these smaller parties of mutineers. By this means, the confusion and concourse continued to augment at this first unfortunate bake-house; for all those whose fingers itched to be at work, and whose hearts were set upon doing some great deed, repaired thither, where their friends were in greatest numbers, and impunity was secure.

Such was the state of things, when Renzo, finishing, as we have related, his piece of bread, came to the suburb of the Porta Orientale, and set off, without being aware of it, exactly to the central scene of the tumult. He continued his way, now urged forward, now hindered, by the crowd; and as he walked, he watched and listened, to gather from the confused murmurs of voices some more positive information of the state of things. The following are nearly the words he caught on his way.

'Now,' said one, 'the infamous imposture of these villains is discovered, who said there was no more bread, nor flour, nor corn. Now we see things clearly and distinctly, and they can no longer deceive us as they have done. Hurrah for plenty!'

'I tell you all this just goes for nothing,' said another; 'it is only like making a hole in water; so that it will be the worse for us, if we don't get full justice done us. Bread will be sold at a low price: but they will put poison in it to kill us poor people like flies. They've said already that we are too many: they said so in the council; and I know it for certain, because I heard it with these ears from an acquaintance of mine, who is the friend of a relation of a scullion of one of these lords.'

'They are not things to be laughed at,' said another poor wretch, who was foaming at the mouth, and holding up to his bleeding head a ragged pocket-handkerchief; some neighbour, by way of consolation, echoing his remark.

'Make way, gentlemen: pray be good enough to make way for a poor father of a family, who is carrying something to eat to five famished children.' These were the words of one who came staggering under the weight of a large sack of flour; and everybody instantly drew back to attend to his request.'

'I,' said another, almost in an under-tone, to his companion, 'I shall take my departure. I am a man of the world, and I know how these things go. These clowns who now make so much noise, to-morrow or next day will be shut up in their houses, cowering with fear. I have already noticed some faces, some worthy fellows, who are going about as spies, and taking note of those who are here and not here; and when all is over they will render in an account, and bring punishment on those who deserve it.'

'He who protects the bakers,' cried a sonorous voice, which attracted Renzo's attention, 'is the superintendent of provisions.'

'They are all rascals,' said a by-stander.

'Yes; but he is at the head of them,' replied the first.

The superintendent of provisions, elected every year by the governor, from a list of six nobles, formed by the council of *decu-rioni*, was the president of this council, as well as of the court of provisions, which, composed of twelve noblemen, had, together with other duties, that of overlooking the distribution of corn in the city.

The person who occupied this post must, necessarily, in times of scarcity and ignorance, have been regarded as the author of the evil, unless he had acted like Ferrer—a course which was not in his power, even had the idea entered his mind.

'Rascals!' exclaimed another: 'could they do worse? They have actually dared to say that the high chancellor is an old fool, to rob him of his credit, and get the government into their own hands. We ought to make a large hen-coop, and put them in, to live upon vetches and cockle-weed, as they would treat us.'

'Bread, eh!' said one who was making as great haste as he could. 'Bread? Blows with stones of a pound weight—stones falling plump, that came down like hail. And such breaking of ribs! I long to be at my own house.'

Among such sentences as these, by which it is difficult to say whether he were more informed or perplexed, and among number-less knocks and pushes, Renzo at last arrived opposite the bake-house. The crowds here had considerably dispersed, so that he could contemplate the dismal scene of recent confusion—the walls unplastered and defaced with stones and bricks, the windows broken, and the door destroyed.

'These are no very fine doings,' thought Renzo to himself: 'if they treat all the bake-houses in this way, where will they make bread? In the ditches?'

From time to time somebody would issue from the house, carry-ing part of a bin, of a tub, or of a bolting hutch, the pole of a kneading instrument, a bench, a basket, a journal, a waste-book, or something belonging to this unfortunate bake-house; and shout-ing 'Make room, make room,' would pass on through the crowd. All these, he observed, went in the same direction, and to some fixed place. Renzo, determined to find out the meaning of this procedure, followed behind a man who, having tied together a bundle of broken planks and chips, carried it off on his back, and, like the others, took the road that runs along the northern side of the cathedral, and receives its name from the flight of steps which was then in existence, and has only lately been removed. The wish of observing what happened, did not prevent our mountaineer, on arriving in sight of this noble pile, from stopping to gaze upwards, with open mouth. He then quickened his pace to overtake his self-chosen guide; and, on turning the corner, gave another glance at the front of the building, at that time in a rude and far-from-finished state, keeping all the while close behind his leader, who advanced towards the middle of the square. The crowds became more dense as he went forward, but they made way for the carrier; and while he cleft the waves of people, Renzo, following in his wake, arrived with him in the very centre of the throng. Here was a space, and in the midst a bonfire, a heap of embers, the relics of the implements before mentioned. Around, the people were dancing and clapping their hands, mingling in the uproar a thousand shouts of triumph and imprecation.

The man with the bundle upset it into the embers; others, with a long half-burnt pole, gathered them up and raked them together from the sides and underneath: the smoke increased and thickened, the flame again burst forth, and with it, the redoubled cries of the by-standers: 'Hurrah for plenty! Death to those who would starve us! Away with the famine! Perish the Court of Provision! Perish the junta! Hurrah for plenty! Hurrah for bread!'

To say the truth, the destruction of sieves and kneading-troughs, the pillaging of bake-houses, and the routing of bakers, are not the most expeditious means of providing a supply of bread; but this is one of those metaphysical subtleties which never enter the mind of the multitude. Renzo, without being of too metaphysical a turn, yet not being in such a state of excitement as the others, could not avoid making this reflection in his mind; he kept it, however, to himself, for this, among other reasons: because, out of so many faces, there was not one that seemed to say, 'My friend, if I am wrong, correct me, and I shall be indebted to you.'

The flame had again sunk; no one was seen approaching with fresh combustibles, and the crowd was beginning to feel impatient, when a rumour was spread that at the *Cordusio* (a small square or cross-way not far distant) they had laid siege to a bake-house. In similar circumstances, the announcement of an event very often produces it. Together with this rumour, a general wish to repair thither gained ground among the multitude: 'I am going; are you going? Let us go, let us go!' were heard in every direction; the crowd broke up, were set in motion, and moved on. Renzo remained behind, almost stationary, except when dragged forward by the torrent; and in the mean while held counsel with himself, whether he should make his escape from the stir, and return to the convent in search of Father Bonaventura, or go and see this affray too. Curiosity prevailed. He resolved, however, not to mingle in the thickest of the crowd, at the risk of broken bones, or something worse; but to keep at a distance and watch. Having determined on his plans, and finding himself tolerably unobserved, he took out the second roll, and, biting off a mouthful, moved forward in the rear of the tumultuous body.

By the outlet at one corner of the square, the multitude had already entered the short and narrow street *Pescheria vecchia*[2] and thence, through the crooked archway, into the *Piazza de' Mercanti*.[3] Very few were there who, in passing the niche which divides, about the centre, the terrace of the edifice then called the College of Doctors, did not cast a slight glance upwards at the great statue that adorns it—at that serious, surly, frowning, morose countenance of Don Filippo II., which, even in marble, enforces a feeling of respect, and seems ready to say, 'I am here, you rabble!'

This niche is now empty, by a singular accident. About a hundred and seventy years after the events we are now relating, one morning, the head of the statue that stood there was exchanged, the sceptre was taken out of his hand, and a dagger placed there instead, and on his statue was inscribed the name of Marcus Brutus. Thus adorned, it remained, perhaps, a couple of years; but, one morning, some persons who had no sympathies with Marcus Brutus, and who must even have borne him a secret grudge, threw a rope around the statue, tore it down, and bestowed upon it a hundred injuries; thus mangled, and reduced to a shapeless trunk, they dragged it along, with a profuse accompaniment of epithets, through the streets, and when they were well tired, threw it—no one knows where. Who would have foretold this to Andrea Biffi, when he sculptured it?

[2] The Old Fish Market.　　[3] The Square of the Merchants.

From the square of the *Mercanti* the clamorous multitude turned into the by-street *de' Fustagnai,* whence they poured into the *Cordusio.* Every one, immediately on entering the square, turned their eyes towards the bake-house that had been indicated to them. But, instead of the crowd of friends whom they expected to find already at work, they saw only a few, irresolutely hovering about at some distance from the shop, which was fastened up, and protected by armed men at the windows, who gave tokens of a determination to defend themselves in case of need. They, therefore, turned back and paused, to inform those who were coming up, and see what course the others would wish to take; some returned, or remained behind. There was a general retreat and detention, asking and answering of questions, a kind of stagnation, sighs of irresolution, then a general murmur of consultation. At this moment an ill-omened voice was heard in the midst of the crowd: 'The house of the superintendent of provisions is close by; let us go and get justice, and lay siege to it.' It seemed rather the common recollection of an agreement already concluded, than the acceptance of a proposal. 'To the superintendent's! to the superintendent's!' was the only cry that could be heard. The crowd moved forward with unanimous fury towards the street where the house, named at such an ill-fated moment, was situated.

CHAPTER XIII

THE unfortunate superintendent was at this moment digesting a poor and scanty dinner, unwillingly eaten with a little stale bread, and awaiting, with much suspense, the termination of this storm, far from suspecting that it was about to fall with such violence upon his own head. Some benevolent person preceded the crowd in urging haste, and entered the house to warn him of his pressing danger. The servants, already attracted to the door by the noise, were looking with much alarm up the street, in the direction of the approaching tumult. While listening to the warning, the vanguard came in sight; they ran in haste and terror to inform their master, and while he was deliberating whether he should fly, and how he should accomplish it, some one else arrived to tell him there was no longer time for flight. Scarcely was there time for the servants to secure the door. They, however, barred and locked it, and then ran to fasten the windows, as when a violent storm is threatening, and the hail is expected to come down every moment. The increasing howls of the people, falling like a thunder-clap, resounded through the empty yard; every corner of the house re-echoed it: and in the midst of the tremendous and mingled uproar, were heard, loudly and repeatedly, the blows of stones upon the door.

'The superintendent! The tyrant! The fellow who would starve us! We'll have him, dead or alive!'

The poor man wandered from room to room, pale and almost breathless with terror, striking his hands together, commending himself to God, and imploring his servants to stand firm, and find him some way of making his escape. But how, and where? He ascended to the garret, and there, through an aperture between the ceiling and the tiles, looked anxiously into the street, and saw it swarming with the enraged populace; more terrified than ever, he then withdrew to seek the most secure and secret hiding-place he could find. Here he crouched down and listened whether the awful burst of fury would ever subside, and the tumult ever abate; but hearing that the uproar rather became more savage and outrageous, and the blows against the door more rapidly repeated, his heart sank within him, and he hastily stopped his ears. Then, as if beside himself, gnashing his teeth and distorting his countenance, he impetuously extended his arms, and shook his fists, as if he would keep the door secure in spite of all the pushes and blows. At last, in absolute despair, he sank down upon the floor, and remained terrified and almost insensible, expecting his death.

Renzo found himself this time in the thickest of the confusion, not now carried there by the throng, but by his own deliberate will. At the first proposal of blood-shedding, he felt his own curdle within him; as to the plundering, he had not exactly determined whether, in this instance, it were right or wrong; but the idea of murder aroused in him immediate and unfeigned horror. And although, by that fatal submission of excited minds to the excited affirmations of the many, he felt as fully persuaded that the superintendent was an oppressive villain, as if he had known, with certainty and minuteness, all that the unhappy man had done, omitted, and thought; yet he had advanced among the foremost, with a determined intention of doing his best to save him. With this resolution, he had arrived close to the door which was assailed in a hundred ways. Some, with flints, were hammering at the nails of the lock to break it open; others, with stakes, chisels, and hammers, set to work with more method and regularity. Others, again, with sharp stones, blunted knives, broken pieces of iron, nails, and even their finger-nails, if they had nothing else, pulled down the plaster and defaced the walls, and laboured hard to loosen the bricks by degrees, so as to make a breach. Those who could not lend a hand, encouraged the others by their cries; but, at the same time, by the pressure of their persons they contributed to impede the work already considerably obstructed by the disorderly contentions of the workers: for, by the favour of Heaven, it sometimes happens in evil undertakings, as too often in good, that the most ardent abettors of a work become its greatest impediments.

The first magistrates who had notice of the insurrection immediately sent off to the commander of the castle, which then bore the name of Porta Giovia, for the assistance of some troops; and he quickly despatched a band of men. But what with the information, and the orders, and the assembling, and getting on their way, and their march, the troops did not arrive till the house was completely surrounded by an immense army of besiegers and they, therefore, halted at a sufficient distance from it, at the extremity of the crowd. The officer who commanded them knew not what course to pursue. Here was nothing but an assembly of idle and unarmed people, of every age and both sexes. On orders being given to disperse and make way, they replied by a deep and prolonged murmur; but no one moved. To fire down upon the crowd seemed to the officer not only a cruel, but a dangerous, course, which, while it offended the less formidable, would irritate the more violent: besides, he had received no such instructions. To push through this first assembly, overthrow them right and left, and go forward to carry war where it was given, would have been the best; but how to succeed was the point. Who knew whether the soldiers would be able to proceed, united and in order? For if, instead of breaking through the crowd, they should be routed on entering, they would be left to the mercy of the people, after having exasperated them. The irresolution of the commander, and the inactivity of the soldiers, appeared, whether justly or not, to proceed from fear. Those who stood next to them contented themselves with looking them in the face with an air, as the Milanese say, of I-don't-care-for-you; those who stood a little farther off, could not refrain from provoking them, by making faces at them, and by cries of mockery; farther on, few knew or cared who was there; the spoilers continued to batter the wall, without any other thought than of succeeding quickly in their undertaking; the spectators ceased not to animate them with shouts.

Amongst these appeared one, who was himself a spectacle, an old and half-starved man, who, rolling about two sunken and fiery eyes, composing his wrinkled face to a smile of diabolical complacency, and with his hands raised above his infamous, hoary head, was brandishing in the air a hammer, a rope, and four large nails, with which he said he meant to nail the vicar to the posts of his own door, alive as he was.

'Fie upon you! for shame!' burst forth from Renzo, horrified at such words, and at the sight of so many faces betokening approbation of them; at the same time encouraged by seeing others, who, although silent, betrayed in their countenances the same horror that he felt. 'For shame! Would you take the executioner's business out of his hand? Murder a Christian! How can you expect that God will give us food, if we do such wicked things? He will send us thunder-bolts instead of bread!'

'Ah, dog! traitor to his country!' cried one of those who could hear, in the uproar, these sacred words, turning to Renzo, with a diabolical countenance. 'Wait, wait! He is a servant of the superintendent's, dressed like a peasant; he is a spy; give it him! give it him!' A hundred voices echoed the cry. 'What is it? where is he? who is he?—A servant of the superintendent!—A spy!—The superintendent disguised as a peasant, and making his escape!—Where is he? where is he? give it him! give it him!'

Renzo became dumb, shrank into a mere nothing, and endeavoured to make his escape; some of his neighbours helped him to conceal himself, and, by louder and different cries, attempted to drown these adverse and homicidal shouts. But what was of more use to him than anything else, was a cry of 'Make way, make way!' which was heard close at hand: 'Make way! here is help: make way; ho, hey!'

What was it? It was a long ladder, that some persons were bringing to rear against the house, so as to gain an entrance through one of the windows. But by great good fortune this means, which would have rendered the thing easy, was not, in itself, so easy of execution. The bearers, who at each end, and here and there at intervals, supported it, pushed it about and impeded by the crowd, reeled to and fro like waves; one, with his head between two steps and the sides resting on his shoulders, groaned beneath the weight, as under a galling yoke; another was separated from his burden by a violent push; the abandoned machine bruised heads, shoulders, and arms: and the reader must imagine the complaints and murmurs of those who thus suffered. Others, raising the dead weight with their hands, crept underneath it, and carried it on their backs, crying, 'It is our turn; let us go!' The fatal machine advanced by bounds and exchanges—now straightforward, now obliquely. It came, however, in time to distract and divert the attention of Renzo's persecutors, and he profited by this confusion within confusion; creeping quietly along at first, and then elbowing his way as well as he could, he withdrew from the post where he found himself in such a perilous situation, with the intention of making the best of his escape from the tumult, and of going, in real earnest, to find or to wait for Father Bonaventura.

All on a sudden, a movement, begun at one extremity, extended itself through the crowd, and a cry was echoed from mouth to mouth, in chorus: 'Ferrer! Ferrer!' Surprise, expressions of favour or contempt, joy and anger, burst forth wherever the name was heard: some echoed it, some tried to drown it; some affirmed, some denied, some blessed, some cursed.

'Is Ferrer here?—It isn't true, it isn't true!—Yes, yes! long live Ferrer; he who gives bread at a low price!—No, no!—He's here, he's here, in his carriage.—What is this fellow going to do? Why does he meddle in it? We don't want anybody!—Ferrer! long live Ferrer! the friend of poor people! he's come to take the superintendent to prison.—No, no: we will get justice ourselves: back, back!—Yes, yes! Ferrer! let Ferrer come! off with the superintendent to prison!'

And everybody, standing on tiptoe, turned towards the part where the unexpected new arrival was announced. But everybody rising, they saw neither more nor less than if they had all remained standing as they were; yet so it was: all arose.

In fact, at the extremity of the crowd, on the opposite side to where the soldiers were stationed, Antonio Ferrer, the high chancellor, was approaching in his carriage; feeling conscious, probably, that by his mistakes and obstinacy, he was the cause, or, at any rate, the occasion, of this outbreak, he now came to try and allay it, and to avert, at least, the most terrible and irreparable effects: he came, in short, to employ worthily a popularity unworthily acquired.

In popular tumults there is always a certain number of men, who, either from overheated passions, or from fanatical persuasion, or from wicked designs, or from an execrable love of destruction, do all they can to push matters to the worst; they propose or second the most inhuman advice, and fan the flame whenever it seems to be sinking: nothing is ever too much for them, and they wish for nothing so much as that the tumult should have neither limits nor end. But, by way of counterpoise, there is always a certain number of very different men, who, perhaps, with equal ardour and equal perseverance, are aiming at a contrary effect: some influenced by friendship or partiality for the threatened objects; others, without further impulse than that of a pious and spontaneous horror of bloodshed and atrocious deeds. Heaven blesses such. In each of these two opposite parties, even without antecedent concert, conformity of inclination creates an instantaneous agreement in operation. Those who make up the mass, and almost the materials of the tumult besides, are a mixed body of men, who, more or less, by infinite gradations, hold to one or the other extreme: partly incensed, partly knavish, a little inclined to a sort of justice, according to their idea of the word, a little desirous of witnessing some grand act of villainy; prone to ferocity or compassion, to adoration or execration, according as opportunities present themselves of indulging to the full one or other of these sentiments; craving every moment to know, to believe, some gross absurdity or improbability, and longing to shout, applaud, or revile in somebody's train. 'Long live,' and 'Down with,' are the words most readily uttered; and he who has succeeded in persuading them that such an one does not deserve to be quartered, has need of very few words to convince them that he deserves to be carried in triumph: actors, spectators, instruments, obstacles, whichever way the wind blows; ready even to be silent, when there is no longer any one to give them the word; to desist, when instigators fail; to disperse, when many concordant and uncontradicted voices have pronounced, 'Let us go;' and to return to their own homes, demanding of each other—What has happened? Since, however, this body has, hence, the greatest power, nay, is, in fact, the power itself; so, each of the two active parties uses every endeavour to bring it to its own side, to engross its services: they are, as it were, two adverse spirits, struggling which shall get possession of, and animate, this huge body. It depends upon which side can diffuse a cry the most apt to excite the passions, and direct their motions in favour of its own schemes; can most seasonably find information which will arouse or allay their indignation, and excite either their terror or their hopes; and can give the word, which, repeated more and more vehemently, will at once express, attest, and create the vote of the majority in favour of one or the other party.

All these remarks are intended as an introduction to the information that, in the struggle of the two parties who were contending for the suffrages of the populace crowded around the house of the superintendent, the appearance of Antonio Ferrer instantly gave a great advantage to the more moderate side, which had evidently been kept in awe, and, had the succour been a little longer delayed, would have had neither power nor scope for combat. This person was acceptable to the multitude on account of the tariff of his own appointment, which had been so favourable to purchasers, and also for his heroic resistance to every argument on the contrary side. Minds already thus biased were now more than ever captivated by the bold confidence of the old man, who, without guards or retinue, ventured thus to seek and confront an angry and ungoverned multitude. The announcement also that he came to take the superintendent prisoner produced a wonderful effect: so that the fury entertained towards the unfortunate man, which would have been rendered more violent, whoever had come to oppose it without making any concessions, was now, with this promise of satisfaction, and, to use a Milanese expression, with this bone in their mouth, a little allayed, and made way for other and far different sentiments which pervaded the minds of the greater part of the crowd.

The favourers of peace, having recovered their breath, seconded Ferrer in a hundred ways: those who were next to him, by exciting and re-exciting the cries of general applause by their own, and endeavouring at the same time to repulse the people so as to make a clear passage for the carriage; the others, by applauding, repeating, and spreading his words, or what appeared to them the best he could utter by silencing the furious and obstinate, and turning against them the new passions of the fickle assembly. 'Who is there that won't say, "Long live Ferrer?" Don't you wish bread to be sold cheap, eh? They are all rascals who don't wish for justice like Christians: they want to make as much noise as they can, to let the vicar escape. To prison with the vicar! Long live Ferrer! Make room for Ferrer!' As those who talked in this strain continued to increase, the courage of the opposite party rapidly cooled; so that the former proceeded from reprimands so far as to lay hands upon the demolishers, to repulse them, and even to snatch the weapons from their grasp. These grumbled, threatened, and endeavoured to regain their implements; but the cause of blood had given way, and the predominating cries were—'Prison! Justice! Ferrer!' After a little struggle, they were driven back: the others possessed themselves of the door, both to defend it from further assaults, and to secure access for Ferrer; and some of them, calling to those within (apertures for such a purpose were not wanting) informed them of the assistance that had arrived, and bid them get the superintendent ready, 'to go directly . . . to prison, ehem, do you hear!'

'Is this the Ferrer who helps to make out proclamations?' demanded our friend, Renzo, of a new neighbour, remembering the *Vidit Ferrer* that the doctor had pointed out to him at the bottom of one of these edicts, and which he had resounded so perseveringly in his ears.

'Yes; the high chancellor,' was the reply.

'He is a worthy man, isn't he?'

'More than that! it is he who fixed bread at a low price; and they wouldn't have it so; and now he is come to take the superintendent prisoner, who has not dealt justice to us.'

It is unnecessary to say that Renzo was instantly for Ferrer. He wished to get a sight of him directly, but this was no easy matter; yet, with the help of sundry breastings and elbowings, like a true Alpine, he succeeded in forcing a passage and reaching the foremost ranks next to the side of the carriage.

The vehicle had proceeded a little way into the crowd, and was at this moment at a stand-still, by one of those inevitable impediments so frequent in a journey of this sort. The aged Ferrer presented himself now at one window of the carriage, now at another with a countenance full of humility, affability, and benevolence—a countenance which he had always reserved, perchance he should ever have an interview with Don Filippo IV.; but he was compelled to display it also on this occasion. He talked too; but the noise and murmur of so many voices, and the *Long lives* which were addressed to him, allowed only few of his words to be heard. He therefore had recourse to gestures, now laying his fingers on his lips to receive a kiss, which his hands, on quickly extending them, distributed right and left, as an acknowledgment of thanks for these public demonstrations of kindness; now spreading them and waving them slowly outside the windows to beg a little room; now politely lowering them to request a moment's silence. When he had partly succeeded in obtaining it, the nearest to the carriage heard and repeated his words: 'Bread, abundance: I come to give you justice: a little room, if you please.' Then overcome, and, as it were, smothered with the buzzing of so many voices, the sight of so many crowded faces, and the consciousness of so many eyes fixed upon him, he drew back for a moment, puffed out his cheeks, sent forth a long-drawn breath, and said to himself, *Por mi vida, que de gente!*[1]

'Long live Ferrer! Don't be afraid. You are a worthy man. Bread, bread!'

'Yes: bread, bread,' replied Ferrer; 'abundance; I promise you,' and he laid his hand on his heart. 'A little room,' added he, in his loudest voice: 'I am coming to take him to prison, and give him just punishment:' continuing, in an under-tone, *'si està culpable.'*[2] Then bending forward towards the coachman, he said, hastily, *'Adelante, Pedro, si puedes.'*[3]

The driver himself also smiled with gracious condescension on the multitudes, as if he were some great personage; and, with ineffable politeness, waved his whip slowly to the right and left, to beg his incommodious neighbours to restrain themselves, and retire a little on either side. 'Be good enough, gentlemen,' said he, at last, 'to make a little room, a very little; just enough to let us pass.'

The most active and benevolent now exerted themselves to make the passage so courteously requested; some before the horses made the people retire by civil words, by putting their hands on their breasts, and by sundry gentle pushes: 'There, there, a little room, gentlemen.' Others pursued the same plan at the sides of the carriage, so that it might proceed without crushing toes, or infring-

---

[1] Upon my life, what a crowd!　　[2] If he be guilty.　　[3] Go on, Peter, if you can.

ing upon mustachios; for, besides injury to others, these accidents would expose the reputation of Antonio Ferrer to great risk.

After having stood a few moments admiring the behaviour of the old man, who, though agitated by perplexity and overcome with fatigue, was yet animated with solicitude, and adorned, so to say, with the hope of rescuing a fellow-creature from mortal anguish, Renzo put aside every thought of going away, and resolved to lend a hand to Ferrer, and not to leave him until he had obtained his purpose. No sooner said than done; he joined with the rest in endeavouring to clear a passage, and certainly was not among the least efficient. A space was cleared: 'Now come forward,' said more than one to the coachman, retiring or going before to make room further on. '*Adelante, presto, con juicio,*'[4] said his master, and the carriage moved on. Ferrer, in the midst of salutations which he lavished at random on the multitude, returned many particular acknowledgments with a smile of marked notice, to those who he saw interesting themselves for him; and of these smiles more than one fell to Renzo's share, who indeed merited them, and rendered more assistance to the high chancellor that day than the bravest of his secretaries could have done. The young mountaineer, delighted with these marks of distinction, almost fancied he had made acquaintance with Antonio Ferrer.

The carriage, once more on its way, continued to advance, more or less slowly, and not without some further trifling delays. The distance to be traversed was not perhaps above a stone's throw; but with respect to the time it occupied, it might have appeared a little journey even to one who was not in such urgent haste as Ferrer. The crowds moved onward, before, behind, and on each side of the carriage, like the mighty billows around a vessel advancing through the midst of a storm. The noise was more shrill, more discordant, more stunning, even than the whistling and howling of a storm itself. Ferrer, looking out first at one side and then at the other, beckoning and making all sorts of gestures to the people, endeavoured to catch something to which he might accommodate his replies; he tried as well as he could to hold a little dialogue with this crowd of friends; but it was a difficult task, the most

[4] Forward, quickly, but carefully.

difficult, perhaps, that he had yet met with during so many years of his high chancellorship. From time to time, however, a single word, or occasionally some broken sentence, repeated by a group in his passage, made itself heard, as the report of a large squib is heard above the continued crackling and whizzing of a display of fireworks. Now endeavouring to give a satisfactory answer to these cries, now loudly ejaculating the words that he knew would be most acceptable, or that some instant necessity seemed to require, he, too, continued to talk the whole way. 'Yes, gentlemen; bread, abundance—I will conduct him to prison: he shall be punished— *si està culpable*. Yes, yes: I will command: bread at a low price. *A si es.* . . . So it is, I mean to say: the King our master would not wish such faithful subjects to suffer from hunger. *Ox! ox! guardaos:* take care we do not hurt you, gentlemen. *Pedro, adelante, con juicio.* Plenty, plenty! A little room, for pity's sake. Bread, bread. To prison, to prison. What?' then demanded he of one who had thrust half his body through the window to shout in his ear some advice or petition or applause, or whatever it might be. But he, without having time to hear the 'what?' was forcibly pulled back by one who saw him on the point of being run over by the wheels. With such speeches and replies, amongst incessant acclamations, and some few grumbles of opposition, which were distinguishable here and there, but were quickly silenced, Ferrer at last reached the house, principally by the aid of these good auxiliaries.

The rest, who, as we have before related, were already here with the same good intentions, had in the mean while laboured to make and maintain a clear space. They begged, exhorted, threatened; and stamping, trampling, and pacing up and down, with that increased ardour and renewed strength which the near approach of a desired result usually excites, had succeeded in dividing the crowd into two, and then in repressing the two parties, so that when the carriage stopped before the door, there was left between it and the house a small empty space. Renzo, who, by acting a little both as a scout and guide, had arrived with the carriage, managed to place himself in one of the two frontiers of worthy people, who served at once both as wings to the carriage, and as a rampart to the too eager crowd of gazing by-standers. And helping to restrain one of these with his own powerful shoulders, he was also conveniently placed for seeing.

Ferrer drew a long deep breath on perceiving this small open space, and the door still shut. 'Shut,' here means not open; for, as to the rest, the hinges were almost wrenched out of the pillars; the door-posts shivered to pieces, crushed, forced, and dissevered; and through a large hole in the door might be seen a piece of a chain, twisted, bent, and almost broken in two, which, if we may say so, still held them together. Some kind-hearted person had placed himself at this opening to call to those within; another ran to let down the steps of the carriage: the old man rose, put out his head, and laying his right hand on the arm of this worthy assistant, came out and stood on the top step.

The crowd on each side stretched themselves up to see him: a thousand faces, a thousand beards pressed forward; and the general curiosity and attention produced a moment of general silence. Ferrer, standing for that moment on the step, cast a glance around, saluted the people with a bow, as if from a rostrum, and laying his left hand on his heart, cried: 'Bread and justice;' then bold, upright, and in his robes, he descended amidst acclamations which rent the skies.

Those within had, in the mean while, opened the door, or, to speak more correctly, had finished the work of wresting out the chain, together with the already more than half-loosened staples. They made an opening, to admit so ardently-desired a guest, taking, however, great care to limit the aperture to a space that his person would occupy. 'Quick, quick,' said he: 'open it wide, and let me in: and you, like brave fellows, keep back the people; don't let them follow me, for Heaven's sake! Make ready a passage, for by and by . . . Eh! eh! gentlemen, one moment,' said he to those within: 'softly with this door, let me pass: oh! my ribs: take care of my ribs. Shut it now: no, eh! eh! my gown, my gown!' It would have remained caught in the door, if Ferrer had not dexterously withdrawn the train, which disappeared from the outside like the tail of a snake that slips into a hiding-place when pursued.

The door pushed to, and closed as it best could be, was then propped up with bars within. Outside, those who constituted themselves Ferrer's body-guard laboured with shoulders, arms, and cries, to keep the space clear, praying from the bottom of their hearts that he would be expeditious.

'Be quick, be quick,' said he, also, as he stood within the portico, to the servants who had gathered round him, and who, almost out of breath, were exclaiming: 'Blessings on you! ah, your Excellency! oh, your Excellency! uh, your Excellency!'

'Quick, quick,' repeated Ferrer; 'where is this poor man?'

The superintendent came down-stairs, half dragged along, and half carried by his servants, as white as a sheet. When he saw his kind helper, he once more breathed freely; his pulse again beat, a little life returned into his limbs, and a little colour into his cheeks: he hastened towards Ferrer, saying, 'I am in the hands of God and your Excellency. But how shall we get out of this house? It is surrounded by the mob, who desire my death.'

'*Venga con migo usted,*[5] and be of good courage: my carriage is outside; quick, quick!' And taking his hand, he led him towards the door, doing his best to encourage him: but in his heart thinking, *Aqui està el busillis! Dios nos valga!*[6]

The door opened; Ferrer led the way, followed by his companion, who, creeping along, clung to the toga of his deliverer, like a little child to its mother's gown. Those who had kept the space clear, now raised their hands and hats so as to form a kind of net or cloud to screen the superintendent from the perilous gaze of the populace, and allow him to enter the carriage, where he concealed himself, by crouching in a corner. Ferrer then got in, and the door was shut. The people knew or guessed what had happened, and sent forth a confused shout of applauses and imprecations.

It may seem that the most difficult and hazardous part of the journey still remained to be performed; but the public desire of letting the superintendent be carried to prison, was sufficiently evident; and during the stay of the chancellor in the house, many of those who had facilitated his arrival had so busied themselves in preparing and maintaining a passage through the midst of the crowd, that on its return the carriage could proceed at a quicker pace, and without further delays. As fast as it advanced, the two crowds, repelled on both sides, fell back and mingled again behind it.

---

[5] Come with me, sir.   [6] Here is the difficult point. God help us!

As soon as Ferrer had seated himself, he bent down, and advised the vicar to keep himself well concealed in the corner, and not show himself for Heaven's sake; but there was no necessity for this warning. He, on the contrary, was obliged to display himself at the window, to attract and engage the attention of the multitude: and through the whole course of this drive he was occupied, as before, in making, to his changeable audience, the most lengthened and most unconnected harangue that ever was uttered; only interrupting it occasionally with some Spanish word or two, which he turned to whisper hastily in the ear of his squatting companion. 'Yes, gentlemen, bread and justice. To the castle, to prison, under my guard. Thank you, thank you; a thousand thanks. No, no; he shall not escape! *Por ablandarlos.*[7] It is too just; we will examine, we will see. I also wish you well, gentlemen. A severe punishment. *Esto lo digo por su bien.*[8] A just tariff, a fair limit, and punishment to those who would starve you. Stand aside, I beg of you.—Yes, yes, I am an honest man, a friend of the people. He shall be punished. It is true, he is a rogue, a rascal. *Perdone usted!*[9] It will go ill with him, it will go ill with him . . . *Si està culpable.*[10] Yes, yes; we will make the bakers plough straightforward. Long live the king, and the good Milanese, his most faithful subjects! It is bad, very bad. *Animo; estamos ya quasi afuera.'* [11]

They had, in fact, traversed the thickest part of the crowd, and were now just on the point of issuing into the open street. Here Ferrer, as he began to give his lungs a little rest, met his tardy allies, those Spanish soldiers, who, towards the end, had not been quite useless, since, supported and directed by some citizen, they had assisted to disperse a few of the mob in quiet, and to keep open a passage for the final exit. On the arrival of the carriage, they made way and presented arms to the high chancellor, who returned the acknowledgment by a bow to the right and left; and to the officer who approached nearer to salute him, he said, accompanying the words with a wave of his right hand *'Beso á usted las manos;'* [12] which the officer took for what it really meant—You have given me fine assistance! In reply, he made another low bow, and shrugged his shoulders. It would have been appropriate enough to add, *Cedant*

[7] It is to coax them.   [8] I say this for your good.   [9] Excuse me, sir.
[10] If he be guilty.   [11] Courage! we are almost out of danger.
[12] Your servant, sir: literally, 'I kiss your hand.'

arma togæ, but Ferrer was not at that moment in a humour for quotations; and had he been, his words would have been wasted on the winds, for the officer did not understand Latin.

Pedro regained his ancient spirit in passing between these two files of puppets and these muskets so respectfully elevated. Having recovered from his consternation, he remembered who he was, and whom he was driving; and shouting 'Ohey! ohey!' without the addition of other complimentary speeches to the mob, now sufficiently reduced in number to allow of his venturing on such treatment, he whipped on his horses, and took the road towards the castle.

'Levantese, levantese; estamos afuera,' [13] said Ferrer to the superintendent, who, reassured by the cessation of the cries, by the rapid motion of the carriage, and by these words, uncovered and stretched himself, rose, and recovering himself a little, began to overwhelm his liberator with thanks. Ferrer, after having condoled with him on his perilous situation, and congratulated him on his safety, exclaimed, running the palm of his hand over his bald pate, 'Ah, *que dirá de esto su Excelencia,*[14] who is already beside himself, for this cursed Casale, that won't surrender? *Que dirà el Conde Duque,*[15] who starts with fear if a leaf makes more noise than usual? *Que dirá el Rey nuestro señor,*[16] who will be sure to hear something of a great tumult? And when will it be over? *Dios lo sabe.*[17]

'Ah! as to myself, I will meddle no more in the business,' said the superintendent: 'I wash my hands of it; I resign my office into your Excellency's hands, and will go and live in a cave, or on a mountain, like a hermit, far, far away from this inhuman rabble.'

'Usted will do what is best *por el servicio de su Magestad,*[18] gravely replied the chancellor.

'His Majesty does not desire my death,' answered the superintendent. 'In a cave, in a cave, far from these people.' What followed afterwards upon this proposal is not recorded by our author, who, after accompanying the poor man to the castle, makes no further mention of his proceedings.

[13] Get up, get up; we are out of danger.
[14] What will his Excellency say of this?   [15] What will the Count Duke say?
[16] What will the King our master say?   [17] God knows.
[18] You will do, sir, what is best for the service of his Majesty.

CHAPTER XIV

THE crowd that was left behind began to disperse, and to branch off to the right and left along the different streets. One went home to attend to his business; another departed that he might breathe the fresh air in a little liberty, after so many hours of crowded confinement; while a third set off in search of acquaintances, with whom he might have a little chat about the doings of the day. The same dispersion was going on at the other end of the street, where the crowd was sufficiently thinned to allow the troop of Spaniards to advance, and approach the superintendent's house, without having to fight their way. Around this, the dregs, so to say, of the insurgents were still congregated—a handful of rascals who, discontented with so quiet and imperfect a termination to such great preparations, grumbled, cursed, and consulted, to encourage themselves in seeking if something further might not be undertaken; and, by way of experiment, began beating and pounding at the unfortunate door, which had been again barred and propped up within. On the arrival of the troop, these, without previous consultation, but with a unanimous resolution, moved off, and departed by the opposite side, leaving the post free to the soldiers, who took possession of it, and encamped as a guard to the house and street. But the neighbouring streets and squares were still full of scattered groups: where two or three were standing, three, four, twenty others would stop; some would depart, others arrive: it was like those little straggling clouds that sometimes remain scattered and shifting over the azure sky after a storm, and make one say, on looking upwards, The weather is not settled yet. There was heard a confused and varying sound of voices: one was relating with much energy the particular incidents he had witnessed; another recounted what he himself had done; another congratulated his neighbours on this peaceable termination, applauded Ferrer, and prognosticated dire evils about to fall on the superintendent; others laughed at the idea, and asserted that no harm would be done him, because a wolf does not prey upon a wolf; while others more angrily murmured because things had not been managed properly—said that it was all a hoax, and that they were fools to have made such a hubbub, only to allow themselves, after all, to be cozened in this manner.

Meanwhile, the sun had set, and twilight spread its uniform sombreness over all objects. Many, wearied with the exertions of the day, and tired of gossiping in the dark, returned to their respective homes. Our youth, after having assisted the progress of the carriage so long as there was need of assistance, and having followed it even between the two files of soldiers, as in triumph, was satisfied when he saw it rolling along, uninterruptedly, out of danger; and accompanying the crowd a little way, he soon deserted it by the first outlet, that he might breathe a little fresh air in quiet. After taking a few steps at large, in the midst of much agitation from so many new scenes, so many passions, and so many recent and confused remembrances, he began to feel his need both of food and rest; and kept looking up from side to side, in hopes of seeing a sign of some inn, since it was too late to go to the convent. As he thus proceeded, gazing upwards, he suddenly lit upon a group of gossips; and stopping to listen, he heard them, as they talked, making conjectures, proposals, and designs for the morrow. After listening a moment or two, he could not resist putting in his word, thinking that he who had *done* so much might, without presumption, join a little in the conversation. Persuaded, from what he had seen during the day, that to accomplish anything, it was only necessary to suggest it to the populace, 'My good sirs,' cried he, by way of exordium: 'may I, too, give my poor opinion? My poor opinion is this: that there are other iniquities besides this of bread. Now we've seen plain enough to-day that we can get justice by making ourselves felt. Then let us proceed until all these grievances are cured, that the world may move forward in a little more Christian fashion. Isn't it true, gentlemen, that there's a set of tyrants who set at nought the Ten Commandments, and search out poor people, (who don't trouble their heads about them), just to do them every mischief they can; and yet they're always in the right? Nay, when they've been acting the rascal more than usual, then hold their heads higher than at other times? Yes, and even Milan has its share of them.'

'Too many,' said a voice.

'So I say,' rejoined Renzo: 'the accounts of them have already reached our ears. And, besides, the thing speaks for itself. Let us suppose, for instance, that one of those I am talking about should have one foot outside and one in Milan: if he's a devil there, he won't be an angel here, I fancy. Yet just tell me, sirs, whether you've ever seen one of these men behind the grating! And the worst of it is (and this I can affirm with certainty), there are proclamations in plenty published, to punish them; and those not proclamations without meaning, but well drawn out; you can't find anything better done: there are all sorts of villanies clearly mentioned, exactly as they happen, and to each one its proper punishment. It says: "Whoever it may be, ignoble or plebeians," and what not besides. Now, just go and ask doctors, scribes, and pharisees, to see justice done to you, as the proclamation warrants, and they will give you as much ear as the Pope does to vagabonds: it's enough to make any honest fellow turn desperate. It is plain enough, then, that the king, and those who command under him, are desirous that knaves should be duly punished; but nothing is done because there is some league between them. We, therefore, ought to break it; we should go to-morrow morning to Ferrer, who is a worthy man, and a tractable signor; we saw to-day how glad he was to be amongst the poor people, and how he tried to hear what was said to him, and answered with such condescension. We should go to Ferrer, and tell him how things stand; and I, for my part, can tell him some fine doings; for I saw with my own eyes a proclamation with ever so many arms at the top, which had been made by three of the rulers, for there was the name of each of them printed plain below, and one of these names was Ferrer, seen by me with my own eyes: now, this edict exactly suited my case; and a doctor, to whom I applied for justice, according to the intention of these three gentlemen, among whom was Ferrer himself, this signor doctor, who had himself shown me the proclamation, and a fine one it is, aha! thought that I was talking to him like a madman! I'm sure that when this worthy old fellow hears some of these fine doings, for he cannot know all, particularly those in the country, he won't be willing to let the world go on this way, but will find some remedy for it. And besides, they who make the proclamations ought to wish that they should be obeyed; for it is an insult to count as nothing an edict with their name fixed to it. And if the powerful ones won't lower their heads, and will still play the fool, we are ready to make them, as we've done to-day. I don't say that he should go about in his carriage, to carry off every powerful and overbearing rascal: eh, eh! it would require Noah's ark for that. But he ought to command all those whose business it is, not only in Milan, but everywhere, to do things as the proclamations require; and draw up an indictment against all those who have committed these iniquities; and where it says, prison,—to prison; where it says, galleys,—to the galleys; and bid the *podestà* do his duty; if he won't, send him about his business, and put a better man in his place; and then besides, as I said, we should be ready to lend a hand. And he ought to order the lawyers to listen to the poor, and to talk reasonably. Don't I say right, my good sirs?'

Renzo had talked so earnestly, that from the beginning a great part of the assemblage had stopped all other conversation, and had turned to listen to him; and, up to a certain point, all had continued his auditors. A confused clamour of applause, of 'Bravo; certainly, he is right; it is too true!' followed his harangue. Critics, however, were not wanting. 'Oh, yes,' said one, 'listen to a mountaineer: they are all advocates;' and he went away. 'Now,' muttered another, 'every ragamuffin must put in his word; and what with having too many irons in the fire, we sha'n't have bread sold cheap, which is what we've made this stir for.' Renzo, however, heard nothing but compliments, one taking him by this hand, another by that. 'I will see you to-morrow.—Where?—At the square of the Cathedral.— Very well.—Very well.—And something will be done.—And something will be done.'

'Which of these good gentlemen will direct me to an inn, where I can get something to eat, and a lodging for the night, that will suit a poor youth's pocket?' said Renzo.

'I am at your service, my brave fellow,' said one who had listened attentively to his harangue, and had not yet said a word. 'I know an inn that will just suit you; and I will introduce you to the landlord, who is my friend, and a very worthy man.'

'Near at hand?' asked Renzo.

'Only a little way off,' replied he.

The assembly dispersed; and Renzo, after several warm shakes of the hand from strangers, went off with his new acquaintance, thanking him heartily for his kindness.

'Not a word, not a word,' said he: one hand washes the other, and both the face. Is it not one's duty to serve one's neighbour?' And as he walked, he kept making of Renzo, in the course of conversation, first one and then another inquiry. 'Not out of curiosity about your doings; but you seem tired: where do you come from?'

'I come,' replied Renzo, 'as far as from Lecco.'

'From Lecco! Are you a native of Lecco?'

'Of Lecco . . . that is, of the territory.'

'Poor fellow! from what I have gathered in your conversation, you seem to have been badly treated.'

'Eh! my dear fellow, I was obliged to speak rather carefully, that I might not publish my affairs to the world; but . . . it's enough; some day it will be known, and then . . . But I see a sign of an inn here; and, to say the truth, I am not inclined to go any further.'

'No, no; come where I told you: it's a very little way further,' said the guide: 'here you won't be comfortable.'

'Very well,' replied the youth: 'I'm not a gentleman, accustomed to down, though: something good to supply the garrison, and a straw mattress, are enough for me: and what I most want is to find both directly. Here we are, fortunately.' And he entered a shabby-looking doorway, over which hung the sign of The Full Moon.

'Well; I will lead you here, since you wish it,' said the incognito; and he followed him in.

'Don't trouble yourself any further,' replied Renzo. 'However,' added he, 'you will do me the favour of taking a glass with me.'

'I accept your kind offer,' replied he: and he advanced, as being better acquainted with the place, before Renzo, through a little court, approached a glass door, lifted up the latch, and, opening it, entered with his companion into the kitchen.

Two lights illuminated the apartment, suspended from two hooks fixed in the beam of the ceiling. Many persons, all of whom were engaged, were lounging on benches which stretched along both sides of a narrow, dirty table, occupying almost the whole of one side of the room: here and there a cloth was spread, and a few dishes set out; at intervals, cards were played, and dice cast, and gathered up; and everywhere were bottles and glasses. On the wet table were to be seen *berlinghe, reali,* and *parpagliole,*[1] which, could they have spoken, would probably have said: This morning we were in a baker's till, or in the pockets of some of the spectators of the tumult; for every one, intent on watching how public matters went, forgot to look after their own private interests. The clamour was great. A boy was going backwards and forwards in haste and bustle, waiting upon this table and sundry chess-boards: the host was sitting upon a small bench under the chimney-piece, occupied, apparently, in making and un-making certain figures in the ashes with the tongs; but, in reality, intent on all that was going on around him. He rose at the sound of the latch, and advanced towards the new comers. When he saw the guide.—Cursed fellow! thought he:—you are always coming to plague me, when I least want you!—Then, hastily glancing at Renzo, he again said to himself:—I don't know you; but, coming with such a hunter, you must be either a dog or a hare; when you have said two words, I shall know which.—However, nothing of this mute soliloquy appeared in the landlord's countenance, which was as immovable as a picture: a round and shining face, with a thick reddish beard, and two bright and staring eyes.

'What are your commands, gentlemen?' said he.

'First of all, a good flask of wine,' said Renzo, 'and then something to eat.' So saying, he sat down on a bench towards the end of the table, and uttered a sonorous 'Ah!' which seemed to say: it does one good to sit down after having been so long standing and working so hard. But immediately the recollection of the bench and the table at which he had last sat with Lucia and Agnese, rushed to his mind, and forced from him a sigh. He shook his head to drive away the thought, and then saw the host coming with the wine. His companion had sat down opposite to Renzo, who poured him out a glass, and

---

[1] Different kinds of Spanish and Milanese coins.

pushed it towards him, saying: 'To moisten your lips.' And filling
the other glass, he emptied it at one draught.

'What can you give me to eat?' then demanded he of the landlord.

'A good bit of stewed meat?' asked he.

'Yes, sir; a bit of stewed meat.'

'You shall be served directly,' said the host to Renzo; and turning
to the boy: 'Attend to this stranger.'

And he retreated to the fire-place. 'But . . .' resumed he, turning
again towards Renzo: 'we have no bread to-day.'

'As to bread,' said Renzo, in a loud voice and laughing, 'Providence has provided that.' And drawing from his pocket the third
and last loaf which he had picked up under the Cross of San Dionigi,
he raised it in the air, exclaiming: 'Behold the bread of Providence!'
Many turned on hearing this exclamation; and, seeing such a trophy
in the air, somebody called out: 'Hurrah for bread at a low price!'

'At a low price?' said Renzo: *Gratis et amore.*'

'Better still, better still.'

'But,' added he, immediately, 'I should not like these gentlemen to
think ill of me. I have not, as they say, stolen it: I found it on the
ground; and if I could find its owner, I am ready to pay him for it.'

'Bravo! bravo!' cried his companions, laughing more loudly, without its entering into one of their minds that these words seriously
expressed a real fact and intention.

'They think I'm joking; but it's just so,' said Renzo, to his guide;
and, turning the loaf over in his hand, he added: 'See how they've
crushed it; it looks like a cake: but there were plenty close by it!
if any of them had had very tender bones they'd have come badly
off.' Then, biting off and devouring three or four mouthfuls, he
swallowed another glass of wine, and added, 'This bread won't go
down alone. I never had so dry a throat. A great shouting there
was!'

'Prepare a good bed for this honest fellow,' said the guide; 'for he
intends to sleep here.'

'Do you wish a bed?' asked the landlord of Renzo, advancing
towards the table.

'Certainly,' replied he: 'a bed, to be sure; only let the sheets be
clean; for, though I'm but a poor lad, I'm accustomed to cleanliness.'

'Oh! as to that,' said the host: and going to a counter that stood in a corner of the kitchen, he returned with an inkstand and a little bit of writing-paper in one hand, and a pen in the other.

'What does this mean?' exclaimed Renzo, gulping down a mouthful of the stew that the boy had set before him, and then smiling in astonishment: 'Is this the white sheet, eh?'

Without making any reply, the landlord laid the paper on the table, and put the inkstand by the paper: then stooping forward, he rested his left arm on the table and his right elbow, and holding the pen in the air, with his face raised towards Renzo, said to him: 'Will you be good enough to tell me your name, surname, and country?'

'What?' said Renzo: 'What has all this to do with my bed?'

'I do my duty,' said the host, looking towards the guide; 'we are obliged to give an account and relation of every one that comes to sleep in our house: *name and surname, and of what nation he is, on what business he comes, if he has any arms with him . . . how long he intends to stay in this city . . .* They are the very words of the proclamation.'

Before replying, Renzo swallowed another glass; it was the third, and from this time forward, I fear we shall not be able to count them. He then said, 'Ah! ah! you have the proclamation! And I pride myself upon being a doctor of law; so I know well enough what importance is attached to edicts.'

'I speak in earnest,' said the landlord, keeping his eye on Renzo's mute companion; and going again to the counter, he drew out a large sheet, an exact copy of the proclamation, and came to display it before Renzo's eyes.

'Ah! see!' exclaimed the youth, raising the re-filled glass in one hand, and quickly emptying it, while he stretched out the other, and pointed with his finger towards the unfolded proclamation; 'Look at that fine sheet, like a missal. I'm delighted to see it. I know those arms; and I know what that heretical face means, with the noose round its neck.' (At the head of the edicts the arms of the governor were usually placed; and in those of Don Gonzalo Fernandez de Cordova appeared a Moorish king, chained by the throat.)

'That face means: Command who can, and obey who will. When that face shall have sent to the galleys Signor don —— never mind, I know who; as another parchment says, like this; when it has provided that an honest youth may marry an honest girl who is willing to be married to him, then I will tell my name to this face, and will give it a kiss into the bargain. I may have very good reasons for not telling my name. Oh, truly! And if a rascal, who had under his command a handful more of rascals; for if he were alone ——' Here he finished his sentence with a gesture: 'If a rascal wanted to know where I am, to do me an ill turn, I ask if that face would move itself to help me. I'm to tell my business! This is something new. Supposing I had come to Milan to confess, I should wish to confess to a Capuchin Father, I beg to say, and not to a landlord.'

The host was silent, and looked towards the guide, who gave no token of noticing what passed. Renzo, we grieve to say, swallowed another glass, and continued: 'I will give you a reason, my dear landlord, which will satisfy you. If those proclamations which speak in favour of good Christians are worth nothing, those which speak against them are worth still less. So carry away all these bothering things, and bring us instead another flask; for this is broken.' So saying, he tapped it lightly with his knuckles, and added: 'Listen, how it sounds like a cracked bottle.'

Renzo's language had again attracted the attention of the party; and when he ceased, there arose a general murmur of approbation.

'What must I do?' said the host, looking at the incognito, who was, however, no stranger to him.

'Away, away with them,' cried many of the guests; 'this countryman has some sense; they are grievances, tricks, impositions; new laws to-day, new laws!'

In the midst of these cries, the incognito, glancing towards the landlord a look of reproof for this too public magisterial summons, said, 'Let him have his own way a little; don't give any offence.'

'I have done my duty,' said the host, in a loud voice; and added, to himself:—Now I have *my shoulders against the wall.*—He then removed the pen, ink, and paper, and took the empty flagon to give it to the boy.

'Bring the same sort of wine,' said Renzo; 'for I find it a worthy fellow, and will send it to sleep with the other, without asking its name or surname, and what is its business, and if it intends to stay any time in the city.'

'Some more of the same sort,' said the landlord, to the boy, giving him the flask; and he returned to his seat under the chimney-piece. —More simple than a hare!—thought he, figuring away in the cinders:—and into what hands hast thou fallen! Thou great ass! If thou wilt drown, drown; but the landlord of the Full Moon isn't obliged to go shares in thy folly!—

Renzo returned thanks to his guide, and to all the rest who had taken his part. 'Brave friends,' said he, 'now I see clearly that honest fellows give each other a hand, and support each other.' Then waving his hand in the air, over the table, and again assuming the air of a speaker, 'Isn't it an admirable thing,' exclaimed he, 'that all our rulers will have pen, ink, and paper, intruding everywhere? Always a pen in the hand! They must have a mighty passion for wielding the pen!'

'Eh! you worthy countryman! would you like to know the reason?' said a winner in one of the games, laughing.

'Let us hear,' replied Renzo.

'The reason is,' said he, 'that as these Signori eat geese, they find they have got so many quills that they are obliged to make something of them.'

All began to laugh, excepting the poor man who had just been a loser.

'Oh,' said Renzo, 'this man is a poet. You have some poets here, then: they are springing up everywhere. I have a little turn that way myself; and sometimes I make some fine verses . . . but that's when things go smoothly.'

To understand this nonsense of poor Renzo's, the reader must know that, amongst the lower orders in Milan, and still more in the country, the term poet did not signify, as among all educated people, a sacred genius, an inhabitant of Pindus, a votary of the Muses; it rather meant a humorous and even giddy-headed person, who in conversation and behaviour had more repartee and novelty than sense. So daring are these mischief-makers among the vulgar, in destroying the meaning of words, and making them express things the most foreign and contrary to their legitimate significa- tion! For what, I should like to know, has a poet to do with a giddy brain?

'But I'll tell you the true reason,' added Renzo; 'It is because they hold the pen in their own hand: and so the words that they utter fly away and disappear; the words that a poor lad speaks, are care- fully noted, and very soon they fly through the air with his pen, and are down upon paper to be made use of at a proper time and place. They've also another trick, that when they would bother a poor fellow who doesn't know letters, but who has a little . . . I know what . . .' and to illustrate his meaning he began tapping, and almost battering his forehead with his forefinger, 'no sooner do they per- ceive that he begins to understand the puzzle, than, forsooth, they must throw in a little Latin, to make him lose the thread, to prevent his defending himself, and to perplex his brain. Well, well! it is our business to do away with these practices! To-day everything has been done reasonably, in our own tongue, and without pen, ink and paper: and to-morrow, if people will but govern themselves, we will do still better; without touching a hair of their heads, though; everything must be done in a fair way.'

In the mean time some of the company had returned to their gam- ing, others to eating, and many to shouting; some went away, and others arrived in their place; the landlord busied himself in attending upon all; but these things have nothing to do with our story.

The unknown guide was impatient to take his departure; yet, though he had not, to all appearance, any business at the house, he would not go away till he had chatted a little with Renzo, individu- ally. He, therefore, turned to him, and renewed the conversation about bread; and after a few of those expressions which had been, for some time, in everybody's mouth, he began to give his own opinion. 'Eh! if I were ruling,' said he, 'I would find a way of mak- ing things right.'

'How would you do?' asked Renzo, fixing on him two eyes more sparkling than usual, and twisting his mouth away, as it were to be more attentive.

'How would I do?' said he; 'I would have bread for all: for poor as well as rich.'

'Ah! so far well,' said Renzo.

'See how I would do. First, I would fix a moderate price, that everybody could reach. Then I would distribute bread according to the number of mouths: for there are some inconsiderate gluttons who would have all to themselves, and strive who can get the most, buying at a high price, and thus there isn't bread enough for the poor people. Therefore, distribute bread. And how should that be done? See: give a note to every family, in proportion to the number of mouths, to go and get bread at the bakehouses. To me, for example, they should give a note of this kind:—Ambrogio Fusella, by trade a sword-cutler, with a wife and four children, all of an age to eat bread (note that well): let them have so much bread; and pay so many pence. But to do things justly it must always be in proportion to the number of mouths. You, we will suppose, ought to have a note for . . . your name?'

'Lorenzo Tramaglino,' said the youth; who, delighted with the plan, never recollected that it was entirely founded on paper, pen and ink, and that to put it in execution the first thing must be to get everybody's name.

'Very well,' said the stranger; 'but have you a wife and children?'

'I ought, indeed . . . children, no . . . too soon . . . but a wife . . . if the world went as it ought . . . '

'Ah! you are single! Well, have patience; but a smaller portion . . .'

'You are right; but if soon, as I hope . . . and by the help of God . . . Enough; and when I've a wife too?'

'Then change the note, and increase the quantity. As I said; always in proportion to the number of mouths,' said the unknown, rising from his seat.

'That is all very good,' cried Renzo; and he continued vociferously, as he struck his hand upon the table: 'And why don't they make a law of this kind?'

'How can I tell? But I must bid you good night, and be off; for I fancy my wife and children have been looking out for me this good while.'

'Just another little drop—another little drop,' cried Renzo, hastily filling his glass; and, rising quickly, he seized the skirt of his doublet, and tried to force him to sit down again. 'Another little drop; don't do me this insult.'

But his friend disengaged himself with a sudden jerk, and leaving Renzo to indulge in importunity and reproaches as he pleased, again said: 'Good night,' and went away. Renzo shouted after him when he had even reached the street, and then sank back upon his seat. He eyed the glass that he had just filled; and seeing the boy passing the table, he detained him with a beckon of his hand, as if he had some business to communicate to him; he then pointed to the glass, and, with a slow and grave enunciation, and pronouncing the words in a peculiar manner, said: 'See, I had prepared it for that worthy gentleman: do you see? full to the brim, fit for a friend; but he wouldn't have it; people have very odd ideas, sometimes. I couldn't do otherwise; I let him see my kind intentions. Now, then, since the thing is done, I mus'n't let it go to waste.' So saying, he took it, and emptied it at a draught.

'I understand,' said the boy, going away.

'Ah! you understand, do you?' replied Renzo; 'then it is true. When reasons are sensible! . . .'

Nothing less than our love of truthfulness would induce us to prosecute a faithful account which does so little credit to so important a person, we may almost say, to the principal hero, of our story. From this same motive of impartiality, however, we must also state, that this was the first time that such a thing happened to Renzo; and it is just because he was not accustomed to such excesses that his first attempt succeeded so fatally. The few glasses that he had swallowed one after another, at first, contrary to his usual habits, partly to cool his parched throat, partly from a sort of excitement of mind which gave him no liberty to do anything in moderation, quickly went to his head; a more practised drinker would probably never have felt them. Our anonymous author here makes an observation which we repeat for the benefit of those of our readers who know how to value it. Temperate and honest habits, says he, bring with them this advantage; that the more they are stablished and rooted in a man, so much the more easily, when he acts contrary to them, does he immediately feel the injury or inconvenience, or, to say the least, the disagreeability of such an action: so that he has something to remember for a time; and thus even a slight fault serves him for a lesson.

However this may be, certain it is that when these first fumes had mounted to Renzo's brain, wine and words continued to flow, one down, the other up, without measure or reason: and at the point where we have left him, he had got quite beyond his powers of self-government. He felt a great desire to talk: auditors, or at least men present whom he could imagine such, were not wanting; and for some time also words had readily occurred to him, and he had been able to arrange them in some sort of order. But by degrees his power of connecting sentences began woefully to fail. The thought that had presented itself vividly and definitively to his mind, suddenly clouded over and vanished; while the word he wanted and waited for, was, when it occurred to him, inapplicable and unseasonable. In this perplexity, by one of those false instincts that so often ruin men, he would again have recourse to the flagon; but any one with a grain of sense will be able to imagine of what use the flagon was to him then.

We will only relate some of the many words he uttered in this disastrous evening; the others which we omit would be too unsuitable; for they not only had no meaning, but made no show of having any—a necessary requisite in a printed book.

'Ah, host, host,' resumed he, following him with his eye round the table, or under the chimney-piece; sometimes gazing at him where he was not, and talking all the time in the midst of the uproar of the party: 'What a landlord you are! I cannot swallow this . . . this trick about the name, surname, and business. To a youth like me! . . . You have not behaved well. What satisfaction now, what advantage, what pleasure . . . to put upon paper a poor youth? Don't I speak sense, gentlemen? Landlords ought to stand by good youths . . . Listen, listen, landlord; I will compare you . . . because . . . Do you laugh, eh! I am a little too far gone, I know . . . but the reasons I would give are right enough. Just tell me, now, who is it that keeps up your trade? Poor fellows, isn't it? See if any of these gentlemen of the proclamations ever come here to wet their lips.'

'They are all people that drink water,' said one of Renzo's neighbours.

'They want to have their heads clear,' added another, 'to be able to tell lies cleverly.'

'Ah!' cried Renzo. 'That was the poet who spoke then. Then you also understand my reason. Answer me, then, landlord; and Ferrer, who is the best of all, has he ever come here to drink a toast, or to spend a quarter of a farthing? And that dog of a villain, Don . . . I'll hold my tongue, because I'm a careful fellow. Ferrer and Father Cr-r-r . . . I know, they are two worthy men; but there are so few worthy men in the world. The old are worse than the young; and the young . . . worse again than the old. However, I am glad there has been no murdering; fye; cruelties that should be left for the hangman's hands. Bread; oh yes! I got some great pushes, but . . . I gave some away too. Room! plenty! long live! . . . However, even Ferrer . . . some few words in Latin . . . *siés baraòs trapolorum* . . . Cursed trick! Long live! . . . justice! bread! Ah, these are fair words! . . . There we wanted these comrades . . . when that cursed ton, ton, ton, broke forth, and then again ton, ton, ton. We did not flee then, do you see, to keep that signor curate there . . . I know what I'm thinking about!'

At these words he bent down his head, and remained some time as if absorbed in some idea; he then heaved a deep sigh, and raised a face with two piteous-looking eyes, and such an expression of disagreeable and stupid grief, that woe to him if the object of it could have seen him at that moment. But the wicked men around him, who had already begun to divert themselves with the impassioned and confused eloquence of Renzo, now hastened to ridicule his countenance tinctured with remorse; the nearest to him said to the others: 'Look at him;' and all turned towards the poor fellow, so that he became the laughing-stock of the unruly company. Not that all of them were in their perfect senses, or in their ordinary senses, whatever they might be; but, to say the truth, none of them had gone so far as poor Renzo: and still more, he was a countryman. They began, first one and then another, to provoke him with foolish and unmannerly questions, and jesting ceremonies. One moment he would seem to be offended, the next, would take the treatment in joke; now, without taking notice of all these voices, he would talk of something quite different, now replying, now interrogating, but always by starts and blunders. Fortunately, in all this extravagance, he had preserved a kind of instinctive carefulness not to mention the names of persons, so that even that which was most likely to be firmly fixed in his memory was not once uttered; for deeply it would have grieved us if that name for which even we entertain a degree of respect and affection, had been bandied about, and become the sport of these abandoned wretches.

CHAPTER XV

THE landlord, seeing the game was lasting too long, and being carried too far, had approached Renzo, and, with the greatest politeness, requesting the others to leave him alone, began shaking him by the arm, and tried to make him understand, and persuade him that he had better go to bed. But Renzo could not forget the old subject of the name, and surname, the proclamations, and worthy youths. However, the words 'bed' and 'sleep,' repeated in his ear, wrought some kind of impression on his mind; they made him feel a little more distinctly his need of what they signified, and produced a momentary lucid interval. The little sense that returned to his mind, made him, in some degree, sensible that most of his companions had gone: as the last glimmering torch in an illumination shows all the others extinguished. He made a resolution; placed his open hands upon the table; tried once or twice to raise himself; sighed, staggered, and at a third attempt, supported by his host, he stood upon his feet. The landlord, steadying him as he walked along, guided him from between the bench and the table, and taking a lamp in one hand, partly conducted, and partly dragged him with the other, towards the door of the stairs. Here, Renzo, on hearing the noise of the salutations which were shouted after him by the company, hastily turned round, and if his supporter had not been very alert, and held him by the arm, the evolution would have ended in a heavy fall: however, he managed to turn back, and, with his unconfined arm, began figuring and describing in the air sundry salutes like a running knot.

'Let us go to bed; to bed,' said the landlord, pushing him forward through the door; and with still more difficulty drawing him to the top of the narrow wooden staircase, and then into the room he had prepared for him. Renzo rejoiced on seeing his bed ready; he looked graciously upon his host, with eyes which one moment glistened more than ever, and the next faded away, like two fire-flies: he endeavoured to steady himself on his legs, and stretched out his hand toward his host's cheek to take it between his first and middle fingers, in token of friendship and gratitude, but he could not succeed. 'Brave landlord,' he at last managed to stammer out: 'now I see that you are a worthy fellow: this is a kind deed, to give a poor youth a bed; but that trick about the name and surname, that wasn't like a gentleman. By good luck, I saw through it . . .'

The landlord, who little thought he could have uttered anything so connected, and who knew, by long experience, how men in such a condition may be induced more easily than usual, suddenly to change their minds, was determined to take advantage of this lucid interval, to make another attempt.

'My dear fellow,' said he, with a most coaxing tone and look, 'I didn't do it to vex you, nor to pry into your affairs. What would you have? There are the laws, and we must obey them; otherwise we are the first to suffer the punishment. It is better to satisfy them, and . . . After all, what is it all about? A great thing, certainly, to say two words! Not, however, for them, but to do me a favour. Here, between ourselves, face to face, let us do our business: tell me your name . . . and then go to bed with a quiet mind.'

'Ah rascal!' exclaimed Renzo: 'Cheat! you are again returning to the charge, with that infamous name, surname, and business!'

'Hold your tongue, simpleton, and go to bed,' said the landlord.

But Renzo pursued more vehemently: 'I understand: you are one of the league. Wait, wait, and I'll settle it.' And directing his voice towards the head of the stairs, he began to shout more vociferously than ever, 'Friends! the landlord is of the . . .'

'I only said it in a joke,' cried he, in Renzo's face, repulsing him, and pushing him towards the bed—'In joke: didn't you understand that I only said it in joke?'

'Ah! in joke: now you speak sensibly. When you say in joke . . . They are just the things to make a joke of.' And he sank upon the bed.

'Here; undress yourself, and be quick,' said the host, adding assistance to his advice; and there was need of it. When Renzo had succeeded in getting off his waistcoat, the landlord took it, and put his hands in the pockets to see if there were any money in them.

His search was successful; and thinking that his guest would have something else to do than to pay him on the morrow, and that this money would probably fall into hands whence a landlord would not easily be able to recover any share, he resolved to risk another attempt.

'You are a good youth, and an honest man, aren't you?' said he.

'Good youth, and honest man,' replied Renzo, vainly endeavouring to undo the buttons of the clothes which he had not yet been able to take off.

'Very well,' rejoined the host: 'just settle, then, this little account; for to-morrow I must go out on some business . . .'

'That's only fair,' said Renzo: 'I'm a fool, but I'm honest . . . But the money? Am I to go look for money now! . . .'

'It's here,' said the innkeeper; and calling up all his practice, patience, and skill, he succeeded in settling the account, and securing the reckoning.

'Lend me a hand to finish undressing, landlord,' said Renzo; 'I'm beginning to feel very sleepy.'

The landlord performed the required office: he then spread the quilt over him, and, almost before he had time to say, disdainfully, 'Good night!' Renzo was snoring fast asleep. Yet, with that sort of attraction which sometimes induces us to contemplate an object of dislike as well as of affection, and which, perhaps, is nothing else than a desire of knowing what operates so forcibly on our mind, he paused, for a moment, to contemplate so annoying a guest, holding the lamp towards his face, and throwing the light upon it with a strong reflection, by screening it with his hand, almost in the attitude in which Psyche is depicted, when stealthily regarding the features of her unknown consort.—Mad blockhead!—said he, in his mind, to the poor sleeper,—you've certainly taken the way to look for it. To-morrow you'll be able to tell me how you've liked it. Clowns, who will stroll over the world, *without knowing whereabouts the sun rises,* just to bring themselves and their neighbours into trouble!—

So saying, or rather thinking, he withdrew the light, and left the room, locking the door behind him. On the landing-place at the top of the stairs, he called the landlady, and bade her leave the children under the care of a young servant girl, and go down into the kitchen, to preside and keep guard in his stead. 'I must go out, thanks to a stranger who has arrived here, to my misfortune,' said he; and he briefly related the annoying circumstance. He then added: 'Have your eyes everywhere; and, above all, be prudent this unfortunate day. There's a group of licentious fellows down below, who, between drink and their own inclination, are ready enough to talk, and will say anything. It will be enough, if a rash . . .'

'Oh, I'm not a child; and I know well enough what's to be done. I think you can't say that, up to this time . . .'

'Well, well; and be sure they pay; and pretend not to hear anything they say about the superintendent of provisions, and the governor, and Ferrer, and the *decurioni,* and the cavaliers, and Spain, and France, and such fooleries; for if you contradict them, you'll come off badly directly; and if you agree with them, you may fare badly afterwards: and *you* know well enough, that sometimes those who say the worst things . . . But enough; when you hear certain sayings, turn away your head, and cry, "I'm coming," as if somebody was calling you from the other side; I'll come back as quick as I can.'

So saying, he went down with her into the kitchen, and gave a glance round, to see if there was anything new of consequence; took down his hat and cloak from a peg, reached a short, thick stick out of the corner, summed up, in one glance at his wife, the instructions he had given her, and went out. But during these preparations, he had again resumed the thread of the apostrophe begun at Renzo's bedside; and continued it, even while proceeding on his walk.

—Obstinate fellow of a mountaineer!—For, however Renzo was determined to conceal his condition, this qualification had betrayed itself in his words, pronunciation, appearance, and actions.—Such a day as this, by good policy and judgment, I thought to have come off clear; and you must just come in at the end of it, to spoil the egg in the hatching. Were there no other inns in Milan, that you must just light upon mine? Would that you had even lit upon it alone! I would then have shut my eyes to it to-night, and to-morrow morning would have given you a hint. But, my good sir, no; you must come in company; and, to do better still, in company with a sheriff.—

At every step the innkeeper met either with solitary passengers, or persons in groups of three or four, whispering together. At this stage of his mute soliloquy, he saw a patrol of soldiers approaching, and, going a little aside, peeped at them from under the corner of his eye as they passed, and continued to himself:—There go the fool-chastisers. And you, great ass, because you saw a few people rambling about and making a noise, it must even come into your brain that the world is turning upside down. And on this fine foundation you have ruined yourself, and are trying to ruin me too; this isn't fair. I did my best to save you; and you, you fool, in return, have very nearly made a disturbance in my inn. Now you must get yourself out of the scrape, and I will look to my own business. As if I wanted to know your name out of curiosity! What does it matter to me, whether it be Thaddeus or Bartholomew? A mighty desire I have to take the pen in hand; but you are not the only people who would have things all their own way. I know, as well as you, that there are proclamations which go for nothing: a fine novelty, that a mountaineer should come to tell me that! But you don't know that proclamations against landlords are good for something. And you pretend to travel over the land, and speak; and don't know that, if one would have one's own way, and carry the proclamations in one's pocket, the first thing requisite is not to speak against them in public. And for a poor innkeeper who was of your opinion, and didn't ask the name of any one who happens to favour him with his company, do you know, you fool, what good things are in store for him? *Under pain of three hundred crowns to any one of the aforesaid landlords, tavern-keepers, and others, as above;* there are three hundred crowns hatched; and now to spend them well; *to be applied, two-thirds to the royal chamber, and the other third to the accuser or informer:* what a fine bait! *And in case of inability, five years in the galleys, and greater punishment, pecuniary or corporal, at the will of his Excellency.* Much obliged for all his favours.—

At these words the landlord reached the door of the court of the high-sheriff.

Here, as at all the other secretaries' offices, much business was going forward. Everywhere they were engaged in giving such orders as seemed most likely to pre-occupy the following day, to take away every pretext for discontent, to overcome the boldness of those who were anxious for fresh tumults, and to confirm power in the hands of those accustomed to exercise it. The soldiery round the house of the superintendent were increased, and the ends of the street were blockaded with timber, and barricaded with carts. They commanded all the bakers to make bread without intermission, and despatched couriers to the surrounding country, with orders to send corn into the city; while noblemen were stationed at every bakehouse, who repaired thither early in the morning to superintend the distribution, and to restrain the factious, by fair words, and the authority of their presence. But to give, as the saying is, one blow to the hoop and another to the cask, and to render their cajolings more efficient by a little awe, they thought also of taking measures to seize some one of the seditious: and this was principally the business of the high-sheriff, whose temper towards the insurrection and the insurgents the reader may imagine, when he is informed of the vegetable fomentation which it was found necessary to apply to one of the organs of his metaphysical profundity. His blood-hounds had been in the field from the beginning of the riot: and this self-styled Ambrogio Fusella was, as the landlord said, a disguised under-sheriff, sent about for the express purpose of catching in the act some one whom he could again recognize, whose motions he could watch, and whom he could keep in mind, so as to seize, either in the quiet of the evening or next morning. He had not heard four words of Renzo's harangue, before he had fixed upon him as a capital object —exactly his man. Finding, afterwards, that he was just fresh from the country, he had attempted the master-stroke of conducting him at once to the prison, as the safest inn in the city; but here he failed, as we have related. He could, however, bring back certain information of his name, surname, and country; besides a hundred other fine conjectural pieces of information; so that when the innkeeper arrived here to tell what he knew of Renzo, they were already better acquainted with him than he. He entered the usual apartment, and deposed that a stranger had arrived at his house to lodge, who could not be persuaded to declare his name.

'You've done your duty in giving us this information,' said a criminal notary, laying down his pen: 'But we know it already.'

—A strange mystery!—thought the host:—they must be wonderfully clever!—

'And we know, too,' continued the notary, 'this revered name!'

—The name, too! how have they managed it?—thought the landlord again.

'But you,' resumed the other, with a serious face, 'you don't tell all, candidly.'

'What more have I to say?'

'Ha! ha! we know very well that this fellow brought to your inn a quantity of stolen bread—plundered, acquired by robbery and sedition.'

'A man comes, with one loaf in his pocket; do you think I know where he went to get it? for, to speak as on my death-bed, I can positively affirm that I saw but one loaf.'

'There! always excusing and defending yourself: one would think, to hear you, everybody was honest. How can you prove that his bread was fairly obtained?'

'Why am I to prove it? I don't meddle with it; I am an innkeeper.'

'You cannot, however, deny that this customer of yours had the temerity to utter injurious words against the proclamations, and to make improper and shameful jokes on the arms of his Excellency.'

'Pardon me, sir: how can he be called my customer, when this is the first time I've ever seen him? It was the devil (under your favour) that sent him to my house: and if I had known him, you, sir, know well enough I should have had no occasion to ask his name.'

'Well: in your inn, in your presence, inflammatory speeches have been uttered, unadvised words, seditious propositions; murmurs, grumbles, outcries.'

'How can you expect, my good sir, that I should attend to the extravagances which so many noisy fellows, talking all at the same time, may chance to utter? I must attend to my interest, for I'm only badly off. And besides, your worship knows well enough that those who are lavish of their tongues are generally ready with their fists too, particularly when there are so many together, and . . .'

'Ay, ay; leave them alone to talk and fight: to-morrow you'll see if their tricks have gone out of their heads. What do you think?'

'I think nothing about it.'

'That the mob will have got the upper hand in Milan?'

'Oh, just so.'

'We shall see, we shall see.'

'I understand very well: the king will be always king; and he that is fined will be fined: but the poor father of a family naturally wishes to escape. Your honours have the power, and it belongs to you.'

'Have you many people still in your house?'

'A world of them.'

'And this customer of yours, what is he doing? Does he still continue to be clamorous, to excite the people, and arouse sedition?'

'That stranger, your worship means: he's gone to bed.'

'Then, you've many people . . . Well, take care not to let them go away.'

—Am I to be a constable?—thought the landlord, without replying either negatively or affirmatively.

'Go home again, and be careful,' resumed the notary.

'I've always been careful. Your honour can say whether I have ever made any opposition to justice.'

'Well, well; and don't think that justice has lost its power.'

'I! For Heaven's sake; I think nothing: I only attend to my business.'

'The old song: you've never anything else to say.'

'What else would your worship have me say? truth is but one.'

'Well, we will remember what you have deposed; if the case comes on, you will have to give more particular information to justice about whatever they may choose to ask you.'

'What can I depose further? I know nothing. I have scarcely head enough to attend to my own business.'

'Take care you don't let him go.'

'I hope that his worship the high-sheriff will be informed that I came immediately to discharge my duty. Your honour's humble servant.'

By break of day, Renzo had been snoring for about seven hours, and was still, poor fellow, fast asleep, when two rough shakes at either arm, and a voice at the foot of the bed, calling, 'Lorenzo Tramaglino!' recalled him to his senses. He shook himself, stretched his arms, and with difficulty opening his eyes, saw a man standing before him at the foot of the bed, dressed in black, and two others armed, one on the right and the other on the left of his pillow. Between surprise, not being fully awake, and the stupidity occasioned by the wine of the night before, he lay, for a moment, as if bewildered; and then, thinking he was dreaming, and not being very well pleased with his dream, he shook himself so as to awake thoroughly.

'Ah! have you heard, for once, Lorenzo Tramaglino?' said the man with the black cloak, the very notary of the night before. 'Up; up, then; get up, and come with us.'

'Lorenzo Tramaglino!' said Renzo: 'What does this mean? What do you want with me? Who's told you my name?'

'Less talk, and up with you directly,' said one of the bailiffs who stood at his side, taking him again by the arm.

'Ah, eh! what oppression is this?' cried Renzo, withdrawing his arm. 'Landlord! ho, landlord!'

'Shall we carry him off in his shirt?' said the bailiff again, looking towards the notary.

'Did you hear that?' said he to Renzo: 'they'll do so, if you don't get up as quick as thought, and come with us.'

'And what for?' asked Renzo.

'The *what for* you will hear from the high-sheriff.'

'I? I'm an honest man; I've done nothing; and I'm astonished . . .'

'So much the better for you—so much the better for you; for then you may be discharged with two words, and may go about your own business.'

'Let me go now,' said Renzo: 'I've nothing to do with justice.'

'Come, let us finish the business,' said one of the bailiffs.

'Shall we carry him off?' said the other.

'Lorenzo Tramaglino!' said the notary.

'How do you know my name, sir?'

'Do your duty,' said the notary to the bailiffs, who immediately laid hands on Renzo to pull him out of bed.

'Hey! don't you touch a hair of an honest fellow, or! . . . I know how to dress myself.'

'Then dress yourself, and get up directly,' said the notary.

'I'm getting up,' replied Renzo; and he began, in fact, to gather up his clothes, which were scattered here and there on the bed, like the relics of a shipwreck on the shore. And beginning to dress himself, he continued: 'But I'm not inclined to go to the high-sheriff, not I. I've nothing to do with him. Since you unjustly put this affront upon me, I should like to be conducted to Ferrer. I know him; I know that he's a gentleman, and he's under some obligation to me.'

'Yes, yes, my good fellow, you shall be conducted to Ferrer,' replied the notary. In other circumstances he would have laughed heartily at such a proposal; but this was not a time for merriment. In coming hither, he had noticed in the streets a movement which could not easily be defined, as the remainder of the old insurrection not entirely suppressed, or the beginning of a new one: the streets were full of people, some walking in parties, some standing in groups. And now, without seeming to do so, or at least trying not to show it, he was anxiously listening, and fancied that the murmur continued to increase. This made him desirous to get off; but he also wished to take Renzo away willingly and quietly; since, if he had declared war against him, he could not have been sure, on reaching the street, of not finding three to one against him. He, therefore, winked at the bailiffs to have patience, and not to irritate the youth, while he also endeavoured to soothe him with fair words. Renzo busied himself, while dressing as quickly as possible, in recalling the confused remembrances of the day before, and at last conjectured, with tolerable certainty, that the proclamation, and the name and surname, must be the cause of this disagreeable occurrence; but how ever did this fellow know his name? And what on earth could have happened that night, for justice to have gained such confidence as come and lay hands on one of those honest youths who, only the day before, had such a voice in the assembly, and who could not all be asleep now? for he also observed the increasing bustle in the street. He looked at the countenance of the notary, and there perceived the irresolution which he vainly endeavoured to conceal. At last, as well to satisfy his conjectures, and sound the officers, as to gain time, and even attempt a blow, he said, 'I understand well enough the origin of all this; it is all from love of the name and surname. Last night I certainly was a little muddled:

these landlords have sometimes very treacherous wines; and some-times, as I say, you know, when wine passes through the medium of words, it will have its say too. But if this is all, I am now ready to give you every satisfaction; and, besides, you know my name already. Who on earth told you it?'

'Bravo, my boy, bravo!' replied the notary, coaxingly; 'I see you've some sense; and believe me, who am in the business, that you're wiser than most. It is the best way of getting out of the difficulty quickly and easily; and with such good dispositions, in two words you will be dismissed and set at liberty. But I, do you see, my good fellow, have my hands tied; I cannot release you, as I should like to do. Come, be quick and come along with a good heart; for when they see who you are . . . and then I will tell . . . Leave it to me . . . Enough; be quick, my good fellow.'

'Ah! you cannot! I understand,' said Renzo; and he continued to dress himself, repulsing, by signs, the intimations of the bailiffs, that they would carry him off if he were not very expeditious.

'Shall we pass by the square of the cathedral?' asked he.

'Wherever you like; the shortest way, to set you the sooner at liberty,' said the notary, vexed in his heart, that he must let this mysterious inquiry of Renzo's pass, which might have served as the subject for a hundred interrogatives.—When one is born to be unfortunate!—thought he.—Just see; a fellow falls into my hands, who, plainly enough, likes nothing better than to talk; and if he could have a little time, he would confess all one wants, without the aid of a rope—*extra formam,* to speak academically, in the way of friendly chit-chat; the very man to take to prison ready examined, without his being at all aware of it; and he must just fall into my hands at this unfortunate moment. Well! there's no help for it,—he continued, listening attentively, and tossing his head backwards —there's no remedy; it's likely to be a worse day than yesterday.— What gave rise to this thought, was an extraordinary noise he heard in the street, and he could not resist opening the window to take a peep at it. He saw that it was a group of citizens, who, on being required by a patrol of soldiers to disperse, had at first given angry words in reply, and had finally separated in murmuring dissatisfac-tion; and, what appeared to the notary a fatal sign, the soldiers behaved to them with much civility. Having closed the window, he stood for a moment in perplexity, whether he should finish his undertaking, or leave Renzo in the care of the two bailiffs, while he ran to the high-sheriff to give him an account of his difficulty.—But,— thought he, directly,—they'll set me down for a coward, a base rascal, who ought to execute orders. We are in the ball-room, and we must dance. Curse the throng! What a miserable business!—

Renzo now stood between the two satellites, having one on each side; the notary beckoned to them not to use too much force, and said to him, 'Courage, like a good fellow; let us be off, and make haste.'

Renzo, however, was feeling, looking, thinking. He was now entirely dressed, excepting his jacket, which he held in one hand, and feeling with the other in his pockets; 'Oho!' said he, looking at the notary with a very significant expression; 'here there were some pence, and a letter, my good sir!'

'Everything shall be punctually restored to you,' said the notary, 'when these few formalities are properly executed. Let us go, let us go.'

'No, no, no,' said Renzo, shaking his head; 'that won't do; I want my money, my good sir. I will give an account of my doings; but I want my money.'

'I'll show you that I trust you; here, and be quick,' said the notary, drawing out of his bosom the sequestered articles, and handing them to Renzo with a sigh. Renzo received them, and put them into his pocket, muttering between his teeth: 'Stand off! you've associated so much with thieves, that you've learnt a little of their business.' The bailiffs could no longer restrain their impatience, but the notary curbed them with a glance, saying to himself,—If thou succeedest in setting foot within that threshold, thou shalt pay for this with interest, that thou shalt.—

While Renzo was putting on his jacket, and taking up his hat, the notary beckoned to one of the bailiffs to lead the way downstairs; the prisoner came next behind him, then the other kind friend, and he himself brought up the rear. On reaching the kitchen, and while Renzo was saying; 'And this blessed landlord, where is he fled to?' the notary made a sign to the two police officers, who, seizing each a hand, proceeded hastily to secure his wrists with certain instruments, called, in the hypocritical figures of euphemism, *ruffles*—in plain language, handcuffs. These consisted—we are sorry that we are obliged to descend to particulars unworthy of historical gravity, but perspicuity requires it—they consisted of a small cord, a little longer than the usual size of a wrist, having at the ends two little bits of wood—two tallies, so to say—two small straight pegs. The cord encircled the wrist of the patient; the pieces of wood, passed through the middle and third fingers, were shut up in the hand of the captor, so that by twisting them, he could tighten the bandage at pleasure; and thus he possessed means, not only of securing his prisoner, but also of torturing the refractory; to do which more effectually, the cord was full of knots.

Renzo struggled, and cried, 'What treachery is this? To an honest man! . . .'

But the notary, who had fair words at hand on every disagreeable occasion, replied, 'Have patience, they only do their duty. What would you have? They are only formalities; and we can't always treat people as we would wish. If we don't do as we're bid, it will fare badly with us, and worse with you. Have patience!'

While he was speaking, the two bailiffs gave a sudden twitch at the handcuffs. Renzo bore it as a restive horse bears the jerk of a severe bit, and exclaimed, 'Patience!'

'Brave youth!' said the notary; 'this is the best way of getting off well. What would you have? It is an annoyance, I know; but if you behave well, you'll very soon be rid of it. And, since I see that you're well-disposed, and I feel inclined to help you, I'll give you another little piece of advice for your good. You may believe me, for I'm practised in these matters;—go straightforward, without looking about, or attracting observation; so no one will notice you, no one will observe what you are, and you will preserve your honour. An hour hence you will be set at liberty. There is so much to be done, that they, too, will be in a hurry to have done with you; and, besides, I will speak . . . You shall go about your own business, and nobody will know that you've been in the hands of justice. And you,' continued he, turning to the two bailiffs with a severe countenance, 'take care you don't do him any harm; for I will protect him. You are obliged to do your duty; but remember that this is an honest man, a civil youth, who will shortly be at liberty, and who has some regard for his honour. Let nothing appear but that you are three honest men walking together.' And, in an imperative tone, and with a threatening look, he concluded: 'You understand me?' He then turned to Renzo, his brow smoothed, and his face rendered, in an instant, more cheerful and pleasant, which seemed to say, 'What capital friends we are!' and whispered to him again, 'Be careful; do as I tell you; don't look about you; trust one who wishes you well; and now let us go.' And the convoy moved off.

Renzo, however, believed none of these fine words; nor that the notary wished him well more than the bailiffs, nor that he was so mighty anxious about his reputation, nor that he had any intention of helping him; not a word of all this did he believe: he understood well enough that the good man, fearing some favourable opportunity for making his escape might present itself in the way, laid before him all these flattering inducements, to divert him from watching for and profiting by it. So that all these exhortations served no other purpose than to determine Renzo more decidedly on a course which he had indistinctly meditated, viz. to act exactly contrary to them.

Let no one hereby conclude that the notary was an inexperienced novice in his trade, for he will be much deceived. Our historian, who seems to have been among his friends, says that he was a matriculated knave; but at this moment his mind was greatly agitated. With a calm mind, I venture to say, he would have laughed at any one who, to induce others to do something which he himself mistrusted, would have gone about to suggest and inculcate it so eagerly, under the miserable pretence of giving him the disinterested advice of a friend. But it is a general tendency of mankind, when they are agitated and perplexed, and discern what another can do to relieve them from their perplexities, to implore it of him eagerly and perseveringly, and under all kinds of pretexts; and when villains are agitated and perplexed, they also fall under this common rule. Hence it is that, in similar circumstances, they generally make so poor a figure. Those masterly inventions, those cunning subtleties, by which they are accustomed to conquer, which have become to them almost a second nature, and which, put in operation at the proper time, and conducted with the necessary tranquillity and serenity of mind, strike a blow so surely and secretly, and, discovered even after the success, receive such universal applause; these, when their unlucky employers are in trouble, are hastily and tumultuously made use of, without either judgment or dexterity; so that a third party, who observes them labouring and busying themselves in this manner, is moved to compassion or provoked to laughter; and those whom they attempt to impose upon, though less crafty than themselves, easily perceive the game they are playing, and gain light from their artifices, which may be turned against them. It can never, therefore, be sufficiently inculcated upon knaves by profession, always to maintain their *sang froid,* or, what is better still, never to get themselves into perplexing circumstances.

No sooner, therefore, were they in the street, than Renzo began to look eagerly in every direction, throwing himself about, bending his head forward, and listening attentively. There was, however, no extraordinary concourse; and though a certain air of sedition might easily be discerned on the face of more than one passer-by, yet every one went straight on his way; and of sedition, properly speaking, there was none.

'Prudence! prudence!' murmured the notary, behind his back: 'Your honour, your reputation, my good fellow!' But when Renzo, listening to three men who were approaching with excited looks, heard them speaking of a bake-house, concealed flour, and justice, he began to make signs at them by his looks, and to cough in such a way as indicated anything but a cold. These looked more attentively at the convoy, and then stopped; others who came up, stopped also; others who had passed by, turned round on hearing the noise, and retracing their steps, joined the party.

'Take care of yourself; prudence, my lad; it is worse for you, you see; don't spoil all: honour, reputation,' whispered the notary. Renzo was still more intractable. The bailiffs, after consulting with each other by a look, and thinking they were doing quite right, (everybody is liable to err), again twisted the manacles.

'Ah! ah! ah!' cried the tortured victim: the by-standers gathered close round at the cry; others arrived from every part of the street, and the convoy came to a stand.' He is a dissolute fellow,' whispered the notary to those who had gathered around: 'A thief taken in the act! Draw back and make way for justice!' But Renzo, seeing this was the moment—seeing the bailiffs turn white, or at least pale,— If I don't help myself now,—thought he,—it's my own fault.—And he immediately called out, 'My friends! they are carrying me off, because yesterday I shouted "Bread and justice!" I've done nothing; I am an honest man! help me; don't abandon me, my friends!'

A murmur of approbation, followed by more explicit cries in his favour, arose in reply; the bailiffs first commanded, then asked, then begged the nearest to make way and let them pass; but the crowd only continued still more to trample and push forward. The bailiffs, seeing their danger, let go of the manacles, and only endeavoured to lose themselves in the throng, so as to escape without observation. The notary earnestly longed to do the same; but this was more difficult on account of his black cloak. The poor man, pale in face and dismayed in heart, tried to make himself as diminutive as possible, and writhed his body about so as to slip away through the crowd; but he could not raise his eyes, without seeing a storm gathering against him. He tried every method of appearing a stranger who, passing there by chance, had found himself entangled in the crowd, like a bit of straw in the ice; and encountering a man face to face, who looked at him fixedly with a more terrible countenance than the others, he, composing his face to a smile, with a look of great simplicity, demanded, 'What is all this stir?'

'Uh! you ugly raven!' replied the man. 'A raven! a raven!' resounded around. Pushes were added to cries, so that, in short, partly with his own legs, partly by the elbows of others, he obtained what lay nearest to his heart at that moment, a safe exit from the pressing multitude.

CHAPTER XVI

'ESCAPE, escape, my good fellow! here is a convent; there is a church; this way, that way,' was heard by Renzo on every side. As to escaping, the reader may judge whether he would have need of advice on this head. From the first moment that the hope of extricating himself from the talons of the police had crossed his mind, he had begun to form his plans, and resolved, if he succeeded in this one, to flee without delay, not only out of the city, but also out of the duchy of Milan.—For,—thought he,—they have my name on their black books, however on earth they've got it; and with my name and surname, they can seize me whenever they like.—As to an asylum, he would not willingly have recourse to one, unless, indeed, he were reduced to extremity;—For, if I can be a bird of the woods,—thought he again,—I won't be a bird of the cage.—He had therefore designed as his limit and place of refuge, a village in the territory of Bergamo, where his cousin Bortolo resided, who, the reader may remember, had frequently solicited Renzo to remove thither. But now the point was how to find his way there. Left in an unknown part of a city almost equally unknown, Renzo could not even tell by which gate he should pass to go to Bergamo; and when he had learnt this, he still did not know the way to the gate. He stood for a moment in doubt whether to ask direction of his liberators; but as, in the short time he had had for reflection on his circumstances, many strong suspicions had crossed his mind of that obliging sword-cutler, the father of four children, he was not much inclined to reveal his intentions to a large crowd, where there might be others of the same stamp; he quickly decided, therefore, to get away from that neighbourhood as fast as he could; and he might afterwards ask his way in a part where nobody would know who he was, or why he asked it. Merely saying, then, to his deliverers, 'Thank you, thank you, my friends:

blessings on you!' and escaping through the space that was immediately cleared for him, he took to his heels, and off he went, up
one little street, and down another, running for some time without
knowing whither. When he thought he was far enough off, he
slackened his pace, not to excite suspicion, and began looking around
to choose some person of whom he could make inquiries—some face
that would inspire confidence. But here, also, there was need of
caution. The inquiry in itself was suspicious; time pressed; the
bailiffs, immediately on making their escape from this rencontre,
would, undoubtedly, renew their search of the fugitive; the rumour
of his flight might even have reached hither: and in such a concourse,
Renzo might carefully scrutinize a dozen physiognomies, before he
could meet with a countenance that seemed likely to suit his purpose. That fat fellow, standing at the door of his shop, with legs
extended, and his hands behind his back, the prominent corpulency
of this person projecting beyond the doorway, and supporting his
great double chin; who, from mere idleness, was employing himself
in alternately raising his tremendous bulk upon his toes, and letting
it sink again upon his heels—he looked too much like an inquisitive
gossip, who would have returned interrogatories instead of replies.
That other, advancing with fixed eyes and a drooping lip, instead of
being able expeditiously and satisfactorily to direct another in his
way, scarcely seemed to know his own. That tall, stout boy, who,
to say the truth, certainly looked intelligent enough, appeared also
rather maliciously inclined, and probably would have taken a mischievous delight in sending a poor stranger exactly the opposite way
to the one he was inquiring after. So true is it that, to a man in
perplexity, almost everything seems to be a new perplexity! At
last, fixing his eyes on one who was approaching in evident haste,
he thought that he, having probably some pressing business in hand,
would give an immediate and direct answer, to get rid of him; and
hearing him talking to himself, he deemed that he must be an
undesigning person. He, therefore, accosted him with the question,
'Will you be good enough to tell me, sir, which direction I should
take to go to Bergamo?'

'To go to Bergamo? The Porta Orientale.'

'Thank you, sir: and to the Porta Orientale?'

'Take this street to the left; you will come out into the square of the cathedral; then . . .'

'That will do, sir; I know the rest. Heaven reward you.' And on he went by the way that had been pointed out to him. His director looked after him for a moment, and comparing in his mind his way of walking, with the inquiry, thought within himself,—Either he is after somebody, or somebody is after him.—

Renzo reached the square of the cathedral, crossed it, passed by a heap of cinders and extinguished combustibles, and recognized the relics of the bonfire at which he had assisted the day before; he then passed along the flight of steps leading up to the cathedral, and saw again the bakehouse of the Crutches half demolished, and guarded by soldiers; still he proceeded onward, and, by the street which he had already traversed with the crowd, arrived in front of the convent of the Capuchins, where, glancing at the square and the church-door, he said to himself with a deep sigh:—That friar yesterday gave me good advice, when he bid me go wait in the church, and employ myself profitably there.—

Here he stopped a moment to reconnoitre the gate through which he had to pass; and seeing, even at that distance, many soldiers on guard, his imagination also being rather overstrained, (one must pity him; for he had had enough to unsettle it), he felt a kind of repugnance at encountering the passage. Here he was, with a place of refuge close at hand, where, with the letter of recommendation, he would have been well received; and he felt strongly tempted to enter it. But he quickly summoned up his courage, and thought:—A bird of the woods, as long as I can. Who knows me? Certainly the bailiffs cannot have divided themselves into enough pieces to come and watch for me at every gate.—He looked behind him to see if they were coming in that direction, and saw neither them, nor any one who seemed to be taking notice of him. He, therefore, set off again, slackened the pace of those unfortunate legs which, with their own good will, would have kept constantly on the run, when it was much better only to walk; and, proceeding leisurely along, whistling in an under-tone, he arrived at the gate. Just at the entrance there was a party of police-officers, together with a rein-forcement of Spanish soldiers; but these all had their attention directed to the outside, to forbid entrance to such as, hearing the news of an insurrection, would flock thither like vultures to a deserted field of battle; so that Renzo, quietly walking on, with his eyes bent to the ground, and with a gait between that of a traveller and a common passenger, passed the threshold without any one speaking a word to him: but his heart beat violently. Seeing a little street to the right, he took that way to avoid the high road, and continued his course for some time before he ventured to look round.

On he went; he came to cottages and villages, which he passed without asking their names: he felt certain of getting away from Milan, and hoped he was going towards Bergamo, and this was enough for him at present. From time to time he kept glancing behind him, while walking onwards, occasionally loooking at and rubbing one or other of his wrists, which were still a little benumbed, and marked with a red line from the pressure of the manacles. His thoughts were, as every one may imagine, a confused medley of repentance, disputes, disquietude, revenge, and other more tender feelings; it was a wearying endeavour to recall what he had said and done the night before, to unravel the mysterious part of his mournful adventures, and, above all, how they had managed to discover his name. His suspicions naturally fell on the sword-cutler, to whom he remembered having spoken very frankly. And retracing the way in which he had drawn him into conversation, together with his whole behaviour, and those proffers which always ended in wishing to know something about him, his suspicions were changed almost to certainty. He had, besides, some faint recollection of continuing to chatter after the departure of the cutler; but with whom? guess it, ye crickets; of what? his memory, spite of his efforts, could not tell him this: it could only remind him that he had not been at all himself that evening. The poor fellow was lost in these speculations: he was like a man who has affixed his signature to a number of blank formulæ, and committed them to the care of one he esteemed honest and honourable, and having discovered him to be a shuffling meddler, wishes to ascertain the state of his affairs. What can he discover? It is a chaos. Another painful speculation was how to form some design for the future that would not be a merely aërial project, or at least a melancholy one.

By and by, however, he became still more anxious about finding his way; and after walking for some distance at a venture, he saw the necessity of making some inquiries. Yet he felt particularly reluctant to utter the word 'Bergamo,' as if there were something suspicious or dangerous in the name, and could not bring himself to pronounce it. He resolved, however, to ask direction, as he had before done at Milan, of the first passenger whose countenance suited his fancy, and he shortly met with one.

'You are out of the road,' replied his guide; and having thought a moment, he pointed out to him, partly by words and partly by gestures, the way he should take to regain the high road. Renzo thanked him for his directions, and pretended to follow them, by actually taking the way he had indicated, with the intention of almost reaching the public road, and then, without losing sight of it, to keep parallel with its course as far as possible, but not to set foot within it. The design was easier to conceive than to effect, and the result was, that, by going thus from right to left in a zigzag course, partly following the directions he obtained by the way, partly correcting them by his own judgment, and adapting them to his intentions, and partly allowing himself to be guided by the lanes he traversed, our fugitive had walked perhaps twelve miles, when he was not more than six distant from Milan; and as to Bergamo, it was a great chance if he were not going away from it. He began at last to perceive that by this method he would never come to an end, and determined to find out some remedy. The plan that occurred to his mind was to get the name of some village bordering on the confines, which he could reach by the neighbouring roads: and by asking his way thither, he could collect information, without leaving behind him the name of Bergamo, which seemed to him to savour so strongly of flight, escape, and crime.

While ruminating on the best way of obtaining these instructions without exciting suspicion, he saw a bush hanging over the door of a solitary cottage just outside a little village. He had for some time felt the need of recruiting his strength, and thinking that this would be the place to serve two purposes at once, he entered. There was no one within but an old woman, with her distaff at her side, and the spindle in her hand. He asked for something to eat, and was offered a little *stracchino*[1] and some good wine; he gladly accepted the food, but excused himself from taking any wine, feeling quite an abhorrence of it, after the errors it had made him guilty of the night before; and then sat down, begging the old woman to make haste. She served up his meal in a moment, and then began to tease her customer with inquiries, both about himself, and the grand doings at Milan, the report of which had already reached here. Renzo not only contrived to parry and elude her inquiries with much dexterity, but even profited by the difficulty, and made the curiosity of the old woman subservient to his intentions, when she asked him where he was going to.

'I have to go to many places,' replied he: 'and if I can find a moment of time, I want to pass a little while at that village, rather a large one, on the road to Bergamo, near the border, but in the territory of Milan . . . What do they call it?'—There must be one there, surely,—thought he, in the mean while.

'Gorgonzola you mean,' replied the old woman.

'Gorgonzola!' repeated Renzo, as if to imprint the word better on his memory. 'Is it very far from here?' resumed he.

'I don't know exactly; it may be ten or twelve miles. If one of my sons were here, he could tell you.'

'And do you think I can go by these pleasant lanes without taking the high road? There is such a dust there! such a shocking dust! It's so long since it rained!'

'I fancy you can: you can ask at the first village you come to, after turning to the right.' And she named it.

'That's well,' said Renzo; and rising, he took in his hand a piece of bread remaining from his scanty meal, of a very different quality to that which he had found the day before at the foot of the cross of San Dionigi; and paying the reckoning, he set off again, following the road to the right hand. By taking care not to wander from it more than was needful, and with the name of Gorgonzola in his mouth, he proceeded from village to village, until, about an hour before sunset, he arrived there.

During his walk, he had resolved to make another stop here, and

[1] A kind of soft cheese.

to take some rather more substantial refreshment. His body also craved a little rest; but rather than gratify this desire, Renzo would have sunk in a swoon upon the ground. He proposed gaining some information at the inn about the distance of the Adda, to ascertain dexterously if there was any cross-road that led to it, and to set off again, even at this hour, immediately after his repast. Born and brought up at the second source, so to say, of this river, he had often heard it said, that at a certain point, and for some considerable distance, it served as a boundary between the Milanese and Venetian states; he had no very distinct idea of where this boundary commenced, or how far it extended; but, for the present, his principal object was to get beyond it. If he did not succeed in reaching it that evening, he resolved to walk as long as the night and his strength would allow him, and afterwards to wait the approaching day in a field, or a wilderness, or wherever God pleased, provided it were not an inn.

After walking a few paces along the street at Gorgonzola, he noticed a sign, entered the inn, and on the landlord's advancing to meet him, ordered something to eat, and a small measure of wine; the additional miles he had passed, and the time of day, having overcome his extreme and fanatical hatred of this beverage. 'I must beg you to be quick,' added he; 'for I'm obliged to go on my way again very soon.' This he said not only because it was the truth, but also for fear the host, imagining that he was going to pass the night there, should come and ask him his name and surname, and where he came from, and on what business . . . But enough!

The landlord replied that he should be waited upon immediately; and Renzo sat down at the end of the table, near the door, the usual place of the bashful.

Some loungers of the village had assembled in this room, who, after having argued over, and discussed, and commented upon, the grand news from Milan of the preceding day, were now longing to know a little how matters were going on; the more so, as their first information was rather fitted to irritate their curiosity than to satisfy it; a sedition, neither subdued nor triumphant; suspended, rather than terminated, by the approach of night; a defective thing; the conclusion of an act, rather than of a drama. One of these detached himself from the party, and seating himself by the new comer, asked him if he came from Milan.

'I?' said Renzo, in a tone of surprise, to gain time for a reply.

'You, if the question is allowable.'

Renzo, shaking his head, compressing his lips, and uttering an inarticulate sound, replied; 'Milan, from what I hear . . . from what they say around . . . is not exactly a place to go at present, unless in case of great necessity.'

'Does the uproar continue, then, to-day?' demanded his inquisitive companion more eagerly.

'I must have been there to know that,' said Renzo.

'But you—don't you come from Milan?'

'I come from Liscate,' replied the youth, promptly, who, in the mean while, had decided upon his reply. Strictly speaking, he had come from there, because he had passed it; and he had learnt the name from a traveller on the road, who had mentioned that village as the first he must pass on his way to Gorgonzola.

'Oh!' said his friend, in that tone which seems to say: You'd have done better if you had come from Milan; but patience. 'And at Liscate,' added he, 'did you hear nothing about Milan?'

'There may very likely have been somebody who knew something about it,' replied the mountaineer, 'but I heard nothing.' And this was proffered in that particular manner which seems to mean: I've finished. The querist returned to his party, and a moment afterwards, the landlord came to set out his meal.

'How far is it from here to the Adda?' asked Renzo, in an undertone, with the air of one who is half asleep, and an indifferent manner, such as we have already seen him assume on some other occasions.

'To the Adda—to cross it?' said the host.

'That is . . . yes . . . to the Adda.'

'Do you want to cross by the bridge of Cassano, or the Ferry of Canonica?'

'Oh, I don't mind where . . . I only ask from curiosity.'

'Well, I mention these, because they are the places gentlemen generally choose, and people who can give an account of themselves.'

'Very well; and how far is it?'

'You may reckon that to either one or the other, it is somewhere about six miles, more or less.'

'Six miles! I didn't know that,' said Renzo. 'Well,' resumed he, with a still greater air of indifference, almost amounting to affectation, 'well, I suppose there are other places for crossing, if anybody is inclined to take a short cut?'

'There are, certainly,' replied the landlord, fixing his eyes upon him with a look full of malicious curiosity. This was enough to silence all the other inquiries which our youth had ready on his lips. He drew his plate before him, and, looking at the small measure of wine which the landlord had set down on the table, said, 'Is the wine pure?'

'As gold,' said the host; 'ask all the people of the village and neighbourhood, for they know it; and, besides, you can taste yourself.' So saying, he turned towards his other customers.

'Plague on these landlords!' exclaimed Renzo in his heart; 'the more I know of them, the worse I find them.' However, he began to eat very heartily, listening at the same time, without appearing to pay any attention, to see what he could learn, to discover what was the general impression here about the great event in which he had had no little share; and, above all, to ascertain if, amongst these talkers, there was one honest man, of whom a poor fellow might venture to make inquiries, without fear of getting into a scrape, and being forced to talk about his own doings.

'But,' said one, 'this time, it seems clear the Milanese wanted to bring about a very good thing. Well; to-morrow, at latest, we shall know something.'

'I'm sorry I didn't go to Milan this morning,' said another.

'If you go to-morrow, I'll go with you,' said a third; 'so will I,' said another; 'and I,' said another.

'What I want to know,' resumed the first, 'is, whether these Milanese gentlemen will think of us poor people out of the city; or if they'll only get good laws made for themselves. Do you know how they do, eh? They are all proud citizens, every one for himself; and we strangers mightn't be Christians.'

'We've mouths, too, either to eat, or to give our own opinions,' said another, with a voice as modest as the proposition was daring; 'and when things have gone a little further . . . ' But he did not think fit to finish the sentence.

'There's corn hidden, not only at Milan,' another was beginning, with a dark and designing countenance, when they heard the trampling of a horse approaching; they ran to the door, and having discovered who it was, they all went out to meet him. It was a Milanese merchant who generally passed the night at this inn, in journeying two or three times a year to Bergamo on business; and as he almost always found the same company there, they were all his acquaintances. They now crowded around him; one took his bridle, another his stirrup, and saluted him with, 'Welcome.'

'I'm glad to see you.'

'Have you had a good journey?'

'Very good; and how are you all?'

'Pretty well, pretty well. What news from Milan?'

'Ah! you are always for news,' said the merchant, dismounting, and leaving his horse in the care of a boy. 'And, besides,' continued he, entering the door with the rest of the party, 'by this time you know it, perhaps, better than I do.'

'I assure you we know nothing,' said more than one, laying his hand on his heart.

'Is it possible?' said the merchant. 'Then you shall hear some fine . . . or rather, some bad news. Hey, landlord, is my usual bed at liberty? Very well; a glass of wine, and my usual meal; be quick, for I must go to bed early, and set off to-morrow morning very early, so as to get to Bergamo by dinner-time. And you,' continued he, sitting down at the opposite end of the table to where Renzo was seated, silently but attentively listening, 'you don't know about all the diabolical doings of yesterday?'

'Yes, we heard something about yesterday.'

'You see now!' rejoined the merchant; 'you know the news. I thought, when you are stationed here all day, to watch and sound everybody that comes by . . .'

'But to-day: how have matters gone to-day?'

'Ah, to-day. Do you know nothing about to-day?'

'Nothing whatever; nobody has come by.'

'Then let me wet my lips; and afterwards I'll tell you about everything. You shall hear.' Having filled his glass, he took it in his right hand, and, lifting up his mustachios with the first two fingers of his left, and then settling his beard with the palm, he drank it off, and continued:—'There was little wanting, my worthy friends, to make to-day as rough a day as yesterday, or worse. I can scarcely believe it true that I am here to tell you about it; for I had once put aside every thought of my journey, to stay and take care of my unfortunate shop.'

'What was the matter, then?' said one of his auditors.

'What was the matter? you shall hear.' And, carving the meat that was set before him, he began to eat, at the same time continuing his narration. The crowd, standing at both sides of the table, listened to him with open mouths; and Renzo, apparently giving no heed to what he said, listened, perhaps, more eagerly than any of the others, as he slowly finished the last few mouthfuls.

'This morning, then, those rascals who made such a horrible up-roar yesterday, repaired to the appointed places of meeting (there was already an understanding between them, and everything was arranged); they united together, and began again the old story of going from street to street, shouting to collect a crowd. You know it is like when one sweeps a house—with respect be it spoken—the heap of dust increases as one goes along. When they thought they had assembled enough people, they set off towards the house of the superintendent of provisions; as if the treatment they gave him yesterday was not enough, to a gentleman of his character—the vil-lains! And the lies they told about him! All inventions: he is a worthy, exact gentleman; and I may say so, for I am very intimate with him, and serve him with cloth for his servants' livery. They proceeded then towards this house; you ought to see what a rabble, and what faces: just fancy their having passed my shop, with faces that . . . the Jews of the *Via Crucis* are nothing to them. And such things as they uttered! enough to make one stop one's ears, if it had not been that it might have turned to account in discovering one. They went forward then with the kind intention of plundering the house, but . . .' Here he raised his left hand and extended it in the air, placing the end of his thumb on the point of his nose.

'But?' said almost all his auditors.

'But,' continued the merchant, 'they found the street blockaded with planks and carts, and behind this barricado, a good file of soldiers, with their guns levelled, and the butt-ends resting on their shoulders. When they saw this preparation . . . What would you have done?'

'Turned back.'

'To be sure; and so did they. But just listen if it wasn't the devil that inspired them. They reached the *Cordusio,* and there saw the bake-house which they wanted to plunder the day before: here they were busy in distributing bread to their customers; there were noblemen there, ay, the very flower of the nobility, to watch that everything went on in good order; but the mob (they had the devil within them, I tell you, and besides, there were some whispering in their ears, and urging them on), the mob rushed in furiously; "seize away, and I will seize too:" in the twinkling of an eye, noblemen, bakers, customers, loaves, benches, counters, troughs, chests, bags, sieves, bran, flour, dough, all were turned upside down.'

'And the soldiers?'

'The soldiers had the vicar's house to defend; one cannot sing and carry the cross at the same time. It was all done in the twinkling of an eye, I tell you: off and away; everything that could be put to any use was carried off. And then they proposed again the beautiful scene of yesterday—dragging the rest to the square, and making a bonfire. They had already begun—the villains!—to carry some things out of the house, when one greater villain than the rest— what do you think was the proposal he made?'

'What?'

'What! to make a pile of everything in the shop, and to set fire to the heap and the house together. No sooner said than done . . .'

'Did they set fire to it?'

'Wait. A worthy man of the neighbourhood had an inspiration from Heaven. He ran up-stairs, sought for a crucifix, found one, and hung it in front of one of the windows; then he took two candles which had been blessed, lit them, and set them outside, on the window-sill, one on each side of the crucifix. The mob looked up. It must be owned, there is still some fear of God in Milan; everybody came to their senses. At least, I mean most of them; there were some, certainly, devils enough to have set fire to Paradise, for the sake of plunder; but, finding that the crowd was not of their opinion, they were obliged to abandon their design, and keep quiet. Just fancy now who arrived—all their Graces of the Cathedral, in procession, with the cross elevated, and in their canonical robes; and my lord the Arch-presbyter began preaching on one side, and my lord the Penitentiary on the other, and others again, scattered here and there: "But, good people; what would you do? is this the example you set your children? go home, go home; you shall have bread at a low price; if you'll only look you'll see that the rate is pasted up at every corner."'

'Was it so?'

'What? was it so? Do you think that their Graces of the Cathedral would come, in their magnificent robes, to tell them falsehoods?'

'And what did the people do?'

'They dispersed by degrees; some ran to the corners of the streets, and for those who could read, there was the fixed rate, sure enough. What do you think of it? eight ounces of bread for a penny.'

'What good luck!'

'*The proof of the pudding is in the eating.* How much flour do you think they have wasted yesterday and this morning? Enough to support the Duchy for two months.'

'Then they've made no good laws for us in the country?'

'What has been done at Milan is entirely at the expense of the city. I don't know what to say to you: it must be as God wills. Fortunately, the sedition is finished, for I haven't told you all yet; here comes the best part.'

'What is there besides?'

'Only, that, last evening, or this morning, I'm not sure which, many of the leaders have been seized, and four of them, it is known, are to be hung directly. No sooner did this get abroad, than everybody went home the shortest way, not to run the risk of becoming number five. When I left Milan, it looked like a convent of friars.'

'But will they really hang them?'

'Undoubtedly, and quickly, too,' replied the merchant.

'And what will the people do?' asked the same interrogator as had put the other question.

'The people will go to see them,' said the merchant. 'They had such a desire to see a Christian hanging in the open air, that they wanted—the vagabonds!—to despatch the superintendent of provisions in that way. By this exchange they will have four wretches, attended with every formality, accompanied by Capuchins, and by friars of the *buona morte*:[2] but they deserve it. It is an interference of Providence, you see; and it's a necessary thing. They were already beginning to divert themselves by entering the shops, and helping themselves without paying; if they'd let them go on so, after bread, wine would have had its turn, and so on from thing to thing. . . . You may imagine whether they would abandon so convenient a practice, of their own free will. And I can tell you, that was no very pleasant thought for an honest man keeping a shop.'

'Certainly not,' said one of his hearers. 'Certainly not,' replied the rest, in chorus.

'And,' continued the merchant, wiping his beard with the table-cloth, 'it had all been projected for some time: there was a league, you know.'

'A league, was there?'

'Yes, there was a league. All cabals formed by the Navarrines, by that French cardinal there, you know, with a half-Turkish name, who every day contrives something fresh to annoy the court of Spain. But, above all, he aims at playing some trick in Milan; for he knows well enough—the knave—that the strength of the king lies there.'

'Ay.'

'Shall I give you a proof of it? Those who've made the greatest noise were strangers; there were faces going about which had never before been seen in Milan. By the by, I forgot to tell you one thing

[2] 'A denomination usually given to the monks of the order of St. Paul, the first hermit. They are called *Brothers of death, Fratres à morte,* on account of a figure of a Death's head which they were always to have with them, to remind them continually of their last end. This order, by its constitutions, made in 1620, does not seem to have been established long before Pope Paul V. Louis XIII., in 1621, permitted them to settle in France. The order was, probably, suppressed by Pope Urban VIII. The fraternity of death buries such dead as are abandoned by their relations, and causes masses to be celebrated for them.'

which was told me for certain. The police had caught one of these fellows in an inn . . . ' Renzo, who had not lost a single syllable of this conversation, was taken with a cold shudder on hearing this chord touched, and almost slipped under the table before he thought of trying to contain himself. No one, however, perceived it; and the speaker, without interrupting his relation for a moment, had continued: 'They don't exactly know where he came from, who sent him, nor what kind of man he was, but he was certainly one of the leaders. Yesterday, in the midst of the uproar, he played the very devil; and then, not content with that, he must begin to harangue the people, and propose—a mere trifle!—to murder all the nobility! The great rascal! Who would support the poor if all the nobles were killed? The police, who had been watching him, laid hands upon him; they found on his person a great bundle of letters, and were leading him away to prison, but his companions, who were keeping guard round the inn, came in great numbers, and delivered him— the villain!'

'And what became of him?'

'It isn't known; he may be fled, or he may be concealed in Milan: they are people who have neither house nor home, and yet find lodging and a place of refuge everywhere; however, though the devil can and will help them, yet they may fall into the hands of justice when they least expect it; for when the pear is ripe it must fall. For the present, it is well known that the letters are in possession of government, and that the whole conspiracy is therein described; and they say that many people are implicated in it. This much is certain, that they have turned Milan upside down, and would have done much worse. It is said that the bakers are rogues: I know they are; but they ought to be hung in the course of justice. They say there is corn hidden; who doesn't know that? But it is the business of the government to keep a good look-out to bring it to light, and to hang the monopolists in company with the bakers. And if government does nothing, the city ought to remonstrate; and if they don't listen the first time, remonstrate again; for by dint of appeals they will get what they want; but not adopt the villainous practice of furiously entering shops and warehouses to get booty.'

Renzo's small meal had turned into poison. It seemed like an age before he could get out of, and away from, the inn and the village; and a dozen times, at least, he had said to himself: 'Now I may surely go.' But the fear of exciting suspicion, now increased beyond measure, and prevailing over every other thought, had kept him still nailed to his seat. In this perplexity, he thought the chatterer *must* at last stop talking about him, and determined in his own mind to make his escape as soon as another subject was started.

'For this reason,' said one of the party, 'knowing how these things go, and that honest men fare but badly in such disturbances, I wouldn't let my curiosity conquer, and have, therefore, remained quietly at home.'

'Neither would I move, for the same reason,' said another.

'I,' added a third, 'if I had happened by chance to be at Milan, I would have left any business whatever unfinished, and have returned home as quickly as possible. I have a wife and children; and, besides, to tell the truth, I don't like such stirs.'

At this moment the landlord, who had been eagerly listening with the rest, advanced towards the other end of the table to see what the stranger was doing. Renzo seized the opportunity, and beckoning to the host, asked for his account, settled it without dispute, though his purse was by this time very low; and without further delay, went directly to the door, passed the threshold, and taking care not to turn along the same road as that by which he had arrived, set off in the opposite direction, trusting to the guidance of Providence.

CHAPTER XVII

ONE wish is often enough to allow a man no peace; what, then, must two have been—one at war with the other? Our poor Renzo, as the reader knows, had had two such conflicting desires in his mind for several hours; the wish to make his escape, with the wish to remain undiscovered; and the unfortunate words of the merchant had increased both one and the other to an extravagant degree. His adventure, then, had got abroad! There were means, then, employed, to seize him! Who knew how many bailiffs were in the field to give him chase! or what orders had been forwarded to keep a watch in the villages, at the inn, on the roads! He reflected, however, that, after all, there were but two bailiffs who knew him, and that his name was not written upon his forehead; but then, again, a hundred stories he had heard rushed into his mind, of fugitives caught and discovered in many strange ways, recognized by their walk, by their suspicious air, and other unthought of tokens: everything excited his alarm. Although, as he left Gorgonzola, the tolling of the Avemaria sounded in his ears, and the increasing darkness every moment diminished his danger, yet it was very unwillingly that he took the high road, proposing to follow the first by-lane which seemed likely to bring him to the point he was so anxious to reach. At first, he occasionally met a traveller; but so full was his imagination of direful apprehensions, that he had not courage to detain any one to inquire his way.— That innkeeper said six miles,—thought he.—If, by taking these foot-paths and by-lanes, I make them eight, or even ten, my legs, which have lasted me so far, will manage these too. I'm certainly not going towards Milan, so I must be going towards the Adda. Walk away, then; sooner or later, I shall get there. The Adda has a good voice; and when once I'm near it, I shan't want anybody to point it out to me. If any boat is there, I'll cross directly; if not, I'll wait till morning, in a field, or on a tree, like the sparrows: better on a tree than in prison.—

Very soon, he saw a lane turning down to the left, and he pursued it.

At this hour, if he had met with any one, he would no longer have hesitated to address him; but he heard not a footstep of living creature. He followed, therefore, the windings of the lane, indulging, the mean while, in such reflections as these:

—I play the devil! I murder all the nobility! A packet of letters— I! My companions keeping guard around me! I'd give something to meet with that merchant face to face, on the other side of the Adda, (ah, when shall I get across that blessed Adda?) I'd make him stand, and ask him, at my convenience, where he had picked up all this fine information. Just please to be informed, my dear sir, that the thing went so and so; and that all the mischief I played was helping Ferrer, as if he had been my brother: know, moreover, that those rascals who to hear you talk, one would think were my friends, because once I said a word or two, like a good Christian, wanted to play me a very rough trick; know, too, that while you were taking care of your own shop, I was endangering my ribs to save your signor, the superintendent of provisions—a man I never either knew or saw in my life. Wait and see if I ever stir again to help gentlemen . . . It is true we ought to do it for our soul's good: they are our neighbours, too. And that great bundle of letters, where all the conspiracy was revealed, and which you know for certain is in the hands of government; sure enough, I couldn't show it you here without the help of the devil. Would you have any curiosity to see this mighty packet? Look here . . . A single letter! . . . Yes, my good sir, one letter only; and this letter, if you'd like to know, was written by a monk capable of instructing you in any point of doctrine you wish,—a monk, without doing you injustice, a single hair of whose beard is worth all yours put together; and this letter, I should like to tell you, is written, you see, to another monk, also a man . . . Just see, now, who my rascally friends are. Learn, if you please, how to talk another time, particularly when you are talking about a fellow-creature.—

After a little time, however, these and similar reflections gave way to others; his present circumstances occupying the whole attention of our poor traveller. The dread of being pursued and discovered, which had so incessantly embittered his day's journey, now no longer gave him any uneasiness; but how many things made his nightly wanderings sufficiently uncomfortable!—darkness; solitude; increasing, and now painful, fatigue; a gentle, but steady and piercing breeze, which would be far from agreeable to a man still dressed in the same clothes which he had put on to go a short distance to a wedding, and quickly to return in triumph to his home, only a few steps off; and, what rendered everything doubly irksome, walking at a venture, in search of a place of rest and security.

If he happened to pass through a village, he would walk as quietly and warily as possible, lest any of the doors should be still open; but he saw no further signs of remaining wakefulness among the inhabitants than occasionally a glancing light in one of the windows. When on the road, away from every abode, he would pause, every now and then, and listen eagerly for the beloved murmur of the Adda; but in vain. He heard no sounds but the distant howling of dogs at some solitary dwelling, which floated through the air, at once mournful and threatening. On approaching any of these abodes, the howling was changed into an irritated, angry bark; and in passing before the door, he heard, and almost fancied he saw, the fierce creatures, with their heads at the crack of the door, reiterating their howls. This quickly removed all temptation to knock and ask shelter, and probably his courage would have failed had there been no such obstacles in his way.—Who's there?—thought he:— what do you want at this hour? How did you come here? Tell who you are. Isn't there an inn where you can get a bed? This, at best, is what they will say to me, if I knock; even if it shouldn't be a cowardly sleeper, who would begin to shout out lustily, 'Help! Thieves!' I must have something ready for an answer; and what could I say? If anybody hears a noise in the night, nothing enters their heads but robbers, villains, and rogues: they never think that an honest man may be benighted, not to say a gentleman in his carriage.—He determined, therefore, to reserve this plan as a last resource in case of necessity, and continued his way, still with the hope of at least discovering the Adda, if not of crossing it, that night, and not being obliged again to go in search of it in broad daylight.

On, therefore, he went, till he reached a part where the country changed from cultivated fields into a heath of ferns and broom. This seemed, if not a sure indication, at least, a kind of argument that there was a river in the neighbourhood; and he advanced across the common, pursuing the path which traversed it. After walking a few paces, he stopped to listen; but in vain. The tediousness of the journey seemed to be increased by the wildness of the place; not a mulberry nor a vine was to be seen, nor any other signs of human culture, which, in the early part of his progress, seemed almost like half-companions to him. However, he still went forward, beguiling the time, and endeavouring to drive away the images and apparitions which haunted his mind—the relics of a hundred wonderful stories he had heard—by repeating, as he went along, some of the prayers for the dead.

By degrees, he entered among larger patches of brushwood, wild plum-trees, dwarf oaks, and brambles. Continuing his way, with more impatience than alacrity, he saw scattered occasionally throughout these patches, a solitary tree; and, still following the guidance of the footpath, perceived that he was entering a wood. He felt a kind of reluctance to proceed; but he conquered it, and unwillingly went forward. The further he went, the more this unwillingness increased, and the more did everything he saw vex and harass his imagination. The bushes he discerned before him assumed strange, marvellous, and uncouth forms; the shadows of the tops of the trees alarmed him, as, slightly agitated by the breeze, they quivered on his path, illuminated by the pale light of the moon; the very rustling of the withered leaves, as he trampled them under foot, had in it something hateful to his ear. His limbs felt a strange impulse to run, and, at the same time, seemed scarcely able to support him. The cold night-breeze blew more chilly and sharply against his forehead and throat; he felt it piercing through his thin clothes to his skin, which shivered in the blast, and, penetrating more subtilely to his very bones, extinguishing the last remains of vigour. At one time, the weariness and undefined horror with which he had so long been struggling, had suddenly almost overwhelmed him. He nearly lost his self-government; but terrified above all things at his own terror, he summoned up his former spirits, and by a great effort, forced them to assume their usual sway. Thus fortified for a moment, he stood still to deliberate, and resolved to leave the wood by the same path as he had traversed, to go straight to the last village he had passed, to return once more among mankind, and there to seek shelter, even at the inn. While he thus stood, the rustling of his feet among the leaves hushed, and, perfectly silent around him, a noise reached his ear, a murmur—a murmur of running water. He listens; assures himself; and exclaims, 'It's the Adda!' It was like the restoration of a friend, of a brother, of a deliverer. His weariness almost disappeared, his pulse again beat; he felt his blood circulate freely and warmly through all his veins; his confidence increased, the gloominess and oppression of his mind, in great part, vanished away; and he no longer hesitated to penetrate farther into the wood, towards the friendly murmur.

At last he reached the extremity of the flat, at the edge of a steep declivity; and, peeping through the bushes that everywhere covered its surface, he discerned, at the bottom, the glittering of the running water. Then, raising his eyes, he surveyed the extensive plain on the opposite side, scattered with villages; beyond this the hills, and on one of these a large, whitish tract, in which he fancied he could distinguish a city—Bergamo, undoubtedly. He descended the steep a little way, separating and pushing aside the brushwood with his hands and arms, and looked down, to see if there were any boat moving on the water, or to listen if he could hear the splashing of oars; but he saw and heard nothing. Had it been any thing less than the Adda, Renzo would have descended at once and attempted to ford it; but this, he well knew, in such a river, was not a matter of very great facility.

He therefore stood to consult with himself what were best to be done. To clamber up into a tree, and there await the dawn of morning, in the chill night-breeze, in a frosty air, and in his present dress, was more than enough to benumb him; to pace up and down, for constant exercise, all that time, besides that it would have been a very inefficacious defence against the severity of the temperature, was also asking too much of those unfortunate limbs which had already done much more than their duty. Suddenly he remembered having seen a *cascinotto* in one of the fields adjoining the unculti-

vated down. Thus the peasants of the Milanese plain designate
certain little cottages, thatched with straw, constructed of the trunks
and branches of trees, fastened together and filled up with mud,
where they are in the habit of depositing their harvest during the
summer season, repairing thither at night to protect it: during the
rest of the year they are usually unoccupied. He quickly fixed upon
this as his resting-place for the night; and again setting off on his
way, re-passed the wood, the tract of bushes, and the heath; and
entering upon the cultivated land, he quickly espied the *cascinotto,*
and went towards it. A worm-eaten and tumble-down door, without
lock or chain, blocked up the entrance; Renzo drew it towards him,
and on entering, saw a hurdle, intended to serve the purpose of a
hammock, suspended in the air, and supported by bands formed of
little twigs; he did not, however, make use of it; but seeing a little
straw lying on the ground, thought that, even there, sleep would be
very welcome.

Before stretching his weary frame on the bed Providence had prepared for him, he knelt down to offer up his thanks for this blessing,
and for all the assistance he had received that terrible day. He then
repeated his usual prayers; and, having finished them, begged pardon
of God for having omitted them the evening before, and gone to
rest, as he said, like a dog, or even worse.—And for this reason,—
added he to himself, resting his hands upon the straw, and, from
kneeling, changing his posture to that of lying,—for this reason I
was awaked by such agreeable visitors in the morning.—He then
gathered up all the straw that was scattered around, and spread
it over him, so as to make the best covering he could to secure himself from the cold, which, even there, under shelter, made itself
sufficiently felt; and crouching beneath it, he tried to get a little
sleep, thinking that he had purchased it, that day, more dearly
than usual.

Scarcely, however, had he closed his eyes, before visions began
to throng his memory, or his fancy (I cannot undertake to indicate
the exact spot)—visions so crowded, so incessant, that they quickly
banished every idea of sleep. The merchant, the notary, the bailiffs,
the sword-cutler, the landlord, Ferrer, the superintendent, the party
at the inn, the crowds in the streets; then Don Abbondio, then

Don Rodrigo: and, among so many, there were none that did not bring some sad remembrances of misfortune or aversion.

There were but three images that presented themselves to his mind, divested of every bitter recollection, clear of every suspicion, pleasing in every aspect; and two, principally—certainly very dissimilar, but closely connected in the heart of the youth,—the black-locked Lucia, and the white-bearded Father Cristoforo. Yet the consolation he felt in contemplating even these objects, was anything but unmixed and tranquil. In picturing to himself the good friar, he felt more keenly than ever the disgrace of his faults, his shameful intemperance, and his neglect of the kind Father's paternal advice; and in contemplating the image of Lucia! we will not attempt to describe what he felt; the reader knows the circumstances, and must imagine it himself. Neither did he forget the poor Agnese; Agnese, who had chosen him for her son-in-law, who had considered him almost as one with her only daughter, and before receiving from him the title of mother, had assumed the language and affection of one, and demonstrated parental solicitude for him by her actions. But it was an additional grief to him, and not the least bitter one, that exactly on account of these affectionate and benevolent intentions, the poor woman was now homeless, and almost houseless, uncertain of the future, and reaping sorrows and troubles from those very circumstances, which he had hoped would be the joy and comfort of her declining years. What a night, poor Renzo! which was to have been the fifth of his nuptials! What a room! What a matrimonial couch! And after such a day! And to precede such a morrow, such a succession of days!—What God wills—replied he, to the thoughts which most tormented him;—What God wills. He knows what He does! it is for our good too. Let it be as a penance for my sins. Lucia is so good! God, surely, will not let her suffer for long—for very long!—

Harassed by such thoughts as these, despairing of obtaining any sleep, and the piercing cold becoming more and more insufferable, so that from time to time his whole frame shook, and his teeth chattered in spite of himself, Renzo longed for the approach of day, and impatiently measured the slow progress of the hours. I say, measured, because every half-hour he heard resounding through the deep silence, the strokes of a large clock, probably that of Trezzo. The first time, the sound reached his ear so unexpectedly, without his having the least idea whence it came, it brought with it something solemn and mysterious to his mind; the feeling of a warning uttered in an unknown voice, by some invisible person.

When, at last, the clock had tolled eleven,[1]—the hour Renzo had determined to get up,—he rose, half benumbed with the cold, and falling upon his knees, repeated his matin prayers with more than ordinary devotion; then, standing up, he stretched his limbs, and shook his body, as if to settle and unite his members, which seemed almost dissevered from each other, breathed upon his hands and rubbed them together, and then opened the door of the *cascinotto,* first taking the precaution to look warily about him, perchance any one might be there. No one being visible, he cast his eye round to discover the path he had followed the preceding evening, and quickly recognizing it, much clearer and more distinct than his memory pictured it, he set off in that direction.

The sky announced a beautiful day: the pale and rayless moon was yet visible near the horizon, in the spacious field of azure, still softened by a tinge of morning grey, which shaded gradually towards the east, into a rosy and primrose hue. Still nearer the horizon, a few irregular clouds stretched out, in lengthened waves, rather azure than grey, their lower sides edged with almost a streak of flame, becoming every moment more vivid and sharply defined; while, higher up, light and fleecy clouds, mingling with each other, and of a thousand nameless hues, floated on the surface of the placid heavens; a true Lombard sky, *so* beautiful when it *is* beautiful—so brilliant, so calm. Had Renzo been here to enjoy himself, he would certainly have looked upwards, and admired a dawn so different to what he had been accustomed to see among his native mountains; but his eyes were bent to the ground, and he walked on rapidly, both to regain a little warmth, and to reach the river as quickly as he could. He retraced the fields, the grove, the bushes; traversed the wood,

---

[1] It must be borne in mind by the reader, that, according to Italian computation of time, the first hour of the day is seven o'clock in the morning—two o'clock answerable to eight with us, and so on, till seven o'clock in the evening becomes one again. This arrangement would make eleven o'clock, in the text, the same as five o'clock in the morning in England.

with a kind of compassion, as he looked around and remembered the horror he had felt there a few hours before; reached the edge of the precipitous bank, and looking down through the crags and bushes, discovered a fisherman's bark slowly making its way against the stream, close by the shore. He hastily descended the shortest way through the bushes, stood upon the bank, and gently called to the fisherman; and with the intention of appearing to ask a favour of little importance, but, without being aware of it, in a half-supplicatory manner, beckoned to him to approach. The fisherman cast a glance along the shore, looked carefully both up and down the river, and then turning the prow towards Renzo, approached the side. Renzo, who stood at the very edge of the stream, almost with one foot in the water, seized the prow as it drew near, and jumped into the boat.

'Be good enough to take me across to the other side, and I'll pay you for it,' said he. The fisherman had already guessed his object, and had turned the prow to the opposite bank. Renzo, seeing another oar at the bottom of the boat, stooped down and took it up.

'Softly, softly,' said the owner; but on seeing how dexterously the youth laid hold of the implement, and prepared to handle it, 'Aha!' added he, 'you know your business.'

'A little,' replied Renzo; and he began to row with a vigour and skill beyond those of an amateur. While thus exerting himself, he cast an occasional dark glance at the shore he had just left, and then a look of anxiety to the one they were approaching. He was annoyed at having to go at all down the stream; but the current here was too rapid to cut directly across it; so that the bark, partly cleaving and partly following the course of the water, was obliged to take a diagonal direction. As it happens in all dark and intricate undertakings, that difficulties present themselves to the mind at first only in general, but in the execution of the enterprise are more minutely observable; so, now that the Adda was forded, so to say, Renzo felt a good deal of disquietude at not knowing for certain whether here it was the boundary of the two states, or whether, when this obstacle was overcome, there might not be others still to surmount. Addressing the fisherman, therefore, and nodding with his head towards the whitish spot which he had noticed the night before, and which now appeared much more distinct, 'Is that Bergamo?' said he—'that town?'

'The city of Bergamo,' replied the fisherman.

'And that shore, there, does it belong to Bergamo?'

'The territory of St. Mark.'

'Long live St. Mark!' exclaimed Renzo.

The fisherman made no reply.

They reached, at length, the opposite shore; Renzo jumped out upon it, and, thanking God in his heart, expressed his gratitude in words to the boatman; then putting his hand in his pocket, he drew out thence a *berlinga*—which, considering his circumstances, was no little loss to him—and handed it to the worthy man, who, giving another glance at the Milanese shore, and along the river in either direction, stretched out his hand, and received the gift. He put it into his pocket, and after compressing his lips, at the same time laying his forefinger across them, with a significant expression of countenance, said, 'A good journey to you!' and turned back.

That the reader may not be surprised at the prompt, yet cautious, civility of this man towards a perfect stranger, it will be necessary to inform him that, frequently requested to perform a similar service to smugglers and banditti, he was accustomed to do so, not so much for the sake of the trifling and uncertain gains which he might thereby obtain, as to avoid making himself enemies among these classes. He afforded this assistance whenever he could assure himself of not being discovered by the custom-house officers, bailiffs, or spies. Thus, without particularly favouring one party more than another, he endeavoured to satisfy all, with that impartiality usually exercised by those who are compelled to deal with a certain set of people, while liable to give account to another.

Renzo paused a moment on the bank, to contemplate the opposite shore—that ground which just before had almost burnt beneath his feet.—Ah! I am really out of it!—was his first thought.—Hateful country that you are!—was his second, bidding it farewell. But the third recurred to those whom he had left there. Then he crossed his arms on his breast, heaved a sigh, bent his eyes on the water which flowed at his feet, and thought,—It has passed under the bridge!—Thus that at Lecco was generally called among his fellow-countrymen, by way of eminence.—Ah! hateful world! Enough: whatever God wills.—

He turned his back upon these mournful objects, and went forward, taking, for a mark, the white tract on the side of the hill, until he met with some one to give him more particular directions in his way. It was amusing to see with what carelessness and disembarrassment he now accosted travellers, and how boldly he pronounced the name of the village where his cousin resided, without hesitation or disguise. From the first person who directed him, he learnt that he had yet nine miles to travel.

His journey was not very blithesome. Independent of his own troubles, his eyes rested every moment on pitiable objects, which told him that he would find in the country he was entering the poverty he had left in his own. All along the way, but more particularly in the villages and large towns, he saw beggars hastening along, mendicants rather from circumstances than profession, who revealed their misery more in their countenances than their clothing: peasants, mountaineers, artisans, entire families, and a mingled murmur of entreaties, disputes, and infants' cries. Besides the mournful pity that it awoke in Renzo's mind, this sight also aroused him to the remembrance of his own circumstances.

—Who knows,—thought he, as he went along,—if I shall find anything to do? if there is any work now to be got, as there used to be? Well; Bortolo is kindly inclined to me; he is a good fellow; he has made some money, and has invited me very often; he, surely, won't forsake me. Besides, Providence has helped me hitherto, and will help me, I hope, for the future.—

In the mean while, his appetite, already considerably sharpened, became, as he went on his way, more and more craving; and though he felt that he could manage very well to the end of his journey, which was now only about two miles, without great inconvenience, yet he reflected that it would not be exactly the thing to make his appearance before his cousin like a beggar, and address him with the salutation, 'Give me something to eat;' so drawing all his riches from his pocket, he counted them over on the palm of his hand, to ascertain the amount. It was an amount that required little calculation, yet still there was more than enough to make a small meal; he, therefore, entered an inn to get a little refreshment; and, on paying the account, found that he had still a few pence remaining.

Just outside, lying in the street, and so close to the door that he would have fallen over them had he not been looking about him, Renzo saw two women, one rather elderly, and the other a younger person, with an infant at her breast, which, after vainly endeavouring to satisfy its hunger, was crying bitterly; they were all three as pale as death; and standing by them was a man, in whose face and limbs there might still be discerned tokens of former robustness, though now broken and almost destroyed by long poverty. The three beggars stretched out their hands to Renzo, as he left the inn with a free step and reinvigorated air, but none of them spoke; what more could language have expressed?

'There's a God-send for you!' said Renzo, as he hastily thrust his hand into his pocket, and, taking out his last pence, put them into the hand that was nearest to him, and went on his way.

The refreshment, and this good work together (since we are made of both soul and body), had gladdened and cheered all his thoughts. Certain it is that he felt more confidence for the future from having thus deprived himself of his last penny, than if he had found ten such. For if Providence had kept in reserve, for the support of three wretched beggars, almost fainting on the road, the last farthing of a stranger, himself a fugitive, far from his own home, and uncertain how to get a living, could he think that that Providence would leave in destitution him whom He had made use of for this purpose, and to whom He had given so vivid, so effective, so self-abandoning an inclination? Such was, in general, the feeling of the youth, though, probably, not so clearly defined as that which we have expressed in words. During the remainder of his walk, as his mind recurred to the different circumstances and contingencies which had hitherto appeared the most dark and perplexing, all seemed to brighten. The famine and poverty must come to an end, for there was a harvest every year: in the mean time, he had his cousin Bortolo, and his own abilities; and, as a help towards his support, a little store of money at home, which he could easily send for. With this assistance, at the worst, he could live from day to day as economically as possible, till better times.—Then, when good

times have come at last,—continued Renzo, in his fanciful dreams,—
the demand for work will be renewed; masters will strive who shall
get Milanese weavers, because they know their trade best; the
Milanese weavers will hold their heads high; they who want clever
workmen must pay for them; we shall make something to live upon
and still have some to spare; we can then furnish a cottage, and
write to the women to come. And besides, why wait so long?
Shouldn't we have lived upon my little store at home, all this
winter? So we can live here. There are curates everywhere. Those
two dear women might come now, and we could keep house together. Oh, what a pleasure, to go walking all together on this very
road! to go as far as the Adda, in a cart, and have a picnic on the
shore; yes, just on the shore! and I'd show them the place where I
embarked, the thorny path I came down, and the spot where I
stood to look if there was a boat!—

At length he reached his cousin's village; and, just at the entrance,
even before he set foot in it, distinguished a house considerably
higher than the rest, with several rows of long windows, one above
another, and separated by a much smaller space than the divisions
between the different stories required: he at once recognized a silk-
mill; and going in, asked in a loud voice, so as to be heard amidst
the noise of the running water and the machinery, if Bortolo
Castagneri lived there.

'The Signor Bortolo! He's there.'

—The Signor! that's a good sign,—thought Renzo; and, seeing
his cousin, he ran towards him. Bortolo turned round, recognized
his relation, as he exclaimed, 'Here I am, myself,' and received
him with an 'Oh!' of surprise, as they mutually threw their arms
round each other's neck. After the first welcome, Bortolo took his
cousin into another room, apart from the noise of the machinery
and the eyes of the curious, and greeted him with, 'I'm very glad
to see you; but you're a pretty fellow. I've invited you so often,
and you never would come; and now you arrive in rather a troubled
time.'

'Since you will have me tell you, I've not come with my own good
will,' said Renzo; and then, as briefly as possible, and not without
some emotion, he related his mournful story.

'That's quite another thing,' said Bortolo. 'Oh, poor Renzo! But you've depended upon me; and I'll not forsake you. Certainly, there's no great demand for workmen just now; indeed, it's all we can do not to turn off those we have, and give up the business; but my master likes me, and he has got some money. And, to tell you the truth, without boasting, he mostly owes it to me; he has the capital, and I give my abilities, such as they are. I'm the head workman, you know; and, besides, between you and me, I'm quite his *factotum*. Poor Lucia Mondella! I remember her as it were but yesterday: a good girl she was! always the best-behaved in church; and whenever one passed her cottage . . . I see that cottage in my mind's eye, outside the village, with a fine fig-tree peeping over the wall . . .'

'No, no; don't let us talk about it.'

'I was only going to say, that whenever one passed that cottage, there was the reel always going, going, going. And that Don Rodrigo! even in my time he was inclined that way, but now he's playing the devil outright, from what I hear, so long as God leaves him to take his own course. Well, as I was saying, here, too, we are suffering a little from the famine . . . Apropos, how are you for appetite?'

'I got something to eat, a little while ago, on the road.'

'And how are you for money?'

Renzo held out one of his hands, and putting it to his mouth, gently puffed upon it.

'Never mind,' said Bortolo: 'I've plenty; pluck up heart, for I hope things will soon change, please God; and then you can repay me, and lay up also a little for yourself.'

'I've a trifling sum at home, and will send for it.'

'Very well; and, in the mean time, you may depend upon me. God has given me wealth, that I might give to others; and whom should I serve so soon as my own relations and friends?'

'I said I should be provided for!' exclaimed Renzo, affectionately pressing his good cousin's hand.

'Then,' rejoined his companion, 'they've had a regular uproar at Milan! I think they're all a little mad. The rumour had already reached here; but I want you to tell me things a little more particularly. Ah! we've plenty to talk about. Here, however, you see, we go about it more quietly, and do things with rather more prudence. The city purchased two thousand loads of corn, from a merchant who lives at Venice: the corn came from Turkey; but when life depends upon it, such things are not looked into very narrowly. See now what this occasioned: the governors of Verona and Brescia stopped up the passes, and said, 'No corn shall pass this way.' What did the Bergamascans do, think you? They despatched a man to Venice, who knew how to talk. The messenger went off in haste, presented himself to the Doge, and asked him what was the meaning of such a trick. And such a speech he made! they say, fit to be printed. What a thing it is to have a man who knows what to say! An order was immediately issued for the free transit of corn, requiring the governors not only to let it pass, but to assist in forwarding it; and now it is on its way. There is provision also for the surrounding country. Another worthy man gave the senate to understand that the people in the country were starving; and they have ordered them four thousand bushels of millet. This helps, you know, to make bread. And then I needn't say, that if there isn't bread for us, we will eat meat. God has given me wealth, as I told you. Now, then, I'll take you to my master: I've often mentioned you to him, and I know he'll welcome you. He's a Bergamascan of the old sort, and a kind-hearted man. Certainly, he doesn't expect you just now; but when he hears your history . . . And besides, he knows how to value good workmen; for the famine must come to an end, and business will go on. But, first of all, I must warn you of one thing. Do you know what they call us Milanese, in this country?'

'No; what is it?'

'They call us blockheads.'

'That's not a very nice name.'

'So it is: whoever is born in the territory of Milan, and would make a living in that of Bergamo, must be content to bear it patiently. It is as common, among these people, to give the name of "blockhead" to a Milanese, as "your illustrious lordship" to a cavalier.'

'They only say so, I fancy, to those who will put up with it.'

'My dear fellow, if you are not disposed continually to brook the title, don't reckon that you can live here. You would be obliged always to have a knife in your hand; and when you have killed, we will suppose, two, three, or four, of your neighbours, you'd meet with somebody who would kill you; and what a nice prospect, to have to appear before God's tribunal with three or four murders on your head!'

'And a Milanese who has a little . . .' here he tapped his forehead with his forefinger, as he had before done at the sign of the Full Moon. 'I mean, one who understands his business?'

'It's all the same; he, too, would be a blockhead. Do you know what my master says when he's talking of me to his friends? "Heaven has sent me this blockhead, to conduct my business; if it were not for this blockhead, I should do very badly." It's the custom to say so.'

'It's a very foolish custom, especially considering what we do; for who was it, in fact, that brought the art here, and now carries it on, but us? Is it possible there's no help for it?'

'Not hitherto; there may be, in the course of time, among the young people who are growing up; but in this generation there is no remedy; they've acquired the habit, and won't leave it off. After all, what is it? It's nothing to the tricks they've played upon you, and that most of our precious fellow-countrymen would still play upon you.'

'Well, that's true: if there's no other evil . . .'

'Now that you are persuaded of this, all will go well. Come, let us go to my master, and be of good heart.'

Everything, in fact, did go well, and so exactly in accordance with Bortolo's promises, that it is needless to give any particular description. And it was truly an ordering of Providence; for we shall soon see how little dependence was to be placed upon the small savings Renzo had left at home.

CHAPTER XVIII

THAT same day, the 13th of November, an express arrived to the Signor *Podestà* of Lecco, and presented him with a despatch from the Signor the high sheriff, containing an order to make every possible strict investigation, to ascertain whether a certain young man, bearing the name of Lorenzo Tramaglino, silk-weaver, who had escaped from the hands *prædicti egregii domini capitanei,* had returned, *palam vel clam,* to his own country, *ignotum* the exact village, *verum in territorio Leuci: quod si compertum fuerit sic esse,* the Signor Podestà must endeavour, *quanta maxima diligentia fieri poterit,* to get him into his hands; and having sufficiently secured him, *videlicet,* with strong handcuffs, (seeing that the insufficiency of smaller manacles for the afore-mentioned person has been proved), must cause him to be conducted to prison, and there detained under strong custody, until he be consigned to the officer, who shall be sent to take him: and in case either of success, or non-success, *accedatis ad domum prædicti Laurentii Tramalini; et facta debita diligentia, quid quid ad rem repertum fuerit auferatis; et informationes de illius prava qualitate, vita, et complicibus, sumatis;* and of all his sayings and doings, what is found and not found, what is taken and not taken, *diligenter referatis.* After humanely assuring himself that the object of inquiry had not returned home, the Signor *Podestà* summoned the village constable, and under his direction, proceeded, with a large retinue of notaries and bailiffs, to the above-mentioned house. The door was locked, and either no one had the key, or he was not to be found. They, therefore, forced the locks with all due and praiseworthy zeal, which is equivalent to saying that they proceeded as if taking a city by assault. The report of this expedition immediately spread in the neighbourhood, and reached the ears of Father Cristoforo, who, no less astonished than grieved, sought for some information as to the cause of so unexpected an event from everybody he met with; he could only, however, gather airy conjectures, and contradictory reports: and, at last, therefore, wrote to Father Bonaventura, from whom he imagined he should be able to acquire some more precise information. In the mean while, Renzo's relations and friends were summoned to depose all that they knew about his *depraved habits:* to bear the name of Tramaglino became a misfortune, a disgrace, a crime; and the village was quite in a commotion. By degrees, it became known that Renzo had escaped from the hands of justice during the disturbance at Milan, and had not since been seen. It was whispered about that he had been guilty of some high crime and misdemeanour, but what it was no one could tell, or they told it in a hundred different ways. The more heinous the offence with which he was charged, the less was it believed in the village, where Renzo was universally known as an honest, respectable youth; and many conjectured and spread the report, that it was merely a machination set on foot by the powerful Don Rodrigo, to bring about the ruin of his unfortunate rival. So true is it that, judging only by induction, and without the necessary knowledge of facts, even the greatest villains are sometimes wrongfully accused.

But we, who have the facts in our possession, as the saying is, can affirm that, if Don Rodrigo had had no share in Renzo's misfortunes, yet that he rejoiced in them as if they had been his own work, and triumphed over them among his confidants, especially with Count Attilio. This friend, according to his first intention, should have been, by this time, at Milan; but, on the first announcement of the disturbances that had arisen there, and of the rabble whom he might encounter in a far different mood than tamely to submit to a beating, he thought it expedient to postpone his journey until he received better accounts; and the more so, because having offended many, he had good reason to fear that some who had remained passive only from impotency, might now be encouraged by circumstances, and judge it a favourable opportunity for taking their revenge. The journey, however, was not long delayed; the order despatched from Milan for the execution against Renzo, had already given some indication that things had returned to their ordinary course, and the positive notices which followed quick upon it, confirmed the truth of these appearances. Count Attilio set off immediately, enjoining his cousin to persist in his undertaking, and bring it to an issue, and promising, on his part, that he would use every means to rid him of the friar, to whom the fortunate accident of his cousin's beggarly rival would be a wonderful blow. Scarcely had Attilio gone, when Griso arrived safe and sound from Monza, and related to his master what he had been able to gather:—that Lucia had found refuge in such a monastery, under the protection of the Signora So-and-so; that she was concealed there as if she were a nun herself, never setting foot outside the threshold, and assisting at the services of the church behind a little grated window: an arrangement which was unsatisfactory to many who, having heard some mention of her adventures, and great reports of her beauty, were anxious, for once, to see what she was like.

This account inspired Don Rodrigo with every evil passion, or, to speak more truly, rendered still more ungovernable those with which he was already possessed. So many circumstances favourable to his design, had only further inflamed that mixture of punctilio, rage, and infamous desire of which his passion was composed. Renzo absent, banished, outlawed—so that any proceedings against him became lawful; and even that his betrothed bride might be considered, in a measure, as the property of a rebel: the only man in the world who would and could interest himself for her, and make a stir that would be noticed in head-quarters, and at a distance— the enraged friar—would himself, probably, be soon incapable of acting for her. Yet here was a new impediment, which not only outweighed all these advantages, but rendered them, it might be said, unavailing. A monastery at Monza, even had there not been a princess in the way, was a bone too hard even for the teeth of a Rodrigo; and wander in his fancy round this retreat as he would, he could devise no way or means of assaulting it, either by force or fraud. He was almost resolved to give up the enterprise, to go to Milan by a circuitous route, so as to avoid passing through Monza, and there to plunge himself into the society of his friends, and their recreations, so as to drown, in thoughts of gaiety, the one idea which had now become so tormenting. But, but, but, his friends!—softly a little with these friends. Instead of diverting his mind, he might reasonably expect to find in their company an incessant renewal and memento of his vexation: for Attilio would certainly have published the affair, and put them all in expectation. Everybody would make inquiries about the mountain girl, and he must give some answer. He had wished, he had tried; and how had he succeeded? He had engaged in an undertaking—rather an unworthy one, certainly; but what of that? One cannot always regulate one's caprices; the point is to satisfy them; and how had he come off in the enterprise? How? Put down by a peasant, and a friar! Uh! and when an unexpected turn of good fortune had rid him of one, and a skilful friend of the other, without any trouble on the part of the principal person concerned, he, like a fool, knew not how to profit by the juncture, and basely withdrew from the undertaking! It would be enough to make him never again dare to hold up his head among men of spirit, or compel him always to keep his hand on his sword. And then, again, how could he ever return to, how ever remain in, that village, and that country, where, let alone the incessant and bitter remembrances of his passion, he should always bear about with him the disgrace of its failure? where public hatred would have increased, while his reputation for power and superiority would have proportionably diminished? where he might read in the face of every ragamuffin, even through the veil of profound reverences, a galling 'You've been gulled, and I'm glad of it!' The path of iniquity, as our manuscript here remarks, is broad, but that does not mean that it is easy; it has its stumbling-blocks, and its thorns, and its course is tedious and wearisome, though it be a downward course.

In this perplexity, unwilling either to give up his purpose, to go back, or to stop, and unable by himself to go forward, a plan occurred to Don Rodrigo's mind, by which he hoped to effect his design. This was to take as a partner and assistant in his enterprise, one whose *hands* could often reach beyond the *views* of others—a man at once, and devil, to whom the difficulty of an undertaking was frequently an incentive to engage in it. But this course also had its inconveniences and its dangers; the more pressing, the less they could be calculated upon beforehand; since it was impossible to foresee where one might be led, when once embarked in an affair with this man: a powerful auxiliary, certainly, but a not less absolute and dangerous guide.

These thoughts kept Don Rodrigo for several days in a state of worse than tedious perplexity. In the mean while, a letter arrived from his cousin, informing him that the plot against the friar was going on very well. Following close upon the lightning bursts forth the thunderclap; one fine morning, Don Rodrigo heard that Father Cristoforo had left the convent at Pescarenico. This success, so prompt, and so complete, together with Attilio's letter, encouraging him onward, and threatening him with intolerable ridicule if he withdrew, inclined Don Rodrigo still more to hazard every thing rather than give up; but that which finally decided him, was the unexpected news that Agnese had returned home, thus removing one obstacle from around Lucia. We will relate how these two circumstances were brought about, beginning with the last.

The two unfortunate women were scarcely settled in their retreat, when the report of the disturbances in Milan spread rapidly over Monza, and, consequently, through the monastery; and following the grand news, came an infinite succession of particulars, which multiplied and varied every moment. The portress, situated just between the street and the monastery, was the channel of information both from within and from without, and, eagerly receiving these reports, retailed them at will to her guests. 'Two, six, eight, four, seven, had been imprisoned: they would hang them, some before the bakehouse *of the Crutches,* some at the end of the street where the Superintendent of provisions lived . . . Ay, ay, just listen, now!— one of them escaped—a man somewhere from Lecco, or thereabouts. I don't know the name; but some one will be passing who will be able to tell me, to see if you know him.'

This announcement, together with the circumstance that Renzo would just have arrived at Milan on the fatal day, occasioned a good deal of disquietude to the women, and especially to Lucia; but what must it have been, when the portress came to tell them—'It is a man from your very village who has escaped being hung—a silk-weaver, of the name of Tramaglino; do you know him?'

Lucia, who was sitting hemming some needlework, immediately

let it fall from her hands; she became extremely pale, and changed countenance so much, that the portress would certainly have observed it, had she been nearer to her. Fortunately, however, she was standing at the door with Agnese, who, though much disturbed, yet not to such a degree as her daughter, preserved a calm countenance, and forced herself to reply, that in a little village, everybody knew everybody; that she was acquainted with him, and could scarcely bring herself to believe that anything of the kind had happened to him, he was so peaceable a youth. She then asked if it was known for certain that he had escaped, and whither.

'Every one says he has escaped, where to, they cannot say; it may be they will catch him again, or it may be he is in safety; but if they do get hold of him, your peaceable youth . . .'

Fortunately, at this juncture, the portress was called away, and left them—the reader may imagine in what state of mind. For more than a day were the poor woman and her afflicted daughter obliged to remain in this painful suspense, imagining the causes, ways, and consequences, of this unhappy event, and commenting, in their own minds, or in a low voice with each other, on the terrible words their informer had left unfinished.

At length, one Thursday, a man arrived at the monastery in search of Agnese. It was a fishmonger, of Pescarenico, going to Milan, as usual, to dispose of his fish; and the good Father Cristoforo had requested him, in passing through Monza, to call in at the monastery, to greet the women in his name, to tell them all he knew about this sad affair of Renzo's, to beseech them to have patience, and put their trust in God; and to assure them that he would certainly not forget them, but would watch his opportunity for rendering them assistance; and, in the mean time, would not fail to send them all the news he could collect every week, either by this means, or a similar one. The messenger could tell nothing new or certain about Renzo, except of the execution put into his house, and the search that was being made for him; but, at the same time, that this had been hitherto in vain, and that it was known for certain that he had reached the territory of Bergamo. Such a certainty, it is unnecessary to say, was a balm to poor Lucia's wounded heart: from that time her tears flowed more freely and calmly; she felt more comforted in her secret bursts of feeling with her mother; and expressions of thankfulness began to be mingled with her prayers.

Gertrude frequently invited her into her private apartment, and sometimes detained her there a long while, feeling a pleasure in the ingenuousness and gentleness of the poor girl, and in hearing the thanks and blessings she poured upon her benefactress. She even related to her, in confidence, a part (the blameless part) of her history, and of what she had suffered, that she might come there to suffer, till Lucia's first suspicious astonishment gradually changed to compassion. In that history she found reasons more than enough to explain what she thought rather strange in the behaviour of her patroness, especially when she brought in to her aid Agnese's doctrine about the characters of the nobility. Nevertheless, though some times induced to return the confidence which Gertrude reposed in her, yet she carefully avoided any mention of her fresh causes of alarm, of her new misfortune, and of the ties which bound her to the escaped silk-weaver, lest she should run any risk of spreading a report so full of her shame and sorrow. She also parried, to the best of her ability, all Gertrude's inquisitive questions about herself previous to her betrothal, but this was not so much from prudential motives, as because such an account appeared to the simple-minded girl more perplexing, more difficult to relate, than all she had heard, or thought it possible to hear, from the Signora. In the history of that lady there was oppression, intrigue, suffering—sad and mournful things, but which, nevertheless, could be named: in her own there was a pervading sentiment, a word, which she did not feel it possible to pronounce, when speaking of herself, and as a substitute for which she could never find a periphrasis that did not seem to her mind indelicate: love!

Gertrude was sometimes tempted to be angry at these repulses; but there always appeared behind them so much affection, so much respect, so much gratitude, and even so much trustfulness! Sometimes, perhaps, that modesty, so delicate, sensitive, and mysterious, displeased her still more on another account; but all was quickly forgotten in the soothing thought that every moment recurred to her mind when contemplating Lucia;—I am doing her good.—And this was true; for, besides the asylum she had provided, these conversations and her familiar treatment were some comfort to Lucia. The poor girl also found another satisfaction in constant employment; she always petitioned for something to do, and when she went into the Signora's parlour, generally took a little needlework with her, to keep her fingers employed: but what melancholy thoughts crowded her mind, wherever she went! While plying her needle,—an occupation to which hitherto she had given little attention,—her reel constantly presented itself to her view; and with the reel, how many other things!

The second Thursday, the same, or another messenger arrived, bringing salutations and encouragement from Father Cristoforo, and an additional confirmation of Renzo's escape; but no more positive information about his misfortunes. The reader may remember that the Capuchin had hoped for some account from his brother-friar at Milan, to whom he had given Renzo a letter of recommendation; he only replied, however, that he had seen neither letter nor person: that a stranger from the country had certainly been to the convent in search of him, but finding him out, had gone away, and had not again made his appearance.

The third Thursday, no messenger came; which was not only depriving the poor women of an anticipated and hoped-for source of consolation; but, as it usually happens, on every trifling occasion, to those in sorrow and suspense, was also a subject of much disquietude, and a hundred tormenting suspicions. Agnese had, for some time, been contemplating a visit to her native village, and this unexpected non-appearance of the promised messenger, determined her upon taking such a step. Lucia felt very strange at the thought of being left without the shelter of her mother's wing; but the longing desire she felt to know something, and her sense of security in that guarded and sacred asylum, conquered her great unwillingness; and it was arranged between them that Agnese should watch in the street the following day for the fishmonger, who must, necessarily pass that way on his return from Milan, and that she would ask him to be so good as to give her a seat in his cart, to take her to her own mountains. She met with him, accordingly, and asked if Father Cristoforo had given him no commission for her. The fishmonger said, that he had been out fishing the whole day before his departure, and had received neither news nor message from the Father. Agnese then made her request, which being granted without hesitation, she took her leave of the Signora and her daughter, with many tears; and promising to send them some news soon, and return as quickly as possible, she set off.

The journey was performed without accident. They passed part of the night in an inn on the road-side, as usual, and setting off on their way before sun-rise, arrived early in the morning at Pescarenico. Agnese alighted on the little square before the convent, dismissed her conductor with many thanks; and, since she was at the place, determined, before going home, to see her benefactor, the worthy friar. She rang the bell; the person who came to open the door was fra Galdino, the nut-seeker.

'Oh, my good woman, what wind has brought you here?'

'I want to see Father Cristoforo.'

'Father Cristoforo? He's not here.'

'Oh! will he be long before he comes back?'

'Long!' said the friar, shrugging his shoulders, so as almost to bury his shorn head in his hood.

'Where has he gone?'

'To Rimini.'

'To . . . ?'

'To Rimini.'

'Where is that?'

'Eh! eh! eh!' replied the friar, vertically waving his extended hand in the air, to signify a great distance.

'Alas me! But why has he gone away so suddenly?'

'Because the Father provincial ordered it.'

'And why have they sent him away at all, when he was doing so much good here? Ah, poor me!'

'If superiors were obliged to render a reason for all the orders they give, where would be our obedience, my good woman?'

'Yes; but this is my ruin.'

'This is the way it will be. They will have wanted a good preacher at Rimini (there are some everywhere, to be sure, but sometimes they want a particular man, on purpose); the Father provincial there will have written to the Father provincial here, to know if he had such and such a person: and the Father provincial will have said, "Father Cristoforo is the man for him;" as, in fact, you see it is.'

'Oh, poor us! When did he go?'

'The day before yesterday.'

'See now; if I had only done as I first wished, and come a few days sooner! And don't you know when he may return? Can't you guess at all?'

'Eh, my good woman! Nobody knows, except the Father provincial, if even he does. When once one of our preaching friars has taken the wing, one can never foresee on what branch he will finally alight. They are sought after here, and there, and everywhere; and we have convents in all the four quarters of the globe. Rest assured, Father Cristoforo will make a great noise with his course of Lent sermons, at Rimini; for he doesn't always preach extempore, as he did here, that the poor people might understand him; for the city pulpits he has his beautiful written sermons, and his best robes. The fame of this great preacher will spread; and they may ask for him at . . . I don't know where. Besides, we ought to give him up, for we live on the charity of the whole world, and it is but just that we should serve the whole world.'

'Oh dear, dear!' again cried Agnese, almost weeping: 'What can I do without him? He was like a father to us! It is the undoing of us.'

'Listen, my good woman; Father Cristoforo was certainly an admirable man; but we have others, you know, full of charity and ability, and who know how to deal with either rich or poor. Will you have Father Atanasio? or Father Girolamo? or Father Zaccaria? Father Zaccaria, you know, is a man of great worth. And don't you wonder, as some ignorant people do, that he is so thin, and has such a weak voice, and such a miserable beard: I don't say that he is a good preacher, because everybody has his particular gifts; but he is just the man to give advice, you know.'

'Oh holy patience!' exclaimed Agnese, with that mixture of gratitude and impatience that one feels at an offer in which there is more good nature than suitableness: 'What does it matter to me what a man is or is not, when that good man, who's no longer here, was he who knew all our affairs, and had made preparations to help us?'

'Then you must have patience.'

'I know that,' replied Agnese: 'forgive me for troubling you.'

'Oh don't say a word, my good woman; I am very sorry for you. And if you determine upon consulting any of the Fathers, the convent is here, and won't go away. I shall see you soon, when I collect the oil.'

'Good-bye,' said Agnese; and she turned towards her little village, forlorn, perplexed, and disconcerted, like a blind man who has lost his staff.

Rather better informed than fra Galdino, we will now relate how things had really happened. Immediately on Attilio's arrival at Milan, he went, as he had promised Don Rodrigo, to pay a visit to their common uncle of the Privy-council. (This was a committee, composed, at that time, of thirteen persons of rank, with whom the governor usually consulted, and who, when he either died or resigned his office, temporarily assumed the command.) Their uncle, the Count, a robed member, and one of the oldest of the Council, enjoyed there a certain authority; but in displaying this authority, and making it felt by those around him, there was not his equal. Ambiguous language, significant silence, abrupt pauses in speaking, a wink of the eye, that seemed to say, 'I may not speak,' flattery without promises, and formal threatenings—all were directed to this end; and all, more or less, produced the desired effect; so that even the positive declaration, 'I can do nothing in this business,' pronounced sometimes in absolute truth, but pronounced so that it was not believed, only served to increase the idea, and, therefore the reality, of his power: like the japanned boxes which may still be occasionally seen in an apothecary's shop, with sundry Arabic characters stamped upon them, actually containing nothing, yet serving to keep up the credit of the shop. That of the Count, which had been for a long time increasing, by very gradual steps, had, at last, made a giant's stride, as the saying is, on an extraordinary occasion; namely, a journey to Madrid, on an embassy to the Court, where the reception that he met with should be related by himself. To mention nothing else the Count Duke had treated him with particular condescension, and admitted him into his confidence so far as to have asked him, in the presence, he might say, of half the Court, how he liked Madrid, and to have told him, another time, when standing in the recess of a window, that the Cathedral of Milan was the largest Christian temple in the king's dominions.

After paying all due ceremony to his uncle, and delivering his cousin's compliments, Attilio addressed him with a look of seriousness, such as he knew how and when to assume: 'I think I am only doing my duty without betraying Rodrigo's confidence, when I acquaint my uncle with an affair, which, unless you interfere, may become serious, and produce consequences . . .'

'One of his usual scrapes, I suppose?'

'I can assure you that the fault is not on Rodrigo's side, but his spirit is roused; and, as I said, no one but you can . . .'

'Well, let us hear, let us hear.'

'There is a Capuchin friar in that neighbourhood, who bears a grudge against my cousin; and things have gone to such a pitch that . . .'

'How often have I told you both to let the monks fry their own fish? It is quite sufficient for those to have to do with them who are obliged . . . whose business it is . . .' and here he sighed. 'But you can avoid them . . .'

'Signor uncle, I am bound to tell you that Rodrigo would have let them alone, had it been possible. It is the friar who is determined to quarrel with him, and has tried in every way to provoke him.'

'What the——has this friar to do with my nephew?'

'First of all, he is well known as a restless spirit, who prides himself upon quarrelling with gentlemen. This fellow, too, has taken under his protection and direction, and I don't know what besides, a country girl of the village, whom he regards with an affection . . . an affection . . . I don't say of what kind; but a very jealous, suspicious, and sullen affection.'

'I understand,' said the Count, and a ray of cunning intelligence shot across the depth of dulness nature had stamped upon his countenance, now, however, partially veiled under the mask of a politician.

'Now, for some time,' continued Attilio, 'this friar has taken a fancy that Rodrigo has, I don't know what designs upon this . . .'

'Taken a fancy, eh, taken a fancy? I know the Signor Don Rodrigo too well; and it needs another advocate besides your lordship to justify him in these matters.'

'That Rodrigo, Signor uncle, may have had some idle jesting with this girl, when he met her on the road, I can easily believe: he is young, and besides, not a Capuchin: but these are mere nonsenses, not worth mentioning to my noble uncle: the serious part of the business is, that the friar has begun to talk of Rodrigo as he would of a common fellow, and has tried to instigate all the country against him.'   -

'And the other friars?'

'They don't meddle with it, because they know him to be a hotheaded fool, and bear a great respect to Rodrigo; but, on the other side, this monk has great reputation among the villagers as a saint, and . . .'

'I fancy he doesn't know that Rodrigo is my nephew . . .'

'Doesn't he, though? It is just this that urges him onward.'

'How? how?'

'Because—and he scruples not to publish it—he takes greater delight in vexing Rodrigo, exactly because he has a natural protector of such authority as your lordship; he laughs at great people and politicians, and says that the cord of St Francis binds even swords and . . .'

'The rash villain! What is his name?'

'Fra Cristoforo, of * * *,' said Attilio; and his uncle, taking a tablet from his desk, and considerably incensed, inscribed within it the unfortunate name. In the mean while Attilio continued: 'This fellow has always had such a disposition: his former life is well known. He was a plebeian, who possessed a little money, and would, therefore, compete with the noblemen of his country; and out of rage at not being able to make them all yield to him, he killed one, and then turned friar to escape the gallows.'

'Bravo! capital! we will see, we will see,' exclaimed the Count, panting and puffing with an important air.

'Lately,' continued Attilio, 'he is more enraged than ever, because he has failed in a design which he was very eager about; and from this my noble uncle will understand what sort of man he is. This fellow wanted to marry his protégée; whether to remove her from the perils of the world, you understand, or whatever it might be, at any rate he was determined to marry her; and he had found the . . . the man, another of his protégés, a person whose name my honoured uncle may not improbably have heard; for I dare say the Privy-council have had some transactions with this worthy subject.'

'Who is he?'

'A silk-weaver, Lorenzo Tramaglino, he who . . .'

'Lorenzo Tramaglino!' exclaimed his uncle. 'Well done, my brave friar! Certainly! . . . indeed . . . he had a letter for a . . . A crime that . . . But it matters not; very well. And why did Don Rodrigo tell me nothing of all this; but let things go so far, without applying to one who is both able and willing to direct and help him?'

'I will be candid with you. On the one hand, knowing how many intrigues and affairs you had in your head . . .' (here his uncle drew a long breath, and put his hand to his forehead, as if to intimate the fatigue he underwent in the settlement of so many intricate undertakings), 'he felt in a manner bound,' continued Attilio, 'not to give you any additional trouble. And besides, I will tell you the whole: from what I can gather, he is so vexed, so angry, so annoyed at the insults offered him by this friar, that he is more desirous of getting justice for himself by some summary means, than of obtaining it in the regular way of prudence by the assistance of your Lordship. I have tried to extinguish the flame; but seeing things taking a wrong course, I thought it my duty to inform your Lordship of everything, who, after all, is the head and chief prop of the house . . .'

'You would have done better to have spoken a little sooner.'

'True; but I continued to hope that the thing would die off of itself, or that the friar would, at last, come to his senses, or would, perhaps, leave the convent, as is often the case among the monks, who are one day here and another there; and then all would have been quietly ended. But . . .'

'Now it is my business to settle it.'

'So I have thought. I said to myself: The Signor, my uncle, with his discretion and authority, will know well enough how to prevent a quarrel, and at the same time secure Rodrigo's honour, which is almost, as it were, his own. This friar, thought I, is always boasting of the girdle of St Francis; but to employ this girdle seasonably, it is not necessary to have it always buckled around one's waist. My noble uncle has many means that I know not of: I only know that the Father provincial has, as is but right, a great respect for him; and if my honoured uncle thought that the best course, in this instance, would be to give the friar a change of air; two words . . .'

'Your Lordship will be pleased to leave the arrangement to the person it belongs to,' said his uncle, rather abruptly.

'Oh, certainly!' exclaimed Attilio, with a toss of his head, and a disguised smile of disdainful compassion. 'I am not intending to give advice to your Lordship! But the regard I have for the reputation of the family made me speak. And I am afraid I have been guilty of another error,' added he, with a thoughtful air; 'I fear I have wronged Rodrigo in your Lordship's opinion. I should have no peace if I were the cause of making you think that Rodrigo had not all the confidence in you, and all the submission to your will, that he ought to have. Believe me, Signor uncle, that, in this instance, it is merely . . .'

'Come, come; you two won't wrong each other, if you can help it; you will be always friends, till one of you becomes prudent. Ever getting into some scrape or other, and expecting me to settle it: for . . . you will force me to say so, you give me more to think about, you two, than . . .' here he heaved a profound sigh—'all these blessed affairs of state.'

Attilio made a few more excuses, promises, and compliments, and then took his leave, accompanied by a—'Be prudent,'—the Count's usual form of dismissal to his nephews.

CHAPTER XIX

IF a weed be discovered in a badly cultivated field, a fine root of sorrel, for example, and the spectator wish to ascertain with certainty whether it has sprung up from seed, either ripened in the field itself, or wafted thither by the wind, or dropped there by a bird in its flight, let him think as he will about it, he will never come to a satisfactory conclusion. For the same reason we are unable to decide whether the resolution formed by the Count of making use of the Father provincial to cut in two, as the best and easiest method, this intricate knot, arose from his own unassisted imagination, or from the suggestions of Attilio. Certain it is, that Attilio had not thrown out the hint unintentionally; and however naturally he might expect that the jealous haughtiness of his noble relative would recoil at so open an insinuation, he was determined at any rate to make the idea of such a resource flash before his eyes, and let him know the course which he desired he should pursue. On the other hand, the plan was so exactly consonant with his uncle's disposition, and so naturally marked out by circumstances, that one might safely venture the assertion, that he had thought of, and embraced it, without the suggestion of any one. It was a most essential point towards the reputation of power which he had so much at heart, that one of his name, a nephew of his, should not be worsted in a dispute of such notoriety. The satisfaction that his nephew would take for himself, would have been a remedy worse than the disease, a foundation for future troubles, which it was necessary to overthrow at any cost, and without loss of time. Command him at once to quit his palace, and he would not obey; and, even should he submit, it would be a surrendering of the contest, a submission of their house to the superiority of a convent. Commands, legal force, or any terrors of that nature, were of no value against an adversary of such a character as Father Cristoforo: the regular and secular clergy were entirely exempt, not only in their persons, but in their places of abode, from all lay-jurisdiction (as must have been observed even by one who has read no other story than the one before him); otherwise they would often have fared very badly. All that could be attempted against such a rival was his removal, and the only means for obtaining this was the Father provincial, at whose pleasure Father Cristoforo was either stationary, or on the move.

Between this Father provincial and the Count of the Privy-council there existed an acquaintanceship of long standing: they seldom saw each other, but whenever they met, it was with great demonstrations of friendship, and reiterated offers of service. It is sometimes easier to transact business advantageously with a person who presides over many individuals than with only one of those same individuals, who sees but his own motives, feels but his own passions, seeks only his own ends; while the former instantly perceives a hundred relations, contingencies, and interests, a hundred objects to secure or avoid, and can, therefore, be taken on a hundred different sides.

When all had been well arranged in his mind, the Count one day invited the Father provincial to dinner, to meet a circle of guests selected with superlative judgment:—an assemblage of men of the highest rank, whose family alone bore a lofty title, and who by their carriage, by a certain native boldness, by a lordly air of disdain, and by talking of great things in familiar terms, succeeded, even without intending it, in impressing, and, on every occasion, keeping up, the idea of their superiority and power; together with a few clients bound to the house by an hereditary devotion, and to its head by the servitude of a whole life; who, beginning with the soup to say 'yes,' with their lips, their eyes, their ears, their head, their whole body, and their whole heart, had made a man, by dessert-time, almost forget how to say 'no.'

At table, the noble host quickly turned the conversation upon Madrid. There are many ways and means of accomplishing one's object, and he tried all. He spoke of the court, the Count-duke, the ministers, and the governor's family; of the bull-baits, which he could accurately describe, having been a spectator from a very advantageous post; and of the Escurial, of which he could give a minute account, because one of the Count-duke's pages had conducted him through every nook and corner of it. For some time the company continued like an audience, attentive to him alone; but, by degrees, they divided into small groups of talkers, and he then proceeded to relate further anecdotes of the great things he had seen, as in confidence, to the Father provincial, who was seated near him, and who suffered him to talk on without interruption. But at a certain point he gave a turn to the conversation, and, leaving Madrid, proceeded from court to court, and from dignitary to dignitary, till he had brought upon the tapis Cardinal Barberini, a Capuchin, and brother to the then reigning Pope, Urban VIII. The Count was at last obliged to cease talking for a while, and be content to listen, and remember that, after all, there were some people in the world who were not born to live and act only for him. Shortly after leaving the table, he requested the Father provincial to step with him into another apartment.

Two men of authority, age, and consummate experience, now found themselves standing opposite to each other. The noble lord requested the reverend Father to take a seat, and, placing himself at his side, began as follows: 'Considering the friendship that exists between us, I thought I might venture to speak a word to your Reverence on a matter of mutual interest, which it would be better to settle between ourselves, without taking any other courses, which might . . . But, without further preface, I will candidly tell you to what I allude, and I doubt not you will immediately agree with me. Tell me: in your convent of Pescarenico there is a certain Father Cristoforo of * * * ?'

The Provincial bowed assent.

'Your Paternity will be good enough then, frankly, like a friend, to tell me . . . this person . . . this Father . . . I don't know him personally; I am acquainted with several Capuchin fathers, zealous, prudent, humble men, who are worth their weight in gold: I have been a friend to the order from my boyhood . . . But in every rather numerous family . . . there is always some individual, some wild . . . And this Father Cristoforo, I know by several occurrences that he is a person . . . rather inclined to disputes . . . who has not all the prudence, all the circumspection . . . I dare say he has more than once given your Paternity some anxiety.'

—I understand; this is a specimen,—thought the Provincial in the meantime.—It is my fault; I knew that that blessed Cristoforo was fitter to go about from pulpit to pulpit, than to be set down for six months in one place, specially in a country convent.—

'Oh!' said he aloud, 'I am really very sorry to hear that your Highness entertains such an opinion of Father Cristoforo; for, as far as I know, he is a most exemplary monk in the convent, and is held in much esteem also in the neighbourhood.'

'I understand perfectly; your Reverence ought . . . However, as a sincere friend, I wish to inform you of a thing which it is important for you to know; and even if you are already acquainted with it, I think, without exceeding my duty, I should caution you against the (I only say) possible consequences. Do you know that this Father Cristoforo has taken under his protection a man of that country, a man . . . of whom your Paternity has doubtless heard mention; him who escaped in such disgrace from the hands of justice, after having done things on that terrible day of St. Martin . . . things . . . Lorenzo Tramaglino?'

—Alas!—thought the Provincial, as he replied: 'This particular is quite new to me, but your Highness is sufficiently aware that it is a part of our office to seek those who have gone astray, to recall them . . .'

'Yes, yes; but intercourse with offenders of a certain kind! . . . is rather a dangerous thing—a very delicate affair . . .' And here, instead of puffing out his cheeks and panting, he compressed his lips, and drew in as much air as he was accustomed to send forth with such profound importance. He then resumed: 'I thought it as well to give you this hint, because if ever his Excellency . . . He may have had some business at Rome . . . I don't know, though . . . and there might come to you from Rome . . .'

'I am much obliged to your Lordship for this information, but I feel confident, that if they would make inquiries on this subject, they would find that Father Cristoforo has had no intercourse with the person you mention, unless it be to try and set him right again. I know Father Cristoforo well.'

'You know, probably, already, better than I do, what kind of a man he was as a layman, and the life he led in his youth.'

'It is one of the glories of our habit, Signor Count, that a man who has given ever so much occasion in the world for men to talk about him, becomes a different person when he has assumed this dress. And ever since Father Cristoforo has worn the habit . . .'

'I would gladly believe it, I assure you—I would gladly believe it; but sometimes . . . as the proverb says . . . "It is not the cowl that makes the friar." '

The proverb was not exactly to the purpose, but the Count had cited it instead of another, which had crossed his mind: 'The wolf changes its skin, but not its nature.'

'I have facts,' continued he; 'I have positive proofs . . .'

'If you know for certain,' interrupted the Provincial, 'that this friar has been guilty of any fault, (and we are all liable to err), you will do me a favour to inform me of it. I am his superior, though unworthily; but it is, therefore, my duty to correct and reprove.'

'I will tell you; together with the unpleasing circumstance of the favour this Father displays towards the person I have mentioned, there is another grievous thing, which may . . . But we will settle all this between ourselves at once. This same Father Cristoforo has begun a quarrel with my nephew, Don Rodrigo * * *'

'Indeed! I am very sorry to hear it!—very sorry indeed!'

'My nephew is young, and hot-tempered; he feels what he is, and is not accustomed to be provoked . . .'

'It shall be my business to make every inquiry on the subject. As I have often told your Lordship, and as you must know, with your great experience in the world, and your noble judgment, far better than I, we are all human, and liable to err . . . some one way, some another; and if our Father Cristoforo has failed . . .'

'Your Reverence must perceive that these are matters, as I said, which had better be settled between ourselves, and remain buried with us—things which, if much meddled with, will only be made worse. You know how it often happens; these strifes and disputes frequently originate from a mere bagatelle, and become more and more serious as they are suffered to proceed. It is better to strike at the root before they grow to a head, or become the causes of a hundred other contentions. Suppress it, and cut it short, most reverend Father; suppress, and cut it short. My nephew is young; the

monk, from what I hear, has still all the spirit—all the . . . inclinations of a young man; and it belongs to us who have some years on
our shoulders—(too many, are there not, most reverend Father?)
it belongs to us, I say, to have judgment for the young, and try to
remedy their errors. Fortunately we are still in good time: the matter has made no stir; it is still a case of a good *principiis obsta*. Let
us remove the straw from the flame. A man who has not done well,
or who may be a cause of some trouble in one place, sometimes gets
on surprisingly in another. Your Paternity, doubtless, knows where
to find a convenient post for this friar. This will also meet the other
circumstance of his having, perhaps, fallen under the suspicions of
one . . . who would be very glad that he should be removed; and
thus, by placing him at a little distance, we shall kill two birds with
one stone; all will be quietly settled, or rather, there will be no harm
done.'

The Father provincial had expected this conclusion from the beginning of the interview.—Ay, ay!—thought he to himself;—I see
well enough what you would bring me to. It's the usual way; if a
poor friar has an encounter with you, or with any one of you, or
gives you any offence, right or wrong, the superior must make him
march immediately.—

When the Count was at last silent, and had puffed forth a long-
drawn breath, which was equivalent to a full stop: 'I understand
very well,' said the Provincial, 'what your noble Lordship would
say; but before taking a step . . .'

'It is a step, and it is not a step, most reverend Father. It is a
natural thing enough—a very common occurrence; and if it does
not come to this, and quickly too, I foresee a mountain of disorders
—an Iliad of woes. A mistake . . . my nephew, I do not believe
. . . I am here, for this . . . But, at the point at which matters have
now arrived, if we do not put a stop to it between ourselves, without
loss of time, by one decided blow, it is not possible that it should
remain a secret . . . and then, it is not only my nephew . . . we
raise a hornet's nest, most reverend Father. You know, we are a
powerful family—we have adherents . . .'

'Plainly enough . . .'

'You understand me: they are all persons who have some blood in their veins, and who . . . count as somebody in the world. Their honour will come in; it will become a common affair; and then . . . even one who is a friend to peace . . . It will be a great grief to me to be obliged . . . to find myself . . . I, who have always had so much kind feeling towards the Capuchin Fathers! You reverend Fathers, to continue to do good, as you have hitherto done, with so much edification among the people, stand in need of peace, should be free from strifes, and in harmony with those who . . . And, besides, you have friends in the world . . . and these affairs of honour, if they go any length, extend themselves, branch out on every side, and draw in . . . half the world. I am in a situation which obliges me to maintain a certain dignity . . . His Excellency . . . my noble colleagues . . . it becomes quite a party matter . . . particularly with that other circumstance . . . You know how these things go.'

'Certainly,' said the Father provincial, 'Father Cristoforo is a preacher; and I had already some thoughts . . . I have just been asked . . . But at this juncture, and under the present circumstances, it might look like a punishment; and a punishment before having fully ascertained . . .'

'Pshaw! punishment, pshaw!—merely a prudential arrangement —a convenient resource for preventing evils which might ensue . . . I have explained myself.'

'Between the Signor Count and me things stand in this light, I am aware; but as your Lordship has related the circumstances, it is impossible, I should say, but that something is known in the country around. There are everywhere firebrands, mischief-makers, or, at least, malicious priers, who take a mad delight in seeing the nobility and the religious orders at variance; they observe it immediately, report it, and enlarge upon it . . . Everybody has his dignity to maintain; and I also, as Superior, (though unworthily,) have an express duty . . . The honour of the habit . . . is not my private concern . . . it is a deposit of which . . . Your noble nephew, since he is so high-spirited as your Lordship describes him, might take it as a satisfaction offered to him, and . . . I do not say boast of it, and triumph over him, but . . .'

'Is your Paternity joking with me? My nephew is a gentleman of some consideration in the world . . . that is, according to his rank and the claims he has; but in my presence he is a mere boy, and will do neither more nor less than I bid him. I will go further, and tell you that my nephew shall know nothing about it. Why need we give any account of what we do? It is all transacted between ourselves, as old friends, and never need come to light. Don't give yourself a thought about this. I ought to be accustomed to be silent.' And he heaved a deep sigh. 'As to gossips,' resumed he, 'what do you suppose they can say? The departure of a monk to preach somewhere else, is nothing so very uncommon! And then, we who see . . . we who foresee . . . we who ought . . . we need not give ourselves any concern about gossipings.'

'At any rate, it would be well to try and prevent them on this occasion, by your noble nephew's making some demonstration, giving some open proof of friendship and deference . . . not for our sakes, as individuals, but for the sake of the habit . . .'

'Certainly, certainly, this is but fair . . . However, there is no need of it; I know that the Capuchins are always received as they ought to be by my nephew. He does so from inclination; it is quite the disposition of the family; and besides, he knows it is gratifying to me. In this instance, however . . . something more marked . . . is only right. Leave me to settle it, most reverend Father; I will order my nephew . . . that is, I must cautiously suggest it to him, lest he should suspect what has passed between us. It would not do, you know, to lay a plaister where there is no wound. And as to what we have determined upon, the quicker the better. If you can find some post at a little distance . . . to obviate every occasion . . .'

'I have just been asked for a preacher at Rimini; and perhaps, even without any other reason, I should have thought of . . .'

'Exactly *apropos,* exactly *apropos.* And when . . .?'

'Since the thing must be done, it had better be done at once.'

'Directly, directly, most reverend Father; better to-day than to-morrow. And,' continued he, as he rose from his seat, 'if I can do anything, I or my friends, for our worthy Capuchin Fathers . . .'

'We know, by experience, the kindness of your house,' said the Father provincial, also rising, and advancing towards the door, behind his vanquisher.

'We have extinguished a spark,' said the Count, walking slowly forward; 'a spark, most reverend Father, which might have been fanned into a wide-spreading and dangerous flame. Between friends, two or three words will often settle great things.'

On reaching the other apartment, he threw open the door, and insisted upon the Father's first entering; then following him in, they mingled with the rest of the company.

This nobleman employed a studied politeness, great dexterity, and fine words, to accomplish his designs; and they produced corresponding effects. In fact, he succeeded, by the conversation we have related, in making Father Cristoforo go, on foot, from Pescarenico to Rimini, which is a very tolerable distance.

One evening, a Capuchin arrived at Pescarenico, from Milan, with a despatch to the Father-guardian. It contained an order for Father Cristoforo to repair at once to Rimini, where he was appointed to preach the course of Lent Sermons. The letter to the guardian contained instructions to insinuate to the said friar, that he must give up all thoughts of any business he might have in hand in the neighbourhood he was about to leave, and was not to keep up any correspondence there: the bearer would be his companion by the way. The guardian said nothing that evening; but next morning he summoned Father Cristoforo, showed him the command, bade him take his wallet, staff, maniple, and girdle, and, with the Father whom he presented to him as a companion, immediately set off on his journey.

What a blow this would be to the poor friar, the reader must imagine. Renzo, Lucia, Agnese, instantly rushed into his mind; and he exclaimed, so to say, to himself:—Oh my God! what will these poor creatures do, when I am no longer here!—But instantly raising his eyes to heaven, he reproached himself for want of faith, and for having supposed that he was necessary in anything. He crossed his hands on his breast, in token of obedience, and bowed his head before the guardian, who, taking him aside, told him the rest of the message, adding a few words of advice, and some sensible precepts. Father Cristoforo then went into his cell, took his basket, and placed therein his breviary, his sermons, and the bread of forgiveness, bound round his waist a leathern girdle, took leave of his brethren whom he found in the convent, went to request the guardian's blessing, and then, with his companion, took the route which had been prescribed for him.

We have said that Don Rodrigo, more than ever resolved to accomplish his praiseworthy undertaking, had determined to seek the assistance of a very formidable character. Of this personage we can give neither the name, surname, nor title, nor can we even venture a conjecture on any one of them; which is the more remarkable, as we find mention of him in more than one published book of those times. That it is the same personage, the identity of facts leaves no room for doubt; but everywhere a studious endeavour may be traced to conceal his name, as if the mention of it would have ignited the pen, and scorched the writer's hand. Francesco Rivola, in his Life of the Cardinal Federigo Borromeo, speaking of this person, says: 'A nobleman, as powerful by wealth as illustrious by birth,' and nothing more. Giuseppe Ripamonti, who, in the fifth book of the fifth decade of his *Storia Patria,* makes more exclusive mention of him, describes him as 'one,' 'this person,' 'that person,' 'this man,' 'that personage.' 'I will relate,' says he, in his elegant Latin, which we translate as follows,—'the case of one, who, being among the first of the great men of the city, took up his residence in the country; where, securing himself by the force of crime, he set at nought justice and judges, all magisterial, and even all sovereign power. Situated on the very confines of the state, he led an independent life; a harbourer of outlaws, an outlaw at one time himself, and then safely returned . . .' We will extract, in the sequel, some other passages from this writer, which will serve to confirm and elucidate the account of our anonymous author, with whom we are travelling onward.

To do what was forbidden by the public laws, or rendered difficult by an opposing power; to be the arbiter, the judge in other people's affairs, without further interest in them than the love of command; to be feared by all, and to have the upper hand among those who were accustomed to hold the same station over others: such had ever been the principal objects and desires of this man. From his youth he had always had a mingled feeling of contempt and impatient envy at the sight or report of the power, rencounters, strifes, or oppressive tyranny of others. Young, and living in a city, he omitted no opportunity, nay, even sought for them, of setting himself up against the most renowned of this profession, either entirely to subdue them, to struggle with them, and keep them in awe, or to induce them to solicit his friendship. Superior to most in riches and retinue, and, perhaps, to all in presumption and intrepidity, he compelled many to retire from competition; some he treated with haughtiness or contempt, some he took as friends; not, however, on an equality with himself, but, as alone would satisfy his proud and arrogant mind, as subordinate friends, who would be content to acknowledge their inferiority, and use their hands in his service. In fact, however, he became at length the grand actor, and the instrument of his companions, who never failed to solicit the aid of so powerful an auxiliary in all their undertakings, while for him to draw back, would be to forfeit his reputation, and come short of what he had assumed. He went on thus, till, on his own service and that of others, he had gone to such a length, that neither his name, family, friends, nor even his own audacity, sufficed to secure him against public proclamations and outlawry, and he was compelled to give way and leave the state. I believe it is to this circumstance that a remarkable incident, related by Ripamonti, refers. 'On one occasion, when obliged to quit the country, the secrecy he used, and the respect and timidity he displayed, were such, that he rode through the city on horseback, followed by a pack of hounds, and accompanied with the sound of the trumpet; and, in passing before the palace of the court, left an insolent message with the guards, for the governor.'

During his absence he continued the same practices, not even intermitting his correspondence with those of his friends who remained united to him (to translate literally from Ripamonti), 'in the secret alliance of atrocious consultations and fatal deeds.' It even appears that he engaged the foreign courts in other new and formidable undertakings, of which the above-cited historian speaks with mysterious brevity. 'Some foreign princes several times availed themselves of his assistance in important murders, and frequently sent him reinforcements of soldiers, from a considerable distance, to act under his orders.'

At length (it is not exactly known how long afterwards) either the

sentence of banishment against him being withdrawn, by some powerful intercession, or the audacity of the man serving him in place
of any other liberation, he resolved to return home, and, in fact,
did return; not, however, to Milan, but to a castle on his manor,
situated on the confines of the Bergamascan territory, at that time,
as most of our readers know, under Venetian government; and here
he fixed his abode. 'This dwelling,' we again quote Ripamonti, 'was,
as it were, a dispensary of sanguinary mandates: the servants were
outlaws and murderers; the very cooks and scullions were not
exempt from homicide; the hands of the children were stained with
blood.' Besides this amiable domestic circle, he had, as the same historian affirms, another set of dependents of a similar character dispersed abroad, and quartered, so to say, at different posts in the
two states on the borders of which he lived, who were always ready
to execute his orders.

All the tyrannical noblemen, for a considerable distance round,
had been obliged, on one occasion or another, to choose between the
friendship or the enmity of this super-eminent tyrant. Those, however, who at first attempted to resist him, came off so badly in the
contest, that no one was ever induced to make a second trial. Neither
was it possible, by maintaining a neutral course, or standing, as the
saying is, in their own shoes, to keep themselves independent of him.
If a message arrived, intimating that such a person must desist from
such an undertaking, or cease to molest such a debtor, or so forth,
it was necessary to give a decided answer one way or other. When
one party came, with the homage of a vassal, to refer any business to
his arbitration, the other party was reduced to the hard alternative
of either abiding by his sentence, or publicly declaring hostilities;
which was equivalent to being, as the saying is, in the last stage
of consumption. Men who were in the wrong had recourse to him
that they might be right in effect; many being in the right, yet
resorted to him to pre-engage so powerful a patronage, and close
the way against their adversaries; thus both bad and good came to
be dependent upon him. It sometimes happened that the weak,
oppressed, harassed, and tyrannized over by some powerful lord,
turned to him for protection; he would then take the part of the
oppressed, and force the oppressor to abstain from further injuries,
to repair the wrongs he had committed, and even to stoop to

apologies; or, in case of his proving stubborn and unbending, he would completely crush his power, constrain him to quit the place where he had exercised such unjust influence, or even make him pay a more expeditious and more terrible penalty. In these cases, his name, usually so dreaded and abhorred, became, for a time, an object of blessing: for (I will not say, this justice, but) this remedy, this recompense of some sort, could not have been expected, under the circumstances of the times, from any other either public or private source. More frequently, and indeed ordinarily, his power and authority ministered to iniquitous desires, atrocious revenge, or outrageous caprice. But the very opposite uses he made of this power produced in the end the self-same effect, that of impressing all minds with a lofty idea of how much he could will and execute in spite of equity or iniquity, those two things which interpose so many impediments to the accomplishment of man's desires, and so often force him to turn back. The fame of ordinary oppressors was for the most part restricted to the limited tract of country where they continually or frequently exercised their oppression: each district had its own tyrant; and these so resembled each other, that there was no reason that people should interfere with those from whom they sustained neither injury nor molestation. But the fame of this man had long been diffused throughout every corner of the Milanese: his life was everywhere the subject of popular stories; and his very name carried with it the idea of something formidable, dark, and fabulous. The suspicions that were everywhere entertained of his confederates and tools of assassination, contributed to keep alive a constant memento of him. They were nothing more than suspicions; since who would have openly acknowledged such a dependence? but every tyrant might be his associate, every robber one of his assassins; and the very uncertainty of the fact rendered the opinion more general, and the terror more profound. At every appearance of an unknown ruffian, more savage-looking than usual; at every enormous crime, the author of which could not be at first pointed out or conjectured, the name of this man was pronounced and whispered about, whom, thanks to the unhappy circumspection, to give it no other epithet, of our author's, we shall be obliged to designate The Unnamed.

The distance between his castle and the palace of Don Rodrigo was not more than seven miles: and no sooner had the latter become a lord and tyrant than he could not help seeing that, at so short a distance from such a personage, it would not be possible to carry on this profession without either coming to blows, or walking hand in hand with him. He had, therefore, offered himself and been accepted, for a friend, in the same way, that is, as the rest: he had rendered him more than one service (the manuscript says nothing further); and had each time been rewarded by promises of requital and assistance in any cases of emergency. He took great pains, however, to conceal such a friendship, or at least of what nature and how strict it was. Don Rodrigo liked well enough to play the tyrant, but not the fierce and savage tyrant: the profession was to him a means, not an end: he wished to live at freedom in the city, to enjoy the conveniences, diversions, and honours of social life; and for this end he was obliged to keep up a certain appearance, make much of his family, cultivate the friendship of persons in place, and keep one hand on the scales of justice, so as on any occasion to make them preponderate in his favour, either removing them altogether from view, or bringing them to bear with double force on the head of some individual, on whom he could thus more easily accomplish his designs than by the arm of private violence. Now, an intimacy, or it would be better to say an alliance, with a person of such notoriety, an open enemy of the public power, would certainly not have advanced his interests in these respects, and particularly with his uncle. However, the slight acquaintance which he was unable to conceal, might pass very well for an indispensable attention towards a man whose enmity was much to be deprecated, and thus it might receive excuse from necessity; since one who assumes the charge of providing for another without the will or the means, in the long run consents that his protégé shall provide for himself up to a certain point in his own affairs; and if he does not expressly give his consent, at least he winks at it.

One morning, Don Rodrigo set off on horseback, in the guise of a hunter, with a small escort of bravoes on foot, Griso at his side, and four others following behind him, and took the road to the castle of the Unnamed.

CHAPTER XX

THE castle of the Unnamed was commandingly situated over a dark and narrow valley, on the summit of a cliff projecting from a rugged ridge of hills, whether united to them or separated from them it is difficult to say, by a mass of crags and rocks, and by a boundary of caverns and abrupt precipices, both flanking it and on the rear. The side which overlooked the valley was the only accessible one; rather a steep acclivity, certainly, but even and unbroken: the summit was used for pasturage, while the lower grounds were cultivated, and scattered here and there with habitations. The bottom was a bed of large stones, the channel, according to the season, of either a rivulet or a noisy torrent, which at that time formed the boundary of the two states. The opposite ridges, forming, so to speak, the other wall of the valley, had a small cultivated tract, gently inclining from the base; the rest was covered with crags, stones, and abrupt risings, untrodden, and destitute of vegetation, excepting here and there a solitary bush in the interstices, or on the edges of the rocks.

From the height of this castle, like an eagle from his sanguinary nest, the savage nobleman surveyed every spot around where the foot of man could tread, and heard no human sound above him. At one view he could overlook the whole vale, the declivities, the bed of the stream, and the practicable paths intersecting the valley. That which approached his terrible abode by a zigzag and serpentine course appeared to a spectator from below like a winding thread; while from the windows and loop-holes on the summit, the Signor could leisurely observe any one who was ascending, and a hundred times catch a view of him. With the garrison of bravoes whom he there maintained, he could even oppose a tolerably numerous troop of assailants, stretching any number of them on the ground, or hurling them to the bottom, before they could succeed in gaining the height. He was not very likely, however, to be put to the trial, since no one who was not on good terms with the owner of the castle would venture to set foot within its walls, or even in the valley or its environs. The bailiff who should have chanced to be seen there would have been treated like an enemy's spy seized within the camp. Tragical stories were related of the last who had dared to attempt the undertaking; but they were then tales of by-gone days; and none of the village youths could remember having seen one of this race of beings, either dead or alive.

Such is the description our anonymous author gives of the place: nothing is said of the name; and for fear of putting us in the way of discovering it, he avoids all notice of Don Rodrigo's journey, bringing him at one jump into the midst of the valley, and setting him down at the foot of the ascent, just at the entrance of the steep and winding footpath. Here stood an inn, which might also be called a guard-house. An antique sign suspended over the door, displayed on each side, in glowing colours, a radiant sun; but the public voice, which sometimes repeats names as they are first pronounced, and sometimes remodels them after its own fashion, never designated this tavern but by the title of the *Malanotte*.[1]

At the sound of a party approaching on horseback, an ill-looking lad appeared at the door-way, well armed with knives and pistols, and after giving a glance at them, re-entered to inform three ruffians, who, seated at table, were playing with a very dirty pack of cards, reversed and laid one upon another like so many tiles. He who seemed to be the leader rose, and advancing towards the door, recognized a friend of his master's, and saluted him with a bow. Don Rodrigo, returning the salutation with great politeness, inquired if his master were in the castle, and receiving for an answer that he believed so, he dismounted from his horse, throwing the reins to Tiradritto, one of his retinue. Then, taking his musket from his shoulder, he handed it to Montanarolo, as if to disencumber himself of a useless weight, and render his ascent easier; but in reality, because he knew well enough that no one was permitted to mount that steep who carried a gun. Then taking out of his purse two or three *berlinghe*, he gave them to Tanabuso, saying: 'Wait for me here; and in the mean time enjoy yourselves with these good

[1] Bad Night.

people.' He then presented the estimable chief of the party with a few gold coins, one half for himself, and the rest to be divided among his companions; and at length, in company with Griso, who had also laid aside his weapons, began to ascend the cliff on foot. In the mean while, the three above-mentioned bravoes, together with their fourth companion, Squinternotto, (what amiable names to be preserved with so much care!) remained behind with the three players, and the unfortunate boy, who was training for the gallows, to game, drink, and relate by turns their various feats of prowess.

Another bravo belonging to the Unnamed shortly overtook Don Rodrigo in his ascent; and after eying him for a moment, recognized a friend of his master's, and bore him company; by this means, sparing him the annoyance of telling his name, and giving a further account of himself, to the many others whom he met, and with whom he was unacquainted. On reaching the castle, and being admitted, (having left Griso, however, outside,) he was conducted a roundabout way through dark corridors, and various apartments hung with muskets, sabres, and partisans, in each of which a bravo stood on guard; and after having waited some time, was at last ushered into the room where the Unnamed was expecting him.

The Signor advanced to meet Don Rodrigo, returning his salutation, and at the same time eying him from head to foot with the closest scrutiny, according to his usual habit, now almost an involuntary one, towards any one who approached him, even towards his oldest and most tried friends. He was tall, sun-burnt, and bald; and at first sight this baldness, the whiteness of his few remaining hairs, and the wrinkles on his face, would have induced the judgment that he was considerably beyond the sixty years he had scarcely yet attained: though on a nearer survey, his carriage and movements, the cutting sarcasm of his features, and the deep fire that sparkled in his eye, indicated a vigour of body and mind which would have been remarkable even in a young man.

Don Rodrigo told him that he came to solicit his advice and assistance; that, finding himself engaged in a difficult undertaking, from which his honour would not now suffer him to retire, he had called to mind the promises of his noble friend, who never promised too much, or in vain; and he then proceeded to relate his infamous enterprise. The Unnamed, who already had some indefinite knowledge of the affair, listened attentively to the recital, both because he was naturally fond of such stories, and because there was implicated in it a name well known and exceedingly odious to him, that of Father Cristoforo, the open enemy of tyrants, not only in word, but, when possible, in deed also. The narrator then proceeded to exaggerate, in evidence, the difficulties of the undertaking:—the distance of the place, a monastery, the Signora! . . . At this word, the Unnamed, as if a demon hidden in his heart had suggested it, abruptly interrupted him, saying that he would take the enterprise upon himself. He took down the name of our poor Lucia, and dismissed Don Rodrigo with the promise: 'You shall shortly hear from me what you are to do.'

If the reader remembers that infamous Egidio whose residence adjoined the monastery where poor Lucia had found a retreat, we will now inform him that he was one of the nearest and most intimate associates in iniquity of the Unnamed; and it was for this reason that the latter had so promptly and resolutely taken upon him to pledge his word. Nevertheless, he was no sooner left alone, than he began to feel, I will not say, repentance, but vexation at having made the promise. For some time past he had experienced, not exactly remorse, but a kind of weariness of his wicked course of life. These feelings, which had accumulated rather in his memory than on his conscience, were renewed each time any new crime was committed, and each time they seemed more multiplied and intolerable: it was like constantly adding and adding to an already incommodious weight. A certain repugnance experienced on the commission of his earlier crimes, afterwards overcome and almost entirely excluded, again returned to make itself felt. But in his first misgivings, the image of a distant and uncertain future, together with the consciousness of a vigorous habit of body and a strong constitution, had only confirmed him in a supine and presumptuous confidence. Now, on the contrary, it was the thoughts of the future that embittered the retrospect of the past.—To grow old! To die! And then?—It is worthy of notice, that the image of death, which in present danger, when facing an enemy, usually only nerved his spirit, and inspired him with impetuous courage,—this same image,

when presented to his mind in the solemn stillness of night, and in
the security of his own castle, was always accompanied with a feeling
of undefined horror and alarm. It was not death threatened by an
enemy who was himself mortal; it was not to be repulsed by
stronger weapons, or a readier arm; it came alone, it was suggested
from within; it might still be distant, but every moment brought it
a step nearer; and even while he was hopelessly struggling to banish
the remembrance of this dreaded enemy, it was coming fast upon
him. In his early days, the frequent examples of violence, revenge,
and murder, which were perpetually exhibited to his view, while
they inspired him with a daring emulation, served at the same time
as a kind of authority against the voice of conscience: now an indistinct but terrible idea of individual responsibility, and judgment
independent of example, incessantly haunted his mind; now the
thought of his having left the ordinary crowd of wicked doers, and
surpassed them all, sometimes impressed him with a feeling of dreadful solitude. That God, of whom he had once heard, but whom he
had long ceased either to deny or acknowledge, solely occupied as
he was in acting as though he existed not, now, at certain moments
of depression without cause, and terror without danger, he imagined
he heard repeating within him, 'Nevertheless, I am.' In the first
heat of youthful passion, the laws which he had heard announced
in His name had only appeared hateful to him; now, when they
returned unbidden to his mind, he regarded them, in spite of himself, as something which would have a fulfilment. But that he might
suffer nothing of this new disquietude to be apparent either in word
or deed, he carefully endeavoured to conceal it under the mask of
deeper and more vehement ferocity; and by this means also he
sought to disguise it from himself, or entirely to stifle it. Envying
(since he could neither annihilate nor forget them) the days in
which he had been accustomed to commit iniquity without remorse,
and without further solicitude than for its success, he used every
endeavour to recall them, and to retain or recover his former unfettered, daring, and undisturbed will, that he might convince himself he was still the same man.

On this occasion, therefore, he had hastily pledged his word to
Don Rodrigo, that he might close the door against all hesitation.

Feeling, however, on his visitor's departure, a failing of the resolution that he had summoned up to make the promise, and gradually overwhelmed with thoughts presenting themselves to his mind, which tempted him to break his word, and which, if yielded to, would have made him sink very low in the eyes of his friend, a secondary accomplice, he resolved at once to cut short the painful conflict, and summoned Nibbio[2] to his presence, one of the most dexterous and venturesome ministers of his enormities, and the one whom he was accustomed to employ in his correspondence with Egidio. With a resolute countenance he ordered him immediately to mount his horse, to go straight to Monza, to inform Egidio of the engagement he had made, and to request his counsel and assistance in fulfilling it.

The worthless messenger returned more expeditiously than his master expected, with Egidio's reply, that the undertaking was easy and secure: if the Unnamed would send a carriage which would not be known as his, with two or three well-disguised bravoes, Egidio would undertake the charge of all the rest, and would manage the whole affair. At this announcement, the Unnamed, whatever might be passing in his mind, hastily gave orders to Nibbio to arrange all as Egidio required, and to go himself, with two others whom he named, upon this expedition.

Had Egidio been obliged to reckon only on ordinary means for the accomplishment of the horrible service he had been requested to undertake, he certainly would not thus readily have given so unhesitating a promise. But in that very asylum, where it would seem all ought to have been an obstacle, the atrocious villain had a resource known only to himself; and that which would have been the greatest difficulty to others became an instrument to him. We have already related how the unhappy Signora on one occasion lent an ear to his addresses; and the reader may have understood that this was not the last time,—that it was but the first step in a career of abomination and bloodshed. The same voice, rendered imperative, and almost authoritative through guilt, now imposed upon her the sacrifice of the innocent creature who had been committed to her care.

The proposal was frightful to Gertrude. To lose Lucia by an

[2] A kite.

unforeseen accident, and without any fault on her part, would have seemed to her a misfortune, a bitter punishment: but now she was enjoined to deprive herself of her society by a base act of perfidy, and to convert a means of expiation into a fresh subject for remorse. The unhappy lady tried every method to extricate herself from the horrible command;—every method, except the only one which would have been infallible, and which still remained in her power. Guilt is a rigid and inflexible tyrant, against whom all are powerless but those who entirely rebel. On this Gertrude could not resolve, and she obeyed.

It was the day fixed; the appointed hour approached; Gertrude retired with Lucia into her private apartment, and there lavished upon her more caresses than usual, which Lucia received and returned with increasing affection: as the lamb, trembling under the hand of the shepherd as he coaxes and gently urges it forward, turns to lick that very hand, unconscious that the butcher waits outside the sheepfold, to whom the shepherd a moment before has sold it.

'I want you to do me a great service; one that nobody but you can do. I have plenty of persons ready to obey me, but none whom I dare trust. On some very important business, which I will tell you about afterwards, I want to speak to the Father-guardian of the Capuchins who brought you here to me, my poor Lucia; but it is absolutely necessary that no one should know I have sent for him. I have nobody but you who can secretly carry this message . . .'

Lucia was terrified at such a request; and with her own native modesty, yet not without a strong expression of surprise, she endeavoured to dissuade her by adducing reasons which the Signora ought to have understood and foreseen: without her mother, without an escort, by a solitary road, in an unknown country . . . But Gertrude, instructed in an infernal school, manifested much surprise and displeasure at finding this stubborn opposition in one whom she had so greatly benefited, and pretended to think her excuses very frivolous. In broad daylight—a mere step—a road Lucia had travelled only a few days before, and which could be so described that even a person who had never seen it could not possibly go astray! . . . In short, she said so much, that the poor girl, touched at once with gratitude and shame, suffered the words to escape: 'Well, what am I to do?'

'Go to the convent of the Capuchins,' and here she again described the road; 'ask for the Father-guardian, and tell him to come to me as quickly as possible; but not to let any one know that he comes at my request.'

'But what shall I say to the portress, who has never seen me go out, and will therefore be sure to ask whither I am going?'

'Try to get out without her seeing you; and if you can't manage it, tell her you are going to such a church, where you have vowed to offer up some prayers.'

Here was a new difficulty for Lucia,—to tell a falsehood; but the Signora again showed herself so vexed by her repulses, and made her so ashamed of herself for interposing a vain scruple in the way of gratitude, that the poor girl, stupefied rather than convinced, and greatly affected by her words, replied: 'Very well; I will go. And may God help me!'

And she set off.

But Gertrude, who from her grated window followed her with a fixed and anxious look, no sooner saw her set foot on the threshold, than, overcome by an irresistible emotion, she exclaimed: 'Listen, Lucia!'

Lucia turned round, and advanced towards the window. But another thought, the thought accustomed to predominate, had already prevailed over Gertrude's unhappy mind. Pretending that she was not yet satisfied with the instructions she had given, she again described to Lucia the road she must follow, and dismissed her, saying: 'Do everything as I have told you, and return quickly.' Lucia departed.

She passed the gate of the cloister unobserved, and took the road along the side of the wall, with her eyes bent to the ground; by the help of the directions she had received, and her own recollection, she found the city gate, and went out. Self-possessed, but still rather trembling, she proceeded along the high road, and shortly reached the turn to the convent, which she immediately recognized. This road was, and still is, buried, like the bed of a river, between two high banks bordered with trees, which spread their branches over it like a vaulted roof. Lucia felt her fears increase, and quickened her steps, as she found herself quite alone on entering it: but a few paces further her courage revived on seeing a travelling carriage standing, and two travellers looking this and that way, as if uncertain of the road. On drawing nearer, she overheard one of them saying: 'Here is a good woman, who will show us the way.' In fact, when she had got opposite the carriage, the same person, with a more courteous manner than countenance, turned and addressed her: 'My good girl, can you tell us which is the way to Monza?'

'You have taken the wrong direction,' replied the poor girl: 'Monza is there . . .' and turning to point it out with her finger, the other companion (it was Nibbio) seized her unexpectedly round the waist, and lifted her from the ground. Lucia, in great alarm, turned her head round, and uttered a scream; the ruffian pushed her into the carriage; a third, who was seated in the back of it, concealed from view, received her and forced her, in spite of her struggles and cries, to sit down opposite to him; while another put a handkerchief over her mouth, and stifled her cries. Nibbio now hastily threw himself into the carriage, shut the door, and they set off at a rapid pace. The other, who had made the treacherous inquiry, remained in the road, and looked hurriedly around: no one was to be seen: he therefore sprang upon the bank, grasped a branch of the hedge which was planted upon the summit, pushed through the fence, and entering a plantation of green oaks, which, for a short distance, ran along the side of the road, stooped down there, that he might not be seen by the people who would probably be attracted by the cries. This man was one of Egidio's villains; he had been to watch near the gate of the monastery, had seen Lucia go out, had noticed her dress and figure, and had then run by a shorter way to wait for her at the appointed spot.

Who can represent the terror, the anguish of the unfortunate girl, or describe what was passing in her mind? She opened her terrified eyes, from anxiety to ascertain her horrible situation, and quickly closed them again with a shudder of fear at the sight of the dreadful faces that met her view: she writhed her body, but found that she was held down on all sides; she collected all her strength, and made a desperate effort to push towards the door; but two sinewy arms held her as if she were nailed to the bottom of the carriage, while four other powerful hands supported her there. At every signal she gave of intending to utter a cry, the handkerchief was instantly stuffed into her mouth to smother the sound, while three infernal mouths, with voices more human than they were accustomed to utter, continued to repeat: 'Be still, be still; don't be afraid, we don't want to do you any harm.' After a few moments of agonized struggle, she seemed to become quieter; her arms sank by her side, her head fell backwards, she half opened her eyelids, and her eyes became fixed; the horrible faces which surrounded her appeared to mingle and flock before her in one monstrous image; the colour fled from her cheek; a cold moisture overspread her face; her consciousness vanished, and she fainted away.

'Come, come, courage,' said Nibbio. 'Courage, courage,' repeated the two other ruffians; but the prostration of every faculty preserved Lucia, at that moment, from hearing the consolations addressed to her by those horrible voices.

'The ——! she seems to be dead,' said one of them: 'if she's really dead!'

'Pshaw!' said the other: 'It's only a swoon, such as women often fall into. I know well enough that when I've wanted to send another, be it man or woman, into the other world, it has required something more than this.'

'Hold your tongues,' said Nibbio. 'Attend to your own business, and mind nothing else. Take your muskets from under the seat, and keep them in readiness; for there are always some villains hidden in the wood we are entering. Not in your hands, the ——! put them behind your backs, and let them lie there; don't you see that she's a cowardly chicken, who faints for nothing? If she sees fire-arms, it will be enough to kill her outright. And when she recovers, take good care you don't frighten her; don't touch her unless I beckon to you; I am enough to manage her. And hold your tongues: leave me to talk to her.'

In the meanwhile, the carriage, which was proceeding at a very rapid pace, entered the wood.

After some time, the unhappy Lucia gradually began to come to her senses, as if awaking from a profound and troubled sleep, and slowly opened her eyes. At first she found it difficult to distinguish the gloomy objects that surrounded her, and collect her scattered thoughts; but she at last succeeded in recalling her fearful situation. The first use she made of her newly recovered, though still feeble, powers, was to rush towards the door, and attempt to throw herself out; but she was forcibly restrained, and had only time to get a glance at the wild solitude of the place through which they were passing. She again uttered a cry; but Nibbio, holding up the handkerchief in his dreaded hand, 'Come,' said he, in the gentlest tone he could command, 'be quiet, and it will be better for you. We don't want to do you any harm; but if you don't hold your tongue, we'll make you.'

'Let me go! Who are you? Where are you taking me? Why have you seized me? Let me go, let me go!'

'I tell you, you needn't be afraid: you're not a baby, and you ought to understand that we don't want to do you any harm. Don't you see that we might have murdered you a hundred times, if we had any bad intentions?—so be quiet.'

'No, no, let me go on my own business; I don't know you.'

'We know you, however.'

'O most holy Virgin! Let me go, for pity's sake. Who are you? Why have you taken me?'

'Because we have been bid to do so.'

'Who? Who? Who can have bid you?'

'Hush!' said Nibbio, with a stern look; 'you mustn't ask me such questions.'

Lucia made a third attempt to throw herself suddenly out of the window; but finding it in vain, she again had recourse to entreaties; and with her head bent, her cheeks bathed with tears, her voice interrupted by sobs, and her hands clasped before her, 'Oh!' cried she, 'for the love of God and the most holy Virgin, let me go! What harm have I done? I am an innocent creature, and have done nobody any harm. I forgive you the wrongs you have done me, from the bottom of my heart, and will pray God for you. If any of you have a daughter, a wife, a mother, think what they would suffer, if they were in this state. Remember that we must all die, and that you will one day want God to be merciful towards you. Let me go; leave me here; the Lord will teach me to find my way.'

'We cannot.'

'You cannot! Oh my God! Why can't you? Where are you taking me? Why?' ...

'We cannot; it's no use asking. Don't be afraid, for we won't harm you: be quiet, and nobody'll touch you.'

Overcome with distress, agony, and terror at finding that her words made no impression, Lucia turned to Him who holds the hearts of men in His hand, and can, when it pleaseth Him, soften the most obdurate. She sank back into the corner where she had been placed, crossed her arms on her breast, and prayed fervently, from the bottom of her heart; then, drawing out her rosary, she began to repeat the prayers with more faith and devotion than she had ever done before in her life. From time to time she would turn to entreat her companions, in hopes that she might gain the mercy she implored; but she implored in vain. Then she fell back, and again became senseless, only to awake to new anguish. But we have not the heart to relate these agonizing vicissitudes more at length; a feeling of overpowering compassion makes us hasten to the close of this mournful journey, which lasted for more than four hours; succeeding which we shall be obliged to describe many hours of still more bitter anguish. We will transport ourselves to the castle where the unhappy girl was expected. She was awaited by the Un-named with a solicitude and anxiety of mind which were very unusual. Strange! that he who had disposed of so many lives with an imperturbed heart, who in so many undertakings had considered as nothing the sufferings he inflicted, unless it were sometimes to glut his appetite with the fierce enjoyment of revenge, should now feel a recoiling, a regret—I might almost say, a feeling of alarm, at the authority he was exercising over this Lucia,—a stranger, a poor peasant-girl! From a lofty window of his castle he had been for some time watching the entrance of the valley; by and by the carriage made its appearance, slowly advancing along the road; for the rapid pace at which they had at first started had curbed the mettle and cooled the ardour of the horses. And although, from the post where he stood to watch, the convoy looked no larger than one of those diminutive vehicles with which children are wont to amuse themselves, yet he hesitated not a moment to recognize it; and his heart began afresh to beat violently.

—Will she be there?—thought he immediately; and he continued to say to himself:—What trouble this creature gives me! I will free myself from it.—

And he prepared to summon one of his men, and despatch him immediately to meet the carriage, with orders to Nibbio to turn round, and conduct her at once to Don Rodrigo's palace. But an imperative *no,* that instantly flashed across his mind, made him at once abandon this design. Wearied at length by the desire of ordering something to be done, and intolerably tired of idly waiting the approach of the carriage, as it advanced slowly, step by step, like a traitor to his punishment, he at length summoned an old woman of his household.

This person was the daughter of a former keeper of the castle, had been born within its walls, and spent all her life there. All that she had seen and heard around her from her very infancy, had contributed to impress upon her mind a lofty and terrible idea of the power of her masters; and the principal maxim that she had acquired from instruction and example was, that they must be obeyed in everything, because they were capable of doing either great good or great harm. The idea of duty, deposited like a germ in the hearts of all men, and mingling in hers with sentiments of respect, dread, and servile devotion, was associated with, and solely directed to, these objects. When the Unnamed became her lord, and began to make such terrible use of his power, she felt, from the first, a kind of horror, and, at the same time, a more profound feeling of subjection. In time she became habituated to what she daily saw and heard around her: the potent and unbridled will of such a Signor was, in her idea, a kind of justice appointed by fate. When somewhat advanced in years, she had married a servant of the household, who, being sent on some hazardous expedition, shortly afterwards left his bones on the highway, and her a widow in the castle. The vengeance which the Signor quickly took on the instruments of his death, yielded her a savage consolation, and increased her pride at being under such protection.

From that time forward she rarely set foot outside the castle, and, by degrees, retained no other ideas of human life than such as she received within its precincts. She was not confined to any particular branch of service, but among such a crowd of ruffians, one or other was constantly finding her some thing to do, which furnished her with a never-failing subject for grumbling. Sometimes she would have clothes to repair, sometimes a meal to provide in haste, for one who had returned from an expedition, and sometimes she was called upon to exercise her medical skill in dressing a wound. The commands, reproaches, and thanks of these ruffians, were generally seasoned with jokes and rude speeches: 'old woman' was her usual appellation; while the adjuncts which were perpetually attached to it, varied according to the circumstances and humour of the speaker. Crossed thus in her idleness, and irritated in her peevish temper, which were her two predominant passions, she sometimes returned these compliments with language in which Satan might have recognized more of his own spirit than in that of her tormentors.

'You see that carriage down there?' said the Signor to this amiable specimen of woman-kind.

'I see it,' replied she, protruding her sharp chin, and staring with her sunken eyes, as if trying to force them out of their sockets.

'Bid them prepare a litter immediately; get into it yourself, and let it be carried to Malanotte instantly, that you may get there before the carriage; it is coming on at a funeral pace. In that carriage there is . . . there ought to be . . . a young girl. If she's there, tell Nibbio it is my order that she should be put into the litter, and that he must come directly to me. You will come up in the litter with the . . . girl; and when you are up here, take her into your own room. If she asks you where you are taking her, whom the castle belongs to, take care . . .'

'Oh!' said the old woman.

'But,' continued the Unnamed, 'try to encourage her.'

'What must I say to her?'

'What must you say to her? Try to encourage her, I tell you. Have you come to this age, and don't know how to encourage others when they want it! Have you ever known sorrow of heart? Have you never been afraid? Don't you know what words soothe and comfort at such moments? Say those words to her; find them in the remembrance of your own sorrows. Go directly.'

As soon as she had taken her departure, he stood for a while at the window, with his eyes fixed on the carriage, which had already considerably increased in size; afterwards he watched the sun, at that moment sinking behind the mountain; then he contemplated the fleecy clouds scattered above the setting orb, and from their usual greyish hue almost instantaneously assuming a fiery tinge. He drew back, closed the window, and began to pace up and down the apartment with the step of a hurried traveller.

CHAPTER XXI

THE old woman immediately hastened to obey, and to give commands, under the sanction of that name, which by whomsoever pronounced, always set the whole household on the alert; for it never entered the imagination of any one, that another person would venture to use it unauthorized. She reached Malanotte shortly before the carriage arrived; and on seeing it approach, got out of the litter, beckoned to the driver to stop, advanced towards the door, and whispered to Nibbio, who put his head out of the window, the wishes of his master.

Lucia aroused herself, on feeling the carriage stop, and, awaking from a kind of lethargy, was seized with renewed terror, as she wildly gazed around her. Nibbio had pushed himself back on the seat, and the old woman, with her chin resting on the door, was looking at Lucia, and saying, 'Come, my good girl; come, you poor thing; come with me, for I have orders to treat you well, and try to comfort you.'

At the sound of a female voice, the poor girl felt a ray of comfort —a momentary flash of courage; but she quickly relapsed into still more terrible fears. 'Who are you?' asked she, in a trembling voice, fixing her astonished gaze on the old woman's face.

'Come, come, you poor creature,' was the unvaried answer she received. Nibbio, and his two companions, gathering from the words, and the unusually softened tones of the old hag, what were the intentions of their lord, endeavoured, by kind and soothing words, to persuade the unhappy girl to obey. She only continued, however, to stare wildly around; and though the unknown and savage character of the place, and the close guardianship of her keepers, forbade her indulging a hope of relief, she nevertheless, attempted to cry out; but seeing Nibbio cast a glance towards the handkerchief, she stopped, trembled, gave a momentary shudder, and was then seized, and placed in the litter. The old woman entered after her;

Nibbio left the other two villains to follow behind as an escort, while he himself took the shortest ascent to attend to the call of his master.

'Who are you?' anxiously demanded Lucia of her unknown and ugly-visaged companion: 'Why am I with you? Where am I? Where are you taking me?'

'To one who wishes to do you good,' replied the aged dame; 'to a great . . . Happy are they to whom he wishes good! You are very lucky, I can tell you. Don't be afraid—be cheerful; he bid me try to encourage you. You'll tell him, won't you, that I tried to comfort you?'

'Who is he?—why?—what does he want with me? I don't belong to him! Tell me where I am! let me go! bid these people let me go— bid them carry me to some church. Oh! you who are a woman, in the name of Mary the Virgin! . . .'

This holy and soothing name, once repeated with veneration in her early years, and now for so long a time uninvoked, and, perhaps, unheard, produced in the mind of the unhappy creature, on again reaching her ear, a strange, confused, and distant recollection, like the remembrance of light and form in an aged person, who has been blind from infancy.

In the meanwhile, the Unnamed, standing at the door of his castle, was looking downwards, and watching the litter, as before he had watched the carriage, while it slowly ascended, step by step; Nibbio rapidly advancing before it at a distance which every moment became greater. When he had at length attained the summit, 'Come this way,' cried the Signor; and taking the lead, he entered the castle, and went into one of the apartments.

'Well?' said he, making a stand.

'Everything exactly right,' replied Nibbio, with a profound obeisance; 'the intelligence in time, the girl in time, nobody on the spot, only one scream, nobody attracted by it, the coachman ready, the horses swift, nobody met with: but . . .'

'But what?'

'But . . . I will tell the truth; I would rather have been commanded to shoot her in the back, without hearing her speak—without seeing her face.'

'What? . . . what? . . . what do you mean?'

'I mean that all this time . . . all this time . . . I have felt too much compassion for her.'

'Compassion! What do you know of compassion? What is compassion?'

'I never understood so well what it was as this time; it is something that rather resembles fear; let it once take possession of you, and you are no longer a man.'

'Let me hear a little of what she did to excite your compassion.'

'O, most noble Signor! such a time! . . . weeping, praying, and looking at one with such eyes! and becoming pale as death! and then sobbing, and praying again, and certain words . . .'

—I won't have this creature in my house,—thought the Unnamed, meanwhile, to himself.—In an evil hour, I engaged to do it; but I've promised—I've promised. When she's far away . . . And raising his face with an imperious air towards Nibbio, 'Now,' said he, 'you must lay aside compassion, mount your horse, take a companion— two, if you like—and ride away, till you get to the palace of this Don Rodrigo, you know. Tell him to send immediately . . . immediately, or else . . .'

But another internal *no,* more imperative than the first, prohibited his finishing. 'No,' said he, in a resolute tone, almost, as it were, to express to himself the command of this secret voice. 'No: go and take some rest; and to-morrow morning . . . you shall do as I will tell you.'

—This girl must have some demon of her own,—thought he, when left alone, standing with his arms crossed on his breast, and his gaze fixed upon a spot on the floor, where the rays of the moon, entering through a lofty window, traced out a square of pale light, chequered like a draught-board by the massive iron bars, and more minutely divided into smaller compartments by the little panes of glass.— Some demon, or . . . some angel who protects her . . . Compassion in Nibbio! . . . To-morrow morning—to-morrow morning, early she must be off from this; she must go to her place of destination; and she shall not be spoken of again, and,—continued he to himself, with the resolution with which one gives a command to a rebellious child, knowing that it will not be obeyed;—and she shall not be *thought* of again, either. That animal of a Don Rodrigo must not come to pester me with thanks; for . . . I don't want to hear her spoken of any more. I have served him because . . . because I promised; and I promised, because . . . it was my destiny. But I'm determined the fellow shall pay me well for this piece of service. Let me see a little . . . —

And he tried to devise some intricate undertaking, to impose upon Don Rodrigo by way of compensation, and almost as a punishment; but the words again shot across his mind—Compassion in Nibbio!—What can this girl have done?—continued he, following out the thought;—I must see her. Yet no—yes, I will see her.—

He went from one room to another, came to the foot of a flight of stairs, and irresolutely ascending, proceeded to the old woman's apartment; here he knocked with his foot at the door.

'Who's there?'

'Open the door.'

The old woman made three bounds at the sound of his voice; the bolt was quickly heard grating harshly in the staples, and the door was thrown wide open. The Unnamed cast a glance round the room, as he paused in the doorway; and by the light of a lamp which stood on a three-legged table, discovered Lucia crouched down on the floor, in the corner farthest from the entrance.

'Who bid you throw her there, like a bag of rags, you uncivil old beldame?' said he to the aged matron, with an angry frown.

'She chose it herself,' replied she, in an humble tone. 'I've done my best to encourage her; she can tell you so herself; but she won't mind me.'

'Get up,' said he to Lucia, approaching her. But she, whose already terrified mind had experienced a fresh and mysterious addition to her terror at the knocking, the opening of the door, his footstep, and his voice, only gathered herself still closer into the corner, and, with her face buried in her hands, remained perfectly motionless, excepting that she trembled from head to foot.

'Get up; I will do you no harm . . . and I can do you some good,' repeated the Signor . . . 'Get up!' thundered he forth at last, irritated at having twice commanded in vain.

As if invigorated by fear, the unhappy girl instantly raised herself upon her knees, and joining her hands, as she would have knelt before a sacred image, lifted her eyes to the face of the Unnamed, and instantly dropping them, said: 'Here I am, kill me if you will.'

'I have told you I would do you no harm,' replied the Unnamed, in a softened tone, gazing at her agonized features of grief and terror.

'Courage, courage,' said the old woman; 'if he himself tells you he will do you no harm . . .'

'And why,' rejoined Lucia, with a voice in which the daringness of despairing indignation was mingled with the tremor of fear, 'why make me suffer the agonies of hell? What have I done to you? . . .'

'Perhaps they have treated you badly? Tell me . . .'

'Treated me badly! They have seized me by treachery—by force! Why—why have they seized me? Why am I here? Where am I? I am a poor harmless girl. What have I done to you? In the name of God . . .'

'God, God!' interrupted the Unnamed, 'always God! They who cannot defend themselves—who have not the strength to do it, must always bring forward this God, as if they had spoken to him. What do you expect by this word? To make me? . . .' and he left the sentence unfinished.

'O Signor, expect! What can a poor girl like me expect, except that you should have mercy upon me? God pardons so many sins for one deed of mercy. Let me go; for charity's sake, let me go. It will do no good to one who must die, to make a poor creature suffer thus. Oh! you who can give the command, bid them let me go! They brought me here by force. Bid them send me again with this woman, and take me to * * * , where my mother is. Oh! most holy Virgin! My mother! my mother!—for pity's sake, my mother. Perhaps she is not far from here . . . I saw my mountains. Why do you give me all this suffering? Bid them take me to a church; I will pray for you all my life. What will it cost you to say one word? Oh, see! you are moved to pity: say one word, oh say it! God pardons so many sins for one deed of mercy!'

—Oh, why isn't she the daughter of one of the rascally dogs that outlawed me!—thought the Unnamed;—of one of the villains who wish me dead; then I should enjoy her sufferings; but instead . . .—

'Don't drive away a good inspiration!' continued Lucia, earnestly, reanimated by seeing a certain air of hesitation in the countenance and behaviour of her oppressor. 'If you don't grant me this mercy, the Lord will do it for me. I shall die, and all will be over with me; but you . . . Perhaps, some day, even you . . . But no, no; I will always pray the Lord to keep you from every evil. What will it cost you to say one word? If you knew what it was to suffer this agony! . . .'

'Come, take courage,' interrupted the Unnamed, with a gentleness that astonished the old woman. 'Have I done you any harm? Have I threatened you?'

'Oh no! I see that you have a kind heart, and feel some pity for an unhappy creature. If you chose, you could terrify me more than all the others: you could kill me with fear; but instead of that, you have . . . rather lightened my heart; God will reward you for it. Finish your deed of mercy: set me free, set me free.'

'To-morrow morning . . .'

'Oh! set me free now—now . . .

'To-morrow morning, I will see you again, I say. Come, in the mean while, be of good courage. Take a little rest; you must want something to eat. They shall bring you something directly.'

'No, no; I shall die, if anybody comes here; I shall die! Take me to a church . . . God will reward you for that step.'

'A woman shall bring you something to eat,' said the Unnamed; and having said so, he stood wondering at himself how such a remedy had entered his mind, and how the wish had arisen to seek a remedy for the sorrows of a poor humble villager.

'And you,' resumed he hastily, turning to the aged matron, 'persuade her to eat something, and let her lie down to rest on this bed; and if she is willing to have you as a companion, well; if not, you can sleep well enough for one night on the floor. Encourage her, I say, and keep her cheerful. Beware that she has no cause to complain of you.'

So saying, he moved quickly towards the door. Lucia sprang up, and ran to detain him, and renew her entreaties; but he was gone.

'Oh, poor me! Shut the door quickly.' And having heard the door closed, and the bolt again drawn, she returned to seat herself in her corner. 'Oh, poor me!' repeated she, sobbing; 'whom shall I implore now? Where am I? Do you tell me—tell me, for pity's sake, who is this Signor . . . he who has been speaking to me?'

'Who is he, eh?—who is he? Do you think I may tell you? Wait till he tells you himself. You are proud, because he protects you; and you want to be satisfied, and make me your go-between. Ask him yourself. If I were to tell you this, I shouldn't get the good words he has just given you. I am an old woman, an old woman,' continued she, muttering between her teeth. 'Hang these young folks, who may make a fine show of either laughing or crying, just as they like, and yet are always in the right.' But hearing Lucia's sobs and the commands of her master returning in a threatening manner to her memory, she stooped toward the poor crouching girl, and, in a gentler and more humane tone, resumed: 'Come, I have said no harm to you; be cheerful. Don't ask me questions which I've no business to answer; but pluck up heart, my good girl. Ah! if you knew how many people would be glad to hear him speak, as he has spoken to you! Be cheerful, for he will send you something to eat just now; and I know . . . by the way he spoke, I'm sure it will be something good. And then you lie down, and . . . you will leave just a little corner for me,' added she, with an accent of suppressed rancour.

'I don't want to eat, I don't want to sleep. Let me alone; don't come near me; but you won't leave the room?'

'No, no, not I,' said the old woman, drawing back, and seating herself on an old arm-chair, whence she cast sundry glances of alarm, and at the same time of envy, towards the poor girl. Then she looked at the bed, vexed at the idea of being, perhaps, excluded from it for the whole night, and grumbling at the cold. But she comforted herself with the thoughts of supper, and with the hope that there might be some to spare for her. Lucia was sensible of neither cold nor hunger, and, almost as if deprived of her senses, had but a confused idea of her very grief and terror, like the undefined objects seen by a delirious patient.

She roused herself, when she heard a knocking at the door; and raising her head, exclaimed, in much alarm, 'Who's there?—who's there? Don't let any one in!'

'Nobody, nobody; good news!' said the old woman; 'it's Martha bringing something to eat.'

'Shut the door, shut the door!' cried Lucia.

'Ay, directly,' replied the old woman; and taking a basket out of Martha's hand, she hastily nodded to her, shut the door, and came and set the basket on a table, in the middle of the room. She then repeatedly invited Lucia to come and partake of the tempting repast, and employing words, which, according to her ideas, were most likely to be efficacious in restoring the poor girl's appetite, broke forth into exclamations on the excellence of the food;—'Morsels which, when common people have once got a taste, they don't forget in a hurry! Wine, which her master drank with his friends . . . when any of them happened to arrive . . . and they wanted to be merry! Hem!' But seeing that all these charms produced no effect—'It is you who *won't* eat,' said she. 'Don't you be saying to-morrow that I didn't try to persuade you. I'll eat something, however; and then there'll be more than enough left for you, when you come to your senses, and are willing to do as you are bid.' So saying, she applied herself with avidity to the refreshments. When she had satisfied herself, she rose, advanced towards the corner, and bending over Lucia, again invited her to take something, and then lie down.

'No, no, I don't want anything,' replied she, with a feeble and almost drowsy voice. Then with more energy she continued; 'Is the door locked?—is it well secured?' And having looked around, she rose, and feeling with her hands, walked with a suspicious step towards the door.

The old woman sprang thither before her, stretched out her hand to the lock, seized the handle, shook it, rattled the bolt, and made it grate against the staple that received and secured it. 'Do you hear? —do you see?—is it well locked? Are you content now?'

'Oh, content! I content here!' said Lucia, again arranging herself in her corner. 'But the Lord knows I'm here!'

'Come to bed; what would you do there, crouching like a dog? Did ever anybody see a person refuse comforts, when he could get them?'

'No, no; let me alone.'

'Well, it's your own wish. See, I'll leave you the best place; I'm lying here on the very edge; I shall be uncomfortable enough, for your sake. If you want to come to bed, you know what you have to do. Remember, I've asked you very often.' So saying, she crept, dressed as she was, under the counterpane, and soon all was silent.

Lucia remained motionless, shrunk up into the corner, her knees drawn close to her breast, her hands resting on her knees, and her face buried in her hands. She was neither asleep nor awake, but worn out with a rapid succession—a tumultuous alternation, of thoughts, anticipations, and heart-throbbings. Recalled, in some degree, to consciousness, and recollecting more distinctly the horrors she had seen and suffered that terrible day, she would now dwell mournfully on the dark and formidable realities in which she found herself involved; then, her mind being carried onward into a still more obscure region, she had to struggle against the phantoms conjured up by uncertainty and terror. In this distressing state she continued for a long time, which we would here prefer to pass over rapidly; but at length, exhausted and overcome, she relaxed her hold on her benumbed limbs, and sinking at full length upon the floor, remained for some time in a state closely resembling real sleep. But suddenly awaking, as at some inward call, she tried to arouse herself completely, to regain her scattered senses, and to remember where she was, and how, and why. She listened to some sound that caught her ear; it was the slow, deep breathing of the old woman. She opened her eyes, and saw a faint light, now glimmering for a moment, and then again dying away: it was the wick of the lamp, which, almost ready to expire, emitted a tremulous gleam, and quickly drew it back, so to say, like the ebb and flow of a wave on the sea-shore; and thus, withdrawing from the surrounding objects ere there was time to display them in distinct colouring and relief, it merely presented to the eye a succession of confused and indistinct glimpses. But the recent impressions she had received quickly returned to her mind, and assisted her in distinguishing what appeared so disorderly to her visual organs. When fully aroused, the unhappy girl recognized her prison; all the recollections of the horrible day that was fled, all the uncertain terrors of the future, rushed at once upon her mind: the very calm in which she now found herself after so much agitation, the sort of repose she had just tasted, the desertion in which she was left, all combined to inspire her with new dread, till, overcome by alarm, she earnestly longed for death. But at this juncture, she remembered that she could still pray; and with that thought there seemed to shine forth a sudden ray of comfort. She once more took out her rosary, and began to repeat the prayers; and in proportion as the words fell from her trembling lips she felt an indefinite confiding faith taking possession of her heart. Suddenly another thought rushed into her mind, that her prayer might, perhaps, be more readily accepted, and more certainly heard, if she were to make some offering in her desolate condition. She tried to remember what she most prized, or rather, what she had once most prized; for at this moment her heart could feel no other affection than that of fear, nor conceive any other desire than that of deliverance. She did remember it, and resolved at once to make the sacrifice. Rising upon her knees, and clasping her hands, from whence the rosary was suspended before her breast, she raised her face and eyes to heaven, and said, 'O most holy Virgin! thou to whom I have so often recommended myself, and who hast so often comforted me!—thou who hast borne so many sorrows, and art now so glorious!—thou who hast wrought so many miracles for the poor and afflicted, help me! Bring me out of this danger; bring me safely to my mother, O Mother of our Lord; and I vow unto thee to continue a virgin! I renounce for ever my unfortunate betrothed, that from henceforth I may belong only to thee!'

Having uttered these words, she bowed her head, and placed the beads around her neck, almost as a token of her consecration, and, at the same time, as a safeguard, a part of the armour for the new warfare to which she had devoted herself. Seating herself again on the floor, a kind of tranquillity, a more childlike reliance, gradually diffused themselves over her soul. The *to-morrow morning,* repeated by the unknown nobleman, came to her mind, and seemed to her ear to convey a promise of deliverance. Her senses, wearied by such struggles, gradually gave way before these soothing thoughts; until at length, towards day-break, and with the name of her protectress upon her lips, Lucia sank into a profound and unbroken sleep.

But in this same castle there was one who would willingly have followed her example, yet who tried in vain. After departing, or rather escaping, from Lucia, giving orders for her supper, and paying his customary visits to several posts in his castle, with her image ever vividly before his eyes, and her words resounding in his ears, the nobleman had hastily retired to his chamber, impetuously shut the door behind him, and hurriedly undressing, had lain down. But that image, which now more closely than ever haunted his mind, seemed at that moment to say: 'Thou shalt not sleep!'—What absurd womanly curiosity tempted me to go see her?—thought he.—That fool of a Nibbio was right: one is no longer a man; yes, one is no longer a man! . . . I? . . . am I no longer a man? What has happened? What devil has got possession of me? What is there new in all this? Didn't I know, before now, that women always weep and implore? Even men do sometimes, when they have not the power to rebel. What the——! have I never heard women cry before?—

And here, without giving himself much trouble to task his memory, it suggested to him, of its own accord, more than one instance in which neither entreaties nor lamentations availed to deter him from the completion of enterprises upon which he had once resolved. But these remembrances, instead of inspiring him with the courage he now needed to prosecute his present design as it would seem he expected and wished they might, instead of helping to dispel his feelings of compassion, only added to them those of terror and consternation, until they compelled him to return to that first image of Lucia, against which he had been seeking to fortify his courage.—She still lives,—said he:—She is here; I am in time; I can yet say to her, Go, and be happy; I can yet see that countenance change; I can even say, Forgive me . . . Forgive me? I ask forgiveness? And of a woman, too? I? . . . Ah, however! if one word, one such word could do me good, could rid me of the demon that now possesses me, I would say it; yes, I feel that I would say it. To what am I reduced! I'm no longer a man; surely, no longer a man! . . . Away! —said he, turning himself with impetuosity on the couch which had now become so hard, under the covering which had now become so intolerable a weight:—Away! these are fooleries which have many a time passed through my head. This will take its flight too.—

And to effect such a riddance, he began seeking some important subject, some of the many which often so busily occupied his mind, in hopes he might be entirely engrossed by it; but he sought in vain. All appeared changed: that which once most urgently stimulated his desires, now no longer possessed any charms for him: his passions, like a steed suddenly become restive at the sight of a shadow, refused to carry him any further. In reflecting on enterprises engaged in, and not yet concluded, instead of animating himself to their completion, and feeling irritated at the obstacles interposed, (for anger at this moment would have been sweet to him,) he felt regret, nay, almost consternation, at the steps already taken. His life presented itself to his mind devoid of all interest, deprived of all will, divested of every action, and only laden with insupportable recollections; every hour resembling that which now rolled so slowly and heavily over his head. He drew out before his fancy all his ruffians in a kind of battle-array, and could contrive nothing of importance in which to employ one of them; nay, the very idea of seeing them again, and mixing among them, was an additional weight, a fresh object of annoyance and detestation. And when he sought an occupation for the morrow, a feasible employment, he could only remember that on the morrow, he might liberate his unfortunate prisoner.

—I will set her free; yes, I will. I will fly to her by day-break, and bid her depart safely. She shall be accompanied by . . . And my promise? My engagement? Don Rodrigo? . . . Who is Don Rodrigo?—

Like one suddenly surprised by an unexpected and embarrassing question from a superior, the Unnamed hastily sought for an answer to the query he had just put to himself, or rather which had been suggested to him by that new voice which had all at once made itself heard, and sprung up to be, as it were, a judge of his former self. He tried to imagine any reasons which could have induced him, almost before being requested, to engage in inflicting so much suffering, without any incentives of hatred or fear, on a poor un-

known creature, only to render a service to this man; but instead
of succeeding in discovering such motives as he would now have
deemed sufficient to excuse the deed, he could not even imagine how
he had ever been induced to undertake it. The willingness, rather
than the determination to do so, had been the instantaneous impulse
of a mind obedient to its old and habitual feelings, the consequence
of a thousand antecedent actions; and to account for this one deed,
the unhappy self-examiner found himself involved in an examination
of his whole life. Backwards from year to year, from engagement
to engagement, from bloodshed to bloodshed, from crime to crime,
each one stood before his conscience-stricken soul, divested of the
feelings which had induced him to will and commit it, and therefore
appearing in all its monstrousness, which those feelings had, at the
time,prevented his perceiving. They were all his own, they made up
himself; and the horror of this thought, renewed with each fresh
remembrance, and cleaving to all, increased at last to desperation.
He sprang up impetuously in his bed, eagerly stretched out his hand
towards the wall at his side, touched a pistol, grasped it, reached
it down, and . . . at the moment of finishing a life which had become insupportable, his thoughts, seized with terror and a (so to say)
superstitious dread, rushed forward to the time which would still
continue to flow on after his end. He pictured with horror his disfigured corpse, lying motionless, and in the power of his vilest sur-
vivor; the astonishment, the confusion of the castle in the morning:
everything turned upside down; and he, powerless and voiceless,
thrown aside, he knew not whither. He fancied the reports that
would be spread, the conversations to which it would give rise, both
in the castle, the neighbourhood, and at a distance, together with
the rejoicings of his enemies. The darkness and silence around him
presented death in a still more mournful and frightful aspect; it
seemed to him that he would not have hesitated in open day, out
of doors, and in the presence of spectators, to throw himself into
the water, and vanish. Absorbed in such tormenting reflections,
he continued alternately snapping and unsnapping the cock of his
pistol with a convulsive movement of his thumb, when another
thought flashed across his mind.—If this other life, of which they
told me when I was a boy, of which everybody talks now, as if it

were a certain thing, if there be not such a thing, if it be an invention of the priests; what am I doing? why should I die? what matters all that I have done? what matters it? It is an absurdity, my . . . But if there really be another life! . . . —

At such a doubt, at such a risk, he was seized with a blacker and deeper despair, from which even death afforded no escape. He dropped the pistol, and lay with his fingers twined among his hair, his teeth chattering, and trembling in every limb. Suddenly the words he had heard repeated a few hours before rose to his remembrance:—God pardons so many sins for one deed of mercy!—They did not come to him with that tone of humble supplication in which they had been pronounced; they came with a voice of authority, which at the same time excited a distant glimmering of hope. It was a moment of relief: he raised his hands from his temples, and, in a more composed attitude, fixed his mind's eye on her who had uttered the words; she seemed to him no longer like his prisoner and suppliant, but in the posture of one who dispenses mercy and consolation. He anxiously awaited the dawn of day, that he might fly to liberate her, and to hear from her lips other words of alleviation and life, and even thought of conducting her himself to her mother. —And then? what shall I do to-morrow for the rest of the day? What shall I do the day after to-morrow? And the day after that again? And at night? the night which will return in twelve hours? Oh, the night! no, no, the night!—And falling again into the weary void of the future, he sought in vain for some employment of time, some way of living through the days and nights. One moment he proposed leaving his castle, and going into some distant country, where he had never been known or heard of; but he felt that he should carry himself with him. Then a dark hope would arise that he should resume his former courage and inclinations, and that this would prove only a transient delirium. Now he dreaded the light which would show him to his followers so miserably changed; then he longed for it, as if it would bring light also to his gloomy thoughts. And, lo! about break of day, a few moments after Lucia had fallen asleep, while he was seated motionless in his bed, a floating and confused murmur reached his ear, bringing with it something joyous and festive in its sound. Assuming a listening posture, he distinguished a distant chiming of bells; and, giving still more attention, could hear the mountain echo, every now and then, languidly repeating the harmony, and mingling itself with it. Immediately afterwards his ear caught another, and still nearer peal: then another, and another.—What rejoicings are these? What are they all so merry about? What is their cause of gladness?—He sprang from his bed of thorns; and, half-dressing himself in haste, went to the window, threw up the sash, and looked out. The mountains were still wrapt in gloom; the sky was not so much cloudy, as composed of one entire lead-coloured cloud; but by the already glimmering light of day, he distinguished in the road, at the bottom of the valley, numbers of people passing eagerly along,—some leaving their dwellings and moving on with the crowd, and all taking the same direction towards the outlet of the vale on the right of the castle; he could even distinguish the joyous bearing and holiday dress of the passengers.—What the——is the matter with these people? What cause of merriment can there be in this cursed neighbourhood?—And calling a confidential bravo who slept in the adjoining room, he asked him what was the cause of this movement. The man replied that he knew no more than his master, but would go directly to make inquiry. The Signor remained with his eyes riveted upon the moving spectacle, which increasing day rendered every moment more distinct. He watched crowds pass by, and new crowds constantly appear; men, women, children, in groups, in couples, or alone; one, overtaking another who was before him, walked in company with him; another, just leaving his door, accompanied the first he fell in with by the way; and so they proceeded together, like friends in a preconcerted journey. Their behaviour evidently indicated a common haste and joy; and the unharmonious, but simultaneous burst of the different chimes, some more, some less contiguous and distinct, seemed, so to say, the common voice of these gestures, and a supplement to the words which could not reach him from below. He looked and looked, till he felt more than common curiosity to know what could communicate so unanimous a will, so general a festivity, to so many different people.

CHAPTER XXII

SHORTLY afterwards the bravo returned with the information, that Cardinal Federigo Borromeo, archbishop of Milan, had arrived the day before at * * *, with the purpose of spending there that which was now just dawning; that the news of his arrival, which had been spread around for a considerable distance the preceding evening, had excited a desire in the people to go and see this great man; and that the bells were ringing, both to express their joy, and more widely to diffuse the glad intelligence. When again alone, the Signor continued to look down into the valley, still more absorbed in thought.—For a man! Everybody eager, everybody joyful, at the sight of a man! And yet, doubtless, each has his own demon that torments him. But none, none will have one like mine! None will have passed such a night as I have! What has this man about him to make so many people merry? Some pence, perhaps, that he will distribute at random among them . . . But all these cannot be going for alms. Well then, a few acknowledgments and salutations—a word or two . . . Oh! if he had any words for me that could impart peace! if! . . . Why shouldn't I go too? Why not? . . . I will go! what else can I do? I will go; and I will talk with him: face to face I'll have some talk with him. What shall I say, though? Well, whatever, whatever . . . I'll hear first what the man has to say for himself!—

Having come to this vague determination, he hastily finished dressing himself, and put on, over all, a great coat, which had something of a military cut about it; he then took up the pistol which lay upon the bed, and secured it on one side of his belt, fastening at the other its fellow, which hung upon a nail in the wall; stuck a dagger into this same girdle; and taking a carabine from the wall, which was almost as famous as himself, swung it across his shoulders: then he put on his hat, quitted the apartment, and repaired at once to that in which he had left Lucia. Setting down his carabine in a

348

corner near the door, he knocked, at the same time letting them know, by his voice, who he was. The old woman sprang out of bed, threw some article of clothing around her, and flew to open the door. The Signor entered, and, casting a glance around the room, saw Lucia lying in her little corner, and perfectly quiet.

'Does she sleep?' asked he, in an under-tone, of the old woman: 'But is she sleeping there? were these my orders, you old hag?'

'I did all I could,' replied the woman; 'but she wouldn't eat, and she wouldn't come . . .'

'Let her sleep quietly; take care you don't disturb her; and when she awakes . . . Martha shall wait in the next room; and you must send her to fetch anything that she may ask for. When she awakes . . . tell her that I . . . that the master has gone out for a little while, that he will be back soon, and that . . . he will do all that she wishes.'

The old woman stood perfectly astonished, thinking to herself:— This girl must surely be some princess!—

The Signor then left the room, took up his carabine, sent Martha to wait in the adjoining apartment, and the first bravo whom he met to keep guard, that no one but this woman might presume to approach Lucia; and then, leaving the castle, took the descent with a rapid step.

The manuscript here fails to mention the distance from the castle to the village where the Cardinal was staying: it cannot, however, have been more than a moderate walk. We do not infer the proximity merely from the flocking thither of the inhabitants of the valley; since we find, in the histories of these times, that people came for twenty miles, or more, to get but one sight of Cardinal Federigo. From the circumstances that we are about to relate, as happening on this day, we may, however, easily conjecture that the distance cannot have been very great. The bravoes whom he met ascending, stopped respectfully as their lord passed, waiting to see if he had any orders to give, or if he wished of them to accompany him on some expedition, and seemed perfectly astonished at his countenance and the glances he returned in answer to their salutations.

When, however, he reached the base, and entered the public road, it was a very different matter. There was a general whispering among the first passengers who observed him, an exchange of suspicious looks, and an endeavour on each side to get out of his reach. For the whole length of the way he could not take two steps by the side of another passenger; for every one who found him quickly gaining upon him, cast an uneasy look around, made him a low bow, and slackened his pace so as to remain behind. On reaching the village, he found a large crowd assembled; his name spread rapidly from mouth to mouth, the moment he made his appearance, and the throng fell back to make way for him. He accosted one of these prudent gentry, and asked where the Cardinal was. 'In the Curate's house,' replied the addressed party, reverently, at the same time pointing out the mansion. The Signor went forward, entered a little court, where many priests were assembled, all of whom regarded him with surprised and doubtful looks, and saw before him an open door, which gave admission into a small hall, where there was also collected a considerable number of priests. Taking his carabine from his shoulders, he deposited it in one corner of the little court, and then entered the hall, where he was received with significant glances, murmurs, and his oft-repeated name; then all was silent. Turning to one of those who surrounded him, he asked where the Cardinal was, and said that he wished to speak to him.

'I am a stranger,' replied the priest; but hastily glancing around, he called the chaplain and cross-bearer, who, seated in a corner of the hall, was saying, in an under-tone, to his companion, 'This man? this notorious character? what can he have to do here? Make way!' However, at this call, which resounded in the general silence, he was obliged to come forward; he made a lowly reverence to the Unnamed, listened to his inquiry, raised his eyes with uneasy curiosity towards his face, and instantly bending them on the ground, stood hesitating for a moment, and then said, or rather stammered out: 'I don't know whether his illustrious Lordship . . . just now . . . is to be . . . can . . . may . . . But I will go and see.' And he very unwillingly carried the message into the adjoining room, where the Cardinal was by himself.

At this point in our story, we cannot do less than pause for a little while; as the traveller, wearied and worn out with a lengthened journey, through a wild and sterile country, retards his pace, and halts for a little time under the shade of a noble tree, reclining on the grassy bank of a stream of running water. We have now fallen upon a person, whose name and memory, occurring when they will to the mind, refresh it with a calm emotion of reverence, and a pleasurable feeling of sympathy; how much more, then, after so many mournful pictures—after the contemplation of such fearful and hateful depravity! On the history of this personage, we must absolutely expend a few words: he who cares not about hearing them, and is anxious to proceed with the story, may pass on at once to the succeeding chapter.

Federigo Borromeo, born in 1564, was among those characters, rare in whatever age, who have employed singular talents, all the resources of great wealth, all the advantages of privileged rank, and an unwearying diligence in the search and exercise of the highest objects and principles. His life resembles a rivulet, which, issuing limpid from the rock, flows in a ceaseless and unruffled, though lengthened course, through various lands, and, clear and limpid still, falls at last into the ocean. Amidst comforts and luxuries, he attended, even from childhood, to those lessons of self-denial and humility, and those maxims on the vanity of worldly pleasures, and the sinfulness of pride, on true dignity and true riches, which, whether acknowledged or not in the heart, have been transmitted from one generation to another in the most elementary instruction in religion. He attended, I say, to these lessons and maxims; he received them in real earnest; he tried them, and found them true; he saw, therefore, that other and contrary lessons and maxims could not possibly be true, which yet were transmitted from age to age, with the same asseveration, and sometimes by the same lips; and he resolved to take, as the rule of his thoughts and actions, those which were indeed right. By these he understood that life was not designed to be a burden to many, and a pleasure to only a few; but was intended as a time of employment for all, of which every one would have to give an account; and he began from a child to consider how he could render his useful and holy.

In 1580 he declared his resolution of dedicating himself to the ministry of the Church, and received ordination from the hands of his cousin Carlo, whom long and universal suffrage had already signalized as a saint. Shortly afterwards, he entered the college founded by this relative in Pavia, which still bears the name of their house; and here, while applying himself with assiduity to the occupations which were prescribed, he added to them two others of his own free will; and these were, to give instruction to the most ignorant and neglected among the population, in the doctrines of the Christian religion; and to visit, assist, comfort, and relieve the sick and needy. He employed the authority conceded to him by all around, in inducing his companions to second him in such works of charity; and set a noble example of spending, in every honest and beneficial employment, a pre-eminence which, considering his superior mind and talents, he would, perhaps, equally have attained had he been the lowest in rank and fortune. The advantages of a different nature, which the circumstances of fortune could have procured for him, he not only sought not after, but studiously neglected. He kept a table rather meagre than frugal, and wore a dress rather mean than decent; while the whole tenor of his life and behaviour was in conformity with these particulars. Nor did he think it necessary to alter it, because some of his relatives exclaimed loudly against such a practice, and complained that by this means he would degrade the dignity of the house. He had also another warfare to maintain against his instructors, who stealthily, and as it were by surprise, endeavoured to place before, behind, and around him, more noble appendages, something which might distinguish him from others, and make him appear the first in the place: either thinking, by this means, to ingratiate themselves with him in the long run; or influenced by that servile attachment which prides itself in, and rejoices at, the splendour of others; or being among the number of those prudent persons who shrink back with alarm from the extreme of virtue as well as vice, are for ever proclaiming that perfection lies in a medium between the two, and fix that medium exactly at the point which they have reached, and where they find themselves very much at their ease. Federigo not only refused these kindly offices, but rebuked the officious instruments: and that between the ages of childhood and youth.

That, during the life of the Cardinal Carlo, his senior by twenty-six years, in his authoritative and, so to say, solemn presence, surrounded by homage and respectful silence, incited by the fame, and impressed with the tokens of sanctity, Federigo, as a boy and a youth, should have endeavoured to conform himself to the behaviour and talents of such a cousin, is certainly not to be wondered at; but it is, indeed, much to be able to say, that, after his death, no one could perceive that Federigo, then twenty years of age, had lost a guide and censor. The increasing fame of his talents, erudition, and piety; the relationship and connection of more than one powerful Cardinal; the credit of his family; his very name, to which Carlo had almost annexed in people's minds an idea of sanctity and sacerdotal pre-eminence; all that should, and all that could, lead men to ecclesiastical dignities, concurred to predict them for him. But he, persuaded in heart of what no one who professes Christianity can deny with the lips, that there is no real superiority of a man over his fellowmen, excepting in so far as he devotes himself to their service, both dreaded exaltation, and sought to avoid it; not, indeed, that he might shrink from serving others—for few lives have been more devoted to this object than his own—but because he considered himself neither worthy enough of so high and perilous a service, nor sufficiently competent for it. For these reasons, the Archbishopric of Milan being offered to him in 1595, by Clement VIII., he seemed much disturbed and refused the charge without hesitation. He yielded afterwards, however, to the express command of the Pope.

Such demonstrations (who knows it not?) are neither difficult nor uncommon; and it requires no greater effort of subtlety for hypocrisy to make them, than for raillery to deride them, and hold them cheap on every occasion. But do they, therefore, cease to be the natural expression of a wise and virtuous principle? One's life is the touch-stone of profession; and the profession of this sentiment, though it may have been on the tongue of all the impostors and all the scoffers in the world, will ever be worthy of admiration, when preceded and followed by a life of disinterested self-sacrifice.

In Federigo, as Archbishop, was apparent a remarkable and con-stant carefulness to devote to himself no more of his wealth, his time, his care—in short, of his whole self, than was absolutely neces-sary. He said, as everybody says, that ecclesiastical revenues are the patrimony of the poor; how he showed he understood such a maxim in reality, will be evident from this fact. He caused an estimate to be taken of the sum required for his own expenditure, and that of those in his personal service; and being told that six hundred *scudi* would be sufficient, (*scudo* was at that time the name of a golden coin which, retaining the same weight and value, was afterwards called a *zecchino,*)[1] he gave orders that this sum should annually be set apart out of his patrimonial estate, for the expenses of the table. So sparing and scrupulous was he in his personal outlay, that he was careful never to leave off a dress which was not completely worn out; uniting, however, as was recorded by contemporary writers, to this habit of simplicity, that of singular neatness; two remarkable qualities, in fact, in this age of ostentation and uncleanliness. That nothing, again, might be wasted of the remnants of his frugal table, he assigned them to a hospital for the poor; one of whom came daily, by his orders, to the dining apartment, to gather up all that remained. Such instances of economy might, perhaps, suggest the idea of a close, parsimonious, over-careful virtue, of a mind wrapt up in attention to minutiæ, and incapable of elevated designs, were it not for the Ambrosian Library, still standing, which Federigo projected with such noble magnificence, and executed, from the foundations upwards, with such munificent liberality; to supply which with books and manuscripts, besides the presentation of those he had already collected with great labour and expense, he sent eight of the most learned and experienced men he could find, to make purchases throughout Italy, France, Spain, Germany, Flanders, Greece, Lebanon, and Jerusalem. By this means, he succeeded in gathering together about thirty thousand printed volumes, and fourteen thousand manuscripts. To this library he united a college of doctors (nine in number at first, and maintained at his charge while he lived; afterwards, the ordinary income not sufficing for this expense, they were reduced to two). Their office was to cultivate various branches of study, theology, history, polite literature, and the Oriental languages, obliging each one to publish some work on the subject assigned to him. To this he also added a college, which he called *Trilingue,* for the study of the Greek, Latin, and Italian languages; a college of

[1] Sequin:—an Italian gold coin, worth about ten shillings of English money.

pupils, for instruction in these several faculties and languages, that they might become professors in their turn; a printing-office for the Oriental languages, for Hebrew, that is to say, Chaldaic, Arabic, Persian, and Armenian; a gallery of paintings, another of statues, and a school for the three principal arts of design. For these last he could find professors already existing; but as to the rest, we have seen the trouble it cost him to collect books and manuscripts. Undoubtedly, it would be more difficult to meet with types in those languages, then much less cultivated in Europe than they are at present; and still more difficult than types, would be men who understood them. Suffice it to say, that, out of nine professors, eight were taken from among the young pupils of the seminary; from which circumstance we may infer what was his opinion of the schools then established, and the celebrity gained in those days; an opinion agreeing with that which posterity seems to have formed of them, by suffering both one and the other to sink into oblivion. In the regulations which he left for the use and government of the library, a provision for perpetual utility is conspicuous, not only admirable in itself, but, in many particulars, judicious and elegant, far beyond the general ideas and habits of the age. He required the librarian to keep up a correspondence with the most learned men in Europe, that he might have information of the state of science, and intelligence of the best works on any subject that should be published, and immediately purchase them. He gave him in charge to point out to the students those works which might assist them in their designs; and ordered that the advantages of consulting the works here preserved should be open to all, whether citizens or strangers. Such a regulation will now appear quite natural—one and the same thing with the founding of a library; but in those days it was not so. In a history of the Ambrosian Library, written (with the precision and elegance usual in that age) by one Pier-paolo Bosca, a librarian, after the death of Federigo, it is expressly noted as a remarkable fact, that, in this library, built by a private individual almost entirely at his own expense, the books were accessible to the view of all, and brought to any one who should demand them, with liberty to sit down and study them, and the provision of pen, ink, and paper, to take notes; while, in some other celebrated public libraries in Italy, the volumes were not only not visible, but concealed in closets, where they were never disturbed, except when the humanity, as he says, of the presidents prompted them sometimes to display them for a moment. As to accommodation and conveniences for study provided for those who frequented it, they had not the least idea of such a thing. So that, to furnish such libraries, was to withdraw books from the use of the public; one of those means of cultivation, many of which were, and still are, employed, that only serve to render the soil more sterile.

It were useless to inquire what were the effects of this foundation of Borromeo on public education: it would be easy enough to demonstrate in two words, according to the general method of demonstration, that they were miraculous, or that they were nothing; but to investigate and explain, up to a certain point, what they really were, would be a work of much difficulty, little advantage, and somewhat ill-timed. Rather let us think what a generous, judicious, benevolent, persevering lover of the improvement of mankind he must have been, who planned such an undertaking—who planned it on so grand a scale, and who executed it in the midst of ignorance, inertness, and general contempt of all studious application, and, consequently, in spite of 'What does it matter?' and 'There's something else to think about;' and, 'What a fine invention!' and, 'This was certainly wanting;' and similar remarks, which, undoubtedly, will have been more in number than the scudi expended by him in the undertaking, amounting to a hundred and five thousand, the greatest part of his property.

To style such a man beneficent and liberal in a high degree, it would be unnecessary, perhaps, that he should have spent much in the immediate relief of the needy; and there are, besides, many in whose opinion expenditure of the character we have described, and, indeed, I may say all expenditure, is the best and more beneficial almsgiving. But in Federigo's opinion, almsgiving, properly speaking, was a paramount duty; and here, as in everything else, his actions were in accordance with his principles. His life was one continual overflowing charity. On occasion of this very scarcity, to which our story has already alluded, we shall have presently to relate several traits which will exhibit the judgment and delicacy he

knew how to employ even in his liberality. Of the many remarkable
examples which his biographers have recorded of this virtue, we will
here cite but one. Having heard that a certain nobleman was using
artifices and compulsion to force into a convent one of his daughters
who wished rather to be married, he had an interview with her
father; and drawing from him the acknowledgment that the true
motive of this oppression was the want of four thousand *scudi,* which,
according to his idea, were necessary towards marrying his daughter
suitably, Federigo immediately presented the required dowry. Some
may perhaps think this an extravagant act of bounty, not well-judged,
and too condescending to the foolish caprices of a vain nobleman;
and that four thousand *scudi* might have been better employed in
this or that manner. To which we have nothing to answer, excepting
that it were devoutly to be wished that one could more frequently
see excesses of a virtue so unfettered by prevailing opinion, (every age
has its own,) and so free from the general tendency, as in this instance
that must have been, which induced a man to give four thousand
scudi, that a young person might not be made a nun.

The inexhaustible charity of this man appeared, not only in his
almsgiving, but in his whole behaviour. Easy of access to all, he
considered a cheerful countenance and an affectionate courtesy particularly due to those in the lower ranks of life; and the more so in
proportion as they were little thought of by the world. Here, therefore, he had to combat with the gentlemen of the *ne quid nimis*
school, who were anxious to keep him within limits, i. e., within their
limits. One of these, on occasion of a visit to a wild and mountain-
ous country, when Federigo was teaching some poor children, and
during the interrogations and instruction was fondly caressing them,
besought him to be more cautious in handling such children, as
they were dirty and repelling: as if the worthy gentleman supposed
that Federigo had not discernment enough to make the discovery,
or acumen enough to suggest this recondite counsel for himself.
Such, in certain circumstances of times and things, is the misfortune
of men exalted to high stations, that while they so seldom find any
one to inform them of their failings, there is no lack of persons
courageous enough to reprove them for doing right. But the good
Bishop, not without anger, replied: 'They are my lambs, and perhaps

may never again see my face; and would you not have me caress them?'

Very seldom, however, did he exhibit any anger, being admired for his mild and imperturbable gentleness of behaviour, which might be attributed to an extraordinarily happy temperament of mind; while, in truth, it was the effect of constant discipline over a naturally hasty and passionate disposition. If ever he showed himself severe, nay, even harsh, it was towards those pastors under his authority whom he discovered guilty of avarice, or negligence, or any other conduct opposed to the spirit of their high vocation. Upon what might affect his own interest or temporal glory, he never betokened either joy, regret, eagerness, or anxiety: wonderful indeed if these emotions were not excited in his mind; more wonderful if they were. Not only in the many conclaves at which he had assisted, did he acquire the reputation of having never aspired to that lofty post so desirable to ambition, and so terrible to piety; but on one occasion, when a colleague, who possessed considerable influence, came to offer him his vote and those of his (so, alas! it was termed) faction, Federigo refused the proposal in such a manner that his friend immediately abandoned the idea, and turned his views elsewhere. This same humility, this dread of pre-eminence, was equally apparent in the more common occurrences of life. Careful and indefatigable in ordering and governing everything, where he considered it his duty to do so, he always shrank from intruding into the affairs of others, and even when solicited, refused, if possible, to interfere;—discretion and temperance far from common, as everybody knows, in men as zealous in the cause of good as Federigo was.

Were we to allow ourselves to prosecute the pleasing task of collecting together the remarkable points in his character, the result would certainly be a complication of virtues in apparent opposition to each other, and assuredly difficult to find combined. We cannot, however, omit to notice one more excellency in his excellent life: replete as it was with action, government, functions, instruction, audiences, diocesan visitations, journeys, and controversies, he not only found time for study, but devoted as much to this object as a professor of literature would have required. Indeed, among many other and various titles of commendation, he possessed in a high degree, among his contemporaries, that of a man of learning.

We must not, however, conceal that he held with firm persuasion, and maintained, in fact, with persevering constancy, some opinions which, in the present day, would appear to every one rather singular than ill-founded; even to such as would be anxious to consider them sound. For any one who would defend him on this head, there is the current and commonly received excuse, that they were the errors of the age, rather than his own; an excuse, to say the truth, which, when it results from the minute consideration of facts, may be valid and significant; but which generally, applied in the usual naked way, and as we must do in this instance, comes in the end to mean exactly nothing at all. And, besides, not wishing to resolve complicated questions with simple formulæ, we will venture to leave this unsolved; resting satisfied with having thus cursorily mentioned, that in a character so admirable as a whole, we do not pretend to affirm that every particular was equally so, lest we should seem to have intended making a funeral oration.

We shall not be doing injustice to our readers to suppose that some of them may inquire, whether this person has left any monument of so much talent and erudition. Whether he has left any! The works remaining from him, great and small, Latin and Italian, published and manuscript, amount to about a hundred volumes, preserved in the library he himself founded: moral treatises, discourses, dissertations on history, sacred and profane antiquities, literature, arts, and various other subjects.

—And however does it happen,—this inquirer may ask,—that so many works are forgotten, or at least so little known, so little sought after? How is it, that with such talents, such learning, such experience of men and things, such profound thought, such a sense of the good and the beautiful, such purity of mind, and so many other qualities which constitute the elegant author; how is it, that out of a hundred works, he has not left even one to be considered excellent by those who approve not of the whole, and to be known by title even by those who have never read it? How is it that all of them together have not sufficed, at least by their number, to procure for his name a literary fame among posterity?—

The inquiry is undoubtedly reasonable, and the question sufficiently interesting: because the reasons of this phenomenon are to be found, or, at least, must be sought for, in many general facts; and when found, would lead to the explanation of other similar phenomena. But they would be many and prolix: and what if they should not prove satisfactory? if they should make the reader turn away in disgust? So that it will be better to resume our 'walk through' the story, and instead of digressing more at length on the character of this wonderful man, proceed to observe him in action under the conduct of our anonymous author.

CHAPTER XXIII

CARDINAL FEDERIGO was employed, according to his usual custom in every leisure interval, in study, until the hour arrived for repairing to the church for the celebration of Divine Service, when the chaplain and cross bearer entered with a disturbed and gloomy countenance.

'A strange visitor, my noble Lord,—strange indeed!'

'Who?' asked the Cardinal.

'No less a personage than the Signor * * *' replied the chaplain; and pronouncing the syllables with a very significant tone, he uttered the name which we cannot give to our readers. He then added: 'He is here outside in person; and demands nothing less than to be introduced to your illustrious Grace.'

'He!' said the Cardinal, with an animated look, shutting his book, and rising from his seat; 'let him come in!—let him come in directly!'

'But . . . ' rejoined the chaplain, without attempting to move, 'your illustrious Lordship must surely be aware who he is: that outlaw, that famous . . .'

'And is it not a most happy circumstance for a bishop, that such a man should feel a wish to come and seek an interview with him?'

'But . . .' insisted the chaplain, 'we may never speak of certain things, because my Lord says that it is all nonsense: but, when it comes to the point, I think it is a duty . . . Zeal makes many enemies, my Lord; and we know positively that more than one ruffian has dared to boast that some day or other . . .'

'And what have they done?' interrupted the Cardinal.

'I say that this man is a plotter of mischief, a desperate character, who holds correspondence with the most violent desperadoes, and who may be sent . . .'

'Oh, what discipline is this,' again interrupted Federigo, smiling, 'for the soldiers to exhort their general to cowardice? then resuming a grave and thoughtful air, he continued: 'Saint Carlo would not have deliberated whether he ought to receive such a man: he would have gone to seek him. Let him be admitted directly: he has already waited too long.'

The chaplain moved towards the door, saying in his heart:—There's no remedy: these saints are all obstinate.—

Having opened the door, and surveyed the room where the Signor and his companions were, he saw that the latter had crowded together on one side, where they sat whispering and cautiously peeping at their visitor, while he was left alone in one corner. The chaplain advanced towards him, eying him guardedly from head to foot, and wondering what weapons he might have hidden under that great coat; thinking, at the same time, that really, before admitting him, he ought at least to have proposed . . . but he could not resolve what to do. He approached him, saying: 'His Grace waits for your Lordship. Will you be good enough to come with me?' And as he preceded him through the little crowd, which instantly gave way for him, he kept casting glances on each side, which meant to say: What could I do? don't you know yourselves that he always has his own way?

On reaching the apartment, the chaplain opened the door, and introduced the Unnamed. Federigo advanced to meet him with a happy and serene look, and his hand extended, as if to welcome an expected guest, at the same time making a sign to the chaplain to go out, which was immediately obeyed.

When thus left alone, they both stood for a moment silent and in suspense, though from widely different feelings. The Unnamed, who had, as it were, been forcibly carried there by an inexplicable compulsion, rather than led by a determinate intention, now stood there, also as it were by compulsion, torn by two contending feelings: on the one side, a desire and confused hope of meeting with some alleviation of his inward torment; on the other, a feeling of self-rebuked shame at having come thither, like a penitent, subdued, and wretched, to confess himself guilty, and to make supplication to a man: he was at a loss for words, and, indeed, scarcely sought for them. Raising his eyes, however, to the Archbishop's face, he became gradually filled with a feeling of veneration, authoritative, and at the same time soothing; which, while it increased his confidence, gently subdued his haughtiness, and, without offending his pride, compelled it to give way, and imposed silence.

The bearing of Federigo was, in fact, one which announced superiority, and, at the same time, excited love. It was naturally sedate, and almost involuntarily commanding, his figure being not in the least bowed or wasted by age; while his solemn, yet sparkling eye, his open and thoughtful forehead, a kind of virginal floridness, which might be distinguished even among grey locks, paleness, and the traces of abstinence, meditation, and labour: in short, all his features indicated that they had once possessed that which is most strictly entitled beauty. The habit of serious and benevolent thought, the inward peace of a long life, the love that he felt towards his fellow-creatures, and the uninterrupted enjoyment of an ineffable hope, had now substituted the beauty (so to say) of old age, which shone forth more attractively from the magnificent simplicity of the purple.

He fixed, for a moment, on the countenance of the Unnamed, a penetrating look, long accustomed to gather from this index what was passing in the mind; and imagining he discovered, under that dark and troubled mien, something every moment more corresponding with the hope he had conceived on the first announcement of such a visit, 'Oh!' cried he, in an animated voice, 'what a welcome visit is this! and how thankful I ought to be to you for taking such a step, although it may convey to me a little reproof!'

'Reproof!' exclaimed the Signor, much surprised, but soothed by his words and manner, and glad that the Cardinal had broken the ice, and started some sort of conversation.

'Certainly, it conveys to me a reproof,' replied the Archbishop, 'for allowing you to be beforehand with me when so often, and for so long a time, I might and ought to have come to you myself.'

'You come to me! Do you know who I am? Did they deliver in my name rightly?'

'And the happiness I feel, and which must surely be evident in my countenance, do you think I should feel it at the announcement and visit of a stranger? It is you who make me experience it; you, I say, whom I ought to have sought; you whom I have, at least, loved and wept over, and for whom I have so often prayed; you, among all my children, for each one I love from the bottom of my heart, whom I should most have desired to receive and embrace, if I had thought I might hope for such a thing. But God alone knows how to work wonders, and supplies the weakness and tardiness of His unworthy servants.'

The Unnamed stood astonished at this warm reception, in language which corresponded so exactly with that which he had not yet expressed, nor, indeed, had fully determined to express; and, affected, but exceedingly surprised, he remained silent. 'Well!' resumed Federigo, still more affectionately, 'you have good news to tell me; and you keep me so long expecting it?'

'Good news! I have hell in my heart; and can I tell you any good tidings? Tell me, if you know, what good news you can expect from such as I am?'

'That God has touched your heart, and would make you His own,' replied the Cardinal, calmly.

'God! God! God! If I could see Him! If I could hear Him! Where is this God?'

'Do *you* ask this? you? And who has Him nearer than you? Do you not feel Him in your heart, overcoming, agitating you, never leaving you at ease, and at the same time drawing you forward, presenting to your view a hope of tranquillity and consolation, a consolation which shall be full and boundless, as soon as you recognize Him, acknowledge, and implore Him?'

'Oh, surely! there is something within that oppresses, that consumes me! But God! If this be God, if He be such as they say, what do you suppose He can do with me?'

These words were uttered with an accent of despair; but Federigo, with a solemn tone, as of calm inspiration, replied: 'What can God do with you? What would He wish to make of you? A token of His power and goodness: He would acquire through you a glory, such as others could not give Him. The world has long cried out against you, hundreds and thousands of voices have declared their detestation of your deeds . . .' (The Unnamed shuddered, and felt for a moment surprised at hearing such unusual language addressed to him, and still more surprised that he felt no anger, but rather, almost a relief.) 'What glory,' pursued Federigo, 'will thus redound to God! *They* may be voices of alarm, of self-interest; of justice, perhaps—a justice so easy! so natural! Some perhaps, yea, too many, may be voices of envy of your wretched power; of your hitherto deplorable security of heart. But when you, yourself, rise up to condemn your past life, to become your own accuser, then! then, indeed, God will be glorified! And you ask what God can do with you. Who am I, a poor mortal, that I can tell you what use such a Being may choose henceforth to make of you; how He can employ your impetuous will, your unwavering perseverance, when He shall have animated and invigorated them with love, with hope, with repentance? Who are you, weak man, that you should imagine yourself capable of devising and executing greater deeds of evil, than God can make you will and accomplish in the cause of good? What can God do with you? Pardon you! save you! finish in you the work of redemption! Are not these things noble and worthy of Him? Oh, just think! if I, an humble and feeble creature, so worthless and full of myself—I, such as I am, long so ardently for your salvation, that, for its sake, I would joyfully give (and He is my witness!) the few days that still remain to me; oh, think what, and how great, must be the love of Him, Who inspires me with this imperfect, but ardent affection; how must He love you, what must He desire for you, Who has bid and enabled me to regard you with a charity that consumes me!'

While these words fell from his lips, his face, his expression, his whole manner, evinced his deep feeling of what he uttered. The countenance of his auditor changed, from a wild and convulsive look, first to astonishment and attention, and then gradually yielded to deeper and less painful emotions; his eyes, which from infancy had been unaccustomed to weep, became suffused; and when the words ceased, he covered his face with his hands, and burst into a flood of tears. It was the only and most evident reply.

'Great and good God!' exclaimed Federigo, raising his hands and eyes to heaven, 'what have I ever done, an unprofitable servant, an idle shepherd, that Thou shouldest call me to this banquet of grace! that Thou shouldest make me worthy of being an instrument in so joyful a miracle!' So saying, he extended his hand to take that of the Unnamed.

'No!' cried the penitent nobleman; 'no! keep away from me: defile not that innocent and beneficent hand. You don't know all that the one you would grasp has committed.'

'Suffer me,' said Federigo, taking it with affectionate violence, 'suffer me to press the hand which will repair so many wrongs, dispense so many benefits, comfort so many afflicted, and be extended, disarmed, peacefully, and humbly, to so many enemies.'

'It is too much!' said the Unnamed, sobbing, 'leave me, my Lord; good Federigo, leave me! A crowded assembly awaits you; so many good people, so many innocent creatures, so many come from a distance, to see you for once, to hear you: and you are staying to talk . . . with whom!'

'We will leave the ninety and nine sheep,' replied the Cardinal; 'they are in safety, upon the mountain: I wish to remain with that which was lost. Their minds are, perhaps, now more satisfied than if they were seeing their poor bishop. Perhaps God, Who has wrought in you this miracle of mercy, is diffusing in their hearts a joy of which they know not yet the reason. These people are, perhaps, united to us without being aware of it: perchance the Spirit may be instilling into their hearts an undefined feeling of charity, a petition which He will grant for you, an offering of gratitude of which you are, as yet, the unknown object.' So saying, he threw his arms round the neck of the Unnamed, who, after attempting to disengage himself, and making a momentary resistance, yielded, completely overcome by this vehement expression of affection, embraced the Cardinal in his turn, and buried in his shoulder his trembling and altered face. His burning tears dropped upon the stainless purple of Federigo, while the guiltless hands of the holy bishop affectionately pressed those members, and touched that garment, which had been accustomed to hold the weapons of violence and treachery.

Disengaging himself, at length, from this embrace, the Unnamed again covered his eyes with his hand, and raising his face to heaven, exclaimed; 'God is, indeed, great! God is, indeed, good! I know myself now, now I understand what I am; my sins are present before me, and I shudder at the thought of myself; yet! . . . yet I feel an alleviation, a joy; yes, even a joy, such as I have never before known during the whole of my horrible life!'

'It is a little taste,' said Federigo, 'which God gives you, to incline you to His service, and encourage you resolutely to enter upon the new course of life which lies before you, and in which you will have so much to undo, so much to repair, so much to mourn over!'

'Unhappy man that I am!' exclaimed the Signor: 'how many, oh, how many . . . things for which I can do nothing besides mourn! But, at least, I have undertakings scarcely set on foot which I can break off in the midst, if nothing more: one there is which I can quickly arrest, which I can easily undo, and repair.'

Federigo listened attentively, while the Unnamed briefly related, in terms of, perhaps, deeper execration than we have employed, his attempt upon Lucia, the sufferings and terrors of the unhappy girl, her importunate entreaties, the frenzy that these entreaties had aroused within him, and how she was still in the castle . . .

'Ah, then! let us lose no time!' exclaimed Federigo, breathless with eagerness and compassion. 'You are indeed blessed! This is an earnest of God's forgiveness! He makes you capable of becoming the instrument of safety to one whom you intended to ruin. God bless you! Nay, He has blessed you! Do you know where our unhappy protégée comes from?'

The Signor named Lucia's village.

'It's not far from this,' said the Cardinal, 'God be praised; and probably . . .' So saying, he went towards a little table, and rang a bell. The cross-bearing chaplain immediately attended the summons with a look of anxiety, and instantly glanced towards the Unnamed. At the sight of his altered countenance, and his eyes still red with weeping, he turned an inquiring gaze upon the Cardinal; and perceiving, amidst the invariable composure of his countenance, a look of solemn pleasure and unusual solicitude, he would have stood with open mouth, in a sort of ecstasy, had not the Cardinal quickly aroused him from his contemplations, by asking whether, among the parish-priests who were assembled in the next room, there were one from * * *.

'There is, your illustrious Grace,' replied the chaplain.

'Let him come in directly,' said Federigo, 'and with him the priest of this parish.'

The chaplain quitted the room, and on entering the hall where the clergy were assembled, all eyes were immediately turned upon him; while, with a look of blank astonishment, and a countenance in which was still depicted the rapture he had felt, he lifted up his hands, and waving them in the air, exclaimed, 'Signori! Signori! *hæc mutatio dexteræ Excelsi.*' And he stood for a moment without uttering another word. Then assuming the tone and language of a message, he added, 'His most noble and very reverend Lordship desires to speak with the Signor Curate of this parish, and the Signor Curate of * * *.'

The first party summoned immediately came forward; and, at the same time, there issued from the midst of the crowd, an 'I' drawled forth with an intonation of surprise.

'Are you not the Signor Curate of * * *?' replied the chaplain. 'I am; but . . .'

'His most noble and very reverend Lordship asks for you.'

'Me?' again replied the same voice, clearly expressing in this monosyllable, 'What *can* they want with me?' But this time, together with the voice, came forth the living being, Don Abbondio himself, with an unwilling step, and a countenance between astonishment and disgust. The chaplain beckoned to him with his hand, as if he meant to say, 'Come, let us go; is it so very alarming?' and escorting them to the door, he opened it, and introduced them into the apartment.

The Cardinal relinquished the hand of the Unnamed, with whom, meanwhile, he had been concerting arrangements, and withdrawing a little aside, beckoned to the curate of the village. Briefly relating the circumstances, he asked whether he could immediately find a trustworthy woman who would be willing to go to the castle in a litter, and fetch away Lucia; a kind and clever person, who would know how to conduct herself in so novel an expedition, and whose manners and language would be most likely to encourage and tranquilize the unfortunate girl, to whom, after so much anguish and alarm, even liberation itself might be an additional cause of apprehension. After a moment's thought, the Curate said that he knew just the very person, and then took his departure. The Cardinal now calling to him the chaplain, desired him to have a litter and bearers immediately prepared and to see that two mules were saddled, for riders; and as soon as he had quitted the apartment, turned to Don Abbondio.

This worthy gentleman, who had kept tolerably close to the Archbishop, that he might be at a respectful distance from the other Signor, and had, in the mean time, been casting side glances, first to one, and then to the other, dubitating the while within himself what ever all this strange manœuvring might mean, now advanced a step forward, and, making a respectful bow, said, 'I was told that your most illustrious Lordship wanted me; but I think there must be some misunderstanding.'

'There is no misunderstanding, I assure you,' replied Federigo; 'I have glad news to give you, and a pleasant and most agreeable task to impose upon you. One of your parishioners, whom you must have lamented as lost, Lucia Mondella, is again found, and is near at hand, in the house of my good friend here; and you will go now with him, and a woman, whom the Signor Curate of this place has gone to seek; you will go, I say, to fetch thence one of your own children, and accompany her hither.'

Don Abbondio did his best to conceal the vexation—the what shall I say?—the alarm, the dismay excited by this proposal, or command; and unable any longer to restrain or dismiss a look of inexpressible discontent already gathering in his countenance, he could only hide it by a profound reverence, in token of obedient acceptance; nor did he again raise his face, but to make another equally profound obeisance to the Unnamed, with a piteous look, which seemed to say, 'I am in your hands, have pity upon me; *Parcere subjectis.*'

The Cardinal then asked him what relations Lucia had.

'Of near relations, with whom she lives, or might live, she has only a mother,' replied Don Abbondio.

'Is she at home?'

'Yes, my Lord.'

'Well,' replied Federigo, 'since this poor girl cannot be so directly restored to her own home, it will be a great consolation to her to see her mother as quickly as possible; so, if the Signor Curate of this village doesn't return before I go to church, I request you will tell him to find a cart, or some kind of conveyance, and despatch a person of discretion to fetch her mother here.'

'Had not *I* better go?' said Don Abbondio.

'No, no, not you; I've already requested you to undertake another commission,' replied the Cardinal.

'I proposed it,' rejoined Don Abbondio, 'to prepare her poor mother for the news. She is a very sensitive woman, and it requires one who knows her disposition, and how to go to work with her the right way, or he will do her more harm than good.'

'And therefore I have requested you to acquaint the Signor Curate of my wish that a proper person should be chosen for this office: you will do better elsewhere,' replied the Cardinal. And he would willingly have added: That poor girl at the castle has far more need of shortly seeing a known and trusted countenance, after so many hours of agony, and in such terrible ignorance as to the future. But this was not a reason to be so clearly expressed before the present third party. Indeed, the Cardinal thought it very strange that it had not immediately occurred to Don Abbondio; that he had not thought of it himself; and the proffer he had made, and so warmly insisted upon, seemed so much out of place, that he could not help suspecting there must be something hidden beneath. He gazed upon his face, and there readily detected his fear of journeying with that terrible person, and of being his guest even for a few moments. Anxious, therefore, entirely to dissipate these cowardly apprehensions, yet unwilling to draw the curate aside and whisper with him in secret, while his new friend formed the third of their party, he judged that the best plan would be to do what, indeed, he would have done without such a motive, that is, address the Unnamed himself; and thus Don Abbondio might at length understand, from his replies, that he was no longer an object of fear. He returned, therefore, to the Unnamed, and addressing him with that frank cordiality which may be met with in a new and powerful affection, as well as in an intimacy of long standing, 'Don't think,' said he, 'that I shall be content with this visit for to-day. You will return, won't you, with this worthy clergyman?'

'Will I return?' replied the Unnamed. 'Should you refuse me, I would obstinately remain outside your door, like the beggar. I want to talk with you; I want to hear you, to see you; I deeply need you!'

Federigo took his hand and pressed it, saying: 'Do the clergyman of this village, then, and me, the favour of dining with us to-day. I shall expect you. In the mean while, I must go to offer up prayers and praises with the people; and you to reap the first-fruits of mercy.'

Don Abbondio, at these demonstrations, stood like a cowardly child, who watches a person boldly petting and stroking a large, surly, shaggy dog, with glaring eyes, and a notoriously bad name for biting and growling, and hears its master say that his dog is a good and very quiet beast: he looks at the owner and neither contradicts nor assents; he looks at the animal, afraid to approach him for fear the 'very gentle beast' should show his teeth, were it only from habit; and equally afraid to run away, lest he should be thought a coward; and can only utter an internal aspiration:—Would that I were safe in my own house!

In quitting the apartment, in company with the Unnamed, whose hand he still grasped, the Cardinal cast another glance upon the poor man who remained behind, looking very awkward and mortified, and with a doleful expression of countenance. Thinking that possibly his vexation arose from being apparently overlooked, and left, as it were, in a corner, particularly in contrast with the notoriously wicked character now so warmly received and welcomed, he turned towards him in passing, and hung back for a moment, and said to him, with a friendly smile: 'Signor Curate, thou wert ever with me in the house of our kind Father, but this . . . this one *perierat, et inventus est.'*

'Oh, how glad I am to hear it!' said Don Abbondio, making a profound reverence to the two together.

The Archbishop then went on, gave a slight push to the door, which was immediately opened from without by two servants who stood outside, and the notable pair stood before the longing eyes of the clergy assembled in the apartment. They gazed with interest upon their two countenances, both of which bore the traces of a very different, but equally profound emotion: a grateful tenderness, an humble joy, on Federigo's venerable features; and on those of the Unnamed, confusion, tempered with consolation, a new and unusual modesty, and a feeling of contrition, through which the vigour of his wild and fiery temper was, nevertheless, still apparent. It was afterwards found that the passage in the prophet Isaiah had occurred to more than one of the spectators: *The wolf and the*

lamb shall feed together, and the lion shall eat straw like the bullock.
(Isa. lxv. 25.) Behind them came Don Abbondio, to whom no one
paid any attention.

When they had reached the middle of the room, the Cardinal's
groom of the chamber entered on the opposite side, and informed
his master that he had executed all the orders communicated to
him by the chaplain; that the litter and mules were in readiness,
and they only waited the arrival of the female whom the curate
was to bring. The Cardinal bid him tell the priest, when he came
back, that Don Abbondio wished to speak with him; and then all
the rest was left under the direction of the latter and the Unnamed,
whom the Cardinal again shook warmly by the hand on taking
leave, saying: 'I shall expect you.' Then, turning to salute Don
Abbondio with a bow, he set off in the direction of the church,
followed by the clergy, half grouped and half in procession, while
the fellow-travellers remained alone in the apartment.

The Unnamed stood wrapt up in his own thoughts, and impatient
for the moment when he might go to liberate his Lucia from her
sufferings and confinement,—*his,* now, in a very different sense
from that in which she was so the day before: and his face expressed
a feeling of intense agitation, which to Don Abbondio's suspicious
eye, might easily appear something worse. He peeped and glanced
at him from the corner of his eye, and longed to start some friendly
conversation:—But what can I say to him?—thought he:—must I
say again, I am glad? Glad of what? that having hitherto been a
devil, he has at last resolved to become a gentleman, like others? A
fine compliment, indeed! Eh, eh, eh! however I may turn the words,
I am glad can mean nothing else. And, after all, will it be true
that he has become a gentleman? so on a sudden! There are so
many displays made in the world, and from so many motives!
What do I know about it? And, in the mean time, I have to go
with him: and to that castle! oh, what a tale! what a tale! what a
tale is this to tell! who would have told me this, this morning! Ah,
if I can but escape in safety, my lady Perpetua shan't soon hear the
end of it from me, for having sent me here by force, when there
was no necessity for it, out of my own parish: with her fine plausible
reasons, that all the priests, for many a mile round, would flock

hither, even those who were further off than I; and that I mustn't be behindhand; and this, that, and the other; and then to embark me in a business of this sort! O, poor me! But I must say something to this man.—And he had just thought of that something, and was on the point of opening his mouth to say:—I never anticipated the pleasure of being thrown into such honourable company,—when the groom of the chamber entered, with the curate of the parish, who announced that the woman was waiting in the litter; and then turned to Don Abbondio, to receive from him the further commission of the Cardinal. Don Abbondio delivered himself as well as he could in the confusion of mind under which he was labouring; and then, drawing up to the groom, said to him: 'Pray give me, at least, a quiet beast; for, to tell the truth, I am but a poor horseman.'

'You may imagine,' replied the groom, with a half smile: 'it is the secretary's mule, who is a very learned man.'

'That will do . . .' replied Don Abbondio, and he continued to ruminate:—Heaven send me a good one.—

The Signor had readily set off the moment he heard the announcement; but on reaching the door, and perceiving that Don Abbondio was remaining behind, he stood still to wait for him. When he came up, hastily, with an apologizing look, the Signor bowed and made him pass on first, with a courteous and humble air, which somewhat reanimated the spirits of the unfortunate and tormented man. But scarcely had he set foot in the court-yard, when he saw a new object of alarm, which quickly dissipated all his reviving confidence; he beheld the Unnamed go towards the corner, take hold of the barrel of his carabine with one hand, and of the strap with the other, and with a rapid motion, as if performing the military exercise, swing it over his shoulder.

—Alas! alas! woe is me!—thought Don Abbondio:—what would he do with that weapon? Suitable sackcloth, truly! fine discipline for a new convert! And supposing some fancy should take him? Oh, what an expedition! what an expedition!—

Could this Signor have suspected for a moment what kind of thoughts they were which were passing through his companion's mind, it is difficult to say what he would not have done to reassure him; but he was far enough away from such a suspicion, and Don Abbondio carefully avoided any movement which would distinctly express—I don't trust your Lordship.—On reaching the door into the street, they found the two animals in readiness: the Unnamed mounted one, which was held for him by an hostler.

'Isn't it vicious?' said Don Abbondio to the valet, as he stood with one foot suspended on the stirrup, and the other still resting on the ground.

'You may go with a perfectly easy mind; it's a very lamb,' replied the man, and Don Abbondio, grasping the saddle, and assisted by the groom, gradually mounted upwards, and, at last, found himself safely seated on the creature's back.

The litter, which stood a few paces in advance, and was borne by two mules, moved forward at the word of the attendant, and the party set off.

They had to pass before the church, which was full to overflowing with people; and through a little square, also swarming with the villagers, and newly arrived visitors, whom the building could not accommodate. The glad news had already spread; and on the appearance of the party, and more especially of him who, only a few hours before had been an object of terror and execration, but was now the object of joyful wonder, there arose from the crowd almost a murmur of applause; and as they made way for him, even their eagerness was hushed in the desire to obtain a near view of him. The litter passed on, the Unnamed followed; and when he arrived before the open door of the church, took off his hat, and bowed his hitherto dreaded forehead, till it almost touched the animal's mane, amidst the murmur of a hundred voices, exclaiming, 'God bless you!' Don Abbondio, also, took off his hat, and bending low, recommended himself to Heaven; but hearing the solemn harmony of his brethren, as they chanted in chorus, he was so overcome with a feeling of envy, a mournful tenderness of spirit, and a sudden fervour of heart, that it was with difficulty he restrained his tears.

When they got beyond the habitations into the open country, and in the often entirely deserted windings of the road, a still darker cloud overspread his thoughts. The only object on which his eye could rest with any confidence, was the attendant on the litter, who, belonging to the Cardinal's household, must certainly be an honest man; and who, besides, did not look like a coward. From time to time passengers appeared, sometimes even in groups, who were flocking to see the Cardinal, and this was a great relief to Don Abbondio; it was, however, but transitory, and he was advancing towards that tremendous valley, where he should meet none but the vassals of his companion; and what vassals! He now more than ever longed to enter into conversation with this companion, both to sound him a little more, and to keep him in good humour; but even this wish vanished on seeing him so completely absorbed in his own thoughts. He must then talk to himself; and we will present the reader with a part of the poor man's soliloquy during his journey, for it would require a volume to record the whole.

—It is a fine thing, truly, that saints as well as sinners must have quicksilver in their compositions, and cannot be content with fussing about and busying themselves, but must also bring into the dance with them the whole world, if they can; and that the greatest busy-bodies must just come upon me, who never meddle with anybody, and drag me by the hair into their affairs; me, who ask for nothing but to be left alone! That mad rascal of a Don Rodrigo! What does he want to make him the happiest man in the world, if he had but the least grain of judgment? He is rich, he is young, he is respected and courted: he is sick with too much prosperity, and must needs go about making trouble for himself and his neighbour. He might follow the ways of Saint Michael; oh, no! my gentleman doesn't choose: he chooses to set up the trade of molesting women, the most absurd, the most vile, the most insane business in the world: he might ride to heaven in his carriage, and chooses rather to walk halting to the devil's dwelling. And this man? . . . And here he looked at him, as if he suspected he could hear his very thoughts.—This man! after turning the world upside down with his wickedness, now he turns it upside down with his conversion . . . if it prove really so. In the mean while, it falls to me to make the trial! . . . So it is, that when people are born with this madness in their veins, they must always be making a noise! Is it so difficult to act an honest part all one's life, as I have done? Oh, no, my

good sir: they must kill and quarter, play the devil . . . oh, poor me!
. . . and then comes a great stir even when doing penance. Repentance, when there is an inclination to it, can be performed at
home, quietly, without so much show, without giving so much
trouble to one's neighbours. And his illustrious Lordship, instantly,
with open arms calling him his dear friend, his dear friend; and
this man listens to all he says as if he had seen him work miracles;
and then he must all at once come to a resolution, and rush into it
hand and foot, one minute here, and the next there; we, at home,
should call this precipitation. And to deliver a poor curate into his
hands without the smallest security! this may be called playing
with a man at great odds. A holy bishop, as he is, ought to value
his curates as the apple of his eye. It seems to me there might be a
little moderation, a little prudence, a little charity along with
sanctity . . . Supposing this should be all a mere show? Who
can tell all the intentions of men? and particularly of such a man
as this? To think that it is my lot to go with him to his own house!
There may be some underwork of the devil here: oh, poor me! it is
best not to think about it. How is Lucia mixed up with all this?
It is plain Don Rodrigo had some designs upon her: what people:
and suppose it is exactly thus, how then has this man got her into
his clutches? Who knows, I wonder? It is all a secret with my
Lord; and to me, whom they are making trot about in this way,
they don't tell a word. I don't care about knowing other people's
affairs; but when I have to risk my skin in the matter, I have a
right to know something. If it be only to go and fetch away this
poor creature, patience! though he could easily enough bring her
straight away himself. And besides, if he is really converted, if he
has become a holy father, what need is there of me? Oh, what a
chaos! Well; it is Heaven's will it should be thus: it will be a very
great inconvenience, but patience! I shall be glad, too, for this
poor Lucia: she also must have escaped some terrible issue: Heaven
knows what she must have suffered: I pity her; but she was born
to be my ruin . . . At least, I wish I could look into his heart, and
see what he is thinking about. Who can understand him? Just
look, now; one minute he looks like Saint Antony in the desert,
the next he is like Holofernes himself. Oh, poor me! poor me!

Well; Heaven is under an obligation to help me, since I didn't get myself into this danger with my own good will.—

In fact, the thoughts of the Unnamed might be seen, so to say, passing over his countenance, as in a stormy day the clouds flit across the face of the sun, producing every now and then an alternation of dazzling light and gloomy shade. His soul, still quite absorbed in reflection upon Federigo's soothing words, and, as it were, renewed and made young again with fresh life, now rose with cheerful hope at the idea of mercy, pardon, and love; and then again sank beneath the weight of the terrible past. He anxiously tried to select those deeds of iniquity which were yet reparable, and those which he could still arrest in the midst of their progress; he considered what remedies would be most certain and expeditious, how to disentangle so many knots, what to do with so many accomplices; but it was all obscurity and difficulty. In this very expedition, the easiest of execution, and so near its termination, he went with a willingness mingled with grief at the thought, that in the mean while the poor girl was suffering, God knew how much, and that he, while burning to liberate her, was all the while the cause of her suffering. At every turn, or fork in the road, the mule-driver looked back for direction as to the way: the Unnamed signified it with his hand, and at the same time beckoned to him to make haste.

They entered the valley. How must Don Abbondio have felt then! That renowned valley, of which he had heard such black and horrible stories, to be actually within it! Those men of notorious fame, the flower of the bravoes of Italy, men without fear and without mercy,—to see them in flesh and blood,—to meet one, two, or three, at every turn of a corner! They bowed submissively to the Signor; but their sunburnt visages! their rough mustachios! their large fierce eyes! they seemed to Don Abbondio's mind to mean,—Shall we dispatch that Priest?—So that, in a moment of extreme consternation, the thought rushed into his mind,—Would that I had married them! worse could not befall me.—In the mean while they went forward along a gravelly path by the side of the torrent: on one hand was a view of isolated and solid rocks; on the other, a population which would have made even a desert seem desirable: Dante was not in a worse situation in the midst of Malebolge.

They passed the front of Malanotte; where bravoes were lounging at the door, who bowed to the Signor, and gazed at his companion and the litter. They knew not what to think; the departure of the Unnamed in the morning by himself had already seemed extraordinary, and his return was not less so. Was it a captive that he was conducting? And how had he accomplished it alone? And what was the meaning of a strange litter? And whose could this livery be? They looked and looked, but no one moved, because such was the command they read in his eye and expression.

They climbed the ascent, and reached the summit. The bravoes on the terrace and round the gate retired on either side to make room for him; the Unnamed motioned to them to retreat no farther, spurted forward and passed before the litter, beckoned to the driver and Don Abbondio to follow him, entered an outer court, and thence into a second, went towards a small postern, made signs to a bravo, who was hastening to hold his stirrup, to keep back, and said to him, 'You there, and no one nearer.' He then dismounted, and holding the bridle, advanced towards the litter, addressed himself to the female who had just drawn back the curtain, and said to her in an undertone: 'Comfort her directly; let her understand at once that she is at liberty, and among friends. God will reward you for it.' He then ordered the driver to open the door, and assist her to get out. Advancing, then, to Don Abbondio, with a look of greater serenity than the poor man had yet seen, or thought it possible he could see, on his countenance, in which there might now be traced joy at the good work which was at length so near its completion, he lent him his arm to dismount, saying to him at the same time, in a low voice: 'Signor Curate, I do not apologize for the trouble you have had on my account; you are bearing it for One who rewards bountifully, and for this His poor creature!'

This look, and these words, once more put some heart into Don Abbondio; and, drawing a long breath, which for an hour past had been striving ineffectually to find vent, he replied, whether or not in a submissive tone it need not be asked: 'Is your Lordship joking with me? But, but, but, but! . . .' And, accepting the hand which was so courteously offered, he slid down from the saddle as he best could. The Unnamed took the bridle, and handed it with his own to the driver, bidding him wait there outside for them. Taking a key from his pocket, he opened the postern, admitted the curate and the woman, followed them in, advanced to lead the way, went to the foot of the stairs, and they all three ascended in silence.

CHAPTER XXIV

LUCIA had aroused herself only a short time before, and part of that time she had been striving to awaken herself thoroughly, and to sever the disturbed dreams of sleep from the remembrances and images of a reality which too much resembled the feverish visions of sickness. The old woman quickly made up to her, and, with a constrained voice of humility, said: 'Ah! have you slept? You might have slept in bed: I told you so often enough last night.' And receiving no reply, she continued, in a tone of pettish entreaty: 'Just eat something; do be prudent. Oh, how wretched you look! You must want something to eat. And then if, when he comes back, he's angry with me!'

'No, no; I want to go away. I want to go to my mother. Your master promised I should; he said, *to-morrow morning*. Where is he?'

'He's gone out; but he said he'd be back soon, and would do all you wished.'

'Did he say so? did he say so? Very well; I wish to go to my mother, directly, directly.'

And behold! the noise of footsteps was heard in the adjoining room; then a tap at the door. The old woman ran to it, and asked, 'Who's there?'

'Open the door,' replied the well-known voice, gently.

The old woman drew back the bolt, and, with a slight push, the Unnamed half opened the door, bid her come out, and hastily ushered in Don Abbondio and the good woman. He then nearly closed the door again, and waiting himself outside, sent the aged matron to a distant part of the castle, as he had before dismissed the other one, who was keeping watch outside.

All this bustle, the moment of expectation, and the first appearance of strange figures, made Lucia's heart bound with agitation; for, if her present condition was intolerable, every change was an additional cause of alarm. She looked up, and beheld a priest and a woman; this somewhat reanimated her; she looked more closely; is it he or not? At last, she recognized Don Abbondio, and remained with her eyes fixed, as if by enchantment. The female then drew near, and bending over her, looked at her compassionately, taking both her hands, as if to caress and raise her at the same time, and saying: 'Oh, my poor girl! come with us, come with us.'

'Who are you?' demanded Lucia; but without listening to the reply, she again turned to Don Abbondio, who was standing two or three yards distant, even his countenance expressing some compassion; she gazed at him again, and exclaimed: 'You! Is it you! The Signor Curate? Where are we? . . . Oh, poor me! I have lost my senses!'

'No, no,' replied Don Abbondio, 'it is indeed I: take courage. Don't you see we are here to take you away? I am really your curate, come hither on purpose on horseback . . .'

As if she had suddenly regained all her strength, Lucia precipitately sprang upon her feet: then again fixing her eyes on those two faces, she said: 'It is the Madonna, then, that has sent you.'

'I believe indeed it is,' said the good woman.

'But can we go away? Can we really go away?' resumed Lucia, lowering her voice, and assuming a timid and suspicious look. 'And all these people? . . .' continued she, with her lips compressed, and quivering with fear and horror: 'And that Lord . . . that man! . . . He did, indeed, promise . . .'

'He is here himself in person, came on purpose with us,' said Don Abbondio; 'he is outside waiting for us. Let us go at once; we mustn't keep a man like him waiting.'

At this moment, he of whom they were speaking opened the door, and showing himself at the entrance, came forward into the room. Lucia, who but just before had wished for him, nay, having no hope in any one else in the world, had wished for none but him, now, after having seen and listened to friendly faces and voices, could not restrain a sudden shudder: she started, held her breath, and throwing herself on the good woman's shoulder, buried her face in her bosom. At the first sight of that countenance, on which, the evening before, he had been unable to maintain a steady gaze, now rendered more pale, languid and dejected, by prolonged suffering and abstinence, the Unnamed had suddenly checked his steps; now, at the sight of her impulse of terror, he cast his eyes on the ground, stood for a moment silent and motionless, and then replying to what the poor girl had not expressed in words, 'It is true,' exclaimed he; 'forgive me!'

'He is come to set you free; he's no longer what he was; he has become good; don't you hear him asking your forgiveness?' said the good woman, in Lucia's ear.

'Could he say more? Come, lift up your head; don't be a baby: we can go directly,' said Don Abbondio. Lucia raised her face, looked at the Unnamed, and seeing his head bent low, and his embarrassed and humble look, she was seized with a mingled feeling of comfort, gratitude, and pity, as she replied, 'Oh, my Lord! God reward you for this deed of mercy!'

'And you a thousandfold, for the good you do me by these words.'

So saying, he turned round, went towards the door, and led the way out of the room. Lucia, completely reassured, followed, leaning on the worthy female's arm, while Don Abbondio brought up the rear. They descended the staircase, and reached the little door that led into the court. The Unnamed opened it, went towards the litter, and, with a certain politeness, almost mingled with timidity, (two novel qualities in him,) offered his arm to Lucia, to assist her to get in; and afterwards to the worthy dame. He then took the bridles of the two mules from the driver's hand, and gave his arm to Don Abbondio, who had approached his gentle steed.

'Oh, what condescension!' said Don Abbondio, as he mounted much more nimbly than he had done the first time; and as soon as the Unnamed was also seated, the party resumed their way. The Signor's brow was raised: his countenance had regained its customary expression of authority. The ruffians whom they passed on their way, discovered, indeed, in his face the marks of deep thought, and an extraordinary solicitude; but they neither understood, nor could understand, more about it. They knew not yet anything of the great change which had taken place in their master; and, undoubtedly, none of them would have divined it merely from conjecture.

The good woman immediately drew the curtains over the little windows; and then, affectionately taking Lucia's hands, she applied herself to comfort her with expressions of pity, congratulation, and tenderness. Seeing, then, that not only fatigue from the suffering she had undergone, but the perplexity and obscurity of all that had happened, prevented the poor girl from being sensible of the joy of her deliverance, she said all she could think of most likely to recall her recollection, and to clear up, and set to rights, so to say, her poor scattered thoughts. She named the village she came from, and to which they were now going.

'Yes!' said Lucia, who knew how short a distance it was from her own. 'Ah, most holy Madonna, I praise thee! My mother! my mother!'

'We will send to fetch her directly,' said the good woman, not knowing that it was already done.

'Yes, yes, and God will reward you for it . . . And you, who are you? How have you come . . .'

'Our Curate sent me,' said the good woman, 'because God has touched this Signor's heart, (blessed be His name!) and he came to our village to speak to the Signor Cardinal Archbishop, for he is there in his visitation, that holy man of God; and he had repented of his great sins, and wished to change his life; and he told the Cardinal that he had caused a poor innocent to be seized, meaning you, at the instigation of another person, who had no fear of God; but the Curate didn't tell me who it could be.'

Lucia raised her eyes to heaven.

'You know who it was, perhaps,' continued the good woman.

'Well; the Signor Cardinal thought that, as there was a young girl in the question, there ought to be a female to come back with her; and he told the Curate to look for one; and the Curate, in his goodness, came to me . . .'

'Oh, the Lord recompense you for your kindness!'

'Well, just listen to me, my poor child! And the Signor Curate bid me encourage you, and try to comfort you directly, and point out to you how the Lord has saved you by a miracle . . .'

'Ah yes, by a miracle indeed; through the intercession of the Madonna!'

'Well, that you should have a right spirit, and forgive him who has done you this wrong, and be thankful that God has been merciful to him, yes, and pray for him too; for, besides that you will be rewarded for it, you will also find your heart lightened.'

Lucia replied with a look which expressed assent as clearly as words could have done, and with a sweetness which words could not have conveyed.

'Noble girl!' rejoined the woman. 'And your Curate, too, being at our village, (for there are numbers assembled from all the country round to elect four public officers,) the Signor Cardinal thought it better to send him with us; but he has been of little use: I had before heard that he was a poor-spirited creature; but, on this occasion, I couldn't help seeing that he was as frightened as a chicken in a bundle of hemp.'

'And this man . . .' asked Lucia, 'this person who has become good . . . who is he?'

'What! don't you know him?' said the good woman, mentioning his name.

'Oh, the mercy of the Lord!' exclaimed Lucia. How often had she heard that name repeated with horror in more than one story, in which it always appeared as, in other stories, that of the monster Orcus! And at the thought of having once been in his dreaded power, and being now under his merciful protection—at the thought of such fearful danger, and such unlooked-for deliverance; and at the remembrance of whose face it was that had at first appeared to her so haughty, afterwards so agitated, and then so humbled, she remained in a kind of ecstasy, only occasionally repeating, 'Oh, what a mercy!'

'It is a great mercy, indeed!' said the good woman. 'It will be a great relief to half the world, to all the country round. To think how many people he kept in fear; and now, as our Curate told me . . . and then, only to see his face, he is become a saint! And the fruits are seen so directly.'

To assert this worthy person did not feel much curiosity to know rather more explicitly the wonderful circumstances in which she was called upon to bear a part, would not be the truth. But we must say, to her honour, that, restrained by a respectful pity for

Lucia, and feeling, in a manner, the gravity and dignity of the charge which had been entrusted to her, she never even thought of putting an indiscreet or idle question; throughout the whole journey, her words were those of comfort and concern for the poor girl.

'Heaven knows how long it is since you have eaten anything!'

'I don't remember . . . not for some time.'

'Poor thing! you must want something to strengthen you?'

'Yes,' replied Lucia, in a faint voice.

'Thank God, we shall get something at home directly. Take heart, for it's not far now.'

Lucia then sank languidly to the bottom of the litter, as if overcome with drowsiness, and the good woman left her quietly to repose.

To Don Abbondio the return was certainly not so harassing as the journey thither not long before; but, nevertheless, even this was not a ride of pleasure. When his overwhelming fears had subsided, he felt, at first, as if relieved from every burden; but very shortly a hundred other fancies began to haunt his imagination; as the ground whence a large tree has been uprooted remains bare and empty for a time, but is soon abundantly covered with weeds. He had become more sensitive to minor causes of alarm; and in thoughts of the present, as well as the future, failed not to find only too many materials for self-torment. He felt now, much more than in coming, the inconveniences of a mode of travelling to which he was not at all accustomed, and particularly in the descent from the castle to the bottom of the valley. The mule-driver, obedient to a sign from the Unnamed, drove on the animals at a rapid pace; the two riders followed in a line behind, with corresponding speed, so that, in sundry steep places, the unfortunate Don Abbondio, as if forced up by a lever behind, rolled forward, and was obliged to keep himself steady by grasping the pommel of the saddle; not daring to request a slower pace, and anxious, also, to get out of the neighbourhood as quickly as he could. Besides this, wherever the road was on an eminence, on the edge of a steep bank, the mule, according to the custom of its species, seemed as if aiming, out of contempt, always to keep on the outside, and to set its feet on the very brink; and Don Abbondio saw, almost perpendicularly beneath him, a good leap, or, as he thought, a precipice.—Even you,—said he to the animal, in his heart,—have a cursed inclination to go in search of dangers, when there is such a safe and wide path.—And he pulled the bridle to the opposite side, but in vain; so that, grumbling with vexation and fear, he suffered himself, as usual, to be guided at the will of others. The ruffians no longer gave him so much alarm, now that he knew for certain how their master regarded them.—But,—reflected he,—if the news of this grand conversion should get abroad among them while we are still here, who knows how these fellows would take it? Who knows what might arise from it? What, if they should get an idea that I am come hither as a missionary! Heaven preserve me! they would martyr me!—The haughty brow of the Unnamed gave him no uneasiness.—To keep those visages there in awe,—thought he,—it needs no less than this one here; I understand that myself; but why has it fallen to my lot to be thrown amongst such people?—

But enough; they reached the foot of the descent, and at length also issued from the valley. The brow of the Unnamed became gradually smoother. Don Abbondio, too, assumed a more natural expression, released his head somewhat from imprisonment between his shoulders, stretched his legs and arms, tried to be a little more at his ease, which, in truth, made him look like a different creature, drew his breath more freely, and, with a calmer mind, proceeded to contemplate other and remoter dangers.—What will that villain of a Don Rodrigo say? To be left in this way, wronged, and open to ridicule; just fancy whether that won't be a bitter dose. Now's the time when he'll play the devil outright. It remains to be seen whether he won't be angry with me, because I have been mixed up with this business. If he has already chosen to send these two demons to meet me on the high road with such an intimation, what will he do now, Heaven knows! He can't quarrel with his illustrious Lordship, for he's rather out of his reach; he'll be obliged to gnaw the bit with *him*. But all the while the venom will be in his veins, and he'll be sure to vent it upon somebody. How will all these things end? The blow must always fall somewhere; the lash must be uplifted. Of course, his illustrious Lordship intends to place Lucia in safety: that other unfortunate misguided youth is beyond reach, and has already had his share; so behold the lash must fall upon my shoulders. It will indeed be cruel, if, after so many inconveniences and so much agitation, without my deserving it, too, in the least, I should have to bear the punishment. What will his most illustrious Grace do now to protect me, after having brought me into the dance? Can he ensure that this cursed wretch won't play me a worse trick than before? And, besides, he has so many things to think of; he puts his hand to so many businesses. How can he attend to all? Matters are sometimes left more entangled than at first. Those who do good, do it in the gross; when they have enjoyed this satisfaction, they've had enough, and won't trouble themselves to look after the consequences; but they who have such a taste for evil-doings, are much more diligent; they follow it up to the end, and give themselves no rest, because they have an ever-devouring canker within them. Must I go and say that I came here at the express command of his illustrious Grace, and not with my own good will? That would seem as if I favoured the wicked side. Oh, sacred Heaven! I favour the wicked side! For the pleasure it gives me! Well; the best plan will be to tell Perpetua the case as it is, and then leave it to her to circulate it, provided my Lord doesn't take a fancy to make the whole matter public, and bring even me into the scene. At any rate, as soon as ever we arrive, if he's out of church, I'll go and take my leave of him as quickly as possible; if he's not, I'll leave an apology, and go off home at once. Lucia is well attended to; there's no need for me; and after so much trouble, I, too, may claim a little repose. And besides . . . what if my Lord should feel some curiosity to know the whole history, and it should fall to me to give an account of that wedding business! This is all that is wanting to complete it. And if he should come on a visit to my parish? . . . Oh, let it be what it will, I will not trouble myself about it beforehand; I have troubles enough already. For the present, I shall shut myself up at home. As long as his Grace is in this neighbourhood, Don Rodrigo won't have the face to make a stir. And afterwards . . . oh, afterwards! Ah, I see that my last years are to be spent in sorrow!—

The party arrived before the services in the church were over; they passed through the still assembled crowd, which manifested no less emotion than on the former occasion, and then separated. The two riders turned aside into a small square, at the extremity of which stood the Curate's residence, while the litter went forward to that of the good woman.

Don Abbondio kept his word: scarcely dismounted, he paid the most obsequious compliments to the Unnamed, and begged him to make an apology for him to his Grace, as he must return immediately to his parish on urgent business. He then went to seek for what he called his horse, that is to say, his walking-stick, which he had left in a corner of the hall, and set off on foot. The Unnamed remained to wait till the Cardinal returned from church.

The good woman, having accommodated Lucia with the best seat in the best place in her kitchen, hastened to prepare a little refreshment for her, refusing, with a kind of rustic cordiality, her reiterated expressions of thanks and apology.

Hastily putting some dry sticks under a vessel, which she had replaced upon the fire, and in which floated a good capon, she quickly made the broth boil; and then, filling from it a porringer, already furnished with sops of bread, she was at length able to offer it to Lucia. And on seeing the poor girl refreshed at every spoonful, she congratulated herself aloud, that all this had happened on a day when, as she said, the cat was not sitting on the hearth-stone. 'Everybody contrives to set out a table to-day,' added she, 'unless it be those poor creatures who can scarcely get bread of vetches, and a *polenta* of millet; however, they all hope to beg something to-day, from such a charitable Signor. We, thank Heaven, are not so badly off: what with my husband's business, and a little plot of ground, we can live very well, so that you needn't hesitate to eat with a good appetite; the chicken will soon be done, and you can then refresh yourself with something better.' And, receiving the little porringer from her hand, she turned to prepare the dinner, and to set out the table for the family.

Invigorated in body, and gradually revived in heart, Lucia now began to settle her dress, from an instinctive habit of cleanliness and modesty: she tied up and arranged afresh her loose and dishevelled tresses, and adjusted the handkerchief over her bosom, and around her neck. In doing this, her fingers became entangled in the chaplet she had hung there: her eye rested upon it; aroused an instantaneous agitation in her heart; the remembrance of her vow, hitherto suppressed and stifled by the presence of so many other sensations, suddenly rushed upon her mind, and presented itself clearly and distinctly to her view. The scarcely recovered powers of her soul were again at once overcome; and had she not been previously prepared by a life of innocence, resignation, and confiding faith, the consternation she experienced at that moment would have amounted to desperation. After a tumultuous burst of such thoughts as were not to be expressed in words, the only ones she could form in her mind were,—Oh, poor me, whatever have I done!—

But scarcely had she indulged the thought, when she felt a kind of terror at having done so. She recollected all the circumstances of the vow, her insupportable anguish, her despair of all human succour, the fervency of her prayer, the entireness of feeling with which the promise had been made. And after having obtained her petition, to repent of her promise seemed to her nothing less than sacrilegious ingratitude and perfidy towards God and the Virgin; she imagined that such unfaithfulness would draw down upon her new and more terrible misfortunes, in which she could not find consolation even in prayer; and she hastened to abjure her momentary regret. Reverently taking the rosary from her neck, and holding it in her trembling hand, she confirmed and renewed the vow, imploring, at the same time, with heartrending earnestness, that strength might be given her to fulfill it; and that she might be spared such thoughts and occurrences as would be likely, if not to disturb her resolution, at least to harass her beyond endurance. The distance of Renzo, without any probability of return, that distance which she had hitherto felt so painful, now seemed to her a dispensation of Providence, who had made the two events work together for the same end; and she thought to find in the one a motive of consolation for the other. And, following up this thought, she began representing to herself that the same Providence, to complete the work, would know what means to employ to induce Renzo himself to be resigned, to think no more . . . But scarcely had such an idea entered her mind, when all was again overturned. The poor girl, feeling her heart still prone to regret the vow, again had recourse to prayer, confirmation of the promise, and inward struggles, from which she arose, if we may be allowed the expression, like the wearied and wounded victor from his fallen enemy.

At this moment she heard approaching footsteps and joyous cries. It was the little family returning from church. Two little girls and a young boy bounded into the house, who, stopping a moment to cast an inquisitive glance at Lucia, ran to their mother, and gathered around her; one inquiring the name of the unknown guest, and how, and why; another attempting to relate the wonderful things they had just witnessed; while the good woman replied to each and all, 'Be quiet, be quiet.' With a more sedate step, but with cordial interest depicted on his countenance, the master of the house then entered. He was, if we have not yet said so, the tailor of the village and its immediate neighbourhood; a man who knew how to read, who had, in fact, read more than once *Il Leggendario de' Santi,* and *I Reali di Francia,* and who passed among his fellow-villagers as a man of talent and learning; a character, however, which he modestly disclaimed, only saying, that he had mistaken his vocation, and that, had he applied himself to study, instead of so many others ... and so on. With all this, he was the best-tempered creature in the world. Having been present when his wife was requested by the Curate to undertake her charitable journey, he had not only given his approbation, but would also have added his persuasion, had it been necessary. And now that the services, the pomp, the concourse, and above all, the sermon of the Cardinal, had, as the saying is, elevated all his best feelings, he returned home with eager anticipations, and an anxious desire to know how the thing had succeeded, and to find the innocent young creature safe.

'See, there she is!' said his good wife, as he entered, pointing to Lucia, who blushed, and rose from her seat, beginning to stammer forth some apology. But he, advancing towards her, interrupted her excuses, congratulating her on her safety, and exclaiming, 'Welcome, welcome! You are the blessing of Heaven in this house. How glad I am to see you here! I was pretty sure you would be brought out safely; for I've never found that the Lord began a miracle without bringing it to a good end; but I'm glad to see you here.

Poor girl! but it is indeed a great thing to have received a miracle!'

Let it not be thought that he was the only person who thus denominated this event, because he had read the Legendary; as long as the remembrance of it lasted, it was spoken of in no other terms in the whole village, and throughout the neighbourhood. And, to say truth, considering its attendant and following consequences, no other name is so appropriate.

Then, sidling up to his wife, who was taking the kettle off the hook over the fire, he whispered, 'Did everything go on well?'

'Very well; I'll tell you afterwards.'

'Yes, yes, at your convenience.'

Dinner now being quickly served up, the mistress of the house went up to Lucia, and leading her to the table, made her take a seat; then cutting off a wing of the fowl, she set it before her, and she and her husband sitting down, they both begged their dispirited and bashful guest to make herself at home, and take something to eat. Between every mouthful, the tailor began to talk with great eagerness, in spite of the interruptions of the children, who stood round the table to their meal, and who, in truth, had seen too many extraordinary things, to play, for any length of time, the part of mere listeners. He described the solemn ceremonies, and then passed on to the miraculous conversion. But that which had made the most impression upon him, and to which he most frequently returned, was the Cardinal's sermon.

'To see him there before the altar,' said he, 'a gentleman like him, like a Curate . . .'

'And that gold thing he had on his head . . .' said a little girl.

'Hush. To think, I say, that a gentleman like him, such a learned man, too, that from what people say, he has read all the books there are in the world; a thing which nobody else has ever done, not even in Milan—to think that he knew how to say things in such a way, that every one understood . . .'

'Even I understood very well,' said another little prattler.

'Hold your tongue; what may you have understood, I wonder?'

'I understood that he was explaining the Gospel, instead of the Signor Curate.'

'Well, be quiet. I don't say those who know something, for then one is obliged to understand; but even the dullest and most ignorant could follow out the sense. Go now and ask them if they could repeat the words that he spoke: I'll engage they could not remember one; but the meaning they will have in their heads. And without ever mentioning the name of that Signor, how easy it was to see that he was alluding to him! Besides, to understand that, one had only to observe him with the tears standing in his eye. And then the whole church began to weep . . .'

'Yes, indeed, they did,' burst forth the little boy; 'but why were they all crying in that way, like children?'

'Hold your tongue. Surely there are some hard hearts in this country. And he made us see so well, that though there is a famine here, we ought to thank God, and be content; do whatever we can, work industriously, help one another, and then be content, because it is no disgrace to suffer and be poor; the disgrace is to do evil. And these are not only fine words; for everybody knows that he lives like a poor man himself, and takes the bread out of his own mouth to give to the hungry, when he might be enjoying good times better than any one. Ah! then it gives one satisfaction to hear a man preach: not like so many others: "Do what I say, and not what I do." And then he showed us that even those who are not what they call gentlemen, if they have more than they actually want, are bound to share it with those who are suffering.'

Here he interrupted himself, as if checked by some thought. He hesitated a moment; then filling a platter from the several dishes on the table, and adding a loaf of bread, he put it into a cloth, and taking it by the four corners, said to his eldest girl: 'Here, take this.' He then put into her other hand a little flask of wine, and added: 'Go down to the widow Maria, leave her these things, and tell her it is to make a little feast with her children. But do it kindly and nicely, you know; that it may not seem as if you were doing her a charity. And don't say anything, if you meet any one; and take care you break nothing.'

Lucia's eyes glistened, and her heart glowed with tender emotion; as from the conversation she had already heard, she had received more comfort than an expressly consolatory sermon could possibly have imparted to her. Her mind, attracted by these descriptions, these images of pomp, and these emotions of piety and wonder, and sharing in the very enthusiasm of the narrator, was detached from the consideration of its own sorrows; and on returning to them, found itself strengthened to contemplate them. Even the thought of her tremendous sacrifice, though it had not lost its bitterness, brought with it something of austere and solemn joy.

Shortly afterwards, the Curate of the village entered, and said that he was sent by the Cardinal to inquire after Lucia, and to inform her that his Grace wished to see her some time during the day; and then, in his Lordship's name, he returned many thanks to the worthy couple. Surprised and agitated, the three could scarcely find words to reply to such messages from so great a personage.

'And your mother hasn't yet arrived?' said the Curate to Lucia.

'My mother!' exclaimed the poor girl. Then hearing from him how he had been sent to fetch her by the order and suggestion of the Archbishop, she drew her apron over her eyes, and gave way to a flood of tears, which continued to flow for some time after the Curate had taken his leave. When, however, the tumultuous feelings which had been excited by such an announcement began to yield to more tranquil thoughts, the poor girl remembered that the now closely impending happiness of seeing her mother again, a happiness so unhoped-for a few hours previous, was what she had expressly implored in those very hours, and almost stipulated as a condition of her vow. *Bring me in safety to my mother,* she had said; and these words now presented themselves distinctly to her memory. She strengthened herself more than ever in the resolution to maintain her promise, and afresh and more bitterly lamented the struggle and regret she had for a moment indulged.

Agnese, indeed, while they were talking about her, was but a very little way off. It may easily be imagined how the poor woman felt at this unexpected summons, and at the announcement, necessarily defective and confused, of an escaped but fearful danger,—an obscure event, which the messenger could neither circumstantiate nor explain, and of which she had not the slightest ground of explanation in her own previous thoughts. After tearing her hair,—after frequent exclamations of 'Ah, my God! Ah, Madonna!'—after putting various questions to the messenger which he had not the means of satisfying, she threw herself impetuously into the vehicle, continuing to utter, on her way, numberless ejaculations and useless inquiries. But at a certain point she met Don Abbondio, trudging on, step after step, and before each step, his walking-stick. After an 'oh!' from both parties, he stopped; Agnese also stopped and dismounted; and drawing him apart into a chestnut-grove on the roadside, she there learnt from Don Abbondio all that he had been able to ascertain and observe. The thing was not clear; but at least Agnese was assured that Lucia was in safety; and she again breathed freely.

After this Don Abbondio tried to introduce another subject, and give her minute instructions as to how she ought to behave before the Archbishop, if, as was likely, he should wish to see her and her daughter; and, above all, that it would not do to say a word about the wedding . . . But Agnese, perceiving that he was only speaking for his own interest, cut him short, without promising, indeed without proposing, anything, for she had something else to think about; and immediately resumed her journey.

At length the cart arrived, and stopped at the tailor's house. Lucia sprang up hastily: Agnese dismounted and rushed impetuously into the cottage, and, in an instant, they were locked in each other's arms. The good dame, who alone was present, tried to encourage and calm them, and shared with them in their joy; then, with her usual discretion, she left them for a while alone, saying that she would go and prepare a bed for them, for which, indeed, she had the means, though, in any case, both she and her husband would much rather have slept upon the ground, than suffer them to go in search of shelter elsewhere for that night.

The first burst of sobs and embraces being over, Agnese longed to hear Lucia's adventures, and the latter began, mournfully, to relate them. But, as the reader is aware, it was a history which no one knew fully; and to Lucia herself there were some obscure passages, which were, in fact, quite inextricable: more particularly the fatal coincidence of that terrible carriage being in the road, just when Lucia was passing on an extraordinary occasion. On this point, both mother and daughter were lost in conjecture, without ever hitting the mark, or even approaching the real cause.

As to the principal author of the plot, neither one nor the other could for a moment doubt but that it was Don Rodrigo.

'Ah, the black villain! ah, the infernal firebrand!' exclaimed Agnese: 'but his hour will come. God will reward him according to his works; and then he, too, will feel . . .'

'No, no, mother; no!' interrupted Lucia; 'don't predict suffering for him; don't predict it to any one! If you knew what it was to suffer! If you had tried it! No, no! rather let us pray God and the Madonna for him: that God would touch his heart, as he has done to this other poor Signor, who *was* worse than he is, and is now a saint.'

The shuddering horror that Lucia felt in retracing such recent and cruel scenes, made her more than once pause in the midst; more than once she said she had not courage to go on; and, after many tears, with difficulty resumed her account. But a different feeling checked her at a certain point of the narration,—at the mention of the vow. The fear of being blamed by her mother as imprudent and precipitate; or that, as in the affair of the wedding, she should bring forward one of her broad rules of conscience, and try to make it prevail; or that, poor woman, she should tell it to some one in confidence, if nothing else, to obtain light and counsel, and thus make it publicly known, from the bare idea of which Lucia shrank back with insupportable shame; together with a feeling of present shame, an inexplicable repugnance to speak on such a subject;—all these things together determined her to maintain absolute silence on this important circumstance, proposing, in her own mind, to open herself first to Father Cristoforo. But what did she feel, when, in inquiring after him, she heard that he was no longer at Pescarenico; that he had been sent to a town far, far away, to a town bearing such and such a name!

'And Renzo?' said Agnese.

'He's in safety, isn't he?' said Lucia, hastily.

'That much is certain, because everybody says so; it is thought, too, pretty surely, that he's gone to the territory of Bergamo; but the exact place nobody knows: and hitherto he has sent no news of himself. Perhaps he hasn't yet found a way of doing so.'

'Ah, if he's in safety, the Lord be praised!' said Lucia; and she was seeking some other subject of conversation, when they were interrupted by an unexpected novelty—the appearance of the Cardinal Archbishop.

This holy prelate, having returned from church, where we last left him, and having heard from the Unnamed of Lucia's safe arrival, had sat down to dinner, placing his new friend on his right hand, in the midst of a circle of priests, who were never weary of casting glances at that countenance, now so subdued without weakness, so humble without dejection, and of comparing him with the idea they had so long entertained of this formidable personage.

Dinner being removed, the two again withdrew together. After a conversation, which lasted much longer than the first, the Unnamed set off anew for his Castle, on the same mule which had borne him thither in the morning; and the Cardinal, calling the priest of the parish, told him that he wished to be guided to the house where Lucia had found shelter.

'Oh, my Lord!' replied the parish priest, 'allow me, and I will send directly to bid the young girl come here, with her mother, if she has arrived, and their hosts too, if my Lord wishes—indeed, all that your illustrious Grace desires to see.'

'I wish to go myself to see them,' replied Federigo.

'There's no necessity for your illustrious Lordship to give yourself that trouble; I will send directly to fetch them: it's very quickly done,' insisted the persevering spoiler of his plans, (a worthy man on the whole), not comprehending that the Cardinal wished by this visit to do honour at once to the unfortunate girl, to innocence, to hospitality, and to his own ministry. But the superior having again expressed the same desire, the inferior bowed, and led the way.

When the two companions were seen to enter the street every one immediately gathered round them; and, in a few moments, people flocked from every direction, forming two wings at their sides, and a train behind. The Curate officiously repeated, 'Come, come, keep back, keep off; fye! fye!' Federigo, however, forbade him; 'Let them alone, let them alone;' and he walked on, now raising his hand to bless the people, now lowering it to fondle the children, who gathered round his feet. In this way they reached the house, and entered, the crowd hedging round the door outside. In this crowd the tailor also found himself, having followed behind, like the rest, with eager eyes and open mouth, not knowing whither they were going. When he saw, however, this unexpected *whither*, he forced the throng to make way, it may be imagined with what bustle, crying over and over again, 'Make way for one who has a right to pass;' and so went into the house.

Agnese and Lucia heard an increasing murmur in the street, and while wondering what it could be, saw the door thrown open, and admit the purple-clad prelate, and the priest of the parish.

'Is this she?' demanded Federigo of the Curate; and on receiving a sign in the affirmative, he advanced towards Lucia, who was holding back with her mother, both of them motionless, and mute with surprise and bashfulness; but the tone of his voice, the countenance, the behaviour, and, above all, the words of Federigo, quickly re-animated them. 'Poor girl,' he began, 'God has permitted you to be put to a great trial; but He has surely shown you that His eye was still over you, that He had not forgotten you. He has restored you in safety, and has made use of you for a great work, to show infinite mercy to one, and to relieve, at the same time, many others.'

Here the mistress of the house came into the apartment, who, at the bustle outside, had gone to the window upstairs, and seeing who was entering the house, hastily ran down, after slightly arranging her dress; and almost at the same moment the tailor made his appearance at another door. Seeing their guests engaged in conversation, they quietly withdrew into one corner, and waited there with profound respect. The Cardinal, having courteously saluted them, continued to talk to the women, mingling with his words of comfort many inquiries, thinking he might possibly gather from their replies some way of doing good to one who had under-gone so much suffering.

'It would be well if all priests were like your Lordship, if they would sometimes take the part of the poor, and not help to put them into difficulties to get themselves out,' said Agnese, emboldened by the kind and affable behaviour of Federigo, and annoyed at the thought that the Signor Don Abbondio, after having sacrificed others on every occasion, should now even attempt to forbid their giving vent to their feelings, and complaining to one who was set in authority over him, when, by an unusual chance, the occasion for doing so presented itself.

'Just say all that you think,' said the Cardinal: 'speak freely.'

'I mean to say, that if our Signor Curate had done his duty, things wouldn't have gone as they have.'

But the Cardinal renewing his request that she should explain herself more fully, she began to feel rather perplexed at having to relate a story in which she, too, had borne a part she did not care to make known, especially to such a man. However, she contrived to manage it, with the help of a little curtailing. She related the intended match, and the refusal of Don Abbondio; nor was she silent on the pretext of *the superiors* which he had brought forward (ah, Agnese!); and then she skipped on to Don Rodrigo's attempt, and how, having been warned of it, they had been able to make their escape. 'But indeed,' added she, in conclusion, 'we only escaped to be again caught in the snare. If instead, the Signor Curate had honestly told us the whole, and had immediately married my poor children, we would have gone away all together directly, privately, and far enough off, to a place where not even the wind would have known us. But, in this way, time was lost; and now has happened what has happened.'

'The Signor Curate shall render me an account of this matter,' said the Cardinal.

'Oh, no, Signor, no!' replied Agnese: 'I didn't speak on that account: don't scold him; for what is done, is done; and, besides, it will do no good; it is his nature; and on another occasion he would do just the same.'

But Lucia, dissatisfied with this way of relating the story, added: 'We have also done wrong: it shows it was not the Lord's will that the plan should succeed.'

'What can you have done wrong, my poor girl?' asked Federigo.

And, in spite of the threatening glances which her mother tried to give her secretly, Lucia, in her turn, related the history of their attempt in Don Abbondio's house; and concluded by saying, 'We have done wrong, and God has punished us for it.'

'Take, as from His hand, the sufferings you have undergone, and be of good courage,' said Federigo; 'for who have reason to rejoice and be hopeful, but those who have suffered, and are ready to accuse themselves?'

He then asked where was the Betrothed; and hearing from Agnese (Lucia stood silent, with her head bent, and downcast eyes) how he had been outlawed, he felt and expressed surprise and dissatisfaction, and asked why it was.

Agnese stammered out what little she knew of Renzo's history.

'I have heard speak of this youth,' said the Cardinal; 'but how happens it that a man involved in affairs of this sort is in treaty of marriage with this young girl?'

'He was a worthy youth,' said Lucia, blushing, but in a firm voice.

'He was even too quiet a lad,' added Agnese; 'and you may ask this of anybody you like, even of the Signor Curate. Who knows what confusion they may have made down there, what intrigues? It takes little to make poor people seem rogues.'

'Indeed, it's too true,' said the Cardinal; 'I'll certainly make inquiries about him;' and learning the name and residence of the youth, he made a memorandum of them on his tablets. He added, that he expected to be at their village in a few days, that then Lucia might go thither without fear, and that, in the mean while, he would think about providing her some secure retreat, till everything was arranged for the best.

Then, turning to the master and mistress of the house, who immediately came forward, he renewed the acknowledgment which he had already conveyed through the priest of the parish, and asked them whether they were willing to receive, for a few days, the guests which God had sent them.

'Oh yes, sir!' replied the woman, in a tone of voice and with a look which meant much more than the bare words seemed to express. But her husband, quite excited by the presence of such an interrogator, and by the wish to do him honour on so important an occasion, anxiously sought for some fine reply. He wrinkled his forehead, strained and squinted with his eyes, compressed his lips, stretched his intellect to its utmost extent, strove, fumbled about in his mind, and there found an overwhelming medley of unfinished ideas and half-formed words: but time pressed; the Cardinal signified that he had already interpreted his silence; the poor man opened his mouth and pronounced the words, 'You may imagine!' At this point not another word would occur to him. This failure not only disheartened and vexed him at the moment, but the tormenting remembrance ever after spoiled his complacency in the great honour he had received. And how often, in the thinking it over, and fancying himself again in the same circumstances, did numberless words crowd upon his mind, as it were, out of spite, any of which would have been better than that silly, *You may imagine!* But are not the very ditches full of wisdom—too late!

The Cardinal took his leave, saying, 'The blessing of God be upon this house.'

The same evening he asked the Curate in what way he could best compensate to the tailor, who certainly could not be rich, for the expenses he must have incurred, especially in these times, by his hospitality. The Curate replied, that, in truth, neither the profits of his business nor the produce of some small fields which the good tailor owned, would be enough this year to allow of his being liberal to others; but that, having laid by a little in the preceding years, he was among the most easy in circumstances in the neighbourhood, and could afford to do a kindness without inconvenience, as he certainly would with all his heart; and that, under any circum·stances, he would deem it an insult to be offered money in compensation.

'He will, probably,' said the Cardinal, 'have demands on people unable to pay.'

'You may judge yourself, my most illustrious Lord: these poor people pay from the overplus of the harvest. Last year there was no overplus; and this one, everybody falls short of absolute necessaries.'

'Very well,' replied Federigo, 'I will take all these debts upon myself; and you will do me the pleasure of getting from him a list of the sums, and discharging them for me.'

'It will be a tolerable sum.'

'So much the better: and you will have, I dare say, many more wretched, and almost destitute of clothing, who have no debts, because they can get no credit.'

'Alas! too many! One does what one can; but how can we supply all in times like these?'

'Tell him to clothe them at my expense, and pay him well. Really, this year, all that does not go for bread seems a kind of robbery; but this is a particular case.'

We cannot close the history of this day, without briefly relating how the Unnamed concluded it.

This time the report of his conversion had preceded him in the valley, and quickly spreading throughout it, had excited among all the inhabitants consternation, anxiety, and angry whisperings. To the first bravoes or servants (it mattered not which) whom he met, he made signs that they should follow him; and so on, on either hand. All fell behind with unusual perplexity of mind, but with their accustomed submission; so that, with a continually increasing train, he at length reached the Castle. He beckoned to those who were loitering about the gate to follow him with the others; entered the first court, went towards the middle, and here, seated all the while on his saddle, uttered one of his thundering calls: it was the accustomed signal at which all his dependents, who were within hearing, immediately flocked towards him. In a moment, all those who were scattered throughout the Castle attended to the summons, and mingled with the already assembled party, gazing eagerly at their master.

'Go, and wait for me in the great hall,' said he; and, from his higher station on horseback, he watched them all move off. He then dismounted, led the animal to the stables himself, and repaired to the room where he was expected. On his appearance, a loud whispering was instantly hushed, and retiring to one side, they left a large space in the hall quite clear for him: there may have been, perhaps, about thirty.

The Unnamed raised his hand, as if to preserve the silence his presence had already created, raised his head, which towered above all those of the assemblage, and said: 'Listen, all of you, and let no one speak unless I bid him. My friends! the path we have hitherto followed leads to the depths of hell. I do not mean to upbraid you, I, who have been foremost of you all, the worst of all; but listen to what I have to say. The merciful God has called me to change my life; and I will change it, I have already changed it: so may He do with you all! Know, then, and hold it for certain, that I am resolved

rather to die than to do anything more against His holy laws. I
revoke all the wicked commands you may any of you have received
from me; you understand me; indeed, I command you not to do
anything I have before commanded. And hold it equally certain,
that no one, from this time forward, shall do evil with my sanction,
in my service. He who will remain with me under these conditions
shall be to me as a son; and I shall feel happy at the close of that
day in which I shall not have eaten, that I may supply the last of
you with the last loaf I have left in the house. He who does not
wish to remain, shall receive what is due of his salary, and an
additional gift: he may go away, but must never again set foot here,
unless it be to change his life; for this purpose he shall always be
received with open arms. Think about it to-night: to-morrow morning I will ask you one by one for your reply, and will then give you
new orders. For the present retire, every one to his post. And God,
who has exercised such mercy towards me, incline you to good
resolutions!'

Here he ceased, and all continued silent. How various and tumultuous soever might be the thoughts at work in their hardened minds,
they gave no outward demonstration of emotion. They were accustomed to receive the voice of their master as the declaration of
a will from which there was no appeal: and that voice, announcing
that the will was changed, in no wise denoted that it was enfeebled.
It never crossed the mind of one of them that, because he was converted, they might therefore assume over him, and reply to him as
to another man. They beheld in him a saint, but one of those saints
who are depicted with a lofty brow, and a sword in their hands.
Besides the fear he inspired, they also entertained for him (especially
those born in his service, and they were a large proportion) the affection of subjects; they had all, besides, a kindly feeling of admiration
for him, and experienced in his presence a species of, I will even say,
modest humility, such as the rudest and most wanton spirits feel
before an authority which they have once recognized. Again, the
things they had just heard from his lips were doubtless odious to
their ears, but neither false, nor entirely alien to their understandings:
if they had a thousand times ridiculed them, it was not because they
disbelieved them; but to obviate, by ridicule, the fear which any

serious consideration of them would have awakened. And now, on seeing the effect of this fear on a mind like that of their master, there was not one who did not either more or less sympathize with him, at least for a little while. In addition to all this, those among them who had first heard the grand news beyond the valley, had at the same time witnessed and related the joy, the exultation of the people, the new favour with which the Unnamed was regarded, and the veneration so suddenly exchanged for their former hatred—their former terror. So that in the man whom they had always regarded, so to say, as a superior being, even while they, in a great measure, themselves constituted his strength, they now beheld the wonder, the idol of a multitude; they beheld him exalted above others, in a different, but not less real, manner; ever above the common throng, ever at the head. They stood now confounded, uncertain one of another, and each one of himself. Some murmured; some began to plan whither they could go to find shelter and employment; some questioned with themselves whether they could make up their minds to become honest men; some even, moved by his words, felt a sort of inclination to do so; others, without resolving upon anything, proposed to promise everything readily, to remain in the mean while where they could share the loaf so willingly offered, and in those days so scarce, and thus gain time for decision: no one, however, uttered a syllable. And when, at the close of his speech, the Unnamed again raised his authoritative hand, and beckoned to them to disperse, they all moved off in the direction of the door as quietly as a flock of sheep. He followed them out, and placing himself in the middle of the courtyard, stood to watch them by the dim evening light, as they separated from each other, and repaired to their several posts. Then, returning to fetch a lantern, he again traversed the courts, corridors, and halls, visited every entrance, and after seeing that all was quiet, at length retired to sleep. Yes, to sleep, because he was sleepy.

Never, though he had always industriously courted them, had he, in any conjuncture, been so overburdened with intricate, and at the same time urgent, affairs, as at the present moment: yet he was sleepy. The remorse, which had robbed him of rest the night before, was not only unsubdued, but even spoke more loudly, more sternly, more absolutely: yet he was sleepy. The order, the kind of government established by him in that Castle for so many years, with so much care, and such a singular union of rashness and perseverance, he had now himself overturned by a few words; the unlimited devotion of his dependents, their readiness for any undertaking, their ruffian-like fidelity, on which he had long been accustomed to depend,—these he had himself shaken; his various engagements had become a tissue of perplexities; he had brought confusion and uncertainty into his household: yet he was sleepy.

He went, therefore, into his chamber, approached that bed, which, the night before, he had found such a thorny couch, and knelt down at its side with the intention of praying. He found, in fact, in a deep and hidden corner of his mind, the prayers he had been taught to repeat as a child; he began to recite them, and the words so long wrapped up, as it were, together, flowed one after another, as if emerging once more to light. He experienced in this act a mixture of undefined feelings; a kind of soothing pleasure, in this actual return to the habits of innocent childhood; a doubly bitter contrition at the thought of the gulf that he had placed between those former days and the present; an ardent desire to attain, by works of expiation, a clearer conscience, a state more nearly resembling that of innocence, to which he could never return; together with a feeling of deep gratitude, and of confidence in that mercy which could lead him towards it, and had already given so many tokens of willingness to do so. Then, rising from his knees, he lay down, and was quickly wrapt in sleep.

Thus ended a day still so much celebrated when our anonymous author wrote: a day of which, had he not written, nothing would have been known, at least nothing of the particulars; for Ripamonti and Rivola, whom we have quoted above, merely record that, after an interview with Federigo, this remarkable tyrant wonderfully changed his course of life, and for ever. And how few are there who have read the works of these authors! Fewer still are there who will read this of ours. And who knows whether in the valley itself, if any one had the inclination to seek, and the ability to find it, there now remains the smallest trace, the most confused tradition, of such an event? So many things have taken place since that time!

CHAPTER XXV

NEXT day, there was no one spoken of in Lucia's village, and throughout the whole territory of Lecco, but herself, the Unnamed, the Archbishop, and one other person, who, however ambitious to have his name in men's mouths, would willingly, on this occasion, have dispensed with the honor: we mean the Signor Don Rodrigo.

Not that his doings had not before been talked about; but they were detached, secret conversations; and that man must have been very well acquainted with his neighbour who would have ventured to discourse with him freely on such a subject. Nay, people did not even exercise those feelings on the subject of which they were capable; for, generally speaking, when men cannot give vent to their indignation without imminent danger, they not only show less than they feel, or disguise it entirely, but they feel less in reality. But now, who could refrain from inquiring and reasoning about so notorious an event, in which the hand of Heaven had been seen, and in which two such personages bore a conspicuous part? One, in whom such a spirited love of justice was united to so much authority; the other who, with all his boldness, had been induced, as it were, to lay down his arms, and submit. By the side of these rivals, Don Rodrigo looked rather insignificant. Now, all understood what it was to torment innocence with the wish to dishonour it; to persecute it with such insolent perseverance, with such atrocious violence, with such abominable treachery. They reviewed, on this occasion, all the other feats of the Signor, and said what they thought about all, each one being emboldened by finding everybody else of the same opinion. There were whisperings, and general murmurs; cautiously uttered, however, on account of the numberless bravoes he had around him.

A large share of public animadversion fell also upon his friends and flatterers. They said of the Signor Podestà what he richly deserved, always deaf, and blind, and dumb, on the doings of this tyrant; but this also cautiously, for the Podestà had bailiffs. With the Doctor *Azzecca-Garbugli,* who had no weapons but gossiping and cabals, and with other flatterers like himself, they did not use so much ceremony; these were pointed at, and regarded with very contemptuous and suspicious glances, so that, for some time, he judged it expedient to keep as much within doors as possible.

Don Rodrigo, astounded at this unlooked-for news, so different to the tidings he had expected day after day, and hour after hour, remained ensconced in his den-like palace, with no one to keep him company but his bravoes, devouring his rage, for two days, and on the third set off for Milan. Had there been nothing else but the murmuring of the people, perhaps since things had gone so far, he would have stayed on purpose to face it, or even to seek an opportunity of making an example to others of one of the most daring; but the certain intelligence that the Cardinal was coming into the neighbourhood fairly drove him away. The Count, his uncle, who knew nothing of the story but what he had been told by Attilio, would certainly expect that on such an occasion, Don Rodrigo should be the first to wait upon the Cardinal, and receive from him in public the most distinguished reception: every one must see how he was on the road to this consummation! The Count expected it, and would have required a minute account of the visit; for it was an important opportunity of showing in what esteem his family was held by one of the head powers. To extricate himself from so odious a dilemma, Don Rodrigo, rising one morning before the sun, threw himself into his carriage, Griso and some other bravoes outside, both in front and behind; and leaving orders that the rest of his household should follow him, took his departure, like a fugitive—like, (it will, perhaps, be allowed us to exalt our characters by so illustrious a comparison)—like Catiline from Rome, fretting and fuming, and swearing to return very shortly in a different guise to execute his vengeance.

In the mean while, the Cardinal proceeded on his visitation among the parishes in the territory of Lecco, taking one each day. On the day in which he was to arrive at Lucia's village, a large part of the inhabitants were early on the road to meet him. At the entrance of the village, close by the cottage of our two poor women, was erected a triumphal arch, constructed of upright stakes, and poles laid cross-wise, covered with straw and moss, and ornamented with green boughs of holly, distinguishable by its scarlet berries, and other shrubs. The front of the church was adorned with tapestry; from every window-ledge hung extended quilts and sheets, and infants swaddling-clothes, disposed like drapery; in short, all the few necessary articles which could be converted, either bodily or otherwise, into the appearance of something superfluous. Towards evening, (the hour at which Federigo usually arrived at the church, on his visitation-tours), all who had remained within doors, old men, women and children, for the most part, set off to meet him, some in procession, some in groups, headed by Don Abbondio, who, in the midst of the rejoicing, looked disconsolate enough, both from the stunning noise of the crowd, and the continual hurrying to and fro of the people, which, as he himself expressed it, quite dimmed his sight, together with a secret apprehension that the women might have been *babbling* and that he would be called upon to render an account of the wedding.

At length the Cardinal came in sight, or, to speak more correctly, the crowd in the midst of which he was carried in his litter, surrounded by his attendants; for nothing could be distinguished of his whole party, but a signal towering in the air above the heads of the people, part of the cross, which was borne by the chaplain, mounted upon his mule. The crowd, which was dancing with Don Abbondio, hurried forward in a disorderly manner to join the approaching party; while he, after ejaculating three or four times, 'Gently; in procession; what are you doing?' turned back in vexation, and muttering to himself, 'It's a perfect Babel, it's a perfect Babel' went to take refuge in the church until they had dispersed; and here he awaited the Cardinal.

The holy prelate in the mean while advanced slowly, bestowing benedictions with his hand, and receiving them from the mouths of the multitude, while his followers had enough to do to keep their places behind him. As Lucia's countrymen, the villagers were anxious to receive the Archbishop with more than ordinary honours, but this was no easy matter; for it had long been customary, where-

ever he went, for all to do the most they could. At the very beginning of his episcopate, on his first solemn entry into the cathedral,
the rush and crowding of the populace upon him were such as to
excite fears for his life; and some of the gentlemen who were nearest
to him, had actually drawn their swords to terrify and repulse the
press. Such were their violent and uncouth manners, that even in
making demonstrations of kindly feeling to a bishop in church, and
attempting to regulate them, it was necessary almost to have recourse
to bloodshed. And that defence would not, perhaps, have proved sufficient, had not two priests, strong in body, and bold in spirit, raised
him in their arms, and carried him at once from the door of the
temple to the very foot of the high altar. From that time forward,
in the many episcopal visits he had to make, his first entrance into
the church might, without joking, be reckoned among his pastoral
labours, and sometimes even among the dangers he had incurred.

On this occasion, he entered as he best could, went up to the altar,
and thence, after a short prayer, addressed, as was his custom, a few
words to his auditors, of his affection for them, his desire for their
salvation, and the way in which they ought to prepare themselves
for the services of the morrow. Then retiring to the parsonage,
among many other things he had to consult about with the Curate,
he questioned him as to the character and conduct of Renzo. Don
Abbondio said that he was rather a brisk, obstinate, hot-headed
fellow. But, on more particular and precise interrogations, he was
obliged to admit that he was a worthy youth, and that he himself
could not understand how he could have played all the mischievous
tricks at Milan, which had been reported of him.

'And about the young girl,' resumed the Cardinal; 'do you think
she may now return in security to her own home?'

'For the present,' replied Don Abbondio, 'she might come and be
as safe—the present, I say—as she wishes; but,' added he with a
sigh, 'your illustrious Lordship ought to be always here, or, at least,
near at hand.'

'The Lord is always near,' said the Cardinal: 'as to the rest, I will
think about placing her in safety.' And he hastily gave orders that,
next morning early, a litter should be despatched, with an attendant,
to fetch the two women.

Don Abbondio came out from the interview quite delighted that the Cardinal had talked to him about the two young people, without requiring an account of his refusal to marry them.—Then he knows nothing about it,—said he to himself:—Agnese has held her tongue. Wonderful! They have to see him again; but I will give them further instructions, that I will.—He knew not, poor man, that Federigo had not entered upon the discussion, just because he intended to speak to him about it more at length when they were disengaged; and that he wished, before giving him what he deserved, to hear his side of the question.

But the intentions of the good prelate for the safe placing of Lucia had, in the mean while, been rendered unnecessary: after he had left her, other circumstances had occurred which we will now proceed to relate.

The two women, during the few days which they had to pass in the tailor's hospitable dwelling, had resumed, as far as they could, each her former accustomed manner of living. Lucia had very soon begged some employment; and, as at the monastery, diligently plied her needle in a small retired room shut out from the gaze of the people. Agnese occasionally went abroad, and at other times sat sewing with her daughter. Their conversations were more melancholy, as well as more affectionate; both were prepared for a separation; since the lamb could not return to dwell so near the wolf's den: and when and what would be the end of this separation? The future was dark, inextricable; for one of them in particular. Agnese, nevertheless, indulged in her own mind many cheerful anticipations, that Renzo, if nothing evil had happened to him, would, sooner or later, send some news of himself, and if he had found some employment to which he could settle, if (and how could it be doubted?) he still intended to keep faith with Lucia; why could they not go and live with him? With such hopes she often entertained her daughter, who found it, it is difficult to say, whether more mournful to listen to them, or painful to reply. Her great secret she had always kept to herself; and uneasy, certainly, at concealing anything from so good a mother, yet restrained, invincibly as it were, by shame, and the different fears we have before mentioned, she went from day to day without speaking. Her designs were very different from those of her mother, or rather, she had no designs; she had entirely given herself up to Providence. She always therefore endeavoured to divert or let drop the conversation; or else said, in general terms, that she had no longer any hope or desire for anything in this world except to be soon restored to her mother; more frequently, however, tears came opportunely instead of words.

'Do you know why it appears so to you?' said Agnese; 'because you've suffered so much, and it doesn't seem possible that it can turn out for good to you. But leave it to God; and if . . . Let a ray come, but *one* ray; and then *I* know whether you will always care about nothing.' Lucia kissed her mother, and wept.

Besides this, a great friendship quickly sprang up between them and their hosts: where, indeed, should it exist, unless between benefactors and the benefited, when both one and the other are worthy, good people? Agnese, particularly, had many long chats with the mistress of the house. The tailor, too, gave them a little amusement with his stories and moral discourses: and, at dinner especially, had always some wonderful anecdote to relate of Buovo d'Antona, or the Fathers of the Desert.

A few miles from this village resided, at their country-house, a couple of some importance, Don Ferrante and Donna Prassede: their family, as usual, is unnamed by our anonymous author. Donna Prassede was an old lady, very much inclined to do good, the most praise-worthy employment, certainly, that a person can undertake; but which, like every other, can be too easily abused. To do good, we must know how to do it; and, like everything else, we can only know this through the medium of our own passions, our own judgment, our own ideas; which not unfrequently are rather as correct as they are capable of being, than as they ought to be. Donna Prassede acted towards her ideas as it is said one ought to do towards one's friends; she had few of them; but to those few she was very much attached. Among the few, there were, unfortunately, many distorted ones; nor was it these she loved the least. Hence it happened, either that she proposed to herself as a good end what was not such in reality, or employed means which would rather produce an opposite effect, or thought them allowable when they were not at all so, from a certain vague supposition, that he who does more than his duty, may also go beyond his right; it happened that she could not see in an event what was actually there, or did see what was not there; and many other similar things, which may and do happen to all, not excepting the best; but to Donna Prassede far too often, and, not unfrequently, all at once.

On hearing Lucia's wonderful case, and all that was reported on this occasion of the young girl, she felt a great curiosity to see her, and sent a carriage, with an aged attendant, to fetch both mother and daughter. The latter shrugged her shoulders, and besought the tailor, who was the bearer of the message, to find some sort of excuse for her. So long as it only related to the common people, who tried to make acquaintance with the young girl who had been the subject of a miracle, the tailor had willingly rendered her that service; but in this instance, resistance seemed in his eyes a kind of rebellion. He made so many faces, uttered so many exclamations, used so many arguments—'that it wasn't customary to do so, and that it was a grand house, and that one shouldn't say "No" to great people, and that it might be the making of their fortune, and that the Signora Donna Prassede, besides all the rest, was a saint too!'—in short, so many things, that Lucia was obliged to give way: more especially, as Agnese confirmed all these reasonings with a corresponding number of ejaculations: 'Certainly, surely.'

Arrived in the lady's presence, she received them with much courtesy and numberless congratulations; questioning and advising them with a kind of almost innate superiority, but corrected by so many humble expressions, tempered by so much interest in their behalf, and sweetened with so many expressions of piety, that Agnese, almost immediately, and Lucia not long afterwards, began to feel relieved from the oppressive sense of awe with which the presence of such a lady had inspired them; nay, they even found something attractive in it. In short, hearing that the Cardinal had undertaken to find Lucia a place of retreat, and urged by a desire to second, and, at the same time, anticipate his good intention, Donna Prassede proposed to take the young girl into her own house, where no other services would be required of her than the use of her needle, scissors, and spindle; adding, that she would take upon herself the charge of informing his Lordship.

Beyond the obvious and immediate good in this work Donna Prassede saw in it, and proposed to herself another, perhaps a more considerable one in her ideas, that of directing a young mind, and of bringing into the right way one who greatly needed it; for, from the first moment she had heard Lucia mentioned, she became instantly persuaded, that, in a young girl who could have promised herself to a scoundrel, a villain, in short, a scape-gallows, there must be some fault, some hidden wickedness lurking within: *Tell me what company you keep, and I'll tell you what you are.* Lucia's visit had confirmed this persuasion: not that, on the whole, as the saying is, she did not seem to Donna Prassede a good girl; but there were many things to favour the idea. That head hung down till her chin was buried in her neck; her not replying at all, or only in broken sentences, as if by constraint, might indicate modesty; but they undoubtedly denoted a great deal of wilfulness: it did not require much discernment to discover that that young brain had its own thoughts on the subject. And those blushes every moment, and those suppressed sighs . . . Two such eyes, too, which did not please Donna Prassede at all. She held it for certain, as if she knew it on good grounds, that all Lucia's misfortunes were a chastisement from Heaven for her attachment to a rascal, and a warning to her to give him up entirely; and these premises being laid down, she proposed to co-operate towards so good an end. Because, as she often said both to herself and others, she made it her object to second the will of Heaven; but she often fell into the misconception of taking for the will of Heaven the fancies of her own brain. However, she took care not to give the least hint of the second intention we have named. It was one of her maxims, that, to bring a good design to a useful issue, the first requisite, in the greater number of instances, is not to let it be discovered.

The mother and daughter looked at each other. Considering the mournful necessity of their separating, the offer seemed to both of them most acceptable, when they had no choice for it, on account of the vicinity of the residence to their village, whither, let the worst come to the worst, they would return, and be able to meet at the approaching festivity. Seeing assent exhibited in each other's eyes, they both turned to Donna Prassede with such acknowledgments as expressed their acceptance of the proposal. She renewed her kind affability and promises, and said that they would shortly have a letter to present to his Lordship. After the women had taken their departure, she got Don Ferrante to compose the letter. He, being a learned person, as we shall hereafter relate more particularly, was always employed by her as secretary on occasions of importance. On one of such magnitude as this, Don Ferrante exerted his utmost stretch of ingenuity; and on delivering the rough draught to his partner to copy, warmly recommended the orthography to her notice; this being one of the many things he had studied, and the few over which he had any command in the house. Donna Prassede copied it very diligently, and then despatched the letter to the tailor's. This was two or three days before the Cardinal sent the litter to convey the two women home.

Arriving at the village before the Cardinal had gone to church, they alighted at the curate's house. There was an order to admit them immediately: the chaplain, who was the first to see them, executed the order, only detaining them so long as was necessary to school them very hastily in the ceremonials they ought to observe towards his Lordship, and the titles by which they should address him, his usual practice wherever he could effect it unknown to his Grace. It was a continual annoyance to the poor man to see the little ceremony that was used towards the Cardinal in this particular. 'All,' said he to the rest of the household, 'through the excess of kindness of that saintly man—from his great familiarity.' And then he related how, with his own ears, he had more than once even heard the reply: 'Yes, sir,' and 'No, sir.'

The Cardinal was, at this moment, busily talking with Don Abbondio on some parish matters: so that the latter had not the desired opportunity of giving *his* instructions also to the women. He could only bestow upon them in passing, as he withdrew and they came forward, a glance, which meant to say how well-pleased he was with them, and conjuring them, like good creatures, to continue silent.

After the first kind greetings on one hand, and the first reverent salutations on the other, Agnese drew the letter from her bosom, and handed it to the Cardinal, saying: 'It is from the Signora Donna

Prassede, who says, she knows your most illustrious Lordship well, my Lord; it's natural enough, among such great people, that they should know each other. When you have read it, you'll see.'

'Very well,' said Federigo, when he had read the letter, and extracted the honey from Don Ferrante's flowers of rhetoric. He knew the family well enough to feel certain that Lucia had been invited thither with good intentions, and that there she would be secure from the machinations and violence of her persecutor. What opinion he entertained of Donna Prassede's head, we have no positive information. Probably she was not the person whom he would have chosen for such a purpose; but, as we have said, or hinted, elsewhere, it was not his custom to undo arrangements made by those whose duty it was to make them, that he might do them over again better.

Take this separation also, and the uncertainty in which you are placed, calmly,' added he; 'trust that it will soon be over, and that God will bring matters to that end to which He seems to have directed them; but rest assured, that whatever He wills shall happen, will be the best for you.' To Lucia, in particular, he gave some further kind advice; another word or two of comfort to both; and then, bestowing on them his blessing, he let them go. At the street-door they found themselves surrounded by a crowd of friends of both sexes, the whole population, we may almost say, who were waiting for them, and who conducted them home, as in triumph. Among the women there was quite a rivalry in congratulations, sympathy, and inquiries; and all exclaimed with dissatisfaction, on hearing that Lucia would leave them the next day. The men vied with each other in offering their services;—every one wished to keep guard at the cottage for that night. Upon this fact, our anonymous author thinks fit to ground a proverb: *Would you have many ready to help you? be sure not to need them.*

So many welcomes confounded and almost stunned Lucia; though, on the whole, they did her good, by somewhat distracting her mind from those thoughts and recollections which, even in the midst of the bustle and excitement, rose only too readily on crossing that threshold, on entering those rooms, at the sight of every object.

When the bells began to ring, announcing the approach of the hour for Divine service, everybody moved towards the church, and, to our newly-returned friends, it was a second triumphal march.

Service being over, Don Abbondio, who had hastened forward to see if Perpetua had everything well arranged for dinner, was informed that the Cardinal wished to speak with him. He went immediately to his noble guest's apartment, who, waiting till he drew near; 'Signor Curate,' he began—and these words were uttered in such a way as to convey the idea, that they were the preface to a long and serious conversation—'Signor Curate, why did you not unite in marriage this Lucia with her betrothed husband?'

—Those people have emptied the sack this morning,—thought Don Abbondio, as he stammered forth in reply,—'Your most illustrious Lordship will, doubtless, have heard speak of the confusions which have arisen out of this affair: it has all been so intricate, that, to this very day, one cannot see one's way clearly in it: as your illustrious Lordship may yourself conclude from this, that the young girl is here, after so many accidents, as it were by miracle; and that the bridegroom, after other accidents, is nobody knows where.'

'I ask,' replied the Cardinal, 'whether it is true that, before all these circumstances took place, you refused to celebrate the marriage, when you were requested to do so, on the appointed day; and if so, why?'

'Really . . . if your illustrious Lordship knew . . . what intimations . . . what terrible injunctions I have received not to speak . . . ' And he paused, without concluding, with a certain manner intended respectfully to insinuate, that it would be indiscreet to wish to know more.

'But,' said the Cardinal, with a voice and look much more serious than usual, 'it is your Bishop who, for his own duty's sake, and for your justification, wishes to learn from you why you have not done what, in your regular duties, you were bound to do?'

'My Lord,' said Don Abbondio, shrinking almost into a nut-shell, 'I did not like to say before . . . But it seemed to me that, things being so entangled, so long gone by, and now irremediable, it was useless to bring them up again . . . However—however, I say, I know your illustrious Lordship will not betray one of your poor priests. For you see, my Lord, your illustrious Lordship cannot be everywhere at once; and I remain here exposed . . . But, when you command it, I will tell you . . . I will tell you all.'

'Tell me: I only wish to find you free from blame.'

Don Abbondio then began to relate the doleful history; but suppressing the principal name, he merely substituted *a great Signor;* thus giving to prudence the little that he could in such an emergency.

'And you had no other motive?' asked the Cardinal, having attentively heard the whole.

'Perhaps I have not sufficiently explained myself,' replied Don Abbondio. 'I was prohibited, under pain of death, to perform this marriage.'

'And does this appear to you a sufficient reason for omitting a positive duty?'

'I have always endeavoured to do my duty, even at very great inconvenience; but when one's life is concerned . . .'

'And when you presented yourself to the Church,' said Federigo, in a still more solemn tone, 'to receive Holy Orders, did she caution you about your life? Did she tell you that the duties belonging to the ministry were free from every obstacle, exempt from every danger? or did she tell you that where danger begins, there duty would end? Did she not expressly say the contrary? Did she not warn you, that she sent you forth as a sheep among wolves? Did you not know that there are violent oppressors, to whom what you are commanded to perform would be displeasing? He from whom we have received teaching and example, in imitation of whom we suffer ourselves to be called, and call ourselves, shepherds; when He descended upon earth to execute His office, did He lay down as a condition the safety of His life? And to save it, to preserve it, I say, a few days longer upon earth, at the expense of charity and duty, did he institute the holy unction, the imposition of hands, the gift of the priesthood? Leave it to the world to teach this virtue, to advocate this doctrine. What do I say? Oh, shame! the world itself rejects it: the world also makes its own laws, which fix the limits of good and evil; it, too, has its gospel, a gospel of pride and hatred; and it will not have it said that the love of life is a reason for transgressing its precepts. It will not, and it is obeyed. And we! children and proclaimers of the promise! What would the Church be, if such language as yours were that of all your brethren? Where would she be, had she appeared in the world with these doctrines?'

Don Abbondio hung his head. His mind during these arguments was like a chicken in the talons of a hawk, which holds its prey elevated to an unknown region, to an atmosphere it has never before breathed. Finding that he must make some reply, he said in an unconvinced tone of submission, 'My Lord, I shall be to blame. When one is not to consider one's life, I don't know what to say. But when one has to do with some people, people who possess power, and won't hear reason, I don't see what is to be gained by it, even if one were willing to play the bravo. This Signor is one whom it is impossible either to conquer, or win over.'

'And don't you know that suffering for righteousness' sake is our conquest? If you know not this, what do you preach? What are you teacher of? What is the *good news* you announce to the poor? Who requires from you that you should conquer force by force? Surely you will not one day be asked, if you were able to overcome the powerful; for this purpose neither your mission nor rule was given to you. But you will assuredly be demanded, whether you employed the means you possessed to do what was required of you, even when they had the temerity to prohibit you.'

—These saints are very odd,—thought Don Abbondio meanwhile: —in substance, to extract the plain meaning, he has more at heart the affections of two young people than the life of a poor priest.— And, as to himself, he would have been very well satisfied had the conversation ended here; but he saw the Cardinal, at every pause, wait with the air of one who expects a reply, a confession, or an apology,—in short, something.

'I repeat, my Lord,' answered he, therefore, 'that I shall be to blame . . . One can't give one's self courage.'

'And why then, I might ask you, did you undertake an office which binds upon you a continual warfare with the passions of the world? But I will rather say, how is it you do not remember that, if in this ministry, however you may have been placed there, courage is necessary to fulfil your obligations, there is One who will infallibly bestow it upon you, when you ask Him? Think you all the millions of martyrs naturally possessed courage? that they naturally held life in contempt? So many young persons, just beginning to enjoy it —so many aged ones, accustomed to regret that it is so near its end— so many children—so many mothers? All possessed courage, because courage was necessary, and they relied upon God. Knowing your own weakness, and the duties to which you were called, have you ever thought of preparing yourself for the difficult circumstances in which you might be placed, in which you actually are placed at present? Ah! if for so many years of pastoral labours you have loved your flock (and how could you *not* love them?)—if you have placed in them your affections, your cares, your happiness, courage ought not to fail you in the moment of need: love is intrepid. Now, surely, if you loved those who have been committed to your spiritual care, those whom you call children, when you saw two of them threatened, as well as yourself, ah, surely! as the weakness of the flesh made you tremble for yourself, so love would have made you tremble for them. You would feel humbled for your former fears, as the effect of your corrupt nature; you would have implored strength to overcome them, to expel them as a temptation. But a holy and noble fear for others, for your children, this you would have listened to, this would have given you no peace; this would have incited—constrained you to think and do all you could to avert the dangers that threatened them . . . With what has this fear, this love, inspired you? What have you done for them? What have you thought for them?'

And he ceased, in token of expectation.

CHAPTER XXVI

A T such a question, Don Abbondio, who had been studying to find some reply in the least precise terms possible, stood without uttering a word. And, to speak the truth, even we, with the manuscript before us, and pen in hand, having nothing to contend with but words, nor anything to fear but the criticisms of our readers, even we, I say, feel a kind of repugnance in proceeding; we feel somewhat strange in this setting forth, with so little trouble, such admirable precepts of fortitude and charity, of active solicitude for others, and unlimited sacrifice of self. But remembering that these things were said by one who also practised them, we will confidently proceed.

'You give me no answer!' resumed the Cardinal. 'Ah, if you had done, on your part, what charity and duty required of you, however things had turned out, you would now have something to answer! You see, then, yourself what you have done. You have obeyed the voice of Iniquity, unmindful of the requirements of duty. You have obeyed her punctually: she showed herself to you to signify her desire; but she wished to remain concealed from those who could have sheltered themselves from her reach, and been on their guard against her; she did not wish to resort to arms, she desired secrecy, to mature her designs of treachery and force at leisure; she required of you transgression and silence. You have transgressed, and kept silence. I ask you, now, whether you have not done more?—you will tell me whether it be true that you alleged false pretexts for your refusal, that you might not reveal the true motive.' And he paused awhile, awaiting a reply.

—The tell-tales have reported this too,—thought Don Abbondio; but as he gave no token in words of having anything to say, the Cardinal continued: 'If it be true, then, that you told these poor people what was not the case, to keep them in the ignorance and darkness in which iniquity wished them to be . . . I must believe it,

419

then; it only remains for me to blush for it with you, and to hope that you will weep for it with me! See, then, to what this solicitude (good God! and but just now you adduced it as a justification!) this solicitude for your temporal life has led you! It has led you . . . repel freely these words, if you think them unjust; take them as a salutary humiliation, if they are not . . . it has led you to deceive the weak, to lie to your own children.'

—Just see now how things go!—thought Don Abbondio again to himself: to that fiend,—meaning the Unnamed,—his arms round his neck; and to me, for a half-lie, uttered for the sole purpose of saving my life, all this fuss and noise. But they are our superiors; they're always in the right. It's my ill star that everybody sets upon me; even saints.—And, speaking aloud, he said: 'I have done wrong; I see that I've done wrong; but what could I do in an extremity of that kind?'

'Do you still ask this? Have not I told you already? Must I tell you again? You should have loved, my son; loved and prayed. Then you would have felt that iniquity may, indeed, have threats to employ, blows to bestow, but not commands to give; you would have united, according to the law of God, those whom man wished to put asunder; you would have extended towards these unhappy innocents the ministry they had a right to claim from you: God Himself would have been surety for the consequences, because you had followed His will: by following another's, *you* have come in as answerable: and for what consequences! But supposing all human resources failed you, supposing no way of escape was open, when you looked anxiously around you, thought about it, sought for it? Then you might have known, that when your poor children were married, they would themselves have provided for their escape, that they were ready to flee from the face of their powerful enemy, and had already designed a place of refuge. But even without this, did you not remember that you had a superior? How would he have this authority to rebuke you for having been wanting in the duties of your office, did he not feel himself bound to assist you in fulfilling them? Why did you not think of acquainting your bishop with the impediment that infamous violence had placed in the way of the exercise of your ministry?

—The very advice of Perpetua!—thought Don Abbondio, pettishly, who, in the midst of this conversation, had most vividly before his eyes the image of the bravoes, and the thought that Don Rodrigo was still alive and well, and that he would, some day or other, be returning in glory and triumph, and furious with revenge. And though the presence of so high a dignitary, together with his countenance and language, filled him with confusion, and inspired him with fear; yet it was not such fear as completely to subdue him, or expel the idea of resistance: because this idea was accompanied by the recollection, that, after all, the Cardinal employed neither musket, nor sword, nor bravoes.

'Why did you not remember,' pursued the bishop, 'that if there were no other retreat open to these betrayed innocents, I at least was ready to receive them, and put them in safety, had you directed them to me—the desolate to a bishop, as belonging to him, as a precious part, I don't say, of his charge, but of his riches? And as to yourself, I should have become anxious for you; I should not have slept till I was sure that not a hair of your head would be injured. Do you think I had not the means of securing your life? Think you, that he who was so very bold, would have remitted nothing of his boldness, when he was aware that his plots and contrivances were known elsewhere, were known to me, that I was watching him, and was resolved to use all the means within my power in your defence? Didn't you know that if men too often promise more than they can perform, so they not unfrequently threaten more than they would attempt to execute? Didn't you know that iniquity depends not only on its own strength, but often also on the fears and credulity of others?'

—Just Perpetua's arguments,—again thought Don Abbondio, never reflecting that this singular concurrence of his servant and Federigo Borromeo, in deciding on what he might and should have done, would tell very much against him.

'But you,' pursued the Cardinal, in conclusion, 'saw nothing, and would see nothing, but your own temporal danger; what wonder that it seemed to you sufficient to outweigh every other consideration?'

'It was because I myself saw those terrible faces,' escaped from

Don Abbondio in reply; 'I myself heard their words. Your illustrious Lordship can talk very well; but you ought to be in a poor priest's shoes, and find yourself brought to the point.'

No sooner, however, had he uttered these words, than he bit his tongue with vexation; he saw that he had allowed himself to be too much carried away by petulance, and said to himself,—Now comes the storm!—But raising his eyes doubtfully, he was utterly astonished to see the countenance of that man, whom he never could succeed in divining or comprehending, pass from the solemn air of authority and rebuke, to a sorrowful and pensive gravity.

' 'Tis too true!' said Federigo; 'such is our miserable and terrible condition. We must rigorously exact from others what God only knows whether *we* should be ready to yield: we must judge, correct, reprove; and God knows what we ourselves should do in the same circumstances, what we actually have done in similar ones! But woe unto me, had I to take my own weakness as the measure of other people's duties, or the rule of my own teaching! Yet I certainly ought to give a good example, as well as good instruction, to others, and not be like the Pharisees, who "lade men with burdens grievous to be borne, while they themselves touch not the burden with one of their fingers." Well then, my son, my brother; as the errors of those in authority are often better known to others than to themselves; if you are aware of my having, from pusillanimity, or from any other motive, failed in any part of my duty, tell me of it candidly, and help me to amend; so that where example has been wanting, confession at least may supply its place. Remonstrate freely with me on my weaknesses; and then my words will acquire more value in my mouth, because you will feel more vividly that they are not mine, but are the words of Him who can give both to you and me the necessary strength to do what they prescribe.'

—Oh, what a holy man! but what a tormentor!—thought Don Abbondio;—he doesn't even spare himself: that I should examine, interfere with, criticize, and accuse even himself—He then said aloud: 'Oh, my Lord, you are joking with me! Who does not know the fortitude of mind, the intrepid zeal of your illustrious Lordship?' And in his heart he added—Even too much so.—

'I did not ask you for praise, which makes me tremble,' said Federigo; 'for God knows my failings, and what I know of them myself is enough to confound me; but I wished that we should humble ourselves together before Him, that we might depend upon Him together. I would, for your own sake, that you should feel how your conduct has been, and your language still is, opposed to the law you nevertheless preach, and according to which you will be judged.'

'All falls upon me,' said Don Abbondio: 'but these people, who have told you this, didn't probably, tell you, too, of their having introduced themselves treacherously into my house, to take me by surprise, and to contract a marriage contrary to the laws.'

'They did tell me, my son: but it is this that grieves, that depresses me, to see you still anxious to excuse yourself; still thinking to excuse yourself by accusing others; still accusing others of what ought to make part of your own confession. Who placed them, I don't say under the necessity, but under the temptation, to do what they have done? Would they have sought this irregular method, had not the legitimate one been closed against them? Would they have thought of snaring their pastor, had they been received to his arms, assisted, advised by him? or of surprising him, had he not concealed himself? And do you lay the blame upon them? And are you indignant, because, after so many misfortunes,—what do I say? in the midst of misfortune,—they have said a word or two, to give vent to their sorrows, to their and your pastor? That the appeals of the oppressed, and the complaints of the afflicted, are odious to the world, is only too true; but we! . . . But what advantage would it have been to you, had they remained silent? Would it turn to your profit that their cause should be left entirely to the judgment of God? Is it not a fresh reason why you should love these persons, (and you have many already), that they have afforded you an opportunity of hearing the sincere voice of your pastor, that they have given you the means of knowing more clearly, and in part discharging, the great debt you owe them? Ah! if they have provoked, offended, annoyed you, I would say to you, (and need I say it?) love them exactly for that reason. Love them, because they have suffered, because they still suffer, because they are yours, because they are weak, because you have need of pardon, to obtain which, think of what efficacy their prayer may be.'

Don Abbondio was silent, but it was no longer an unconvinced and scornful silence: it was that of one who has more things to think about than to say. The words he had heard were unexpected consequences, novel applications, of a doctrine he had nevertheless long believed in his heart, without a thought of disputing it. The misfortunes of others, from the contemplation of which his fear of personal misfortune had hitherto diverted his mind, now made a new impression upon him.

And if he did not feel all the contrition which the address was intended to produce (for this same fear was ever at hand to execute the office of defensive advocate), yet he felt it in some degree; he experienced dissatisfaction with himself, a kind of pity for others,— a mixture of compunction and shame. It was, if we may be allowed the comparison, like the crushed and humid wick of a candle, which, on being presented to the flame of a large torch, at first smokes, spirts, crackles, and will not ignite; but it lights at length, and, well or ill, burns. He would have accused himself bitterly, he would even have wept, had it not been for the thought of Don Rodrigo; and, as it was, betrayed sufficient emotion to convince the Cardinal that his words had not been entirely without effect.

'Now,' pursued he, 'the one a fugitive from his home, the other on the point of abandoning it, both with too good reasons for absenting themselves, and without a probability of ever meeting again here, even if God purposes to re-unite them; now, alas! they have too little need of you, now you have no opportunity of doing them any service; nor can our limited foresight predict any for the future. But who knows whether a God of mercy may not be preparing some for you? Ah! suffer them not to escape! Seek them, be on the watch for them; beseech Him to create them for you.'

'I will not fail, my Lord, I will not fail, I assure you,' replied Don Abbondio, in a tone that showed it came from the heart.

'Ah yes, my son, yes!' exclaimed Federigo; and with a dignity full of affection, he concluded, 'Heaven knows how I should have wished to hold a different conversation with you. We have both lived long; Heaven knows if it has not been painful to me to be obliged thus to grieve your gray hairs with reprimands; how much more gladly I would have shared with you our common cares and sorrows, and conversed with you on the blessed hope to which we have so nearly approached. God grant that the language which I have been compelled to use, may be of use to us both. You would not wish that He should call me to account at the last day, for having countenanced you in a course of conduct in which you have so unhappily fallen short of your duty. Let us redeem the time; the hour of midnight is at hand; the Bridegroom cannot tarry; let us, therefore, keep our lamps burning. Let us offer our hearts, miserable and empty as they are, to God that He may be pleased to fill them with that charity which amends the past, which is a pledge of the future, which fears and trusts, weeps and rejoices, with true wisdom; which becomes, in every instance, the virtue of which we stand in need.'

So saying, he left the room, followed by Don Abbondio.

Here our anonymous author informs us, that this was not the only interview between these two persons, nor Lucia the only subject of these interviews; but that he has confined himself to the mention of this one, that he might not digress too far from the principal object of his narrative. And, for the same reason, he does not make mention of other notable things, said and done by Federigo, throughout the whole course of his visitation; or of his liberality, or of the dissensions composed, and the ancient feuds between individuals, families, and entire towns, extinguished, or (which was, alas! far more frequent) suppressed; or of sundry ruffians, and petty tyrants, tamed either for life, or for some time;—all of them things which occurred more or less in every part of the diocese where this excellent man made any stay.

He then goes on to say how, next morning, Donna Prassede came, according to agreement, to fetch Lucia, and to pay her respects to the Cardinal, who spoke in high terms of the young girl, and recommended her warmly to the Signora. Lucia parted from her mother, it may be imagined with what tears, left her cottage, and a second time said farewell to her native village, with that sense of doubly bitter sorrow, which is felt on leaving a spot which was once dearly loved, and can never be so again. But this parting from her mother was not the last; for Donna Prassede had announced that she should still reside some time at their country house, which was not very far off; and Agnese had promised her daughter to go thither, to give and receive a more mournful adieu.

The Cardinal was himself just starting for another parish, when the Curate of that in which the castle of the Unnamed was situated, arrived, and requested to speak to him. On being admitted, he presented a packet and a letter from that nobleman, wherein he besought Federigo to prevail upon Lucia's mother to accept a hundred *scudi* of gold, which were contained in the parcel, to serve either as a dowry for the young girl, or for any other use which the two women might deem more suitable; requesting him at the same time to tell them, that if ever, on any occasion, they thought he could render them any service, the poor girl knew too well where he lived; and that, for him, this would be one of the most desirable events that could happen. The Cardinal immediately sent for Agnese, who listened with equal pleasure and amazement to the courteous message, and suffered the packet to be put into her hand without much scrupulous ceremony. 'May God reward this Signor for it,' said she; 'and will your illustrious Lordship thank him very kindly? And don't say a word about it to anybody, because this is a kind of country . . . Excuse me, Sir; I know very well that a gentleman like you won't chatter about these things; but . . . you understand me.'

Home she went as quickly as possible; shut herself up in her room, unwrapped the parcel, and, however prepared by anticipation, beheld with astonishment so many of those coins all together, and all her own, of which she had, perhaps, never seen more than one at once before, and that but seldom; she counted them over, and then had some trouble in putting them together again, and making the whole hundred stand up upon their edges; for every now and then, they would jut out, and slide from under her inexpert fingers; at length, however, she succeeded in rolling them up, after a fashion, put them in a handkerchief, so as to make quite a large parcel, and wrapping a piece of cord several times round it, went and tucked it into a corner of her straw mattress. The rest of the day was spent in castle-building, devising plans for the future, and longing for the morrow. After going to bed, she lay for a long time awake, with the thought of the hundred *scudi* she had beneath her to keep her company; and when asleep she saw them in her dreams. By break of day she arose, and set off in good time towards the villa where her daughter was residing.

Though Lucia's extreme reluctance to speak of her vow was in no degree diminished, she had, on her part, resolved to force herself to open her mind to her mother in this interview, as it would be the last they should have for a long time.

Scarcely were they left alone, when Agnese, with a look full of animation, and, at the same time, in a suppressed tone of voice, as if there were some one present who she was afraid would hear, began: 'I've a grand thing to tell you;' and proceeded to relate her unexpected good fortune.

'God bless this Signor,' said Lucia: 'now you have enough to be well off yourself, and you can also do good to others.'

'Why!' replied Agnese, 'don't you see how many things we may do with so much money? Listen; I have nobody but you—but you two, I may say; for, from the time that he began to address you, I've always considered Renzo as my son. The whole depends upon whether any misfortune has happened to him, seeing he gives no sign of being alive: but oh! surely all won't go ill with us? We'll hope not, we'll hope not. For me, I should have liked to lay my bones in my native country; but now that you can't be there, thanks to that villain! and when I remember that he is near, even my country has become hateful to me; and with you two I can be happy anywhere. I was always inclined to go with you both to the very end of the world, and have ever been in readiness; but how could we do it without money? Do you understand, now? The little sum that the poor fellow had been scarcely able to lay by, with all his frugality, justice came, and cleared it away; but the Lord has sent us a fortune to make up for it. Well, when he has found a way of letting us know that he's alive, where he is, and what are his intentions, I'll come to Milan and fetch you; ay, I'll come myself. Once upon a time, I should have thought twice about such a thing, but misfortunes make one experienced and independent; I've gone as far as Monza, and know what it is to travel. I'll bring with me a proper companion,—a relation, as I may say,—Alessio, of Maggianico; for, to say the truth, a fit person isn't to be found in the country at all. I'll come with him; we will pay the expense, and . . . do you understand?'

But perceiving that, instead of cheering up, Lucia became more and more dejected, and only exhibited emotion unmixed with pleasure, she stopped abruptly in the midst of her speech, and said, 'But what's the matter with you? Don't you see it?'

'Poor mamma!' exclaimed Lucia, throwing her arm round her neck, and burying her weeping face in her bosom.

'What *is* the matter?' again asked her mother, anxiously.

'I ought to have told you at first,' said Lucia, raising her head, and composing herself, 'but I never had the heart to do it: pity me.'

'But tell me then, now.'

'I can no longer be that poor fellow's wife!'

'How? how?'

With head hung down, a beating heart, and tears rolling down her cheeks, like one who relates something which, though a misfortune, is unalterable, Lucia disclosed her vow; and, at the same time, clasping her hands, again besought her mother's forgiveness for having hitherto concealed it from her; she implored her not to speak of such a thing to any living being, and to give her help, and facilitate the fulfilment of what she had promised.

Agnese remained stupefied with consternation. She would have been angry with her for her silence to her mother, but the more serious thoughts the case itself aroused stifled this personal vexation; she would have reproached her for the act, but it seemed to her that that would be a murmuring against Heaven; the more so, as Lucia began to depict, more vividly than ever, the horrors of that night, the absolute desolation, and the unhoped-for deliverance, between which the promise had been so expressly, so solemnly made. And all the while, example after example rose to the recollection of the listener, which she had often heard repeated, and had repeated herself to her daughter, of strange and terrible punishments following upon the violation of a vow. After a few moments of astonishment, she said, 'And what will you do now?'

'Now,' replied Lucia, 'it is the Lord who must think for us; the Lord, and the Madonna. I have placed myself in their hands; they have not forsaken me hitherto; they will not forsake me now, that . . . The mercy I ask for myself of the Lord, the only mercy, after the salvation of my soul, is, that He will let me rejoin you; and He will grant it me—yes, I feel sure He will. That day . . . in that carriage . . . Ah, most holy Virgin! . . . those men! . . . who would have told me that they were bringing me to this, that they would bring me to join my mother the next day?'

'But not to tell your mother of it at once!' said Agnese, with a kind of anger, subdued by affection and pity.

'Oh, pity me! I had not the heart . . . and what use would it have been to grieve you so long ago?'

'And Renzo?' said Agnese, shaking her head.

'Ah!' exclaimed Lucia, with a sudden start, 'I must think nothing more of that poor fellow. Long ago God had not destined . . . See how it appears that it was His will we should be kept asunder. And who knows? . . . but no, no; the Lord will have preserved him from danger, and will make him even happier without me.'

'But now, you see,' replied Agnese, 'if it were not that you are bound for ever, for all the rest, if no misfortune has happened to Renzo, I might have found a remedy with so much money.'

'But should we have got this money,' replied Lucia, 'if I had not passed through such a night? . . . It is the Lord who has ordered everything as it is; His will be done.' And here her voice was choked with tears.

At this unexpected argument, Agnese remained silent and thoughtful. In a few moments, however, Lucia, suppressing her sobs, resumed: 'Now that the deed is done, we must submit to it with cheerfulness; and you, my poor mother, you can help me, first, by praying to the Lord for your unhappy daughter, and then . . . that poor fellow must be told of it, you know. Will you see to this, and do me also this kindness; for *you* can think about it. When you can find out where he is, get some one to write to him; find a man . . . Oh, your cousin, Alessio, is just the man, a prudent and kind person, who has always wished us well, and won't gossip and tell tales; get him to write the thing just as it is, where I have been, how I have suffered, and that God has willed it should be thus; and that he must set his heart at rest, and that I can never, never be anybody's wife!

And tell him of it in a kind and clever way; explain to him that I have promised, that I have really made a vow . . . When he knows that I have promised the Madonna . . . he has always been good and religious . . . And you, the moment you have any news of him, get somebody to write to me; let me know that he is well, and then . . . let me never hear anything more.'

Agnese, with much feeling, assured her daughter that everything should be done as she desired.

'There's one thing more I have to say,' resumed Lucia; 'this poor fellow . . . if he hadn't had the misfortune to think of me, all that has happened to him never would have happened. He's a wanderer in the wide world; they've ruined him on setting out in life; they've carried away all he had, all those little savings he had made, poor fellow; you know why . . . And we have so much money! Oh, mother! as the Lord has sent us so much wealth, and you look upon this poor fellow, true enough, as belonging to you . . . yes, as your son, oh! divide it between you; for, most assuredly, God won't let us want. Look out for the opportunity of a safe bearer, and send it him; for Heaven knows how much he wants it!'

'Well, what do you think?' replied Agnese: 'I'll do it, indeed. Poor youth! Why do you think I was so glad of this money? But! . . . I certainly came here very glad, so I did. Well, I'll send it him; poor youth! But he, too . . . I know what I would say; certainly, money gives pleasure to those who want it; but it isn't this that will make him rich.'

Lucia thanked her mother for her ready and liberal assent, with such deep gratitude and affection, as would have convinced an observer that her heart still secretly clung to Renzo, more, perhaps, than she herself believed.

'And what shall I, a poor solitary woman, do without you?' said Agnese, weeping in her turn.

'And I without you, my poor mother! and in a stranger's house! and down there in Milan! . . . But the Lord will be with us both, and afterwards will bring us together again. Between eight and nine months hence, we shall see each other once more here; and by that time, or even before it, I hope, He will have disposed matters to our comfort. Leave it to Him. I will ever, ever beseech the Madonna for this mercy. If I had anything else to offer her, I would do it; but she is so merciful, that she will obtain it for me as a gift.'

With these, and other similar and oft-repeated words of lamentation and comfort, of opposition and resignation, of interrogation and confident assurance, with many tears, and after long and renewed embraces, the women tore themselves apart, promising, by turns, to see each other the next autumn, at the latest; as if the fulfilment of these promises depended upon themselves, and as people always do, nevertheless, in similar cases.

Meanwhile, a considerable time passed away, and Agnese could hear no tidings of Renzo. Neither letter nor message reached her from him; and among all those whom she could ask from Bergamo, or the neighbourhood, no one knew anything at all about him.

Nor was she the only one who made inquiries in vain: Cardinal Federigo, who had not told the poor woman merely out of compliment that he would seek for some information concerning the unfortunate man, had, in fact, immediately written to obtain it. Having returned to Milan after his visitation, he received a reply, in which he was informed, that the address of the person he had named could not be ascertained; that he had certainly made some stay in such a place, where he had given no occasion for any talk about himself; but that, one morning, he had suddenly disappeared; that a relative of his, with whom he had lodged there, knew not what had become of him, and could only repeat certain vague and contradictory rumours which were afloat, that the youth had enlisted for the Levant, had passed into Germany, or had perished in fording a river; but that the writer would not fail to be on the watch, and if any better authenticated tidings came to light, would immediately convey them to his most illustrious and very reverend Lordship.

These, and various other reports, at length spread throughout the territory of Lecco, and, consequently, reached the ears of Agnese. The poor woman did her utmost to discover which was the true account, and to arrive at the origin of this and that rumour; but she never succeeded in tracing it further than *they say,* which, even at the present day, suffices, by itself, to attest the truth of facts. Sometimes she had scarcely heard one tale, when some one would come and tell her not a word of it was true; only, however, to give her another in compensation, equally strange and disastrous. The truth is, all these rumours were alike unfounded.

The Governor of Milan, and Captain-General in Italy, Don Gonzalo Fernandez de Cordova, had complained bitterly to the Venetian minister, resident at Milan, because a rogue, and public robber, a promoter of plundering and massacre, the famous Lorenzo Tramaglino, who, while in the very hands of justice, had excited an insurrection to force his escape, had been received and harboured in the Bergamascan territory. The minister in residence replied, that he knew nothing about it; he would write to Venice, that he might be able to give his Excellency any explanation that could be procured on the subject.

It was a maxim of Venetian policy to second and cultivate the inclination of Milanese silk-weavers to emigrate into the Bergamascan territory, and, with this object, to provide many advantages for them, more especially that without which every other was worthless; we mean, security. As, however, when two great diplomatists dispute, in however trifling a matter, third parties must always have a taste in the shape of consequences, Bortolo was warned, in confidence, it was not known by whom, that Renzo was not safe in that neighbourhood, and that he would do wisely to place him in some other manufacture for a while, even under a false name. Bortolo understood the hint, raised no objections, explained the matter to his cousin, took him with him in a carriage, conveyed him to another new silk-mill, about fifteen miles off, and presented him, under the name of Antonio Rivolta, to the owner, who was a native of the Milanese, and an old acquaintance. This person, though the times were so bad, needed little entreaty to receive a workman who was recommended to him as honest and skilful by an intelligent man like Bortolo. On the trial of him afterwards, he found he had only reason to congratulate himself on the acquisition; excepting that, at first, he thought the youth must be naturally rather stupid, because, when any one called *Antonio,* he generally did not answer.

Soon after, an order came from Venice, in peaceable form, to the sheriff of Bergamo, requiring him to obtain and forward information, whether, in his jurisdiction, and more expressly in such a village, such an individual was to be found. The sheriff, having made the necessary researches in the manner he saw was desired, transmitted a reply in the negative, which was transmitted to the minister at Milan, who transmitted it to Don Gonzalo Fernandez de Cordova.

There were not wanting inquisitive people who tried to learn from Bortolo why this youth was no longer with him, and where he had gone. To the first inquiry he replied, 'Nay, he has disappeared!' but afterwards, to get rid of the most pertinacious without giving them a suspicion of what was really the case, he contrived to entertain them, some with one, some with another, of the stories we have before mentioned: always, however, as uncertain reports, which he also had heard related, without having any positive accounts.

But when inquiries came to be made of him by commission from the Cardinal, without mentioning his name, and with a certain show of importance and mystery, merely giving him to understand that it was in the name of a great personage, Bortolo became the more guarded, and deemed it the more necessary to adhere to his general method of reply; nay, as a great personage was concerned, he gave out by wholesale all the stories which he had published, one by one, of his various disasters.

Let it not be imagined that such a person as Don Gonzalo bore any personal enmity to the poor mountain silk-weaver; that informed, perhaps, of his irreverence and ill-language towards his Moorish king, chained by the throat, he would have wreaked his vengeance upon him; or that he thought him so dangerous a subject as to be worth pursuing even in flight, and not suffered to live even at a distance, like the Roman senate with Hannibal. Don Gonzalo had too many and too important affairs in his head to trouble himself about Renzo's doings; and if it seems that he did trouble himself about them, it arose from a singular combination of circumstances, by which the poor unfortunate fellow, without desiring it, and without being aware of it, either then, or ever afterwards, found himself linked, as by a very subtile and invisible chain, to these same too many and too important affairs.

CHAPTER XXVII

IT has already occurred to us more than once to make mention of the war which was at this time raging, for the succession to the states of the Duke Vincenzo Gonzaga, the second of that name; but it has always occurred in a moment of great haste, so that we have never been able to give more than a cursory hint of it. Now, however, for the due understanding of our narrative, a more particular notice of it is required. They are matters which any one who knows anything of history must be acquainted with; but as, from a just estimate of ourselves, we must suppose that this work can be read by none but the ignorant, it will not be amiss that we should here relate as much as will suffice to give some idea of them to those who need it.

We have said that on the death of this duke, the first in the line of succession, Carlo Gonzaga, head of a younger branch now established in France, where he possessed the duchies of Nevers and Rhetel, had entered upon the possession of Mantua, and we may now add, of Monferrat: for our haste made us leave this name on the point of the pen. The Spanish minister, who was resolved at any compromise (we have said this too) to exclude the new prince from these two fiefs, and who, to exclude him, wanted some pretext (because wars made without any pretext would be unjust), had declared himself the upholder of the claims which another Gonzaga Ferrante, prince of the Guastalla, pretended to have upon Mantua; and Carlo Emanuele I., duke of Savoy, and Margherita Gonzaga, duchess dowager of Lorraine, upon Monferrat. Don Gonzalo, who was of the family of the great commander, and bore his name, who had already made war in Flanders, and was extremely anxious to bring one into Italy, was perhaps the person who made most stir that this might be undertaken: and in the mean while, interpreting the intentions, and anticipating the orders of the above-named minister, he concluded a treaty with the Duke of Savoy for the invasion

and partition of Monferrat; and afterwards readily obtained a ratifi-
cation of it from the Count Duke, by persuading him that the acquisition of Casale would be very easy, which was the most strongly
defended point of the portion assigned to the King of Spain. He protested, however, in the king's name, against any intention of occupying the country further than under the name of a deposit, until the
sentence of the Emperor should be declared; who, partly from the
influence of others, partly from private motives of his own, had,
in the mean while, denied the investiture to the new duke, and
intimated to him that he should give up to him in sequestration the
controverted states: afterwards, having heard the different sides,
he would restore them to him who had the best claim. To these
conditions the Duke of Nevers would not consent.

He had, however, friends of some eminence in the Cardinal de
Richelieu, the Venetian noblemen, and the Pope. But the first of
these, at that time engaged in the siege of La Rochelle, and in a war
with England, and thwarted by the party of the queen-mother,
Maria de' Medici, who, for certain reasons of her own, was opposed
to the house of Nevers, could give nothing but hopes. The Venetians
would not stir, nor even declare themselves in his favour, unless a
French army were first brought into Italy; and while secretly aiding
the duke as they best could, they contented themselves with putting
off the Court of Madrid and the Governor of Milan with protests,
propositions, and peaceable or threatening admonitions, according
to circumstances. Urban VIII. recommended Nevers to his friends,
interceded in his favour with his enemies, and designed projects of
accommodation; but would not hear a word of sending men into
the field.

By this means the two confederates for offensive measures were
enabled the more securely to begin their concerted operations. Carlo
Emanuele invaded Monferrat from his side; Don Gonzalo willingly
laid siege to Casale, but did not find in the undertaking all the
satisfaction he had promised himself: for it must not be imagined
that war is a rose without a thorn. The Court did not provide him
with nearly all the means he demanded; his ally, on the contrary,
assisted him too much: that is to say, after having taken his own
portion, he went on to take that which was assigned to the King

of Spain. Don Gonzalo was enraged beyond expression; but fearing that, if he made any noise about it, this duke, as active in intrigues and fickle in treaty, as bold and valiant in arms, would revolt to the French, he was obliged to shut his eyes to it, gnaw the bit, and put on a satisfied air. The siege, besides, went on badly, being protracted to a great length, and sometimes thrown back, owing to the steady, cautious, and resolute behaviour of the besieged, the lack of sufficient numbers on the part of the besiegers, and, according to the report of some historian, the many false steps taken by Don Gonzalo; on which point we leave truth to choose her own side, being inclined even, were it really so, to consider it a very happy circumstance, if it were the cause that in this enterprise there were some fewer than usual slain, beheaded, or wounded; and, *cæteris paribus,* rather fewer tiles injured in Casale. In the midst of these perplexities, the news of the sedition at Milan arrived, to the scene of which he repaired in person.

Here, in the report which was given him, mention was also made of the rebellious and clamorous flight of Renzo, and of the real or supposed doings which had been the occasion of his arrest; and they could also inform him that this person had taken refuge in the territory of Bergamo. This circumstance arrested Don Gonzalo's attention. He had been informed from another quarter, that great interest had been felt at Venice in the insurrection at Milan; that they had supposed he would be obliged on this account to abandon the siege of Casale; and that they imagined he was reduced to great despondency and perplexity about it: the more so, as shortly after this event, the tidings had arrived, so much desired by these noblemen, and dreaded by himself, of the surrender of La Rochelle. Feeling considerably annoyed, both as a man and a politician, that they should entertain such an opinion of his proceedings, he sought every opportunity of undeceiving them, and persuading them, by induction, that he had lost none of his former boldness; for to say, explicitly, I have no fear, is just to say nothing. One good plan is to show displeasure, to complain, and to expostulate: accordingly, the Venetian ambassador having waited upon him to pay his respects, and at the same time to read in his countenance and behaviour how he felt within, Don Gonzalo, after having spoken lightly of the tumult, like a man who had already provided a remedy for every-thing, made those complaints about Renzo which the reader already knows; as he is also acquainted with what resulted from them in consequence. From that time, he took no further interest in an affair of so little importance, which, as far as he was concerned, was terminated; and when, a long time afterwards, the reply came to him at the camp at Casale, whither he had returned, and where he had very different things to occupy his mind, he raised and threw back his head, like a silkworm searching for a leaf; reflected for a moment, to recall more clearly to his memory a fact of which he only retained a shadowy idea; remembered the circumstance, had a vague and momentary recollection of the person; passed on to something else, and thought no more about it.

But Renzo, who, from the little which he had darkly com-prehended, was far from supposing so benevolent an indifference, had, for a time, no other thought, or rather, to speak more cor-rectly, no other care, than to keep himself concealed. It may be imagined whether he did not ardently long to send news of himself to the women, and receive some from them in exchange; but there were two great difficulties in the way. One was, that he also would have been forced to trust to an amanuensis, for the poor fellow knew not how to write, nor even read, in the broad sense of the word; and if, when asked the question, as the reader may perhaps re-member, by the Doctor Azzecca-Garbugli, he replied in the affirma-tive, it was not, certainly, a boast, a mere bravado, as they say; it was the truth, that he could manage to read print, when he could take his time over it: writing, however, was a different thing. He would be obliged, then, to make a third party the depositary of his affairs, and of a secret so jealously guarded: and it was not easy in those times to find a man who could use his pen, and in whom con-fidence could be placed, particularly in a country where he had no old acquaintances. The other difficulty was to find a bearer; a man who was going just to the place he wanted, who would take charge of the letter, and really recollect to deliver it; all these, too, qualifica-tions rather difficult to be met with in one individual.

At length, by dint of searching and sounding, he found somebody to write for him; but ignorant where the women were, or whether they were still at Monza, he judged it better to enclose the letter directed to Agnese under cover to Father Cristoforo, with a line or two also for him. The writer undertook the charge, moreover, of forwarding the packet, and delivered it to one who would pass not far from Pescarenico; this person left it with many strict charges, at an inn on the road, at the nearest point to the monastery; and, as it was directed to a convent, it reached this destination; but what became of it afterwards was never known. Renzo, receiving no reply, sent off a second letter, nearly like the first, which he enclosed in another to an acquaintance or distant relation of his at Lecco. He sought for another bearer, and found one; and this time the letter reached the person to whom it was addressed. Agnese posted off to Maggianico, had it read and interpreted to her by her cousin Alessio; concerted with him a reply, which he put down in writing for her, and found means of sending it to Antonio Rivolta in his present place of abode: all this, however, not quite so expeditiously as we have recounted it. Renzo received the reply, and in time sent an answer to it. In short, a correspondence was set on foot between the two parties, neither frequent nor regular, but still kept up by starts, and at intervals.

To form some idea, however, of this correspondence, it is necessary to know a little how such things went on in those days—indeed, how they go on now; for in this particular, I believe, there is little or no variation.

The peasant who knows not how to write, and finds himself reduced to the necessity of communicating his ideas to the absent, has recourse to one who understands the art, taking him, as far as he can, from among those of his own rank,—for, with others, he is either shamefaced, or afraid to trust them; he informs them, with more or less order and perspicuity, of past events; and in the same manner, describes to him the thoughts he is to express. The man of letters understands part, misunderstands part, gives a little advice, proposes some variation, says, 'Leave it to me;' then he takes the pen, transfers the idea he has received, as he best can, from speaking to writing, corrects it his own way, improves it, puts in flourishes, abbreviates, or even omits, according as he deems most suitable for his subject; for so it is, and there is no help for it, he who knows more than his neighbours will not be a passive instrument in their hands; and when he interferes in other people's affairs, he will force them to do things his own way. In addition to all this, it is not always quite a matter of course that the above-named literate himself expresses all that he intended; nay, sometimes it happens just the reverse, as, indeed, it does even to us who write for the press. When the letter thus completed reaches the hands of the correspondent, who is equally unpractised in his a, b, c, he takes it to another learned genius of that tribe, who reads and expounds it to him. Questions arise on the matter of understanding it, because the person interested, presuming upon his acquaintance with the antecedent circumstances, asserts that certain words mean such and such a thing; the reader, resting upon his greater experience in the art of composition, affirms that they mean another. At last, the one who does not know, is obliged to put himself into the hands of the one who does, and trusts to him the task of writing a reply; which, executed like the former example, is liable to a similar style of interpretation. If, in addition, the subject of the correspondence be a rather delicate topic, if secret matters be treated of in it, which it is desirable should not be understood by a third party, in case the letter should go astray; if with this view there be a positive intention of not expressing things quite clearly, then, however short a time the correspondence is kept up, the parties invariably finish by understanding each other as well as the two schoolmen who had disputed for four hours upon abstract mutations; not to take our simile from living beings, lest we expose ourselves to have our ears boxed.

Now, the case of our two correspondents was exactly what we have described. The first letter written in Renzo's name, contained many subjects. Primarily, besides an account of the flight, by far more concise, but, at the same time, more confused, than that which we have given, was a relation of his actual circumstances, from which both Agnese and her interpreter were very far from deriving any lucid or tolerably correct idea. Then he spoke of secret intelligence, change of name, his being in safety, but still requiring concealment; things in themselves not very familiar to their understandings, and related in the letter rather enigmatically. Then followed warm and impassioned inquiries about Lucia's situation, with dark and mournful hints of the rumours which had reached even his ears. There were, finally, uncertain and distant hopes and plans in reference to the future; and for the present promises and entreaties to keep their plighted faith, not to lose patience or courage, and to wait for better days.

Some time passed away, and Agnese found a trusty messenger, to convey an answer to Renzo, with the fifty *scudi* assigned to him by Lucia. At the sight of so much gold, he knew not what to think; and, with a mind agitated by wonder and suspense, which left no room for gratification, he set off in search of his amanuensis, to make him interpret the letter, and find the key to so strange a mystery.

Agnese's scribe, after lamenting, in the letter, the want of perspicuity in Renzo's epistle, went on to describe, in a way at least quite as much to be lamented, the tremendous history of that person (so he expressed himself); and here he accounted for the fifty *scudi;* then he went on to speak of the vow, employing much circumlocution in the expression of it, but adding, in more direct and explicit terms, the advice to set his heart at rest, and think no more about it.

Renzo very nearly quarrelled with the reader; he trembled, shuddered, became enraged with what he had understood, and with what he could not understand. Three or four times did he make him read over the melancholy writing, now comprehending better, now finding what had at first appeared clear, more and more incomprehensible. And, in this fervour of passion, he insisted upon his amanuensis immediately taking pen in hand, and writing a reply. After the strongest expressions imaginable of pity and horror at Lucia's circumstances—'Write,' pursued he, as he dictated to his secretary, 'that I won't set my heart at rest, and that I never will; and that this is not advice to be giving to a lad like me; and that I won't touch the money; that I'll put it by, and keep it for the young girl's dowry; that she already belongs to me; and that I know nothing about a vow; and that I have often heard say that the Madonna interests herself to help the afflicted, and obtains favours for them; but that she encourages them to despise and break their word, I never heard; and that this vow can't hold good; and that with this money we have enough to keep house here; and that I am somewhat in difficulties now, it's only a storm which will quickly pass over;' and other similar things. Agnese received this letter also, and replied to it; and the correspondence continued in the manner we have described.

Lucia felt greatly relieved when her mother had contrived, by some means or other, to let her know that Renzo was alive, safe, and acquainted with her vow, and desired nothing more than that he should forget her; or, to express it more exactly, that he should try to forget her. She, on her part, made a similar resolution a hundred times a day with respect to him; and employed, too, every means she could think of to put it into effect. She continued to work indefatigably with her needle, trying to apply her whole mind to it; and when Renzo's image presented itself to her view, would begin to repeat or chant some prayers to herself. But that image, just as if it were actuated by pure malice, did not generally come so openly; it introduced itself stealthily behind others, so that the mind might not be aware of having harboured it, till after it had been there for some time. Lucia's thoughts were often with her mother; how should it have been otherwise? and the ideal Renzo would gently creep in as a third party, as the real person had so often done. So, with everybody, in every place, in every remembrance of the past, he never failed to introduce himself. And if the poor girl allowed herself sometimes to penetrate in fancy into the obscurity of the future, there, too, he would appear, if it were only to say: I, ten to one, shall not be there. However, if not to think of him at all were a hopeless undertaking, yet Lucia succeeded up to a certain point, in thinking less about him, and less intensely than her heart would have wished. She would even have succeeded better, had she been alone in desiring to do so. But there was Donna Prassede, who, bent on her part, upon banishing the youth from her thoughts, had found no better expedient than constantly talking about him. 'Well,' she would say, 'have you given up thinking of him?'

'I am thinking of nobody,' replied Lucia.

Donna Prassede, however, not to be appeased by so evasive an answer, replied that there must be deeds, not words; and enlarged upon the usual practices of young girls, 'who,' said she, 'when they have set their hearts upon a dissolute fellow, (and it is just to such they have a leaning), won't consent to be separated from them. An honest and rational contract to a worthy man, a well-tried character, which, by some accident, happens to be frustrated,—they are quickly resigned; but let it be a villain, and it is an incurable wound.' And then she commenced a panegyric upon the poor absentee, the rascal who had come to Milan to plunder the town, and massacre the inhabitants; and tried to make Lucia confess all the knavish tricks he had played in his own country.

Lucia, with a voice tremulous with shame, sorrow, and such indignation as could find place in her gentle breast and humble condition, affirmed and testified that the poor fellow had done nothing in his country to give occasion for anything but good to be said of him; 'she wished,' she said, 'that some one were present from his neighbourhood, that the lady might hear his testimony.' Even on his adventures at Milan, the particulars of which she could not learn, she defended him merely from the knowledge she had had of him and his behaviour, from his very childhood. She defended him, or intended to defend him, from the simple duty of charity, from her love of truth, and, to use just the expression by which she described her feelings to herself, as her neighbour. But Donna Prassede drew fresh arguments from these apologies, to convince Lucia that she had quite lost her heart to this man. And, to say the truth, in these moments it is difficult to say how the matter stood. The disgraceful picture the old lady drew of the poor youth, revived, from opposition, more vividly and distinctly than ever in the mind of the young girl, the idea which long habit had established there; the recollections she had stifled by force, returned in crowds upon her; aversion and contempt recalled all her old motives of esteem and sympathy, and blind and violent hatred only excited stronger feelings of pity. With these feelings, who can say how much there might or might not be of another affection which follows upon them, and introduces itself so easily into the mind? Let it be imagined what it would do in one whence it was attempted to eject it by force. However it may be, the conversation, on Lucia's side, was never carried to any great length, for words were very soon resolved into tears.

Had Donna Prassede been induced to treat her in this way from some inveterate hatred towards her, these tears might, perhaps, have vanquished and silenced her; but as she spoke with the intention of doing good, she went on without allowing herself to be moved by them, as groans and imploring cries may arrest the weapons of an enemy, but not the instrument of the surgeon. Having, however, discharged her duty for that time, she would turn from reproaches and denunciations to exhortation and advice, sweetened also by a little praise; thus designing to temper the bitter with the sweet, the better to obtain her purpose, by working upon the heart under every state of feeling. These quarrels, however, (which had always nearly the same beginning, middle, and end), left no resentment, properly speaking, in the good Lucia's heart against the harsh sermonizer, who, after all, treated her, in general, very kindly; and even in this instance, evinced a good intention. Yet they left her in such agitation, with such a tumult of thoughts and affections, that it required no little time, and much effort, to regain her former degree of calmness.

It was well for her that she was not the only one to whom Donna Prassede had to do good; for, by this means, these disputes could not occur so frequently. Besides the rest of the family, all of whom were persons more or less needing amendment and guidance—besides all the other occasions which offered themselves to her, or she contrived to find, of extending the same kind office, of her own free will, to many to whom she was under no obligations; she had also five daughters, none of whom were at home, but who gave her much more to think about than if they had been. Three of these were nuns, two were married: hence Donna Prassede naturally found herself with three monasteries and two houses to superintend; a vast and complicated undertaking, and the more arduous, because two husbands, backed by fathers, mothers, and brothers; three abbesses, supported by other dignitaries, and by many nuns, would not accept her superintendence. It was a complete warfare, *alias* five warfares, concealed, and even courteous, up to a certain point, but ever active, ever vigilant. There was in every one of these places a continued watchfulness to avoid her solicitude, to close the door against her counsels, to elude her inquiries, and to keep her in the dark, as far as possible, on every undertaking. We do not mention the resistance, the difficulties she encountered in the management of other still more extraneous affairs: it is well known that one must generally do good to men by force. The place where her zeal could best exercise itself, and have full play, was in her own house: here everybody was subject in everything, and for everything, to her authority, saving Don Ferrante, with whom things went on in a manner entirely peculiar.

A man of studious turn, he neither loved to command nor obey. In all household matters, his wife was the mistress, with his free consent; but he would not submit to be her slave. And if, when requested, he occasionally lent her the assistance of his pen, it was because it suited his taste; and after all, he knew how to say no, when he was not convinced of what she wished him to write. 'Use your own sense,' he would say, in such cases; 'do it yourself, since it seems so clear to you.' Donna Prassede, after vainly endeavouring for some time to induce him to recant, and do what she wanted, would be obliged to content herself with murmuring frequently against him, with calling him one who hated trouble, a man who would have his own way, and a scholar: a title which, though pronounced with contempt, was generally mixed with a little complacency.

Don Ferrante passed many hours in his study, where he had a considerable collection of books, scarcely less than three hundred volumes: all of them choice works, and the most highly esteemed on their numerous several subjects, in each of which he was more or less versed. In astrology, he was deservedly considered as more than a *dilettante;* for he not only possessed the generical notions and common vocabulary of influences, aspects, and conjunctions; but he knew how to talk very aptly, and as it were *ex cathedra,* of the twelve houses of the heavens, of the great circles, of lucid and obscure degrees, of exultation and dejection, of transitions and revolutions—in short, of the most assured and most recondite principles of the science. And it was for perhaps twenty years that he maintained, in long and frequent disputes, the system of Cardano against another learned man who was staunchly attached to that of Alcabizio, from mere obstinacy, as Don Ferrante said; who, readily acknowledging the superiority of the ancients, could not, however, endure that unwillingness to yield to the moderns, even when they evidently have reason on their side. He was also more than indifferently acquainted with the history of the science; he could, on an occasion, quote the most celebrated predictions which had been verified, and reason clearly and learnedly on other celebrated predictions which had failed, showing that the fault was not in the science, but in those who knew not how to apply it.

He had learnt as much of ancient philosophy as might have sufficed him, but still went on acquiring more from the study of Diogenes Laertius. As, however, these systems, how beautiful soever they may be, cannot all be held at once; and as, to be a philosopher, it is necessary to choose an author, so Don Ferrante had chosen Aristotle, who, he used to say, was neither ancient nor modern; he was the philosopher, and nothing more. He possessed also various works of the wisest and most ingenious disciples of that school among the moderns: those of its impugners he would never read, not to throw away time, as he said; nor buy, not to throw away money. Surely, by way of exception, did he find room in his library for those celebrated two-and-twenty volumes De Subtilitate, and for some other antiperipatetic work of Cardano's, in consideration of his value in astrology. He said, that he who could write the treatise De Restitutione temporum et motuum cœlestium, and the book Duodecim geniturarum, deserved to be listened to even when he erred; that the great defect of this man was, that he had too much talent; and that no one could conceive what he might have arrived at, even in philosophy, had he kept himself in the right way. In short, although, in the judgment of the learned, Don Ferrante passed for a consummate peripatetic, yet he did not deem that he knew enough about it himself; and more than once he was obliged to confess, with great modesty, that essence, universals, the soul of the world, and the nature of things, were not so very clear as might be imagined.

He had made a recreation rather than a study of natural philosophy; the very works of Aristotle on this subject he had rather read than studied: yet, with this slight perusal, with the notices incidentally gathered from treatises on general philosophy, with a few cursory glances at the *Magia naturale* of Porta, at the three histories, *lapidum, animalium, plantarum,* of Cardano, at the treatise on herbs, plants, and animals, by Albert Magnus, and a few other works of less note, he could entertain a party of learned men, for a while, with dissertations on the most wonderful virtues and most remarkable curiosities of many medicinal herbs; he could minutely describe the forms and habits of sirens and the solitary phœnix; and explain how the salamander exists in the fire without burning; how the remora, that diminutive fish, has strength and ability completely to arrest a ship of any size in the high seas; how drops of dew become pearls in the shell; how the chameleon feeds on air; how ice, by being gradually hardened, is formed into crystal, in the course of time; with many other of the most wonderful secrets of nature.

Into those of magic and witchcraft he had penetrated still more deeply, as it was a science, says our anonymous author, much more necessary and more in vogue in those days, in which the facts were of far higher importance, and it was more within reach to verify them. It is unnecessary to say that he had no other object in view in such a study, than to inform himself, and to become acquainted with the very worst arts of the sorcerers, in order that he might guard against them and defend himself. And, by the guidance principally of the great Martino Delrio (a leader of the science), he was capable of discoursing *ex professo* upon the fascination of love, the fascination of sleep, the fascination of hatred, and the infinite varieties of these three principal genuses of enchantment, which are only too often, again says our anonymous author, beheld in practice at the present day, attended by such lamentable effects.

Not less vast and profound was his knowledge of history, particularly universal history, in which his authors were Tarcagnota, Dolce, Bugatti, Campana, and Guazzo; in short, all the most highly esteemed.

'But what is history,' said Don Ferrante, frequently, 'without politics?—A guide who walks on and on, with no one following to learn the road, and who consequently throws away his steps; as politics without history is one who walks without a guide.' There was therefore a place assigned to statistics on his shelves; where, among many of humbler rank and less renown, appeared, in all their glory, Bedino, Cavalcanti, Sansovino, Paruta, and Boccalini. There were two books, however, which Don Ferrante infinitely preferred above all others on this subject; two which, up to a certain time, he used to call the first, without ever being able to decide to which of the two this rank should exclusively belong: one was the *Principe* and *Discorsi* of the celebrated Florentine secretary; 'a great rascal, certainly,' said Don Ferrante, 'but profound': the other, the *Ragion di Stato* of the no less celebrated Giovanni Botero; 'an honest man, certainly,' said he again, 'but shrewd.' Shortly after, however, just at the period which our story embraces, a work came to light which terminated the question of pre-eminence, by surpassing the works of even these two *Matadores,* said Don Ferrante; a book in which was enclosed and condensed every trick of the system, that it might be known, and every virtue, that it might be practised; a book of small dimensions, but all of gold; in one word, the *Statista Regnante* of Don Valeriano Castiglione, that most celebrated man, of whom it might be said that the greatest scholars rivalled each other in sounding his praises, and the greatest personages in trying to rob him of them; that man, whom Pope Urban VIII. honoured, as is well known, with magnificent encomiums; whom the Cardinal Borghese and the Viceroy of Naples, Don Pietro di Toledo, entreated to relate,—one, the doings of Pope Paul V., the other, the wars of his Catholic Majesty in Italy, and both in vain; that man, whom Louis XIII., King of France, at the suggestion of Cardinal de Richelieu, nominated his historiographer; on whom Duke Carlo Emanuele, of Savoy, conferred the same office; in praise of whom, not to mention other lofty testimonials, the Duchess Cristina, daughter of the most Christian King Henry IV., could, in a diploma, among many other titles, enumerate 'the certainty of the reputation he is obtaining in Italy of being the first writer of our times.'

But if, in all the above-mentioned sciences, Don Ferrante might be considered a learned man, one there was in which he merited and enjoyed the title of Professor—the science of chivalry. Not only did he argue on it in a really masterly manner, but, frequently requested to interfere in affairs of honour, always gave some decision. He had in his library, and one may say, indeed, in his head, the works of the most renowned writers on this subject: Paris del

Pozzo, Fausto da Longiano, Urrea, Muzio, Romei, Albergato, the first and second *Forno* of Torquato Tasso, of whose other works, 'Jerusalem Delivered,' as well as 'Jerusalem Taken,' he had ever in readiness, and could quote from memory, on occasion, all the passages which might serve as a text on the subject of chivalry. The author, however, of all authors, in his estimation, was our celebrated Francesco Birago, with whom he was more than once associated in giving judgment on cases of honour; and who, on his side, spoke of Don Ferrante in terms of particular esteem. And from the time that the *Discorsi Cavallereschi* of this renowned writer made their appearance, he predicted, without hesitation, that this work would destroy the authority of Olevano, and would remain, together with its other noble sisters, as a code of primary authority among posterity: and every one may see, says our anonymous author, how this prediction has been verified.

From this he passes on to the study of belles lettres; but we begin to doubt whether the reader has really any great wish to go forward with us in this review, and even to fear that we may already have won the title of servile copyist for ourselves, and that of a *bore,* to be shared with the anonymous author, for having followed him out so simply, even thus far, into a subject foreign to the principal narrative, and in which, probably, he was only so diffuse, for the purpose of parading erudition, and showing that he was not behind his age. However, leaving written what is written, that we may not lose our labour, we will omit the rest to resume the thread of our story: the more willingly, as we have a long period to traverse without meeting with any of our characters, and a longer still, before finding those in whose success the reader will be most interested, if anything in the whole story has interested him at all.

Until the autumn of the following year, 1629, they all remained, some willingly, some by force, almost in the state in which we left them, nothing happening to any one, and no one doing anything worthy of being recorded. The autumn at length approached, in which Agnese and Lucia had counted upon meeting again; but a great public event frustrated that expectation: and this certainly was one of its most trifling effects. Other great events followed, which, however, made no material change in the destinies of our characters. At length, new circumstances, more general, more influential, and more extensive, reached even to them,—even to the lowest of them, according to the world's scale. It was like a vast, sweeping, and irresistible hurricane, which, uprooting trees, tearing off roots, levelling battlements, and scattering their fragments in every direction, stirs up the straws hidden in the grass, pries into every corner for the light and withered leaves, which a gentler breeze would only have lodged there more securely, and bears them off in its headlong course of fury.

Now, that the private events which yet remain for us to relate may be rendered intelligible, it will be absolutely necessary for us, even here, to promise some kind of account of these public ones, and thus make a still further digression.

CHAPTER XXVIII

AFTER the sedition of St. Martin's, and the following day, it seemed that abundance had returned to Milan, as by enchantment. The bread shops were plentifully supplied; the price as low as in the most prolific years, and flour in proportion. They who during those two days had employed themselves in shouting, or doing something worse, had now (excepting a few who had been seized) reason to congratulate themselves: and let it not be imagined that they spared these congratulations, after the first fear of being captured had subsided. In the squares, at the corners of the streets, and in the taverns, there was undisguised rejoicing, a general murmur of applauses, and half-uttered boasts of having found a way to reduce bread to a moderate price.

In the midst, however, of this vaunting and festivity, there was (and how could it be otherwise?) a secret feeling of disquietude, and presentiment that the thing could not last long. They besieged the bakers and meal-sellers, as they had before done in the former artificial and transient abundance procured by the first tariff of Antonio Ferrer; he who had a little money in advance, invested it in bread and flour, which were stored up in chests, small barrels, and iron vessels. By thus emulating each other in enjoying present advantage, they rendered (I do not say, its long duration impossible, for such it was of itself already, but even) its continuance from moment to moment ever more difficult. And lo! on the 15th November, Antonio Ferrer, *De orden de su Excelencia,* issued a proclamation, in which all who had any corn or flour in their houses were forbidden to buy either one or the other, and every one else to purchase more than would be required for two days, *under pain of pecuniary and corporal punishments, at the will of his Excellency.* It contained, also, intimations to the elders, (a kind of public officer), and insinuations to all other persons, to inform against offenders; orders to magistrates to make strict search in any houses which might be reported to them; together with fresh commands to the bakers to keep their shops well furnished with bread, *under pain, in case of failure, of five years in the galleys, or even greater penalties, at the will of his Excellency.* He who can imagine such a proclamation executed, must have a very clever imagination; and, certainly, had all those issued at that time taken effect, the duchy of Milan would have had at least as many people on the seas as Great Britain itself may have at present.

At any rate, as they ordered the bakers to make so much bread, it was also necessary to give some orders that the materials for making it should not fail. They had contrived, (as, in times of scarcity, the endeavour is always renewed to reduce into bread different alimentary materials, usually consumed under another form), they had contrived, I say, to introduce rice into a composition, called mixed bread. On the 23rd November, an edict was published, to limit to the disposal of the superintendent, and the twelve members who constituted the board of provision, one-half of the dressed rice (*risone* it was then, and is still, called there) which every one possessed; with the threat, to any one who should dispose of it without the permission of these noblemen, of the loss of the article, and a fine of three crowns a bushel. The honesty of this proceeding every one can appreciate.

But it was necessary to pay for this rice, and at a price very disproportioned to that of bread. The burden of supplying the enormous inequality had been imposed upon the city; but the Council of the *Decurioni,* who had undertaken to discharge the debt in behalf of the city, deliberated the same day, 23rd November, about remonstrating with the governor on the impossibility of any longer maintaining such an engagement; and the governor, in a decree of the 7th December, fixed the price of the above-named rice at twelve livres per bushel. To those who should demand a higher price, as well as to those who should refuse to sell, he threatened the loss of the article, and a fine of equal value, *and greater pecuniary, and even corporal punishment, including the galleys, at the will of his Excellency, according to the nature of the case, and the rank of the offender.*

The price of undressed rice had been already limited before the insurrection; as the tariff, or, to use that most famous term of modern annals, the *maximum* of wheat, and other of the commonest grains, had probably been established in different decrees, which we have not happened to meet with.

Bread and flour being thus reduced to a moderate price at Milan, it followed of consequence that people flocked thither in crowds to obtain a supply. To obviate this inconvenience, as he said, Don Gonzalo, in another edict of the 15th December, prohibited carrying bread out of the city, beyond the value of twenty pence, under penalty of the loss of the bread itself, and twenty-five crowns; *or, in case of inability, of two stripes in public, and greater punishment still,* as usual, *at the will of his Excellency.* On the 22nd of the same month, (and why so late, it is difficult to say), a similar order was issued with regard to flour and grain.

The multitude had tried to procure abundance by pillage and incendiarism; the legal arm would have maintained it with the galleys and the scourge. The means were convenient enough in themselves, but what they had to do with the end, the reader knows; how they actually answered their purpose, he will see directly. It is easy, too, to see, and not useless to observe, the necessary connection between these stranger measures; each was an inevitable consequence of the antecedent one; and all of the first, which fixed a price upon bread so different to that which would have resulted from the real state of things. Such a provision ever has, and ever must have, appeared to the multitude as consistent with justice, as simple and easy of execution: hence, it is quite natural that, in the deprivations and grievances of a famine, they should desire it, implore it, and, if they can, enforce it. In proportion, then, as the consequences begin to be felt, it is necessary that they whose duty it is should provide a remedy for each, by a regulation, prohibiting men to do what they were impelled to do by the preceding one. We may be permitted to remark here in passing a singular coincidence. In a country and at a period by no means remote, a period the most clamorous and most renowned of modern history, in similar circumstances, similar provisions obtained (the same, we might almost say, in substance, with the sole difference of proportions, and in nearly the same succession); they obtained, in spite of the march of intellect, and the knowledge which had spread over Europe, and in that country, perhaps, more than any other; and this, principally, because the great mass of the people, whom this knowledge had not yet reached, could, in the long run, make their judgment prevail, and, as it were there said, compel the hands of those who made the laws.

But to return to our subject. On a review of the circumstances, there were two principal fruits of the insurrection: destruction and actual loss of provision, in the insurrection itself, and a consumption, while the tariff lasted, immense, immeasurable, and, so to say, jovial, which rapidly diminished the small quantity of grain that was to have sufficed till the next harvest. To these general effects may be added, the punishment of four of the populace, who were hung as ringleaders of the tumult, two before the bake-house of the Crutches, and two at the end of the street where the house of the superintendent of provisions was situated.

As to the rest, the historical accounts of those times have been written so much at random, that no information is to be found as to how and when this arbitrary tariff ceased. If, in the failure of positive notices, we may be allowed to form a conjecture, we are inclined to believe that it was withdrawn shortly before, or soon after, the 24th December, which was the day of the execution. As to the proclamations, after the last we have quoted, of the 22nd of the same month, we find no more on the subject of provisions; whether it be that they have perished, or have escaped our researches, or, finally, that the government discouraged, if not instructed, by the inefficiency of these its remedies, and quite overwhelmed with different matters, abandoned them to their own course. We find, indeed, in the records of more than one historian, (inclined, as they were, rather to describe great events, than to note the causes and progress of them), a picture of the country, and chiefly of the city, in the already advanced winter, and following spring, when the cause of the evil, the disproportion, *i. e.,* between food and the demand for it, (which, far from being removed, was even increased, by the remedies which temporarily suspended its effects), when the true cause, I say, of the scarcity, or, to speak more correctly, the scarcity itself, was operating without a check, and exerting its full force. It was not even checked by the introduction of a sufficient supply of corn from without, to which remedy were opposed the, insufficiency of public and private means, the poverty of the surrounding countries, the prevailing famine, the tediousness and restrictions of commerce, and the laws themselves, tending to the production and violent maintenance of moderate prices. We will give a sketch of the mournful picture.

At every step, the shops closed; manufactories for the most part deserted; the streets presenting an indescribable spectacle, an incessant train of miseries, a perpetual abode of sorrows. Professed beggars of long standing, now become the smallest number, mingled and lost in a new swarm, and sometimes reduced to contend for alms with those from whom, in former days, they had been accustomed to receive them. Apprentices and clerks dismissed by shopkeepers and merchants, who, when their daily profits diminished, or entirely failed, were living sparingly on their savings, or on their capital; shopkeepers and merchants themselves, to whom the cessation of business had brought failure and ruin; workmen, in every trade and manufacture, the commonest as well as the most refined, the most necessary as well as those more subservient to luxury, wandering from door to door, and from street to street, leaning against the corners, stretched upon the pavement, along the houses and churches, begging piteously, or hesitating between want and a still unsubdued shame, emaciated, weak, and trembling, from long fasting, and the cold that pierced through their tattered and scanty garments, which still, however, in many instances, retained traces of having been once in a better condition; as their present idleness and despondency ill disguised indications of former habits of industry and courage. Mingled in the deplorable throng, and forming no small part of it, were servants dismissed by their masters, who either had sunk from mediocrity into poverty, or otherwise, from wealthy and noble citizens, had become unable in such a year, to maintain their accustomed pomp of retinue. And for each one, so to say, of these different needy objects, was a number of others, accustomed, in part, to live by their gains; children, women, and aged relatives, grouped around their old supporters, or dispersed in search of relief elsewhere.

There were, also, easily distinguishable by their tangled locks, by the relics of their showy dress, or even by something in their carriage and gestures, and by that expression which habits impress upon the countenance, the more marked and distinct as the habits are strange and unusual,—many of that vile race of bravoes, who, having lost in the common calamity their wickedly acquired substance, now went about imploring it for charity. Subdued by hunger, contending with others only in entreaties, and reduced in person, they dragged themselves along through the streets, which they had so often traversed with a lofty brow, and a suspicious and ferocious look, dressed in sumptuous and fantastic liveries, furnished with rich arms, plumed, decked out, and perfumed; and humbly extended the hand which had so often been insolently raised to threaten, or treacherously to wound.

But the most frequent, the most squalid, the most hideous spectacle, was that of the country people, alone, in couples, or even in entire families; husbands and wives, with infants in their arms, or tied up in a bundle upon their backs, with children dragged along by the hand, or with old people behind. Some there were who, having had their houses invaded and pillaged by the soldiery, had fled thither, either as residents or passengers, in a kind of desperation; and among these there were some who displayed stronger incentives to compassion, and greater distinction in misery, in the scars and bruises from the wounds they had received in the defence of their few remaining provisions; while others gave way to a blind and brutal licentiousness. Others, again, unreached by that particular scourge, but driven from their homes by those two, from which the remotest corner was not exempt, sterility and prices more exorbitant than ever, to meet what were called the necessities of war, had come, and were continually pouring into the city, as to the ancient seat and ultimate asylum of plenty and pious munificence. The newly arrived might be distinguished, not only by a hesitating step, and novel air, but still more by a look of angry astonishment, at finding such an accumulation, such an excess, such a rivalry of misery, in a place where they had hoped to appear singular objects of compassion, and to attract to themselves all assistance and notice. The others, who, for more or less time, had haunted the streets of the city, prolonging life by the scanty food obtained, as it were, by chance, in such a disparity between the supply and the demand, bore expressed in their looks and carriage still deeper and more anxious consternation. Various in dress, (or rather rags), as well as appearance, in the midst of the common prostration, there were the pale faces of the marshy districts, the bronzed countenances of the open and hilly country, and the ruddy complexion of the mountaineer, all alike wasted and emaciated, with sunken eyes, a stare between sternness and idiocy, matted locks, and long and ghastly beards; bodies, once plump and inured to fatigue, now exhausted by want; shrivelled skin on their parched arms, legs, and bony breasts, which appeared through their disordered and tattered garments; while different from, but not less melancholy than, this spectacle of wasted vigour, was that of a more quickly subdued nature; of languor, and a more self-abandoning debility, in the weaker sex and age.

Here and there, in the streets and cross-ways, along the walls, and under the eaves of the houses, were layers of trampled straw and stubble, mixed with dirty rags. Yet such revolting filth was the gift and provision of charity; they were places of repose prepared for some of those miserable wretches, where they might lay their heads at night. Occasionally, even during the day, some one might be seen lying there, whom faintness and abstinence had robbed of breath, and the power of supporting the weight of his body. Sometimes these wretched couches bore a corpse; sometimes a poor exhausted creature would suddenly sink to the ground, and remain a lifeless body upon the pavement.

Bending over some of these prostrated sufferers, a neighbour or passer-by might frequently be seen, attracted by a sudden impulse of compassion. In some places assistance was tendered, organized with more distant foresight, and proceeding from a hand rich in the means, and experienced in the exercise, of doing good on a large scale;—the hand of the good Federigo. He had made choice of six priests, whose ready and persevering charity was united with, and ministered to by, a robust constitution; these he divided into pairs, and assigned to each a third part of the city to perambulate, followed by porters laden with various kinds of food, together with other more effective and more speedy restoratives, and clothing

Every morning these three pairs dispersed themselves through the streets in different directions, approached those whom they found stretched upon the ground, and administered to each the assistance he was capable of receiving. Some in the agonies of death, and no longer able to partake of nourishment, received at their hands the last succours and consolations of religion. To those whom food might still benefit, they dispensed soup, eggs, bread, or wine; while to others, exhausted by longer abstinence, they offered jellies and stronger wines, reviving them first, if need were, with cordials and powerful acids. At the same time they distributed garments to those who were most indecorously and miserably clothed.

Nor did their assistance end here: it was the good bishop's wish that, at least where it could be extended, efficacious and more permanent relief should be administered. Those poor creatures, who felt sufficiently strengthened by the first remedies to stand up and walk, were also provided, by the same kindly ministry, with a little money, that returning need, and the failure of further succour, might not bring them again immediately into their first condition; for the rest, they sought shelter and maintenance in some of the neighbouring houses. Those among the inhabitants who were well off in the world, afforded hospitality out of charity, and on the recommendation of the Cardinal; and where there was the will, without the means, the priests requested that the poor creature might be received as a boarder, agreed upon the terms, and immediately defrayed a part of the expense. They then gave notice of those who were thus lodged to the parish priests, that they might go to see them; and they themselves would also return to visit them.

It is unnecessary to say that Federigo did not confine his care to this extremity of suffering, nor wait till the evil had reached its height, before exerting himself. His ardent and versatile charity must feel all, be employed in all, hasten where it could not anticipate, and take, so to say, as many forms as there were varieties of need. In fact, by bringing together all his means, saving with still more rigorous economy, and applying sums destined to other purposes of charity, now, alas! rendered of secondary importance, he had tried every method of making money, to be expended entirely in alleviating poverty. He made large purchases of corn, which he despatched to the most indigent parts of his diocese; and as the succours were far from equalling the necessity, he also sent plentiful supplies of salt, 'with which,' says Ripamonti, relating the circumstances, 'the herbs of the field, and bark from the trees, might be converted into human sustenance.' He also distributed corn and money to the clergy of the city; he himself visited it by districts, dispensing alms; he relieved in secret many destitute families; in the archiepiscopal palace large quantities of rice were daily cooked; and according to the account of a contemporary writer, (the physician, Alessandro Tadino, in his *Ragguaglio,* which we shall frequently have occasion to quote in the sequel), two thousand porringers of this food were here distributed every morning.

But these fruits of charity, which we may certainly specify as wonderful, when we consider that they proceeded from one individual, and from his sole resources, (for Federigo habitually refused to be made a dispenser of the liberality of others), these, together with the bounty of other private persons, if not so copious, at least more numerous, and the subsidies granted by the Council of the *Decurioni* to meet this emergency, the dispensation of which was committed to the Board of Provision, were, after all, in comparison of the demand, scarce and inadequate. While some few mountaineers and inhabitants of the valleys, who were ready to die of hunger, had their lives prolonged by the Cardinal's assistance, others arrived at the extremest verge of starvation; the former, having consumed their measured supplies, returned to the same state; in other parts, not forgotten, but considered as less straitened by a charity which was compelled to make distinctions, the sufferings became fatal; in every direction they perished, from every direction they flocked to the city. Here two thousand, we will say, of famishing creatures, the strongest and most skilful in surmounting competition, and making way for themselves, obtained, perhaps, a bowl of soup, so as not to die that day; but many more thousands remained behind, envying those, shall we say, more fortunate ones, when among them who remained behind, were often their wives, children, or parents? And while, in two or three parts of the city, some of the most destitute and reduced were raised from the ground, revived, recovered, and provided for, for some time, in a hundred other quarters, many more sank, languished, or even expired, without assistance, without alleviation.

Throughout the day a confused humming of lamentable entreaties was to be heard in the streets; at night, a murmur of groans, broken now and then by howls, suddenly bursting upon the ear, by loud and long accents of complaint, or by deep tones of invocation, terminating in wild shrieks.

It is worthy of remark, that in such an extremity of want, in such a variety of complaints, not one attempt was ever made, not one rumour ever raised, to bring about an insurrection: at least, we find not the least mention of such a thing. Yet, among those who lived and died in this way, there was a great number of men brought up to anything rather than patient endurance; there were, indeed, in hundreds, those very same individuals who, on St. Martin's-day, had made themselves so sensibly felt. Nor must it be imagined that the example of those four unhappy men, who bore in their own persons the penalty of all, was what now kept them in awe: what force could, not the sight, but the remembrance, of punishments have, on the minds of a dispersed and reunited multitude, who saw themselves condemned, as it were, to a prolonged punishment, which they were already suffering? But so constituted are we mortals in general, that we rebel indignantly and violently against medium evils, and bow in silence under extreme ones; we bear, not with resignation, but stupefaction, the weight of what at first we had called insupportable.

The void daily created by mortality in this deplorable multitude, was every day more than replenished: there was an incessant concourse, first from the neighbouring towns, then from all the country, then from the cities of the state, to the very borders, even, of others. And in the meanwhile, old inhabitants were every day leaving Milan; some to withdraw from the sight of so much suffering; others, being driven from the field, so to say, by new competitors for support, in a last desperate attempt to find sustenance elsewhere, anywhere—anywhere, at least, where the crowds and rivalry in begging were not so dense and importunate. These oppositely bound travellers met each other on their different routes, all spectacles of horror, and disastrous omens of the fate that awaited them at the end of their respective journeys. They prosecuted, however, the way they had once undertaken, if no longer with the hope of changing their condition, at least not to return to a scene which had become odious to them, and to avoid the sight of a place where they had been reduced to despair. Some, even, whose last vital powers were destroyed by abstinence, sank down by the way, and were left where they expired, still more fatal tokens to their brethren in condition,—an object of horror, perhaps of reproach, to other passengers. 'I saw,' writes Ripamonti, 'lying in the road surrounding the wall, the corpse of a woman . . . Half-eaten grass was hanging out of her mouth, and her contaminated lips still made almost a convulsive effort . . . She had a bundle at her back, and, secured by bands to her bosom, hung an infant, which with bitter cries was calling for the breast . . . Some compassionate persons had come up, who, raising the miserable little creature from the ground, brought it some sustenance, thus fulfilling in a measure the first maternal office.'

The contrast of gay clothing and rags, of superfluity and misery, the ordinary spectacle of ordinary times, had, in these peculiar ones, entirely ceased. Rags and misery had invaded almost every rank; and what now at all distinguished them was but an appearance of frugal mediocrity. The nobility were seen walking in becoming and modest, or even dirty and shabby, clothing; some, because the common causes of misery had affected their fortunes to this degree, or even given a finishing hand to fortunes already much dilapidated; others, either from fear of provoking public desperation by display, or from a feeling of shame at thus insulting public calamity. Petty tyrants, once hated and looked upon with awe, and accustomed to wander about with an insolent train of bravoes at their heels, now walked almost unattended, crestfallen, and with a look which seemed to offer and entreat peace. Others who, in prosperity also, had been of more humane disposition and more civil bearing, appeared nevertheless confused, distracted, and, as it were, overpowered by the continual view of a calamity, which excluded not only the possibility of relief, but, we may almost say, the powers of commiseration. They who were able to afford any assistance, were obliged to make a melancholy choice between hunger and hunger, between extremity and extremity. And no sooner was a compassionate hand seen to drop anything into the hand of a wretched beggar, than a strife immediately rose between the other miserable wretches; those who retained still a little strength, pressed forward to solicit with more importunity; the feeble, aged people, and children, extended their emaciated hands; mothers, from behind, raised and held out their weeping infants, miserably clad in their tattered swaddling-clothes, and reclining languidly in their arms.

Thus passed the winter and the spring: for some time the Board of Health had been remonstrating with the Board of Provision, on the danger of contagion which threatened the city from so much suffering, accumulated in, and spread throughout it; and had proposed, that all the vagabond mendicants should be collected together into the different hospitals. While this plan was being debated upon and approved; while the means, methods, and places, were being devised to put it into effect, corpses multiplied in the streets, every day bringing additional numbers; and in proportion to this, followed all the other concomitants of loathsomeness, misery, and danger. It was proposed by the Board of Provision as more practicable and expeditious, to assemble all the mendicants, healthy or diseased, in one place, the Lazzaretto, and there to feed and maintain them at the public expense; and this expedient was resolved upon, in spite of the Board of Health, which objected that, in such an assemblage, the evil would only be increased which they wished to obviate.

The Lazzaretto at Milan (perchance this story should fall into the hands of any one who does not know it, either by sight or description), is a quadrilateral and almost equilateral enclosure, outside the city, to the left of the gate called the Porta Orientale, and separated from the bastions by the width of the fosse, a road of circumvallation, and a smaller moat running round the building itself. The two larger sides extend to about the length of five hundred paces; the other two, perhaps, fifteen less; all, on the outside, divided into little rooms on the ground floor; while, running round three sides of the interior, is a continuous, vaulted portico, supported by small light pillars. The number of the rooms was once two hundred and eighty-eight, some larger than others; but in our days, a large aperture made in the middle, and a smaller one in one corner of the side that flanks the highway, have destroyed I know not how many.

At the period of our story there were only two entrances, one in the centre of the side which looked upon the city-wall, the other facing it in the opposite side. In the midst of the clear and open space within, rose a small octagonal temple, which is still in existence. The primary object of the whole edifice, begun in the year 1489, with a private legacy, and afterwards continued with the public money, and that of other testators and donors, was, as the name itself denotes, to afford a place of refuge, in cases of necessity, to such as were ill of the plague; which, for some time before that epoch, and for a long while after it, usually appeared two, four, six, or eight times a century, now in this, now in that European country, sometimes taking a great part of it, sometimes even traversing the whole, so to say, from one end to the other. At the time of which we are speaking, the Lazzaretto was merely used as a repository for goods suspected of conveying infection.

To prepare it on this occasion for its new destination, the usual forms were rapidly gone through; and having hastily made the necessary cleansings and prescribed experiments, all the goods were immediately liberated. Straw was spread out in every room, purchases were made of provisions, of whatever kind and in whatever quantities they could be procured; and, by a public edict, all beggars were invited to take shelter there.

Many willingly accepted the offer; all those who were lying ill in the streets or squares were carried thither; and in a few days there was altogether more than three thousand who had taken refuge there. But far more were they who remained behind. Whether it were that each one expected to see others go, and hoped that there would thus be a smaller party left to share the relief which could be obtained in the city, or from a natural repugnance to confinement, or from the distrust felt by the poor of all that is proposed to them by those who possess wealth or power (a distrust always proportioned to the common ignorance of those who feel it and those who inspire it—to the number of the poor, and the strictness of the regulations), or from the actual knowledge of what the offered benefit was in reality, or whether it were all these put together, or whatever else it might be, certain it is that the greater number, paying no attention to the invitation, continued to wander about begging through the city. This being perceived, it was considered advisable to pass from invitation to force. Bailiffs were sent round, who drove all the mendicants to the Lazzaretto, who even brought those bound who made any resistance; for each one of whom a premium of ten *soldi* [1] was assigned to them; so true is it that, even in the scarcest times, public money may always be found to be employed foolishly. And though, as it had been imagined, and even expressly intended by the provision, a certain number of beggars made their escape from the city to go and live or die elsewhere, if it were only in freedom, yet the compulsion was such, that in a short time the number of refugees, what with guests and prisoners, amounted to nearly ten thousand.

We must naturally suppose that the women and children were lodged in separate quarters, though the records of the time make no mention of it. Regulations, besides, and provisions for the maintenance of good order, would certainly not be wanting; but the reader may imagine what kind of order could be established and maintained, especially in those times, and under such circumstances, in so vast and diversified an assemblage, where the unwilling inmates associated with the willing,—those to whom mendicity was a mournful necessity, and subject of shame, with those whose trade and custom it had long been; many who had been trained to honest industry in the fields or warehouses, with many others who had been brought up in the streets, taverns, or some other vile resorts, to idleness, roguery, scoffing, and violence.

How they fared all together for lodging and food, might be sadly conjectured, had we no positive information on the subject; but we have it. They slept crammed and heaped together, by twenty and thirty in each little cell, or lying under the porticoes, on pallets of putrid and fetid straw, or even on the bare ground: it was ordered, indeed, that the straw should be fresh and abundant, and frequently changed; but, in fact, it was scarce, bad, and never renewed. There were orders, likewise, that the bread should be of a good quality; for what administration ever decreed that bad com-

[1] Tenpence.

modities should be manufactured and dispensed? But how obtain, under the existing circumstances, and in such confusion, what in ordinary cases could not have been procured, even for a less enormous demand? It was affirmed, as we find in the records of the times, that the bread of the Lazzaretto was adulterated with heavy but unnutritious materials; and it is too likely that this was not a mere unfounded complaint. There was also a great deficiency of water, that is to say, of wholesome spring-water: the common beverage must have been from the moat that washed the walls of the enclosure, shallow, slow, in places even muddy; and become, too, what the use and the vicinity of such and so vast a multitude must have rendered it.

To all these causes of mortality, the more effective as they acted upon diseased or enfeebled bodies, was added the most unpropitious season; obstinate rains, followed by a drought still more obstinate, and with it, an anticipated and violent heat. To these evils were added a keen sense of them; the tedium and frenzy of captivity; a longing to return to old habits; grief for departed friends; anxious remembrances of absent ones; disgust and dread, inspired by the misery of others; and many other feelings of despair, or madness, either brought with them, or first awakened there; together with the apprehension and constant spectacle of death, which was rendered frequent by so many causes, and had become itself a new and powerful cause. Nor is it to be wondered at, that mortality increased and prevailed in this confinement, to such a degree, as to assume the aspect, and with many the name, of pestilence. Whether it were that the union and augmentation of all these causes only served to increase the activity of a merely epidemic influenza, or (as it seems frequently to happen in less severe and prolonged famines) that a real contagion had gained ground there, which, in bodies disposed and prepared for it by the scarcity and bad quality of food, by unwholesome air, by uncleanliness, by exhaustion, and by consternation, found its own temperature, so to say, and its own season;— the conditions, in short, necessary for its birth, preservation, and multiplication; (if one unskilled in these matters may be allowed to put forth these sentiments, after the hypothesis propounded by certain doctors of medicine, and re-propounded at length, with many arguments, and much caution, by one as diligent as he is talented;[2]) or whether, again, the contagion first broke out in the Lazzaretto itself, as, according to an obscure and inexact account, it seems was thought by the physicians of the Board of Health; or whether it were actually in existence and hovering about before that time, (which seems, perhaps, the most likely, if we recollect that the scarcity was already universal, and of long date, and the mortality frequent), and that, when once introduced there, it spread with fresh and terrible rapidity, owing to the accumulation of bodies, which were rendered still more disposed to receive it, from the increasing efficacy of the other causes; whichever of these conjectures be the true one, the daily number of deaths in the Lazzaretto shortly exceeded a hundred.

While all the rest here was languor, suffering, fear, lamentations, and horror, in the Board of Provision there was shame, stupefaction, and incertitude. They consulted and listened to the advice of the Board of Health, and could find no other course than to undo what had been done with so much preparation, so much expense, and so much unwillingness. They opened the Lazzaretto, and dismissed all who had any strength remaining, who made their escape with a kind of furious joy. The city once more resounded with its former clamour, but more feeble and interrupted; it again saw that more diminished, and 'more miserable' crowd, says Ripamonti, when remembering how it had been thus diminished. The sick were transported to Santa Maria della Stella, at that time an hospital for beggars; and here the greater part perished.

In the mean while, however, the blessed fields began to whiten. The mendicants from the country set off, each one to his own parts, for this much-desired harvest. The good Federigo dismissed them with a last effort and new invention of charity; to every countryman who presented himself at the archiepiscopal palace, he gave a *giulio*,[3] and a reaping sickle.

With the harvest, the scarcity at length ceased; the mortality, however, whether epidemic or contagious, though decreasing from day to day, was protracted even into the season of autumn. It was

[2] *On the Spotted Plague . . . and on other contagions in general,* by the learned F. Enrico Acerbi, Ch. iii. § 1 and 2.

[3] A piece of money, in value about sixpence sterling.

on the point of vanishing, when, behold, a new scourge made its appearance.

Many important events, of that kind which are more peculiarly denominated historical facts, had taken place during this interval. The Cardinal Richelieu having, as we have said, taken La Rochelle, and having patched up an accommodation with the King of England, had proposed and carried by his potential voice in the French Council, that some effectual succour should be rendered to the Duke of Nevers, and had, at the same time, persuaded the King himself to conduct the expedition in person. While making the necessary preparations, the Count de Nassau, imperial commissary, suggested at Mantua to the new Duke, that he should give up the states into Ferdinand's hands, or that the latter would send an army to occupy them. The Duke, who, in more desperate circumstances, had scorned to accept so hard and little-to-be-trusted a condition, and encouraged now by the approaching aid from France, scorned it so much the more; but in terms in which the *no* was wrapped up and kept at a distance, as much as might be, and with even more apparent, but less costly, proposals of submission.

The commissary took his departure, threatening that they would come to decide it by force. In the month of March the Cardinal Richelieu made a descent, with the King, at the head of an army; he demanded a passage from the Duke of Savoy, entered upon a treaty, which, however, was not concluded; and after an encounter, in which the French had the advantage, again negotiated and concluded an agreement, in which the Duke stipulated, among other things, that Cordova should raise the siege of Casale; pledging himself, in case of his refusal, to join with the French, for the invasion of the Duchy of Milan. Don Gonzalo, reckoning it, too, a very cheap bargain, withdrew his army from Casale, which was immediately entered by a body of French to reinforce the garrison.

It was on this occasion that Achillini addressed to King Louis his famous sonnet:—

'Sudate, o, fochi, a preparar metalli;'

and another, in which he exhorted him to repair immediately to the deliverance of Terra-Santa. But there is a fatal decree, that the advice of poets should not be followed; and if any doings happen to be found in history, in conformity with their suggestions, we may safely affirm that they were resolved upon beforehand. The Cardinal Richelieu determined, instead, to return to France on affairs which he considered more urgent. Girolamo Soranzo, the Venetian envoy, urged, indeed, much stronger reasons to divert his resolution; but the King and the Cardinal, paying no more attention to his prose than to the verses of Achillini, returned with the greater part of the army, leaving only six thousand men in Susa, to occupy the pass, and maintain the treaty.

While this army was retiring on one hand, that of Ferdinand, headed by the Count di Collalto, approached on the other; it invaded the country of Grisons and Valtelline, and prepared to descend upon the Milanese. Besides all the terrors to which the announcement of such a migration gave rise, the alarming rumour got abroad, and was confirmed by express tidings, that the plague was lurking in the army, of which there were always some symptoms at that time in the German troops, according to Varchi, in speaking of that which, a century before, had been introduced into Florence by their means. Alessandro Tadino, one of the Conservators of the public health, (there were six, besides the president; four magistrates and two physicians), was commissioned by the Board, as he himself relates in his *Ragguaglio* already quoted,[4] to remonstrate with the governor on the fearful danger which threatened the country, if that vast multitude obtained a passage through it to Mantua, as the report ran. From the whole behaviour of Don Gonzalo, it appears he had a great desire to make a figure in history, which, in truth, cannot avoid giving an account of some of his doings; but (as often happens) it knew not, or took no pains to record, an act of his, the most worthy of remembrance and attention—the answer he gave to the physician Tadino on this occasion. He replied, 'That he knew not what to do; that the reasons of interest and reputation which had caused the march of that army, were of greater weight than the represented danger; but that, nevertheless, he must try to remedy it as well as he could, and must then trust in Providence.'

[4] Account of the Origin and Daily Progress of the great Plague, communicated by infection, poison, and sorcery, which visited the City of Milan, &c.—*Milan*, 1648, p. 16.

To remedy it, therefore, as well as he could, the two physicians of the Board of Health (the above-mentioned Tadino, and Senatore Settala, son of the celebrated Lodovico), proposed in this committee to prohibit, under severe penalties, the purchase of any kind of commodities whatsoever from the soldiers who were about to pass; but it was impossible to make the president understand the advantage of such a regulation; 'A kind-hearted man,' says Tadino,[5] 'who would not believe that the probability of the death of so many thousands must follow upon traffic with these people and their goods.' We quote this extract, as one of the singularities of those times: for certainly, since there have been Boards of Health, no other president of one of them ever happened to use such an argument—if argument it be.

As to Don Gonzalo, this reply was one of his last performances here; for the ill success of the war, promoted and conducted chiefly by himself, was the cause of his being removed from his post, in the course of the summer. On his departure from Milan, a circumstance occurred which, by some contemporary writer, is noticed as the first of that kind that ever happened there to a man of his rank. On leaving the palace, called the City Palace, surrounded by a great company of noblemen, he encountered a crowd of the populace, some of whom preceded him in the way, and others followed behind, shouting, and upbraiding him with imprecations, as being the cause of the famine they had suffered, by the permission, they said, he had given to carry corn and rice out of the city. At his carriage, which was following the party, they hurled worse missiles than words: stones, bricks, cabbage-stalks, rubbish of all sorts—the usual ammunition, in short, of these expeditions. Repulsed by the guards, they drew back; but only to run, augmented on the way by many fresh parties, to prepare themselves at the Porta Ticinese, through which gate he would shortly have to pass in his carriage. When the equipage made its appearance, followed by many others, they showered down upon them all, both with hands and slings, a perfect torrent of stones. The matter, however, went no further.

The Marquis Ambrogio Spinola was despatched to supply his

5 Page 17.

place, whose name had already acquired, in the wars of Flanders, the military renown it still retains.

In the mean while, the German army had received definite orders to march forward to Mantua, and, in the month of September, they entered the Duchy of Milan.

The military forces in those days were still chiefly composed of volunteers, enlisted under commanders by profession, sometimes by commission from this or that prince; sometimes, also, on their own account, that they might dispose of themselves and their men together. These were attracted to this employment, much less by the pay, than by the hopes of plunder, and all the gratifications of military license. There is no fixed and universal discipline in an army so composed; nor was it possible easily to bring into concordance the independent authority of so many different leaders. These too, in particular, were not very nice on the subject of discipline, nor, had they been willing, can we see how they could have succeeded in establishing and maintaining it; for soldiers of this kind would either have revolted against an innovating commander, who should have taken it into his head to abolish pillage, or, at least, would have left him by himself to defend his colours. Besides, as the princes who hired these troops sought rather to have hands enough to secure their undertakings, than to proportion the number to their means of remuneration, which were generally very scanty, so the payments were for the most part late, on account, and by little at a time; and the spoils of the countries they were making war upon, or over-ran, became, as it were, a compensation tacitly accorded to them. It was a saying of Wallenstein's, scarcely less celebrated than his name, that it was easier to maintain an army of a hundred thousand men, than one of twelve thousand. And that of which we are speaking, was in great part, composed of men who, under his command, had desolated Germany in that war, so celebrated among other wars both for itself and for its effects, which afterwards took its name from the thirty years of its duration; it was then the eleventh year. There was, besides, his own special regiment, conducted by one of his lieutenants; of the other leaders, the greatest part had commanded under him; and there were, also, more than one of those who, four years afterwards, had to assist in bringing him to that evil end which everybody knows.

There were twenty-eight thousand foot, and seven thousand horse; and in descending from Valtelline to reach the territory of Mantua, they had to follow, more or less closely, the course of the Adda where it forms two branches of a lake, then again as a river to its junction with the Po, and afterwards for some distance along the banks of this river; on the whole eight days' march in the Duchy of Milan.

A great part of the inhabitants retired to the mountains, taking with them their most valuable effects, and driving their cattle before them; others stayed behind, either to tend upon some sick person, or to defend their houses from the flames, or to keep an eye upon precious things which they had concealed under-ground; some because they had nothing to lose; and a few villains, also, to make acquisitions. When the first detachment arrived at the village where they were to halt, they quickly spread themselves through this and the neighbouring ones, and plundered them directly; all that could be eaten or carried off, disappeared: not to speak of the destruction of the rest, of the fields laid waste, of the houses given to the flames, the blows, the wounds, the rapes, committed.

All the expedients, all the defences employed to save property, often proved useless, sometimes even more injurious to the owners. The soldiers, far more practised in the stratagems of this kind of war, too, rummaged every corner of the dwellings; tore down walls; easily discovered in the gardens the newly disturbed soil; penetrated even to the hills, to carry off the cattle; went into caves, under the guidance of some villain, as we have said, in search of any wealthy inhabitant who might be concealed there; despoiled his person, dragged him to his house, and, by dint of threats and blows, compelled him to point out his hidden treasure.

At length, however, they took their departure, and the distant sounds of drums or trumpets gradually died away on the ear: this was followed by a few hours of death-like calm: and then a new hateful clashing of arms, a new hateful rumbling, announced another squadron. These, no longer finding anything to plunder, applied themselves with the more fury to make destruction and havoc of the rest, burning furniture, door-posts, beams, casks, wine-vats, and sometimes even the houses; they seized and ill-used the inhabitants with double ferocity;—and so on, from worse to worse, for twenty days; for into this number of detachments the army was divided.

Colico was the first town of the Duchy invaded by these fiends; afterwards, they threw themselves into Belano; thence they entered and spread themselves through Valsassina, and then poured down into the territory of Lecco.

CHAPTER XXIX

A**ND** here we find that persons of our acquaintance were
sharers in the wide-spread alarm.

One who saw not Don Abbondio, the day that the news
were suddenly spread of the descent of the army, of its near approach, and destructive proceedings, knows very little of what embarrassment and consternation really are. They are coming! there are
thirty, there are forty, there are fifty thousand! they are devils, here-
tics, antichrists! they've sacked Cortenuova! they've set fire to Prim-
aluna! they've devastated Introbbio, Pasturo, Barsio! they've been
seen at Balabbio! they'll be here to-morrow!—such were the reports
that passed from mouth to mouth; some hurrying to and fro, others
standing in little parties; together with tumultuous consultations,
hesitation whether to fly or remain, the women assembling in groups,
and all utterly at a loss what to do. Don Abbondio, who had resolved
before any one else, and more than any one else, to fly, by any possible
mode of flight, and to any conceivable place of retreat, discovered
insuperable obstacles and fearful dangers. 'What shall I do?' exclaimed he: 'Where shall I go?' The mountains, letting alone the
difficulty of getting there, were not secure: it was well known that
the German foot soldiers climbed them like cats, where they had
the least indication or hope of finding booty. The lake was wide;
there was a very high wind: besides, the greater part of the boatmen,
fearing they might be compelled to convey soldiers or baggage, had
retreated with their boats to the opposite side: the few that had
remained, were gone off overladen with people, and, distressed by
their own weight and the violence of the storm, were considered
in greater peril every moment. It was impossible to find a vehicle,
horse, or conveyance of any kind, to carry him away from the road
the army had to traverse; and on foot Don Abbondio could not
manage any great distance, and feared being overtaken by the way.
The confines of the Bergamascan territory were not so very far off

but that his limbs could have borne him thither at a stretch; but a report had been already spread, that a squadron of *cappelletti* had been
despatched from Bergamo in haste, who were occupying the borders
to keep the German troops in order; and those were neither more
nor less devils incarnate than these, and on their part did the worst
they could. The poor man ran through the house with eyes starting
from his head, and half out of his senses; he kept following Perpetua
to concert some plan with her; but Perpetua, busied in collecting the
most valuable household goods, and hiding them under the floor,
or in any other out-of-the-way place, pushed by hurriedly, eager and
pre-occupied, with her hands or arms full, and replied: 'I shall have
done directly putting these things away safely, and then we'll do what
others do.' Don Abbondio would have detained her, and discussed
with her the different courses to be adopted; but she, what with
her business, and her hurry, and the fear which she, too, felt within,
and the vexation which that of her master excited, was, in this juncture, less tractable than she had ever been before. 'Others do the best
they can; and so will we. I beg your pardon: but you are good for
nothing but to hinder one. Do you think that others haven't skins
to save, too? That the soldiers are only coming to fight with you?
You might even lend a hand at such a time, instead of coming
crying and bothering at one's feet.' With these and similar answers
she at length got rid of him, having already determined, when this
bustling operation was finished as well as might be, to take him by
the arm like a child, and to drag him along to one of the mountains.
Left thus alone, he retreated to the window, looked, listened; or,
seeing some one passing, cried out in a half-crying and half-reproach-
ful tone: 'Do your poor Curate this kindness, to seek some horse,
some mule, some ass, for him! Is it possible that nobody will help
me! Oh, what people! Wait for me, at least, that I may go with you!
wait till you are fifteen or twenty, to take me with you, that I may
not be quite forsaken! Will you leave me in the hand of dogs?
Don't you know they are nearly all Lutherans, who think it a meri-
torious deed to murder a priest? Will you leave me here to be
martyred? Oh, what a set! Oh, what a set!'

But to whom did he address these words? To men who were
passing along bending under the weight of their humble furniture,

and their thoughts turned towards that which they were leaving at home exposed to plunder; one driving before him a young cow, another dragging after him his children, also laden as heavily as they could bear, while his wife carried in her arms such as were unable to walk. Some went on their way without replying or looking up; others said, 'Eh, sir, you too must do as you can! happy you, who have no family to think for! you must help yourself, and do the best you can.'

'Oh, poor me!' exclaimed Don Abbondio; 'oh, what people! what hard hearts! There's no charity: everybody thinks of himself; but nobody'll think for me!' And he set off again in search of Perpetua.

'Oh, I just wanted you!' said she. 'Your money?'

'What shall we do?'

'Give it me, and I'll go and bury it in the garden here by the house, together with the silver and knives and forks.'

'But . . .'

'But, but; give it here; keep a few pence for whatever may happen; and then leave it to me.'

Don Abbondio obeyed, went to his trunk, took out his little treasure, and handed it to Perpetua, who said: 'I'm going to bury it in the garden, at the foot of the fig-tree;' and went out. Soon afterwards she reappeared with a packet in her hand containing some provision for the appetite, and a small empty basket, in the bottom of which she hastily placed a little linen for herself and her master, saying, at the same time, 'You'll carry the breviary, at least!'

'But where are we going?'

'Where are all the rest going? First of all, we'll go into the street; and there we shall see and hear what's best to be done.'

At this moment Agnese entered, also carrying a basket slung over her shoulder, and with the air of one who comes to make an important proposal.

Agnese herself, equally resolved not to await guests of this sort, alone as she was in the house, and with a little of the money of the Unnamed still left, had been hesitating for some time about a place of retreat. The remainder of those *scudi,* which in the months of famine had been of such use to her, was now the principal cause of her anxiety and irresolution, from having heard how, in the already

invaded countries, those who had any money had found themselves
in a worse condition than anybody else, exposed alike to the violence
of the strangers and the treachery of their fellow-countrymen. True
it was that she had confided to no one, save Don Abbondio, the
wealth that had fallen, so to say, into her lap; to him she had applied,
from time to time, to change her a *scudo* into silver, always leaving
him something to give to some one who was poorer than herself.
But hidden riches, particularly with one who is not accustomed to
handle much, keep the possessor in continual suspicion of the suspicion of others. While, however, she was going about hiding here
and there, as she best could, what she could not manage to take with
her, and thinking about the *scudi,* which she kept sewn up in her
stays, she remembered that, together with them, the Unnamed had
sent her the most ample proffers of service; she remembered what
she had heard related about his castle's being in so secure a situation,
where nothing could reach it, against its owner's will, but birds; and
she resolved to go and seek an asylum there. Wondering how she
was to make herself known to the Signor, Don Abbondio quickly
occurred to her mind; who, after the conversation we have related
with the Archbishop, had always shown her particular marks of
kindness; the more heartily, as he could do so without committing
himself to any one, and, the two young people being far enough
off, the probability was also distant that a request would be made
him which would have put this kindness to a very dangerous test.
Thinking that in such confusion the poor man would be still more
perplexed and dismayed than herself, and that this course might
appear desirable also to him, she came to make the proposal. Finding him with Perpetua, she suggested it to them both together.

'What say you to it, Perpetua?' asked Don Abbondio.

'I say that it is an inspiration from Heaven, and that we mustn't
lose time, but set off at once on our journey.'

'And then . . .'

'And then, and then, when we get there, we shall find ourselves
very well satisfied. It is well known now that the Signor desires
nothing more than to benefit his fellow-creatures; and I've no doubt
he'll be glad to receive us. There, on the borders, and as it were in the
air, the soldiers certainly won't come. And then, and then, we shall

find something to eat there; for up in the mountains, when this little store is gone,' and, so saying, she placed it in the basket upon the linen, 'we should find ourselves very badly off.'

'He's converted, he's really converted, isn't he?'

'Why should we doubt it any longer, after all that's known about him, nay, after what you yourself have seen?'

'And supposing we should be going to put ourselves in prison?'

'What prison? I declare, with all your silly objections, (I beg your pardon), you'd never come to any conclusion. Well done, Agnese! it was certainly a capital thought of yours!' And setting the basket on a table, she passed her arms through the straps, and lifted it upon her back.

'Couldn't we find some man,' said Don Abbondio, 'who would come with us as a guard to his Curate? If we should meet any ruffians, for there are plenty of them roving about, what help could you two give me?'

'Another plan, to waste time!' exclaimed Perpetua. 'To go now and look for a man, when everybody has to mind himself! Up with you; go and get your breviary and hat, and let us set off.'

Don Abbondio obeyed, and soon returned with the breviary under his arm, his hat on his head, and his staff in his hand; and the three companions went out by a little door which led into the churchyard. Perpetua locked it after her, rather not to neglect an accustomed form, than from any faith she placed in bolts and door-posts, and put the key in her pocket. Don Abbondio cast a glance at the church in passing, and muttered between his teeth: 'It's the people's business to take care of it, for it's they who use it. If they've the least love for their church, they'll see to it; if they've not, why, it's their own look-out.'

They took the road through the fields, each silently pursuing his way, absorbed in thought on his own particular circumstances, and looking rather narrowly around; more particularly Don Abbondio, who was in continual apprehension of the apparition of some suspicious figure, or something not to be trusted. However, they encountered no one: all the people were either in their houses to guard them, to prepare bundles, and to put away goods, or on the roads which led directly to the mountain-heights.

After heaving a few deep sighs, and then giving vent to his vexation in an interjection or two, Don Abbondio began to grumble more connectedly. He quarrelled with the duke of Nevers, who might have been enjoying himself in France, and playing the prince there, yet was determined to be duke of Mantua in spite of the world; with the Emperor, who ought to have sense for the follies of others, to let matters take their own course, and not stand so much upon punctilio; for, after all, he would always be Emperor, whether Titius or Sempronius were duke of Mantua; and, above all, with the governor, whose business it was to do everything he could to avert these scourges of the country, while, in fact, he was the very person to invite them—all from the pleasure he took in making war. 'I wish,' said he, 'that these gentry were here to see and try how pleasant it is. They will have a fine account to render! But, in the mean while, we have to bear it who have no blame in the matter.'

'Do let these people alone, for they'll never come to help us,' said Perpetua. 'This is some of your usual prating, (I beg your pardon), which just comes to nothing. What rather gives me uneasiness . . .'

'What's the matter?'

Perpetua, who had been leisurely going over in her mind, during their walk, her hasty packing and stowing away, now began her lamentations at having forgotten such a thing, and badly concealed such another; here she had left traces which might serve as a clue to the robbers, there . . .

'Well done!' cried Don Abbondio, gradually sufficiently relieved from fear for his life to allow of anxiety for his worldly goods and chattels: 'Well done! Did you really do so? Where was your head?'

'What!' exclaimed Perpetua, coming to an abrupt pause for a moment, and resting her hands on her sides, as well as the basket she carried would allow: 'What! do you begin now to scold me in this way, when it was you who almost turned my brain, instead of helping and encouraging me? I believe I've taken more care of the things of the house than of my own; I'd not a creature to lend me a hand; I've been obliged to *play the parts of both Martha and Magdalene;* if anything goes wrong, I've nothing to say: I've done more than my duty now.'

Agnese interrupted these disputes, by beginning, in her turn, to talk about her own grievances; she lamented not so much the trouble and damage, as finding all her hopes of soon meeting her Lucia dashed to the ground: for, the reader may remember, this was the very autumn on which they had so long calculated. It was not at all likely that Donna Prassede would come to reside in her country-house in that neighbourhood, under such circumstances: on the contrary, she would more probably have left it, had she happened to be there, as all the other residents in the country were doing.

The sight of the different places they passed brought these thoughts to Agnese's mind more vividly, and increased the ardour of her desires. Leaving the footpath through the fields, they had taken the public road, the very same along which Agnese had come when bringing home her daughter for so short a time, after having stayed with her at the tailor's. The village was already in sight.

'We will just say "how d'ye do" to these good people,' said Agnese.

'Yes, and rest there a little; for I begin to have had enough of this basket; and to get a mouthful to eat too,' said Perpetua.

'On condition we don't lose time; for we are not journeying for our amusement,' concluded Don Abbondio.

They were received with open arms, and welcomed with much pleasure; it reminded them of a former deed of benevolence. 'Do good to as many as you can,' here remarks our author, 'and you will the more frequently happen to meet with countenances which bring you pleasure.'

Agnese burst into a flood of tears on embracing the good woman, which was a great relief to her; and could only reply with sobs to the questions which she and her husband put about Lucia.

'She is better off than we are,' said Don Abbondio; 'she's at Milan, out of all danger, and far away from these diabolical dangers.'

'Are the Signor Curate, and his companion, making their escape, then?' asked the tailor.

'Certainly,' replied both master and servant, in one breath.

'Oh, how I pity you both!'

'We are on our way,' said Don Abbondio, 'to the Castle of * * *.'

'That's a very good thought; you'll be as safe there as in Paradise.'

'And you've no fear here?' said Don Abbondio.

'I'll tell you, Signor Curate: they won't have to come here to halt, or, as you know the saying is, in polite language, *in ospitazione:* we are too much out of their road, thank Heaven. At the worst, there'll only be a little party of foragers, which God forbid!—but, in any case, there's plenty of time. We shall first hear the intelligence from the other unfortunate towns, where they go to take up their quarters.'

It was determined to stop here and take a little rest; and as it was just the dinner-hour, 'My friends,' said the tailor, 'will do me the favour of sharing my poor table: at any rate, you will have a hearty welcome.'

Perpetua said she had brought some refreshment with them; and after exchanging a few complimentary speeches, they agreed to put all together, and dine in company.

The children gathered with great glee round their old friend Agnese. Very soon, however, the tailor desired one of his little girls (the same that had carried that gift of charity to the widow Maria; who knows if any reader remembers it?) to go and shell a few early chestnuts, which were deposited in one corner, and then put them to roast.

'And you,' said he to a little boy, 'go into the garden, and shake the peach-tree till some of the fruit falls, and bring them all here; go. And you,' said he to another, 'go, climb the fig-tree, and gather a few of the ripest figs. You know that business too well already.' He himself went to tap a little barrel of wine; his wife to fetch a clean table-cloth; Perpetua took out the provisions; the table was spread; a napkin and earthenware plate were placed at the most honourable seat for Don Abbondio, with a knife and fork which Perpetua had in the basket; the dinner was dished, and the party seated themselves at the table, and partook of the repast, if not with great merriment, at least with much more than any of the guests had anticipated enjoying that day.

'What say you, Signor Curate, to a turn out of this sort?' said the tailor; 'I could fancy I was reading the history of the Moors in France.'

'What say I? To think that even this trouble should fall to my lot!'

'Well, you've chosen a good asylum,' resumed his host; 'people would be puzzled to get up there by force. And you'll find company there; it's already reported that many have retreated thither, and many more are daily arriving.'

'I would fain hope,' said Don Abbondio, 'that we shall be well received. I know this brave Signor; and when I once had the pleasure of being in his company, he was so exceedingly polite.'

'And he sent word to me,' said Agnese, 'by his most illustrious Lordship, that if ever I wanted anything, I had only to go to him.'

'A great and wonderful conversion!' resumed Don Abbondio: 'and does he really continue to persevere?'

'Oh yes,' said the tailor; and he began to speak at some length upon the holy life of the Unnamed, and how, from being a scourge to the country, he had become its example and benefactor.

'And all those people he kept under him . . . that household . . .' rejoined Don Abbondio, who had more than once heard something about them, but had never been sufficiently assured of the truth.

'They are most of them dismissed,' replied the tailor; 'and they who remain have altered their habits in a wonderful way! In short, this castle has become like the Thebaid. You, Signor, understand these things.'

He then began to recall, with Agnese, the visit of the Cardinal. 'A great man,' said he, 'a great man! Pity that he left us so hastily; for I did not, and could not, do him any honour. How often I wish I could speak to him again, a little more at my ease.'

Having left the table, he made them observe an engraved likeness of the Cardinal, which he kept hung up on one of the door-posts, in veneration for the person, and also that he might be able to say to any visitor, that the portrait did not resemble him; for he himself had had an opportunity of studying the Cardinal, close by, and at his leisure, in that very room.

'Did they mean this thing here for him?' said Agnese. 'It's like him in dress; but . . .'

'It doesn't resemble him, does it?' said the tailor. 'I always say so, too; but it bears his name, if nothing more; it serves as a remembrance.'

Don Abbondio was in a great hurry to be going; the tailor undertook to find a conveyance to carry them to the foot of the ascent, and having gone in search of one, shortly returned to say that it was coming. Then, turning to Don Abbondio, he added, 'Signor Curate, if you should ever like to take a book with you up there to pass away the time, I shall be glad to serve you in my poor way; for I sometimes amuse myself a little with reading. They're not things to suit you, being all in the vulgar tongue; but, perhaps . . .'

'Thank you, thank you,' replied Don Abbondio; 'under present circumstances, one has hardly brains enough to attend to what we are bid to read.'

While offering and refusing thanks, and exchanging condolence, good wishes, invitations, and promises to make another stay there on their return, the cart arrived at the front door. Putting in their baskets, the travelling party mounted after them, and undertook, with rather more ease and tranquillity of mind, the second half of their journey.

The tailor had related the truth to Don Abbondio about the Unnamed. From the day on which we left him, he had steadily persevered in the course he had proposed to himself, atoning for wrongs, seeking peace, relieving the poor, and performing every good work for which an opportunity presented itself. The courage he had formerly manifested in offence and defence now showed itself in abstaining from both one and the other. He had laid down all his weapons, and always walked alone, willing to encounter the possible consequences of the many deeds of violence he had committed, and persuaded that it would be the commission of an additional one to employ force in defence of a life which owed so much to so many creditors; and persuaded, too, that every evil which might be done to him would be an offence offered to God, but, with respect to himself, a just retribution; and that he, above all, had no right to constitute himself a punisher of such offences. However, he had continued not less inviolate than when he had kept in readiness for his security, so many armed hands, and his own. The remembrance of his former ferocity, and the sight of his present meekness, one of which, it might have been expected, would have left so many longings for revenge, while the other rendered that revenge so easy, conspired, instead, to procure and maintain for him an admiration, which was the principal guarantee for his safety. He was that very man whom no one could humble, and who had now humbled himself. Every feeling of rancour, therefore, formerly irritated by his contemptuous behaviour, and by the fears of others, vanished before this new humility: they whom he had offended had now obtained, beyond all expectation, and without danger, a satisfaction which they could not have promised themselves from the most complete revenge—the satisfaction of seeing such a man mourning over the wrongs he had committed, and participating, so to say, in their indignation. More than one, whose bitterest and greatest sorrow had been, for many years, that he saw no probability of ever finding himself, in any instance, stronger than this powerful oppressor, that he might revenge himself for some great injury, meeting him afterwards alone, unarmed, and with the air of one who would offer no resistance, felt only an impulse to salute him with demonstrations of respect. In his voluntary abasement, his countenance and behaviour had acquired, without his being aware of it, something more lofty and noble; because there was in them, more clearly than ever, the absence of all fear. The most violent and pertinacious hatred felt, as it were, restrained and held in awe by the public veneration for so penitent and beneficent a man. This was carried to such a length, that he often found it difficult to avoid the public expression of it which was addressed to him, and was obliged to be careful that he did not evince too plainly in his looks and actions the inward compunction he felt, nor abuse himself too much, lest he should be too much exalted. He had selected the lowest place in church, and woe to any one who should have attempted to pre-occupy it! it would have been, as it were, usurping a post of honour. To have offended him, or even to have treated him disrespectfully, would have appeared not so much a criminal or cowardly, as a sacrilegious act: and even they who would scarcely have been restrained by this feeling on ordinary occasions, participated in it, more or less.

These and other reasons sheltered him also from the more remote animadversions of public authority, and procured for him, even in this quarter, the security to which he himself had never given a thought. His rank and family, which had at all times been some protection to him, availed him more than ever, now that personal recommendations, the renown of his conversion, was added to his already illustrious and famous, or rather infamous, name. Magistrates and nobles publicly rejoiced with the people at the change; and it would have appeared very incongruous to come forward irritated against a man who was the subject of so many congratulations. Besides, a government occupied with a protracted, and often unprosperous, war against active and oft-renewed rebellions, would have been very well satisfied to be freed from the most indomitable and irksome, without going in search of another: the more so, as this conversion produced reparations which the authorities were not accustomed to obtain, nor even to demand. To molest a saint seemed no very good means to ward off the reproach of having never been able to repress a villain; and the example they would have made of him would have had no other effect than to dissuade others, like him, from following his example. Probably, too, the share that Cardinal Federigo had had in his conversion, and the association of his name with that of the convert, served the latter as a sacred shield. And, in the state of things and ideas of those times, in the singular relations between the ecclesiastical authority and the civil power, which so frequently contended with each other without at all aiming at mutual destruction, nay, were always mingling expressions of acknowledgment, and protestations of deference, with hostilities, and which not unfrequently co-operated towards a common end, without ever making peace,—in such a state of things, it might almost seem, in a manner, that the reconciliation of the first carried along with it, if not the absolution, at least the forgetfulness, of the second; when the former alone had been employed to produce an effect equally desired by both.

Thus that very individual, who, had he fallen from his eminence, would have excited emulation among small and great in trampling him under-foot, now, having spontaneously humbled himself to the dust, was reverenced by many, and spared by all.

True it is, that there were, indeed, many to whom this much-talked-of change brought anything but satisfaction: many hired perpetrators of crime, many other associates in guilt, who thereby lost a great support on which they had been accustomed to depend, and who beheld the threads of a deeply-woven plot suddenly snapped, at the moment, perhaps, when they were expecting the intelligence of its completion.

But we have already seen what various sentiments were awakened by the announcement of this conversion in the ruffians who were with their master at the time, and heard it from his own lips: astonishment, grief, depression, vexation; a little, indeed, of everything, except contempt and hatred. The same was felt by the others whom he kept dispersed at different posts, and the same by his accomplices of higher rank, when they first learned the terrible tidings; and by all for the same reasons. Much hatred, however, as we find in the passage elsewhere cited from Ripamonti, fell to the share of the Cardinal Federigo. They regarded him as one who had intruded like an enemy into their affairs; the Unnamed would see to the salvation of his own soul; and nobody had any right to complain of what he did.

From time to time, the greater part of the ruffians in his household, unable to accommodate themselves to the new discipline, and seeing no probability that it would ever change, gradually took their departure. Some went in search of other masters, and found employment, perchance, among the old friends of the patron they had left; others enlisted in some *terzo*[1] of Spain or Mantua, or any other belligerent power; some infested the highways, to make war on a smaller scale, and on their own account; and others, again, contented themselves with going about as beggars at liberty. The same courses were pursued by the rest who had acted under his orders in different countries. Of those who had contrived to assimilate themselves to his new mode of life, or had embraced it of their own free will, the greater number, natives of the valley, returned to the fields, or to the trades which they had learnt in their early years, and had afterwards abandoned for a life of villany; the strangers remained in the castle as domestic servants; and both natives and strangers, as if blessed at the same time with their master, lived contentedly, as he did, neither giving nor receiving injuries, unarmed, and respected.

But when, on the descent of the German troops, several fugitives

[1] A regiment consisting of three thousand soldiers.

from the threatened or invaded dominions arrived at his castle to request an asylum, he, rejoiced that the weak and oppressed sought refuge within his walls, which had so long been regarded by them at a distance as an enormous scarecrow, received these exiles with expressions of gratitude rather than courtesy; he caused it to be proclaimed that his house would be open to any one who should choose to take refuge there; and soon proposed to put, not only his castle, but the valley itself, into a state of defence, if ever any of the German or Bergamascan troops should attempt to come thither for plunder. He assembled the servants who still remained with him (like the verses of Torti, few and valiant); addressed them on the happy opportunity that God was giving both to them and himself of employing themselves for once in aid of their fellow-creatures, whom they had so often oppressed and terrified; and with that ancient tone of command which expressed a certainty of being obeyed, announced to them in general what he wished them to do, and, above all, impressed upon them the necessity of keeping a restraint over themselves, that they who took refuge there might see in them only friends and protectors. He then had brought down from one of the garrets all the fire-arms, and other warlike weapons, which had been for some time deposited there, and distributed them among his household; ordered that all the peasants and tenants of the valley, who were willing to do so, should come with arms to the castle; provided those who had none with a sufficient supply; selected some to act as officers, and placed others under their command; assigned to each his post at the entrance, and in various parts of the valley, on the ascent, and at the gates of the castle; and established the hours and methods of relieving the guards, as in a camp, or as he had been accustomed to do in that very place during his life of rebellion.

In one corner of this garret, divided from the rest, were the arms which he alone had borne, his famous carabine, muskets, swords, pistols, huge knives, and poniards, either lying on the ground, or set up against the wall. None of the servants laid a finger on them; but they determined to ask the Signor which he wished to be brought to him. 'Not one of them,' replied he; and whether from a vow or intentional design, he remained the whole time unarmed, at the head of this species of garrison.

He employed, at the same time, other men and women of his household or dependents, in preparing accommodation in the castle for as many persons as possible, in erecting bedsteads, and arranging straw beds, mattresses, and sacks stuffed with straw, in the apartments which were now converted into dormitories. He also gave orders that large stores of provisions should be brought in for the maintenance of the guests whom God should send him, and who thronged in in daily increasing numbers. He, in the mean while, was never stationary; in and out of the castle, up and down the ascent, round about through the valley, to establish, to fortify, to visit the different posts, to see and to be seen, to put and to keep all in order by his directions, oversight, and presence. Indoors, and by the way, he gave hearty welcomes to all the new comers whom he happened to meet; and all, who had either seen this wonderful person before, or now beheld him for the first time, gazed at him in rapture, forgetting for a moment the misfortunes and alarm which had driven them thither, and turning to look at him, when, having severed himself from them, he again pursued his way.

CHAPTER XXX

THOUGH the greatest concourse was not from the quarter by which our three fugitives approached the valley, but rather at the opposite entrance; yet in this second half of their journey, they began to meet with fellow-travellers, companions in misfortune, who, from cross-roads or by-paths, had issued, or were issuing, into the main road. In circumstances like these all who happen to meet each other are acquaintances. Every time that the cart overtook a pedestrian traveller, there was an exchanging of questions and replies. Some had made their escape, like our friends, without awaiting the arrival of the soldiers; some had heard the clanging of arms and kettle-drums; while others had actually beheld them, and painted them as the terror-stricken usually paint the objects of their terror.

'We are fortunate, however,' said the two women: 'let us thank Heaven for it. Our goods must go; but, at least, we are out of the way.'

But Don Abbondio could not find so much to rejoice at; even this concourse, and still more the far greater one which he heard was pouring in from the opposite direction, began to throw a gloom over his mind. 'Oh, what a state of things!' muttered he to the women, at a moment when there was nobody at hand: 'oh, what a state of things! Don't you see, that to collect so many people into one place is just the same thing as to draw all the soldiers here by force? Everybody is hiding, everybody carries off his things! nothing's left in the houses: so they'll think there must be some treasures up here. They'll surely come! Oh poor me! What have I embarked in?'

'What should they have to come here for?' said Perpetua: 'they are obliged to go straight on their way. And besides, I've always heard say, that it's better to be a large party when there's any danger.'

'A large party? a large party?' replied Don Abbondio. 'Foolish

487

woman! Don't you know that a single German soldier could devour a hundred of such as they? And then, if they should take into their heads to play any pranks, it would be a fine thing, wouldn't it, to find ourselves in the midst of a battle? Oh poor me! It would have been less dangerous to have gone to the mountains. Why should everybody choose to go to one place? ... Tiresome folks!' muttered he in a still lower voice. 'All here: still coming, coming, coming; one after the other, like sheep that have no sense.'

'In this way,' said Agnese, 'they might say the same of us.'

'Hush, hush!' said Don Abbondio, 'all this talk does no good. What's done is done: we are here, and now we must stay here. It will be as Providence wills: Heaven send it may be good!'

But his horror was greatly increased when, at the entrance of the valley, he saw a large body of armed men, some at the door of a house, and others quartered in the lower rooms. He cast a side glance at them: they were not the same faces which it had been his lot to see on his former melancholy entrance, or if there were any of the same, they were strangely altered; but, with all this, it is impossible to say what uneasiness this sight gave him.—Oh poor me!—thought he.—See, now, if they won't play pranks! It isn't likely it could be otherwise; I ought to have expected it from a man of this kind. But what will he want to do? Will he make war? will he play the king, eh? Oh poor me! In circumstances when one would wish to bury oneself under-ground, and this man seeks every way of making himself known, and attracting attention; it seems as if he wished to invite them!—

'You see now, Signor master,' said Perpetua, addressing him, 'there are brave people here who will know how to defend us. Let the soldiers come now: these people are not like our clowns, who are good for nothing but to drag their legs after them.'

'Hold your tongue,' said Don Abbondio, in a low and angry tone, 'hold your tongue; you don't know what you are talking about. Pray Heaven that the soldiers may make haste, or that they may never come to know what is doing here, and that the place is being fortified like a fortress. Don't you know it's the soldiers' business to take fortresses? They wish nothing better; to take a place by storm is to them like going to a wedding; because all they find they take to themselves, and the inhabitants they put to the edge of the sword. Oh poor me! Well, I'll surely see if there's no way of putting oneself in safety on some of these peaks. They won't reach me there in a battle! oh, they won't reach me there!'

'If you're afraid, too, of being defended and helped . . .' Perpetua was again beginning; but Don Abbondio sharply interrupted her, though still in a suppressed tone: 'Hold your tongue; and take good care you don't report what we've said: woe unto us if you do! Remember that we must always put on a pleasant countenance here, and approve all we see.'

At Malanotte they found another watch of armed men, to whom Don Abbondio submissively took off his hat, saying, in the meanwhile, in his heart—Alas! alas! I've certainly come to an encampment!—Here the cart stopped; they dismounted; Don Abbondio hastily paid and dismissed the driver; and with his two companions silently mounted the steep. The sight of those places recalled to his imagination and mingled with his present troubles the remembrance of those which he had suffered here once before. And Agnese, who had never seen these scenes, and who had drawn to herself an imaginary picture, which presented itself to her mind whenever she thought of the circumstances that had occurred here, on seeing them now as they were in reality, experienced a new and more vivid feeling of these mournful recollections. 'Oh, Signor Curate!' exclaimed she, 'to think that my poor Lucia has passed along this road! . . .'

'Will you hold your tongue, you absurd woman?' cried Don Abbondio in her ear. 'Are those things to be bringing up here? Don't you know we are in his place? It was well for us nobody heard you then; but if you talk in this way . . .'

'Oh!' said Agnese; 'now that he's a saint! . . .'

'Well, be quiet!' replied Don Abbondio again in her ear. 'Do you think one may say without caution, even to saints, all that passes through one's mind? Think rather of thanking him for his goodness to you.'

'Oh, I've already thought of that: do you think I don't know even a little civility?'

'Civility is, not to say things that may be disagreeable to a person, particularly to one who is not accustomed to hear them. And understand well, both of you, that this is not a place to go chattering about, and saying whatever may happen to come into your heads. It is a great Signor's house, you know that already: see what a household there is all around: people of all sorts come here: so be prudent, if you can; weigh your words; and above all, let there be few of them, and only when there is a necessity: one can't get wrong when one is silent.'

'You do far worse, with all your . . .' Perpetua began: but, 'Hush!' cried Don Abbondio, in a suppressed voice, at the same time hastily taking off his hat, and making a profound bow: for, on looking up, he had discovered the Unnamed coming down to meet them. He, on his part, had noticed and recognized Don Abbondio, and was now hastening to welcome him.

'Signor Curate,' said he, when he had reached him, 'I should have liked to offer you my house on a pleasanter occasion; but, under any circumstances, I am exceedingly glad to be able to be of some service to you.'

'Trusting in your illustrious Lordship's great kindness,' replied Don Abbondio, 'I have ventured to come, under these melancholy circumstances, to intrude upon you: and, as your illustrious Lordship sees, I have also presumed to bring company with me. This is my housekeeper . . .'

'She is welcome,' said the Unnamed.

'And this,' continued Don Abbondio, 'is a woman to whom your Lordship has already been very good: the mother of that . . . of that . . .'

'Of Lucia,' said Agnese.

'Of Lucia!' exclaimed the Unnamed, turning with a look of shame towards Agnese. 'Been very good, I! Immortal God! You are very good to me, to come here . . . to me . . . to this house. You are most heartily welcome. You bring a blessing with you.'

'Oh, sir,' said Agnese, 'I come to give you trouble. I have, too,' continued she, going very close to his ear, 'to thank you . . .'

The Unnamed interrupted these words, by anxiously making inquiries about Lucia: and having heard the intelligence they had to give, he turned to accompany his new guests to the castle, and persisted in doing so, in spite of their ceremonious opposition. Agnese cast a glance at the Curate, which meant to say,—You see, now, whether there's any need for you to interpose between us with your advice!—

'Have they reached your parish?' asked the Unnamed, addressing Don Abbondio.

'No, Signor; for I would not willingly await the arrival of these devils,' replied he. 'Heaven knows if I should have been able to escape alive out of their hands, and come to trouble your illustrious Lordship.'

'Well, well, you may take courage,' resumed the nobleman, 'for you are now safe enough. They'll not come up here; and if they should wish to make the trial, we're ready to receive them.'

'We'll hope they won't come,' said Don Abbondio. 'I hear,' added he, pointing with his finger towards the mountains which enclosed the valley on the opposite side, 'I hear that another band of soldiers is wandering about in that quarter too, but . . . but . . .'

'True,' replied the Unnamed; 'but you need have no fear: we are ready for them also.'—Between two fires; in the mean while said Don Abbondio to himself,—exactly between two fires. Where have I suffered myself to be drawn? and by two silly women! And this man seems actually in his element in it all! Oh, what people there are in the world!—

On entering the castle, the Signor had Agnese and Perpetua conducted to an apartment in the quarter assigned to the women, which occupied three of the four sides of the inner court, in the back part of the building, and was situated on a jutting and isolated rock, overhanging a precipice. The men were lodged in the sides of the other court to the right and left, and in that which looked on the esplanade. The central block, which separated the two quadrangles, and afforded a passage from one to the other through a wide archway opposite the principal gate, was partly occupied with provisions, and partly served as a depository for any little property the refugees might wish to secure in this retreat. In the quarters appropriated to the men, was a small apartment destined for the use of any clergy who might happen to take refuge there. Hither the Unnamed himself conducted Don Abbondio, who was the first to take possession of it.

Three or four and twenty days our fugitives remained at the castle, in a state of continual bustle, forming a large company, which at first received constant additions, but without any incidents of importance. Perhaps, however, not a single day passed without their resorting to arms. Lansquenets were coming in this direction; *cappelletti* had been seen in that. Every time this intelligence was brought, the Unnamed sent men to reconnoitre; and, if there were any necessity, took with him some whom he kept in readiness for the purpose, and accompanied them beyond the valley, in the direction of the indicated danger. And it was a singular thing to behold a band of brigands, armed *cap-à-pié,* and conducted like soldiers by one who was himself unarmed. Generally it proved to be only foragers and disbanded pillagers, who contrived to make off before they were taken by surprise. But once, when driving away some of these, to teach them not to come again into that neighbourhood, the Unnamed received intelligence that an adjoining village was invaded and given up to plunder. They were soldiers of various corps, who, having loitered behind to hunt for booty, had formed themselves into a band, and made a sudden irruption into the lands surrounding that where the army had taken up its quarters; despoiling the inhabitants, and even levying contributions from them. The Unnamed made a brief harangue to his followers, and bid them march forward to the invaded village.

They arrived unexpectedly: the plunderers, who had thought of nothing but taking the spoil, abandoned their prey in the midst, on seeing men in arms, and ready for battle, coming down upon them, and hastily took to flight, without waiting for one another, in the direction whence they had come. He pursued them a little distance; then, making a halt, waited awhile to see if any fresh object presented itself, and at length returned homewards. It is impossible to describe the shouts of applause and benediction which accompanied the troop of deliverers and its leader, on passing through the rescued village.

Among the multitude of refugees assembled in the castle, strangers to each other, and differing in rank, habit, sex, and age, no disturbance of any moment occurred. The Unnamed had placed guards in various posts, all of whom endeavoured to ward off any unpleasantness with the care usually exhibited by those who are held accountable for any misdemeanours.

He had also requested the clergy, and others of most authority among those to whom he afforded shelter, to walk round the place, and keep a watch; and, as often as he could, he himself went about to show himself in every direction, while, even in his absence, the remembrance of who was in the house served as a restraint to those who needed it. Besides, they were all people that had fled from danger, and hence generally inclined to peace: while the thoughts of their homes and property, and in some cases, of relatives and friends whom they had left exposed to danger, and the tidings they heard from without, depressed their spirits, and thus maintained and constantly increased this disposition.

There were, however, some unburdened spirits, some men of firmer mould and stronger courage, who tried to pass these days merrily. They had abandoned their homes because they were not strong enough to defend them; but they saw no use in weeping and sighing over things that could not be helped, or in picturing to themselves, and contemplating beforehand, in imagination, the havoc they would only too soon witness with their own eyes. Families acquainted with each other had left their homes at the same time, and had met with each other again in this retreat; new friendships were formed; and the multitude were divided into parties, according to their several habits and dispositions. They who had money and consideration went to dine down in the valley, where eating-houses and inns had been hastily run up for the occasion: in some, mouthfuls were interchanged with lamentations, or no subject but their misfortunes was allowed to be discussed; in others, misfortunes were never remembered, unless it were to say that they must not think about them. To those who either could not, or would not, bear part of the expenses, bread, soup, and wine were distributed, in the castle; besides other tables which were laid out daily for those whom the Signor had expressly invited to partake of them; and our acquaintances were among this number.

Agnese and Perpetua, not to eat the bread of idleness, had begged to be employed in the services which, in so large an establishment, must have been required; and in these occupations they spent a great part of the day, while the rest was passed in chatting with some friends, whose acquaintance they had made, or with the unfortunate Don Abbondio. This individual, though he had nothing to do, was, nevertheless, never afflicted with ennui: his fears kept him company. The direct dread of an assault had, I believe subsided: or, if it still remained, it was one which gave him the least uneasiness; because, whenever he bestowed upon it the slightest thought, he could not help seeing how unfounded it was. But the idea of the surrounding country, inundated on both sides with brutal soldiers, the armour and armed men he had constantly before his eyes, the remembrance that he was in a castle, together with the thought of the many things that might happen any moment in such a situation, all contributed to keep him in indistinct, general, constant alarm; let alone the anxiety he felt when he thought of his poor home. During the whole time he remained in this asylum, he never once went more than a stone's throw from the building, nor ever set foot on the descent: his sole walk was to go out upon the esplanade, and pace up and down, sometimes to one, sometimes to the other side of the castle, there to look down among the cliffs and precipices, in hopes of discovering some practicable passage, some kind of footpath, by which he might go in search of a hiding-place, in case of being very closely pressed. On meeting any of his companions in this asylum, he failed not to make a profound bow, or respectful salutation, but he associated with very few; his most frequent conversations were with the two women, as we have related; and to them he poured out all his griefs, at the risk of being sometimes silenced by Perpetua, and completely put to shame even by Agnese. At table, however, where he sat but little, and talked still less, he heard the news of the terrible march which arrived daily at the castle, either reported from village to village, and from mouth to mouth, or brought thither by some one who had at first determined to remain at home, and had, after all, made his escape, without having been able to save anything, and probably, also, after receiving considerable ill-treatment; and every day brought with it some fresh tale of misfortune. Some, who were newsmongers by profession, diligently collected the different rumours, weighed all **the** various accounts, and then gave the substance of them to the others. They disputed which were the most destructive regiments, and whether infantry or cavalry were the worst; they reported, as well as they could, the names of some of the leaders; related some of their past enterprises, specified the places of halting, and the daily marches. That day such a regiment would spread over such a district; to-morrow, it would ravage such another, where, in the mean while, another had been playing the very devil, and worse. They chiefly, however, sought information and kept count of the regiments which from time to time crossed the bridge of Lecco, because these might be considered as fairly gone, and really out of the territory. The cavalry of Wallenstein passed it, and the infantry of Marradas; the cavalry of Anzlalt, and the infantry under Brandeburgo; the troops of Montecuccoli, then those of Ferrari; then followed Altringer, then Furstenburg, then Colloredo; after them came the Croatians, Torquato Conti, and this, that, and the other leader; and last of all, in Heaven's good time, came at length Galasso. The flying squadron of Venetians made their final exit; and the whole country, on either hand, was once more set at liberty. Those belonging to the invaded villages which were first cleared of their ravagers, had already begun to evacuate the castle, and every day people continued to leave the place: as after an autumnal storm, the birds may be seen issuing on every side from the leafy branches of a great tree, where they had sought a shelter from its fury. Our three refugees were, perhaps, the last to take their departure, owing to Don Abbondio's extreme reluctance to run the risk, if they returned home immediately, of meeting some straggling soldiers who might still be loitering in the rear of the army. It was in vain Perpetua repeated and insisted, that the longer they delayed, the greater opportunities they afforded to the thieves of the neighbourhood to enter the house and finish the business: whenever the safety of life was at stake, Don Abbondio invariably gained the day; unless, indeed, the imminence of the danger were such as to deprive him of the power of self-defence.

On the day fixed for their departure, the Unnamed had a carriage in readiness at Malanotte, in which he had already placed a full supply of clothes for Agnese. Drawing her a little aside, he also forced her to accept a small store of *scudi,* to compensate for the damages she would find at home; although, striking her breast, she kept repeating that she had still some of the first supply left.

'When you see your poor good Lucia . . .' said he, the last thing: 'I am already convinced she prays for me, because I have done her so much wrong; tell her, then, that I thank her, and trust in God her prayers will return, also, in equal blessings upon her own head.'

He then insisted upon accompanying his three guests to the carriage. The obsequious and extravagant acknowledgments of Don Abbondio, and the complimentary speeches of Perpetua, we leave to the reader's imagination. They set off, made a short stay, according to agreement, at the tailor's cottage, and there heard a hundred particulars of the march, the usual tale of theft, violence, destruction, and obscenity; but there, fortunately, none of the soldiery had been seen.

'Ah, Signor Curate!' said the tailor, as he offered him his arm to assist him again into the carriage, 'they'll have matter enough for a printed book in a scene of destruction like this.'

As they advanced a little on their journey, our travellers began to witness, with their own eyes, something of what they had heard described; vineyards despoiled, not as by the vintager, but as though a storm of wind and hail combined had exerted their utmost energies; branches strewn upon the earth, broken off, and trampled under-foot; stakes torn up, the ground trodden and covered with chips, leaves, and twigs; trees uprooted, or their branches lopped; hedges broken down; stiles carried away. In the villages, too, doors shivered to pieces, windows destroyed, straw, rags, rubbish of all kinds, lying in heaps, or scattered all over the pavement; a close atmosphere, and horrid odours of a more revolting nature proceeding from the houses; some of the villagers busy in sweeping out the accumulation of filth within them; others in repairing the doors and windows as they best could; some again weeping in groups, and indulging in lamentations together; and as the carriage drove through, hands stretched out on both sides at the doors of the vehicle imploring alms.

With these scenes, now before his eyes, now pictured in their minds, and with the expectation of finding their own houses in just the same state, they at length arrived there, and found that their expectations were indeed realized.

Agnese deposited her bundles in one corner of her little yard, the cleanest spot that remained about the house; she then set herself to sweep it thoroughly, and collect and rearrange the little furniture which had been left her; she got a carpenter and blacksmith to come and mend the doors and window frames, and then, unpacking the linen which had been given her, and secretly counting over her fresh store of coins, she exclaimed to herself,—I've fallen upon my feet! God, and the Madonna, and that good Signor, be thanked! I may indeed say, I've fallen upon my feet!—

Don Abbondio and Perpetua entered the house without the aid of keys, and at every step they took in the passage encountered a fetid odour, a poisonous effluvia, which almost drove them back. Holding their noses, they advanced to the kitchen-door; entered on tip-toe, carefully picking their way to avoid the most disgusting parts of the filthy straw which covered the ground, and cast a glance around. Nothing was left whole; but relics and fragments of what once had been, both here and in other parts of the house, were to be seen in every corner: quills and feathers from Perpetua's fowls, scraps of linen, leaves out of Don Abbondio's calendars, remnants of kitchen utensils; all heaped together, or scattered in confusion upon the floor. On the hearth might be discovered tokens of a riotous scene of destruction, like a multitude of ordinary ideas scattered through a widely diffused period by a professional orator. There were the vestiges of extinguished faggots and billets of wood, which showed them to have been once the arm of a chair, a table-foot, the door of a cupboard, a bed-post, or a stave of the little cask which contained the wine, so beneficial to Don Abbondio's stomach. The rest was cinders and coal; and with some of these very coals, the spoilers, by way of recreation, had scrawled on the walls distorted figures, doing their best, by the help of sundry square caps, shaven crowns, and large bands, to represent priests studiously exhibited in all manner of horrible and ludicrous attitudes: an intention, certainly, in which such artists could not possibly have failed.

'Ah, the dirty pigs!' exclaimed Perpetua. 'Ah, the thieves!' cried Don Abbondio; and, as if making their escape, they went out by another door, that led into the garden. Once more drawing their breath, they went straight up to the fig-tree; but, even before reaching it, they discovered that the ground had been disturbed, and both together uttered an exclamation of dismay, and, on coming up, they found in truth, instead of the dead, only the empty tomb. This gave rise to some disputes. Don Abbondio began to scold Perpetua for having hidden it so badly: it may be imagined whether she would fail to retort: and after indulging in mutual recrimination till they were tired, they returned, with many a lingering look cast back at the empty hole, grumbling into the house. They found things nearly in the same state everywhere. Long and diligently they worked to cleanse and purify the house, the more so as it was then extremely difficult to get any help; and they remained for I know not what length of time, as if in encampment, arranging things as they best could—and bad was the best—and gradually restoring doors, furniture, and utensils, with money lent to them by Agnese.

In addition to these grievances, this disaster was, for some time afterwards, the source of many other very ticklish disputes; for Perpetua, by dint of asking, peeping, and hunting out, had come to know for certain that some of her master's household goods, which were thought to have been carried off or destroyed by the soldiers, were, instead, safe and sound with some people in the neighbourhood; and she was continually tormenting her master to make a stir about them, and claim his own. A chord more odious to Don Abbondio could not have been touched, considering that his property was in the hands of ruffians, of that species of persons, that is to say, with whom he had it most at heart to remain at peace.

'But if I don't want to know about these things . . . ' said he. 'How often am I to tell you that what is gone, is gone? Am I to be harassed in this way, too, because my house has been robbed?'

'I tell you,' replied Perpetua, 'that you would let the very eyes be eaten out of your head. To rob others is a sin, but with you, it is a sin *not* to rob you.'

'Very proper language for you, certainly!' answered Don Abbondio. 'Will you hold your tongue?'

Perpetua did hold her tongue, but not so directly; and even then everything was a pretext for beginning again; so that the poor man was at last reduced to the necessity of suppressing every lamentation on the lack of this or that article of furniture, at the moment he most wanted to give vent to his regrets; for more than once he had been doomed to hear: 'Go seek it at such a one's, who has it, and who wouldn't have kept it till now, if he hadn't had to deal with such an easy man.'

Another and more vivid cause of disquietude, was the intelligence that soldiers continued daily to be passing in confusion, as he had too well conjectured; hence he was ever in apprehension of seeing a man, or even a band of men, arriving at his door, which he had had repaired in haste the first thing, and which he kept barred with the greatest precaution; but, thank Heaven! this catastrophe never occurred. These terrors, however, were not appeased, when a new one was added to their number.

But here we must leave the poor man on one side: for other matters are now to be treated of than his private apprehensions, the misfortunes of a few villages, or a transient disaster.

CHAPTER XXXI

THE plague, which the Board of Health had feared might enter with the German troops into the Milanese, had entered it indeed, as is well known; and it is likewise well known, that it paused not here, but invaded and ravaged a great part of Italy. Following the thread of our story, we now come to relate the principal incidents of this calamity in the Milanese, or rather in Milan almost exclusively: for almost exclusively of the city do the records of the times treat, nearly as it always and everywhere happens, for good reasons or bad. And, to say the truth, it is not only our object, in this narrative, to represent the state of things in which our characters will shortly be placed; but at the same time to develop, as far as may be in so limited a space, and from our pen, an event in the history of our country more celebrated than well known.

Of the many contemporary accounts, there is not one which is sufficient by itself to convey a distinct and connected idea of it; as there is not, perhaps, one which may not give us some assistance in forming that idea. In every one, not excepting that of Ripamonti,[1] which considerably exceeds all the rest, both in copiousness and in its selection of facts, and still more in its method of viewing them, essential facts are omitted which are recorded in others; in every one there are errors of material importance, which may be detected and rectified with the help of some other, or of the few printed or manuscript acts of public authority which still remain; and we may often discover in one, those causes, the effects of which were found partially developed in another. In all, too, a strange confusion of times and things prevailed, and a perpetual wandering backward and forward, as it were at random, without design, special or general: the character, by the by, of books of all classes in those days, chiefly among such as were written in the vulgar tongue, at least in Italy;

[1] Josephi Ripamontii, canonici scalensis, chronistæ urbis Mediolani, de Peste quæ fuit anno 1630, Lib. V. Mediolani, 1640. Apud Malatestas.

whether, also, in the rest of Europe, the learned will know, and we shrewdly suspect it so to have been. No writer of later date has attempted to examine and compare these memoirs, with the view of extracting thence a connected series of events, a history of this plague; so that the idea generally formed of it must necessarily be very uncertain and somewhat confused, a vague idea of great evils and great errors, (and assuredly there were both one and the other beyond what can possibly be imagined,)—an idea composed more of opinions than of facts, mingled, indeed, with a few scattered events, but unconnected, sometimes, with their most characteristic circumstances, and without distinction of time, that is to say, without perception of cause and effect, of course and progress. We, having examined and compared, with at least much diligence, all the printed accounts, more than one unpublished one, and (in comparison of the few that remain on the subject) many official documents, have endeavoured to do, not, perhaps, all that is needed, but something which has not hitherto been done. We do not purpose relating every public act, nor all the results worthy, in some degree, of remembrance. Still less do we pretend to render needless to such as would gain a more complete acquaintance with the subject, the perusal of the original writings: we are too well aware what lively, peculiar, and, so to say, incommunicable force invariably belongs to works of that kind, in whatever manner designed and executed. We have merely endeavoured to distinguish and ascertain the most general and important facts, to arrange them in their real order of succession, so far as the matter and the nature of them will allow, to observe their reciprocal effect, and thus to give, for the present, and until some one else shall do better, a succinct, but plain and continuous, account of this calamity.

Throughout the whole track, then, of the territory traversed by the army, corpses might be found either in the houses, or lying upon the highway. Very shortly, single individuals, or whole families, began to sicken and die of violent and strange complaints, with symptoms unknown to the greater part of those who were then alive. There were only a few who had ever seen them before: the few, that is, who could remember the plague which, fifty-three years previously, had desolated a great part of Italy indeed, but especially the Milanese, where it was then, and is still, called the plague of San Carlo. So powerful is Charity! Among the various and awful recollections of a general calamity, she could cause that of one individual to predominate; because she had inspired him with feelings and actions more memorable even than the evils themselves; she could set him up in men's minds as a symbol of all these events, because in all she had urged him onward, and held him up to view as guide, and helper, example, and voluntary victim; and could frame for him, as it were, an emblematical device out of a public calamity, and name it after him as though it had been a conquest or discovery.

The oldest physician of his time, Lodovico Settala, who had not only seen that plague, but had been one of its most active and intrepid, and, though then very young, most celebrated successful opponents; and who now, in strong suspicion of this, was on the alert, and busily collecting information, reported, on the 20th of October, in the Council of the Board of Health, that the contagion had undoubtedly broken out in the village of Chiuso, the last in the territory of Lecco, and on the confines of the Bergamascan district. No resolution, however, was taken on this intelligence, as appears from the 'Narrative' of Tadino.[2]

Similar tidings arrived from Lecco and Bellano. The Board then decided upon, and contented themselves with, despatching a commissioner, who should take a physician from Como by the way, and accompany him on a visit to the places which had been signified. 'Both of them, either from ignorance or some other reason, suffered themselves to be persuaded by an old ignorant barber of Bellano that this sort of disease was not the pestilence;'[3] but in some places the ordinary effect of the autumnal exhalations from the marshes, and elsewhere, of the privations and sufferings undergone during the passage of the German troops. This affirmation was reported to the Board, who seem to have been perfectly satisfied with it.

But additional reports of the mortality in every quarter pouring in without intermission, two deputies were despatched to see and provide against it—the above-named Tadino, and an auditor of the committee. When these arrived, the evil had spread so widely, that

[2] Tadino, p. 24.   [3] Ibid.

proofs offered themselves to their view without being sought for.
They passed through the territory of Lecco, the Valsassina, the
shores of the Lake of Como, and the districts denominated Il Monte
di Brianza and La Gera d'Adda; and everywhere found the towns
barricaded, others almost deserted, and the inhabitants escaped and
encamped in the fields, or scattered throughout the country; 'who
seemed,' says Tadino, 'like so many wild savages, carrying in their
hands, one a sprig of mint, another of rue, another of rosemary,
another, a bottle of vinegar.'[4] They made inquiries as to the number
of deaths, which was really fearful; they visited the sick and dead,
and everywhere recognized the dark and terrible marks of the
pestilence. They then speedily conveyed the disastrous intelligence
by letter to the Board of Health, who, on receiving it, on the 30th of
October, 'prepared,' says Tadino, 'to issue warrants to shut out of the
city any persons coming from the countries where the plague had
shown itself; and while preparing the decree,'[5] they gave some summary orders beforehand to the custom-house officers.

In the mean while, the commissioners, in great haste and precipitation, made what provisions they knew, or could think of, for
the best, and returned with the melancholy consciousness of their
insufficiency to remedy or arrest an evil already so far advanced,
and so widely disseminated.

On the 14th of November, having made their report, both by word
of mouth and afresh in writing, to the Board, they received from
this committee a commission to present themselves to the governor,
and to lay before him the state of things. They went accordingly,
and brought back word, that he was exceedingly sorry to hear such
news, and had shown a great deal of feeling about it; but the
thoughts of war were more pressing: '*Sed belli graviores esse curas.*'
So says Ripamonti,[6] after having ransacked the records of the Board
of Health, and compared them with Tadino, who had been specially
charged with this mission: it was the second, if the reader remembers,
for this purpose, and with this result. Two or three days afterwards,
the 18th of November, the governor issued a proclamation, in which
he prescribed public rejoicings for the birth of the Prince Charles,
the first-born son of the king, Philip IV., without thinking of, or

[4] Tadino, p. 26.   [5] *Ibid.*, p. 27.   [6] Ripamonti, p. 245.

without caring for, the danger of suffering a large concourse of people under such circumstances: everything as in common times, just as if he had never been spoken to about anything.

This person was, as we have elsewhere said, the celebrated Ambrogio Spinola, sent for the very purpose of adjusting this war, to repair the errors of Don Gonzalo, and, incidentally, to govern; and we may here incidentally mention, that he died a few months later in that very war which he had so much at heart; not wounded in the field of battle, but on his bed, of grief and anxiety occasioned by reproaches, affronts, and ill-treatment of every kind, received from those whom he had served. History has bewailed his fate, and remarked upon the ingratitude of others; it has described with much diligence his military and political enterprises, and extolled his foresight, activity, and perseverance; it might also have inquired what he did with all these, when pestilence threatened and actually invaded a population committed to his care, or rather entirely given up to his authority.

But that which, leaving censure, diminishes our wonder at his behaviour, which even creates another and greater feeling of wonder, is the behaviour of the people themselves; of those, I mean, who, unreached as yet by the contagion, had so much reason to fear it. On the arrival of the intelligence from the territories which were so grievously infected with it, territories which formed almost a semi-circular line round the city, in some places not more than twenty, or even eighteen, miles distant from it, who would not have thought that a general stir would have been created, that they would have been diligent in taking precautions, whether well or ill selected, or at least have felt a barren disquietude? Nevertheless, if in anything the records of the times agree, it is in attesting that there were none of these. The scarcity of the antecedent year, the violence of the soldiery, and their sufferings of mind, seemed to them more than enough to account for the mortality: and if any one had attempted, in the streets, shops, and houses, to throw out a hint of danger, and mention the plague, it would have been received with incredulous scoffs, or angry contempt. The same incredulity, or, to speak more correctly, the same blindness and perversity, prevailed in the senate, in the Council of the *Decurioni,* and in all the magistrates.

I find that Cardinal Federigo, immediately on learning the first cases of a contagious sickness, enjoined his priests, in a pastoral letter, among other things, to impress upon the people the importance and obligation of making known every similar case, and delivering up any infected or suspected goods:[7] and this, too, may be reckoned among his praiseworthy peculiarities.

The Board of Health solicited precautions and co-operation: it was all but in vain. And in the Board itself their solicitude was far from equaling the urgency of the case; it was the two physicians, as Tadino frequently affirms, and as appears still better from the whole context of his narrative, who, persuaded and deeply sensible of the gravity and imminence of the danger, urged forward that body, which was then to urge forward others.

We have already seen how, on the first tidings of the plague, there had been indifference and remissness in acting, and even in obtaining information: we now give another instance of dilatoriness not less portentous, if indeed it were not compelled by obstacles interposed by the superior magistrates. That proclamation in the form of warrants, resolved upon on the 30th of October, was not completed till the 23rd of the following month, nor published till the 29th. The plague had already entered Milan.

Tadino and Ripamonti would record the name of the individual who first brought it thither, together with other circumstances of the person and the fact: and, in truth, in observing the beginnings of a wide-spread destruction, in which the victims not only cannot be distinguished by name, but their numbers can scarcely be expressed with any degree of exactness, even by the thousand, one feels a certain kind of interest in ascertaining those first and few names which could be noted and preserved: it seems as if this sort of distinction, a precedence in extermination, invests them, and all the other minutiæ, which would otherwise be most indifferent, with something fatal and memorable.

But one and the other historian say that it was an Italian soldier

[7] Life of Federigo Borromeo, compiled by Francesco Rivola. Milan: 1666. P. 584.

in the Spanish service; but in nothing else do they agree, not even in the name. According to Tadino, it was a person of the name of Pietro Antonio Lovato, quartered in the territory of Lecco: according to Ripamonti, a certain Pier Paolo Locati, quartered at Chiavenna. They differ also as to the day of his entrance into Milan; the first placing it on the 22nd of October, the second, on the same day in the following month; yet it cannot be on either one or the other. Both the dates contradict others which are far better authenticated. Yet Ripamonti, writing by order of the General Council of the *Decurioni,* ought to have had many means at his command of gaining the necessary information; and Tadino, in consideration of his office, might have been better informed than any one else on a subject of this nature. In short, comparing other dates, which, as we have said, appear to us more authentic, it would seem that it was prior to the publication of the warrants; and if it were worth while, it might even be proved, or nearly so, that it must have been very early in that month: but the reader will, doubtless, excuse us the task.

However it may be, this soldier, unfortunate himself, and the bearer of misfortune to others, entered the city with a large bundle of clothes purchased or stolen from the German troops; he went to stay at the house of one of his relatives in the suburbs of the Porta Orientale, near to the Capuchin Convent. Scarcely had he arrived there, when he was taken ill; he was conveyed to the hospital; here, a spot, discovered under one of the armpits, excited some suspicion in the mind of the person who tended him, of what was in truth the fact; and on the fourth day he died.

The Board of Health immediately ordered his family to be kept separate, and confined within their own house; and his clothes, and the bed on which he had lain at the hospital, were burned. Two attendants, who had there nursed him, and a good friar, who had rendered him his assistance, were all three, within a few days, seized with the plague. The suspicions which had here been felt, from the beginning, of the nature of the disease, and the precautions taken in consequence, prevented the further spread of the contagion from this source.

But the soldier had left seed outside, which delayed not to spring up, and shoot forth. The first person in whom it broke out was the master of the house where he had lodged, one Carlo Colonna, a lute-player. All the inmates of the dwelling were then, by order of the Board, conveyed to the Lazzaretto; where the greater number took to their beds, and many shortly died of evident infection.

In the city, that which had been already disseminated there by intercourse with the above-mentioned family, and by clothes and furniture belonging to them preserved by relations, lodgers, or servants, from the searches and flames prescribed by the Board, as well as that which was afresh introduced by defectiveness in the regulations, by negligence in executing them, and by dexterity in eluding them, continued lurking about, and slowly insinuating itself among the inhabitants, all the rest of the year, and in the earlier months of 1630, the year which followed. From time to time, now in this, now in that quarter, some one was seized with the contagion, some one was carried off with it: and the very infrequency of the cases contributed to lull all suspicions of pestilence, and confirmed the generality more and more in the senseless and murderous assurance that plague it was not, and never had been, for a moment. Many physicians, too, echoing the voice of the people, (was it, in this instance also, the voice of Heaven?) derided the ominous predictions and threatening warnings of the few; and always had at hand the names of common diseases to qualify every case of pestilence which they were summoned to cure, with what symptom or token soever it evinced itself.

The reports of these instances, when they reached the Board of Health at all, reached it, for the most part, tardily and uncertainly. Dread of sequestration and the Lazzaretto sharpened every one's wits; they concealed the sick, they corrupted the grave-diggers and elders, and obtained false certificates, by means of bribes, from subalterns of the Board itself, deputed by it to visit and inspect the dead bodies.

As, however, on every discovery they succeeded in making, the Board ordered the wearing apparel to be committed to the flames, put the houses under sequestration, and sent the inmates to the

Lazzaretto, it is easy to imagine what must have been the anger and dissatisfaction of the generality 'of the nobility, merchants, and lower orders,'[8] persuaded, as they all were, that they were mere causeless vexations without any advantage. The principal odium fell upon the two doctors, our frequently mentioned Tadino and Senatore Settala, son of the senior physician, and reached such a height, that thenceforward they could not publicly appear without being assailed with opprobrious language, if not with stones. And, certainly, the situation in which these individuals were placed for several months, is remarkable, and worthy of being recorded, seeing a horrible scourge advancing towards them, labouring, by every method, to repulse it, yet meeting with obstacles, not only in the arduousness of the task, but from every quarter, in the unwillingness of the people, and being made the general object of execration, and regarded as the enemies of their country: *'Pro patriæ hostibus,'* says Ripamonti.[9]

Sharers, also, in the hatred were the other physicians, who, convinced like them of the reality of the contagion, suggested precautions, and sought to communicate to others their melancholy convictions. The most knowing taxed them with credulity and obstinacy; while, with the many, it was evidently an imposture, a planned combination, to make a profit by the public fears.

The aged physician, Lodovico Settala, who had almost attained his eightieth year, who had been Professor of Medicine in the University of Pavia, and afterwards of Moral Philosophy at Milan, the author of many works at that time in very high repute, eminent for the invitations he had received to occupy the chairs of other universities, Ingolstadt, Pisa, Bologna, and Padua, and for his refusal of all these honours, was certainly one of the most influential men of his time. To his reputation for learning was added that of his life; and to admiration of his character, a feeling of good-will for his great kindness in curing and benefiting the poor. Yet there is one circumstance, which, in our minds, disturbs and overclouds the sentiment of esteem inspired by these merits, but which at that time must have rendered it stronger and more general: the poor man participated in the commonest and most fatal prejudices of

[8] Tadino, p. 73.   [9] Ripamonti, p. 261.

his contemporaries: he was in advance of them, but not distinguished from the multitude; a station which only invites trouble, and often causes the loss of an authority acquired by other means. Nevertheless, that which he enjoyed in so great a degree, was not only insufficient to overcome the general opinion on this subject of the pestilence, but it could not even protect him from the animosity and the insults of that part of the populace, which most readily steps from opinions to their exhibition by actual deeds.

One day, as he was going in a litter to visit his patients, crowds began to assemble round him, crying out that he was the head of those who were determined, in spite of everything, to make out that there was a plague; that it was he who put the city in alarm, with his gloomy brow, and shaggy beard; and all to give employment to the doctors! The multitude and their fury went on increasing; so that the bearers, seeing their danger, took refuge with their master in the house of a friend, which fortunately happened to be at hand. All this occurred to him for having foreseen clearly, stated what was really the fact, and wished to save thousands of his fellow-creatures from the pestilence: when having, by his deplorable advice, co-operated in causing a poor unhappy wretch to be put to the torture, racked, and burnt as a witch, because one of her masters had suffered extraordinary pains in his stomach, and another, some time before, had been desperately enamoured of her,[10] he had received from the popular voice additional reputation for wisdom, and, what is intolerable to think of, the additional title of the well-deserving.

Towards the latter end of March, however, sickness and deaths began rapidly to multiply, first in the suburbs of the Porta Orientale, and then in all the other quarters of the city, with the unusual accompaniments of spasms, palpitation, lethargy, delirium, and those fatal symptoms, livid spots and sores; and these deaths were, for the most part, rapid, violent, and not unfrequently sudden, without any previous tokens of illness. Those physicians who were opposed to the belief of contagion, unwilling now to admit what they had hitherto derided, yet obliged to give a generical name to the new malady, which had become too common and too evident to go with-

[10] History of Milan, by Count Pietro Verri. Milan: 1825. Vol. iv. p. 155.

out one, adopted that of malignant or pestilential fevers;—a miserable expedient, a mere play upon words, which was productive of much harm; because, while it appeared to acknowledge the truth, it only contributed to the disbelief of what it was most important to believe and discern, viz., that the infection was conveyed by means of the touch. The magistrates, like one awakening from a deep sleep, began to lend a little more ear to the appeals and proposals of the Board of Health, to support its proclamations, and second the sequestrations prescribed, and the quarantines enjoined by this tribunal. The Board was also constantly demanding money to provide for the daily expenses of the Lazzaretto, now augmented by so many additional services; and for this they applied to the *Decurioni,* while it was being decided (which was never done, I believe, except by practice) whether such expenses should be charged to the city, or to the royal exchequer. The high chancellor also applied importunately to the *Decurioni,* by order, too, of the governor, who had again returned to lay siege to the unfortunate Casale; the senate likewise applied to them, imploring them to see to the best method of victualing the city, before they should be forbidden, in case of the unhappy dissemination of the contagion, to have any intercourse with other countries; and to find means of maintaining a large proportion of the population which was now deprived of employment. The *Decurioni* endeavoured to raise money by loans and taxes; and of what they thus accumulated they gave a little to the Board of Health, a little to the poor, purchased a little corn, and thus, in some degree, supplied the existing necessity. The severest sufferings had not yet arrived.

In the Lazzaretto, where the population, although decimated daily, continued daily on the increase, there was another arduous undertaking, to insure attendance and subordination, to preserve the enjoined separations, to maintain, in short, or rather to establish, the government prescribed by the Board of Health: for, from the very first, everything had been in confusion, from the ungovernableness of many of the inmates, and the negligence or connivance of the officials. The Board and the *Decurioni,* not knowing which way to turn, bethought themselves of applying to the Capuchins, and besought the Father Commissary, as he was called, of the province, who occupied the place of the Father Provincial, lately deceased, to give them a competent person to govern this desolate kingdom. The commissary proposed to them as their governor, one Father Felice Casati, a man of advanced age, who enjoyed great reputation for charity, activity, and gentleness of disposition, combined with a strong mind—a character which, as the sequel will show, was well deserved; and as his coadjutor and assistant, one Father Michele Pozzobonelli, still a young man, but grave and stern in mind as in countenance. Gladly enough were they accepted; and on the 30th of March they entered the Lazzaretto. The President of the Board of Health conducted them round, as it were, to put them in possession; and having assembled the servants and officials of every rank, proclaimed Father Felice, in their presence, governor of the place, with primary and unlimited authority. In proportion as the wretched multitude there assembled increased, other Capuchins resorted thither; and here were superintendents, confessors, administrators, nurses, cooks, overlookers of the wardrobes, washerwomen, in short, everything that was required. Father Felice, ever diligent, ever watchful, went about day and night, through the porticoes, chambers, and open spaces, sometimes carrying a spear, sometimes armed only with hair-cloth; he animated and regulated every duty, pacified tumults, settled disputes, threatened, punished, reproved, comforted, dried and shed tears. At the very outset he took the plague; recovered, and with fresh alacrity resumed his first duties. Most of his brethren here sacrificed their lives, and all joyfully.

Such a dictatorship was certainly a strange expedient; strange as was the calamity, strange as were the times; and even did we know no more about it, this alone would suffice as an argument, as a specimen, indeed, of a rude and ill-regulated state of society. But the spirit, the deeds, the self-sacrifice, of these friars, deserve no less than that they should be mentioned with respect and tenderness, and with that species of gratitude which one feels, *en masse* as it were, for great services rendered by men to their fellows. To die in a good cause is a wise and beautiful action, at any time, under any state of things whatsoever. 'For had not y^se Fathers repayred hither,' says Tadino, 'assuredly ye whole Citie would have been annihilated; for it was a miraculous thing that y^se Fathers effected so much for ye publick Benefit in so short a space of Time, and, receiving no Assistance, or at least, very little, from ye Citie, contrived, by their Industrie and Prudence, to maintain so many thousands of Poore in ye Lazzaretto.' [11]

Among the public, also, this obstinacy in denying the pestilence gave way naturally, and gradually disappeared, in proportion as the contagion extended itself, and extended itself, too, before their own eyes, by means of contact and intercourse; and still more when, after having been for some time confined to the lower orders, it began to take effect upon the higher. And among these, as he was then the most eminent, so by us now, the senior physician Settala, deserves express mention. People must at least have said: The poor old man was right! But who knows? He, with his wife, two sons, and seven persons in his service, all took the plague. One of these sons and himself recovered; the rest died. 'These Cases,' says Tadino, 'occurring in the Citie in the first families, disposed the Nobilitie and common People to think; and the incredulous Physicians, and the ignorant and rash lower Orders, began to bite their Lips, grind their Teeth, and arch their Eyebrows in Amazement.' [12]

But the revolutions, the reprisals, the vengeance, so to say, of convinced obstinacy, are sometimes such as to raise a wish that it had continued unshaken and unconquered, even to the last, against reason and evidence: and this was truly one of these occasions. They who had so resolutely and perseveringly impugned the existence of a germ of evil near them, or among them, which might propagate itself by natural means, and make much havoc, unable now to deny its propagation, and unwilling to attribute it to those means (for this would have been to confess at once a great delusion and a great error), were so much the more inclined to find some other cause for it, and make good any that might happen to present itself. Unhappily, there was one in readiness in the ideas and traditions common at that time, not only here, but in every part of Europe, of magical arts, diabolical practices, people sworn to disseminate the plague by means of contagious poisons and witchcraft. These and similar things had already been supposed and believed during many other plagues; and at Milan, especially, in that of half a century

[11] Tadino, p. 98.   [12] Ib., p. 96.

before. It may be added, that, even during the preceding year, a despatch, signed by King Philip IV., had been forwarded to the governor, in which he was informed that four Frenchmen had escaped from Madrid, who were sought upon suspicion of spreading poisonous and pestilential ointments; and requiring him to be on the watch, perchance they should arrive at Milan. The governor communicated the despatch to the Senate and the Board of Health; and thenceforward, it seems, they thought no more about it. When, however, the plague broke forth, and was recognized by all, the return of this intelligence to memory may have served to confirm and support the vague suspicion of an iniquitous fraud; it may even have been the first occasion of creating it.

But two actions, one of blind and undisciplined fear, the other of I know not what malicious mischief, were what converted this vague suspicion of a possible attempt, into more than suspicion (and, with many, a certain conviction) of a real plot. Some persons who fancied they had seen people, on the evening of the 17th of May, in the cathedral, anointing a partition which was used to separate the spaces assigned to the two sexes, had this partition, and a number of benches enclosed within it, brought out during the night; although the President of the Board of Health, having repaired thither with four members of the committee, and having inspected the screen, the benches, and the stoups of holy water, and found nothing that could confirm the ignorant suspicion of a poisonous attempt, had declared, to humour other people's fancies, and *rather to exceed in caution, than from any conviction of necessity,* that it would be sufficient to have the partition washed. This mass of piled-up furniture produced a strong impression of consternation among the multitude, to whom any object so readily became an argument. It was said, and generally believed, that all the benches, walls, and even the bell-ropes in the cathedral, had been rubbed over with unctuous matter. Nor was this affirmed only at the time: all the records of contemporaries (some of them written after a lapse of many years) which allude to this incident, speak of it with equal certainty of asseveration: and we should be obliged to conjecture its true history, did we not find it in a letter from the Board of Health to the governor, preserved in the archives of San

Fedele, from which we have extracted it, and whence we have quoted the words we have written in italics.

Next morning, a new, stranger, and more significant spectacle, struck the eyes and minds of the citizens. In every part of the city they saw the doors and walls of the houses stained and daubed with long streaks of I know not what filthiness, something yellowish and whitish, spread over them as if with a sponge. Whether it were a base inclination to witness a more clamorous and more general consternation, or a still more wicked design to augment the public confusion, or whatever else it may have been, the fact is attested in such a manner, that it seems to us less rational to attribute it to a dream of the imagination, than to a wickedly malicious trick, not entirely new, indeed, to the wit of man,—not, alas, deficient in corresponding effects, in every place, so to say, and every age. Ripamonti, who frequently on this subject of the anointing, ridicules, and still more frequently deplores, the popular credulity, here affirms that he had seen this plastering, and then describes it.[13] In the above-quoted letter, the gentlemen of the Board of Health relate the circumstance in the same terms; they speak of inspections, of experiments made with this matter upon dogs, without any injurious effect; and add, that they believe *such temerity proceeded rather from insolence than from any guilty design:* an opinion which evinces that, up to this time, they retained sufficient tranquillity of mind not to see what really did not exist. Other contemporary records, not to reckon their testimony as to the truth of the fact, signify, at the same time, that it was at first the opinion of many, that this beplastering had been done in joke, in a mere frolic; none of them speak of any one who denied it; and had there been any, they certainly would have mentioned them, were it only to call them irrational. I have deemed it not out of place to relate and put together these particulars, in part little known, in part entirely unknown, of a celebrated popular delirium; because in errors, and especially in the errors of a multitude, what seems to me most interesting and most useful to observe, is, the course they

[13] . . . 'Et nos quoque ivimus visere. Maculæ erant sparsim inæqualiterque manantes, veluti si quis haustam spongia saniem adspersissit, impressissetve parieti: et ianuæ passim ostiaque ædium eadem adspergine contaminata cernebantur.'—Page 75.

have taken, their appearances, and the ways by which they could enter men's minds, and hold sway there.

The city, already tumultuously inclined, was now turned upside down: the owners of the houses, with lighted straw, burned the besmeared spots; and passers-by stopped, gazed, shuddered, murmured. Strangers, suspected of this alone, and at that time easily recognized by their dress, were arrested by the people in the streets, and consigned to prison. Here interrogations and examinations were made of captured, captors, and witnesses; no one was found guilty: men's minds were still capable of doubting, weighing, understanding. The Board of Health issued a proclamation, in which they promised reward and impunity to any one who would bring to light the author or authors of the deed. *'In any wise, not thinking it expedient,'* say these gentlemen in the letter we have quoted, which bears date the 21st of May, but which was evidently written on the 19th, the day signified in the printed proclamation, *'that this crime should by any means remain unpunished, speciallie in times so perilous and suspicious, we have, for the consolation and peace of the people, this daie published an edicte,'* &c. In the edict, however, there is no mention, at least no distinct one, of that rational and tranquillizing conjecture they had suggested to the governor: a reservation which indicates at once a fierce prejudice in the people, and in themselves a degree of obsequiousness, so much the more blamable as the consequences might prove more pernicious.

While the Board was thus making inquiries, many of the public, as is usually the case, had already found the answer. Among those who believed this to be a poisonous ointment, some were sure it was an act of revenge of Don Gonzalo Fernandez de Cordova, for the insults received at his departure; some, that it was an idea of Cardinal Richelieu's to desolate Milan, and make himself master of it without trouble; others, again—it is not known with what motives—would have that the Count Collalto was the author of the plot, or Wallenstein, or this or that Milanese nobleman. There wanted not too, as we have said, those who saw nothing in this occurrence but a mischievous jest, and attributed it to students, to gentlemen, to officers who were weary of the siege of Casale. It did not appear, however, as had been dreaded, that infection and universal slaughter immediately ensued: and this was probably the cause that this first fear began by degrees to subside, and the matter was, or seemed to be, forgotten.

There was, after all, a certain number of persons not yet convinced that it was indeed the plague; and because, both in the Lazzaretto and in the city, some were restored to health, 'it was affirmed,' (the final arguments for an opinion contradicted by evidence are always curious enough), 'it was affirmed by the common people, and even yet by many partial physicians, that it was not really the plague, or all would have died.' [14] To remove every doubt, the Board of Health employed an expedient conformable to the necessity of the case, a means of speaking to the eye, such as the times may have required or suggested. On one of the festal days of Whitsuntide, the citizens were in the habit of flocking to the cemetery of San Gregorio, outside the Porta Orientale, to pray for the souls of those who had died in the former contagion, and whose bodies were there interred; and borrowing from devotion an opportunity of amusement and sightseeing, every one went thither in his best and gayest clothing. One whole family, amongst others, had this day died of the plague. At the hour of the thickest concourse, in the midst of carriages, riders on horseback, and foot-passengers, the corpses of this family were, by order of the Board, drawn naked on a car to the above-named burying-ground; in order that the crowd might behold in them the manifest token, the revolting seal and symptom, of the pestilence. A cry of horror and consternation arose wherever the car was passing; a prolonged murmur was predominant where it had passed, another murmur preceded it. The real existence of the plague was more believed: besides, every day it continued to gain more belief by itself; and that very concourse would contribute not a little to propagate it.

First, then, it was not the plague, absolutely not—by no means: the very utterance of the term was prohibited. Then, it was pestilential fevers: the idea was indirectly admitted in an adjective. Then, it was not the true nor real plague; that is to say, it was the plague, but only in a certain sense; not positively and undoubtedly the plague, but something to which no other name could be affixed.

[14] Tadino, p. 93.

Lastly, it was the plague without doubt, without dispute: but even then another idea was appended to it, the idea of poison and witch-craft, which altered and confounded that conveyed in the word they could no longer repress.

There is no necessity, I imagine, to be well versed in the history of words and ideas, to perceive that many others have followed a similar course. Heaven be praised that there have not been many of such a nature, and of so vast importance, which contradict their evidence at such a price, and to which accessories of such a character may be annexed! It is possible, however, both in great and trifling concerns, to avoid, in great measure, so lengthened and crooked a path, by following the method which has been so long laid down, of observing, listening, comparing, and thinking, before speaking.

But speaking—this one thing by itself—is so much easier than all the others put together, that even we, I say, we men in general, are somewhat to be pitied.

CHAPTER XXXII

THE difficulty of providing for the mournful exigencies of the times becoming daily greater, it was resolved, on the 4th of May, in the Council of the *Decurioni,* to have recourse for aid and favour to the governor; and accordingly, on the 22nd, two members of that body were despatched to the camp, who represented to him the sufferings and poverty of the city: the enormous expenditure, the treasury exhausted and involved in debt, its future revenue in pledge, and the current taxes unpaid, by reason of the general impoverishment, produced by so many causes, and especially by the havoc of the military; they submitted to his consideration that, according to laws and customs, which had never been repealed, and by a special decree of Charles V., the expenses of the pestilence ought to be defrayed from the king's exchequer: that, in the plague of 1576, the governor, the Marquis of Ayamonte, had not indeed remitted all the taxes of the Chamber, but had relieved the city with forty thousand *scudi* from that same Chamber; and, finally, they demanded four things:—that, as once before already, the taxes should not be exacted; that the Chamber should grant some supplies of money; that the governor should acquaint the king with the misery of the city and the territory; and that the duchy should be exempted from again quartering the military, as it had been already wasted and destroyed by the former troops. Spinola gave in reply condolences and fresh exhortations: he said he was sorry he did not happen to be in the city, that he might use all his endeavours for its relief; but he hoped that all would be compensated for by the zeal of these gentlemen: that this was the time to expend without parsimony, and to do all they could by every means: and as to the express demands, he would provide for them in the best way the times and existing necessities would allow. Nor was there any further result: there were, indeed, more journeys to and fro, new requisitions and replies; but I do not find that they came to any more determinate conclusions. Some time later, when the plague was at its greatest height, the governor thought fit to transfer his authority, by letters patent, to the High Chancellor Ferrer, he having, as he said, to attend to the war.

Together with this resolution, the *Decurioni* had also taken another, to request the Cardinal Archbishop to appoint a solemn procession, bearing through the city the body of San Carlo. The good prelate refused, for many reasons. This confidence in an arbitrary measure displeased him; and he feared that if the effect should not correspond to it, which he had also reason to fear, confidence would be converted into offence.[1] He feared further, that, *if indeed there were poisoners about,* the procession would afford too convenient opportunities for crime; *if there were not,* such a concourse of itself should not fail to disseminate the contagion more widely: *a danger far more real.*[2] For the suppressed suspicions of poisonous ointments had, meanwhile, revived more generally and more violently than ever.

People had again seen, or this time they fancied they had seen anointed walls, entrances to public buildings, doors of private houses, and knockers. The news of these discoveries flew from mouth to mouth; and, as it happens even more than usually in great prepossessions, the report produced the same effect that the sight of it would have done. The minds of the populace, ever more and more embittered by the actual presence of suffering, and irritated by the pertinacity of the danger, embraced this belief the more willingly; for anger burns to execute its revenge, and, as a very worthy man acutely observes on this same subject,[3] would rather attribute evils to human wickedness, upon which it might vent its tormenting energies, than acknowledge them from a source which leaves no other remedy than resignation. A subtle, instantaneous, exceedingly penetrating poison, were words more than enough to explain the

[1] Memoirs of successive Remarkable Events in Milan about the time of the Plague, in the year 1630, &c., compiled by D. Pio la Croce, Milan, 1730. It is evidently taken from an unpublished writing of an author who lived at the time of the pestilence; if indeed it be not a simple edition, rather than a new compilation.

[2] 'Si unguenta scelerata et unctores in urbe essent . . . Si non essent . . . Certiusque adeo malum.'—*Ripamonti,* p. 185.

[3] P. Verri. Observations on Torture: Italian Writers on Modern Political Economy, vol. xvii. p. 205.

virulence, and all other most mysterious and unusual accompaniments of the contagion. It was said that this venom was composed of toads, of serpents, of saliva and matter from infected persons, of worse still, of everything, in short, that wild and perverse fancy could invent which was foul and atrocious. To these was added witchcraft, by which any effect became possible, every objection lost its force, every difficulty was resolved. If the anticipated effects had not immediately followed upon the first anointing, the reason was now clear—it had been the imperfect attempt of novices in the art of sorcery; now it was more matured, and the wills of the perpetrators were more bent upon their infernal project. Now, had any one still maintained that it had been a mere trick, had any one still denied the existence of a conspiracy, he would have passed for a deluded or obstinate person; if, indeed, he would not have fallen under the suspicion of being interested in diverting public scrutiny from the truth, of being an accomplice, a *poisoner*. The term very soon became common, solemn, tremendous. With such a persuasion, that poisoners there were, some must almost infallibly be discovered: all eyes were on the look-out; every act might excite jealousy; and jealousy easily became certainty, and certainty fury.

Ripamonti relates two instances, informing us that he had selected them, not as the most outrageous among the many which daily occurred, but because, unhappily, he could speak of both as an eye-witness.[4]

In the church of Sant' Antonio, on the day of I know not what solemnity, an old man, more than eighty years of age, was observed, after kneeling in prayer, to sit down, first, however, dusting the bench with his cloak. 'That old man is anointing the benches!' exclaimed with one voice some women, who witnessed the act. The people who happened to be in church, (in church!) fell upon the old man; they tore his gray locks, heaped upon him blows and kicks, and dragged him out half dead, to convey him to prison, to the judges, to torture. 'I beheld him dragged along in this way,' says Ripamonti, 'nor could I learn anything further about his end; but, indeed, I think he could not have survived many moments.'

The other instance, which occurred the following day, was equally

[4] Page 96.

strange, but not equally fatal. Three French youths, in company, one a scholar, one a painter, and the third a mechanic, who had come to see Italy, to study its antiquities, and to try and make money, had approached I know not exactly what part of the exterior of the cathedral, and stood attentively surveying it. One, two, or more passers-by, stopped, and formed a little group, to contemplate and keep their eye on these visitors, whom their costume, their headdress, and their wallets, proclaimed to be strangers, and, what was worse, Frenchmen. As if to assure themselves that it was marble, they stretched out their hands to touch it. This was enough. They were surrounded, seized, tormented, and urged by blows to prison. Fortunately, the hall of justice was not far from the cathedral, and by still greater good fortune, they were found innocent, and set at liberty.

Nor did such things happen only in the city; the frenzy had spread like the contagion. The traveller who was met by peasants out of the highway, or on the public road was seen loitering and amusing himself, or stretched upon the ground to rest; the stranger in whom they fancied they saw something singular and suspicious in countenance or dress—these were poisoners; at the first report of whomsoever it might be—at the cry of a child—the alarm was given, and the people flocked together; the unhappy victims were pelted with stones, or, if taken, were violently dragged to prison. And the prison, up to a certain period, became a haven of safety.[5]

But the *Decurioni,* not discouraged by the refusal of the judicious prelate, continued to repeat their entreaties, which were noisily seconded by the popular vote. The Bishop persevered for some time, and endeavoured to dissuade them: so much and no more could the discretion of one man do against the judgment of the times, and the pertinacity of the many. In this state of opinion, with the idea of danger, confused as it was at that period, disputed, and very far from possessing the evidence which we have for it, it will not be difficult to comprehend how his good reasons might, even in his own mind, be overcome by the bad ones of others. Whether, besides, in his subsequent concession, a feebleness of will had or had not any share, is a mystery of the human heart. Cer-

[5] Ripamonti, pp. 91, 92.

tainly if, in any case, it be possible to attribute error wholly to the intellect, and to relieve the conscience of responsibility, it is when one treats of those rare persons, (and, assuredly, the Cardinal was of the number), throughout whose whole life is seen a resolute obedience to conscience, without regard to temporal interests of any kind. On the repetition of the entreaties, then, he yielded, gave his consent to the procession, and further, to the desire, the general eagerness, that the urn which contained the relics of San Carlo should afterwards remain exposed for eight days to the public concourse, on the high altar of the cathedral.

I do not find that the Board of Health, or the other authorities, made any opposition or remonstrance of any kind. The above-named Board merely ordered some precautions, which, without obviating the danger, indicated their apprehension of it. They gave more strict regulations about the admission of persons into the city, and to insure the execution of them, kept all the gates shut: as also, in order to exclude from the concourse, as far as possible, the infected and suspected, they caused the doors of the condemned houses to be nailed up; which, so far as the bare assertion of a writer—and a writer of those times—is to be valued in such matters, amounted to about five hundred.[6]

Three days were spent in preparations; and on the 11th of June, which was the day fixed, the procession started by early dawn from the cathedral. A long file of people led the way, chiefly women, their faces covered with ample silken veils, and many of them barefoot, and clothed in sackcloth. Then followed bands of artificers, preceded by their several banners, the different fraternities, in habits of various shades and colours; then came the brotherhoods of monks, then the secular clergy, each with the insignia of his rank, and bearing a lighted wax taper. In the centre, amidst the brilliancy of still more numerous torches, and the louder tones of the chanting, came the coffin, under a rich canopy, supported alternately by four canons, most pompously attired. Through the crystal sides appeared the venerated corpse, the limbs enveloped in splendid pontifical robes, and the skull covered with a mitre; and under the mutilated and decomposed features, some traces might

[6] Alleviation of the State of Milan, &c., by C. G. Cavatio della Somaglia. Milan, 1653, p. 248.

still be distinguished of his former countenance, such as it was represented in pictures, and as some remembered seeing and honouring it during his life. Behind the mortal remains of the deceased pastor, (says Ripamonti,[7] from which we chiefly have taken this description), and near him in person, as well as in merit, blood, and dignity, came the Archbishop Federigo. Then followed the rest of the clergy, and close behind them the magistrates, in their best robes of office; after them the nobility, some sumptuously apparelled, as for a solemn celebration of worship, others in token of humiliation, clothed in mourning, or walking barefoot, covered with sackcloth, and the hoods drawn over their faces, all bearing large torches. A mingled crowd of people brought up the rear.

The whole street was decked out as at a festival; the rich had brought out their most showy decorations; the fronts of the poorer houses were ornamented by their wealthier neighbours, or at the public expense; here and there, instead of ornaments, or over the ornaments themselves, were leafy branches of trees; everywhere were suspended pictures, mottoes, and emblematical devices; on the window-ledges were displayed vases, curiosities of antiquity, and valuable ornaments; and in every direction were torches. At many of these windows the sick, who were put under sequestration, beheld the pomp, and mingled their prayers with those of the passengers. The other streets were silent and deserted, save where some few listened at the windows to the floating murmur in the distance; while others, and among these even nuns might be seen, mounted on the roofs, perchance they might be able to distinguish afar off the coffin, the retinue—in short, something.

The procession passed through all quarters of the city; at each of the crossways, or small squares, which terminate the principal streets in the suburbs, and which then preserved the ancient name of *carrobii,* now reduced to only one, they made a halt, depositing the coffin near the cross which had been erected in every one by San Carlo, during the preceding pestilence, some of which are still standing; so that they returned not to the cathedral till considerably past midday.

But lo! the day following, just while the presumptuous confidence,

[7] Pages 62–66.

nay, in many, the fanatical assurance prevailed, that the procession must have cut short the progress of the plague, the mortality increased in every class, in every part of the city, to such a degree, and with so sudden a leap, that there was scarcely any one who did not behold in the very procession itself, the cause and occasion of this fearful increase. But, oh wonderful and melancholy force of popular prejudices! the greater number did not attribute this effect to so great and so prolonged a crowding together of persons, nor to the infinite multiplication of fortuitous contact, but rather to the facilities afforded to the poisoners of executing their iniquitous designs on a large scale. It was said that, mixing in the crowd, they had infected with their ointment everybody they had encountered. But as this appeared neither a sufficient nor appropriate means for producing so vast a mortality, which extended itself to every rank; as, apparently, it had not been possible, even for an eye the most watchful, and the most quick-sighted from suspicion, to detect any unctuous matter, or spots of any kind, during the march, recourse was had for the explanation of the fact to that other fabrication, already ancient, and received at that time into the common scientific learning of Europe, of magical and venomous powders; it was said that these powders, scattered along the streets and chiefly at the places of halting, had clung to the trains of the dresses, and still more to the feet of those who had that day, in great numbers, gone about barefoot. 'That very day, therefore, of the procession,' says a contemporary writer,[8] 'saw piety contending with iniquity, perfidy with sincerity, and loss with acquisition.' It was, on the contrary, poor human sense contending with the phantoms it had itself created.

From that day, the contagion continued to rage with increasing violence; in a little while, there was scarcely a house left untouched; and the population of the Lazzaretto, according to Somaglia, above quoted, amounted to from two to twelve thousand. In the course of time, according to almost all reports, it reached sixteen thousand. On the fourth of July, as I find in another letter from the conservators of health to the Governor, the daily mortality exceeded five hundred. Still later, when the plague was at its height,

<hr>

[8] Agostino Lampugnano: Of the Pestilence that happened in Milan, in the year 1630. Milan, 1634, p. 44.

it reached, and for some time remained at, twelve or fifteen hundred, according to the most common computation; and if we may credit Tadino,[9] it sometimes even exceeded three thousand five hundred.

It may be imagined what must now have been the difficulties of the *Decurioni,* upon whom was laid the burden of providing for the public necessities, and repairing what was still reparable in such a calamity. They were obliged every day to replace, every day to augment, public officers of numerous kinds: *Monatti,* by which denomination (even then at Milan of ancient date, and uncertain origin,) were designated those who were devoted to the most painful and dangerous services of a pestilence, viz. taking corpses from the houses, out of the streets, and from the Lazzaretto, transporting them on carts to the graves, and burying them; carrying or conducting the sick to the Lazzaretto, overlooking them there, and burning and cleansing infected or suspected goods: *Apparitori,*[10] whose special office it was to precede the carts, warning passengers, by the sound of a little bell, to retire: and *Commissarii,* who superintended both the other classes, under the immediate orders of the Board of Health. The Council had also to keep the Lazzaretto furnished with physicians, surgeons, medicines, food, and all the other necessaries of an infirmary; and to provide and prepare new quarters for the newly arising needs. For this purpose, they had cabins of wood and straw hastily constructed, in the unoccupied space within the Lazzaretto; and another Lazzaretto was erected, also of thatched cabins, with an enclosure of boards, capable of containing four thousand persons. These not being sufficient, two others were decreed; they even began to build them, but, from the deficiency of means of every kind, they remained uncompleted. Means, men, and courage failed, in proportion as the necessity for them increased. And not only did the execution fall so far short of the projects and decrees—not only were many too clearly acknowledged necessities deficiently provided for, even in words, but they arrived at such a pitch of impotency and desperation, that many of the most deplorable and urgent cases were left without succour of any kind. A great number of infants, for example, died of absolute neglect, their mothers having been carried off by the pestilence. The

[9] Pages 115–117.   [10] A bailiff of the meanest kind.

Board of Health proposed that a place of refuge should be founded for these, and for destitute lying-in women, that something might be done for them, but they could obtain nothing. 'The *Decurioni* of the Citie,' says Tadino, 'were no less to be pitied, who found themselves harassed and oppressed by the Soldierie without any Bounds or Regarde whatsoever, as well as those in the unfortunate Duchy, seeing that they could get no Help or Prouision from the Gouernor, because it happened to be a Tyme of War, and they must needs treat the Soldierie well.' [11] So important was the taking of Casale! so glorious appeared the fame of victory, independent of the cause, of the object for which they contended!

So, also, an ample but solitary grave which had been dug near the Lazzaretto being completely filled with corpses; and fresh bodies, which became day by day more numerous, remaining therefore in every direction unburied, the magistrates, after having in vain sought for hands to execute the melancholy task, were compelled to acknowledge that they knew not what course to pursue. Nor was it easy to conjecture what would be the end, had not extraordinary relief been afforded. The President of the Board of Health solicited it almost in despair, and with tears in his eyes, from those two excellent friars who presided at the Lazzaretto; and Father Michele pledged himself to clear the city of dead bodies in the course of four days. At the expiration of eight days he had not only provided for the immediate necessity, but for that also which the most ominous foresight could have anticipated for the future. With a friar for his companion, and with officers granted him for this purpose by the President, he set off out of the city in search of peasants; and partly by the authority of the Board of Health, partly by the influence of his habit and his words, he succeeded in collecting two hundred, whom he distributed in three separate places, to dig the ample graves. He then despatched *monatti* from the Lazzaretto to collect the dead, and on the day appointed his promise was fulfilled.

On one occasion, the Lazzaretto was left destitute of physicians; and it was only by offers of large salaries and honours, with much labour, and considerable delay, that they could procure them; and

[11] Page 117.

even then their number was far from sufficient for the need. It was often so reduced in provisions as to raise fears that the inmates would actually have to die of starvation; and more than once, while they were trying every method of raising money or supplies, with scarcely a hope of procuring them,—not to say of procuring them in time,—abundant assistance would most opportunely be afforded by the unexpected gift of some charitable private individual; for, in the midst of the common stupefaction and indifference to others, arising from continual apprehensions for themselves, there were yet hearts ever awake to the call of charity, and others in whom charity first sprang up on the failure of all earthly pleasures; as, in the destruction and flight of many whose duty it was to superintend and provide, there were others, ever healthy in body and unshaken in courage, who were always at their posts; while some there even were who, urged by compassion, assumed, and perseveringly sustained, cares to which their office did not call them.

The most general and most willing fidelity to the trying duties of the times, was conspicuously evinced by the clergy. In the Lazzarettoes, and throughout the city, their assistance never failed; where suffering was, there were they; they were always to be seen mingled with and interspersed among the faint and dying—faint and dying sometimes themselves. Together with spiritual succours, they were lavish, as far as they could be, of temporal ones, and freely rendered whatever services happened to be required. More than sixty parish-priests, in the city alone, died of the contagion: about eight out of every nine.

Federigo, as was to be expected from him, gave to all encouragement and example. Having seen almost the whole of his archiepiscopal household perish around him, solicited by relatives, by the first magistrates, and by the neighbouring princes, to withdraw from danger to some solitary country-seat, he rejected this counsel and entreaties in the spirit with which he wrote to his clergy: 'Be ready to abandon this mortal life, rather than the family, the children, committed to us; go forward into the plague, as to life, as to a reward, when there is one soul to be won to Christ.' [12] He neglected no precautions which did not impede him in his duty; on which

[12] Ripamonti, p. 164.

point he also gave instructions and regulations to his clergy; and, at the same time, he minded not, nor appeared to observe, danger, where it was necessary to encounter it, in order to do good. Without speaking of the ecclesiastics, whom he was constantly with, to commend and regulate their zeal, to arouse such as were lukewarm in the work, and to send them to the posts where others had perished, it was his wish that there should always be free access for any one who had need of him. He visited the Lazzarettoes, to administer consolation to the sick, and encouragement to the attendants; he traversed the city, carrying relief to the poor creatures sequestrated in their houses, stopping at the doors and under the windows to listen to their lamentations, and to offer in exchange words of comfort and encouragement. In short, he threw himself into, and lived in the midst of the pestilence, and was himself astonished, at the end, that he had come out uninjured.

Thus, in public calamities and in long-continued disturbances of settled habits, of whatever kind, there may always be beheld an augmentation, a sublimation of virtue; but, alas! there is never wanting, at the same time, an augmentation, far more general in most cases, of crime. This occasion was remarkable for it. The villains, whom the pestilence spared and did not terrify, found in the common confusion, and in the relaxation of all public authority, a new opportunity of activity, together with new assurances of impunity; nay, the administration of public authority itself came, in a great measure, to be lodged in the hands of the worst among them. Generally speaking, none devoted themselves to the offices of *monatti* and *apparitori* but men over whom the attractions of rapine and license had more influence than the terror of contagion, or any natural object of horror.

The strictest orders were laid upon these people; the severest penalties threatened to them; stations were assigned them; and commissaries, as we have said, placed over them: over both, again, magistrates and nobles were appointed in every district, with authority to enforce good government summarily on every opportunity. Such a state of things went on and took effect up to a certain period; but, with the increase of deaths and desolation, and the terror of the survivors, these officers came to be, as it were, exempted from all supervision; they constituted themselves, the *monatti* especially, arbiters of everything. They entered the houses like masters, like enemies; and, not to mention their plunder, and how they treated the unhappy creatures reduced by the plague to pass through such hands, they laid them—these infected and guilty hands —on the healthy—children, parents, husbands, wives, threatening to drag them to the Lazzaretto, unless they redeemed themselves, or were redeemed, with money. At other times they set a price upon their services, refusing to carry away bodies already corrupted, for less than so many *scudi.* It was believed (and between the credulity of one party and the wickedness of the other, belief and disbelief are equally uncertain), it was believed, and Tadino asserts it,[13] that both *monatti* and *apparitori* purposely let fall from their carts infected clothes, in order to propagate and keep up the pestilence, which had become to them a means of living, a kingdom, a festival. Other wretches, feigning to be *monatti,* and carrying little bells tied to their feet, as these officers were required to do, to distinguish themselves and to give warning of their approach, introduced themselves into houses, and there exercised all kinds of tyranny. Some of these, open and void of inhabitants, or inhabited only by a feeble or dying creature, were entered by thieves in search of booty, with impunity; others were surprised and invaded by bailiffs, who there committed robberies and excesses of every description.

Together with the wickedness, the folly of the people increased: every prevailing error received more or less additional force from the stupefaction and agitation of their minds, and was more widely and more precipitately applied: while every one served to strengthen and aggravate that special mania about poisonings, which, in its effects and ebullitions, was often, as we have seen, itself another crime. The image of this supposed danger beset and tortured the minds of the people far more than the real and existing danger.

'And while,' says Ripamonti, 'corpses, scattered here and there, or lying in heaps, ever before the eyes and surrounding the steps of the living, made the whole city like one immense sepulchre, a still more appalling symptom, a more intense deformity, was their mutual animosity, their licentiousness, and their extravagant sus-

[13] Page 102.

picions. . . . Not only did they mistrust a friend, a guest; but those names which are the bonds of human affection, husband and wife, father and son, brother and brother, were words of terror, and, dreadful and infamous to tell! the domestic board, the nuptial bed, were dreaded as lurking-places, as receptacles of poison.' [14]

The imaginary vastness and strangeness of the plot distracted people's understandings, and subverted every reason for reciprocal confidence. Besides ambition and cupidity, which were at first supposed to be the motives of the poisoners, they fancied, they even believed at length, that there was something of diabolical, voluptuous delight in this anointing—an attraction predominating over the will. The ravings of the sick, who accused themselves of what they had apprehended from others, were considered as revelations, and rendered anything, so to say, credible of any one. And it would have far greater weight even than words, if it happened that delirious patients kept practising those manœuvres which it was imagined must be employed by the poisoners: a thing at once very probable, and tending to give better grounds for the popular persuasion and the assertions of numerous writers. In the same way, during the long and mournful period of judicial investigation on the subject of witchcraft, the confessions and those not always extorted of the accused, served not a little to promote and uphold the prevailing opinion on this matter; for when an opinion obtains a prolonged and extensive sway, it is expressed in every manner, tries every outlet, and runs through every degree of persuasion; and it is difficult for all, or very many, to believe for a length of time that something extraordinary is being done, without some one coming forward who believes that he has done it.

Among the stories which this mania about poisoning gave rise to, one deserves to be mentioned for the credit it acquired, and the extended dissemination it met with. It was related, not, however, by everybody in the same way (for that would be too remarkable a privilege for stories), but nearly so, that such a person, on such a day, had seen a carriage and six standing in the Square of the Cathedral, containing some great personage with a large suite, of lordly aspect, but dark and sunburnt, with fiery eyes, hair standing

[14] Page 81.

on end, and a threatening expression about the mouth. The spectator, invited to enter the equipage, complied; and after taking a turn or two, stopped and dismounted at the gate of a palace, where, entering with the rest, he beheld horrors and delights, deserts and gardens, caverns and halls; and in these were phantoms seated in council. Lastly, huge chests of money were shown to him, and he was told that he might take as much as he liked, if, at the same time, he would accept a little vessel of unctuous matter, and go about, anointing with it, through the city. Having refused to agree to the terms, he instantly found himself in the place whence he had been taken.

This story, generally believed there by the people, and, according to Ripamonti, not sufficiently ridiculed by many learned men,[15] travelled through the whole of Italy, and even further: an engraving of it was made in Germany; and the electoral Archbishop of Mayence wrote to Cardinal Federigo, to ask what he must believe of the wonderful prodigies related at Milan, and received for answer that they were mere dreams.

Of equal value, if not exactly of the same nature, were the dreams of the learned; and equally disastrous were they in their effects. Most of them saw the announcement at once and cause of their troubles, in a comet which appeared in the year 1628, and in a conjunction of Saturn with Jupiter; 'the aforesaide Conjunction,' writes Tadino, 'inclining so clearlie over this Yeare 1630, that every Bodie could understand it. *Mortales parat morbos, miranda videntur.*'[16] This prediction, fabricated I know not when nor by whom, was upon the tongue, as Ripamonti informs us,[17] of everybody who was able to utter it. Another comet, which unexpectedly appeared in the June of the very year of the pestilence, was looked upon as a fresh warning, as an evident proof, indeed, of the anointing. They ransacked books, and found only in too great abundance examples of pestilence produced, as they said, by human efforts; they quoted Livy, Tacitus, Dionysius, Homer, and Ovid, and the numberless other ancients who have related or alluded to similar events; and of modern writers they had a still greater abundance. They cited a hundred other authors, who have treated theoretically, or incidentally

[15] Page 77.   [16] Page 56.   [17] Page 273.

spoken, of poisons, sorceries, unctions, and powders; Cesalpino was quoted, Cardano, Grevino, Salio, Pareo, Schenchio, Zachia, and finally, that fatal Delrio, who, if the renown of authors were in proportion to the good or evil produced by their works, would assuredly be one of the most eminent; that Delrio, whose *Disquisitions on Magic* (a digest of all that men, up to his time, had wildly devised on this subject), received as the most authoritative and irrefragable text-book, was, for more than a century, the rule and powerful impulse of legal, horrible, and uninterrupted murders.

From the inventions of the illiterate vulgar, educated people borrowed what they could accommodate to their ideas; from the inventions of the educated the vulgar borrowed what they could understand, and as they best could; and of all, an undigested, barbarous jumble was formed of public irrationality.

But that which still further excites our surprise is to see the physicians, those physicians, I say, who from the beginning had believed in the plague, and especially Tadino, who had predicted it, beheld it enter, and kept his eye, so to say, on its progress; who had affirmed and published that it was the plague, and was propagated by contact, and that if no opposition were made to it, it would become a general infection,—to see him, I say, draw a certain argument from these very consequences, for poisonous and magical unctions: to behold him, who in Carlo Colonna, the second that died in Milan, had marked delirium as an accompaniment of the malady, afterwards adduce in proof of unctions and a diabolical plot an incident such as this:—two witnesses deposed to having heard one of their friends, under the influence of the contagion, relate how some persons came one night into his room, to proffer him health and riches, if he would anoint the houses in the vicinity, and how, on his repeated refusal, they had taken their departure, and left in their stead a wolf under the bed, and three great cats upon it, 'which remained there till break of day.' [18] Had such a method of drawing conclusions been confined to one individual, it might have been attributed to his own extreme simplicity and want of common sense, and it would not have been worth our while

[18] Pp. 123, 124.

to mention it; but, as it was received by many, it is a specimen of the human mind; and may serve to show how a well-regulated and reasonable train of ideas may be disordered by another train of ideas thrown directly across it. In other respects this Tadino was one of the most renowned men of his time at Milan.

Two illustrious and highly deserving writers have asserted that Cardinal Federigo entertained some doubt about these poisonings.[19] We would gladly give still more complete commendation to the memory of this excellent and benevolent man, and represent the good prelate in this, as in many other things, distinguished from the multitude of his contemporaries; but we are constrained, instead, to remark in him another example of the powerful influence of public opinion, even on the most exalted minds. It is evident,—from the way, at least, in which Ripamonti relates his thoughts on the subject, —that from the beginning he had some doubts about it; and throughout he always considered that credulity, ignorance, fear, and a wish to excuse their long negligence in guarding against the contagion, had a considerable share in this opinion: that there was a good deal of exaggeration in it; but at the same time something of truth. There is a small work on this pestilence, written by his own hand, preserved in the Ambrosian Library; and the following is one among many instances where such a sentiment is expressed:—'On the method of compounding and spreading such poisonous ointments many and various things are reported, some of which we consider as true, while others appear to us entirely imaginary.' [20]

Some there were who, to the very last, and ever afterwards, thought that it was all imagination; and we learn this, not from themselves, for no one had ever sufficient hardihood to expose to the public an opinion so opposed to that of the public; but from those writers who deride it, or rebuke it, or confute it, as the prejudice of a few, an error which no one had ever dared to make the subject of open dispute, but which nevertheless existed; and we

[19] Muratori, on the Treatment of the Pestilence, Modena, 1714, p. 117. P. Verri, in the treatise before quoted, p. 261.

[20] 'Unguenta vero hæc aiebant componi conficique multifariam, fraudisque vias esse complures: quarum sane fraudum et artium, aliis quidem assentimur, alias vero fictas fuisse commentitiasque arbitramur.'—De Peste quæ, Mediolani, anno 1630, magnam stragem edidit. cap. v.

learnt it, too, from one who had derived it from tradition. 'I have met with sensible and well-informed people in Milan,' says the good Muratori in the above-quoted passage, 'who had received trustworthy accounts from their ancestors, and who were by no means persuaded of the truth of the facts concerning these poisonous ointments.' It seems there was a secret outlet for truth, some remaining domestic confidence; good sense still existed; but it was kept concealed, for fear of the popular sense.

The magistrates, reduced in number daily, and disheartened and perplexed in everything, turned all their little vigilance, so to say, all the little resolution of which they were any longer capable, in search of these poisoners. And too easily did they think they had found them.

The judicial sentences which followed in consequence were not, certainly, the first of such a nature; nor, indeed, can they be considered as uncommon in the history of jurisprudence. For, to say nothing of antiquity, and to mention only some instances in times more nearly approaching those of which we are treating, in Palermo, in 1526; in Geneva, in 1530, afterwards in 1545, and again in 1574; in Casale Monferrato, in 1536; in Padua, in 1555; in Turin, in 1599; and again in Turin, this same year 1630; here one, there many unhappy creatures were tried, and condemned to punishments the most atrocious, as guilty of having propagated the plague by means of powders, ointments, witchcraft, or all these together. But the affair of the so-called anointings at Milan, as it was, perhaps, the longest remembered and the most widely talked of, so, perhaps, it is the most worthy of observation; or, to speak more exactly, there is further room to make observations upon it, from the remaining existence of more circumstantial and more extensive documents. And although a writer we have, not long ago, commended,[21] has employed himself on them, yet, his object having been, not so much to give the history, properly speaking, as to extract thence political suggestions, for a still more worthy and important purpose, it seemed to us that the history of the plague might form the subject of a new work. But it is not a matter to be passed over in a few words; and to treat it with the copiousness it deserves would carry

[21] P. Verri, work before mentioned.

us too far beyond our limits. Besides, after we should have paused upon all these incidents, the reader would certainly no longer care to know those that remain in our narrative. Reserving, therefore, for another publication the account of the former, we will, at length, return to our characters, not to leave them again till we reach the end.

CHAPTER XXXIII

ONE night, towards the end of August, exactly during the very height of the pestilence, Don Rodrigo returned to his residence at Milan, accompanied by the faithful Griso, one of the three or four who remained to him out of his whole household. He was returning from a company of friends, who were accustomed to assemble at a banquet, to divert the melancholy of the times; and on each occasion, some new friends were there, some old ones missing. That day he had been one of the merriest of the party; and among other things, had excited a great deal of laughter among the company, by a kind of funeral eulogium on the Count Attilio, who had been carried off by the plague two days before.

In walking home, however, he felt a languor, a depression, a weakness in his limbs, a difficulty of breathing, and an inward burning heat, which he would willingly have attributed entirely to the wine, to late hours, to the season. He uttered not a syllable the whole way; and the first word was, when they reached the house, to order Griso to light him to his room. When they were there, Griso observed the wild and heated look of his master's face, his eyes almost starting from their sockets, and peculiarly brilliant: he kept, therefore, at a distance; for, in these circumstances every ragamuffin was obliged to look for himself, as the saying is, with a medical eye.

'I'm well, you see,' said Don Rodrigo, who read in Griso's action the thoughts which were passing in his mind. 'I'm very well; but I've taken . . . I've taken, perhaps, a little too much to drink. There was some capital wine! . . . But with a good night's sleep, it will go off. I'm very sleepy . . . Take that light away from before my eyes, it dazzles me . . . it teases me! . . .'

'It's all the effects of the wine,' said Griso, still keeping at a distance; 'but lie down quickly, for sleep will do you good.'

'You're right; if I can sleep . . . After all, I'm well enough. Put that little bell close by my bed, if I should want anything in the night: and be on the watch, you know, perchance you should hear me ring. But I shan't want anything . . . Take away that cursed light directly,' resumed he, while Griso executed the order, approaching him as little as possible. 'The ——! it plagues me excessively!' Griso then took the light, and wishing his master good night, took a hasty departure, while Rodrigo buried himself under the bed-clothes.

But the counterpane seemed to him like a mountain. He threw it off, and tried to compose himself to rest; for, in fact, he was dying of sleep. But scarcely had he closed his eyes, when he awoke again with a start, as if some wickedly disposed person were giving him a shake; and he felt an increase of burning heat, an increase of delirium. His thoughts recurred to the season, the wine, and his debauchery; he would gladly have given them the blame of all; but there was constantly substituted, of its own accord, for these ideas, that which was then associated with all, which entered, so to say, by every sense, which had been introduced into all the conversations at the banquet, since it was much easier to turn it into ridicule than to get out of its reach—the pestilence.

After a long battle, he at length fell asleep, and began to dream the most gloomy and disquieting dreams in the world. He went on from one thing to another, till he seemed to find himself in a large church, in the first ranks, in the midst of a great crowd of people; there he was wondering how he had got there, how the thought had ever entered his head, particularly at such a time; and he felt in his heart excessively vexed. He looked at the bystanders; they had all pale, emaciated countenances, with staring and glistening eyes, and hanging lips; their garments were tattered, and falling to pieces; and through the rents appeared livid spots, and swellings. 'Make room, you rabble!' he fancied he cried, looking towards the door, which was far, far away; and accompanying the cry with a threatening expression of countenance, but without moving a limb; nay, even drawing up his body to avoid coming in contact with those polluted creatures, who crowded only too closely upon him on every side. But not one of the senseless beings seemed to move, nor even to have heard him; nay, they pressed still more upon him;

and, above all, it felt as if some one of them with his elbow, or whatever it might be, was pushing against his left side, between the heart and the armpit, where he felt a painful and, as it were, heavy pressure. And if he writhed himself to get rid of this uneasy feeling, immediately a fresh unknown something began to prick him in the very same place. Enraged, he attempted to lay his hand on his sword and then it seemed as if the thronging of the multitude had raised it up level with his chest, and that it was the hilt of it which pressed so in that spot; and the moment he touched it he felt a still sharper stitch. He cried out, panted, and would have uttered a still louder cry, when behold! all these faces turned in one direction. He looked the same way, perceived a pulpit, and saw slowly rising above its edge something round, smooth, and shining; then rose, and distinctly appeared, a bald head; then two eyes, a face, a long and white beard, and the upright figure of a friar, visible above the sides down to the girdle; it was friar Cristoforo. Darting a look around upon his audience, he seemed to Don Rodrigo to fix his gaze on him, at the same time raising his hand in exactly the attitude he had assumed in that room on the ground floor in his palace. Don Rodrigo then himself lifted up his hand in fury, and made an effort, as if to throw himself forward and grasp that arm extended in the air; a voice, which had been vainly and secretly struggling in his throat, burst forth in a great howl; and he awoke. He dropped the arm he had in reality uplifted, strove, with some difficulty, to recover the right meaning of everything, and to open his eyes, for the light of the already advanced day gave him no less uneasiness than that of the candle had done; recognized his bed and his chamber; understood that all had been a dream; the church, the people, the friar, all had vanished—all, but one thing—that pain in his left side. Together with this, he felt a frightful acceleration of palpitation at the heart, a noise and humming in his ears, a raging fire within, and a weight in all his limbs, worse than when he lay down. He hesitated a little before looking at the spot that pained him; at length, he uncovered it, and glanced at it with a shudder:— there was a hideous spot, of a livid purple hue.

The man saw himself lost; the terror of death seized him, and, with perhaps still stronger feeling, the terror of becoming the prey of *monatti,* of being carried off, of being thrown into the Lazzaretto. And as he deliberated on the way of avoiding this horrible fate, he felt his thoughts become more perplexed and obscure; he felt the moment drawing near that would leave him only consciousness enough to reduce him to despair. He grasped the bell, and shook it violently. Griso, who was on the alert, immediately answered its summons. He stood at some distance from the bed, gazed attentively at his master, and was at once convinced of what he had conjectured the night before.

'Griso!' said Don Rodrigo, with difficulty, raising himself, and sitting up in his bed, 'you have always been my trusty servant.'

'Yes, Signor.'

'I have always dealt well by you.'

'Of your bounty.'

'I think I may trust you . . .'

'The——!'

'I am ill, Griso.'

'I had perceived it.'

'If I recover, I will heap upon you more favours than I have ever yet done.'

Griso made no answer, and stood waiting to see to what all these preambles would lead.

'I will not trust myself to anybody but you,' resumed Don Rodrigo; 'do me a kindness, Griso.'

'Command me,' said he, replying with this usual formula to that unusual one.

'Do you know where the surgeon, Chiodo, lives?'

'I know very well.'

'He is a worthy man, who, if he is paid, will conceal the sick. Go and find him; tell him I will give him four, six *scudi* a visit; more, if he demands more. Tell him to come here directly; and do the thing cleverly, so that nobody may observe it.'

'Well thought of,' said Griso; 'I go, and return.'

'Listen, Griso; give a drop of water first. I am so parched with thirst, I can bear it no longer.'

'Signor, no,' replied Griso; 'nothing without the doctor's leave. These are ticklish complaints; there is no time to be lost. Keep quiet —in the twinkling of an eye I'll be here with Chiodo.'

So saying, he went out, impatiently shutting the door behind him.

Don Rodrigo lay down, and accompanied him, in imagination, to Chiodo's house, counting the steps, calculating the time. Now and then he would turn to look at his left side, but quickly averted his face with a shudder. After some time, he began to listen eagerly for the surgeon's arrival; and this effort of attention suspended his sense of illness, and kept his thoughts in some degree of order. All of a sudden, he heard a distant sound, which seemed, however, to come from the rooms, not the street. He listened still more intently; he heard it louder, more quickly repeated; and with it a trampling of footsteps. A horrid suspicion rushed into his mind. He sat up, and gave still greater attention; he heard a dead sound in the next room as if a weight were being cautiously set down. He threw his legs out of bed, as if to get up; peeped at the door, saw it open, and beheld before his eyes, and advancing towards him, two ragged and filthy red dresses, two ill-looking faces—in one word, two *monatti*. He distinguished, too, half of Griso's face, who, hidden behind the almost closed door, remained there on the lookout.

'Ah, infamous traitor! . . . Begone, you rascal! Biondino! Carlotto! help! I'm murdered!' shouted Don Rodrigo. He thrust one hand under the bolster in search of a pistol; grasped it; drew it out; but, at his first cry, the *monatti* had rushed up to the bed; the foremost is upon him before he can do anything further; he wrenches the pistol out of his hand, throws it to a distance, forces him to lie down again, and keeps him there, crying with a grin of fury mingled with contempt, 'Ah, villain! against the *monatti*! against the officers of the Board! against those who perform works of mercy!'

'Hold him fast till we carry him off,' said his companion, going towards a trunk. Griso then entered, and began with him to force open the lock.

'Scoundrel!' howled Don Rodrigo, looking at him from under the fellow who held him down, and writhing himself under the grasp of his sinewy arms. 'First let me kill that infamous rascal!'

said he to the *monatti,* 'and afterwards do with me what you will.'
Then he began to shout with loud cries to his other servants: but in
vain he called; for the abominable Griso had sent them all off with
pretended orders from their master himself, before going to propose
to the *monatti* to come on this expedition, and divide the spoil.

'Be quiet, will you,' said the villain who held him down upon
the bed to the unfortunate Don Rodrigo. And turning his face to
the two who were seizing the booty, he cried to them, 'Do your work
like honest fellows.'

'You! you!' roared Don Rodrigo to Griso, whom he beheld busying himself in breaking open, taking out money and clothes, and
dividing them. 'You! after! . . . Ah, fiend of hell! I may still
recover! I may still recover!' Griso spoke not, nor, more than he
could help, even turned in the direction whence these words
proceeded.

'Hold him fast,' said the other *monatto;* 'he's frantic.'

The miserable being became so indeed. After one last and more
violent effort of cries and contortions, he suddenly sank down
senseless in a swoon; he still, however, stared fixedly, as if spell-
bound; and from time to time gave a feeble struggle, or uttered a
kind of howl.

The *monatti* took him, one by the feet and the other by the
shoulders, and went to deposit him on a hand-barrow which they
had left in the adjoining room; afterwards one returned to fetch
the booty; and then, taking up their miserable burden, they carried
all away.

Griso remained behind to select in haste whatever more might be
of use to him; and making them up into a bundle, took his departure. He had carefully avoided touching the *monatti,* or being
touched by them; but in the last hurry of plunder, he had taken
from the bed-side his master's clothes and shaken them, without
thinking of anything but of seeing whether there were money in
them. He was forced to think of it, however, the next day; for,
while making merry in a public-house, he was suddenly seized
with a cold shiver, his eyes became clouded, his strength failed him,
and he sank to the ground. Abandoned by his companions, he fell
into the hands of the *monatti,* who, despoiling him of whatever he

had about him worth having, threw him upon a car, on which he expired before reaching the Lazzaretto, whither his master had been carried.

Leaving the latter, for the present, in this abode of suffering, we must now go in search of another, whose history would never have been blended with his, if it had not been forced upon him whether he would or not; indeed we may safely say, that neither one nor the other would have had any history at all:—I mean Renzo, whom we left in the new silk-mill under the assumed name of Antonio Rivolta.

He had been there about five or six months, if I am not mistaken, when, enmity having been openly declared between the Republic and the King of Spain, and therefore every apprehension of ill-offices and trouble from that quarter having ceased, Bortolo eagerly went to fetch him away, and take him again into his own employment, both because he was fond of him, and because Renzo, being naturally intelligent, and skilful in the trade, was of great use to the *factotum* in a manufactory, without ever being able to aspire at that office himself, from his inability to write. As this reason weighed with him in some measure, we were obliged, therefore, to mention it. Perhaps the reader would rather have had a more ideal Bortolo: but what can I say? he must imagine one for himself. We describe him as he was.

From that time Renzo continued to work with him. More than once or twice, and especially after having received one of those charming letters from Agnese, he had felt a great fancy to enlist as a soldier, and make an end of it; nor were opportunities wanting; for just during that interval, the Republic often stood in need of men. The temptation had sometimes been the more pressing to Renzo, because they even talked of invading the Milanese; and it naturally appeared to him that it would be a fine thing to return in the guise of a conqueror to his own home, to see Lucia again, and for once come to an explanation with her. But, by clever management, Bortolo had always contrived to divert him from the resolution. 'If they have to go there,' he would say, 'they can go well enough without you, and you can go there afterwards at your convenience; if they come back with a broken head, won't it be better to have been out of the fray? There won't be wanting des-

perate fellows on the highway for robberies. And before they set
foot there! . . . As for me, I am somewhat incredulous; these fellows
bark; but let them; the Milanese is not a mouthful to be so easily
swallowed. Spain is concerned in it, my dear fellow: do you know
what it is to deal with Spain? St. Mark is strong enough at home:
but it will take something more than that. Have patience; ar'n't
you well off here? . . . I know what you would say to me; but if
it be decreed above that the thing succeed, rest assured it will
succeed better by your playing no fooleries. Some saint will help
you. Believe me, it's no business of yours. Do you think it would
suit you to leave winding silk to go and murder? What would
you do among such a set of people? It requires men who are made
for it.'

At other times Renzo resolved to go secretly, disguised, and under
a false name. But from this project, too, Bortolo always contrived to
divert him with arguments that may be too easily conjectured.

The plague having afterwards broken out in the Milanese territory, and even, as we have said, on the confines of the Bergamascan,
it was not long before it extended itself hither, and . . . be not dismayed, for I am not going to give another history of this: if any
one wishes it, it may be found in a work by one Lorenzo Ghirardelli,
written by public order; a scarce and almost unknown work, however, although it contains, perhaps, more fully than all the rest put
together, the most celebrated descriptions of pestilences: on so many
things does the celebrity of books depend! What I would say is,
that Renzo also took the plague, and cured himself, that is to say,
he did nothing; he was at the point of death, but his good constitution conquered the strength of the malady: in a few days he
was out of danger. With the return of life, its cares, its wishes,
hopes, recollections, and designs, were renewed with double poign-
ancy and vigour; which is equivalent to saying that he thought
more than ever of Lucia. What had become of her, during the
time that life was, as it were, an exception? And at so short a distance from her, could he learn nothing? And to remain, God knew
how long! in such a state of uncertainty! And even when this
should be removed, when all danger being over, he should learn
that Lucia still survived; there would always remain that other

knot, that obscurity about the vow.—I'll go myself; I'll go and learn about everything at once,—said he to himself, and he said it before he was again in a condition to steady himself upon his feet.—Provided she lives! Ah, if she lives! I'll find her, that I will; I'll hear once from her own lips what this promise is, I'll make her see that it cannot hold good, and I'll bring her away with me, her, and that poor Agnese, if she's living! who has always wished me well, and I'm sure she does so still. The capture! aha! the survivors have something else to think about now. People go about safely, even here, who have on them . . . Will there have been a safe-conduct only for bailiffs? And at Milan, everybody says that there are other disturbances there. If I let so good an opportunity pass—(the plague! Only see how that revered instinct of referring and making subservient everything to ourselves, may sometimes lead us to apply words!)—I may never have such another!—

It is well to hope, my good Renzo. Scarcely could he drag himself about, when he set off in search of Bortolo, who had so far succeeded in escaping the pestilence, and was still kept in reserve. He did not go into the house, but, calling to him from the street, made him come to the window.

'Aha!' said Bortolo: 'you've escaped it, then! It's well for you!'

'I'm still rather weak in my limbs, you see, but as to the danger, it's all over.'

'Ay, I'd gladly be in your shoes. It used to be everything to say, "I'm well;" but now it counts for very little. He who is able to say, "I'm better," can indeed say something!'

Renzo expressed some good wishes for his cousin, and imparted to him his resolution.

'Go, this time, and Heaven prosper you!' replied he. 'Try to avoid justice, as I shall try to avoid the contagion; and, if it be God's will that things should go well with us both, we shall meet again.'

'Oh, I shall certainly come back: God grant I may not come alone! Well; we will hope.'

'Come back in company; for, if God wills, we will all work together, and make up a good party. I only hope you may find me alive, and that this odious epidemic may have come to an end!'

'We shall see each other again, we shall see each other again; we must see each other again!'

'I repeat, God grant it!'

For several days Renzo practised taking a little exercise, to assay and recruit his strength; and no sooner did he deem himself capable of performing the journey, than he prepared to set out. Under his clothes he buckled a girdle round his waist, containing those fifty *scudi* upon which he had never laid a finger, and which he had never confided to any one, not even to Bortolo; he took a few more pence with him, which he had saved day after day, by living very economically; put under his arm a small bundle of clothes, and in his pocket a character, with the name of Antonio Rivolta, which had been very willingly given him by his second master; in one pocket of his trowsers he placed a large knife, the least that an honest man could carry in those days; and set off on his peregrinations, on the last day of August, three days after Don Rodrigo had been carried to the Lazzaretto. He took the way towards Lecco, wishing, before venturing himself in Milan, to pass through his village, where he hoped to find Agnese alive, and to begin by learning from her some of the many things he so ardently longed to know.

The few who had recovered from the pestilence were, among the rest of the population, indeed like a privileged class. A great proportion of the others languished or died; and those who had been hitherto untouched by the contagion lived in constant apprehension of it. They walked cautiously and warily about, with measured steps, gloomy looks, and haste at once and hesitation: for everything might be a weapon against them to inflict a mortal wound. These, on the contrary, almost certain of safety (for to have the plague twice was rather a prodigious than a rare instance), went about in the midst of the contagion, freely and boldly, like the knights during one part of the middle ages; who, encased in steel, wherever steel might be, and mounted on chargers, themselves defended as impenetrably as possible, went rambling about at hazard (whence their glorious denomination of knights-errant), among a poor pedestrian herd of burghers and villagers, who, to repel and ward off their blows, had nothing on them but rags. Beautiful, sapient, and useful profession! a profession fit to make the first figure in a treatise on political economy!

With such security, tempered, however, by the anxiety with which our readers are acquainted, and by the frequent spectacle and perpetual contemplation of the universal calamity, Renzo pursued his homeward way, under a beautiful sky and through a beautiful country, but meeting nothing, after passing wide tracts of most mournful solitude, but some wandering shadow rather than a living being, or corpses carried to the grave, unhonoured by funeral rites, unaccompanied by the funeral dirge. About noon he stopped in a little wood, to eat a mouthful of bread and meat which he had brought with him. Of fruit, he had only too much at his command the whole length of the way—figs, peaches, plums, and apples at will; he had only to enter a vineyard, and extend his arm to gather them from the branches, or to pick them up from the ground, which was thickly strewn with them; for the year was extraordinarily abundant in fruit of every kind, and there was scarcely any one to take any care of it. The grapes even hid themselves beneath the leaves, and were left for the use of the first comer.

Towards evening he discovered his own village. At this sight, though he must have been prepared for it, he felt his heart begin to beat violently; he was at once assailed by a host of mournful recollections and presentiments: he seemed to hear ringing in his ears those inauspicious tolls of the bell which had, as it were, accompanied and followed him in his flight from the village; and, at the same time, he heard, so to say, the deathlike silence which actually reigned around. He experienced still stronger agitation on entering the churchyard; and worse still awaited him at the end of his walk; for the spot he had fixed upon as his resting-place, was the dwelling which he had once been accustomed to call Lucia's cottage. Now it could not be, at the best, more than Agnese's; and the only favour he begged of Heaven was, that he might find her living and in health. And in this cottage he proposed asking for a bed, rightly conjecturing that his own would no longer be a place of abode for anything but rats and polecats.

To reach that point, therefore, without passing through the village, he took a little by-path that ran behind it, the very one along which he had gone, in good company, on that notorious night when he tried to surprise the Curate. About half-way stood, on one side, his own house, and on the other, his vineyard; so that he could enter both for a moment in passing, to see a little how his own affairs were going on.

He looked forward, as he pursued his way, anxious, and at the same time afraid, to meet with any one; and after a few paces, he saw a man seated in his shirt on the ground, resting his back against a hedge of jessamine, in the attitude of an idiot; and from this, and afterwards from his countenance, he thought it was that poor simpleton Gervase, who had gone as the second witness in his ill-fated expedition. But going a little nearer, he perceived that it was, instead, the sprightly Tonio, who had brought his brother with him on that occasion. The contagion, robbing him at once of mental as well as bodily vigour, had developed in his look and every action the slight and veiled germ of likeness which he bore to his half-witted brother.

'Oh Tonio!' said Renzo, stopping before him, 'is it you?'

Tonio raised his eyes, without moving his head.

'Tonio, don't you know me?'

'Whoever has got it, has got it,' answered Tonio, gazing at him with open mouth.

'It's on you, eh? poor Tonio: but don't you know me again?'

'Whoever has got it, has got it,' replied he, with a kind of idiotic smile. Seeing he could draw nothing further from him, Renzo pursued his way, still more disconsolate. Suddenly he saw, turning the corner, and advancing towards him, a black object, which he quickly recognized as Don Abbondio. He walked slowly, carrying his stick like one who is alternately carried by it; and the nearer he approached, the more plainly might it be discerned, in his pale and emaciated countenance, and in every look, that he, too, had had to pass through his share of the storm. He looked askance at Renzo; it seemed, and it did not seem, like him; there was something like a stranger in his dress; but it was a stranger from the territory of Bergamo.

—It is he, and nobody else!—said he to himself, raising his hands to Heaven, with a motion of dissatisfied surprise, and the staff he

carried in his right hand suddenly checked in its passage through
the air; and his poor arms might be seen shaking in his sleeves,
where once there was scarcely room for them. Renzo hastened to
meet him, and made a low reverence; for, although they had quitted
each other in the way the reader knows, he was always, nevertheless,
his Curate.

'Are you here—you?' exclaimed the latter.

'I am indeed, as you see. Do you know anything of Lucia?'

'What do you suppose I can know? I know nothing. She's at
Milan, if she's still in this world. But you . . .'

'And Agnese, is she alive?'

'She may be; but who do you suppose can tell? She's not here.
But . . .'

'Where is she?'

'She's gone to live at Valsassina, among her relations at Pasturo,
you know; for they say the plague doesn't make the havoc there it
does here. But you, I say . . .'

'Oh, I'm very sorry. And Father Cristoforo? . . .'

'He's been gone for some time. But . . .'

'I know that, they wrote and told me so much; but I want to
know if he hasn't yet returned to these parts.'

'Nay; they've heard nothing further about him. But you . . .'

'I'm very sorry to hear this too.'

'But you, I say, what, for Heaven's sake, are you coming to do
in this part of the world? Don't you know about that affair of
your apprehension?'

'What does it matter? They've something else to think about.
I was determined to come for once, and see about my affairs. And
isn't it well enough known? . . .'

'What would you see about, I wonder? for now there's no longer
anybody, or anything. And is it wise of you, with that business of
your apprehension, to come hither exactly to your own village, into
the wolf's very mouth? Do as an old man advises you, who is
obliged to have more judgment than you, and who speaks from the
love he bears you; buckle on your shoes well, and set off, before any
one sees you, to where you came from; and if you've been seen

already, return only the more quickly. Do you think that this is the air for you? Don't you know they've been to look for you? that they've ransacked everything, and turned all upside down? . . .'

'I know it too well, the scoundrels!'

'But then . . .'

'But if I tell you I don't care! And is that fellow alive yet? is he here?'

'I tell you nobody's here; I tell you, you musn't think about things here; I tell you . . .'

'I ask if he's here?'

'Oh, sacred Heaven! Speak more quietly. Is it possible you've all that fieriness about you after so many things have happened?'

'Is he here, or is he not?'

'Well, well, he's not here. But the plague, my son, the plague! Who would go travelling about in such times as these?'

'If there was nothing else but the plague in this world . . . I mean for myself: I've had it, and am free.'

'Indeed, indeed! what news is this? When one has escaped a danger of this sort, it seems to me he should thank Heaven, and . . .'

'And so I do.'

'And not go to look for others, I say. Do as I advise.'

'You've had it too, Signor Curate, if I mistake not.'

'I had it! Obstinate and bad enough it was! I'm here by miracle; I need only say it has left me in the state you see. Now, I had just need of a little quiet, to set me to rights again. I was beginning to be a little better . . . In the name of Heaven, what have you come to do here? Go back . . .'

'You're always at me with that *go back*. As for going back, I have reasons enough for not stirring. You say, what are you come for? what are you come for? I've come home.'

'Home . . .'

'Tell me, are many dead here? . . .'

'Alas, alas!' exclaimed Don Abbondio; and beginning with Perpetua, he entered upon a long enumeration of individuals and entire families. Renzo had certainly expected something of the kind, but, on hearing so many names of acquaintances, friends, and relatives, (he had lost his parents many years before,) he stood overcome with grief, his head hung down, and only exclaiming from time to time, 'Poor fellow! poor girl! poor creatures!'

'You see,' continued Don Abbondio; 'and it isn't yet over. If those who are left don't use their senses this time, and drive the whims out of their brains, there's nothing for it but the end of the world.'

'Don't be afraid; I've no intentions of stopping here.'

'Ah! thank Heaven, you at last understand! And you'd better make up your mind to return . . .'

'Don't you trouble yourself about that.'

'What! didn't you once want to do something more foolish than this even?'

'Never mind me, I say; that is my business; I'm more than seven years old. I hope, at any rate, you won't tell anybody you've seen me. You are a priest; I am one of your flock; you won't betray me?'

'I understand,' said Don Abbondio, sighing pettishly, 'I understand. You would ruin yourself and me too. You haven't gone through enough already, I suppose; and I haven't gone through enough either. I understand, I understand.' And continuing to mutter these last words between his teeth, he again resumed his way.

Renzo stood there, chagrined and discontented, thinking where he could find a lodging. In the funereal list recounted by Don Abbondio, there was a family of peasants, who had been all swept off by the pestilence, excepting one youth, about Renzo's own age, who had been his companion from infancy; the house was out of the village, a very little way off. Hither he determined to bend his steps and ask for a night's lodging.

He had nearly reached his own vineyard, and was soon able to infer from the outside in what state it was. Not a single tree, not a single leaf, which he had left there was visible above the wall. If anything blossomed there, it was all what had grown during his absence. He went up to the opening, (of a gate there was no longer the least sign); he cast a glance around: poor vineyard! For two successive winters the people of the neighbourhood had gone to chop firewood 'in the garden of that poor fellow,' as they used to say. Vines, mulberry-trees, fruits of every kind, all had been rudely torn up, or cut down to the trunk. Vestiges, however, of former cultivation still appeared; young shoots, in broken lines, which retained, nevertheless, traces of their now desolated rows; here and there stumps and sprouts of mulberry, fig, peach, cherry, and plum-trees; but even these seemed overwhelmed and choked by a fresh, varied, and luxuriant progeny, born and reared without the help of man. There was a thick mass of nettles, ferns, tares, dog-grass, rye-grass, wild oats, green amaranths, succory, wild sorrel, fox-glove, and other similar plants; all those, I mean, which the peasant of every country has included in one large class at his pleasure, denominating them weeds. There was a medley of stalks, each trying to out-top the others in the air, or rivalling its fellow in length upon the ground—aiming, in short, to secure for itself the post of honour in every direction; a mixture of leaves, flowers, and fruit, of a hundred colours, forms, and sizes; ears of corn, Indian corn, tufts, bunches, and heads of white, yellow, red and blue. In the midst of this medley, other taller and more graceful, though not, for the most part, more valuable plants, were prominently conspicuous; the Turkish vine soared above all the rest, with its long and reddish branches, its large and magnificent dark-green leaves, some already fringed with purple at the top, and its bending clusters of grapes; adorned below with berries of bluish-grey tinge, higher up of a purple hue, then green, and at the very top with whitish little flowers. There was also the bearded yew, with its large rough leaves down to the ground, the stem rising perpendicularly to the sky, and the long pendent branches scattered, and, as it were, bespangled with bright yellow blossoms; thistles, too, with rough and prickly leaves and calyxes, from which issued little tufts of white or purple flowers, or else light and silvery plumes, which were quickly swept away by the breeze. Here a little bunch of bindweed, climbing up and twining around fresh suckers from a mulberry-tree, had entirely covered them with its pendent leaves, which pointed to the ground, and adorned them at the top with its white and delicate little bells. There a red-berried bryony had twisted itself among the new shoots of a vine, which, seeking in vain a firmer support, had reciprocally entwined its tendrils around its companion, and, mingling their feeble stalks, and their not very dissimilar leaves, they mutually drew each other upward, as often happens with the weak, who take one another for their stay. The bramble intruded everywhere; it stretched from one bough to another; now mounting, and again turning downward, it bent the branches, or straightened them, according as it happened; and crossing before the very threshold, seemed as if it were placed there to dispute the passage even with the owner.

But he had no heart to enter such a vineyard, and probably did not stand as long looking at it as we have taken to make this little sketch. He went forward; a little way off stood his cottage; he passed through the garden, trampling underfoot by hundreds the intrusive visitors with which, like the vineyard, it was peopled and overgrown. He just set foot within the threshold of one of the rooms on the ground floor; at the sound of his footsteps, and on his looking in, there was a hubbub, a scampering to and fro of rats, a rush under the rubbish that covered the whole floor; it was the relics of the German soldiers' beds. He raised his eyes, and looked round upon the walls; they were stripped of plaster, filthy, blackened with smoke. He raised them to the ceiling—a mass of cobwebs. Nothing else was to be seen. He took his departure, too, from this desolate scene, twining his fingers in his hair; returned through the garden, retracing the path he had himself made a moment before, took another little lane to the left, which led into the fields, and without seeing or hearing a living creature, arrived close to the house he had designed as his place of lodging. It was already evening; his friend was seated outside the door on a small wooden bench, his arms crossed on his breast, and his eyes fixed upon the sky, like a man bewildered by misfortunes, and rendered savage by long solitude. Hearing a footstep, he turned round, looked who was coming, and to what he fancied he saw in the twilight, between the leaves and branches, cried in a loud voice, as he stood up and raised both his hands, 'Is there nobody but me? didn't I do enough yesterday? Let me alone a little, for that, too, will be a work of charity.'

Renzo, not knowing what this meant, replied to him, calling him by name.

'Renzo . . .' said he, in a tone at once of exclamation and interrogation.

'Myself,' said Renzo, and they hastened to meet each other.

'Is it really you?' said his friend, when they were near. 'Oh, how glad I am to see you? Who would have thought it? I took you for Paolin de' Morti,[1] who is always coming to torment me to go and bury some one. Do you know I am left alone?—alone! alone! as a hermit!'

'I know it too well,' said Renzo. And interchanging in this manner, and crowding upon one another, welcomings, and questions, and answers, they went into the house together. Here, without interrupting the conversation, his friend busied himself in doing some little honour to his guest, as he best could on so sudden a warning, and in times like those. He set some water on the fire, and began to make the *polenta;* but soon gave up the pestle to Renzo, that he might proceed with the mixing, and went out, saying, 'I'm all by myself, you see, all by myself!'

By and by he returned with a small pail of milk, a little salt meat, a couple of cream-cheeses, and some figs and peaches; and all being ready, and the *polenta* poured out upon the trencher, they sat down to table, mutually thanking each other, one for the visit, the other for the reception he met with. And, after an absence of nearly two years, they suddenly discovered that they were much greater friends than they ever thought they were when they saw each other almost every day; for, as the manuscript here remarks, events had occurred to both which make one feel what a cordial to the heart is kindly feeling, both that which one experiences oneself, and that which one meets with in others.

True, no one could supply the place of Agnese to Renzo, nor console him for her absence, not only on account of the old and special affection he entertained for her, but also because, among the things he was anxious to clear up, one there was of which she alone possessed the key. He stood for a moment in doubt whether he should not first go in search of her, since he was so short a distance off; but, considering that she would know nothing of Lucia's health, he kept to his first intention of going at once to assure himself of this, to confront the one great trial, and afterwards to bring the news to her mother. Even from his friend, however, he learnt

---

[1] One of the friars of the Order of Death.

many things of which he was ignorant, and gained some light on many points with which he was but partially acquainted, both about Lucia's circumstances, the prosecutions instituted against himself, and Don Rodrigo's departure thence, followed by his whole suite, since which time he had not been seen in the neighbourhood; in short, about all the intricate circumstances of the whole affair. He learnt also (and to him it was an acquisition of no little importance) to pronounce properly the name of Don Ferrante's family; Agnese, indeed, had written it to him by her secretary; but Heaven knows how it was written, and the Bergamascan interpreter had read it in such a way,—had given him such a word,—that, had he gone with it to seek direction to his house in Milan, he would probably have found no one who could have conjectured for whom he was making inquiry. Yet this was the only clue he possessed that could put him in the way of learning tidings of Lucia. As to justice, he was ever more and more convinced that this was a hazard remote enough not to give him much concern: the Signor *Podestà* had died of the plague; who knew when a substitute would be appointed? the greater part of the bailiffs were carried off; and those that remained had something else to do than look after old matters. He also related to his friend the vicissitudes he had undergone, and heard in exchange a hundred stories about the passage of the army, the plague, the poisoners, and other wonderful matters. 'They are miserable things,' said his friend, accompanying Renzo into a little room which the contagion had emptied of occupants; 'things which we never could have thought to see, and after which we can never expect to be merry again all our lives; but nevertheless, it is a relief to speak of them to one's friends.'

By break of day they were both down-stairs; Renzo equipped for his journey, with his girdle hidden under his doublet, and the large knife in his pocket, but otherwise light and unencumbered, having left his little bundle in the care of his host. "If all goes well with me,' said he; 'if I find her alive; if . . . enough . . . I'll come back here; I'll run over Pasturo to carry the good news to poor Agnese, and then, and then . . . But if, by ill-luck, by ill-luck which God forbid! . . . then I don't know what I shall do; I don't know where I shall go: only, assuredly, you will never see me again in these parts!'

And, as he said so, standing in the doorway which led into the fields, he cast his eyes around, and contemplated, with a mixed feeling of tenderness and bitter grief, the sun-rising of his own country, which he had not seen for so long a time. His friend comforted him with bright hopes and prognostications, and made him take with him some little store of provision for that day; then, accompanying him a mile or two on his way, he took his leave with renewed good wishes.

Renzo pursued his way deliberately and easily, as all he cared for was to reach the vicinity of Milan that day, so that he might enter next morning early, and immediately begin his search. The journey was performed without accident; nor was there anything which particularly attracted his attention, except the usual spectacles of misery and sorrow. He stopped in due time, as he had done the day before, in a grove, to refresh himself and take breath. Passing through Monza, before an open shop where bread was displayed for sale, he asked for two loaves, that he might not be totally un-provided for under any circumstances. The shopkeeper, beckoning to him not to enter, held out to him, on a little shovel, a small basin containing vinegar and water, into which he desired him to drop the money in payment; he did so; and then the two loaves were handed out to him, one after another, with a pair of tongs, and deposited by Renzo one in each pocket.

Towards evening he arrived at Greco, without, however, knowing its name; but, by the help of some little recollection of the places which he retained from his former journey, and his calculation of the distance he had already come from Monza, he guessed that he must be tolerably near the city, and therefore left the high-road and turned into the fields in search of some *cascinotto,* where he might pass the night; for with inns he was determined not to meddle. He found more than he looked for: for seeing a gap in a hedge which surrounded the yard of a cow-house, he resolved at any rate to enter. No one was there: he saw in one corner a large shed with hay piled up beneath it, and against this a ladder was reared; he once more looked round, and then, mounting at a venture, laid himself down to pass the night there, and quickly fell asleep, not to awake till morning. When he awoke he crawled towards the edge of this great bed, put his head out, and seeing no one, descended as he had gone up, went out where he had come in, pursued his way through little by-paths, taking the cathedral for his polar star; and, after a short walk, came out under the walls of Milan, between the Porta Orientale and the Porta Nuova, and rather nearer to the latter.

CHAPTER XXXIV

AS to the way of entering the city, Renzo had heard, in general terms, that there were very strict orders not to admit persons without a certificate of health; but that, in fact, it was easy enough for any one to effect an entrance who at all knew how to help himself, and to seize opportunities. So it was; and, letting alone the general causes why every order, in those days, was so imperfectly executed; letting alone the particular ones, which rendered the rigorous execution of this so impracticable, Milan was now reduced to such a pass that no one could see of what use it was to defend it, or against what it was to be defended; and whoever came thither might be considered rather to risk his own health than to endanger that of the inhabitants.

Upon this information, Renzo's intention was to attempt a passage at the first gate upon which he might happen to light; and if any obstacle presented itself, to go round outside, until he found another more easy of access. And Heaven knows how many gates he thought Milan must have!

Arrived, then, before the walls, he stood still to look about him, as one does who, not knowing which way will be the best way to bend his steps, seems as if he awaited and asked direction from anything. But he could discover nothing either way but two reaches of a winding road, and before him a part of the wall: in no quarter was there a symptom of a human being, except that in one spot, on the platform, might be seen a dense column of black and murky smoke, which expanded itself as it mounted, and curled into ample circles, and afterwards dispersed itself through the gray and motionless atmosphere. They were clothes, beds, and other articles of infected furniture which were being committed to the flames: and such melancholy conflagrations were constantly to be seen, not only here, but on every side of the wall.

The weather was close, the air thick and heavy, the whole sky veiled by a uniform sluggish cloud of mist, which seemed to forbid the sun, without giving promise of rain; the country round was partly uncultivated, and the whole looked parched; vegetation was stunted, and not a drop of dew moistened the drooping and withered leaves. This solitude, this deep silence, so near a large mass of habitations, added new consternation to Renzo's disquietude, and rendered his thoughts still more gloomy.

Having stood thus for a moment, he took the right hand, at a venture, directing his steps, without being aware of it, towards the Porta Nuova, which, though close at hand, he had not been able to perceive, on account of a bastion behind which it was concealed. After taking a few steps, a tinkling of little bells fell upon his ear, which ceased and was renewed at intervals, and then the voices of men. He went forward; and having turned the corner of the bastion, the first thing that met his eye on the esplanade before the gate was a small wooden house, or sentry-box, at the doorway of which stood a guard, leaning on his musket with a languid and negligent air; behind was a fence, composed of stakes, and beyond that the gate, that is to say, two wings of the wall connected by a roof above, which served to shelter the door, both leaves of which were wide open, as was also the wicket of the palisade. Exactly before the opening, however, stood a melancholy impediment—a handbarrow, placed upon the ground, on which two *monatti* were laying out a poor creature to bear him away: it was the head of the customhouse officers, in whom the plague had been discovered just before. Renzo stood still where he was, awaiting the issue. The party being gone, and no one appearing to shut the gate again, now seemed to be his time, he hastened forward; but the ill-looking sentinel called out to him: 'Holla!' He instantly stopped, and winking at the man drew out a half-ducat, and showed it to him. The fellow, either having already had the pestilence, or fearing it less than he loved half-ducats, beckoned to Renzo to throw it to him; and soon seeing it roll at his feet, muttered, 'Go forward, quickly.' Renzo gave him no occasion to repeat the order; he passed the palisade, entered the gate, and went forward without any one observing or taking any notice of him; except that when he had gone perhaps forty paces, he heard another 'holla' from a toll-gatherer who was calling after him. This he pretended not to hear, and instead of turning round only quickened his pace. 'Holla!' cried the collector again, in a tone, however, which rather indicated vexation than a determination to be obeyed; and finding he was not obeyed, he shrugged his shoulders and returned into the house, like one who was more concerned about not approaching too near to passengers, than inquiring into their affairs.

The street inside this gate, at that time, as now, ran straight forward as far as the canal called the *Naviglio:* at the sides were hedges or walls of gardens, churches, convents, and a few private dwellings; and at the end of this street, in the middle of that which ran along the brink of the canal, was erected a cross, called the Cross of Sant' Eusebio. And, let Renzo look before him as he would, nothing but this cross ever met his view. Arrived at the cross road, which divided the street about half way, and looking to the right and left, he perceived in the right hand one, which bore the name of Santa Teresa, a citizen who was coming exactly towards him.—A Christian, at last! —said he to himself, and he immediately turned into the street, with the intention of making some inquiries of him. The man stared at and eyed the stranger who was advancing towards him, with a suspicious kind of look, even at a distance; and still more, when he perceived, that, instead of going about his own business, he was making up to him. Renzo, when he was within a little distance, took off his hat, like a respectful mountaineer, such as he was; and holding it in his left hand, put the whole fist of his right into the empty crown, and advanced more directly towards the unknown passenger. But he, wildly rolling his eyes, gave back a step, uplifted a knotty stick he carried, with a sharp spike at the end like a rapier, and pointing it at Renzo's breast, cried, 'Stand off! stand off!'

'Oho!' cried the youth in his turn, putting on his hat again; and willing to do anything, as he afterwards said in relating the matter, rather than pick a quarrel at that moment, he turned his back upon the uncourteous citizen, and pursued his way, or to speak more correctly, that in which he happened to have set off.

The citizen also continued *his* route, trembling from head to foot, and every now and then looking behind him. And having reached home, he related how a poisoner had come up to him, with a meek and humble air, but with the look of an infamous impostor, and with a box of ointment or a paper of powder (he was not exactly certain which) in his hand in the crown of his hat, with the intention of playing a trick upon him, if he hadn't known how to keep him at a distance. 'If he had come one step nearer,' added he, 'I'd have run him through before he'd had time to touch me, the scoundrel! The misfortune was that we were in so unfrequented a place; had it been in the heart of Milan, I'd have called people, and bid them seize him. I'm sure we should have found that infamous poison in his hat. But there, all alone, I was obliged to be content with saving myself, without running the risk of getting the infection; for a little powder is soon thrown, and these people are remarkably dexterous: besides, they have the devil on their side. He'll be about Milan now: who knows what murders he is committing!' And as long as he lived, which was many years, every time that poisoners were talked of, he repeated his own instance, and added: 'They who still maintain that it wasn't true, don't let them talk to me: for absolute facts one couldn't help seeing.'

Renzo, far from imagining what a stab he had escaped, and more moved with anger than fear, reflected, in walking, on this reception, and pretty nearly guessed the opinion which the citizen had formed of his actions; yet the thing seemed to him so beyond all reason, that he came to the conclusion that the man must have been half a fool.—It's a bad beginning,—thought he, however;—it seems as if there were an evil star for me at this Milan. Everything seconds me readily enough in entering; but afterwards, when I am in, I find disagreeabilities all prepared for me. Well . . . with God's help . . . if I find . . . if I succeed in finding . . . Oh! all will have been nothing!—

Having reached the foot of the bridge, he turned without hesitation to the left, along a road called San Marco's Street, as it seemed to him this must lead into the heart of the city. As he went along, he kept constantly on the look-out, in hopes of discovering some human creature; but he could see none, except a disfigured corpse in the little ditch which runs between the few houses (which were then still fewer) and the street, for a part of the way. Having passed this part, he heard some cries which seemed to be addressed to him; and turning his eyes upwards in the direction whence the sound came, he perceived, at a little distance, on the balcony of an isolated dwelling, a poor woman, with a group of children around her, who, calling to him, was beckoning also with her hand to entreat him to approach. He ran towards her; and when he came near, 'O young man,' said the woman, 'in the name of the friends you've lost, have the charity to go and tell the commissary that we are here forgotten! They've shut us up in the house as suspected persons, because my poor husband is dead; they've nailed up the door, as you see; and since yesterday morning nobody has brought us anything to eat: for the many hours I've stood here, I haven't been able to find a single Christian who would do me this kindness: and these poor little innocents are dying of hunger!'

'Of hunger!' exclaimed Renzo; and putting his hands into his pocket, 'See here!' said he, drawing out the two loaves: 'send something down to take them.'

'God reward you for it! wait a moment,' said the woman; and she went to fetch a little basket, and a cord by which to lower it for the bread. Renzo at this moment recollected the two loaves he had found near the Cross on his first instance into Milan, and thought to himself:—See! it's a restitution, and perhaps better than if I'd found the real owner; for this surely is a deed of charity!—

'As to the commissary you mention, my good woman,' said he putting the bread into the basket, 'I'm afraid I can't serve you at all; for, to tell you the truth, I'm a stranger, and have no acquaintance with any one in this country. However, if I meet any one at all civil and human to speak to, I'll tell him.'

The woman begged he would do so, and told him the name of the street, by which he might describe the situation.

'You, too, I think,' resumed Renzo, 'can do me a service, a real kindness, without any trouble. A family of high rank, very great signors here in Milan, the family of * * *; can you tell me where they live?'

'I know very well there is such a family,' replied the woman: 'but where it is I haven't the least idea. If you go forward into the city, in this direction, you'll find somebody who will show you the way. And don't forget to tell him about us!'

'Don't fear it,' said Renzo; and he pursued his way.

At every step he heard increasing, and drawing nearer, a noise which he had already begun to distinguish as he stood talking with the woman: a noise of wheels and horses, with a tinkling of little bells, and every now and then a cracking of whips, and loud vociferations. He looked before him, but saw nothing. Having reached the end of this winding street, and got a view of the square of San Marco, the objects which first met his eye were two erect beams, with a rope and sundry pulleys, which he failed not immediately to recognize (for it was a familiar spectacle in those days) as the abominable instrument of torture. It was erected in that place, (and not only there, but in all the squares and most spacious streets,) in order that the deputies of every quarter, furnished with this most arbitrary of all means, might be able to apply it immediately to any one whom they should deem deserving of punishment, whether it were sequestrated persons who left their houses, or officers rebelling against orders, and whatever else it might be: it was one of those extravagant and inefficacious remedies, of which, in those days, and at that particular period especially, they were so extremely prodigal.

While Renzo was contemplating this machine, wondering why it was erected in that place, and listening to the closely approaching sound, behold, he saw appearing from behind the corner of the church a man ringing a little bell: it was an *apparitore;* and behind him two horses, which, stretching their necks and pawing with their hoofs, could with difficulty make their way; and drawn by these a cart full of dead bodies, and after that another, and then another, and another; and on each hand *monatti* walking by the side of the horses, hastening them on with whips, blows, and curses. These corpses were for the most part naked, while some were miserably enveloped in tattered sheets, and were heaped up and twined together, almost like a nest of snakes slowly unfolding themselves to the warmth of a mild spring day; so that at every trifling obstacle, at every jolt, these fatal groups were seen quivering and falling into horrible confusion, heads dangling down, women's long tresses dishevelled, arms torn off and striking against the wheels, exhibiting to the already horror-stricken view how such a spectacle may become still more wretched and disgraceful.

The youth had paused at the corner of the square, by the side of the railing of the canal, and was praying, meanwhile, for these unknown dead. A horrible thought flashed across his mind:—Perhaps there, amongst these, beneath them! . . . Oh Lord! let it not be true! help me not to think of it!—

The funeral procession having disappeared, he moved on, crossing the square, and taking the street along the left-hand side of the canal, without other reason for his choice than because the procession had taken the opposite direction. After going a few steps between the side of the church and the canal, he saw to the right the bridge Marcellino; he crossed it, and by that unique passage arrived in the street of the Borgo Nuovo. Casting his eyes forward, on the constant look-out for some of whom he might ask direction, he saw at the other end of the street a priest clothed in a doublet, with a small stick in his hand, standing near a half-open door, with his head bent, and his ear at the aperture; and very soon afterwards he saw him raise his hand to pronounce a blessing. He guessed,—what in fact was the case,—that he had just finished confessing some one; and said to himself:—This is my man. If a priest, in the exercise of his functions, hasn't a little charity, a little good-nature and kindness, I can only say there is none left in the world.—

In the mean while, the priest, leaving the door-way, advanced towards Renzo, walking with much caution in the middle of the road. When he was within four or five paces of him, Renzo took off his hat and signified that he wanted to speak to him, stopping, at the same time, so as to let him understand that he would not approach too indiscreetly. The priest also paused, with the air of one prepared to listen, planting his stick, however, on the ground before him, to serve, as it were, for a kind of bulwark. Renzo proposed his inquiries, which the good priest readily satisfied, not only telling him the name of the street where the house was situated, but giving him also, as he saw the poor fellow had need of it, a little direction as to his way; pointing out to him, *i.e.* by the help of right and left hands, crosses and churches, those other six or eight streets he had yet to traverse before reaching the one he was inquiring after.

'God keep you in good health, both in these days and always!' said Renzo: and as the priest prepared to go away, 'Another favour,' added he; and he told him of the poor forgotten woman. The

worthy priest thanked him for having given him this opportunity
of conveying assistance where it was so much needed; and saying
that he would go and inform the proper authorities, took his departure.

Renzo, making a bow, also pursued his way, and tried, as he went
along, to recapitulate the instructions he had received, that he might
be obliged as seldom as possible to ask further directions. But it
cannot be imagined how difficult he found the task; not so much
on account of the perplexity of the thing, as from a fresh uneasiness
which had arisen in his mind. That name of the street, that tracing
of the road, had almost upset him. It was the information he had
desired and requested, without which he could do nothing; nor had
anything been said to him, together with it, which could suggest a
presage, not to say a suspicion, of misfortune. Yet how was it? The
rather more distinct idea of an approaching termination to his doubts,
when he might hear either, 'She is living;' or, on the other hand,
'She is dead'—that idea had come before him with so much force,
that at that moment he would rather have been in ignorance about
everything, and have been at the beginning of that journey of which
he now found himself so near the end. He gathered up his courage,
however:—Ah!—said he to himself,—if we begin now to play the
child, how will things go on?—Thus re-emboldened as best might
be, he pursued his way, advancing further into the city.

What a city? and who found time in those days to recollect what
it had been the year before, by reason of the famine!

Renzo happened to have to pass through one of its most unsightly
and desolated quarters; that junction of streets known by the name
of the *Carrobio* of the Porta Nuova. (Here, at that time, was a
cross at the head of the street, and opposite to it, by the side of the
present site of San Francesco di Paola, an ancient church, bearing
the name of San Anastasia.) Such had been the virulence of the
contagion, and the infection of the scattered corpses in this neighbourhood, that the few survivors had been obliged to remove; so that
while the passer-by was stunned with such a spectacle of solitude
and desertion, more than one sense was only too grievously incommoded and offended by the tokens and relics of recent habitation.
Renzo quickened his steps, consoling himself with the thought that

the end of his search could not yet be at hand, and hoping that before he arrived at it, he would find the scene, at least in part, changed; and, in fact, a little further on, he came out into a part which might still be called the city of the living—but what a city, and what living! All the doorways into the streets kept shut from either suspicion or alarm, except those which were left open because deserted or invaded; others nailed up and sealed outside, on account of the sick, or dead, who lay within; others marked with a cross drawn with coal, as an intimation to the *monatti* that there were dead to be carried away: all more a matter of chance than otherwise, according as there happened to be here, rather than there, a commissary of health, or other officer, who was inclined either to execute the regulations, or to exercise violence and oppression. Everywhere were rags and corrupted bandages, infected straw, or clothes, or sheets, thrown from the windows; sometimes bodies, which had suddenly fallen dead in the streets, and were left there till a cart happened to pass by and pick them up, or shaken from off the carts themselves, or even thrown from the windows. To such a degree had the obstinacy and virulence of the contagion brutalized men's minds and divested them of all compassionate care, of every feeling of social respect! The stir of business, the clatter of carriages, the cries of sellers, the talking of passengers, all were everywhere hushed; and seldom was the death-like stillness broken but by the rumbling of funeral cars, the lamentations of beggars, the groans of the sick, the shouts of the frantic, or the vociferations of the *monatti*. At daybreak, midday, and evening, one of the bells of the cathedral gave the signal for reciting certain prayers proposed by the Archbishop; its tones were responded to by the bells of the other churches; and then persons might be seen repairing to the windows to pray in common; and a murmur of sighs and voices might be heard which inspired sadness, mingled at the same time with some feeling of comfort.

Two-thirds, perhaps, of the inhabitants being by this time carried off, a great part of the remainder having departed, or lying languishing at home, and the concourse from without being reduced almost to nothing, perhaps not one individual among the few who still went about, would be met with in a long circuit, in whom something strange, and sufficient in itself to infer a fatal change in circumstances, was not apparent. Men of the highest rank might be seen without cape or cloak, at that time a most essential part of any gentleman's dress; priests without cassocks, friars without cowls; in short, all kinds of dress were dispensed with which could contract anything in fluttering about, or give (which was more feared than all the rest) facilities to the poisoners. And besides this carefulness to go about as trussed up and confined as possible, their persons were neglected and disorderly; the beards of such as were accustomed to wear them grown much longer, and suffered to grow by those who had formerly kept them shaven; their hair, too, long and undressed, not only from the neglect which usually attends prolonged depression, but because suspicion had been attached to barbers ever since one of them, Giangiacomo Mora, had been taken and condemned as a famous poisoner; a name which, for a long while afterwards, preserved throughout the duchy a pre-eminent celebrity in infamy, and deserved a far more extensive and lasting one in commiseration. The greater number carried in one hand a stick, some even a pistol, as a threatening warning to any one who should attempt to approach them stealthily; and in the other, perfumed pastils, or little balls of metal or wood, perforated and filled with sponges steeped in aromatic vinegar, which they applied from time to time, as they went along, to their noses, or held there continually. Some carried a small vial hung round their neck, containing a little quick-silver, persuaded that this possessed the virtue of absorbing and arresting every pestilential effluvia; this they were very careful to renew from time to time. Gentlemen not only traversed the streets without their usual attendants, but even went about with a basket on their arms, providing the common necessaries of life. Even friends, when they met in the streets alive, saluted each other at a distance, with silent and hasty signs. Every one, as he walked along, had enough to do to avoid the filthy and deadly stumbling-blocks with which the ground was strewn, and in some places even encumbered. Every one tried to keep the middle of the road, for fear of some other obstacle, some other more fatal weight, which might fall from the windows; for fear of venomous powders, which it was affirmed were often thrown down thence upon the passengers;

for fear, too, of the walls, which might, perchance, be anointed. Thus ignorance, unseasonably secure, or preposterously circumspect, now added trouble to trouble, and incited false terrors in compensation for the reasonable and salutary ones which it had withstood at the beginning.

Such were the less disfigured and pitiable spectacles which were everywhere present; the sight of the whole, the wealthy: for after so many pictures of misery, and remembering that still more painful one which it remains for us to describe, we will not now stop to tell what was the condition of the sick who dragged themselves along, or lay in the streets—beggars, women, children. It was such that the spectator could find a desperate consolation, as it were, in what appears at first sight, to those who are far removed in place and time, the climax of misery; the thought, I mean,—the constant observation, that the survivors were reduced to so small a number.

Renzo had already gone some distance on his way through the midst of this desolation, when he heard, proceeding from a street a few yards off, into which he had been directed to turn, a confused noise, in which he readily distinguished the usual horrible tinkling.

At the entrance of the street, which was one of the most spacious, he perceived four carts standing in the middle; and as in a cornmarket there is a constant hurrying to and fro of people, and an emptying and filling of sacks, such was the bustle here; *monatti* intruding into houses, *monatti* coming out, bearing a burden upon their shoulders, which they placed upon one or other of the carts; some in red livery, others without that distinction: many with another still more odious, plumes and cloaks of various colours, which these miserable wretches wore in the midst of the general mourning, as if in honour of a festival. From time to time the mournful cry resounded from one of the windows: 'Here, *monatti!*' And, with a still more wretched sound, a harsh voice rose from this horrible source in reply: 'Coming directly!' Or else there were lamentations nearer at hand, or entreaties to make haste; to which the *monatti* responded with oaths.

Having entered the street, Renzo quickened his steps, trying not to look at these obstacles further than was necessary to avoid them; his attention, however, was arrested by a remarkable object of pity, such pity as inclines to the contemplation of its object; so that he came to a pause almost without determining to do so.

Coming down the steps at one of the door-ways, and advancing towards the convoy, he beheld a woman, whose appearance announced still-remaining, though somewhat advanced youthfulness; a veiled and dimmed, but not destroyed beauty, was still apparent, in spite of much suffering, and a fatal languor—that delicate, and, at the same time, majestic, beauty, which is conspicuous in the Lombard blood. Her gait was weary, but not tottering; no tears fell from her eyes, though they bore tokens of having shed many; there was something peaceful and profound in her sorrow, which indicated a mind fully conscious and sensitive enough to feel it. But it was not only her own appearance which, in the midst of so much misery, marked her out so especially as an object of commiseration, and revived in her behalf a feeling now exhausted—extinguished, in men's hearts. She carried in her arms a little child, about nine years old, now a lifeless body; but laid out and arranged, with her hair parted on her forehead, and in a white and remarkably clean dress, as if those hands had decked her out for a long-promised feast, granted as a reward. Nor was she lying there, but upheld and adjusted on one arm, with her breast reclining against her mother's like a living creature; save that a delicate little hand, as white as wax, hung from one side with a kind of inanimate weight, and the head rested upon her mother's shoulder with an abandonment deeper than that of sleep; her mother, for even if their likeness to each other had not given assurance of the fact, the countenance which still depicted any feeling would have clearly revealed it.

A horrible-looking *monatto* approached the woman, and attempted to take the burden from her arms, with a kind of unusual respect, however, and with involuntary hesitation. But she, slightly drawing back, yet with the air of one who shows neither scorn nor displeasure, said, 'No! don't take her from me yet; I must place her myself on this cart: here.' So saying, she opened her hand, displayed a purse which she held in it, and dropped it into that which the *monatto* extended towards her. She then continued: 'Promise me not to take a thread from around her, nor to let any one else attempt to do so, and to lay her in the ground thus.'

The *monatto* laid his right hand on his heart; and then zealously, and almost obsequiously, rather from the new feeling by which he was, as it were, subdued, than on account of the unlooked for reward, hastened to make a little room on the car for the infant dead. The lady, giving it a kiss on the forehead, laid it on the spot prepared for it, as upon a bed, arranged it there, covering it with a pure white linen cloth, and pronounced the parting words: 'Farewell, Cecilia! rest in peace! This evening we, too, will join you, to rest together for ever. In the meanwhile, pray for us; for I will pray for you and the others.' Then, turning to the *monatto,* 'You,' said she, 'when you pass this way in the evening, may come to fetch me too, and not me only.'

So saying, she re-entered the house, and, after an instant, appeared at the window, holding in her arms another more dearly-loved one, still living, but with the marks of death on its countenance. She remained to contemplate these so unworthy obsequies of the first child, from the time the car started until it was out of sight, and then disappeared. And what remained for her to do, but to lay upon the bed the only one that was left to her, and to stretch herself beside it, that they might die together? as the flower already full blown upon the stem, falls together with the bud still enfolded in its calyx, under the scythe which levels alike all the herbage of the field.

'Oh Lord!' exclaimed Renzo, 'hear her! take her to Thyself, her and that little infant one: they have suffered enough! surely, they have suffered enough!'

Recovered from these singular emotions, and while trying to recall to memory the directions he had received, to ascertain whether he was to turn at the first street, and whether to the right or left, he heard another and a different sound proceeding from the latter, a confused sound of imperious cries, feeble lamentations, prolonged groans, sobs of women, and children's moans.

He went forward, oppressed at heart by that one sad and gloomy foreboding. Having reached the spot where the two streets crossed, he beheld a confused multitude advancing from one side, and stood still to wait till it had passed. It was a party of sick on their way to the Lazzaretto; some driven thither by force, vainly offering re- sistance, vainly crying that they would rather die upon their beds, and replying with impotent imprecations to the oaths and commands of the *monatti* who were conducting them; others who walked on in silence, without any apparent grief and without hope, like insensible beings; women with infants clinging to their bosoms; children terrified by the cries, the mandates, and the crowd, more than by the confused idea of death, with loud cries demanding their mother and her trusted embrace, and imploring that they might remain at their well-known homes. Alas! perhaps their mother, whom they supposed they had left asleep upon her bed, had there thrown herself down senseless, subdued in a moment by the disease, to be carried away on a cart to the Lazzaretto,—or the grave, if perchance the cart should arrive a little later. Perhaps—oh misfortune deserving of still more bitter tears—the mother, entirely taken up by her own sufferings, had forgotten everything, even her own children, and had no longer any wish but to die in quiet.

In such a scene of confusion, however, some examples of constancy and piety might still be seen: parents, brothers, sons, husbands, supporting their loved ones, and accompanying them with words of comfort; and not adults only, but even boys and little girls escorting their younger brothers and sisters, and, with manly sense and compassion, exhorting them to obedience, and assuring them that they were going to a place where others would take care of them and try to restore them to health.

In the midst of the sadness and emotions of tenderness excited by these spectacles, a far different solicitude pressed more closely upon our traveller, and held him in painful suspense. The house must be near at hand, and who knew whether among these people . . . But the crowd having all passed by, and this doubt being removed, he turned to a *monatto* who was walking behind, and asked him for the street and dwelling of Don Ferrante. 'It's gone to smash, clown,' was the reply he received. Renzo cared not to answer again; but perceiving a few yards distant, a commissary who brought up the convoy, and had a little more Christian-like countenance, he re-repeated to him the same inquiry. The commissary, pointing with a stick in the direction whence he had come, said, 'The first street to the right, the last gentleman's house on the left.'

With new and still deeper anxiety of mind, the youth bent his steps thitherward, and quickly distinguished the house among others more humble and unpretending; he approached the closed door, placed his hand on the knocker, and held it there in suspense, as in an urn, before drawing out the ticket upon which depends life or death. At length he raised the hammer, and gave a resolute knock.

In a moment or two a window was slightly opened, and a woman appeared at it to peep out, looking towards the door with a suspicious countenance, which seemed to say,—*Monatti?* robbers? commissaries? poisoners? devils?—

'Signora,' said Renzo, looking upwards, in a somewhat tremulous tone, 'is there a young country girl here at service, of the name of Lucia?'

'She's here no longer, go away,' answered the woman, preparing to shut the window.

'One moment, for pity's sake! She's no longer here? Where is she?'

'At the Lazzaretto;' and she was again about to close the window.

'But one moment, for Heaven's sake! With the pestilence?'

'To be sure. Something new, eh? Get you gone.'

'Oh stay! Was she very ill? How long is it? . . .'

But this time the window was closed in reality.

'Oh Signora! Signora! one word, for charity! for the sake of your poor dead! I don't ask you for anything of yours: alas! oh!' But he might as well have talked to the wall.

Afflicted by this intelligence, and vexed with the treatment he had received, Renzo again seized the knocker, and standing close to the door, kept squeezing and twisting it in his hand, then lifted it to knock again, in a kind of despair, and paused, in act to strike. In this agitation of feeling, he turned to see if his eye could catch any person near at hand, from whom he might, perhaps, receive some more sober information, some direction, some light. But the first, the only person he discovered was another woman, distant, perhaps, about twenty yards; who, with a look full of terror, hatred, impatience, and malice, with a certain wild expression of eye which betrayed an attempt to look at him and something else at a distance at the same time, with a mouth opened as if on the point of shouting as loud as she could; but holding even her breath, raising two thin, bony arms, and extending and drawing back two wrinkled and clenched hands, as if reaching to herself something, gave evident signs of wishing to call people without letting somebody perceive it. On their eyes encountering each other, she, looking still more hideous, started like one taken by surprise.

'What the ——?' began Renzo, raising his fist towards the woman; but she, having lost all hope of being able to have him unexpectedly seized, gave utterance to the cry she had hitherto restrained: 'The poisoner! seize him! seize him! seize him! the poisoner!'

'Who? I! ah, you lying old witch! hold your tongue there!' cried Renzo; and he sprang towards her to frighten her and make her be silent. He perceived, however, at this moment, that he must rather look after himself. At the screams of the woman people flocked from both sides; not the crowds, indeed, which, in a similar case, would have collected three months before; but still more than enough to crush a single individual. At this very instant, the window was again thrown open, and the same woman who had shown herself so uncourteous just before, displayed herself this time in full, and cried out, 'Take him, take him; for he must be one of those wicked wretches who go about to anoint the doors of gentlefolks.'

Renzo determined in an instant that it would be a better course to make his escape from them, than stay to clear himself; he cast an eye on each side to see where were the fewest people; and in that direction took to his legs. He repulsed, with a tremendous push, one who attempted to stop his passage; with another blow on the chest he forced a second to retreat eight or ten yards, who was running to meet him; and away he went at full speed, with his tightly clenched fist uplifted in the air, in preparation for whomsoever should come in his way. The street was clear before him; but behind his back he heard resounding more and more loudly the savage cry: 'Seize him! seize him! a poisoner!' he heard, drawing nearer and nearer, the footsteps of the swiftest among his pursuers. His anger became fury, his anguish was changed into desperation; a cloud seemed gathering over his eyes; he seized hold of his poniard, unsheathed it, stopped, drew himself up, turned round a more fierce and savage face than he had ever put on in his whole life; and, brandishing in the air, with outstretched arm, the glittering blade, exclaimed, 'Let him who dares come forward, you rascals! and I'll anoint him with this, in earnest.'

But, with astonishment and a confused feeling of relief, he perceived that his persecutors had already stopped at some distance, as if in hesitation, and that while they continued shouting after him, they were beckoning with uplifted hands, like people possessed and terrified out of their senses, to others at some distance beyond him. He again turned round, and beheld before him, and a very little way off, (for his extreme perturbation had prevented his observing it a moment before), a cart advancing, indeed a file of the usual funeral carts with their usual accompaniments; and beyond them another small band of people, who were ready, on their part, to fall upon the poisoner, and take him in the midst; these, however, were also restrained by the same impediment. Finding himself thus between two fires, it occurred to him that what was to them a cause of terror might be for himself a means of safety; he thought that this was not a time for squeamish scruples; so again sheathing his poniard, he drew a little on one side, resumed his way towards the carts, and passing by the first, remarked in the second a tolerably empty space. He took aim, sprang up and lit with his right foot in the cart, his left in the air, and his arms stretched forward.

'Bravo! bravo!' exclaimed the *monatti* with one voice, some of whom were following the convoy on foot, others were seated on the carts; and others, to tell the horrible fact as it really was, on the dead bodies, quaffing from a large flask which was going the round of the party. 'Bravo! a capital hit!'

'You've come to put yourself under the protection of the *monatti*: you may reckon yourself as safe as in church,' said one of the two who were seated on the cart upon which he had thrown himself.

The greater part of his enemies had, on the approach of the train, turned their backs upon him and fled, crying at the same time, 'Seize him! seize him! a poisoner!' Some few of them, however, retired more deliberately, stopping every now and then, and turning with a hideous grin of rage and threatening gestures towards Renzo; who replied to them from the cart by shaking his fist at them.

'Leave it to me,' said a *monatto;* and tearing a filthy rag from one of the bodies, he hastily tied it in a knot, and taking it by one of its ears, raised it like a sling towards these obstinate fellows, and pretended to hurl it at them, crying, 'Here, you rascals!' At this action they all fled in horror; and Renzo saw nothing but the backs of his enemies and heels which bounded rapidly through the air, like the hammers in a clothier's mill.

A howl of triumph arose among the *monatti,* a stormy burst of laughter, a prolonged 'Eh!' as an accompaniment, so to say, to this fugue.

'Aha! look if we don't know how to protect honest fellows!' said the same *monatto* to Renzo: 'one of us is worth more than a hundred of those cowards!'

'Certainly, I may say I owe you my life,' replied he; 'and I thank you with all my heart.'

'Not a word, not a word,' answered the *monatto:* 'you deserve it; one can see you're a brave young fellow. You do right to poison these rascals; anoint away, extirpate all those who are good for nothing, except when they're dead; for in reward for the life we lead, they only curse us, and keep saying that when the pestilence is over, they'll have us all hanged. They must be finished before the pestilence; the *monatti* only must be left to chant victory and revel in Milan.'

'Long live the pestilence, and death to the rabble!' exclaimed the other; and with this beautiful toast he put the flask to his mouth, and holding it with both his hands amidst the joltings of the cart, took a long draught, and then handed it to Renzo, saying, 'Drink to our health.'

'I wish it you all, with my whole heart,' said Renzo, 'but I'm not thirsty: I don't feel any inclination to drink just now.'

'You've had a fine fright, it seems,' said the *monatto.* 'You look like a harmless creature enough; you should have another face than that to be a poisoner.'

'Let everybody do as he can,' said the other.

'Here, give it me,' said one of those on foot at the side of the car, 'for I, too, want to drink another cup to the health of his honour, who finds himself in such capital company . . . there, there, just there, among that elegant carriage-full.'

And with one of his hideous and cursed grins he pointed to the cart in front of that upon which our poor Renzo was seated. Then, composing his face to an expression of seriousness still more wicked and revolting, he made a bow in that direction, and resumed: 'May it please you, my lord, to let a poor wretch of a *monatto* taste a little of this wine from your cellar? Mind you, sir: our way of life is only so so: we have taken you into our carriage to give you a ride into the country; and then it takes very little wine to do harm to your lordships: the poor *monatti* have good stomachs.'

And amidst the loud laughs of his companions, he took the flask, and lifted it up, but, before drinking, turned to Renzo, and fixed his eyes on his face, and said to him, with a certain air of scornful compassion: 'The devil, with whom you have made agreement, must be very young; for if we hadn't been by to rescue you, he'd have given you mighty assistance.' And amidst a fresh outburst of laughter, he applied the flagon to his lips.

'Give us some! What! give us some!' shouted many voices from the preceding car. The ruffian, having swallowed as much as he wished, handed the great flask with both hands into those of his fellow-ruffians, who continued passing it round, until one of them, having emptied it, grasped it by the neck, slung it round in the air two or three times, and dashed it to atoms upon the pavement, crying, 'Long live the pestilence!' He then broke into one of their licentious ballads, and was soon accompanied by all the rest of this depraved chorus. The infernal song, mingled with the tinkling of the bells, the rattle of the cart, and the trampling of men and horses, resounded through the silent vacuity of the streets, and echoing in the houses, bitterly wrung the hearts of the few who still inhabited them.

But what cannot sometimes turn to advantage? What cannot appear good in some case or another? The extremity of a moment before had rendered more than tolerable to Renzo the company of these dead and living companions; and now the sounds that relieved him from the awkwardness of such a conversation, were, I had almost said, acceptable, music to his ears. Still half bewildered, and in great agitation, he thanked Providence in his heart, as he best could, that he had escaped such imminent danger without receiving or inflicting injury; he prayed for assistance to deliver himself now from his deliverers; and for his part kept on the look-out, watching his companions, and reconnoitring the road, that he might seize the proper moment to slide quietly down without giving them an opportunity of making any disturbance or uproar, which might stir up mischief in the passers-by.

And lo! on turning a corner, he seemed to recognize the place along which they were about to pass: he looked more attentively, and at once knew it by more certain signs. Does the reader know where he was? In the direct course to the Porta Orientale, in that very street along which he had gone so slowly, and returned so speedily, about twenty months before. He quickly remembered that from thence he could go straight to the Lazzaretto; and this finding of himself in the right way without any endeavour of his own, and without direction, he looked upon as a special token of Divine guidance, and a good omen of what remained. At that moment a commissary came to meet the cars, who called out to the *monatti* to stop, and I know not what besides: it need only be said that they came to a halt, and the music was changed into clamorous dialogues. One of the *monatti* seated on Renzo's car jumped down: Renzo said to the other, 'Thank you for your kindness; God reward you for it!' and sprang down at the opposite side.

'Get you gone, poor poisoner,' replied the man: 'you'll not be the fellow that'll ruin Milan!'

Fortunately there was no one at hand who could overhear him. The party had stopped on the left hand of the street: Renzo hastily crossed over to the opposite side; and, keeping close to the wall, trudged onward towards the bridge; crossed it; followed the well-known street of the Borgo, and recognized the Convent of the Capuchins; he comes close to the gate, sees the projecting corner of the Lazzaretto, passes through the palisade, and the scene outside the enclosure is laid open to his view; not so much an indication and specimen of the interior, as itself a vast, diversified, and indescribable scene.

Along the two sides, which are visible to a spectator from this point, all was bustle and confusion; there was a great concourse; an influx and reflux of people; sick flocking in crowds to the Lazzaretto; some sitting or lying on the edge of one or other of the moats that flanked the road, whose strength had proved insufficient to carry them within their place of retreat, or, when they had abandoned it in despair, had equally failed to convey them further away. Others were wandering about as if stupefied; and not a few were absolutely beside themselves: one would be eagerly relating his fancies to a miserable creature labouring under the malady; another would be actually raving; while a third appeared with a smiling countenance, as if assisting at some gay spectacle. But the strangest and most clamorous kind of so melancholy a gaiety, was a loud and continual singing, which seemed to proceed from that wretched assembly, and even drowned all the other voices—a popular song of love, joyous and playful, one of those which are called rural; and following this sound by the eye to discover who could possibly be so cheerful, yonder, tranquilly seated in the bottom of the ditch that washes the walls of the Lazzaretto, he perceived a poor wretch, with upturned eyes, singing at the very stretch of his voice!

Renzo had scarcely gone a few yards along the south side of the edifice, when an extraordinary noise arose in the crowd, and a distant cry of 'Take care!' and 'Stop him!' He stood upon tiptoe, looked forward, and beheld a jaded horse galloping at full speed, impelled forward by a still more wretched looking rider: a poor frantic creature, who, seeing the beast loose and unguarded, standing by a cart, had hastily mounted his bare back, and striking him on the neck with his fists, and spurring him with his heels, was urging him impetuously onward; *monatti* were following, shouting and howling; and all were enveloped in a cloud of dust, which whirled around their heads.

Confounded and weary with the sight of so much misery, the youth arrived at the gate of that abode where perhaps more was concentrated than had been scattered over the whole space it had yet been his fortune to traverse. He walked up to the door, entered under the vaulted roof, and stood for a moment without moving in the middle of the portico.

CHAPTER XXXV

LET the reader imagine the enclosure of the Lazzaretto peopled with sixteen thousand persons ill of the plague; the whole area encumbered, here with tents and cabins, there with carts, elsewhere with people; those two interminable ranges of portico to the right and left, covered, crowded, with dead or dying, stretched upon mattresses, or the bare straw; and throughout the whole of this, so to say, immense den, a commotion, a fluctuation, like the swell of the sea; and within, people coming and going, stopping and running, some sinking under disease, others rising from their sick beds, either convalescent, frantic, or to attend upon others. Such was the spectacle which suddenly burst upon Renzo's view, and forced him to pause there, horror-struck and overpowered. We do not intend to describe this spectacle by itself, for which, doubtless, none of our readers would thank us; we will only follow our youth in his painful walk, stop where he stopped, and relate what he happened to witness, so far as is necessary to explain what he did, and what chanced to occur to him.

From the gate where he stood, up to the temple in the middle, and from that again to the opposite gate, ran a kind of pathway, free from cabins, and every other substantial impediment; and, at a second glance, he observed a great bustle of removing carts, and making the way clear; and discovered officers and Capuchins directing this operation, and at the same time dismissing all those who had no business there. Fearing lest he also should be turned out in this manner, he slipped in between the pavilions, on the side to which he had casually turned—the right.

He went forward, according as he found room to set his foot down, from cabin to cabin, popping his head into each, casting his eye upon every one who lay outside, gazing upon countenances broken down by suffering, contracted by spasm, or motionless in death, perchance he might happen to find that one which, nevertheless, he dreaded to find. He had already, however, gone some considerable distance, and often and often repeated this melancholy inspection, without having yet seen a single woman; he concluded, therefore, that these must be lodged in a separate quarter. So far he guessed; but of the whereabouts he had no indication, nor could he form the least conjecture. From time to time he met attendants, as different in appearance, dress, and behaviour, as the motive was different and opposite which gave to both one and the other strength to live in the exercise of such offices: in the one, the extinction of all feelings of compassion; in the other, compassion more than human. But from neither did he attempt to ask directions, for fear of creating for himself new obstacles; and he resolved to walk on by himself till he succeeded in discovering women. And as he walked along, he failed not to look narrowly around, though from time to time he was compelled to withdraw his eyes, overcome, and, as it were, dazzled by the spectacle of so great miseries. Yet, whither could he turn them, where suffer them to rest, save upon other miseries as great?

The very air and sky added, if anything could add, to the horror of these sights. The fog had condensed by degrees, and resolved itself into large clouds, which, becoming darker and darker, made it seem like the tempestuous closing in of evening; except that towards the zenith of this deep and lowering sky, the sun's disk was visible as from behind a thick veil, pale, emitting around a very feeble light, which was speedily exhaled, and pouring down a death-like and oppressive heat. Every now and then, amidst the vast murmur that floated around, was heard a deep rumbling of thunder, interrupted, as it were, and irresolute; nor could the listener distinguish from which side it came. He might, indeed, easily have deemed it a distant sound of cars, unexpectedly coming to a stand. In the country round, not a twig bent under a breath of air, not a bird was seen to alight or fly away; the swallow alone, appearing suddenly from the eaves of the enclosure, skimmed along the ground with extended wing, sweeping, as it were, the surface of the field; but, alarmed at the surrounding confusion, rapidly mounted again into the air, and flew away. It was one of those days in which, among a party of travellers, not one of them breaks the silence; and the

hunter walks pensively along, with his eyes bent to the ground; and
the peasant, digging in the field, pauses in his song, without being
aware of it; one of those days which are the forerunners of a tem-
pest, in which nature, as if motionless without, while agitated by
internal travail, seems to oppress every living thing, and to add an
undefinable weight to every employment, to idleness, to existence
itself. But in that abode specially assigned to suffering and death,
men hitherto struggling with their malady might be seen sinking
under this new pressure; they were to be seen by hundreds rapidly
becoming worse; and at the same time, the last struggle was more
distressing, and, in the augmentation of suffering, the groans were
still more stifled; nor, perhaps, had there yet been in that place an
hour of bitterness equal to this.

The youth had already threaded his way for some time without
success through this maze of cabins, when, in the variety of lamentations and confused murmurs, he began to distinguish a singular
intermixture of bleatings and infants' cries. He arrived at length
before a cracked and disjointed wooden partition, from within
which this extraordinary sound proceeded; and peeping through a
large aperture between two boards, he beheld an enclosure scattered
throughout with little huts, and in these, as well as in the spaces
of the small camp between the cabins, not the usual occupants of
an infirmary, but infants, lying upon little beds, pillows, sheets, or
cloths spread upon the ground, and nurses and other women busily
attending upon them; and, which above everything else attracted
and engrossed his attention, she-goats mingled with these, and acting as their coadjutrices: a hospital of innocents, such as the place
and times could afford them. It was, I say, a novel sight, to behold
some of these animals standing quietly over this or that infant,
giving it suck, and another hastening at the cry of a child, as if en-
dued with maternal feeling, and stopping by the side of the little
claimant, and contriving to dispose itself over the infant, and bleat-
ing, and fidgeting, almost as if demanding some one to come to the
assistance of both.

Here and there nurses were seated with infants at the breast;
some employing such expressions of affection as raised a doubt in
the mind of the spectator whether they had been induced to repair

thither by the promises of reward, or by that voluntary benevolence which goes in search of the needy and afflicted. One of these, with deep sorrow depicted in her countenance, drew from her breast a poor weeping little creature, and mournfully went to look for an animal which might be able to supply her place; another regarded with a compassionate look the little one asleep on her bosom, and gently kissing it, went to lay it on a bed in one of the cabins; while a third, surrendering her breast to the stranger suckling, with an air not of negligence, but of pre-occupation, gazed fixedly up to heaven. What was she thinking of, with that gesture, with that look, but of one brought forth from her own bowels, who, perhaps only a short time before, had been nourished at that breast, perchance had expired on that bosom!

Other women, of more experience, supplied different offices. One would run at the cry of a famished child, lift it from the ground, and carry it to a goat, feeding upon a heap of fresh herbage; and applying it to the creature's paps, would chide, and, at the same time, coax the inexperienced animal with her voice, that it might quietly lend itself to its new office; another would spring forward to drive off a goat which was trampling under-foot a poor babe, in its eagerness to suckle another; while a third was carrying about her own infant, and rocking it in her arms, now trying to lull it to sleep by singing, now to pacify it with soothing words, and calling it by a name she had herself given it. At this moment a Capuchin, with a very white beard, arrived, bringing two screaming infants, one in each arm, which he had just taken from their dying mothers; and a woman ran to receive them, and went to seek among the crowd, and in the flocks, some one that would immediately supply the place of a mother.

More than once, the youth, urged by his anxiety, had torn himself from the opening to resume his way; and, after all, had again peeped in to watch another moment or two.

Having at length left the place, he went on close along the partition, until a group of huts, which were propped against it, compelled him to turn aside. He then went round the cabins, with the intention of regaining the partition, turning the corner of the enclosure, and making some fresh discoveries. But while he was looking forward to reconnoitre his way, a sudden, transient, instantaneous apparition, struck his eye, and put him in great agitation. He saw, about a hundred yards off, a Capuchin threading his way and quickly becoming lost among the pavilions: a Capuchin, who, even thus passingly, and at a distance, had all the bearing, motions, and figure of Father Cristoforo. With the frantic eagerness the reader can imagine, he sprang forward in that direction, looking here and there, winding about, backward, forward, inside and out, by circles, and through narrow passages, until he again saw, with increased joy, the form of the self-same friar; he saw him at a little distance, just leaving a large boiling pot, and going with a porringer in his hands towards a cabin; then he beheld him seat himself in the doorway, make the sign of the cross on the basin he held before him, and, looking around him, like one constantly on the alert, begin to eat. It was, indeed, Father Cristoforo.

The history of the friar, from the point at which we lost sight of him up to the present meeting, may be told in a few words. He had never removed from Rimini, nor even thought of removing, until the plague, breaking out in Milan, afforded him the opportunity he had long so earnestly desired, of sacrificing his life for his fellow-creatures. He urgently entreated that he might be recalled from Rimini to assist and attend upon the infected patients. The Count, Attilio's uncle, was dead; and besides, the times required tenders of the sick rather than politicians; so that his request was granted without difficulty. He came immediately to Milan, entered the Lazzaretto, and had now been there about three months.

But the consolation Renzo felt in thus again seeing his good friar was not for a moment unalloyed; together with the certainty that it was he, he was also made painfully aware of how much he was changed. His stooping, and, as it were, laborious carriage, his wan and shrivelled face, all betokened an exhausted nature, a broken and sinking frame, which was assisted and, as it were, upheld from hour to hour only by the energy of his mind.

He kept his eye fixed on the youth who was approaching him, and who was seeking by gestures, (not daring to do so with his voice,) to make him distinguish and recognize him. 'O, Father

Cristoforo!' said he, at last, when he was near enough to be heard without shouting.

'You here!' said the friar, setting the porringer on the ground, and rising from his seat.

'How are you, Father?—how are you?'

'Better than the many poor creatures you see,' replied the friar; and his voice was feeble, hollow, and as changed as everything else about him. His eye alone was what it always was, or had something about it even more bright and resplendent; as if Charity, elevated by the approaching end of her labours, and exulting in the consciousness of being near her source, restored to it a more ardent and purer fire than that which infirmity was every hour extinguishing. 'But you,' pursued he, 'how is it you're in this place? What makes you come thus to brave the pestilence?'

'I've had it, thank Heaven! I come . . . to seek for . . . Lucia.'

'Lucia! Is Lucia here?'

'She is; at least, I hope in God she may still be here.'

'Is she your wife?'

'Oh, my dear father! My wife! no, that she's not. Don't you know anything of what has happened?'

'No, my son; since God removed me to a distance from you, I've never heard anything further; but now that he has sent you to me, I'll tell you the truth, that I wish very much to know. But . . . and the sentence of outlawry?'

'You know, then, what things they've done to me?'

'But you, what had you done?'

'Listen: if I were to say that I was prudent that day in Milan, I should tell a lie; but I didn't do a single wicked action.'

'I believe you; and I believed it too before.'

'Now, then, I may tell you all.'

'Wait,' said the friar; and, going a few yards out of the hut, he called, 'Father Vittore!' In a moment or two, a young Capuchin appeared, to whom Cristoforo said, 'Do me the kindness, Father Vittore, to take my share, too, of waiting upon our patients, while I am absent for a little while; and if any one should ask for me, will you be good enough to call me. That one, particularly; if ever he gives the least sign of returning consciousness, let me be informed of it directly, for charity's sake.'

The young friar answered that he would do as he requested; and then Cristoforo, turning to Renzo, said, 'Let us go in here. But . . .' added he directly, stopping, 'you seem to me very tired; you must want something to eat.'

'So I do,' said Renzo: 'now that you've reminded me, I remember I'm still fasting.'

'Stay,' said the friar; and taking another porringer, he went to fill it from the large boiler; he then returned, and offered it, with a spoon, to Renzo; made him sit down on a straw mattress which served him for a bed; went to a cask that stood in one corner, and drew a glass of wine, which he set on a little table near his guest; and then, taking up his own porringer, seated himself beside him.

'Oh, Father Cristoforo!' said Renzo, 'is it your business to do all this? But you are always the same. I thank you with all my heart.'

'Don't thank me,' said the friar: 'that belongs to the poor; but you too are a poor man just now. Now, then, tell me what I don't know; tell me about our poor Lucia, and try to do it in a few words, for time is scarce, and there is plenty to be done, as you see.'

Renzo began, between one spoonful and another, to relate the history of Lucia, how she had been sheltered in the monastery at Monza, how she had been forcibly carried off . . .

At the idea of such sufferings and such dangers, and at the thought that it was he who had directed the poor innocent to that place, the good friar became almost breathless with emotion; but he was quickly relieved on hearing how she had been miraculously liberated, restored to her mother, and placed by her with Donna Prassede.

'Now I will tell you about myself,' pursued the narrator; and he briefly sketched the day he spent in Milan, and his flight, and how he had long been absent from home, and now, everything being turned upside down, he had ventured to go thither; how he had not found Agnese there; and how he had learned at Milan that Lucia was at the Lazzaretto. 'And here I am,' he concluded; 'here I am to look for her, to see if she's still living, and if . . . she'll still have me . . . because . . . sometimes . . .'

'But how were you directed here?' asked the friar. 'Have you any information whereabouts she was lodged, or at what time she came?'

'None, dear Father; none, except that she *is* here, if, indeed, she be still living, which may God grant!'

'Oh, you poor fellow! But what search have you yet made here?'

'I've wandered and wandered about, but hitherto I've scarcely seen anything but men. I thought that the women must be in a separate quarter, but I haven't yet succeeded in finding it; if it is really so, now you can tell me.'

'Don't you know, my son, that men are forbidden to enter that quarter, unless they have some business there?'

'Well, and what could happen to me?'

'The regulation is just and good, my dear son; and if the number and weight of sorrows forbid the possibility of its being respected with full rigour, is that a reason why an honest man should transgress it?'

'But, Father Cristoforo,' said Renzo, 'Lucia ought to be my wife; you know how we've been separated; it's twenty months that I've suffered and borne patiently; I've come as far as here, at the risk of so many things, one worse than the other; and now then . . .'

'I don't know what to say,' resumed the friar, replying rather to his own thoughts than to the words of the young man. 'You are going with a good intention; and would to God that all who have free access to that place would conduct themselves as I can feel sure you will do! God, who certainly blesses this your perseverance of affection, this your faithfulness in wishing and seeking for her whom He has given you, God, who is more rigorous than men, yet more indulgent, will not regard what may be irregular in your mode of seeking for her. Only remember, that for your behaviour in this place we shall both have to render an account, not, probably, to men, but, without fail, at the bar of God. Come this way.' So saying, he rose: Renzo followed his example; and, without neglecting to listen to his words, had, in the mean time, determined in himself not to speak, as he had at first intended, about Lucia's vow.—If he hears this, too,—thought he,—he will certainly raise more difficulties. Either I will find her, and then there will be time enough to discuss it, or . . . and then! what will it matter?—

Leading him to the door of the cabin, which faced towards the north, the friar resumed: 'Listen to me; Father Felice, the president of the Lazzaretto, will to-day conduct the few who have recovered to perform their quarantine elsewhere. You see that church there in the middle . . .' and raising his thin and tremulous hand, he pointed out to the left, through the cloudy atmosphere, the cupola of the little temple rising above the miserable tents, and continued: 'About there they are now assembling, to go out in procession through the gate by which you must have entered.'

'Ah! it was for this, then, that they were trying to clear the passage.'

'Just so: and you must also have heard some tollings of the bell.'

'I heard one.'

'It was the second: when the third rings, they will all be assembled: Father Felice will address a few words to them; and then they will set off. At this signal, do you go thither; contrive to place yourself behind the assembly on the edge of the passage, where, without giving trouble, or being observed, you can watch them pass; and look . . . look . . . look if she is there. If it be not God's will that she should be there, that quarter . . .' and he again raised his hand, and pointed to the side of the edifice which faced them, 'that quarter of the building, and part of the field before it, are assigned to the women. You will see some paling that divides this from that enclosure, but here and there broken and interrupted, so that you'll find no difficulty in gaining admittance. Once in, if you do nothing to give offence, no one probably will say anything to you; if, however, they should make any opposition, say that Father Cristoforo of * * * knows you, and will answer for you. Seek her there; seek her with confidence and . . . with resignation. For you must remember it is a great thing you have come to ask here: a person alive within the Lazzaretto! Do you know how often I have seen my poor people here renewed? how many I have seen carried off! how few go out recovered! . . . Go, prepared to make a sacrifice . . .'

'Ay! I understand!' interrupted Renzo, his eyes rolling wildly, and his face becoming very dark and threatening: 'I understand! I'll go: I'll look in one place or another, from top to bottom of the Lazzaretto . . . and if I don't find her! . . .'

'If you don't find her?' said the friar, with an air of grave and serious expectation, and an admonishing look.

But Renzo, whose anger had for some time been swelling in his bosom, and now clouded his sight, and deprived him of all feelings of respect, repeated and continued: 'If I don't find her, I'll succeed in finding somebody else. Either in Milan, or in his detestable palace, or at the end of the world, or in the abode of the devil, I'll find that rascal who separated us; that villain, but for whom Lucia would have been mine twenty months ago; and if we had been doomed to die, we would at least have died together. If that fellow still lives, I'll find him . . .'

'Renzo!' said the friar, grasping him by one arm, and gazing on him still more severely.

'And if I find him,' continued he, perfectly blinded with rage, 'if the plague hasn't already wrought justice . . . This is no longer a time when a coward, with his bravoes at his heels, can drive people to desperation, and then mock at them: a time is come when men meet each other face to face . . . I'll get justice!'

'Miserable wretch!' cried Father Cristoforo, in a voice which had assumed its former full and sonorous tone: 'Miserable wretch!' And he raised his sunken head, his cheeks became flushed with their original colour, and the fire that flashed from his eyes had something terrible in it. 'Look about you, miserable man!' And while with one hand he grasped, and strongly shook, Renzo's arm, he waved the other before him, pointing, as well as he could, to the mournful scene around them. 'See who is He that chastises! Who is He that judges, and is not judged! He that scourges, and forgives! But you, a worm of the earth, you would get justice! You! do you know what justice is? Away, unhappy man; away with you! I hoped . . . yes, I did hope that, before my death, God would have given me the comfort of hearing that my poor Lucia was alive; perhaps of seeing her, and hearing her promise me that she would send one prayer towards the grave where I shall be laid. Go, you have robbed me of this hope! God has not let her remain upon earth for you; and you, surely, cannot have the hardihood to believe yourself worthy that God should think of comforting you. He will have thought of *her,* for she was one of those souls for whom eternal consolations are reserved. Go! I've no longer time to listen to you.'

And so saying, he threw from him Renzo's arm, and moved towards a cabin of sick.

'Ah, Father!' said Renzo, following him with a supplicating air, 'will you send me away in this manner?'

'What!' rejoined the Capuchin, relaxing nothing of his severity; 'dare you require that I should steal the time from these poor afflicted ones, who are awaiting for me to speak to them of the pardon of God, to listen to your words of fury, your propositions of revenge? I listened to you when you asked consolation and direction; I neglected one duty of charity for the sake of another; but now you have vengeance in your heart: what do you want with me? Begone! I have beheld those die here who have been offended and have forgiven; offenders who have mourned that they could not humble themselves before the offended: I have wept with both one and the other; but what have I to do with you?'

'Ah! I forgive him! I forgive him, indeed, and for ever!' exclaimed the youth.

'Renzo!' said the friar, with more tranquil sternness: 'bethink yourself, and just say how often you have forgiven him.'

And having waited a moment without receiving a reply, he suddenly bent his head, and with an appeased voice resumed: 'You know why I bear this habit?'

Renzo hesitated.

'You know it!' resumed the old man.

'I do,' answered Renzo.

'I too have hated, and therefore I have rebuked you for a thought, for a word; the man whom I hated, whom I cordially hated, whom I had long hated, that man I murdered!'

'Yes, but a tyrant! one of those . . .'

'Hush!' interrupted the friar: 'think you that if there were a good reason for it, I shouldn't have found it in thirty years? Ah! if I could now instil into your heart the sentiment I have ever since had, and still have, for the man I hated! If I could! I? But God can: may He do so! . . . Listen, Renzo; He wishes you more good than you even wish yourself: you have dared to meditate revenge; but

He has power and mercy enough to prevent you; He bestows upon
you a favour of which another was too unworthy. You know, and
you have often and often said it, that He can arrest the hand of the
oppressor: but, remember, He can also arrest that of the revengeful;
and think you that, because you are poor, because you are injured,
He cannot defend against your vengeance a man whom He has
created in His own image? Did you think that He would suffer
you to do all you wished? No! but do you know what He can do?
You may hate and be lost for ever; you may, by such a temper of
mind as this, deprive yourself of every blessing. For, however things
may go with you, whatever condition you may be placed in, rest assured that all will be punishment until you have forgiven—forgiven
in such a way, that you may never again be able to say, I forgive
him.'

'Yes, yes,' said Renzo, with deep shame and emotion: 'I see now
that I have never before really forgiven him; I see that I have spoken
like a beast, and not like a Christian: and now, by the grace of God, I
will forgive him; yes, I'll forgive him from my very heart.'

'And supposing you were to see him?'

'I would pray the Lord to give *me* patience, and to touch *his*
heart.'

'Would you remember that the Lord has not only commanded us
to forgive our enemies, but also to love them? Would you remember
that *He* so loved him as to lay down His life for him?'

'Yes, by His help, I would.'

'Well, then; come and see him. You have said, "I'll find him;"
and you shall find him. Come, and you shall see against whom you
would nourish hatred; to whom you could wish evil, and be ready
to do it; of what life you would render yourself master!'

And, taking Renzo's hand, which he grasped as a healthy young
man would have done, he moved forward. Renzo followed, without daring to ask anything further.

After a short walk, the friar stopped near the entrance of a cabin,
fixed his eyes on Renzo's face with a mixture of gravity and tenderness, and drew him in.

The first thing he observed on entering, was a sick person, seated
on some straw, in the background, who did not, however, seem very

ill, but rather recovering from illness. On seeing the Father, he shook his head, as if to say *No:* the Father bent his with an air of sorrow and resignation. Renzo, mean while, eyeing the surrounding objects with uneasy curiosity, beheld three or four sick persons, and distinguished one against the wall, lying upon a bed, and wrapped in a sheet, with a nobleman's cloak laid upon him as a quilt: he gazed at him, recognized Don Rodrigo, and involuntarily shrank back; but the friar, again making him feel the hand by which he held him, drew him to the foot of the bed, and stretching over it his other hand, pointed to the man who there lay prostrate. The unhappy being was perfectly motionless; his eyes were open, but he saw nothing; his face was pale and covered with black spots; his lips black and swollen; it would have been called the face of a corpse, had not convulsive twitchings revealed a tenacity of life. His bosom heaved from time to time with painfully short respiration; and his right hand, laid outside the cloak, pressed it closely to his heart with a firm grasp of his clenched fingers, which were of a livid colour, and black at the extremities.

'You see,' said the friar, in a low and solemn voice. 'This may be a punishment, or it may be mercy. The disposition you now have towards this man, who certainly has offended you, that disposition will God, whom assuredly you have offended, have towards you at the great day. Bless him, and be blessed. For four days has he lain there, as you see him, without giving any signs of consciousness. Perhaps the Lord is ready to grant him an hour of repentance, but waits for you to ask it: perhaps it is His will that you should pray for it with that innocent creature; perhaps he reserves the mercy for your solitary prayer, the prayer of an afflicted and resigned heart. Perhaps the salvation of this man and your own depend at this moment upon yourself, upon the disposition of your mind to forgiveness, to compassion . . . to love!' He ceased; and joining his hands, bent his head over them both, as if in prayer. Renzo did the same.

They had been for a few moments in this position, when they heard the third tolling of the bell. Both moved together, as if by agreement, and went out. The one made no inquiries, the other no protestations: their countenances spoke.

'Go now,' resumed the friar, 'go prepared to make a sacrifice, and to bless God, whatever be the issue of your researches. And, whatever it be, come and give me an account of it: we will praise Him together.'

Here, without further words, they parted; the one returned to the place he had left, the other set off to the little temple, which was scarcely more than a stone's throw distant.

CHAPTER XXXVI

WHO would ever have told Renzo, a few hours before, that in the very crisis of his search, at the approach of the moment of greatest suspense which was so soon to be decisive, his heart would have been divided between Lucia and Don Rodrigo? Yet so it was; that figure he had just beheld, came and mingled itself in all the dear or terrible pictures which either hope or fear alternately brought before him in the course of his walk; the words he had heard at the foot of that bed blended themselves with the conflicting thoughts by which his mind was agitated, and he could not conclude a prayer for the happy issue of this great experiment, without connecting with it that which he had begun there, and which the sound of the bell had abruptly terminated.

The small octagonal temple, which stood elevated from the ground by several steps, in the middle of the Lazzaretto, was, in its original construction, open on every side, without other support than pilasters and columns—a perforated building, so to say. In each front was an arch between two columns; within, a portico ran round that which might more properly be called the church, but which was composed only of eight arches supported by pilasters, surmounted by a small cupola, and corresponding to those on the outside of the arcade; so that the altar, erected in the centre, might be seen from the window of each room in the enclosure, and almost from any part of the encampment. Now, the edifice being converted to quite a different use, the spaces of the eight fronts are walled up; but the ancient framework, which still remains uninjured, indicates with sufficient clearness the original condition and destination of the building.

Renzo had scarcely started, when Father Felice made his appearance in the portico of the temple, and advanced towards the arch in the middle of the side which faces the city, in front of which the assembly were arranged at the foot of the steps, and along the course prepared for them; and shortly he perceived by his manner that he

had begun the sermon. He therefore went round by some little by-
paths, so as to attain the rear of the audience, as had been suggested
to him. Arrived there, he stood still very quietly, and ran over the
whole with his eye; but he could see nothing from his position, except a mass, I had almost said, a pavement of heads. In the centre
there were some covered with handkerchiefs, or veils; and here he
fixed his eyes more attentively; but, failing to distinguish anything
more clearly, he also raised them to where all the others were directed. He was touched and affected by the venerable figure of the
speaker; and, with all the attention he could command in such a
moment of expectation, listened to the following portion of his
solemn address:—

'Let us remember for a moment the thousands and thousands who
have gone forth thither;' and raising his finger above his shoulder,
he pointed behind him towards the gate which led to the cemetery
of San Gregorio, the whole of which was then, we might say, one
immense grave: 'let us cast an eye around upon the thousands and
thousands who are still left here, uncertain, alas! by which way they
will go forth; let us look at ourselves, so few in number, who are
about to go forth restored. Blessed be the Lord! Blessed be He
in His justice, blessed in His mercy! blessed in death, and blessed in
life! blessed in the choice He has been pleased to make of us! Oh!
why has He so pleased, my brethren, if not to preserve to Himself
a little remnant, corrected by affliction, and warmed with gratitude?
if not in order that, feeling more vividly than ever how life is His gift,
we may esteem it as a gift from His hands deserves, and employ
it in such works as we may dare to offer Him? if not in order that
the remembrance of our own sufferings may make us compassionate
towards others, and ever ready to relieve them? In the mean while,
let those in whose company we have suffered, hoped, and feared;
among whom we are leaving friends and relatives, and who are all,
besides, our brethren; let those among them who will see us pass
through the midst of them, not only derive some relief from the
thought that others are going out hence in health, but also be edified by our behaviour. God forbid that they should behold in us a
clamorous festivity, a carnal joy, at having escaped that death against
which they are still struggling. Let them see that we depart in

thanksgivings for ourselves and prayers for them; and let them be able to say, "Even beyond these walls they will not forget us, they will continue to pray for us poor creatures!" Let us begin from this time, from the first steps we are about to take, a life wholly made up of love. Let those who have regained their former vigour lend a brotherly arm to the feeble; young men, sustain the aged; you who are left without children, look around you how many children are left without parents! be such to them! And this charity, covering the multitude of sins, will also alleviate your own sorrows.'

Here a deep murmur of groans and sobs, which had been increasing in the assembly, was suddenly suspended, on seeing the preacher put a rope round his neck, and fall upon his knees; and, in profound silence, they stood awaiting what he was about to say.

'For me,' continued he, 'and the rest of my companions who, without any merit of our own, have been chosen out for the high privilege of serving Christ in you, I humbly implore your forgiveness, if we have not worthily fulfilled so great a ministry. If slothfulness, if the ungovernableness of the flesh, has rendered us less attentive to your necessities, less ready to answer your calls; if unjust impatience, or blameworthy weariness, has sometimes made us show you a severe and dispirited countenance; if the miserable thought that we were necessary to you, has sometimes induced us to fail in treating you with that humility which became us; if our frailty has led us hastily to commit any action which has been a cause of offence to you; forgive us! And so may God forgive you all your trespasses, and bless you.' Then, making the sign of a large cross over the assembly, he rose.

We have succeeded in relating, if not the actual words, at least the sense and burden of those which he really uttered; but the manner in which they were delivered it is impossible to describe. It was the manner of one who called it a privilege to attend upon the infected, because he felt it to be so; who confessed that he had not worthily acted up to it, because he was conscious he had not done so; who besought forgiveness, because he was convinced he stood in need of it. But the people who had beheld these Capuchins as they went about, engaged in nothing but waiting upon them; who had seen so many sink under the duty, and him who was now addressing them ever the foremost in toil, as in authority, except, indeed, when he himself was lying at the point of death; think with what sighs and tears they responded to such an appeal. The admirable friar then took a large cross which stood resting against a pillar, elevated it before him, left his sandals at the edge of the outside portico, and, through the midst of the crowd, which reverently made way for him, proceeded to place himself at their head.

Renzo, no less affected than if he had been one of those from whom this singular forgiveness was requested, also withdrew a little further, and succeeded in placing himself by the side of a cabin. Here he stood waiting, with his body half concealed and his head stretched forward, his eyes wide open, and his heart beating violently, but at the same time with a kind of new and particular confidence, arising, I think, from the tenderness of spirit which the sermon and the spectacle of the general emotion had excited in him.

Father Felice now came up, barefoot, with the rope round his neck, and that tall and heavy cross elevated before him; his face was pale and haggard, inspiring both sorrow and encouragement; he walked with slow, but resolute steps, like one who would spare the weakness of others; and in everything was like a man to whom these super-numerary labours and troubles imparted strength to sustain those which were necessary, and inseparable from his charge. Immediately behind him came the taller children, barefooted for the most part, very few entirely clothed, and some actually in their shirts. Then came the women, almost every one leading a little child by the hand, and alternately chanting the *Miserere;* while the feebleness of their voices, and the paleness and languor of their countenances, were enough to fill the heart of any one with pity who chanced to be there as a mere spectator. But Renzo was gazing and examining, from rank to rank, from face to face, without passing over one; for which the extremely slow advance of the procession gave him abundant leisure. On and on it goes; he looks and looks, always to no purpose; he keeps glancing rapidly over the crowd which still remains behind, and which is gradually diminishing: now there are very few rows;—we are at the last;—all are gone by; —all were unknown faces. With drooping arms, and head reclining on one shoulder, he suffered his eye still to wander after that

little band, while that of the men passed before him. His attention
was again arrested, and a new hope arose in his mind, on seeing
some carts appear behind these, bearing those convalescents who
were not yet able to walk. Here the women came last; and the
train proceeded at so deliberate a pace, that Renzo could with equal
ease review all these without one escaping his scrutiny. But what
then? he examined the first cart, the second, the third, and so on,
one by one, always with the same result, up to the last, behind which
followed a solitary Capuchin, with a grave countenance, and a stick
in his hand, as the regulator of the cavalcade. It was that Father
Michele whom we have mentioned as being appointed coadjutor in
the government with Father Felice.

Thus was this soothing hope completely dissipated; and, as it
was dissipated, it not only carried away the comfort it had brought
along with it, but, as is generally the case, left him in a worse condition than before. Now the happiest alternative was to find Lucia ill.
Yet, while increasing fears took the place of the ardour of present
hope, he clung with all the powers of his mind to this melancholy
and fragile thread, and issuing into the road, pursued his way
towards the place the procession had just left. On reaching the foot
of the little temple, he went and knelt down upon the lowest step,
and there poured forth a prayer to God, or rather a crowd of unconnected expressions, broken sentences, ejaculations, entreaties, complaints, and promises; one of those addresses which are never made
to men, because they have not sufficient quickness to understand
them, nor patience to listen to them; they are not great enough to feel
compassion without contempt.

He rose somewhat more re-animated; went round the temple,
came into the other road which he had not before seen, and which
led to the opposite gate, and after going on a little way, saw on both
sides the paling the friar had told him of, but full of breaks and
gaps, exactly as he had said.

He entered through one of these, and found himself in the quarter
assigned to the women. Almost at the first step he took, he saw lying
on the ground a little bell, such as the *monatti* wore upon their feet,
quite perfect, with all its straps and buckles; and it immediately
struck him that perhaps such an instrument might serve him as

a passport in that place. He therefore picked it up, and, looking round to see if any one were watching him, buckled it on. He then set himself to his search, to that search, which, were it only for the multiplicity of the objects, would have been extremely wearisome, even had those objects been anything but what they were. He began to survey, or rather to contemplate, new scenes of suffering, in part so similar to those he had already witnessed, in part so dissimilar: for, under the same calamity, there was here a different kind of suffering, so to say, a different languor, a different complaining, a different endurance, a different kind of mutual pity and assistance, there was, too, in the spectator, another kind of compassion, so to say, and another feeling of horror. He had now gone I know not how far, without success, and without accidents, when he heard behind him a 'Hey!'—a call, which seemed to be addressed to him. He turned round, and saw at a little distance a commissary, who, with uplifted hand, was beckoning to none other but him, and crying, 'There, in those rooms, you're wanted: here we've only just finished clearing away.'

Renzo immediately perceived whom he was taken for, and that the little bell was the cause of the mistake; he called himself a great fool for having thought only of the inconveniences which this token might enable him to avoid, and not of those which it might draw down upon him; and at the same instant devised a plan to free himself from the difficulty. He repeatedly nodded to him in a hurried manner, as if to say that he understood and would obey; and then got out of his sight by slipping aside between the cabins.

When he thought himself far enough off, he began to think about dismissing this cause of offence; and to perform the operation without being observed, he stationed himself in the narrow passage between two little huts, which had their backs turned to each other. Stooping down to unloose the buckles, and in this position resting his head against the straw wall of one of the cabins, a voice reached his ear from it . . . Oh heavens! is it possible? His whole soul was in that ear; he held his breath . . . Yes, indeed! it is that voice! . . . 'Fear of what?' said that gentle voice: 'we have passed through much worse than a storm. He who has preserved us hitherto, will preserve us even now.'

If Renzo uttered no cry, it was not for fear of being discovered, but because he had no breath to utter it. His knees failed beneath him, his sight became dim; but it was only for the first moment; at the second he was on his feet, more alert, more vigorous than ever; in three bounds he was round the cabin, stood at the doorway, saw her who had been speaking, saw her standing by a bedside, and bending over it. She turned on hearing a noise; looked, fancied she mistook the object, looked again more fixedly, and exclaimed: 'Oh, blessed Lord!'

'Lucia! I've found you! I've found you! It's really you! You're living!' exclaimed Renzo, advancing towards her, all in a tremble.

'Oh, blessed Lord!' replied Lucia, trembling far more violently. 'You? What is this? What way? Why? The plague!'

'I've had it. And you! . . .'

'Ah! and I too. And about my mother? . . .'

'I haven't seen her, for she's at Pasturo; I believe, however, she's very well. But you . . . how pale you still are! how weak you seem! You're recovered, however, aren't you?'

'The Lord has been pleased to leave me a little longer below. Ah Renzo! why are you here?'

'Why?' said Renzo, drawing all the time nearer to her; 'do you ask why? Why I should come here! Need I say why? Who is there I ought to think about? Am I no longer Renzo? Are you no longer Lucia?'

'Ah, what are you saying! What are you saying! Didn't my mother write to you? . . .'

'Ay: that indeed she did! Fine things to write to an unfortunate, afflicted, fugitive wretch—to a young fellow who has never offered you a single affront, at least!'

'But Renzo! Renzo! since you knew . . . why come? why?'

'Why come? Oh Lucia! Why come, do you say? After so many promises! Are we no longer ourselves? Don't you any longer remember? What is wanting?'

'Oh Lord!' exclaimed Lucia, piteously, clasping her hands, and raising her eyes to heaven, 'Why hast Thou not granted me the mercy of taking me to Thyself! . . . Oh Renzo, whatever have you done? See; I was beginning to hope that . . . in time . . . you would have forgotten me . . .'

'A fine hope, indeed! Fine things to tell me to my face!'

'Ah, what have you done? and in this place! among all this misery! among these sights! here, where they do nothing but die, you have! . . .'

'We must Pray God for those who die, and hope that they will go to a good place; but it isn't surely fair, even for this reason, that they who live should live in despair . . .'

'But Renzo! Renzo! you don't think what you're saying. A promise to the Madonna!—a vow!'

'And I tell you they are promises that go for nothing.'

'Oh Lord! What do you say? where have you been all this time? whom have you mixed with? how are you talking?'

'I'm talking like a good Christian; and I think better of the Madonna than you do; for I believe she doesn't wish for promises that injure one's fellow-creatures. If the Madonna had spoken, then, indeed! But what has happened? a mere fancy of your own. Don't you know what you ought to promise the Madonna? promise her that the first daughter we have, we'll call her Maria; for that I'm willing to promise too: these are things that do much more honour to the Madonna; these are devotions that have some use in them, and do no harm to any one.'

'No, no; don't say so: you don't know what you are saying; you don't know what it is to make a vow; you've never been in such circumstances; you haven't tried. Leave me, leave me, for Heaven's sake!'

And she impetuously rushed from him, and returned towards the bed.

'Lucia!' said he, without stirring, 'just tell me this one thing: if there was not this reason . . . would you be the same to me as ever?'

'Heartless man!' replied Lucia, turning round, and with difficulty restraining her tears: 'when you've made me say what's quite use-less, what would do me harm, and what, perhaps, would be sinful, will you be content then? Go away—oh, do go! think no more of me; we were not intended for each other. We shall meet again above; now we cannot have much longer to stay in this world. Ah, go! try to let my mother know that I'm recovered; that here, too, God has always helped me: and that I've found a kind creature, this good lady, who's like a mother to me; tell her I hope she will be preserved from this disease, and that we shall see each other again, when and how God pleases. Go away, for Heaven's sake, and think no more about me . . . except when you say your prayers.'

And, like one who has nothing more to say, and wishes to hear nothing further,—like one who would withdraw herself from danger, she again retreated closer to the bed where lay the lady she had mentioned.

'Listen, Lucia, listen,' said Renzo, without, however, attempting to go any nearer.

'No, no; go away, for charity's sake!'

'Listen: Father Cristoforo . . .'

'What?'

'He's here.'

'Here! Where? How do you know?'

'I've spoken to him a little while ago; I've been with him for a short time: and a religious man like him, it seems to me . . .'

'He's here! to assist the poor sick, I dare say. But he? has he had the plague?'

'Ah Lucia! I'm afraid, I'm sadly afraid . . .' And while Renzo was thus hesitating to pronounce the words which were so distressing to himself, and he felt must be equally so to Lucia, she had again left the bedside, and was once more drawing near him: 'I'm afraid he has it now!'

'Oh, the poor holy man! But why do I say, Poor man? Poor me! How is he? is he in bed? is he attended?'

'He's up, going about, and attending upon others; but if you could see his looks, and how he totters! One sees so many, that it's too easy . . . to be sure there's no mistake!'

'Oh, and he's here indeed.'

'Yes, and only a little way off; very little further than from your house to mine . . . if you remember! . . .'

'Oh, most holy Virgin!'

'Well, very little further. You may think whether we didn't talk about you. He said things to me . . . And if you knew what he showed me! You shall hear; but now I want to tell you what he said to me first, he, with his own lips. He told me I did right to come and look for you, and that the Lord approves of a youth's acting so, and would help me to find you; which has really been the truth: but surely he's a saint. So, you see!'

'But if he said so, it was because he didn't know a word . . .'

'What would you have him know about things you've done out of your own head, without rule, and without the advice of any one? A good man, a man of judgment, as he is, would never think of things of this kind. But oh, what he showed me; . . .' And here he related his visit to the cabin; while Lucia, however her senses and her mind must have been accustomed, in that abode, to the strongest impressions, was completely overwhelmed with horror and compassion.

'And there, too,' pursued Renzo, 'he spoke like a saint; he said that perhaps the Lord has designed to show mercy to that poor fellow . . . (now I really cannot give him any other name) . . . and waits to take him at the right moment, but wishes that we should pray for him together. . . . Together! did you hear?'

'Yes, yes; we will pray for him, each of us where the Lord shall place us; He will know how to unite our prayers.'

'But if I tell you his very words! . . .'

'But, Renzo, he doesn't know . . .'

'But don't you see that when it is a saint who speaks, it is the Lord that makes him speak? and that he wouldn't have spoken thus, if it shouldn't really be so . . . And this poor fellow's soul! I have indeed prayed, and will still pray, for him; I've prayed from my heart, just as if it had been for a brother of mine. But how do you wish the poor creature to be, in the other world, if this matter be not settled here below, if the evils he has done be not undone? For, if you'll return to reason, then all will be as at first; what has been, has been; he has had his punishment here . . .'

'No, Renzo, no; God would not have us do evil that He may

show mercy; leave Him to do this; and for us, our duty is to pray to Him. If I had died that night, could not God, then, have forgiven him? And if I've not died, if I've been delivered . . .'

'And your mother, that poor Agnese, who has always wished me well, and who strove so to see us husband and wife, has she never told you that it was a perverted idea of yours? She, who has made you listen to reason, too, at other times; for, on certain subjects, she thinks more wisely than you . . .'

'My mother! do you think my mother would advise me to break a vow! But, Renzo! you're not in your proper senses.'

'Oh, will you have me say so? You women cannot understand these things. Father Cristoforo told me to go back and tell him whether I had found you. I'm going: we'll hear what he says; whatever he thinks . . .'

'Yes, yes; go to that holy man; tell him that I pray for him, and ask him to do so for me, for I need it so much, so very much! But for Heaven's sake, for your own soul's sake, and mine, never come back here, to do me harm, to . . . tempt me. Father Cristoforo will know how to explain things to you, and bring you to your proper senses; he will make you set your heart at rest.'

'My heart at rest! Oh, you may drive this idea out of your head. You've already had those abominable words written to me; and I know what I've suffered from them; and now you've the heart to say so to me. I tell you plainly and flatly that I'll never set my heart at rest. You want to forget me; but I don't want to forget you. And I assure you—do you hear?—that if you make me lose my senses, I shall never get them again. Away with my business, away with good rules. Will you condemn me to be a madman all my life? and like a madman I shall be . . . And that poor fellow! The Lord knows whether I've not forgiven him from my heart; but you . . . Will you make me think, for the rest of my life, that if he had not? . . . Lucia, you have bid me forget you: forget you! How can I? Whom do you think I have thought about for all this time? . . . And after so many things! after so many promises! What have I done to you since we parted? Do you treat me in this way because I've suffered? because I've had misfortunes? because the world has persecuted me? because I've spent so long a time from home, unhappy, and far from you? because the first moment I could, I came to look for you?'

When Lucia could sufficiently command herself to speak, she exclaimed again, joining her hands, and raising her eyes to heaven, bathed in tears: 'O most holy Virgin, do thou help me! Thou knowest that, since that night I have never passed such a moment as this. Thou didst succour me then; oh, succour me also now!'

'Yes, Lucia, you do right to invoke the Madonna; but why will you believe that she, who is so kind, the mother of mercy, can have pleasure in making us suffer . . . me, at any rate . . . for a word that escaped you at a moment when you knew not what you were saying? Will you believe that she helped you then, to bring us into trouble afterwards? . . . If, after all, this is only an excuse;—if the truth is, that I have become hateful to you . . . tell me so . . . speak plainly.'

'For pity's sake, Renzo, for pity's sake, for the sake of your poor dead, have done, have done, don't kill me quite! . . . That would not be a good conclusion. Go to Father Cristoforo, commend me to him; and don't come back here, don't come back here.'

'I go; but you may fancy whether I shall return or not! I'd come back if I was at the end of the world; that I would.' And he disappeared.

Lucia went and sat down, or rather suffered herself to sink upon the ground, by the side of the bed; and resting her head against it, continued to weep bitterly. The lady, who until now had been attentively watching and listening, but had not spoken a word, asked what was the meaning of this apparition, this meeting, these tears. But perhaps the reader, in his turn, may ask who this person was; we will endeavour to satisfy him in a few words.

She was a wealthy tradeswoman, of about thirty years of age. In the course of a few days she had witnessed the death of her husband, in his own house, and every one of her children; and being herself attacked shortly afterwards with the common malady, and conveyed to the Lazzaretto, she had been accommodated in this little cabin, at the time that Lucia, after having unconsciously surmounted the virulence of the disease, and, equally unconsciously, changed her companions several times, was beginning to recover and regain her senses, which she had lost since the first commencement of her attack in Don Ferrante's house. The hut could only contain two patients; and an intimacy and affection had very soon sprung up between these associates in sickness, bereavement, and depression, alone as they were in the midst of so great a multitude, such as could scarcely have arisen from long intercourse under other circumstances. Lucia was soon in a condition to lend her services to her companion, who rapidly became worse. Now that she, too, had passed the crisis, they served as companions, encouragement, and guards to each other, had made a promise not to leave the Lazzaretto except together, and had, besides, concerted other measures to prevent their separation after having quitted it.

The merchant-woman, who, having left her dwelling, warehouse, and coffers, all well furnished, under the care of one of her brothers, a commissioner of health, was about to become sole and mournful mistress of much more than she required to live comfortably, wished to keep Lucia with her, like a daughter or sister; and to this Lucia had acceded, with what gratitude to her benefactress and to Providence the reader may imagine; but only until she could hear some tidings of her mother, and learn, as she hoped, what was her will. With her usual reserve, however, she had never breathed a syllable about her intended marriage, nor of her other remarkable adventures. But now, in such agitation of feelings, she had at least as much need to give vent to them, as the other a wish to listen to them. And, clasping the right hand of her friend in both hers, she immediately began to satisfy her inquiries, without further obstacles than those which her sobs presented to the melancholy recital.

Renzo, meanwhile, trudged off in great haste, towards the quarters of the good friar. With a little care, and not without some steps thrown away, he at length succeeded in reaching them. He found the cabin: its occupant, however, was not there; but, rambling and peeping about in its vicinity, he discovered him in a tent, stooping towards the ground, or, indeed, almost lying upon his face, administering consolation to a dying person. He drew back, and waited in silence. In a few moments he saw him close the poor creature's eyes, raise himself upon his knees, and after a short prayer, get up. He then went forward, and advanced to meet him.

'Oh!' said the friar, on seeing him approach: 'Well?'

'She's there: I've found her!'

'In what state?'

'Recovered, or at least out of her bed.'

'The Lord be praised!'

'But . . .' said Renzo, when he came near enough to be able to speak in an under-tone, 'there's another difficulty.'

'What do you mean?'

'I mean that . . . You know already what a good creature this young girl is; but she's sometimes rather positive in her opinions. After so many promises, after all you know of, now she actually tells me she can't marry me, because she says,—how can I express it?—in that night of terror, her brain became heated—that is to say, she made a vow to the Madonna. Things without any foundation, aren't they? Good enough for those who have knowledge, and grounds for doing them; but for us common people, that don't well know what we ought to do . . . aren't they things that won't hold good?'

'Is she very far from here?'

'Oh, no: a few yards beyond the church.'

'Wait here for me a moment,' said the friar; 'and then we'll go together.'

'Do you mean that you'll give her to understand . . .'

'I know nothing about it, my son; I must first hear what she has to say to me.'

'I understand,' said Renzo; and he was left, with his eyes fixed on the ground, and his arms crossed on his breast, to ruminate in still-unallayed suspense. The friar again went in search of Father Vittore, begged him once more to supply his place, went into his cabin, came forth with a basket on his arm, and returning to his expectant companion, said: 'Let us go.' He then went forward, leading the way to that same cabin which, a little while before, they had entered together. This time he left Renzo outside; he himself entered, and reappeared in a moment or two, saying: 'Nothing! We must pray; we must pray. Now,' added he, 'you must be my guide.'

And they set off without further words. The weather had been for some time gradually becoming worse, and now plainly announced a not very distant storm. Frequent flashes of lightning broke in upon the increasing obscurity, and illuminated with momentary brilliancy the long, long roofs and arches of the porticoes, the cupola of the temple, and the more humble roofs of the cabins; while the claps of thunder, bursting forth in sudden peals, rolled rumbling along from one quarter of the heavens to the other. The young man went forward intent upon his way, and his heart full of uneasy expectations, as he compelled himself to slacken his pace, to accommodate it to the strength of his follower; who, wearied by his labours, suffering under the pressure of the malady, and oppressed by the sultry heat, walked on with difficulty, occasionally raising his pale face to heaven, as if to seek for freer respiration.

When they came in sight of the little cabin, Renzo stopped, turned round, and said with a trembling voice: 'There she is.'

They enter . . . 'See: they're there!' exclaimed the lady from her bed. Lucia turned, sprang up precipitately, and advanced to meet the aged man, crying: 'Oh, whom do I see? Oh, Father Cristoforo!'

'Well, Lucia! from how many troubles has the Lord delivered you! You must indeed rejoice that you have always trusted in Him.'

'Oh yes, indeed! But you, Father? Poor me, how you are altered! How are you? tell me, how are you?'

'As God wills, and as, by His grace, I will also,' replied the friar, with a placid look. And drawing her on one side, he added; 'Listen: I can only stay here a few moments. Are you inclined to confide in me, as you have done hitherto?'

'Oh! are you not always my Father?'

'Then, my daughter, what is this vow that Renzo has been telling me about?'

'It's a vow that I made to the Madonna not to marry.'

'But did you recollect at the time, that you were already bound by another promise?'

'When it related to the Lord and the Madonna! . . . No; I didn't think about it.'

'My daughter, the Lord approves of sacrifices and offerings when we make them of our own. It is the heart that He desires,—the will;

but you could not offer him the will of another, to whom you had already pledged yourself.'

'Have I done wrong?'

'No, my poor child, don't think so: I believe, rather, that the holy Virgin will have accepted the intention of your afflicted heart, and have presented it to God for you. But tell me: have you never consulted with any one on this subject?'

'I didn't think it was a sin I ought to confess; and what little good one does, one has no need to tell.'

'Have you no other motive that hinders you from fulfilling the promise you have made to Renzo?'

'As to this . . . for me . . . what motive? . . . I cannot say . . . nothing else,' replied Lucia, with a hesitation so expressed that it announced anything but uncertainty of thought; and her cheeks, still pale from illness, suddenly glowed with the deepest crimson.

'Do you believe,' resumed the old man, lowering his eyes, 'that God has given to His Church authority to remit and retain, according as it proves best, the debts and obligations that men may have contracted to Him?'

'Yes, indeed I do.'

'Know, then, that we who are charged with the care of the souls in this place, have, for all those who apply to us, the most ample powers of the Church; and consequently, that I can, when you request it, free you from the obligation, whatever it may be, that you may have contracted by this your vow.'

'But is it not a sin to turn back, and to repent of a promise made to the Madonna? I made it at the time with my whole heart . . .' said Lucia, violently agitated by the assault of so unexpected a *hope,* for so I must call it, and by the uprising, on the other hand, of a terror, fortified by all the thoughts which had so long been the principal occupation of her mind.

'A sin, my daughter?' said the Father, 'a sin to have recourse to the Church, and to ask her minister to make use of the authority which he has received from her, and she has received from God? I have seen how you two have been led to unite yourselves; and, assuredly, if ever it would seem that two were joined together by God, you were—you are those two; nor do I now see that God may wish you to be put asunder. And I bless Him that He has given me, unworthy as I am, the power of speaking in His name, and returning to you your plighted word. And if you request me to declare you absolved from this vow, I shall not hesitate to do it; nay, I wish you may request me.'

'Then! . . . then! . . . I do request you,' said Lucia, with a countenance no longer agitated, except by modesty.

The friar beckoned to the youth, who was standing in the furthest corner, intently watching (since he could do nothing else) the dialogue in which he was so much interested; and, on his drawing near, pronounced, in an explicit voice, to Lucia, 'By the authority I have received from the Church, I declare you absolved from the vow of virginity, annulling what may have been unadvised in it, and freeing you from every obligation you may thereby have contracted.'

Let the reader imagine how these words sounded in Renzo's ears. His eyes eagerly thanked him who had uttered them, and instantly sought those of Lucia; but in vain.

'Return in security and peace to your former desires,' pursued the Capuchin, addressing Lucia; 'beseech the Lord again for those graces you once besought to make you a holy wife; and rely upon it, that He will bestow them upon you more abundantly, after so many sorrows. And you,' said he, turning to Renzo, 'remember, my son, that if the Church restores to you this companion, she does it not to procure for you a temporal and earthly pleasure, which, even could it be complete, and free from all intermixture of sorrow, must end in one great affliction at the moment of leaving you; but she does it to lead you both forward in that way of pleasantness which shall have no end. Love each other as companions in a journey, with the thought that you will have to part from one another, and with the hope of being reunited for ever. Thank Heaven that you have been led to this state, not through the midst of turbulent and transitory joys, but by sufferings and misery, to dispose you to tranquil and collected joy. If God grants you children, make it your object to bring them up for Him, to inspire them with love to Him, and to all men; and then you will train them rightly in everything else. Lucia! has he told you,' and he pointed to Renzo, 'whom he has seen here?'

'Oh yes, Father, he has!'

'You will pray for him! Don't be weary of doing so. And you will pray also for me; . . . My children! I wish you to have a remembrance of the poor friar.' And he drew out of his basket a little box of some common kind of wood, but turned and polished with a certain Capuchin precision, and continued; 'Within this is the remainder of that loaf . . . the first I asked for charity; that loaf, of which you must have heard speak! I leave it to you: take care of it; show it to your children! They will be born into a wretched world, into a miserable age, in the midst of proud and exasperating men: tell them always to forgive, always!—everything, everything! and to pray for the poor friar!'

So saying, he handed the box to Lucia, who received it with reverence, as if it had been a sacred relic. Then, with a calmer voice, he added, 'Now then, tell me; what have you to depend upon here in Milan? Where do you propose to lodge on leaving this? And who will conduct you to your mother, whom may God have preserved in health?'

'This good lady is like a mother to me: we shall leave this place together, and then she will provide for every thing.'

'God bless you,' said the friar, approaching the bed.

'I, too, thank you,' said the widow, 'for the comfort you have given these poor creatures; though I had counted upon keeping this dear Lucia always with me. But I will keep her in the meanwhile; I will accompany her to her own country, and deliver her to her mother; and,' added she, in a lower tone, 'I should like to provide her wardrobe. I have too much wealth, and have not one left out of those who should have shared it with me.'

'You may thus,' said the friar, 'make an acceptable offering to the Lord, and at the same time benefit your neighbour. I do not recommend this young girl to you, for I see already how she has become your daughter: it only remains to bless God, who knows how to show Himself a father even in chastisement, and who, by bringing you together, has given so plain a proof of His love to both of you. But come!' resumed he, turning to Renzo, and taking him by the hand, 'we two have nothing more to do here: we have already been here too long. Let us go.'

'Oh, Father!' said Lucia: 'Shall I see you again? I, who am of no service in this world have recovered; and you! . . .'

'It is now a long time ago,' replied the old man, in a mild and serious tone, 'since I besought of the Lord a very great mercy, that I might end my days in the service of my fellow-creatures. If He now vouchsafes to grant it me, I would wish all those who have any love for me, to assist me in praising Him. Come, give Renzo your messages to your mother.'

'Tell her what you have seen,' said Lucia to her betrothed; 'that I have found another mother here, that we will come to her together as quickly as possible, and that I hope, earnestly hope, to find her well.'

'If you want money,' said Renzo, 'I have about me all that you sent, and . . .'

'No, no,' interrupted the widow; 'I have only too much.'

'Let us go,' suggested the friar.

'Good-bye, till we meet again, Lucia! . . . and to you too, kind lady,' said Renzo, unable to find words to express all that he felt in such a moment.

'Who knows whether the Lord, in His mercy, will allow us all to meet again!' exclaimed Lucia.

'May He be with you always, and bless you,' said Friar Cristoforo to the two companions; and, accompanied by Renzo, he quitted the cabin.

The evening was not far distant, and the crisis of the storm seemed still more closely impending. The Capuchin again proposed to the houseless youth to take shelter for that night in his humble dwelling. 'I cannot keep you company,' added he; 'but you will at least be under cover.'

Renzo, however, was burning to be gone, and cared not to remain any longer in such a place, where he would not be allowed to see Lucia again, nor even be able to have a little conversation with the good friar. As to the time and weather, we may safely say that night and day, sunshine and shower, zephyr and hurricane, were all the same to him at that moment. He therefore thanked his kind friend, but said that he would rather go as soon as possible in search of Agnese.

When they regained the road, the friar pressed his hand, and said, 'If (as may God grant!) you find that good Agnese, salute her in my name; and beg her, and all those who are left, and remember Friar Cristoforo, to pray for him. God go with you, and bless you for ever!'

'Oh, dear Father! . . . We shall meet again?—we shall meet again?'

'Above, I hope.' And with these words he parted from Renzo, who, staying to watch him till he beheld him disappear, set off hastily towards the gate casting his farewell looks of compassion on each side over the melancholy scene. There was an unusual bustle, carts rolling about, *monatti* running to and fro, people securing the curtains of the tents, and numbers of feeble creatures groping about among these, and in the porticoes, to shelter themselves from the impending storm.

CHAPTER XXXVII

SCARCELY had Renzo crossed the threshold of the Lazzaretto, and taken the way to the right, to find the narrow road by which, in the morning, he had come out under the walls, when a few large and scattered drops began to fall, which lighting upon, and rebounding from, the white and parched road, stirred up a cloud of very fine dust; these soon multiplied into rain; and before he reached the by-path, it poured down in torrents. Far from feeling any disquietude, Renzo luxuriated in it, and enjoyed himself in that refreshing coolness, that murmur, that general motion of the grass and leaves, shaking, dripping, revived, and glistening, as they were; he drew in several deep and long breaths; and in that relenting of nature, felt more freely and more vividly, as it were, that which had been wrought in his own destiny.

But, how far fuller and more unalloyed would have been this feeling, could he have divined what actually was beheld a few days afterwards, that that rain carried off,—washed away, so to say,— the contagion; that, from that day forward, the Lazzaretto, if it was not about to restore to the living all the living whom it contained, would engulf, at least, no others; that, within one week, doors and shops would be seen re-opened; quarantine would scarcely be spoken of any longer; and of the pestilence only a solitary token or two remain here and there; that trace which every pestilence had left behind it for some time.

Our traveller, then, proceeded with great alacrity, without having formed any plans as to where, how, when, or whether at all, he should stop for the night, and anxious only to get forward, to reach his own village quickly, to find somebody to talk to, somebody to whom he might relate his adventures, and, above all, to set off again immediately on his way to Pasturo, in search of Agnese. His mind was quite confused by the events of the day; but from beneath all the misery, the horrors, and the dangers he recalled, one little thought always rose to the surface:—I've found her; she's recovered; she's mine!—And then he would give a spring which scattered a drizzling shower around, like a spaniel coming up out of the water; at other times he would content himself with rubbing his hands: and then, on he would go more cheerily than ever. With his eyes fixed upon the road, he gathered up, so to say, the thoughts he had left there in the morning, and the day before, as he came; and with the greatest glee, those very same which he had then most sought to banish from his mind—the doubts, the difficulty of finding her, of finding her alive, amidst so many dead and dying!—And I have found her alive!—he concluded. He recurred to the most critical moments, the most terrible obscurities, of that day; he fancied himself with that knocker in his hand: will she be here or not? and a reply so little encouraging; and before he had time to digest it, that crowd of mad rascals upon him; and that Lazzaretto, that sea? there I wished to find her! And to have found her there! He recalled the moment when the procession of convalescents had done passing by: what a moment! what bitter sorrow at not finding her! and now it no longer mattered to him. And that quarter for the women! And there, behind that cabin, when he was least expecting it, to hear that voice, that very voice! And to see her! To see her standing! But what then? There was still that knot about the vow, and drawn tighter than ever. This too untied. And that madness against Don Rodrigo, that cursed canker which exasperated all his sorrows, and poisoned all his joys, even that rooted out. So that it would be difficult to imagine a state of greater satisfaction, had it not been for the uncertainty about Agnese, his grief for Father Cristoforo, and the remembrance that he was still in the midst of a pestilence.

He arrived at Sesto as evening was coming on, without any token of the rain being about to stop. But feeling more than ever disposed to go forward; considering, too, the many difficulties of finding a lodging, and saturated as he was with wet, he would not even think of an inn. The only necessity that made itself felt was a very craving appetite; for success, such as he had met with, would have enabled him to digest something more substantial than the Capuchin's little bowl of soup. He looked about to see if he could discover a baker's shop, quickly found one, and received two loaves with the tongs, and the other ceremonies we have described. One he put into his pocket, the other to his mouth; and on he went.

When he passed through Monza, the night had completely closed in: he managed, however, to leave the town in the direction that led to the right road. But except for this qualification, which, to say the truth, was a great compensation, it may be imagined what kind of a road it was, and how it was becoming worse and worse every moment. Sunk (as were all; and we must have said so elsewhere) between two banks, almost like the bed of a river, it might then have been called, if not a river, at least in reality a watercourse; and in many places were holes and puddles from which it was difficult to recover one's shoes, and sometimes one's footing. But Renzo extricated himself as he could, without impatience, without bad language, and without regrets; consoling himself with the thought that every step, whatever it might cost him, brought him further on his way, that the rain would stop when God should see fit, that day would come in its own time, and that the journey he was meanwhile performing, would then be performed.

Indeed, I may say, he never even thought of this, except in the moments of greatest need. These were digressions: the grand employment of his mind was going over the history of the melancholy years that had passed, so many perplexities, so many adversities, so many moments in which he had been about to abandon even hope, and give up everything for lost; and then to oppose to these the images of so far different a future, the arrival of Lucia, and the wedding, and the setting up house, and the relating to each other past vicissitudes, and, in short, their whole life.

How he fared at forks of the road, for some indeed there were; whether his little experience, together with the glimmering twilight, enabled him always to find the right road, or whether he always turned into it by chance, I am not able to say; for he himself, who used to relate his history with great minuteness, rather tediously than otherwise (and everything leads us to believe that our anonymous author had heard it from him more than once), he himself declared, at this place, that he remembered no more of that night than if he had spent it in bed, dreaming. Certain it is, however, that towards its close, he found himself on the banks of the Adda.

It had never ceased raining a moment; but at a certain stage it had changed from a perfect deluge to more moderate rain, and then into a fine, silent, uniform drizzle: the lofty and rarefied clouds formed a continual, but light and transparent, veil; and the twilight dawn allowed Renzo to distinguish the surrounding country. Within this tract was his own village; and what he felt at the thought it is impossible to describe. I can only say that those mountains, that neighbouring *Resegone,* the whole territory of Lecco, had become, as it were, his own property. He glanced, too, at himself, and discovered that he looked, to say the truth, somewhat of a contrast to what he felt, to what he even fancied he ought to look: his clothes shrunk up and clinging to his body: from the crown of his head to his girdle one dripping, saturated mass: from his girdle to the soles of his feet, mud and splashes: the places which were free from these might themselves have been called spots and splashes. And could he have seen his whole figure in a looking-glass, with the brim of his hat unstiffened and hanging down, and his hair straight and sticking to his face, he would have considered himself a still greater beauty. As to being tired, he may have been so; but, if he were, he knew nothing about it; and the freshness of the morning, added to that of the night and of his trifling bath, only inspired him with more energy, and a wish to get forward on his way more rapidly.

He is at Pescate; he pursues his course along the remaining part of the road that runs by the side of the Adda, giving a melancholy glance, however, at Pescarenico; he crosses the bridge; and, through fields and lanes, shortly arrives at his friend's hospitable dwelling. He, who, only just risen, was standing in the doorway to watch the weather, raised his eyes in amazement at that strange figure, so drenched, bespattered, and, we may say, dirty, yet at the same time, so lively and at ease: in his whole life he had never seen a man worse equipped, and more thoroughly contented.

'Aha!' said he: 'here already? and in such weather! How have things gone?'

'She's there,' said Renzo: 'she's there, she's there.'

'Well?'

'Recovered, which is better. I have to thank the Lord and the

Madonna for it as long as I live. But oh! such grand things, such wonderful things! I'll tell you all afterwards.'

'But what a plight you are in!'

'I'm a beauty, am I not?'

'To say the truth, you might employ the overplus above to wash off the overplus below. But wait a minute, and I'll make you a good fire.'

'I won't refuse it, I assure you. Where do you think it caught me? just at the gate of the Lazzaretto. But never mind! let the weather do its own business, and I mine.'

His friend then went out, and soon returned with two bundles of faggots: one he laid on the ground, the other on the hearth, and with a few embers remaining over from the evening, quickly kindled a fine blaze. Renzo, meanwhile, had taken off his hat, and giving it two or three shakes, he threw it upon the ground; and, not quite so easily, had also pulled off his doublet. He then drew from his breeches' pocket his poniard, the sheath of which was so wet that it seemed to have been laid in soak; this he put upon the table, saying, 'This, too, is in a pretty plight; but there's rain! there's rain! thank God . . . I've had some hair-breadth escapes; . . . I'll tell you by and by.' And he began rubbing his hands. 'Now do me another kindness,' added he: 'that little bundle that I left upstairs, just fetch it for me, for before these clothes that I have on dry . . .'

Returning with the bundle, his friend said, 'I should think you must have a pretty good appetite: I fancy you haven't wanted enough to drink by the way; but something to eat . . .'

'I bought two rolls yesterday towards evening; but, indeed, they haven't touched my lips.'

'Leave it to me,' said his friend; he then poured some water into a kettle, which he suspended upon the hook over the fire; and added, 'I'm going to milk: when I come back the water will be ready, and we'll make a good *polenta*. You, meanwhile, can dress yourself at your leisure.'

When left alone, Renzo, not without some difficulty took off the rest of his clothes, which were almost as if glued to his skin; he then dried himself, and dressed himself anew from head to foot. His

friend returned, and set himself to make the *polenta,* Renzo, meanwhile, sitting by in expectation.

'Now I feel that I'm tired,' said he. 'But it's a fine long stretch!
That's nothing, however. I've so much to tell you it will take the
whole day. Oh, what a state Milan's in! What one's obliged to see!
what one's obliged to touch! Enough to make one loathe oneself. I
dare say I wanted nothing less than the little washing I've had.
And what those gentry down there would have done to me! You
shall hear. But if you could see the Lazzaretto! It's enough to make
one lose oneself in miseries. Well, well, I'll tell you all . . . And
she's there, and you'll see her here, and she'll be my wife, and you
must be a witness, and, plague or no plague, we'll be merry, at least
for a few hours.'

In short, he verified what he had told his friend, that it would
take all the day to relate everything; for, as it never ceased drizzling,
the latter spent the whole of it under cover, partly seated by the side
of his friend, partly busied over one of his wine-vats and a little
cask, and in other occupations preparatory to the vintage and the
dressing of the grapes, in which Renzo failed not to lend a hand;
for, as he used to say, he was one of those who are sooner tired of
doing nothing than of working. He could not, however, resist taking
a little run up to Agnese's cottage, to see once more a certain window,
and there, too, to rub his hands with glee. He went and returned
unobserved, and retired to rest in good time. In good time, too, he
rose next morning; and finding that the rain had ceased, if settled
fine weather had not yet returned, he set off quickly on his way to
Pasturo.

It was still early when he arrived there; for he was no less willing
and in a hurry to bring matters to an end, than the reader probably
is. He inquired for Agnese, and heard that she was safe and well;
a small cottage standing by itself was pointed out to him as the
place where she was staying. He went thither, and called her by
name from the street. On hearing such a call, she rushed to the
window; and while she stood, with open mouth, on the point of
uttering I know not what sound or exclamation, Renzo prevented
her by saying, 'Lucia's recovered: I saw her the day before yester-

day: she sends you her love, and will be here soon. And beside these, I've so many, many things to tell you.'

Between the surprise of the apparition, the joy of these tidings, and the burning desire to know more about it, Agnese began one moment an exclamation, the next a question, without finishing any; then, forgetting the precautions she had long been accustomed to take, she said, 'I'll come and open the door for you.'

'Wait: the plague!' said Renzo: 'you've not had it, I believe?'

'No, not I: have you?'

'Yes, I have; you must therefore be prudent. I come from Milan; and you shall hear that I've been up to the eyes in the midst of the contagion. To be sure, I've changed from head to foot; but it's an abominable thing that clings to one sometimes like witchcraft. And since the Lord has preserved you hitherto, you must take care of yourself till this infection is over; for you are our mother; and I want us to live together happily for a long while, in compensation for the great sufferings we have undergone, I at least.'

'But . . .' began Agnese.

'Eh!' interrupted Renzo, 'there's no *but* that will hold. I know what you mean; but you shall hear, you shall hear that there are no longer any *buts* in the way. Let us go into some open space, where we can talk at our ease, without danger, and you shall hear.'

Agnese pointed out to him a garden behind the house; if he would go in, and seat himself on one of the two benches which he would find opposite each other, she would come down directly, and go and sit on the other. Thus it was arranged; and I am sure that if the reader, informed as he is of preceding events, could have placed himself there as a third party, to witness with his own eyes that animated conversation, to hear with his own ears those descriptions, questions, explanations, ejaculations, condolences, and congratulations; about Don Rodrigo, and Father Cristoforo, and everything else, and those descriptions of the future, as clear and certain as those of the past;—I am sure, I say, he would have enjoyed it exceedingly, and would have been the last to come away. But to have this conversation upon paper, in mute words written with ink, and without meeting with a single new incident, I fancy he would not care much for it, and would rather that we should leave him

to conjecture it. Their conclusion was that they would go to keep
house all together, in the territory of Bergamo, where Renzo had
already gained a good footing. As to the time, they could decide
nothing, because it depended upon the plague and other circumstances; but no sooner should the danger be over, than Agnese would
return home to wait there for Lucia, or Lucia would wait there for
her; and in the mean time Renzo would often take another trip to
Pasturo, to see his mother, and to keep her acquainted with whatever might happen.

Before taking his leave, he offered money to her also, saying, 'I
have them all here, you see, those *scudi* you sent: I, too, made a vow
not to touch them, until the mystery was cleared up. Now, however,
if you want any of them, bring me a little bowl of vinegar and
water, and I'll throw in the fifty *scudi,* good and glittering as you
sent them.'

'No, no,' said Agnese; 'I've more than I need still by me; keep
yours untouched, and they'll do nicely to set up house with.'

Renzo took his departure, with the additional consolation of having found one so dear to him safe and well. He remained the rest
of that day, and for the night, at his friend's house, and on the
morrow was again on his way, but in another direction, towards his
adopted country.

Here he found Bortolo, still in good health, and in less apprehension of losing it; for in those few days, things had there also
rapidly taken a favourable turn. New cases of illness had become
rare, and the malady was no longer what it had been; there were no
longer those fatal blotches, nor violent symptoms; but slight fevers,
for the most part intermittent, with, at the worst, a discoloured spot,
which was cured like an ordinary tumour. The face of the country
seemed already changed; the survivors began to come forth to reckon
up their numbers, and mutually to exchange condolences and congratulations. There was already a talk of resuming business again;
such masters as survived already began to look out for and bespeak
workmen, and principally in those branches of art where the number
had been scarce even before the contagion, as was that of silk-
weaving. Renzo, without any display of levity, promised his cousin
(with the proviso, however, that he obtained all due consent) to

resume his employment, when he could come in company to settle himself in the country. In the meanwhile he gave orders for the most necessary preparations: he provided a more spacious dwelling, a task become only too easy to execute at a small cost, and furnished it with all necessary articles, this time breaking into his little treasure, but without making any very great hole in it, for of everything there was a superabundance at a very moderate price.

In the course of a few days he returned to his native village, which he found still more signally changed for the better. He went over immediately to Pasturo; there he found Agnese in good spirits again, and ready to return home as soon as might be, so that he accompanied her thither at once: nor will we attempt to describe what were their feelings and words on again beholding those scenes together. Agnese found everything as she had left it; so that she was forced to declare, that, considering it was a poor widow and her daughter, the angels had kept guard over it.

'And that other time,' added she, 'when it might have been thought that the Lord was looking elsewhere, and thought not of us, since he suffered all our little property to be carried away, yet, after all, He showed us the contrary; for He sent me from another quarter that grand store of money which enabled me to restore everything. I say everything, but I am wrong; because Lucia's wedding-clothes, which were stolen among the rest, good and complete as they were at first, were still wanting; and behold, now they come to us in another direction. Who would have told me, when I was working so busily to prepare those others, You think you are working for Lucia: nay, my good woman! you are working for you know not whom. Heaven knows what sort of being will wear this veil, and all those clothes: those for Lucia,—the real wedding-dress which is to serve for her, will be provided by a kind soul whom you know not, nor even that there is such a person.'

Agnese's first care was to prepare for this kind soul the most comfortable accommodations her poor little cottage could afford; then she went to procure some silk to wind, and thus, employed with her reel, beguiled the wearisome hours of delay.

Renzo, on his part, suffered not these days, long enough in themselves, to pass away in idleness: fortunately he understood two trades, and of these two chose that of a labourer. He partly helped his kind host, who considered it particularly fortunate, at such a time, to have a workman frequently at his command, and a workman, too, of his abilities; and partly cultivated and restored to order Agnese's little garden, which had completely run wild during her absence. As to his own property, he never thought about it at all, because, he said, it was too entangled a periwig, and wanted more than one pair of hands to set it to rights again. He did not even set foot into it; still less into his house: it would have pained him too much to see its desolation; and he had already resolved to dispose of everything, at whatever price, and to spend in his new country all that he could make by the sale.

If the survivors of the plague were to one another resuscitated, as it were, he, to his fellow-countrymen, was, so to say, doubly so: every one welcomed and congratulated him, every one wanted to hear from him his history. The reader will perhaps say, how went on the affair of his outlawry? It went on very well: he scarcely thought anything more about it, supposing that they who could have enforced it would no longer think about it themselves; nor was he mistaken. This arose not merely from the pestilence, which had thwarted so many undertakings; but, as may have been seen in more than one place in this story, it was a common occurrence in those days, that special as well as general orders against persons (unless there were some private and powerful animosity to keep them alive and render them availing), often continued without taking effect, if they had not done so on their first promulgation; like musket-balls, which, if they strike no blow, lie quietly upon the ground without giving molestation to any one. A necessary consequence of the extreme facility with which these orders were flung about, both right and left. Man's activity is limited; and whatever excess there was in the making of regulations, must have produced so much greater a deficiency in the execution of them. What goes into the sleeves cannot go into the skirt.' [1]

If any one wants to know how Renzo got on with Don Abbondio, during this interval of expectation, I need only say that they kept at a respectful distance from each other; the latter for fear of hear-

---

[1] 'Quel che va nelle maniche non può andar ne' gheroni.'

ing a whisper about the wedding; and at the very thought of such a thing, his imagination conjured up Don Rodrigo with his bravoes on the one side, and the Cardinal with his arguments on the other; and the former, because he had resolved not to mention it to him till the very last moment, being unwilling to run the risk of making him restive beforehand, of stirring up—who could tell?—some difficulty, and of entangling things by useless chit-chat. All his chit-chat was with Agnese. 'Do you think she'll come soon?' one would ask. 'I hope so,' would the other reply; and frequently the one who had given the answer would not long afterwards make the same inquiry. With these and similar cheats they endeavoured to beguile the time, which seemed to them longer and longer in proportion as more passed away.

We will make the reader, however, pass over all this period in one moment, by briefly stating that, a few days after Renzo's visit to the Lazzaretto, Lucia left it with the kind widow; that, a general quarantine having been enjoined, they kept it together in the house of the latter, that part of the time was spent in preparing Lucia's wardrobe, at which, after sundry ceremonious objections, she was obliged to work herself; and that the quarantine having expired, the widow left her warehouse and dwelling under the custody of her brother, the commissioner, and prepared to set off on her journey with Lucia. We could, too, speedily add,—they set off, arrived, and all the rest; but, with all our willingness to accommodate ourselves to this haste of the reader's, there are three things appertaining to this period of time, which we are not willing to pass over in silence; and with two, at least, we believe the reader himself will say that we should have been to blame in so doing.

The first is, that when Lucia returned to relate her adventures to the good widow more in particular, and with greater order than she could do in her agitation of mind when she first confided them to her, and when she more expressly mentioned the Signora who had given her shelter in the monastery at Monza, she learnt from her friend things which, by giving her the key of many mysteries, filled her mind with melancholy and fearful astonishment. She learnt from the widow that the unhappy lady, having fallen under suspicion of most atrocious conduct, had been conveyed, by order of the Cardinal, to a monastery at Milan; that there, after long indulgence in rage and struggles, she had repented, and confessed her faults, and that her present life was one of such voluntary inflictions, that no one, except by depriving her of that life entirely, could have invented a severer punishment for her. Should any one wish to be more particularly acquainted with this melancholy history, he will find it in the work and at the place which we have elsewhere quoted in relation to this same person.[2]

The other fact is, that Lucia, after making inquiries about Father Cristoforo of all the Capuchins she could meet with in the Lazzaretto, heard there, with more sorrow than surprise, that he had died of the pestilence.

Lastly, before leaving Milan, she wished also to ascertain something about her former patrons, and to perform, as she said, an act of duty, if any yet remained. The widow accompanied her to the house, where they learned that both one and the other had been carried off with the multitude. When we have said of Donna Prassede that she was dead, we have said all; but Don Ferrante, considering that he was a man of erudition, is deemed by our anonymous author worthy of more extended mention; and we, at our own risk, will transcribe, as nearly as possible, what he has left on record about him.

He says, then, that, on the very first whisper of pestilence, Don Ferrante was one of the most resolute, and ever afterwards one of the most persevering, in denying it, not indeed with loud clamours, like the people, but with arguments, of which, at least, no one could complain that they wanted concatenation.

'In rerum natura,' he used to say, 'there are but two species of things, substances and accidents; and if I prove that the contagion cannot be either one or the other, I shall have proved that it does not exist—that it is a mere chimera. Here I am, then. Substances are either spiritual or material. That the contagion is a spiritual substance, is an absurdity no one would venture to maintain; it is needless, therefore, to speak of it. Material substances are either simple or compound. Now, the contagion is not a simple substance; and this may be shown in a few words. It is not an ethereal sub-

---

[2] Ripamonti, Hist. Pat. Dec. V. lib. vi. cap. iii.

stance; because, if it were, instead of passing from one body to another, it would fly off as quickly as possible to its own sphere. It is not aqueous: because it would wet things, and be dried up by the wind. It is not igneous; because it would burn. It is not earthy; because it would be visible. Neither is it a compound substance; because it must by all means be sensible to the sight and the touch; and who has seen this contagion? who has touched it? It remains to be seen whether it can be an accident. Worse and worse. These gentlemen, the doctors, say that it is communicated from one body to another; for this is their Achilles, this the pretext for issuing so many useless orders. Now, supposing it an accident, it comes to this, that it must be a transitive accident, two words quite at variance with each other; there being no plainer and more established fact in the whole of philosophy than this, that an accident cannot pass from one subject to another. For if, to avoid this Scylla, we shelter our-selves under the assertion that it is an accident produced, we fly from Scylla and run upon Charybdis: because, if it be produced, then it is not communicated, it is not propagated, as people go about affirming. These principles being laid down, what use is it to come talking to us so about weals, pustules, and carbuncles? . . .'

'All absurdities,' once escaped from somebody or other.

'No, no,' resumed Don Ferrante, 'I don't say so: science is science; only we must know how to employ it. Weals, pustules, carbuncles, parotides, violaceous tumours, black swellings, are all respectable words, which have their true and legitimate signification: but I say that they don't affect the question at all. Who denies that there may be such things, nay, that there actually are such? All depends upon seeing where they come from.'

Here began the woes even of Don Ferrante. So long as he confined himself to declaiming against the opinion of a pestilence, he found everywhere willing, obliging, and respectful listeners; for it cannot be expressed how much authority the opinion of a learned man by profession carries with it, while he is attempting to prove to others things of which they are already convinced. But when he came to distinguish, and to try and demonstrate that the error of these physicians did not consist in affirming that there was a terrible and prevalent malady, but in assigning its rules and causes; then (I am speaking of the earliest times, when no one would listen to a word about pestilence), then, instead of listeners, he found rebellious and intractable opponents; then there was no room for speechifying, and he could no longer put forth his doctrines but by scraps and piecemeal.

'There's the true reason only too plainly, after all,' said he; 'and even they are compelled to acknowledge it, who maintain that other empty proposition besides . . . Let them deny, if they can, that fatal conjunction of Saturn with Jupiter. And when was it ever heard say that influences may be propagated . . . And would these gentlemen deny the existence of influences? Will they deny that there are stars, or tell me that they are placed up there for no purpose, like so many pin-heads stuck into a pin-cushion? . . . But what I cannot understand about these doctors is this; to confess that we are under so malignant a conjunction, and then to come and tell us, with eager face, 'Don't touch this, and don't touch that, and you'll be safe!' As if this avoiding of material contact with terrestrial bodies could hinder the virtual effect of celestial ones! And such anxiety about burning old clothes! Poor people! will you burn Jupiter, will you burn Saturn?'

His fretus, that is to say, on these grounds, he used no precautions against the pestilence; took it, went to bed, and went to die, like one of Metastasio's heroes, quarrelling with the stars.

And that famous library of his? Perhaps it is still there, distributed around his walls.

CHAPTER XXXVIII

ONE fine evening, Agnese heard a carriage stop at the door. —It is she, and none other!—It was indeed Lucia, with the good widow: the mutual greetings we leave the reader to imagine.

Next morning Renzo arrived in good time, totally ignorant of what had happened, and with no other intentions than of pouring out his feelings a little with Agnese about Lucia's long delay. The gesticulations he made, and the exclamations he uttered, on finding her thus before his eyes, we will also refer to our reader's imagination. Lucia's exhibitions of pleasure towards him were such, that it will not take many words to give an account of them. 'Good morning, Renzo: how do you do?' said she, with downcast eyes, and an air of composure. Nor let the reader think that Renzo considered this mode of reception too cold, and took it at all amiss. He entered fully into the meaning of her behaviour; and as among educated people one knows how to make allowance for compliments, so he understood very well what feelings lay hidden beneath these words. Besides, it was easy enough to perceive that she had two ways of proffering them, one for Renzo, and another for all those she might happen to know.

'It does me good to see you,' replied the youth, making use of a set phrase, which he himself, however, had invented on the spur of the moment.

'Our poor Father Cristoforo! . . .' said Lucia: 'pray for his soul; though one may be almost sure that he is now praying for us above.'

'I expected no less, indeed,' said Renzo. Nor was this the only melancholy chord touched in the course of this dialogue. But what then? Whatever subject was the topic of conversation, it always seemed to them delightful. Like a capricious horse, which halts and plants itself in a certain spot, and lifts first one hoof and then another, and sets it down again in the self-same place, and cuts a

hundred capers before taking a single step, and then all on a sudden
starts on its career, and speeds forward as if borne on the wings of
the wind; such had time become in his eyes: at first minutes had
seemed hours; now hours seemed to him like minutes.

The widow not only did not spoil the party, but entered into it
with great spirit: nor could Renzo, when he saw her lying on that
miserable bed in the Lazzaretto, have imagined her of so companion-
able and cheerful a disposition. But the Lazzaretto and the country,
death and a wedding, are not exactly one and the same thing. With
Agnese she was very soon on friendly terms; and it was a pleasure
to see her with Lucia, so tender, and, at the same time, playful,
rallying her gracefully and without effort, just so much as was
necessary to give more courage to her words and motions.

At length Renzo said that he was going to Don Abbondio, to
make arrangements about the wedding.

He went, and with a certain air of respectful raillery, 'Signor
Curate,' said he, 'have you at last lost that headache, which you told
me prevented your marrying us? We are now in time; the bride
is here, and I've come to know when it will be convenient to you:
but this time, I must request you to make haste.'

Don Abbondio did not, indeed, reply that he would not; but he
began to hesitate, to bring forward sundry excuses, to throw out
sundry insinuations: and why bring himself into notice and publish
his name, with that proclamation for his seizure still out against
him? and that the thing could be done equally well elsewhere;
and this, that, and the other argument.

'Oh, I see!' said Renzo: 'you've still a little pain in your head.
But listen, listen.' And he began to describe in what state he had
beheld poor Don Rodrigo; and that by that time he must undoubtedly be gone. 'Let us hope,' concluded he, 'that the Lord will
have had mercy on him.'

'This has nothing to do with us,' said Don Abbondio. 'Did I
say no? Certainly I did not; but I speak . . . I speak for good
reasons. Besides, don't you see, as long as a man has breath in his
body . . . Only look at me: I'm somewhat sickly; I too have been
nearer the other world than this: and yet I'm here; and . . . if
troubles don't come upon me . . . why . . . I may hope to stay here

a little longer yet. Think, too, of some people's constitutions. But, as I say, this has nothing to do with us.'

After a little further conversation neither more nor less conclusive, Renzo made an elegant bow, returned to his party, made his report of the interview, and concluded by saying: 'I've come away, because I've had quite enough of it, and that I mightn't run the risk of losing my patience, and using bad words. Sometimes he seemed exactly like what he was that other time; the very same hesitation, and the very same arguments: I'm sure, if it had lasted a little longer, he'd have returned to the charge with some words in Latin. I see there must be another delay: it would be better to do what he says at once, and go and get married where we're about to live.'

'I'll tell you what we'll do,' said the widow: 'I should like you to let us women go make the trial, and see whether we can't find rather a better way to manage him. By this means, too, I shall have the pleasure of knowing this man, whether he's just such as you describe him. After dinner I should like to go, not to assail him again too quickly. And now, Signor bridegroom, please to accompany us two in a little walk, while Agnese is so busily employed: I will act the part of Lucia's mother. I want very much to see these mountains, and this lake of which I've heard so much, rather more at large, for the little I've already seen of them seems to me a charmingly fine view.'

Renzo escorted them first to the cottage of his hospitable friend, where they met with a hearty welcome; and they made him promise that, not that day only, but, if he could, every day, he would join their party at dinner.

Having returned from their ramble, and dined, Renzo suddenly took his departure, without saying where he was going. The women waited a little while to confer together, and concert about the mode of assailing Don Abbondio; and at length they set off to make the attack.

—Here they are, I declare,—said he to himself; but he put on a pleasant face, and offered warm congratulations to Lucia, greetings to Agnese, and compliments to the stranger. He made them sit down; then he entered upon the grand subject of the plague, and wanted to hear from Lucia how she had managed to get over it in

the midst of so many sorrows: the Lazzaretto afforded an opportunity of bringing her companion into conversation; then, as was
but fair, Don Abbondio talked about his share in the storm; then
followed great rejoicings with Agnese, that she had come forth un-
harmed. The conversation was carried to some length: from the
very first moment the two elders were on the watch for a favourable
opportunity of mentioning the essential point; and at length one of
the two, I am not sure which, succeeded in breaking the ice. But
what think you? Don Abbondio could not hear with that ear. He
took care not to say no, but behold! he again recurred to his usual
evasions, circumlocutions, and hoppings from bush to bush. 'It
would be necessary,' he said, 'to get rid of that order for Renzo's
arrest. You, Signora, who come from Milan, will know more or
less the course these matters take; you would claim protection—
some cavalier of weight for with such means every wound may be
cured. If then, we may jump to the conclusion, without perplexing
ourselves with so many considerations; as these young people, and
our good Agnese here, already intend to expatriate themselves, (but
I'm talking at random; for one's country is wherever one is well off),
it seems to me that all may be accomplished there, where no proclamation interposes. I don't myself exactly see that this is the
moment for the conclusion of this match, but I wish it well concluded, and undisturbedly. To tell the truth: here, with this edict
in force, to proclaim the name of Lorenzo Tramaglino from the
altar, I couldn't do it with a quiet conscience: I too sincerely wish
them well; I should be afraid I were doing them an injury. You see,
ma'am, and they too.'

Here Agnese and the widow, each in their own way, broke in to
combat these arguments: Don Abbondio reproduced them in another shape: it was a perpetual recommencement: when lo, enter
Renzo with a determined step, and tidings in his face.

'The Signor Marquis has arrived,' said he.

'What does this mean? Arrived where?' asked Don Abbondio.

'He has arrived at his palace, which was once Don Rodrigo's;
because this Signor Marquis is the heir by preferment in trust, as
they say; so that there's no longer any doubt. As for myself, I
should be very glad of it, if I could hear that that poor man had

died in peace. At any rate, I've said Paternosters for him hitherto; now I will say the *De profundis*. And this Signor Marquis is a very fine man.'

'Certainly,' said Don Abbondio, 'I've heard him mentioned more than once as a really excellent Signor, a man of the old stamp. But is it positively true? . . .'

'Will you believe the sexton?'

'Why?'

'Because he's seen him with his own eyes. I've only been in the neighbourhood of the castle; and, to say the truth, I went there on purpose, thinking they must know something there. And several people told me about it. Afterwards, I met Ambrogio, who had just been up there, and had seen him, I say, take possession. Will you hear Ambrogio's testimony? I made him wait outside on purpose.'

'Yet, let him come in,' said Don Abbondio. Renzo went and called the sexton, who, after confirming every fact, adding fresh particulars, and dissipating every doubt, again went on his way.

'Ah! he's dead, then! he's really gone!' exclaimed Don Abbondio. 'You see, my children, how Providence overtakes some people. You know what a grand thing that is! what a great relief to this poor country! for it was impossible to live with him here. This pestilence has been a great scourge, but it has also been a *good broom;* it has swept away some, from whom, my children, we could never have freed ourselves. Young, blooming, and in full vigour, we might have said that they who were destined to assist at their funeral, were still writing Latin exercises at school; and in the twinkling of an eye they've disappeared, by hundreds at a time. We shall no longer see him going about with those cut-throat looking fellows at his heels, with such an ostentatious and supercilious air, looking as if he had swallowed a ramrod, and staring at people as if they were all placed in the world to be honoured by his condescension. Well, he's here no longer, and we are. He'll never again send such messages to honest men. He's given us all a great deal of disquietude, as you see; for now we may venture to say so.'

'I've forgiven him from my heart,' said Renzo.

'And you do right! it's your duty to do so,' replied Don Abbondio;

'but one may thank Heaven, I suppose, who has delivered us from
him. But to return to ourselves; I repeat, do what you like best.
If you wish me to marry you, here I am: if it will be more convenient
to you to go elsewhere, do so. As to the order of arrest, I likewise
think that, as there is now no longer any who keeps his eye on you,
and wishes to do you harm, it isn't worth giving yourself any great
uneasiness about it, particularly as this gracious decree, on occasion
of the birth of the most serene Infanta, is interposed. And then the
plague! the plague! Oh, that plague has put to flight many a grand
thing! So that, if you like . . . to-day is Thursday . . . on Sunday
I'll ask you in church; because what may have been done in that way
before will count for nothing, after so long an interval; and then I
shall have the pleasure of marrying you myself.'

'You know we came about this very thing,' said Renzo.

'Very well; I shall attend you: and I must also write immediately
and inform his Eminence.'

'Who is his Eminence?'

'His Eminence,' replied Don Abbondio, 'is our Signor Cardinal
the Archbishop, whom may God preserve!'

'Oh, I beg your pardon,' answered Agnese; 'but though I'm a
poor ignorant creature, I can assure you he's not called so; because,
the second time we were about to speak to him, just as I'm speaking
to you, sir, one of the priests drew me aside, and instructed me how
to behave to a gentleman like him; and that he ought to be called,
your illustrious Lordship, and my Lord.'

'And now, if he had to repeat his instructions, he'd tell you that
he is to have the title of Eminence: do you understand now? Because
the Pope, whom may God likewise preserve, has ordered, ever since
the month of June, that Cardinals are to have this title. And why
do you think he has come to this resolution? because the word illustrious, which once belonged to them and certain princes, has now
become,—even you know what, and to how many it is given; and
how willingly they swallow it! And what would you have done?
Take it away from all? Then we should have complaints, hatred,
troubles, and jealousies without end, and after all, they would go
on just as before. So the Pope has found a capital remedy. By
degrees, however, they will begin to give the title of Eminence to

Bishops; then Abbots will claim it; then Provosts; for men are made so: they must always be advancing, always be advancing; then Canons . . .'

'And Curates?' said the widow.

'No, no,' pursued Don Abbondio, 'the Curates must draw the cart: never fear that "your Reverence" will sit ill upon Curates to the end of the world. Farther, I shouldn't be surprised if cavaliers, who are accustomed to hear themselves called Illustrious, and to be treated like Cardinals, should some day or other want the title of Eminence themselves. And if they want it, you know, depend upon it they'll find somebody to give it them. And then, whoever happens to be Pope then, will invent something else for the Cardinals. But come, let us return to our own affairs. On Sunday, I'll ask you in church; and, meanwhile, what do you think I've thought of to serve you better? Meanwhile, we'll ask for a dispensation for the two other times. They must have plenty to do up at Court in giving dispensations, if things go on everywhere as they do here. I've already . . . one . . . two . . . three . . . for Sunday, without counting yourselves; and some others may occur yet. And then you'll see afterwards; the fire has caught, and there'll not be left one person single. Perpetua surely made a mistake to die now; for this was the time that even she would have found a purchaser. And I fancy, Signora, it will be the same at Milan.'

'So it is, indeed; you may imagine it, when, in my parish only, last Sunday, there were fifty weddings.'

'I said so; the world won't come to an end yet. And you, Signora, has no *bumble fly* begun to hover about you?'

'No, no; I don't think about such things, nor do I wish to.'

'Oh yes, yes; for you will be the only single one. Even Agnese, you see—even Agnese . . .'

'Poh! you are inclined to be merry!' said Agnese.

'I am, indeed; and I think, at length, it's time. We've passed through some rough days, haven't we, my young ones? Some rough ones we've passed indeed; and the few days we have yet to live, we may hope will be a little less melancholy. But, happy you, who, if no misfortunes happen, have still a little time left to talk over bygone sorrows! I, poor old man . . . villains may die; one may recover of the plague, but there is no help for old age; and, as they say, *senectus ipsa est morbus.'*

'Now, then,' said Renzo, 'you may talk Latin as long as you like, it makes no difference to me.'

'You're at it again with that Latin, are you? Well, well, I'll settle it with you: when you come before me with this little creature here, just to hear you pronounce certain little words in Latin, I'll say to you— You don't like Latin; good-bye. Shall I?'

'Ah! but I know what I mean,' replied Renzo; 'it isn't at all that Latin there that frightens me—that is honest sacred Latin, like that in the mass. And, besides, it is necessary there that you should read what is in the book. I'm talking of that knavish Latin, out of church, that comes upon one treacherously, in the very pith of a conversation. For example, now that we are here, and all is over, that Latin you went on pouring forth, just here in this corner, to give me to understand that you couldn't, and that other things were wanting, and I know not what besides; please now to translate it a little for me.'

'Hold your tongue, you wicked fellow, hold your tongue; don't stir up these things; for if we were now to make up our accounts, I don't know which would be creditor. I've forgiven all; let us talk about it no longer; but you certainly played me some tricks. I don't wonder at you, because you're a downright young scoundrel; but fancy this creature, as quiet as a mouse, this little saint, whom one would have thought it a sin to suspect and guard against. But after all, I know who set her up to it, I know, I know.' So saying, he pointed and waved towards Agnese the finger he had at first directed to Lucia; and it is impossible to describe the good-temper and pleasantry with which he made these reproaches. The tidings he had just heard had given him a freedom and a talkativeness to which he had long been a stranger; and we should be still far enough from a conclusion, if we were to relate all the rest of this conversation, which he continued to prolong, more than once detaining the party when on the point of starting, and afterwards stopping them again for a little while at the very street door, each time to make some jocose speech.

The day following, he received a visit as unexpected as it was gratifying, from the Signor Marquis we have mentioned; a person beyond the prime of manhood, whose countenance was, as it were, a seal to what report had said of him; open, benevolent, placid, humble, dignified, and with something that indicated a resigned sadness.

'I come,' said he, 'to bring you the compliments of the Cardinal Archbishop.'

'Ah, what condescension of you both!'

'When I was about to take leave of that incomparable man, who is good enough to honour me with his friendship, he mentioned to me two young betrothed persons of this parish, who have had to suffer on account of the unfortunate Don Rodrigo. His Lordship wishes to have some tidings of them. Are they living? and are their affairs settled?'

'Everything is settled. Indeed, I was intending to write about them to his Eminence; but now that I have the honour . . .'

'Are they here?'

'They are; and they will be man and wife as soon as possible.'

'And I request you to be good enough to tell me if I can be of any service to them, and also to instruct me in the best way of being so. During this calamity, I have lost the only two sons I had, and their mother, and have received three considerable inheritances. I had a superfluity even before; so that you see it is really rendering me a service to give me an opportunity of employing some of my wealth, and particularly such an opportunity as this.'

'May Heaven bless you! Why are not all . . . Enough; I thank you most heartily, in the name of these my children. And since your illustrious Lordship gives me so much encouragement, it is true, my Lord, that I have an expedient to suggest which perhaps may not displease your Lordship. Allow me to tell you, then, that these worthy people are resolved to go and settle themselves elsewhere, and to sell what little property they have here: the young man a vineyard of about nine or ten perches, if I'm not mistaken, but neglected and completely overgrown. Besides, he also has a cottage, and his bride another, now both, you will see, the abode of rats. A nobleman like your Lordship cannot know how the poor fare, when they are reduced to the necessity of disposing of their goods. It always ends by falling into the hands of some knave, who, if occasion offers, will make love to the place for some time, and as soon as he finds that its owner wants to sell it, draws back, and pretends not to wish for it so that he is obliged to run after him, and give it him for a piece of bread; particularly, too, in such circumstances as these. My Lord Marquis will already have seen the drift of my remarks. The best charity your most illustrious Lordship can afford to these people is, to relieve them from this difficulty by purchasing their little property. To say the truth, I have an eye to my own interest, my own advantage, in making this suggestion, the acquisition in my parish of a fellow-ruler like my Lord Marquis; but your Lordship will decide according to your own judgment; I have only spoken from obedience.'

The Marquis highly commended the suggestion, returned thanks for it, begged Don Abbondio to be the judge of the price, and to charge it exorbitantly, and completed the Curate's amazement by proposing to go together immediately to the bride's house, where they should probably also find the bridegroom.

By the way, Don Abbondio, in high glee, as may be imagined, thought of and mentioned another proposal. 'Since your illustrious Lordship is so inclined to benefit these poor people, there is another service which you might render them. The young man has an order of arrest out against him, a kind of sentence of outlawry, for some trifling fault he committed in Milan two years ago, on that day of the great insurrection, in which he chanced to be implicated, without any malicious intentions, indeed quite ignorantly, like a mouse caught in a trap. Nothing serious, I assure you; mere boyish tricks, mischievous pranks; indeed, he is quite incapable of committing an actual crime. I may say so, for I baptized him, and have seen him grow up under my eyes. Besides, if your Lordship would take any pleasure in it, as gentlemen sometimes do in hearing these poor people's rude language, you can make him relate the account himself, and you will hear. At present, as it refers to old matters, no one gives him any molestation; and, as I have said, he thinks of leaving the state; but in the course of time, or in case of returning here, or going elsewhere, some time or other, you will agree with me that it is always better to find oneself clear. My Lord Marquis has influence in Milan, as is just, both as a noble cavalier, and as the great man he really is . . . No, no, allow me to say it, for truth will have its way. A recommendation, a word from a person like yourself, is more than is necessary to obtain a ready acquittal.'

'Are there not heavy charges against this young man?'

'Pshaw, pshaw! I would not believe them. They made a great stir about it at the moment; but I don't think there's anything now beyond the mere formalities.'

'If so, the thing will be easy; and I willingly take it upon me.'

'And yet you will not let it be said that you are a great man. I say it, and I will say it; in spite of your Lordship, I will say it. And even if I were to be silent, it would be to no purpose, because everybody says so: and *vox populi, vox Dei.*'

They found Renzo and the three women together, as they expected. How these felt we leave the reader to imagine; but for my part, I think that the very rough and bare walls, and the windows, and the tables, and the kitchen utensils, must have marvelled at receiving among them so extraordinary a guest. He encouraged the conversation, by talking of the Cardinal and their other matters with unreserved cordiality, and at the same time with great delicacy. By and by he came to the proposal. Don Abbondio, being requested by him to name the price, came forward; and, after a few gestures and apologies,—that it wasn't in his line, and that he could only guess at random, and that he spoke out of obedience, and that he left it to him, mentioned what he thought a most extravagant sum. The purchaser said that, for his part, he was extremely well satisfied, and, as if he had misunderstood, repeated double the amount. He would not hear of rectifying the mistake, and cut short and concluded all further conversation, by inviting the party to dinner at his palace the day after the wedding, when the deeds should be properly drawn out.

—Ah!—said Don Abbondio afterwards to himself, when he had returned home:—if the plague did things in this way always and everywhere, it would really be a sin to speak ill of it: we might almost wish for one every generation; and be content that people should be in league to produce a malady.—

The dispensation arrived, the acquittal arrived, that blessed day arrived: the bride and bridegroom went in triumphal security to that very church, where, with Don Abbondio's own mouth, they were declared man and wife. Another, and far more singular triumph, was the going next day to the palace; and I leave my readers to conjecture the thoughts which must have passed through their minds on ascending that acclivity, on entering that doorway; and the observations that each must have made, according to his or her natural disposition. I will only mention that, in the midst of their rejoicing, one or other more than once made the remark, that poor Father Cristoforo was still wanting to complete their happiness. 'Yet for himself,' added they, 'he is assuredly better off than we are.'

The nobleman received them with great kindness, conducted them into a fine large servants'-hall, and seated the bride and bridegroom at table with Agnese and their Milanese friend; and before withdrawing to dine elsewhere with Don Abbondio, wished to assist a little at this first banquet, and even helped to wait upon them. I hope it will enter into no one's head to say that it would have been a more simple plan to have made at once but one table. I have described him as an excellent man, but not as an original, as it would now-a-days be called; I have said that he was humble, but not that he was a prodigy of humility. He possessed enough of this virtue to put himself beneath these good people, but not on an equality with them.

After the two dinners, the contract was drawn out by the hands of a lawyer, not, however, *Azzecca-Garbugli*. He, I mean his outward man, was, and still is, at Canterelli. And for those who are unacquainted with that neighbourhood, I suppose some explanation of this information is here necessary.

A little higher up than Lecco, perhaps half a mile or so, and almost on the confines of another country, named Castello, is a place called Canterelli, where two ways cross; and at one corner of the square space is seen an eminence, like an artificial hillock, with a cross on the summit. This is nothing else but a heap of the bodies of those who died in this contagion. Tradition, it is true, simply says, died of *the* contagion: but it must be this one, and none other, as it was the last and most destructive of which any memory remains. And we know that unassisted traditions always say too little by themselves.

They felt no inconvenience on their return, except that Renzo was rather incommoded by the weight of the money he carried away with him. But, as the reader knows, he had had far greater troubles in his life than this. I say nothing of the disquiet of his mind, which was by no means trifling, in deciding upon the best means of employing it. To have seen the different projects that passed through that mind,—the fancies—the debates; to have heard the *pros* and *cons* for agriculture or business, it was as if two academies of the last century had there met together. And the affair was to Renzo far more overwhelming and perplexing, because, since he was but a solitary individual, it could not be said to him,—Why need you choose at all? both one and the other, each in its own turn; for in substance they are the same; and, like one's legs, they are two things which go better together than one alone.

Nothing was now thought of, but packing up and setting off on their journey; the Tramaglino family to their new country, and the widow to Milan. The tears, the thanks, the promises of going to see each other, were many. Not less tender, even to tears, was the separation of Renzo and the family from his hospitable friend: nor let it be thought that matters went on coldly even with Don Abbondio. The three poor creatures had always preserved a certain respectful attachment to their curate; and he, in the bottom of his heart, had always wished them well. Such happy circumstances as these entangle the affections.

Should any one ask if there was no grief felt in thus tearing themselves from their native country,—from their beloved mountains; it may be answered that there was: for sorrow, I venture to say, is mingled, more or less, with everything. We must, however, believe that it was not very profound, since they might have spared themselves from it by remaining at home, now that the two great obstacles, Don Rodrigo and the order for Renzo's apprehension, were both taken away. But all three had been for some time accustomed to look upon the country to which they were going as their own. Renzo had recommended it to the women, by telling them of the facilities which it afforded to artificers, and a hundred things about the fine way in which they could live there. Besides, they had all experienced some very bitter moments in that home upon which they were now turning their backs; and mournful recollections always end in spoiling to the mind the places which recall them. And if these should be its native home, there is, perhaps, in such recollections, something still more keen and poignant. Even an infant, says our manuscript, reclines willingly on his nurse's bosom, and seeks with confidence and avidity the breast which has hitherto sweetly nourished him; but if, in order to wean him, she tinctures it with wormwood, the babe withdraws the lip, then returns to try it once more, but at length, after all, refuses it—weeping, indeed, but still refusing it.

What, however, will the reader now say, on hearing that they had scarcely arrived, and settled themselves in their adopted country, before Renzo found there annoyances all prepared for him! Do you pity him? but so little serves to disturb a state of happiness! This is a short sketch of the matter.

The talk that had been there made about Lucia, for some time before her arrival; the knowledge that Renzo had suffered so much for her sake, and had always been constant and faithful; perhaps a word or two from some friend who was partial to him and all belonging to him,—had created a kind of curiosity to see the young girl, and a kind of expectation of seeing her very beautiful. Now we know what expectation is: imaginative, credulous, confident; afterwards, when the trial comes, difficult to satisfy, disdainful; never finding what she had counted upon, because, in fact, she knew not her own mind; and pitilessly exacting severe payment for the loveliness so unmeaningly lavished on her object.

When this Lucia appeared, many who had perhaps thought that she must certainly have golden locks, and cheeks blushing like the rose, and a pair of eyes one more beautiful than the other, and what not besides, began to shrug their shoulders, turn up their noses, and say, 'Is this she? After such a time, after so much talk, one expected something better! What is she, after all? A peasant, like hundreds more. Why, there are plenty everywhere as good as she is, and far better too.' Then, descending to particulars, one remarks one defect, and another, another; nor were there wanting some who considered her perfectly ugly.

As, however, no one thought of telling Renzo these things to his face, so far there was no great harm done. They who really did harm, they who widened the breach, were some persons who reported them to him: and Renzo—what else could be expected?—took them very much to heart. He began to muse upon them, and to make them matters of discussion, both with those who talked to him on the subject, and more at length in his own mind.—What does it matter to you? And who told you to expect anything? did I ever talk to you about her? did I ever tell you she was beautiful? And when you asked me if she was, did I ever say anything in answer, but that she was a good girl? She's a peasant! Did I ever tell you that I would bring you here a princess? She displeases you! Don't look at her, then. You've some beautiful women: look at them.—

Only look how a trifle may sometimes suffice to decide a man's state for his whole life. Had Renzo been obliged to spend his in that neighbourhood, agreeably to his first intentions, he would have got on but very badly. From being himself displeased, he had now become displeasing. He was on bad terms with everybody, because everybody might be one of Lucia's criticizers. Not that he actually offended against civility; but we know how many sly things may be done without transgressing the rules of common politeness: quite sufficient to give vent to one's spleen. There was something sardonic in his whole behaviour; he, too, found something to criticize in everything: if only there were two successive days of bad weather, he would immediately say, 'Ay indeed, in this country!' In short, I may say, he was already only borne with by a certain number of persons, even by those who had at first wished him well; and in course of time, from one thing to another, he would have gone on till he had found himself, so to say, in a state of hostility with almost the whole population, without being able, probably, himself, to assign the primary cause, or ascertain the root from which such an evil had sprung.

But it might be said that the plague had undertaken to amend all Renzo's errors. That scourge had carried off the owner of another silk-mill, situated almost at the gates of Bergamo; and the heir, a dissolute young fellow, finding nothing in this edifice that could afford him any diversion, proposed, or rather was anxious, to dispose of it, even at half its value; but he wanted the money down upon the spot, that he might instantly expend it with unproductive prodi-

gality. The matter having come to Bortolo's ears, he immediately
went to see it: tried to treat about it: a more advantageous bargain
could not have been hoped for; but that condition of ready money
spoiled all, because his whole property, slowly made up out of his
savings, was still far from reaching the required sum. Leaving the
question, therefore, still open, he returned in haste, communicated
the affair to his cousin, and proposed to take it in partnership. So
capital an agreement cut short all Renzo's economical dubitations,
so that he quickly decided upon business, and complied with the
proposal. They went together, and the bargain was concluded.
When, then, the new owners came to live upon their own possessions,
Lucia, who was here expected by no one, not only did not go thither
subjected to criticisms, but, we may say, was not displeasing to
anybody; and Renzo found out that it had been said by more than
one, 'Have you seen that pretty she-blockhead who has come hither?'
The substantive was allowed to pass in the epithet.

And even from the annoyance he had experienced in the other
country, he derived some useful instruction. Before that time he
had been rather inconsiderate in criticizing other people's wives, and
all belonging to them. Now he understood that words make one
impression in the mouth, and another in the ear; and he accustomed
himself rather more to listen within to his own before uttering them.

We must not, however, suppose that he had no little vexations
even here. Man, (says our anonymous author—and we already
know, by experience, that he had rather a strange pleasure in drawing similes—but bear with it this once, for it is likely to be the last
time), man, so long as he is in this world, is like a sick person lying
upon a bed more or less uncomfortable, who sees around him other
beds nicely made to outward appearance, smooth, and level, and
fancies that they must be most comfortable resting-places. He suc-
ceeds in making an exchange; but scarcely is he placed in another,
before he begins, as he presses it down, to feel in one place a sharp
point pricking him, in another a hard lump: in short, we come to
almost the same story over again. And for this reason, adds he, we
ought to aim rather at doing well, than being well; and thus we
should come, in the end, even to be better. This sketch, although
somewhat parabolic, and in the style of the seventeenth century, is,

in substance, true. However, (continues he again), our good friends had no longer any sorrows and troubles of similar kind and severity to those we have related; their life was, from this time forward, one of the calmest, happiest, and most enviable of lives; so that, were I obliged to give an account of it, it would tire the reader to death. Business went on capitally. At the beginning there was a little difficulty from the scarcity of workmen, and from the ill-conduct and pretensions of the few that still remained. Orders were published, which limited the price of labour: in spite of this help, things rallied again; because, after all, how could it be otherwise? Another rather more judicious order arrived from Venice—exemption, for ten years, from all charges, civil and personal, for foreigners who would come to reside in the State. To our friends this was another advantage.

Before the first year of their marriage was completed a beautiful little creature came to light; and, as if it had been made on purpose to give Renzo an early opportunity of fulfilling that magnanimous promise of his, it was a little girl. It may be believed that it was named Maria. Afterwards, in the course of time, came I know not how many others, of both sexes; and Agnese was busy enough in carrying them about, one after the other, calling them little rogues, and imprinting upon their faces hearty kisses, which left a white mark for ever so long afterwards. They were all very well inclined; and Renzo would have them all learn to read and write, saying, that since this amusement was in fashion, they ought at least to take advantage of it.

The finest thing was to hear him relate his adventures: and he always finished by enumerating the great things he had learnt from them, for the better government of himself in future. 'I've learnt,' he would say, 'not to meddle in disturbances: I've learnt not to make speeches in the street; I've learnt not to drink more than I want; I've learnt not to hold the knocker of a door in my hand, when crazy-headed people are about: and I've learnt not to buckle a little bell to my foot, before thinking of the consequences.' And a hundred other things.

Lucia did not find fault with the doctrine itself, but she was not satisfied with it; it seemed to her, in a confused way, that something was still wanting to it. By dint of hearing the same song over and over again, and meditating on it every time, 'And I,' said she one day to her moralizer, 'what ought I to have learnt? I did not go to look for troubles: it is they that came to look for me. Though you wouldn't say,' added she, smiling sweetly, 'that my error was in wishing you well, and promising myself to you.'

Renzo at first was quite puzzled. After a long discussion and inquiry together, they concluded that troubles certainly often arise from occasion afforded by ourselves; but that the most cautious and blameless conduct cannot secure us from them; and that, when they come, whether by our own fault or not, confidence in God alleviates them, and makes them conducive to a better life. This conclusion, though come to by poor people, seemed to us so right and just, that we have resolved to put it here, as the moral of our whole story.

If this same story has given the reader any pleasure, he must thank the anonymous author, and, in some measure, his reviser, for the gratification. But if, instead, we have only succeeded in wearying him, he may rest assured that we did not do so on purpose.

VE RI
TAS

VE RI
TAS

VE RI
TAS